**Historical and
Contemporary Perspectives**

ONE WEEK LOAN

D1421290

AUSTRALIA

Law Book Company
Sydney

CANADA AND USA

Carswell
Toronto

NEW ZEALAND

Brookers
Auckland

SINGAPORE AND MALAYSIA

Sweet & Maxwell Asia
Singapore and Kuala Lumpur

UK ASYLUM LAW AND POLICY

Historical and Contemporary Perspectives

DALLAL STEVENS

London
Sweet & Maxwell
2004

Published by
Sweet & Maxwell Limited of
100 Avenue Road,
Swiss Cottage, London, NW3 3PF
Typeset by J&L Composition, Filey, North Yorkshire
Printed and bound in Wales by Creative Print and Design Group

A CIP catalogue record for this book
is available from the British Library

ISBN 0421 763507

No natural forests were destroyed to make this product,
only farmed timber was used and re-planted

To my parents
Mary and Paul

Acknowledgements

A decade ago, a book on UK asylum law might have raised eyebrows. Now it is a subject seldom out of the press and receiving unprecedented political attention. Few fields of law can claim such a level of activity over the past decade, not only nationally but also on the European and international stages. While this has made research exciting, it has also been immensely challenging, particularly as the aim of the present book is to place contemporary asylum law in a wider historical perspective. Without the resources of a number of libraries and collections, my task would have been much more difficult. In particular, I should like to thank the following for access to their holdings: the University of Warwick Library, the Centre for Research in Ethnic Relations, the Refugee Council, the Refugee Studies Centre, Oxford, and the Public Records Office.

I am indebted to the Arts and Humanities Research Board for its generous award of a term's Research Leave to work on the book. I should also like to express my gratitude to the University of Warwick, and to the Law School, for granting other periods of research leave.

A special mention is due to Hugh Beale for his support in the early years of my career, and for encouraging me to embark on this project. A number of colleagues at Warwick, past and present, have offered general advice along the way, which has been much appreciated: Lesley Hitchens, Danièle Joly, and Istvan Pogany. I have also benefited from discussions with – and the support of – many colleagues associated with the field of asylum law, among them Keith Best, Peter Billings, Conor Gearty, Guy Goodwin-Gill, Colin Harvey and Judge David Pearl. My thanks also to the team at Sweet & Maxwell, and especially to Nicola Thurlow, Madelaine Overton and Elaine Tuffery for their commitment to the project.

Finally, I am extremely grateful to a number of friends and members of my family, but in particular to: Lena and Johnny for their constant interest; my parents for their patience and understanding, even when my research activities deprived them of visits home; Patrick for unfailing support, encouragement and cheerfulness in the later stages of writing; and, lastly, Jim for years of guidance, wisdom and friendship. Without him this book would never have been written.

Dallal Stevens
University of Warwick
August 31, 2003

Contents

Table of Cases

Table of Statutes

Table of Statutory Instruments

Table of Treaties and Conventions

Selected Abbreviations

AC	Appeal Cases
ACSA	Anti-terrorism, Crime and Security Act 2001
AI	Amnesty International
AIA	Asylum and Immigration Act 1996
AIAA	Asylum and Immigration Appeals Act 1993
All ER	All England Law Reports
ALO	Airline Liaison Officer
API	Asylum Policy Instruction
ARC	Application Registration Card
ASU	Asylum Screening Unit
ATC	Authority to Carry
BCRC	British Committee for Refugees from Czechoslovakia
BDIL	*British Digest of International Law*
BNA	British Nationality Act 1981
CA	Court of Appeal
CAT	Convention against Torture
CEAS	Common European Asylum System
CIPU	Country Information and Policy Unit
CLS	Community Legal Service
CML Rev	*Common Market Law Review*
CRC	Convention on the Rights of the Child
CRTF	Czech Refugee Trust Fund
DL	Discretionary Leave
EC	European Community
ECHR	European Convention on Human Rights
ECJ	European Court of Justice
ECRE	European Council for Refugees and Exiles
ECtHR	European Court of Human Rights
EHRLR	*European Human Rights Law Review*
ELR	Exceptional Leave to Remain
EL Rev	*European Law Review*
EPC	European Political Co-operation
ERF	European Refugee Fund
ERRC	European Roma Rights Centre
EU	European Union
ExCOM	Executive Committee of the Programme of the UNHCR

HC Deb.	House of Commons Parliamentary Debates
HC	House of Commons
HCR	High Commissioner for Refugees
HL	House of Lords
HL Deb.	House of Lords Parliamentary Debates
HP	Humanitarian Protection
IA	Immigration Act 1971
IAA	Immigration and Asylum Act 1999
IANL	*Tolley's Journal of Immigration Asylum and Nationality Law*
IAS	Immigration Advisory Service
IAT	Immigration Appeal Tribunal
ICCPR	International Covenant on Civil and Political Rights 1966
I(CL)A	Immigration (Carriers' Liability) Act 1987
ICD	Integrated Casework Directorate
ICESCR	International Covenant on Economic, Social and Cultural Rights 1966
ICLQ	*International Comparative Law Quarterly*
IFA	Internal Flight Alternative
IGC	Intergovernmental Conference
IGCR	Intergovernmental Committee on Refugees
IJRL	*International Journal of Refugee Law*
Imm AR	Immigration Appeal Reports
ILO	International Labour Organisation
ILPA	Immigration Law Practitioners' Association
ILR	Indefinite Leave to Remain
IND	Immigration and Nationality Directorate
INLR	Immigration and Nationality Law Reports
IOM	International Organisation for Migration
IR	Internal Relocation
IRA	Internal Relocation Alternative
IRO	International Refugee Organisation
JCWI	Joint Council for the Welfare of Immigrants
JHA	Justice and Home Affairs
KB	Kings Bench
KPMG	KPMG Peat Marwick
LSC	Legal Services Commission
MLR	*Modern Law Review*
NASS	National Asylum Support Service
NGO	Non-Governmental Organisation
NIAA	Nationality, Immigration and Asylum Act 2002
OAU	Organisation of African Unity
OJ	Official Journal of the European Community
PACE	Police and Criminal Evidence Act 1984
PAQ	Political Asylum Questionnaire

RLC	Refugee Legal Centre
SAL	Standard Acknowledgement Letter
SEA	Single European Act 1986
SEF	Statement of Evidence Form
SIAC	Special Immigration Appeals Commission
SIACA	Special Immigration Appeals Commission Act 1997
SIS	Schengen Information System
TCU	Third Country Unit
TEU	Treaty on European Union
TPC	Transit Processing Centre
UDHR	Universal Declaration of Human Rights
UK	United Kingdom
UN	United Nations
UNHCR	Office of the United Nations High Commissioner for Refugees
UNRRA	United Nations Relief and Rehabilitation Administration
UNRWA	United Nations Relief and Works Agency for Palestine Refugees in the Near East
WLR	Weekly Law Reports

UK Asylum Law and Policy: Historical and Contemporary Perspectives

Introduction

The past decade has witnessed unprecedented activity in the field of asylum law in the United Kingdom. Four Acts, largely focusing on asylum, were introduced in the space of nine years, where previously none had existed.[1] Consecutive British governments were not alone in their impulse to legislate in this field: new legislation was implemented across Europe, the result of growing concern among European Union Member States over the rise in asylum applications, and of increasing uniformity in European policy on asylum seekers. Such heightened legislative activity has given rise, in some senses, to a new legal discipline and to the subject of this book: UK asylum law and policy within the wider context of Europe.

In international law, asylum has been described as 'the protection accorded by a State [. . .] to an individual who comes to seek it'.[2] It is the process of seeking asylum that leads to the grant of refuge. Asylum law deals then with the stage prior to the grant of refugee status; it is a vital component of refugee law, yet distinct from it. If refugee law is to be viewed as the body of law dealing with refugees, and asylum law the body of law relating to asylum seekers, then the question of definition assumes further importance. The term 'refugee' has been described as 'a term of art, that is, a term with a content verifiable according to principles of general international law'.[3] In its modern and strictly legal sense, it owes its derivation to an international agreement: the 1951 United Nations Convention Relating to the Status of Refugees ('the 1951 Convention'), and 1967 Protocol.[4] It is declaratory by nature: a refugee does not become a refugee because

---

[1] Asylum and Immigration Appeals Act 1993; Asylum and Immigration Act 1996; Immigration and Asylum Act 1999; Nationality, Immigration and Asylum Act 2002.

[2] A. Grahl-Madsen, *Territorial Asylum* (AWI Oceana, 1980), p. 1.

[3] G. Goodwin-Gill, *The Refugee in International Law* (Clarendon, Oxford, 1996), p. 3.

[4] References to the 1951 Convention should be taken to include the 1967 Protocol, unless otherwise indicated.

of recognition, but is recognised because he or she is a refugee.[5] 'Asylum seeker', by contrast, has no such foothold in international law; yet it, too, has become a term of art. To the layperson, there is very little to distinguish the asylum seeker from the refugee. The labels are used interchangeably and the perceptions of both are, on the whole, negative. For the asylum seeker, however, the difference is vast. Assumption to refugee status brings with it recognition and acceptance; it assures protection; it guarantees specific rights. In the limbo status of 'asylum seeker', little is certain; there are few rights and limited protection; and there is always the fear of return.

Through the act of seeking asylum, an individual relinquishes power over his or her destiny to a third party: the host state. Though it may be popular to speak of a 'right of asylum', suggesting a right of the individual, it is the state that retains the right to grant asylum. The individual's right is subject to the state's discretion and, in the context of international law, pertains to no more than a right to seek and enjoy asylum from persecution.[6] It is the state that determines who may enter and who is to be rejected, the state, through its own municipal law, that excludes or includes. By seeking asylum, an individual loses his or her identity, and is defined anew by the host nation. Interpretation of the law, representation in the media, political discourse, and wider economic or cultural factors all lead to the creation of new identities for the asylum seeker, who may be seen as 'alien', 'refugee', 'de facto refugee', 'unaccompanied child', 'economic migrant', or 'bogus asylum seeker'. These identities are more than mere labels; they carry with them the judgement of the host nation; they can, at the extreme, be the difference between freedom and persecution or torture.

Asylum law is about exclusion and inclusion; it is about shifting conceptions of persecution and protection within an ever-changing world. It is a complex subject influenced by numerous factors, some external, some internal. This book discusses the development of asylum law in light of a few of these factors – history, international law, European policy –, and ways in which they have informed the definition (and on going re-definition) of the asylum seeker. The themes of inclusion and exclusion will carry through the book; so too the changes effected in the treatment of asylum seekers from arrival to acceptance or rejection. By combining historical and contemporary perspectives, and taking account of national, European and international determinants, the book seeks to provide a useful conspectus of major developments and issues in UK asylum law and policy.

---

[5] UNHCR, *Handbook on Procedures and Criteria for Determining Refugee Status* (Geneva, 1992), para. 28.

[6] Universal Declaration of Human Rights, Art. 14(1).

OUTLINE OF CHAPTERS

The book is divided, broadly, into two parts. Part 1 (Chapters 1 to 4) places current asylum law and policy in their historical context; part 2 (Chapters 5 to 9) focuses on contemporary aspects of UK and EU asylum and refugee law.

Covering a wide span of time from the twelfth to the late nineteenth centuries, Chapter 1 examines how early asylum seekers and refugees were perceived and treated by the English, and later by the British. It discusses the first legal attempts to control refugees arriving on this country's shores, and considers the role of law in these earlier periods in constructing the identity of the asylum seeker and refugee. Chapter 2 continues the historical analysis, opening with the passing of the Aliens Act 1905, the first statute to incorporate a provision dealing specifically with the plight of refugees, and going on to cover the critical years up to 1945, during which the foundations were laid for modern-day asylum law. Revealing striking parallels with current policy, the chapter discusses how the UK governments of the day adopted restrictive measures when faced with a perceived threat of increasing numbers in the pre-Second World War years. The end of the war in 1945 can be regarded as the start of a new human rights era in the international context. The implementation of the 1951 Convention helped guide national law and policy in relation to refugees, and, to some extent, asylum seekers. Chapter 3 considers the emergence of a national refugee law in the UK in the post-war era and reflects on the treatment of various groups of refugees who made their way to the UK up until 1993.

The development of international refugee law from 1945 to the present day is examined in Chapter 4. It reviews the antecedent to the 1951 Convention, the 1933 Convention Relating to the International Status of Refugees, as well as specific regional instruments. It discusses the relationship between international refugee law and asylum-seeking, and ends with an analysis of the core provisions of the 1950 European Convention on Human Rights and their relevance to asylum law.

Initiating the discussion of contemporary UK asylum and refugee law, Chapter 5 provides an overview of the four asylum-specific Acts: Asylum and Immigration Appeals Act 1993, Asylum and Immigration Act 1996, Immigration and Asylum Act 1999, and, finally, Nationality, Immigration and Asylum Act 2002. The actual application of the law is dealt with in Chapters 6 and 7, which concentrate in particular on Home Office policy towards the asylum seeker from the point of departure from country of origin to the final decision on the asylum claim in the UK. The analysis takes account of governmental policy, asylum law and rules, media reporting and public perceptions, all of which have played a role in the formulation of current attitudes towards and treatment of asylum seekers. The judicial impact is weighed up in Chapter 8. It focuses on a number of key judgments in relation to specific areas of concern, and explores two sides to the development of case-law in the asylum field: judicial activism and judicial restraint. The final chapter offers an overview of the development of EU asylum policy. It tracks the various stages on the road to greater harmonisation of asylum law from early intergovernmental discussions to the post-Amsterdam and Tampere advances, and discusses the influence of EU initiatives on municipal law. Consideration is given here to tensions that run through the other Chapters, between liberalism and restrictionism, unilateralism and co-operation, the letter of the law and its spirit.

Chapter One

Constructing the 'Asylum Seeker': A Historical Analysis

INTRODUCTION

The history of United Kingdom asylum policy falls into several broad **1.1**
phases. Though the term 'asylum seeker' is a relatively recent designation,[1] the practice of granting refuge has a long tradition. While
the development of law and policy in relation to asylum has been subject to the vagaries of a changing social and political environment, it
has been informed throughout by the state's categorisation, or
labelling, of the asylum seeker. Thus the latter has been, by turns,
'alien', '*réfugié*', '*émigré*', 'political exile', 'immigrant', 'refugee', and
'bogus asylum seeker', depending on the political, social, economic or
cultural pressures brought to bear.

   The purpose of this chapter is to examine the historical perception
of asylum seekers by the authorities, by the public and, to some
extent, by themselves. It will attempt to show how such perceptions
helped to define the identities of the new arrivals; to map out the circumstances in which legislation was introduced to deal with asylum
seekers; and to explain how, in certain cases, the law contributed to
the construction, and reconstruction, of asylum seekers. In addressing these issues, the chapter will consider a number of critical periods
between the twelfth and twentieth centuries.

   In modern-day legal parlance, to describe an individual as a
'refugee' suggests compliance with the definition contained in the
United Nations 1951 Convention Relating to the Status of
Refugees/1967 Protocol. For the period under consideration in this
chapter, no such well-defined criteria apply. The terms 'asylum
seeker' and 'refugee' should therefore be read in their wider, and historically more appropriate, sense: that is, any individual dispersed

---

[1] The term 'asylum' is derived from the Greek 'a' (not) and 'sylon' ('right of seizure');
literally, asylum therefore means 'freedom from seizure'.

from his or her homeland who seeks protection or a safe haven in another country, for religious or political reasons.[2] No distinction is drawn at this stage between the asylum seeker and the refugee, since those who arrived on England's shores in search of asylum were generally granted refuge.

ASYLUM AS 'ALIENAGE': FROM THE MIDDLE AGES TO 'EVIL MAY DAY'

1.2   'Every man is either *alienigena*, an alien born, or *subditus*, a subject born. Every alien is either a friend that is in league, &c. or an enemy that is in open war, &c. Every alien enemy is either *pro tempore*, temporary for a time, or *perpetuus*, perpetual, or *specialiter permissus*, permitted especially' (Chief Justice Coke, *Calvin's Case*, 1608).[3]

Calvin's Case was a monumental decision in the field of nationality law. It was the first attempt by the courts to restate the rules on subjects and aliens, in existence from the Middle Ages, and apply them to a modern state.[4] It laid down a general principle for the acquisition of the status of natural born subject which was to apply for centuries after the decision: birth within the king's domains. In so doing, the decision reaffirmed the status of the alien as 'other' and the different treatment that he or she was to be accorded. Coke himself was acutely conscious that the judgement was breaking new ground: 'This case was as elaborately, substantially, and judicially argued by the Lord Chancellor, and by my brethren the Judges, as I ever read or heard of any; [. . .] for though it was one of the shortest and least that ever we argued in this Court, yet was it the longest and weightiest that ever was argued in any Court, the shortest in syllables, and the longest in substance; the least for the value [. . .] but the weightiest for the consequent, both for the present, and for all posterity.'[5]

---

[2] There are many views as to the correct definition of the term 'refugee'. For example, A. Zolberg *et al* define refugees as 'persons whose presence abroad is attributable to a well-founded fear of violence' and adopt a broad definition of violence to include 'coercive circumstances' that have 'threatening effects': *Escape from Violence – Conflict and the Refugee Crisis in the Developing World* (Oxford: OUP, 1989), pp. 31, 33. Zolberg *et al* argue that, in certain circumstances, those fleeing famine – for example, the Irish in 1846 and 1854 – constitute refugees because they flee from 'life-threatening violence' (p. 32). It is submitted that this interpretation of 'violence' is too wide. Consequently, the Irish are not deemed refugees for the purposes of this chapter and are excluded from the discussion.

[3] 7 Co. Rep. 1a, 17a.

[4] See W. Holdsworth, *A History of English Law*, Vol. IX (Sweet & Maxwell/Methuen, 1966), p. 72.

[5] 7 Co. Rep. 1a, 4a.

Coke's distinction between 'alien' and 'subject' has its roots in the Middle Ages; deriving from the Latin for 'other', the 'alien' was the outsider, the foreigner, the individual not born on English soil. As a definition, it was all-encompassing. It included the traveller and trader as well as the fugitive and asylum seeker. It mattered not that an individual was escaping pestilence or persecution – first and foremost, he was foreign. Though, as Coke indicated, an alien might be 'a friend' or might be 'permitted especially', there was no special category of alien denoting entry to England on the basis of persecution.

The importance attached to the concept of alienage over that of refuge can be traced to the Norman invasion when the majority of aliens were drawn to England for economic reasons.[6] Amongst their number was a scattering of refugees, who were also identified as 'alien'.[7] This use of 'alien' as a generic term precluded any need to distinguish the persecuted. It justified circumspection, sanctioned exclusion and paved the way for intolerance. Such exclusion and intolerance were particularly visible in medieval England in the form of persecution and expulsions.

The group to suffer most were the Jews. Throughout the twelfth **1.3** century, English Jewry was subjected to increasing discrimination, culminating in the massacres of 1189–1190.[8] Once crusading fever took hold, the situation worsened. Jews were forced to wear a special badge; they came under attack from local rioters; they were excluded from certain towns; and, from the age of twelve, they were required to pay a special poll tax.[9] By the end of the thirteenth century, many Jews had been financially bankrupted. Though England under Edward I had benefited economically from their presence, their increasing poverty rendered them of limited value to the royal treasury. With this in mind, Edward finally succumbed in 1290 to baronial and burghal pressure and issued a decree of expulsion against all Jews. The exact numbers forced to quit are unknown; some estimate that, as a result of previous pressures, there were scarcely 3,000 Jews

---

[6] See W. Cunningham, *Alien Immigrants to England*, (London: Sonnenschein, 1897), Ch. 2 for a discussion of economic migration following the Norman Conquest.

[7] It is suspected that the original Jews in England were refugees from the butchery of the Crusaders in Rouen and the Rhineland: C. Roth, *A History of the Jews* (Oxford: Clarendon Press, 1978), p. 6.

[8] V. Kiernan, 'Britons Old and New', in C. Holmes ed., *Immigrants and Minorities in British Society* (Allen & Unwin, 1978), p. 27. A number of incidents occurred in 1189 and 1190 in which Jews lost their lives or were the victims of extreme violence; for example, in March 1190, in excess of 150 Jews were burned to death in York castle: C. Roth, *A History of the Jews* (Oxford: Clarendon Press, 1978), pp. 20–25.

[9] S.W. Baron, *A Social and Religious History of the Jews*, Vol. XI (Jewish Publication Society/Columbia University Press, 1967), pp. 201–211.

remaining to face expulsion;[10] others advance a considerably higher figure – in excess of 15,000 for those Jews expelled from England in 1290.[11] They were not to return in numbers until the seventeenth century.[12]

The preoccupation with the Jews, and the extent of animosity towards them, had negative repercussions for aliens. While the Jews' foreignness was accentuated by the voluntary wearing of conical hats and the enforced display of badges,[13] making them an easy target for xenophobic attacks, the non-Jewish alien, whose outward appearance was generally less conspicuous, was increasingly subjected to similar treatment. This was particularly true in the later Middle Ages, when, despite active encouragement by Edward III of Flemish immigration to help bolster English towns in decline, growing resentment at the alien's industry and craftsmanship led to riots against foreign artisans and merchants.[14] The Peasants' Revolt of 1381, though rooted in feudal malaise, unmasked an underlying xenophobia: accounts from the period report the massacre by rebels of at least thirty-five Flemings on the grounds that they were alien.[15] There is every possibility that these Flemings were refugees.[16] Over a century later, the position had not much improved: in a major riot in 1517, popularly known as 'Evil May Day', foreign artisans and merchants were singled out and attacked. Such expressions of intolerance were not confined to the streets; legislative restrictions were regularly imposed by the Crown

---

[10] V. Kiernan, 'Britons Old and New', in C. Holmes ed. *Immigrants and Minorities in British Society* (Allen & Unwin, 1978), p. 27.

[11] W. Cunningham, *Alien Immigrants to England*, (London: Sonnenschein, 1897), p. 70; H. Henriques, *The Jews and English Law* (London: Bibliophile Press, 1908), p. 59.

[12] This is with the exception of the Iberian Marranos, crypto-Jews, who escaped the worst excesses of the Inquisition from 1492. They established small communities in London and Bristol but were finally expelled by James 1 in 1609: see C. Roth, *A History of the Jews* (Oxford: Clarendon Press, 1978), pp. 135–148.

[13] S.W. Baron, *A Social and Religious History of the Jews*, Vol. XI (Jewish Publication Society/Columbia University Press, 1967), p. 203.

[14] T.W.E. Roche, *The Key in the Lock – A History of Immigration Control in England from 1066 to the Present Day* (London: John Murray, 1969), p. 27.

[15] *Anonimalle Chronicle 1333 to 1381*, edited by V.H. Galbraith (Manchester University Press, 1970), pp. 145–6. For a translation, see C. Osman, *The Great Revolt of 1381* (Oxford University Press, 1969), p. 199.

[16] Some commentators are of the view that the Flemish migrants arriving after 1337 could be classified as 'refugees' due to political oppression suffered in the Low Countries: F. Wilson, *They came as Strangers – The Story of Refugees to Great Britain* (London: Hamish Hamilton, 1959), pp. 1–2. Smiles reports that Flemings frequently sought refuge in England from the 'dynastic quarrels of the Burgundian princes' and the 'constant turmoil' of the Low Countries: S. Smiles, *The Huguenots: Their Settlements, Churches and Industries in England and Ireland* (London: John Murray, 1870), p. 2; 4. It is, however, more generally accepted that there was a strong economic motivation for their migration to England.

against alien merchants. Thus at the hands of both the authorities and the public, the alien was constantly reminded of his difference, of his identity as 'other', and of his precariousness within English society.

Not only were foreign asylum seekers potentially at risk from abuse and attack; they were also subject to possible extradition. Contrary to the view expressed by Chief Justice Coke in the seventeenth century that there was no duty to surrender fugitive offenders under mediaeval law,[17] recent academic research has revealed that there were a number of extradition treaties in existence from the twelfth century, and that individuals were frequently passed between countries 'as an exchange in political bargaining'.[18] In contrast to many extradition treaties in the nineteenth century, which exempted political offences,[19] extradition treaties of the Middle Ages actually focused on political offenders, as well as criminals, as the very subjects for surrender.[20] The Treaty of Paris 1303 between England and France, for example, contained a clause of mutual surrender of 'traitors' and 'felons'.[21] With the existence of such treaties, no political asylum seeker could be assured that his quest for asylum in England would be upheld.

This early period laid the foundation for later attitudes towards asylum. There was no legal notion of refugee status; with the exception of the Jews, all foreigners, whether refugees or not, were labelled 'alien' or, more specifically, 'alien friend' and 'alien enemy'.[22] English

---

[17] 3rd Inst, 188; see *British Digest of International Law*, Vol. 6, p. 444.

[18] C. Van den Wijngaert, *The political offence exception to extradition* The Netherlands: Kluwer, 1980), p. 5.

[19] The first such treaty entered into by Great Britain was the Extradition Treaty 1852 with France, which was never implemented by Parliament due mainly to disquiet about the burden of proof provision.

[20] P. O'Higgins, 'The history of extradition in British practice, 1174–1794', (1964) 13 *Indian Yb Int'l Aff.*, 78.

[21] C. Van den Wijngaert, *The political offence exception to extradition* The Netherlands: Kluwer, 1980), p. 6.

[22] A distinction developed between 'alien friend' and 'alien enemy'. Alien friends came by licence and with safe conduct; alien enemies were naturally in a somewhat precarious position. By the 15th century, alien friends seemed able to sue at common law, though they continued to be prevented from acquiring rights in land: Pollock & Maitland, *The History of English Law before Edward I*, Vol.1 (Cambridge University Press, 1911); W. Holdsworth, *A History of English Law*, Vol. IX (Sweet & Maxwell/Methuen, 1966), pp. 95, 97. The position was, however, not altogether clear: Littleton claimed that no alien could bring an action, whether real or personal: Littleton, sec. 198; Commentator Littleton, 129b. This view is contested; it is suspected that greater protection was afforded by the courts than is suggested by Littleton and that alien friends were not barred from pursuing personal actions: see, e.g., W. Holdsworth, *A History of W. English Law*, Vol. IX (Sweet & Maxwell/Methuen, 1966), pp. 94–95.

Jewry suffered the consequences of a double identity: that of both Jew and alien. Non-Jewish asylum seekers, though foreign and therefore exposed to the prevailing anti-alien sentiment, had not yet been singled out for an independent policy. Their numbers were low and the 'problem' was contained. This was soon to change. By the dawn of the sixteenth century, political and religious upheaval in Europe altered the nature of migration. The Reformation created a new phenomenon: the Protestant exile. Here was an individual who, by force rather than choice, was obliged to seek safer havens, and thousands fell into this category. The impact upon England was to be dramatic and enduring.

TOWARDS A CONCEPT OF THE REFUGEE: PROTESTANTS IN THE REIGN OF ELIZABETH I

1.4   The history of the Protestant exiles, the Huguenots, may be divided into two periods. The first significant migration to England occurred in the wake of the St Bartholomew's Day massacre of 1572;[23] the second, as a result of the revocation of the Edict of Nantes by Louis XIV in 1685. In three respects, the experiences of the Protestant fugitives provide an instructive historical record of English attitudes towards asylum seekers. Firstly, the Protestants were real refugees in the modern sense – that is, they had a well-founded fear of being persecuted for reasons of religion.[24] Secondly, here was a group of people with unusually close religious and cultural ties with the host population. Thirdly, England's position as one of the leading Protestant countries of Europe ensured that acceptance of the new migrants would have significant political repercussions. These three factors – genuine suffering, religious affinity and politics – laid the ground for admission to the country. Though acceptance by the people and assimilation within the community could be less readily ensured, here was an opportunity to break with the anti-alien sentiment of the preceding centuries and to recognise a new form of migrant warranting humanitarian treatment.

The trickle of Protestants which started early in the sixteenth century developed into a surge by the end of the seventeenth.[25] Not only

---

[23] See, for a discussion of the background to the massacre, R. Gwynn, *Huguenot Heritage – The History and Contribution of the Huguenots in Britain* (London: Routledge, 1985), pp. 15–16; Gwynn suggests that an estimated 10,000 lost their lives in Paris and the provinces.

[24] 1951 Convention Relating to the Status of Refugees, Art. 1A(2).

[25] Despite Henry VIII's fearsome reputation for burning Protestant heretics as well as Catholics, which had an obvious impact on refugees to England, he is said to have

did England provide a refuge for the French-speaking Huguenots; it was also the first port of call for many Walloons escaping the Low Countries and the 'frightful war of extermination and persecution' waged by the Duke of Alva.[26] It thus fell to Queen Elizabeth I to develop a workable policy on refugees. There is evidence that the notion of asylum was supported in principle by many Elizabethan advisors, though not all of Elizabeth's subjects endorsed a pro-Huguenot line.[27] The Queen herself appears to have confronted something of a dilemma. While she was undoubtedly sensitive to the plight of fellow Protestants, who hailed England as 'Asylum Christi',[28] the atmosphere of suspicion and intrigue that surrounded all international relations advised caution. Two incidents highlight the difficulties encountered by the Crown in coming to terms with the new arrivals. Following the St Bartholomew's Day Massacre, Elizabeth is said to have refused for several days to receive the French Ambassador. When he was finally given an audience, he is reported to have encountered a monarch and court completely attired in black and silent; as he neared the reproachful Queen, the courtiers averted their gaze as an expression of their disapproval.[29] This public display of Protestant solidarity was at odds with the more ambivalent attitude articulated in private by Elizabeth and some of her advisors. In a letter to the Archbishop of Canterbury, Elizabeth complained that some of the new arrivals were 'infected with Dangerous opinions, contrary to the faith of christs church as Anabaptists and such other Sectarys or that be gilty of sum other horrible crymes of rebellion murder, Boggerys or such like.'[30] Elizabeth's animosity towards the Anabaptists was so profound that, in 1561, she ordered that they leave the realm within 20 days or face imprisonment and confiscation of their belongings.[31]

Despite such reservations, the Queen recognised the potential economic value of the Dutch and French and allowed them to enter the

granted forty-five naturalisation papers to Huguenots between 1535 and 1536, indicating a degree of tolerance. Following the Revocation, it is estimated that about 80,000 Huguenots escaped to England: F. Wilson, *They came as Strangers – The Story of Refugees to Great Britain* (London: Hamish Hamilton, 1959), pp. 18, 22.

[26] S. Smiles, *The Huguenots: Their Settlements, Churches and Industries in England and Ireland* (London: John Murray, 1870), p. 55.

[27] L. Yungblut, *Strangers settled here amongst Us – Policies, Perceptions and the Presence of Aliens in Elizabethan England* (London: Routledge, 1996), p. 36.

[28] S. Smiles, *The Huguenots: Their Settlements, Churches and Industries in England and Ireland* (London: John Murray, 1870), p. 56.

[29] C. Weiss, *History of the French Protestant Refugee* (Blackwood & Sons, 1854), p. 198.

[30] Cited in L. Yungblut, *Strangers settled here amongst Us – Policies, Perceptions and the Presence of Aliens in Elizabethan England* (London: Routledge, 1996), p. 85.

[31] A. Dummett and A. Nicol, *Subjects, Citizens, Aliens and Others* (London: Weidenfeld & Nicolson, 1990), p. 57.

country in accordance with a policy of controlled settlement. The inter-town movement of aliens was generally authorised by royal grant; some towns, such as Canterbury, were compelled to take refugees; numerous surveys of the alien population were carried out in an attempt to quantify the numbers of aliens present on English soil,[32] and to control the xenophobia which resulted from the occasional circulation of exaggerated statistics on alien numbers.[33] Already in the late 1560s, the government had begun to suspect the motives of the new arrivals. Aliens were asked whether they had arrived on grounds of religion or not. There was concern that foreigners were falsely claiming religious persecution in order to enter the country and that there were amongst their number ill-intentioned individuals.[34] In 1573, the year following the St Bartholomew Massacre, the return for aliens in London suggested that many foreign Protestants had come 'not for religion, as by their owne confession dothe appeare' but 'to seeke lyvinge'.[35] In fact, 2,561 of the 7,143 strangers found to be living in the City and surrounds admitted that they had come to England to seek work.[36]

1.5   Despite the existence of alien surveys, it is difficult to calculate exact numbers of religious refugees in England during the Elizabethan period. The indications are that between 10,000 and 15,000 foreign Protestants were present at any one time, the peak occurring in the 1590s.[37] Concern over numbers was clear when local officials in the port of Rye contacted the Privy Council for advice on entry requirements. The Council suggested that the refugees could be permitted to stay if 'they be cume out of their countrye for religion and for safegard of their conscience, and that they be such as may be benificiall to that towne, and be also comprised within the nomber of straingers limited by the Queen's Majestie to inhabite there.'[38] Thus, in an early adumbration of current asylum procedures, it fell to the

---

[32] L. Yungblut, *Strangers settled here amongst Us – Policies, Perceptions and the Presence of Aliens in Elizabethan England* (London: Routledge, 1996), p. 80.

[33] O. P. Grell, *Calvinist Exiles in Tudor and Stuart England* (Hampshire: Scolar Press, 1996), p. 3.

[34] L. Yungblut, *Strangers settled here amongst Us – Policies, Perceptions and the Presence of Aliens in Elizabethan England* (London: Routledge, 1996), p. 85

[35] Cited in R. Gwynn, 'Patterns in Study of Huguenot Refugees in Britain: Past, Present and Future' in I. Scouloudi (ed.), *Huguenots in Britain and their French Background, 1550–1800* (Hampshire: Macmillan Press, 1987), p. 223.

[36] I. Scouloudi, 'The Stranger Community in the Metropolis 1558–1640' in I. Scouloudi (ed.), *Huguenots in Britain and their French Background, 1550–1800* (Hampshire: Macmillan Press, 1987), p. 44.

[37] R. Gwynn, *Huguenot Heritage – The History and Contribution of the Huguenots in Britain* (London: Routledge, 1985), pp. 29; 33.

[38] *Acts of the Privy Council of England*, New Series, Vol. VII, 1558–1570, (HM Stationery Office, London, 1893), p. 380.

port officer to interview the asylum seeker to gauge his or her true intentions. Refugees were not to be admitted purely on the grounds of religious persecution; public benefit and weight of numbers were important additional factors.

While Elizabeth and her counsellors pondered their policy on the Protestant fugitives, the actual day-to-day treatment of foreigners continued to be problematic. Their industry and growing wealth, though contributing to the regeneration of many impoverished English towns, rankled with the indigenous population. The Queen was petitioned on various occasions to expel the refugees from certain sites. Faced with local hostility, some moved of their own accord. Extracts from the journals of foreign visitors to England are testament to consistent abuse of foreigners,[39] as are contemporary English records. In 1593, an anonymous leaflet or 'libel' was distributed, unsparing in its invective against foreign fugitives:

> 'Doth not the world see that you, beastly brutes, the Belgians or rather drunken drones, and faint-hearted Flemings; and you, fraudulent fathers, Frenchmen, by your cowardly flight from your own natural countries, have abandoned the same into the hands of your proud, cowardly enemies, and have by a feigned hypocrisy and counterfeit show of religion placed yourselves here in a most fertile soil under a most gracious and merciful Prince; who had been contented, to the great prejudice of her own natural subjects, to suffer you to live here in better case and more freedom than her own people?

> Be it known to all Flemings and Frenchmen, that it is best for them to depart out of the realm of England [. . .] If not, then to take what follows. For there shall be many a sore stripe. Apprentices will rise to the number of 2336. And all prentices and journeymen will down with Flemings and Strangers.'[40]

Though the government attempted to clamp down on such 'libels against strangers', and was prepared to use torture to extract confessions from suspects, anti-alien agitation continued to be recorded. As one commentator notes, 'actual attacks, anticipated attacks, or investigations of threatening materials (such as anti-alien pamphlets or broadsheets) are recorded for 1493, 1517, 1573, 1575, 1581, 1586, 1587, 1593, and 1595.'[41] Violence or its threat was not the only

---

[39] See, e.g., W. Rye, *England as seen by Foreigners in the days of Elizabeth and James the First* (London, 1865), p. 7, n. 13.

[40] G.B. Harrison, *The Elizabethan Journals – being a record of those things most talked of during the years 1591–1603* (London: Routledge & Kegan Paul Ltd, 1965), pp. 236–7.

[41] L. Yungblut, *Strangers settled here amongst Us – Policies, Perceptions and the Presence of Aliens in Elizabethan England* (London: Routledge, 1996), p. 40.

method employed to frighten the exiles; resort was made on occasion to Parliament. Following complaints in 1592 by London freemen and shopkeepers that foreign artisans were spoiling their trades, a bill was introduced to restrain the foreigners; it failed to become law on the dissolution of Parliament, but not before receiving strong support from influential Elizabethans, such as Sir Walter Raleigh.[42]

This conflict between sanctuary and intolerance dogged the alien issue throughout Elizabeth's reign and has given rise to a somewhat confusing picture of the refugee in Tudor England. It is often claimed that England became a 'haven' and a 'sure refuge' under Elizabeth I,[43] but this view is subject to qualification. It is clear that England's refugee policy was hesitant and haphazard. The charged political atmosphere and depressed economic climate did not foster a consistent approach. The word 'refugee' did not, in fact, exist until the 1680s,[44] and the Elizabethan asylum seekers tended still to be referred to as 'aliens', emphasising their foreignness, or 'fugitives'. The government, wary of the implications for national security resulting from the increased presence of foreigners, maintained a close watch on alien statistics, supervised areas of settlement, and occasionally ordered expulsions.[45] It had also to contend with a suspicious and increasingly antagonistic indigenous population in a time of economic hardship.[46] Any suggestion of widespread tolerance at this time is simply not borne out by the available evidence.

From a contemporary perspective, the most remarkable aspect of Elizabeth's handling of the refugee crisis is the extent to which it anticipates current asylum policy. Not only was the government acutely conscious of the potential liabilities of asylum seekers in terms of their numbers, their possible financial burden, and public hostility; it was also keen to exploit the exiles for political and economic benefit, a role to which they were conspicuously well suited. They helped bolster England's image as one of Europe's key Protestant states at a time of heightened Catholic and Protestant tension, and brought with them key technological advancements, notably in the field of armaments manufacture, to an industrially

---

[42] S. Smiles, *The Huguenots: Their Settlements, Churches and Industries in England and Ireland* (London: John Murray, 1870), p. 89.

[43] See, *e.g.*, R. Gwynn, *Huguenot Heritage – The History and Contribution of the Huguenots in Britain* (London: Routledge, 1985), p. 29.

[44] M. Marrus, *The Unwanted – European Refugees in the Twentieth Century* (New York: Oxford University Press, 1985), p. 8.

[45] In 1573 and 1574, strangers who professed no religion were expelled: L. Yungblut, *Strangers settled here amongst Us – Policies, Perceptions and the Presence of Aliens in Elizabethan England* (London: Routledge, 1996), p. 91.

[46] Particularly at the time of Elizabeth's accession to the crown in 1558.

underdeveloped England.[47] Humanitarianism was advocated so long as the country benefited.

THE ORIGINAL 'REFUGEES': FRENCH HUGUENOTS OF THE SEVENTEENTH CENTURY

The second 'wave' of Protestant Huguenots was brought about by the **1.6** Revocation of the Edict of Nantes by Louis XIV in 1685.[48] Initially, the presence of the Catholic James II on the English throne acted as a deterrent to the Huguenots escaping from France; however, James' Declaration of Indulgence, which promised the free exercise of religion, persuaded many of a sympathetic reception in England.[49] It is claimed that, as a result of the Revocation and the brutality of the *dragonnades*,[50] at least 80,000 fled to England,[51] though the figure could be as high as 100,000.[52] Of these, between 40,000 and 50,000 eventually settled in Britain, the rest moving on to North America and Ireland.[53] In the immediate wake of the Revocation, 200,000 quit France, while the total number to leave in the forty years following the Revocation is estimated at one million.[54] There is no doubt that, on the basis of these statistics, the Huguenots constituted the first major refugee problem for Western Europe.

Though James II, like his predecessor Elizabeth, may have resented the refugees in private, he remained true to his word and did not persecute them. His attitude too seems to have been motivated by political expediency. In accordance with the expectations of his Protestant subjects, James permitted the refugees to enter without hindrance and even authorised collections on their behalf. Yet his

---

[47] L. Yungblut, *Strangers settled here amongst Us – Policies, Perceptions and the Presence of Aliens in Elizabethan England* (London: Routledge, 1996), p. 90.

[48] For an account of some of the atrocities inflicted upon the French Protestants, see S. Smiles, *The Huguenots: Their Settlements, Churches and Industries in England and Ireland* (London: John Murray, 1870), Ch. 10.

[49] R. Gwynn, *Huguenot Heritage – The History and Contribution of the Huguenots in Britain* (London: Routledge, 1985), p. 40.

[50] The *dragonnades* were troops used to 'persuade' Protestants to convert; they employed a combination of methods, including sequestration of possessions, intimidation and extreme force.

[51] F. Wilson, *They came as Strangers – The Story of Refugees to Great Britain* (London: Hamish Hamilton, 1959), p. 22.

[52] V. Kiernan, 'Britons Old and New', in C. Holmes ed., *Immigrants and Minorities in British Society* (Allen & Unwin, 1978), p. 38.

[53] R. Gwynn, *Huguenot Heritage – The History and Contribution of the Huguenots in Britain* (London: Routledge, 1985), p. 35.

[54] D. Greer, *The Incidence of the Emigration During the French Revolution* (Massachusetts: Peter Smith, 1951), pp. 20–21.

generosity clearly had its limits. It is claimed that he sought to prevent benefits from reaching the refugee community,[55] and that, in an expression of his true allegiance, and in order perhaps to appease the French, James commanded the public burning of the popular book, *The Complaints of the Protestants cruelly persecuted in the Kingdom of France.*[56] There is evidence to suggest that his censorship was responsible for the unusual silence of *The London Gazette* on the brutal events occurring in France in 1685.[57] Furthermore, in contrast to Elizabeth I, James extended his welcome to the French ambassador, Barrillon, and to the Marquis of Bonrepaus, who was sent to England to exhort Protestants to return to France.[58]

While anti-French sentiment undoubtedly existed at this time, largely related to competitive jealousies, the English were, on the whole, much more supportive of the Huguenots than of any previous aliens. The appeals for money were well-supported: in 1686, a sum of between £40,000 and £50,000 is said to have been collected;[59] following a further collection in 1687, the 'royal bounty' possibly amounted to as much as £200,000.[60] Gwynn suggests that such unusual generosity towards the refugees may have been on account of the wide publicity their sufferings had received; from 1679, accounts in certain newsletters of French persecutions were frequent and detailed, conditioning the public towards an increasingly pro-refugee stance.[61] This attitude was in line with an argument put forward as early as 1625 by Hugo Grotius in his ground-breaking work *De jure belli ac pacis*, where he had come close to suggesting that there was a right for victims of expulsion to be granted asylum: 'A permanent residence ought not to be denied to foreigners who, expelled from their homes, are seeking a refuge, provided that they submit themselves to the established government and observe any regulations which are necessary to avoid strifes.'[62] This so long as the individual had not committed offences which affected public order, were atrociously

---

[55] C. Weiss, *History of the French Protestant Refugee* (Blackwood & Sons, 1854), p. 225.

[56] *ibid.*

[57] R. Gwynn, *Huguenot Heritage – The History and Contribution of the Huguenots in Britain* (London: Routledge, 1985), p. 135.

[58] Bonrepaus apparently took his job most seriously, employing bribes, threats and promises to win over his countrymen; he had some success, managing to send home 507 fugitives: C. Weiss, *History of the French Protestant Refugee* (Blackwood & Sons, 1854), p. 229.

[59] W. Cunningham, *Alien Immigrants to England*, (London: Sonnenschein, 1897), p. 231.

[60] C. Weiss, *History of the French Protestant Refugee* (Blackwood & Sons, 1854), p. 223.

[61] R. Gwynn, *Huguenot Heritage – The History and Contribution of the Huguenots in Britain* (London: Routledge, 1985), pp. 125–126.

[62] II, § xvi. For a translation, see J. Brown Scott ed., *The Classics of International Law* (New York: Oceana Publications, 1964).

criminal, or were crimes by which another state or its sovereign were particularly injured.[63] A further important reason for an apparent shift in attitudes, in contrast to the sixteenth century, was that England was experiencing a period of prosperity; artisans did not need to feel quite so threatened by the arrival of outsiders. Many of the English now recognised and appreciated the contribution that the Huguenots had made to the wealth of the country since the Elizabethan era.[64] In addition, the dogged commitment of the French Protestants to William of Orange, and their contributions on the battlefields,[65] earned them particular respect amongst the English. Further evidence for this view is offered by the contrasting treatment handed out to a near-forgotten group of refugees, the German Palatines.

Like James II, the Elector Palatine[66] offered shelter to the Huguenots. He was, however, to pay dearly for his generosity when, in revenge, Louis XIV devastated much of the Palatinate territory. Once again, the French fugitives found themselves on the move and, although many were received in German towns, a few reached England. Following a second attack by French forces in 1693, native Germans of the Palatinate were themselves forced into exile and poverty. While England was not the first port of call, this was to change. In 1708, an Act for Naturalizing Foreign Protestants was passed. This Act made it possible for any alien to become naturalised if he or she was prepared to take certain oaths and communion, and to state publicly in court his or her support for the Protestant succession to the throne.[67] Thousands chose to do so. At the same time, increasing numbers of displaced Palatines found their way to England and by October 1709, approximately 13,000 German Palatines had arrived in England.[68] Unlike their French counterparts, the majority of Palatines were poor agriculturists with little to offer their host nation.

1.7

---

[63] Grotius, Book II, Ch. XXI, § v.

[64] A number of historians have documented the substantial contribution made by the Huguenots to the English economy: R. Gwynn, *Huguenot Heritage – The History and Contribution of the Huguenots in Britain* (London: Routledge, 1985); W.C. Scoville, 'The Huguenots and the Diffusion of Technology. I', (1952) 60 *Journal of Political Economy*, pp. 294–311; Baron F. de Schickler, *Eglises du refuge en Angleterre* (Paris, 1892); W.C. Scoville, *The Persecution of Huguenots and French Economic Development 1680–1720* (Berkeley and Los Angeles, 1960).

[65] Their contribution to William III's decisive victory over his father-in-law, James II, at the Battle of the Boyne in Ireland is best known.

[66] The Palatinate was the leading Protestant German state and head of the Protestant Union but was considerably weakened by the Thirty Years War (1618–1648) and by France (after 1685). In 1871, it was finally absorbed into the German Reich.

[67] A. Dummett and A. Nicol, *Subjects, Citizens, Aliens and Others* (London: Weidenfeld & Nicolson, 1990), p. 72.

[68] W. Cunningham, *Alien Immigrants to England*, (London: Sonnenschein, 1897), p. 252.

Though the British managed to send a proportion to New York, a significant number remained. These new migrants were decidedly unwelcome, despite their very evident suffering. Their poverty and dependence on their hosts debarred them from the hospitality accorded to the Huguenots. Many were despatched to a special camp erected on Blackheath and the considerable cost of maintenance was borne by the public purse.[69] Attempts to place some of the Palatines in a Kentish town resulted in displays of public disorder.[70]

The 1708 Naturalization Act, seen as the 'signal for a large incursion of destitute aliens' from the Palatinate,[71] was repealed in 1711 on the basis that 'divers mischiefs and inconveniences have been found by experience to follow from [the Naturalization Act], to the discouragement of natural-born subjects of this kingdom, and to the detriment of the trade and welfare thereof'.[72] Four decades later, memory of these events still lived on. In a House of Commons debate in 1748, the promoter of a second Bill on the Naturalization of Foreign Protestants invoked the Palatine incident as a salutary lesson: 'I do not desire that we should run into such an extravagant fit of charity as we ran into in the year 1708, when we not only passed a Bill for a general Naturalization of foreign Protestants, but put ourselves to a great expence in bringing over a number of poor Palatines, who could not be at the expence of transporting themselves; and who, when they arrived, were found to have neither industry nor ingenuity.'[73] Asylum, it was clear, had its price.

PROBLEMS OF REFUGEE STATUS: THE CASE OF THE JEWS

1.8   Having been the source of the term 'refugee', or '*réfugié*', the Huguenots had to some extent appropriated the refugee identity. The seventeenth century was not, however, simply a period of Protestant exiles; this is evident from the case of the German Palatines and also from the experience of the Jews. Despite their expulsion in 1290, Jews had still chosen, on occasion, to make their way to England; but their numbers were small and, in the light of Edward's decree and Elizabeth's laws against recusants, they were a secretive community.[74]

---

[69] In excess of £135,000 is the stated expenditure: W. Cunningham, *Alien Immigrants to England*, (London: Sonnenschein, 1897), p. 253.

[70] R. Gwynn, *Huguenot Heritage – The History and Contribution of the Huguenots in Britain* (London: Routledge, 1985), p. 124.

[71] W. Cunningham, *Alien Immigrants to England*, (London: Sonnenschein, 1897), p. 250.

[72] 10 Anne c. 5.

[73] *Parliamentary History of England*, February 4, 1748, cols. 138–139.

[74] See, *e.g.*, 35 Eliz. c. 1, which required conformity to and attendance at the English Church on pain of expulsion from the kingdom.

This was especially true of the Spanish and Portuguese, 'crypto-Jews' or New Christians, who gave the outward appearance of being Catholic but were in fact still true to their Jewish religion. From the fifteenth century onwards, this community was forced into exile by the Inquisition, though their chances of a happy existence in England under the reign of Henry VIII were severely jeopardised when the King assured the Spanish of his intention to prosecute any Jewish fugitive of the Inquisition found in his realm.[75] Under Elizabeth, the clandestine colony was apparently able to expand, only to be once more expelled by James I in 1609 following an internecine quarrel. The real period of their resurgence in England was during the reign of Charles I (1625–49), when Portugal recommenced its persecution of Marranos and many were once again forced to flee.[76] Though in theory still excluded from England, it is very probable that the majority of Spanish and Portuguese merchants living in the City of London were Marranos.[77]

Cromwell was evidently aware of the Marrano community, but chose to concentrate on the commercial advantages of their presence rather than follow an anti-Semitic course. Hopeful of formal legal and political endorsement, leading Marrano Jews petitioned the Lord Protector, calling for a repeal of the laws against Jews and the free exercise of Judaism. In November 1655, the Lord Protector laid the petition before the Council of State and, in the following month, the Council entered into a heated debate over the Jewish question (the 'Whitehall Conference'). In spite of Cromwell's indulgence towards the Marrano Jews,[78] the petition failed, due, once more, to protest voiced by English merchants and theologians. Merchants claimed that the readmission of Jews would harm English tradesmen whilst enriching the foreigner; theologians insisted that the public exercise of Judaism in a Christian country was blasphemous.[79]

It is notable that, at this time, there seems to have been some confusion as to the right of Jews to enter the British Isles. Some in the anti-Jewish lobby were of the view that Edward's expulsion order had been authorised by Act of Parliament and was therefore still applicable, the only problem being that the Act had disappeared and there

---

[75] C. Roth, *A History of the Jews* (Oxford: Clarendon Press, 1978), p. 136.

[76] *ibid.*, p. 158.

[77] However, see below for discussion on the legality of the supposed continued exclusion.

[78] Cromwell's support of the Marranos is best exemplified by his appeal to the King of Portugal for compensation on behalf of Manuel Martinez Dormido, a Marrano merchant ruined by Portugal's reconquest of Brazil: C. Roth, *A History of the Jews* (Oxford: Clarendon Press, 1978), p. 157.

[79] C. Roth, *A History of the Jews* (Oxford: Clarendon Press, 1978), p. 163.

was no record of its existence; it is likely, however, that there was never any Act and that the King issued a royal decree.[80] As stated by the Whitehall Conference, on the other hand, the legal position seemed clear: there was no law that forbade the Jews' return to England.[81] In reality, the bar to their admission was the inability to practise their religion freely. Furthermore, Chief Justice Coke's statement in *Calvin's Case* had not offered them much hope of a favourable reception: 'All infidels are in law *perpetui inimici*, perpetual enemies (for the law presumes not that they will be converted, that being *remota potentia*, a remote possibility) for between them, as with the devils, whose subjects they be, and the Christian, there is perpetual hostility, and can be no peace.'[82] As alien enemies, their rights were limited. Although Coke's comments were arguably *obiter dicta*, they were for some time applied as legal precedent and continued to discourage Jewish settlement in England, despite claims to persecution abroad.[83]

Relief came to the Jewish community in an unusual guise. Since the autumn of 1655, England had been at war with Spain. This placed the New Christians in a particularly precarious position since, as supposed Catholics, they faced possible reprisals from the native Protestants. However, the betrayal to the authorities in 1656 of a wealthy Marrano merchant, Antonio Rodrigues Robles, and the seizure of his property, led to an unanticipated upturn of fortune for the Marranos. Realising that their very existence could be threatened, the Marrano community decided on a united course of action, openly acknowledging their Jewishness and begging for Cromwell's protection. Relying on the deep anti-Catholic sentiment pervading the country at the time, Robles provided the Council of State with explicit details of the Inquisition's persecution of members of his family and their consequent death or injury. The Council yielded; Robles' identity as a refugee proved more important than his identity as a Jew. His property was returned, and the Jews assumed a legitimacy which had eluded them for centuries,[84] though it was another

---

[80] See, *e.g.*, H. Henriques, *The Jews and English Law* (London: Bibliophile Press, 1908), pp. 58–62.

[81] *ibid.*, p. 1.

[82] 7 Co. Rep. 1a, 17a.

[83] Coke's theory was overruled by the courts in 1697: H. Henriques, *The Jews and English Law* (London: Bibliophile Press, 1908), p. 189.

[84] C. Roth, *A History of the Jews* (Oxford: Clarendon Press, 1978), p. 166. This view is disputed by Henriques who suggests that Robles succeeded because it had not been proved that he was a Spaniard, and that the position of the Jews was wholly unaffected by the decision: pp. 105–106.

thirty years before they would be granted the free exercise of Judaism.[85]

The war with Spain was fundamental to the Robles decision. In other circumstances, it is doubtful whether the Council would have reached the same conclusion. Only months before, the Jewish petition had confronted a tide of protest. The Robles case attests to the importance of politics in the accord of refugee status. Where arguments based on humanity had failed, the power of politics prevailed.

INCREASING POLITICISATION: FROM '*RÉFUGIÉ*' TO '*ÉMIGRÉ*'

Political rather than religious strife was to provide the source of the   **1.9**
next notable group of asylum seekers: the exiles of revolutionary France. The French exiles, or *émigrés* as they were more commonly known, formed a diverse group. Described by one historian as 'émigrés of hatred, émigrés of faith, émigrés of fear, [. . .] émigrés of hunger, of accident, of pleasure, and, [. . .] émigrés without reason',[86] their motivations for leaving were diverse and they may not all have been in search of asylum. Furthermore, the very fact that these new migrants were described as '*émigrés*' rather than '*réfugiés*' is telling. There are two possible explanations for the emergence of this new term. Since '*réfugiés*' still described the Protestant Huguenots, expelled by Louis XIV, and many of the *émigrés* were Catholic Royalists, faithful to the French throne, they did not see their choice to leave France in the same light as the enforced removal of the Protestant Huguenots in the seventeenth century.[87] According to this view, these individuals assumed control over their new identity and chose a word that was less suggestive of vulnerability than '*réfugié*'. The second view asserts that the description '*émigré*' was imposed upon those departing by the revolutionary authorities in France and was thus 'a term of opprobrium'.[88] Whichever view is adopted, there is one major distinction between the '*émigrés*' and the earlier '*réfugiés*': almost all *émigrés* chose to return to France between July 27, 1794 (the fall of Robespierre) and April 26, 1802 (the general amnesty

[85] In the case of *De Wilton* v *Montefiore* [1900] 2 Ch 481, at 489–90, the judge refers to the legal time of resettlement of the Jews as 1685, following an order by the King to that effect.

[86] D. Greer, *The Incidence of the Emigration During the French Revolution* (Massachusetts: Peter Smith, 1951), p. 108.

[87] M. Marrus, *The Unwanted – European Refugees in the Twentieth Century* (New York: Oxford University Press, 1985), p. 9.

[88] A. Zolberg, A. Suhrke & S. Aguayo, *Escape from Violence: Conflict and the Refugee Crisis in the Developing World* (New York: Oxford University Press, 1989), p. 9.

offered by Bonaparte to the exiles). It is probable that 'the great majority of the *émigrés* were in France by the autumn of 1800'.[89] That so many returned differentiates the *émigré* from earlier asylum seekers; unlike the Huguenot, there was no intention permanently to sever links with their country of origin.[90]

Statistically, the Revolution was not of the same magnitude as the Edict of Nantes. Though the figures cannot be determined with absolute precision, Greer's careful study estimates that there were 129,099 official fugitives, and probably between 20,000 and 30,000 unofficial *émigrés*.[91] The British Isles appear to have borne the brunt, accepting about 40,000.[92] The first exodus from France was of the Royalists in 1789. They were soon followed by members of the militia, and the clergy. The *émigrés* were initially well-received by the British public which, on hearing tales of mob-rule and violence, and witnessing the abject poverty into which many *émigrés* were thrown,[93] were sympathetic towards their plight. Prime Minister Pitt's government also adopted a pro-royalist line, but for economic and political reasons. Battling against the crippling financial effects of the American Revolution, the government was anxious to avoid war and held that European peace was best preserved by the restoration of France's monarchy.[94]

Despite this stance, the government increasingly harboured a suspicion that undesirables were being sent over to England, claiming to be *émigrés* but whose real intent was 'to raise an insurrection, and overthrow the government'.[95] Thus by 1792, talk was of the need for aliens' legislation, the first in English history. During the debate on the ensuing Aliens Bill, Edmund Burke, the notable anti-revolutionary, captured the mood in a theatrical performance which saw him produce a dagger and hurl it to the floor:

---

[89] D. Greer, *The Incidence of the Emigration During the French Revolution* (Massachusetts: Peter Smith, 1951), p. 104.
[90] This notion of return is an early example of Joly's dual categorisation of refugees as those with a 'collective project in the land or origin' who view exile as a temporary measure, and those who choose to 'sever links with the society of origin'. D. Joly, *Haven or Hell? – Asylum Policies and Refugees in Europe* (London: Macmillan Press, 1996), pp. 154–9.
[91] D. Greer, *The Incidence of the Emigration During the French Revolution* (Massachusetts: Peter Smith,1951), p. 20.
[92] F. Wilson, *They came as Strangers – The Story of Refugees to Great Britain* (London: Hamish Hamilton, 1959), p. 101.
[93] See, *e.g.*, Comtesse de Boigne, *Memoirs* (Heinemann, 1907); Vicomte F. de Chateaubriand, *Mémoires D'Outre-tombe* (Paris, 1849–50).
[94] W. Cunningham, *Alien Immigrants to England*, (London: Sonnenschein, 1897), p. 256.
[95] *Parliamentary History of England*, December 21, 1792, Vol. XXX, col. 158.

'It is my object [. . .] to keep the French infection from this country; their principles from our minds, and their daggers from our hearts. I vote for this bill, because I consider it the means of saving my life and all our lives, from the hands of assassins [. . .]. When they smile, I see blood trickling down their faces; I see their insidious purposes; I see that the object of all their cajoling is – blood!'[96]

This despite any concrete evidence of actual violence initiated by the French refugees.[97] The few dissenting voices were drowned in the rush for legislation and, in 1793, an Act was implemented 'for establishing regulations respecting aliens arriving in this kingdom, or resident therein, in certain cases'.[98] No recognition was given to the peculiar plight of these asylum seekers, and they received neither mention nor dispensation under the law.

This Aliens Act has an important place in the history of British asylum policy. It was the first major statute enacted generally on the right of entry of aliens, and introduced certain concepts that were to be reflected in alien and asylum legislation over the next two hundred years. Included amongst its provisions were the power to refuse permission to land to 'aliens of any description'; registration of personal details with the Chief Magistrate by all aliens; the possibility of bail for any person who was 'not within the description limited by [the] act in the different cases [. . .] mentioned';[99] and a right of appeal within six days.[100] Since one of the main objectives of the Act was to ensure that foreigners were policed on entry and monitored during their stay in Britain, those arriving after January 10, 1793 gave to the port officer a written declaration of their names, rank or occupation as well as details on their place of residence while in the country. Failure to give such a declaration, or giving a false declaration, could lead to expulsion, transportation for life, or death if found within the realm after being sentenced to transportation.[101]

In a further notable precursor to twentieth century carriers' liability legislation, where carriers are fined if their passengers are not in possession of valid documentation, masters of vessels were required to declare on arrival the numbers, names and occupations of any foreigners on board their vessels. Failure to do so could incur a fine of £10.[102] Thus, as early as 1793, carriers were being called upon by the government to act as quasi-police in the area of migration. The Act

1.10

[96] *Parliamentary History of England*, December 28, 1792, vol. XXX, col. 189.
[97] *ibid.*, cols. 194–195.
[98] 33 Geo. 3, c. 4.
[99] Para. XXIII.
[100] Para. XXXIX and XL.
[101] Para. III and XXXVIII.
[102] Para. II.

went on to empower the King by proclamation or by order in council to direct that 'aliens of any description' be refused permission to
land if it were 'necessary for the safety or tranquillity of the kingdom'.[103] The wide range of powers in the Act – refusal to disembark,
fines, expulsion, and capital punishment – could prevent individuals
in genuine need of a safe haven from being granted asylum. The
potential impact of the legislation therefore went some way beyond
the original objective of protecting 'publick tranquillity'.

Though the Act itself was devoid of any reference to asylum, there
are signs that a change in attitude towards 'refugees' was taking place
at this time. In 1796, the third edition of the *Encyclopaedia Britannica*,
while ascribing the original application to the Huguenots, recognised
that the term 'refugee' had now 'been extended to all such as leave
their country in times of distress, and hence, since the revolt of the
British colonies in America, we have frequently heard of American
refugees'.[104] While the French persisted in distinguishing between the
Calvinist victims of the Edict of Nantes and the mainly Catholic
escapees of the Revolution, the process was already underway which
would see asylum develop into a uniform concept of international
application.

Academic contributions on the foundations of international law
and on asylum played an important role in guiding legal thinking.
Grotius' seventeenth-century *De jure belli ac pacis*, still an influential
text, supported a right to asylum, while Vattel, writing in 1758 in *Le
droit des gens ou principes de la loi naturelle*, was more guarded, offering a
judgement in some ways akin to present-day perceptions:

> '[. . .] a nation, whose territory could scarcely supply the needs of its citi-
> zens, is not bound to receive a body of fugitives or exiles. It ought even to
> refuse them absolutely if they are infected with some contagious disease.
> So also it has the right to send them off elsewhere if it has good reason to
> fear that they will corrupt the morals of its citizens, or cause religious dis-
> turbances or any form of disorder hurtful to the public welfare. In a word,
> it has the right, and is even obliged, to follow in this matter the rules of pru-
> dence. But this prudence should not take the form of suspicion nor be
> pushed to the point of refusing an asylum to the outcast on slight grounds
> and from unreasonable or foolish fears.'[105]

In maintaining its sovereign right to exclude the *émigrés*, the 1793
Act was in line with Vattel's assertion that any threat to the public

---

[103] Para. VII.
[104] Cited in M. Marrus, *The Unwanted – European Refugees in the Twentieth Century* (New York: Oxford University Press, 1985), p. 8.
[105] Vattel, iii, 92 [§ 231], cited in A. Grahl-Madsen, *The Status of Refugees in International Law*, Vol. II (Leiden: Sijthoff, 1972), p. 14.

good justifies a refusal to enter; the unanswered question is whether the Act was itself introduced on the basis of 'unreasonable or foolish fears'. Prior to the legislation, there had been no French-inspired insurrection or any evidence of a genuine threat to the United Kingdom's security. Accordingly, the acceptance of approximately 40,000 *émigrés* suggests that the new law was not abused and that individuals were on the whole authorised to disembark. A number of expulsions were, however, made: between 1793 and 1800, 436 aliens were removed from the kingdom.[106] It is known that Talleyrand, ex-President of the French Assembly, was banished from England and spent the rest of his exile in America. It was his own view that he was expelled simply to prove the effectiveness of the Aliens Act.[107]

The omission of any reference to asylum in the statute of 1793 was remedied in subsequent legislation on aliens.[108] By 1798, the growing acknowledgement of a right of asylum was reflected in the new Act for Establishing Regulations Respecting Aliens.[109] In its lengthy preamble, the Act noted:

'[. . .] and whereas the refuge and asylum which on grounds of humanity and justice, have been granted to persons flying from the oppression and tyranny exercised in France, and in countries invaded by the armies of France, [. . .] may [. . .] be abused by persons coming to this kingdom for purposes dangerous to the interests and safety thereof; [. . .] it is therefore necessary to make further provisions for the safety of this kingdom with respect to aliens, and particularly to the end that a just distinction may be made between persons who either really seek refuge and asylum from oppression and tyranny, [. . .] and persons who, pretending to claim the benefit of such refuge and asylum [. . .] have or shall come to [. . .] this kingdom with hostile purposes [. . .].'

The recognition of the importance of a safe refuge is clearly offset here by talk of 'abuse' of the asylum process. That eighteenth-century legislators should be employing terminology now widely used to justify stringent asylum laws is striking. Other than in the preamble, no further mention is made of refuge and asylum, and there is no adoption in the Act of the word 'refugee'; the term 'aliens' continued to be applied to all non-British subjects, whatever their motivation for entry.

---

[106] Return of number of Resident Aliens, 1793–1816. In 1803, it was reported that the King issued a proclamation ordering 1,700 French aliens to quit the country but not being permitted to land on the continent, they returned and were allowed to remain.

[107] W. Cunningham, *Alien Immigrants to England*, (London: Sonnenschein, 1897), p. 257.

[108] The 1793 Act only lasted for one year but was replaced at frequent intervals by similar statutes.

[109] 38 Geo. III c. 50.

1.11   This 1798 Act nonetheless marks a significant advance in recognising the importance of the principle of asylum for those who 'really seek refuge [. . .] from oppression and tyranny'. Communications between the governments of the United Kingdom and France provide further evidence of an evolving 'right' of asylum at this time. In 1802, the Secretary of State, Lord Hawkesbury, writing to his government's Paris representative, set out the UK's position. Responding to calls by the French for the removal of notable *émigrés*, and in particular the Bourbon princes, Hawkesbury stated: 'His majesty has no desire that they should continue to reside in this country, if they are disposed, or can be induced, to quit it; but he feels it to be inconsistent with his honour, and his sense of justice, to withdraw from them the rights of hospitality, as long as they conduct themselves peaceably and quietly.'[110] Though reference to the King's 'honour' and 'sense of justice' sets the refusal in a highly subjective frame, this may be regarded as an early example of the twentieth-century principle of international refugee law known as *non-refoulement*.[111]

Whereas fugitives in the reign of Elizabeth I had been primarily religious exiles, the specifically political nature of the claims for refuge by the *émigrés* added a new dimension to asylum policy. Britain, by accepting such asylum seekers, sought to point up the divide between the freedom exercised by its own subjects and the oppression faced by many French men and women. Asylum assumed importance not only as a humanitarian principle, but also as a mark of the democratic and civilised state, as evidenced by Lord Hawkesbury's response in 1802 to France's request for the expulsion of *émigrés*:

'But the French government must have formed a most erroneous judgment of the disposition of the British nation, and of the character of its government, if they have been taught to expect that any representation of a foreign power will ever induce them to consent to a violation of those rights on which the liberties of the people of this country are founded [. . .].'[112]

---

[110] Cited in *British Digest of International Law*, Vol. 6, p. 47.
[111] 1951 Convention Relating to the Status of Refugees, Art. 33(1): 'No Contracting State shall expel or return ("refouler") a refugee in any manner whatsoever to the frontiers of territories where his life or freedom would be threatened on account of his race, religion, nationality, membership of a particular social group or political opinion.'
[112] Cited in *BDIL*, Vol. 6, p. 48.

GREAT BRITAIN'S ASYLUM POLICY: AN EXPRESSION OF
NINETEENTH-CENTURY LIBERALISM?

Legislative change

In keeping with Lord Hawkesbury's remarks, various debates on alien   **1.12**
laws in the early nineteenth century reveal a slow change in attitude
towards asylum. This was particularly evident in the case of deportation. During the Napoleonic Wars with France (1800–1815), there
was considerable support for continuing the statutory restrictions on
aliens. Cessation of hostilities did not lead to an immediate revision
of alien policy; rather, the Alien Acts were repeatedly repealed and
re-introduced in amended form until 1826. At this time, statistics suggested that provision for deportation in the Alien Acts was becoming
redundant; from 1801 to 1815, only 218 aliens were removed; for the
period 1816 to 1823, the figure fell to just 17.[113] From 1816, it was
clear that a difference of opinion was emerging between the Tory
government and Whig opposition over the need for alien legislation:
the government supported the continuation of the Alien Act, while
opposition members of Parliament argued for the removal of all
measures against foreigners, including expulsion:

> 'In 1802, the measure had been defended on account of the establishment
> of Bonaparte in his power; in 1814 the "revolutionary demon" was still
> abroad; in 1818 the evacuation of the French fortresses was the neces-
> sity, on account of the restoration of the Bourbons; and in 1820, lord
> Londonderry had argued for its enactment on account of certain elements
> of mischief which he had stated were at work on the continent. All these
> causes had now ceased [. . .].'[114]

The argument for revocation finally won the day and, in 1826, an
act was introduced for the Registration of Aliens.[115] Though it contained provisions similar to the act of 1793, no expulsion power was
included. In 1836, the act was repealed and replaced by yet another
Alien Registration Act.[116] Similar in kind to its predecessor, its distinguishing feature was its durability; it remained on the statute books
until repeal in 1905.[117] This reluctance in the1820s and 30s to retain

---

[113] Return of Number of Resident Aliens, 1793–1816; Return of Number of Persons
sent out of UK under Alien Act, 1816–1819; Return of Number of Aliens directed
to depart Realm, 1850. Note: the statistics conflict for some years.

[114] HC Deb. Vol. 1023, March 1824, cols. 1350–51.

[115] 7 Geo. IV c. 54.

[116] 6 & 7 Will. IV, c. 11.

[117] Aliens Act 1905, s.10(2).

the power of deportation developed into antipathy in subsequent decades towards any form of restrictive legislation on aliens. By the 1850s, political – and, it seems, public – opinion was against an alien act;[118] the attempt in 1858 by Lord Palmerston to implement a Conspiracy Bill, aimed at refugees plotting attacks on European rulers, succeeded in bringing down the government. In a country where the treatment of foreigners had historically oscillated between grudging acceptance and violent hostility, the trend now seemed to be in favour of a liberal policy on refugees.

Public perceptions of exile

1.13   From Porter's detailed analysis, *The Refugee Question in Mid-Victorian Politics*, it is clear that the reasons for changing British attitudes towards the alien, and the refugee in particular, were multifaceted and complex.[119] Part of the issue was that the refugees themselves constituted a highly disparate group. Many were engaged in political struggles in their home countries; a minority were not. Porter notes:

> 'Some of them were exiles by decree – "*proscrits*". Others were deposed kings and royalists, or the remnants of failed revolutionary armies, or escapees from prisons abroad. A few of them were refugees more by choice: men who had chosen to live elsewhere rather than obey régimes they disagreed with, or who anticipated that harm would come to them if they stayed, and so fled before the need arose.'[120]

While religion was not again to be the impetus for mass migration until the last decades of the nineteenth century, the political ground for flight had become an important component of Britain's liberal policy on asylum. The United Kingdom at this time contrasted its own democracy and prosperity with the turbulent state of affairs in many countries on the continent.[121] Britain was 'advancing' while across the Channel there was a 'downward and backward movement'.[122] Any policy that distinguished it from unruly Europe was therefore to be encouraged. Despite frequent warnings from the continent of the dangers of harbouring political criminals, the British seemed now to consider their country immune to subversion by

---

[118] B. Porter, *The Refugee Question in Mid-Victorian Politics* (Cambridge: Cambridge University Press, 1979), pp. 119–120.

[119] *ibid.*

[120] *ibid.*, p. 1.

[121] *ibid.*, pp. 104–5.

[122] HC Deb. Vol. 148, February 19, 1858, col. 1819

foreigners.[123] 'A really good Government,' declared *The Times* in 1853 'can afford not to mind them'.[124] Of course, it was easier to ignore the refugees when their numbers were relatively few: in 1851, 50,289 foreigners (excluding Irish and Scots) were recorded resident in England and Wales, rising to 100,638 in 1871.[125] According to Porter, their limited numbers ensured that they did not 'present any great social problems which were not easily and locally resolvable'.[126]

This last proposition is open to some qualification. Without doubt, the majority of refugees faced poverty and hardship while in Britain. Perhaps the most wretched group were the Poles, refugees from the struggles for independence against Russia. In a statement to the House of Commons in 1838, Viscount Sandon reported that:

> '[. . .] on railroads and public works, Colonels and others of high rank might be found working as common labourers, but being strangers, speaking a strange language, and having few facilities of obtaining employment, the great majority were left to wander starving about the streets. In the police reports accounts would be found of Poles taken in the act of sleeping under our porticos and at our hall doors and such other places of shelter as chance threw in their way.'[127]

In 1834, the government had offered an annual grant of £10,000 for relief of the Poles; over time, however, the amount diminished.[128] Monetary appeals were made to the public but they were not well supported. It would seem that in two-nation Victorian Britain, there was little to distinguish between the poverty of the foreign refugees and that of the poorer elements of the British; though they swelled the population of the destitute, they did not do so in sufficient numbers to warrant a public outcry or any specific policy to address their plight.

By 1850, however, public patience was wearing thin, as evidenced by a contribution to *The Times* criticising preparations for a charity ball in aid of Polish refugees:

---

[123] B. Porter, *The Refugee Question in Mid-Victorian Politics* (Cambridge: Cambridge University Press, 1979), pp. 91; 104.

[124] *The Times*, February 28, 1853, p. 4.

[125] *1851 Census Great Britain, Ages, Civil Condition, Occupations and Birthplaces*, Vol. I. P. ci; *1871 Census England & Wales, Ages, Civil Condition, Occupations and Birthplaces*, p. l.

[126] B. Porter, *The Refugee Question in Mid-Victorian Politics* (Cambridge: Cambridge University Press, 1979), p. 4.

[127] HC Deb. Vol. 44, July 27, 1838, col. 731.

[128] HC Deb. Vol. 55, August 3, 1840, col. 1221; The maximum granted was £15,000 in 1837. By 1862, only £3,062 was offered to Polish refugees and distressed Spaniards: HC Deb. Vol. 168, July 21, 1862, col. 592.

'The truth is that the strong sympathy which has always been felt for the wrongs and ruin of Poland does not, and very justly does not, embrace the Polish refugees for whose benefit this ball is to be given. It is now nineteen years since the termination of the war of independence. Those who sought this country as an asylum from the unrelenting persecution of Russia have had ample time to adapt themselves to their new situation, and to turn their energies to the less brilliant but equally honourable career of private industry.'[129]

1.14   In highlighting the waning compassion for the refugees, the commentator also points to an aspect of British attitudes towards asylum seekers in the mid-nineteenth century, as in earlier periods. There is a hint that the true sympathy lay not with the exiles and their sufferings, but with the *causes* for which they fought. The greater the romanticism surrounding their exploits, the better their reception in the United Kingdom. Certain celebrated revolutionary figures of the period were revered by the British as heroes; the Italian Garibaldi and the Hungarian Kossuth were particularly fêted. Yet neither Garibaldi[130] nor Kossuth[131] could be described as true refugees; their trips to Britain were as visitors rather than asylum seekers. 'He was adored by the gentry and middle classes,' writes Francesca Wilson of Garibaldi, 'and by the common people, for he was a commoner like themselves. In the north of England, where the miners had flocked onto his ship to hand him a sword, my Quaker grandmother wrote him fan-mail letters and received a lock of his hair [. . .] Over our nursery mantelpiece there was a huge portrait of him standing defiantly on the rock of Caprera.'[132]

Such idolatry was the exception. The Russian refugee, Alexander Herzen, provided detailed accounts of the strained relationship that existed between the British and refugee. 'The Englishman,' he noted, 'has no special love for foreigners, still less for exiles, whom he regards as guilty of poverty, a vice he does not forgive – but he clings to his right of asylum; he does not permit it to be touched with impunity, any more than the right of public meeting and the freedom of the

---

[129] *The Times*, October 28, 1850, p. 4.

[130] Garibaldi was required to leave Italy after attempting to seize Genoa in 1834, and again in 1849 after joining the revolutionary government in Rome. In May 1860, he sailed with his 'thousand volunteers' and helped Mazzini's rebels to free Sicily from Neapolitan control; it was a decisive moment in the creation of the Kingdom of Italy.

[131] Kossuth had been appointed governor of Hungary following the revolution of 1848–9 when Hungary attempted to secede from Austria. He was forced into flight when Austria, with the aid of the Russians, was able to quell the uprising.

[132] F. Wilson, *They came as Strangers – The Story of Refugees to Great Britain* (London: Hamish Hamilton, 1959), p. 109.

press.'[133] Herzen went on to observe acidly that England was 'an alien and inimical country that did not conceal that it maintained its right of asylum for the sake of its own self respect, and not for the sake of those who sought it.'[134] *The Times* of the period exemplified the prevailing dichotomy. On the one hand, it carried articles brimming with self-congratulation: 'Every civilised people on the face of the earth must be fully aware that this country is the asylum of nations, and that it will defend the asylum to the last ounce of its treasure, and the last drop of its blood. There is no point on which we are prouder or more resolute. [. . .] We are a nation of refugees.'[135] On the other hand, *The Times* was equally capable of publishing invectives against refugees assumed to be propagating their revolutionary message: 'If England is still to be the favoured receptacle of all the scum and refuse which the continental revolutions have thrown up, it will be just as well, by a few stringent measures of sanitary precaution, to provide against the moral pestilence which a neglected accumulation of such refuse must inevitably produce.'[136]

Government policy

Until 1848, and the outbreak of revolution across Europe, the continent had been forced into grudging acceptance of British intransigence over the asylum issue. The harbouring of political exiles following the 1848 uprisings gave rise to more direct confrontation. Unable to comprehend the United Kingdom's refusal to deport on request certain notorious political figures, European states began to suspect an ulterior motive: Britain, intent on causing widespread disruption, was forming an alliance with the refugees against the continent. The perceived aim was the liberalisation of Europe.[137] Paradoxically, while these suspicions were brewing overseas, Britain, for the first time in over forty years, began to anticipate the threat of revolution. In this period of unease, a new Alien Act was rushed through parliament with large majorities in both houses. It granted power to the government to expel any alien 'when and so often as

1.15

---

[133] Alexander Herzen, *My Past and Thoughts – The Memoirs of Alexander Herzen*, Vol. III (London: Chatto & Windus, 1968), p. 1112.

[134] *ibid.*, p. 1052.

[135] *The Times*, February 28, 1853, p. 4.

[136] *The Times*, November 28, 1849, p. 8. In this letter, an irate correspondent lambasted a certain German refugee who, it was suggested, had been attempting to incite revolution.

[137] B. Porter, *The Refugee Question in Mid-Victorian Politics* (Cambridge: Cambridge University Press, 1979), pp. 50; 57.

One of Her Majesty's Principal Secretaries [had] Reason to believe
[. . .] that for the Preservation of the Peace and Tranquillity of any
Part of this Realm it [was] expedient to remove therefrom any
Alien.'[138] The concern proved unwarranted. The Act lapsed in the
summer of 1850 and was, during its lifetime, never implemented.[139]

Austria, particularly aggrieved at Kossuth's rapturous welcome in
Britain, attempted to push France and Prussia into more radical
action. France, though sympathetic towards Austria, was not willing
to engage in outright hostilities against Britain, at least not until
the Orsini Plot of 1858. On January 14, 1858, a bomb exploded in
the Rue Lepelletier in Paris; the target had been Napoleon III. The
Emperor survived, but a number of Parisians were killed or maimed.
The chief protagonists, Orsini and Pierri, had lived in England just
prior to the assassination attempt and had used bombs constructed in
Birmingham. From across Europe, letters of condemnation poured
into Britain. France's reaction was, understandably, the most violent.
As Britain's erstwhile ally in the Crimean War, France complained in
bitter terms to the Foreign Office through its Foreign Affairs Minister,
Count Walewski:

'[. . .] assassination [has been] elevated to doctrine, preached openly,
practised in repeated attempts, the most recent of which has just struck
Europe with amazement. Ought, then, the right of asylum to protect
such a state of things? Is hospitality due to assassins? Ought the English
legislation to contribute to favour their designs and their plans, and can
it continue to shelter persons who, by their flagrant acts, place themselves beyond the pale of common right and under the banner of
humanity?'[140]

The government now confronted its most serious crisis over the
refugee issue – a real possibility of war. On the one hand, the authorities had no special love of foreigners, particularly in view of the
problems they could cause in international relations; on the other
hand, members of the government still adhered strongly to a liberal
asylum policy and lacked the power to deport. Though an extradition
agreement had been entered into with France in 1852, containing a
list of extraditable offences, it included an exception for political
offences; it failed, in any event, to be incorporated into English law

---

[138] 11 & 12 Vict., c. 20, Preamble.
[139] It was re-enacted for Ireland alone in 1882 for three years: Prevention of Crime
(Ireland) Act 1882, 45 & 46 Vict., c. 25, s. 15.
[140] Count Walewski, French Minister of Foreign Affairs, to Lord Clarendon, Foreign
Office, January 20, 1858: Papers respecting Foreign Refugees, Presented to
Parliament, 1858, cited in *BDIL*, Vol. 6, p. 57.

and was therefore unenforceable.[141] With patience wearing thin on the continent, a placatory gesture was urgently required. Any suggestion that a new, punitive alien act ought to be introduced was, however, swiftly dismissed. Lord Brougham, in a House of Lords debate on the state of public affairs, reiterated Parliament's strong commitment to the principle of *non-refoulement*: 'The old Alien Act was attended with many abuses and grievances, one of which was the sending parties abroad to the very places from which they had escaped, so that they were hurled, as it were, into the lion's mouth.'[142] Yet some legislation was called for and it appeared in the form of the Conspiracy to Murder Bill, drafted only two weeks after the Orsini *attentat*.[143]

Though Palmerston was keen to stress that this was not an alien bill,[144] and though there was no provision for expulsion, the Conspiracy Bill was viewed as a capitulation to France's demands for action, and in particular to Walewski's indignant pleas for 'measures' to be enacted by the Cabinet.[145] If the Bill were passed, argued Sir Robert Peel (son) for the Opposition, it would 'entail shame and degradation on [the] House and on the country'.[146] It did not assist the Cabinet that, in its haste to pass the Bill, it apparently failed to respond formally in writing to Walewski's despatch, thereby compounding the impression that the Bill did constitute the government's response. Seizing his opportunity to discredit Palmerston, a member of the opposition benches introduced an amendment in the following terms: 'This House, [. . .] deems it inexpedient to legislate in compliance with the demand made in Count Walewski's despatch of January 20, until further information is before it of the communications between the two governments subsequent to the date of that despatch.'[147] This device drew across to the opposition 135 Members of Parliament who had supported the Bill on its first reading.[148] The Bill collapsed and the following day Palmerston's government resigned. For the first time in British history, the question of the right to asylum had

1.16

---

[141] Parliament objected to a clause waving the need to provide evidence before the committing magistrate: *BDIL*, Vol. 6, p. 447.

[142] HL Deb. Vol. 148, February 4, 1858, col. 711.

[143] The Conspiracy to Murder Bill was in fact relatively benign, aiming to increase the sanction for conspiracy to murder to between five years and life for penal servitude.

[144] HC Deb. Vol. 148, February 19, 1858, col. 1741–3.

[145] Count Walewski, French Minister of Foreign Affairs, to Lord Clarendon, Foreign Office, January 20, 1858, cited in *BDIL*, Vol. 6, p. 57.

[146] HC Deb. Vol. 148, February 19, 1858, col. 1792.

[147] HC Deb. Vol. 148, February 8, 1858, col. 939.

[148] B. Porter, *The Refugee Question in Mid-Victorian Politics* (Cambridge: Cambridge University Press, 1979), p. 183.

assumed sufficient political importance to result in the fall of a government.

Appeasement of France now fell to the newly elected government, under Lord Derby. Without any recourse to alien legislation, the government fell back on its existing internal laws to deal with the crisis. In February 1858, the police arrested a French refugee doctor, Simon Bernard, who was based in England and who was suspected of major involvement in the Orsini Affair. He was charged with being an accessory to murder, which, if proved, carried the death penalty. The trial was a *cause célèbre*. The political consequences of the verdict were potentially far-reaching. Alexander Herzen, who was present throughout the trial, notes that 'The French Government and the English Ministry took colossal steps to secure Bernard's conviction; the trial cost the two governments as much as thirty thousand pounds sterling, that is 750,000 francs. A gang of French spies stayed in London [. . .].'[149] It seems that few thought Bernard would escape.[150] But the defence, in the hands of Edwin James, concentrated their efforts on the political aspects of the case rather than on the factual evidence. This ploy worked. A verdict of 'not guilty' was returned, and the court erupted with cheers and applause, a spectacle rarely witnessed at the Old Bailey. As Herzen put it, this marked 'a fresh triumph of her [England's] liberty'.[151]

The French authorities realised that Britain would now remain intransigent on the refugee question. Faced with war as the only remaining alternative, France backed down. Anglo-French relations were temporarily soured by the whole Orsini fiasco but its significance faded with time. The lasting legacy of the Orsini Affair lay not in its harm to international diplomacy but in its impact on domestic policy. Asylum had undoubtedly become a political issue of some import. The Affair sent a clear message to the government: 'to try to change or even to enforce English laws against refugees at the request of continental governments was just not worth the candle.'[152] For the next twenty years, no British government took steps to propose new aliens' legislation. An Extradition Act entered into in 1870 specifically guaranteed the protection of political offenders against extradition: 'A fugitive criminal shall not be surrendered if the offence in respect of

---

[149] Alexander Herzen, *My Past and Thoughts – The Memoirs of Alexander Herzen*, Vol. III (London: Chatto & Windus, 1968), p. 1116.
[150] *ibid.*, p. 1117.
[151] *ibid.*, p. 1123.
[152] B. Porter, *The Refugee Question in Mid-Victorian Politics* (Cambridge: Cambridge University Press, 1979), p. 199.

which his surrender is demanded is one of a political character [. . .]'.[153]

This apparent readiness of the British government to push its European neighbours to the brink of war over the refugee question is perhaps the most remarkable episode in nineteenth-century asylum policy. More than just being, as Porter puts it, part of the whole laissez-faire philosophy of Victorian society,[154] it arose from a combination of four vital elements: the political expediency of maintaining liberal asylum laws; a sense of difference and superiority over continental neighbours; unusual economic growth and stability; and the numerical insignificance of refugees to Britain. There was little prospect that all four factors would continue to co-exist; change was therefore inevitable, as was the consequent impact on asylum policy.

CONCLUSION

Sometimes viewed with scepticism or fear, sometimes accepted   **1.17** grudgingly, always perceived as alien, asylum seekers to the British Isles have, throughout history, faced an uncertain welcome. From the apparent inconsistency of their treatment one constant emerges: that the real motive for admission of refugees has been grounded in politics or economics rather than in humanity. Elizabeth I chose to admit those with whom her country held a religious affinity, recognising in time the advantages of their industry and technological skills. The acceptance of the Marrano Jews during the time of Cromwell had more to do with entrenched anti-Catholicism than with protection of an oppressed minority. Political exiles of the nineteenth century provided an opportunity for an increasingly powerful Britain to advance the principle of asylum as a measure of the superiority and stability of its own democratic structures.

The industrious and beneficial Huguenots, to whom we owe the term 'refugee', set a high standard for those who follow. Refugee status had to be earned and failure to do so resulted in a different designation – '*émigré*', 'alien' or 'immigrant' – and even exclusion. Thus one sees the poverty of the Palatines leading to resentment and ultimately restrictive legislation. The claim by so many politicians over the past two hundred years that this country accepts refugees as a moral duty[155] owes more to nostalgic imagining than fact. As Arthur

---

[153] Extradition Act 1870, 33 & 34 Vict. c. 52, s. 3(1).
[154] B. Porter, *The Refugee Question in Mid-Victorian Politics* (Cambridge: Cambridge University Press, 1979), pp. 8–9.
[155] See, *e.g.*, Roy Hattersley, HC Deb. Vol. 198, November 5, 1991, col. 373.

James Balfour observed, with incisive honesty, to the House of
Commons in 1905, 'The truth [is] that the only immemorial right of
asylum given by this country was to allow aliens in with whom the
country agreed.'[156]

---

[156] HC Deb. Vol. 147, July 10, 1905, col. 156.

Chapter Two

UK Asylum Law 1900–1945: Piecemeal Control

INTRODUCTION

As the twentieth century dawned, it became clear that the UK was **2.1** facing one of its most difficult migration issues ever – the arrival of Jews from Eastern Europe and Russia. The liberal approach to asylum, which was so much in evidence in the nineteenth century, no longer seemed appropriate. Nor did the somewhat redundant statutes, legacies of a bygone era, appear capable of responding to a rapid rise in the numbers of new arrivals. New legislation and more restrictive entry policies were soon accepted as the only viable options. Despite various attempts at aliens legislation in the past, the forging of a modern and effective law was a novel departure and one fraught with difficulty.

How such law was implemented, and how a new policy emerged in relation to refugees in the first few decades of the twentieth century, is the subject of this chapter. It will trace the development of a modern form of UK refugee law from the tentative beginnings of the Aliens Act 1905 through the growing restrictionism of the 1930s and 40s to the immigration-focused post-war framework. Through the analysis of statutory material, relevant case-law, parliamentary debates and Home Office practice, it will consider legal and political reactions to various groups of twentieth-century asylum seekers arriving in the UK. The chapter will conclude with an assessment of the UK's record in relation to asylum seekers and refugees in this early period.[1]

---

[1] As in Chapter 1, the terms 'asylum seeker' and 'refugee' are used in their broader, non-legal sense, unless otherwise indicated.

THE DAWN OF THE MODERN ERA: ASYLUM SEEKERS AS A
NEW CHALLENGE

2.2   The combined effects of a weakening British economy and political
upheavals in Eastern Europe in the 1870s and 1880s were to have a
dramatic impact on migration and on the generosity of British asylum policy. The first major wave of the new emigration occurred in
1881, following the assassination of Tsar Alexander II of Russia by a
Polish student and the onset of a series of pogroms against the Jews.
The migrants were Germans, Russians and Poles, mainly of Jewish
extraction. It is estimated that approximately 2.5 million Jews left
Eastern Europe for the West between the early 1880s and 1914.[2]
Marrus, in his study of European refugees in the twentieth century,
cautions against labelling these Jewish emigrants as 'refugees', since
their circumstances and motivations for leaving their homelands varied widely.[3] Yet it seems clear that a large number chose to seek new
havens as a result of increasing anti-Semitic activities. For this reason,
other commentators do ascribe the definition 'refugee' to the East
European and Russian Jews who reached Britain.[4] The numbers
arriving in the UK between 1880 and 1914 are difficult to quantify.
One estimate stands at 120,000 East European Jews;[5] another suggests that net immigration from 1881 to 1883 was some 5,000 to
6,000 per year, falling to between 2,000 and 3,000 by 1884, and that,
with the exception of 1886, numbers remained low until 1890, when
Jews were expelled from Moscow and other major cities.[6]

A census conducted in 1901 revealed that foreigners constituted a
tiny percentage of the total population of England and Wales:
339,000 out of 32,000,000.[7] Yet the popular impression was of a
'horde' or 'invasion'. Sir Howard Vincent, MP for Sheffield and vocif-
erously anti-alien, is reported to have claimed that the immigrants
were setting foot on British soil 'in battalions and taking the bread out
of the mouths [. . .] of English wives and children'.[8] It is clear that

---

[2] M. Marrus, *The Unwanted – European Refugees in the Twentieth Century* (New York: Oxford
University Press, 1985), p. 27.

[3] *ibid.*

[4] B. Gainer, *The Alien Invasion – the Origins of the Aliens Act of 1905* (London: Heinemann,
1972), preface.

[5] M. Marrus, *The Unwanted – European Refugees in the Twentieth Century* (New York: Oxford
University Press, 1985), pp. 36–37.

[6] B. Gainer, *The Alien Invasion – the Origins of the Aliens Act of 1905* (London: Heinemann,
1972), p. 3.

[7] *ibid.*, p. 2.

[8] *Evening News*, May 9, 1891, cited in B. Gainer, *The Alien Invasion* (London: Heinemann,
1972), p. 6.

there was confusion and disagreement about the statistics, despite the call by the 1888–89 Select Committee on Emigration and Immigration (Foreigners) for the reintroduction of measures similar to those contained in the 1836 Alien Registration Act to record the arrivals and details of alien passengers.[9] These, it was claimed, had 'to a very great extent been allowed to fall into desuetude'.[10] The Board of Trade, responsible for compiling the figures, published two sets: the first, a complete list of annual emigration and immigration; the second, a monthly list of arrivals and departures from the European continent, known as the Alien List. Much of the disagreement centred on the use of the Alien List, particularly in relation to transmigration traffic. The anti-restriction lobby pointed out that, though the Alien List divided migrants into those *en route* to countries outside the UK and those not stated to be *en route*, the division was fallacious: a large number of so-called settlers emigrated despite stating that they were not *en route*. One anti-restriction campaigner claimed that, from 1896 to 1902, 423,681 foreigners were entered on the Alien List as *en route*, while 702,891 were ascertained to have proceeded to countries outside Europe, the implication being that 279,210 foreigners, who had been labelled as settlers, 'belied their name by proceeding abroad'.[11] Even the Home Secretary of 1904, Aretas Akers-Douglas, who announced the immigration figures for 1901 and 1902 as 81,000 and 82,000 respectively,[12] was accused of showing 'a deplorable ignorance of the very Government statistics which he purported to quote'.[13] His figures had been taken from the Alien Lists, and had failed to identify all passengers *en route* to countries outside Europe. Arguably, the more accurate statistics were 8,950 for 1901 and 8,700 for 1902, once account was taken of all immigration to and emigration from the UK, and of sailors who left the country as crew.[14]

While the 'numbers game' was used to effect by those opposed to the arrival of foreigners, it was not the only factor which led to the further politicisation of the alien issue: unemployment, poverty, overcrowding and the sweating system all had a major part to play.[15] As

2.3

---

[9] Second report, Proceedings and Minutes of Evidence, 1889 (311) Vol. X, p. xi.

[10] *ibid.*, p. iv.

[11] F. Bradshaw & C. Emanual, *Alien Immigration – Should Restrictions be imposed?* (London: Isbister & Co., 1904), p. 142.

[12] HC Deb. Vol. 133, April 25, 1904, col. 1065.

[13] F. Bradshaw & C. Emanual, *Alien Immigration – Should Restrictions be imposed?* (London: Isbister & Co., 1904), p. 136.

[14] HC Deb. Vol. 133, April 25, 1904, cols. 1065–66; see, for a general discussion on statistical misinterpretation, HC Deb. Vol. 145, May 2, 1905, cols. 689–698.

[15] Sweating was the system by which cheap factory clothing was handed over for completion to sub-contractors who hired small numbers of employees for long hours and very low wages.

the long-standing site of small trades such as cheap tailoring, and one of the worst slums in Western Europe even prior to immigration,[16] the East End of London, and particularly the Borough of Stepney, acted as a focal point for new arrivals. As unemployment grew, especially in the years 1885–7 and 1892, an easy target for blame was sought and found: migration. Shoemakers and tailors, two major trades of the East European community, were cited as typical examples. The argument ran as follows: the advent of large numbers of Jews into the East End had resulted in the introduction of sweating[17] and the production of goods of low quality; this, in turn, had led to a decline in export of shoes and clothes as well as the displacement of the native population employed in such trades. Unemployed Jewish cobblers and tailors, in their search for employment, were further blamed for taking the jobs of other workers, such as dockers. In fact, in so far as export trade was concerned, the opposite was true: exports from the mid-1870s onwards grew steadily.[18] The impact on job displacement of migration to the East End is more difficult to establish. In his book, *The Alien Invasion*, Gainer argues that immigrant labour had a minimal effect on the East End worker and that sweating did not contribute to growing unemployment:

'The confusion of displacement with the sweating system – which was no system, but a catch-all term for every abuse which victimized the worker – caused much of the bitterness and misconceptions in the mind of the East End working man. The most pernicious misconception of all was that sweating among aliens injured British artisans.'[19]

Displacement was not only the charge in relation to employment but was also pressed on the issue of housing. From evidence given to the Royal Commission on Alien Immigration in 1903, it is clear that some British residents blamed the foreigner for the rise in rents and rates, for driving out British families from certain areas, and for the problems of overcrowding.[20] Overcrowding was, for many, the major complaint against the alien; the Royal Commission itself described overcrowding as 'the most difficult question to be dealt with in

---

[16] C. Nicolson, *Strangers to England – Immigration to England 1100–1952* (London: Wayland Publishers, 1974), p. 100.

[17] For contemporary views on sweating, see the Royal Commission on Alien Immigration, 1903, II, Minutes of Evidence, Cd. 1742.

[18] B. Gainer, *The Alien Invasion – the Origins of the Aliens Act of 1905* (London: Heinemann, 1972), p. 24.

[19] *ibid.*, p. 26.

[20] See, *e.g.*, the evidence of Alderman James Lawson Silver, the Royal Commission on Alien Immigration, 1903, II, Minutes of Evidence, Cd. 1742, Mins. 2614–2628.

connection with Alien Immigration'.[21] Frederick Bradshaw, proposing the case for restriction in 1904, summed up thus the plethora of evils which came to be placed at the door of the immigrant:

> 'Perhaps enough has been said to prove that the foreigner is not a very desirable person as a neighbour. He first displaces the native and causes him to pay more rent. He demoralises the Englishman's children by filthy habits and general disregard of decency, and, finally, as fast as the magistrates improve the character of any district the alien comes in, and with him a host of prostitutes and criminals fleeing from justice abroad.'[22]

Faced with such animosity, it is unsurprising that the Royal Commission recommended the repeal of the now redundant Alien Registration Act 1836 and the implementation of new legislation which would empower a specially created Immigration Department to examine all immigrants on arrival to establish whether they were 'desirable' or not. Undesirables were classified as 'criminals, prostitutes, idiots, lunatics, persons of notoriously bad character, or likely to become a charge upon public funds'.[23] Despite reference in the Royal Commission's Report to the 'oppressive measures' adopted against and the 'persecution' of the Russian Jews,[24] no mention was made in the Report's recommendations of the particular plight of the refugee. In fact, the Report describes all new arrivals as 'immigrants' and the issue before the Royal Commission was clearly seen as one of immigration and not of asylum.

Though an Aliens Bill introduced in 1904 to tackle the immigrant problem failed to become law, the government continued to hold that legislation was required. In the next parliamentary session, a new Aliens Bill was published incorporating not only the Royal Commission's proposals in relation to aliens, but also an exempting provision on political grounds: **2.4**

> '[. . .] in the case of an immigrant who proves that he is seeking admission to this country solely to avoid prosecution for an offence of a political character, leave to land shall not be refused on the ground merely of want of means, or the probability of his becoming a charge on the rates.'[25]

---

[21] Royal Commission on Alien Immigration, 1903, II, Report, Cd. 1741, point 145.
[22] F. Bradshaw & C. Emanual, *Alien Immigration – Should Restrictions be imposed?* (London: Isbister & Co., 1904), p. 69.
[23] Royal Commission on Alien Immigration, 1903, II, Report, Cd. 1741, Recommendation 4(c).
[24] *ibid.*, points 22–23.
[25] Aliens Bill 1905 (Bill 187), s.1(3).

This concession, absent from the 1904 Bill, did little to assuage the concerns of the Liberal Party. Repeating the criticisms voiced against the earlier Bill, and in particular its disregard for the right of asylum, Sir Charles Dilke reminded the House that the 1905 Bill excluded victims of political and religious persecution:

> 'The Bill does not touch these victims. There are the religious refugees who are hounded from Russia by fear of mob violence, and there are the political refugees – those who are not prosecuted but arrested by Administration Order . . .[and] who disappear clean into space as if they had never existed and are never heard of again.'[26]

The Secretary of State for the Home Department, Akers-Douglas, responded by arguing that there was 'no such thing as a "right" of asylum' and stressed the differences between the 'class of undesirable aliens which this Bill proposes to deal with and the additions made to our population' since the Middle Ages.[27] He went on to add, with revealing candour:

> 'Not only were they not undesirable in the present sense of the word, but they brought with them arts and crafts, and set up many manufactures which have been of the greatest benefit to this country. [. . .] Many of them, at all events the Huguenots – brought a considerable amount of money into this country [. . .] I do not think that they would have been caught by the meshes of this Bill, because they would have been able to show that they were skilled artisans, or were perfectly able to maintain themselves, and that they would not in any way become a charge on the country.' [28]

By this statement, Akers-Douglas set the tone of asylum policy throughout the twentieth century. Though delivered in 1905, his views could well reflect cross-party attitudes towards asylum in the late 1990s and early twenty-first century: the willingness to protect refugees so long as they brought with them tangible benefits and did not become a burden on the state, with a concern also to distinguish between genuine and bogus applicants: '[. . .] we must be careful in framing words [. . .] not to allow the whole Act to be evaded by people coming here and saying that they are suffering from political persecution.' [29]

Despite concerted opposition, the Bill passed through Committee and received Royal Assent on August 11, 1905. The government had,

---

[26] HC Deb. Vol. 145, May 2, 1905, col. 699.
[27] *ibid.*, col. 751.
[28] *ibid.*, cols. 751–752.
[29] *ibid.*

however, accepted the argument in favour of victims of religious as well as political persecution, and had amended the crucial exempting provision to read:

> '[. . .] in the case of an immigrant who proves that he is seeking admission to this country solely to avoid prosecution or punishment on religious or political grounds or for an offence of a political character, or persecution, involving danger of imprisonment or danger to life or limb, on account of religious belief, leave to land shall not be refused on the ground merely of want of means, or the probability of his becoming a charge on the rates [. . .].'[30]

For the first time in British history, the asylum applicant now had to prove his or her status as a refugee. Yet the statute itself did not speak of the 'refugee'; as was explicit in the exemption, anyone who succeeded in proving persecution was still perceived as an 'immigrant', albeit one accorded exceptional treatment.

1905 TO 1914: RELUCTANT ENFORCEMENT

With the arrival of the Aliens Act 1905 came the apparent end of open-door immigration and the beginning of a new approach towards refugees, in which the legal process was to play a major role. While refugees were still regarded as a type of immigrant subject to control and to the same procedures as other aliens, they had, through the Act's exception, been defined for the first time in statutory form. The connection between the refugee and 'persecution' for religious belief, or 'prosecution' on political grounds, though articulated throughout the preceding centuries, had now been set down in written form. Though an undoubted advance, this statutory provision on asylum seekers gave no assurances on how the law would be implemented or on future government policy.

    On its face, the 1905 Act provided a system of controlled immigration: it established criteria for exclusion of 'undesirable immigrants' who had arrived on 'immigrant ships'; it granted significant powers to the Home Secretary, unparalleled since the Napoleonic Wars, and to the courts in relation to expulsion;[31] it put in place an independent administrative regime, comprising immigration officers, medical inspectors and port Immigration Boards; and it provided the noted exception for immigrants on religious or political grounds. While it was the Home Secretary's task to expel unwanted aliens,

2.5

---

[30] Aliens Act 1905, s. 1(2).
[31] s. 3(1)(a).

subject to a court recommendation, and to appoint members of the Immigration Boards based in every port, it was the unenviable role of the immigration officer, alongside a medical inspector, to identify those immigrants deemed 'undesirable', and those for whom the refugee exception applied. A right of appeal on basic questions was available to the Immigration Board (comprised of three members with 'magisterial, business or administrative experience'),[32] but where a more complex issue was raised on appeal – such as whether an individual was an 'immigrant', whether a crime was an extradition crime, or whether an offence was of a political nature –, the matter had to be referred to the Home Secretary, whose decision was binding on the Board.[33] Amongst these issues of importance, extradition was perhaps the most significant. The decision to extradite, albeit on a court recommendation, placed in the hands of the Secretary of State an unusual and potentially dangerous power. Before expulsion could take place, it had to be certified that (a) the aliens were criminals convicted of imprisonable offences or prostitutes, and that (b) either they were found wandering without ostensible means of support, or were living under insanitary conditions due to overcrowding, or they had entered the UK having been sentenced for a non-political offence in a foreign country with which there was an extradition treaty.[34] This last proviso, a repetition of the principle set down in the Extradition Treaty 1870,[35] offered protection for the political refugee but did not exclude from expulsion those who had fled religious persecution.

While the Aliens Act had been a 'last gasp' attempt by the Conservative Party to win the 1905 election, and had in fact been popular among the electorate, it failed in its objective. The arrival of a Liberal government in 1906, and a new Secretary of State for the Home Department in Herbert Gladstone, heralded a potential change of policy in the implementation of the Act. Though the Liberal Party chose not to repeal the statute, a somewhat surprising decision in view of its pre-enactment opposition, a lighter touch to enforcement was adopted.[36] While Gladstone was careful to adhere to the terminology of the Act, he enjoined immigration officers and appellate boards to act humanely in the case of asylum seekers. Thus he proposed that 'immigrants' be accorded 'the benefit of the doubt':

---

[32] s. 2.
[33] s. 8(5).
[34] ss 3(1)(a) and (b).
[35] See Ch. 1.
[36] See, for striking parallels, Ch. 5 and New Labour's refusal to repeal the much opposed 1993 and 1996 Acts.

'In all cases in which the immigrants, coming from the parts of the Continent which are at present in a disturbed condition, allege that they are flying from political or religious persecution, the benefit of the doubt, where any doubt exists, as to the truth of the allegation will be allowed, and leave to land will be given.'[37]

Though official references to refugees were rare, the Inspector appointed under the Act commented in his 1910 report:

'It is sometimes assumed, though I have never seen any evidence produced in its support, that under the cloak of this provision crowds of undesirable aliens – violent criminals of every sort and anarchists – have passed into this country without let or hindrance. This assumption is not supported by the facts. The number of immigrants admitted on the sole ground that they were political or religious refugees during the five years was 603, of whom 505 were admitted in 1906 (the year of very disturbed conditions in Russia), 43 in 1907, 20 in 1908, 30 in 1909, and 5 in 1910.'[38]

Despite accusations by William Evans-Gordon MP, who fought **2.6** hard against alien admission, that Gladstone had emasculated the Act through amendments and directions such as the 'benefit of the doubt' order, it is clear from these statistics that few arrivals succeeded in being granted *asylum*. There are three arguable explanations for this low success rate: first, few may have chosen to claim asylum; second, the immigration officers deciding such matters may have applied a restrictive policy, refusing to recognise applicants as refugees; finally, it is possible that the majority of applicants were unable to establish that they fell within the requirements of the Act, even when given the benefit of the doubt.

The stigma of poor enforcement was to hound Gladstone throughout his office and beyond. Writing in 1925 on the workings of the Home Office, a former Permanent Under-Secretary of State, Sir Edward Troup, described the 'imperfect' Act as follows:

'Whatever opinion may be held of the merits or demerits of the policy of the Act, it was from the administrative point of view one of the worst ever passed. [. . .] even where the Aliens Officers found good reason to refuse leave to land, their decisions were constantly over-ridden by the statutory appeal boards in a way that made effective enforcement of the restrictions almost impossible. Yet for nine years the Home Office struggled to prevent the Act of Parliament being reduced to a farce, and undoubtedly some

---

[37] Instruction to Immigration Officers, March 9, 1906, in Regulations Made by the Secretary of State for the Home Department with Regard to the Administration of the Aliens Act 1905, Cd. 2879.
[38] Annual Report for the Aliens Act 1905 for 1910, Cd. 5789.

effect was produced in the direction of stopping the mass immigration of aliens, however easy it was for the individual undesirables to evade the requirements.'[39]

This opinion that the Act proved largely ineffectual has been contradicted by one legal commentator:

'In so far as this criticism implies that the activities of the appeals tribunals prevented the Home Office from stopping "the mass immigration of aliens," it is fallacious – the Act did not attempt this but imposed instead a qualitative test. In so far as it is suggested that the institution permitted "individual undesirables" to enter the country, it is grossly exaggerated: the Act was so limited in scope that no individual determined upon entry was obliged to present himself to an immigration officer. In 1909, for example, 422,548 aliens arrived from the Continent; of these, only 35,254 fell within the definition of "immigrant" for the purposes of the Act and thus became liable to inspection.'[40]

Statistics on appeals also suggest that Troup's comments were wildly exaggerated. During the eight years in which the appeals system was in operation, 1906–13, '51% of all rejected immigrants appealed, 38% of all appeals were successful, and 19% of all decisions of refused leave to land were reversed on appeal.'[41] Since a total of only 9,421 aliens actually appealed, these figures are hardly evidence of a serious undermining of the Act or of a constant reversal of decisions by the appeals boards, as claimed.

By 1914, in the face of impending war, immigration was no longer a priority on the political agenda and faded into the background. Yet the Aliens Act of 1905 had managed to make an enduring impression: it established an administrative and legal framework for deciding refugee cases, and it linked the issue of immigration with that of asylum. In the new climate of war, this legacy would prove damaging to future asylum seekers.

REFUGEES AND WAR: 1914–18

2.7   On August 6, 1914, the United Kingdom declared war on Germany. In the days preceding the declaration, the country had witnessed mounting war fever; on August 4, at least 21 suspected spies were

---

[39] E. Troup, *The Home Office* (London: G.P. Putnam's Sons, 1925), pp. 143–4.

[40] C. Thornberry, 'Dr. Soblen and the Alien Law of the United Kingdom' (1968) 12 *ICLQ*, p. 467.

[41] Home Office, *Report of the Committee on Immigration Appeals* ('the Wilson Report'), August 1967, Cmnd. 3387, p. 73.

arrested in various places around the country, giving added momentum to the emergency tabling of an Aliens Restriction Bill on August 5, 1914.[42] Comprising a mere four-and-a-half columns in the parliamentary debates – two columns of which contained the wording of the Act –, the Bill passed all stages of the House in one afternoon, including Royal Assent, and was ready for enforcement by the morning of August 6.[43] What was even more remarkable was the absolute nature of the Act. Sweeping powers were granted to the Crown, and consequently to the Home Secretary through Orders in Council, to control landing and embarkation, to deport, to set down residence and registration restrictions, to search, detain and arrest, and to impose sanctions.[44] All appeal rights to the independent tribunals were summarily removed, as was the religious and political refugee exception contained in the 1905 Act. Sir William Byles MP expressed disquiet. Byles, in his lone attempt to point out that the power being placed in the hands of the Home Secretary was 'very dangerous', was met with the cry 'Sit Down!'.[45] There was no repeat of the anguished debate over the 'right of asylum' and the country's noble tradition. Since the 1905 Act remained in force, it was, in theory, possible to come within in its terms; in practice, however, the reality was quite different, and there was felt to be no need to apply the 1905 Act under wartime conditions. As the H.M. Inspector noted in 1914, 'The two Acts are based on such widely different principles that there is no similarity in their operation and no continuity in their effects.'[46] This was tantamount to an admission that the 1905 Act had, at least for the remainder of 1914, ceased to have any practical effect. This did not mean that refugees were excluded altogether under the new legislation. The Home Secretary clarified that one of the objects of the Act was to draw a distinction between alien friends and alien enemies.[47] Refugees would naturally fall within the category of alien friends.

Belgian refugees

The UK's wartime policy on refugees was soon put to the test.   **2.8**
Belgium's catastrophic failure to resist the German invasion gave rise to an immediate influx of Belgian refugees in the autumn of

[42] HC Deb. Vol. 65, August 5, 1914, cols.1986–1990.
[43] E. Troup, *The Home Office* (London: G.P. Putnam's Sons, 1925), p. 144.
[44] Aliens Restriction Act 1914, 4 & 5 Geo. 5, Ch. 12, s. 1.
[45] HC Deb. Vol. 65, August 5, 1914, col. 1990.
[46] Annual Report of the Aliens Acts 1905 for 1914, Cd. 7969, p. 21.
[47] HC Deb. Vol. 65, August 5, 1914, col. 1989.

1914, which continued to the end of 1915.[48] Although it has been difficult to estimate the exact numbers who reached the UK, Holmes suggests that by 1919, there were '240,000 refugees scattered throughout Britain' and that 'some 19,000 wounded Belgian soldiers came to Britain during the war'.[49] Admission of these refugees appears to have been generous. Speaking in the House of Commons in September 1914, the President of the Local Government Board, Herbert Samuel, acknowledged that Britain was already offering hospitality to large numbers of Belgians, with the aid of the War Refugees Committee,[50] and called upon the public to join the government 'in offering an asylum here until conditions in Belgium enable the refugees to return'.[51] Home Secretary McKenna explained that Belgians would be treated as friends under the Aliens Restriction Act 1914, and that no difficulty would be put in the way of their landing if they could satisfy the Aliens Officer that they were in fact Belgians and not Germans or Austrians.[52]

A noteworthy aspect to the government's policy on the Belgians is the failure to question whether they were refugees in the true sense (of suffering from persecution) or whether they were simply victims of war. In fact, no distinction was drawn between the two. Samuel, for example, uses both expressions in his short statement to the House. From the Belgian perspective, there was no doubt. In the words of the Official Committee of Belgians (a body of appointed Belgians based in the UK and tasked with co-operating with the British government in the interests of Belgian refugees):

'[. . .] when the German hordes broke into Belgium, when they gradually invaded the whole of her territory, when they destroyed her churches and houses, ravaged her fields and slaughtered her peaceful citizens, [. . .] Great Britain then welcomed the Belgian fugitives to her own towns and country sides and homes. Great Britain brought to her own country all who had streamed to the coasts to escape cold, famine, fire and murder.'[53]

---

[48] C. Holmes, *John Bull's Island – Immigration and British Society, 1871–1971* (London: Macmillan, 1994), p. 87.

[49] *ibid.*

[50] Formed on August 24, 1914 by Lady Lugard, Mrs Alfred Lyttelton, and Viscount Gladstone for the purpose of arranging for the reception and maintenance of refugees.

[51] HC Deb. Vol. LXVI, September 9, 1914, col. 558.

[52] P. Cahalan, *Belgian Refugee Relief in England during the Great War* (New York: Garland, 1982), pp. 58–9.

[53] Government Belgian Refugees Committee, *First Report of the Departmental Committee to consider and report on questions arising in connection with the reception and employment of the Belgian refugees in this country*, 1914, Cd. 7750, p. 42 (Handbook of suggestions and advice issued to the Belgian refugees in the United Kingdom by the Official Committee of Belgians, December 1914).

All that the British government asked of Belgium was that all Belgian subjects claiming to be refugees comply with three conditions: (1) that they had lost their homes owing to the war; (2) that they were of good character; and (3) that they should be medically examined. The Belgian government was happy to comply.

Statements such as those by the Official Committee of Belgians, urging Belgians to 'behave properly', 'not to be idle but to be *good workers*' and not to apply for jobs for which a British labourer could be employed, alongside expressions of immense gratitude to the British people, helped to ensure that Belgian refugees were, to a large extent, welcomed.[54] Certainly, in the initial stages of the influx, there were few problems, though unspoken resentment may have remained close to the surface. As Kushner notes:

'[. . .] in these early months, both the Belgian refugees and the British were eager to contribute to a mutually-reinforcing mythology which avoided mention of the difficulties between host and newcomer or, indeed, any reference to past difficulties between the two nations which, as with the issue of Belgian atrocities in the Congo, had caused diplomatic friction and general unease.'[55]

Government policy, though outwardly positive towards the refugees, was in fact much more ambiguous than this suggests. The Home Secretary, McKenna, was doubtful whether it was to the advantage of anyone, including the refugees, to come to the UK. Furthermore, he feared that should their numbers be large, 'they might after time become a considerable source of embarrassment'.[56] This explains in part the clear message imparted by the Official Committee of Belgians to their compatriots that they were not to consider remaining in the UK after the War: 'The time of refuge in Great Britain must prepare the Belgians for the heavy task which awaits them on their return. No one should think of avoiding this task, or should dream of settling abroad, unless for exceptional and various reasons.'[57] It also explains the admission by the Departmental Committee established to look into the reception and employment of Belgian refugees that it was characteristic for this country to assign

[54] *ibid.*, pp. 43–4.

[55] T. Kushner & K. Knox, *Refugees in an Age of Genocide* (London: Frank Cass, 1999), p. 52.

[56] P. Cahalan, *Belgian Refugee Relief in England during the Great War* (New York: Garland, 1982), p. 59.

[57] Government Belgian Refugees Committee, *First Report of the Departmental Committee to consider and report on questions arising in connection with the reception and employment of the Belgian refugees in this country*, 1914, Cd. 7750, p. 44 (Handbook of suggestions and advice issued to the Belgian refugees in the United Kingdom by the Official Committee of Belgians, December 1914).

the duty of attending to refugees to voluntary organisations, thus relieving the government of this onerous task.[58] Despite the enormous role played by members of the public in caring for and supporting the Belgian refugees,[59] and the care which was taken to ensure minimum conflict with the local population, by 1919, the government was being urged to remove any remaining refugees as quickly as possible.[60] This did not prevent Prime Minister Lloyd George from praising the War Refugees Committees and associated relief organisations for their 'great act of humanity',[61] nor subsequent commentators from acknowledging that, during the war, 'England proved a generous island of refuge for the Belgians'.[62] It is all the more surprising, then, that this episode in British refugee law was soon forgotten, even receiving relatively little attention from academics interested in the field.[63]

Other refugees

2.9   The Belgian refugees constituted a tiny proportion of a huge Europe-wide refugee problem. Armenians, Serbs, Romanians, Greeks, Turks, Germans, Jews, displaced Poles and Russians, 'White Russians' – the list seemed endless.[64] The group to suffer the most were undoubtedly the Armenians. In a systematic attempt to wipe out a nation, the Turks engaged in full-scale massacres of the Armenians during the years 1915 and 1916, and perhaps beyond. No one can be certain of the numbers killed but it is estimated that between 1 and 1.5 million died.[65] Some Armenians managed to escape and sought refuge in neighbouring countries. Despite the call by one Member of Parliament, Aneurin Williams, for greater assistance to be afforded the Armenians and for their rescue wherever possible, Lord Robert Cecil, Under-Secretary of State for Foreign Affairs, made it clear that he preferred to devote the resources of the British army and navy to

---

[58]   1914, Cd. 7750, p. 4.

[59]   For a detailed account of treatment of the Belgian refugees, see T. Kushner & K. Knox, *Refugees in an Age of Genocide* (London: Frank Cass, 1999), Ch. 2.

[60]   HC Deb. Vol. 122, December 3, 1919, cols. 421–2.

[61]   *1920 Report*, Appendix 6, copy of letter issued by the Prime Minister in May 1919, cited in P. Cahalan, *Belgian Refugee Relief during the Great War* (New York: Garland Publishing, 1982), p. 499.

[62]   *ibid.*, p. 511.

[63]   *ibid.*, pp. 1–2.

[64]   M. Marrus, *The Unwanted – European refugees in the Twentieth Century* (New York: OUP, 1985), Chs. 1 & 2.

[65]   *ibid.*, p. 77; T. Kushner & K. Knox, *Refugees in an Age of Genocide* (London: Frank Cass, 1999), p. 68.

destroying the enemy. He added, however, that he had telegraphed the Commander of the British forces and 'asked him to communicate with the Arab tribes and induce them, as far as possible, to assist these unhappy fugitives wherever they [could]'.[66] The token nature of this gesture in the face of genocide is hard to excuse.

Faced with governmental disinterest, it fell once more to voluntary organisations and to members of the public to offer help. Walker reports that:

> 'Several charities offered assistance, the chief ones being the Armenian Refugees (Lord Mayor's) Fund, the Armenia Red Cross and Relief Fund, and the Armenian Refugees Relief Fund. In British cathedrals and churches [. . .] it became the practice to designate a Sunday in February as 'Armenia Sunday', and give the proceeds of the collections to Armenian relief. By the time of the armistice the total receipts for all the charities amounted to approximately £15,000.'[67]

In August 1918, the British army played its part by erecting a camp to the north of Baghdad to house Assyrian and Armenian refugees. Of an estimated 40,000 occupants, Armenians comprised about 16,000.[68] However, when compared with the efforts of other countries, Britain's contribution to the Armenian cause was paltry. From 1915 to 1925, the United States managed to raise and spend just under $100 million;[69] by contrast, the Lord Mayor's Armenian Fund, from 1915 to 1937, only reached £300,000.[70] Whereas France received some 63,000 Armenian refugees in the 1930s,[71] the UK would accept only 200 Armenians, and none as true refugees.[72]

The role of the courts

While the government was urging caution in its refugee policy, (and voluntary organisations or members of the public were offering practical assistance to refugees), the courts were beginning to develop their own jurisprudence in the migration field. The involvement of the courts in alien matters was, of course, not unknown and had been

2.10

---

[66] HC Deb. Vol. 75 (November 16, 1915), cols. 1760–1778.

[67] C. Walker, 'Armenian refugees: accidents of diplomacy or victims of ideology?', in M. Marrus & A Bramwell, eds., *Refugees in the Age of Total War* (London: Unwin Hyman, 1988), p. 44.

[68] *ibid.*, p. 45.

[69] *ibid.*

[70] T. Kushner & K. Knox, *Refugees in an Age of Genocide* (London: Frank Cass, 1999), p. 71.

[71] J.H. Simpson, *The Refugee Problem: Report of a Survey* (London: OUP, 1939), p. 319.

[72] *ibid.*, p. 340.

part of English law-making for some time. Whereas earlier cases had revolved around definitions of 'alien friend' and 'alien enemy' and their various rights and liabilities, towards the end of the nineteenth century, judges were contending with the thorny issue of Crown prerogative. In a number of important decisions, the courts addressed either directly or indirectly the right of the Crown to admit or exclude aliens. It is to these cases that one must turn for a true understanding of judicial attitudes towards immigration in the post-aliens legislation era of the early twentieth century.

In 1891, in the case of *Musgrove v Chun Teeong Toy*, the House of Lords, while considering a Victorian statute limiting the number of Chinese immigrants who could be carried on a vessel, declared – *obiter* – that an alien had no legal right, enforceable by action, to enter British territory.[73] *Musgrove* was followed by *Poll v Lord Advocate*, which stated that 'the sovereign power – the supreme executive – of every state must be held to be absolute', except in a question with its own subjects, and that a friendly alien could not sue the state.[74] Finally, in 1906, in the case of *A-G for Canada v Cain*, the Privy Council, citing Vattel, assumed unquestioningly that there existed a Crown prerogative to expel aliens.[75] This trilogy of cases has been adduced, by some, as evidence that a Crown prerogative existed both to exclude and to expel aliens without statute.[76] However, this fails to take account of the immense uncertainty surrounding the whole issue of the Crown prerogative relating to aliens. While Blackstone, in his *Commentaries*, apparently favoured the right of the king to send home aliens whenever he saw fit,[77] Dicey was of the opinion that the Crown's former prerogative of excluding or expelling aliens had fallen into desuetude.[78] The debate gave rise to considerable academic discussion at the turn of the century without much clarification.[79] Nevertheless, subsequent to *Musgrove*, *Poll* and *Cain*, it appears that the courts abdicated any right to review the grounds on which

---

[73] [1891] AC 272

[74] (1899) 1 F. (Ct. of Sess.) 823, at 827–28.

[75] [1906] AC 542.

[76] For further discussion of these cases, see S. Legomsky, *Immigration and the Judiciary – Law and Politics in Britain and America* (Oxford: Clarendon Press, 1987), pp. 87–95.

[77] Blackstone, *Commentaries*, Vol. I, cited in W. Holdsworth, *A History of English Law*, Vol. X (London: Methuen, Sweet and Maxwell, 1966), p. 398.

[78] A.V. Dicey, *Introduction to the Study of the Law of the Constitution* (1880), p. 341, cited in C. Thornberry, 'Dr. Soblen and the Alien Law of the United Kingdom', (1968) 12 *ICLQ*, p. 424.

[79] See, in favour of the prerogative's continued application , T. Haycraft, 'Alien Legislation and the Prerogative of the Crown', (1897) 13 *LQR*, p. 165, against, W. Craies, 'The Right of Aliens to Enter British Territory', (1890) 6 *LQR*, p. 27.

the Crown prerogative had been exercised, believing the continued application of the prerogative to be established law.[80]

While the arrival of legislation controlling the entry and exit of aliens removed the controversy surrounding the existence or otherwise of the Crown prerogative, it gave rise to a new question: the exercise of executive discretion. The enormous power which had been placed in the hands of the Home Secretary by both the Aliens Act 1905 and the Aliens Restriction Act 1914 was undoubtedly open to abuse; how far the courts could or would interfere to restrain that power remained uncertain, but was soon put to the test. In a line of post-war cases, it became clear that the Crown prerogative, while no longer relevant in view of legislation, was playing a residual role in judicial thinking. In the first, *R. v Governor of Brixton Prison, ex parte Sarno*, the Home Secretary had issued an order, under the powers conferred by the Aliens Restriction Act 1914 and Art. 12 of the Aliens Restriction (Consolidation) Order 1914, that Sarno be deported from the UK.[81] Sarno was arrested and detained in Brixton prison prior to completion of the deportation. In support of his application, Sarno stated in an affidavit that he had 'escaped [Russia] for political reasons in or about the year 1900'.[82] Lord Reading C.J. acknowledged the significance of the questions raised with regard to the powers of the Secretary of State under the Aliens Restriction (Consolidation) Order 1914, describing them as 'undoubtedly of supreme importance, in reference to the right or power of the Secretary of State to send back to the country where he was born a person who has sought asylum in this country by reason of his having, or being suspected of having, committed a political offence in his own country'.[83] The judge was, however, unimpressed by the affidavit and was not satisfied that Sarno was 'in the ordinary sense, a political refugee'.[84] More importantly, the court made it clear that although Art. 12 of the Order was an extraordinary power, it was not ultra vires the statute; nor were the powers it conferred upon the executive, and on the Home Secretary in particular, being misused. Lord Reading added significantly, but *obiter*: 'If we were of opinion that the powers were being misused, we should be able to deal with the matter. In other words, if it was clear that an act was done by the Executive with the intention of misusing those powers, this Court would have

---

[80] See S. Legomsky, *Immigration and the Judiciary – Law and Politics in Britain and America* (Oxford: Clarendon Press, 1987), p. 92.

[81] [1916] 2 KB 742.

[82] *ibid.*, at 743.

[83] *ibid.*, at 747.

[84] *ibid.*, at 750.

jurisdiction to deal with the matter'.[85] Thus the *Sarno* decision not only accepted that the Home Secretary had an unfettered right to deport, but also that the courts could review any abuse of the deportation powers. However, while bold in their utterance of the *power* of review, they seemed less decisive as to the extent of that power: '[. . .] this decision must not be thought to determine the question as to what this Court could do if there were a deliberate attempt by the exercise of the powers conferred by the statute and regulations to enforce the return of a real, genuine, political refugee to the country of his origin'.[86]

2.11   *Sarno* may be regarded as a decision moving away from those of *Musgrove* and *Poll*, where the courts did not accept the right of an alien to submit to judicial scrutiny any refusal of admission to British territory. However, *R. v Secretary of State for Home Affairs, ex parte Duke of Château Thierry*[87] was soon to set the record straight. Once again, the Court was faced with a deportation order issued under Art. 12 of the Aliens Restriction (Consolidation) Order, now of 1916. The Home Secretary appealed against an order of the King's Bench Division that made absolute a rule for a certiorari to quash the deportation order. The respondent was a French subject, liable to military service in France but who had been resident in England for some years. He argued that the deportation order should be quashed on the grounds that 'he was a political refugee from France; that there were no facts or materials before the Secretary of State to justify the making of the order; and that there was no power to order his expulsion to France'.[88] In a majority verdict, the Court of Appeal held that the Home Secretary had an absolute discretion to order deportation, one that the court was unwilling to question:

> 'The power given to the Secretary of State is quite unqualified. If the person ordered to be deported be in fact an alien, the Secretary of State has an absolute discretion to order him to be deported, and I do not think that discretion can be questioned in a Court of law. Assuming, therefore, that the respondent proved that he was a political refugee and unfit for military service, these facts would not affect the validity of the order, but would only be matters to be considered by the Secretary of State as affecting the exercise of his discretion. It may be noticed that the Aliens Restriction Act of 1914 contains no provisions as to political refugees similar to those in the Aliens Act 1905, but it was stated by the Attorney-General that the British

---

[85]   [1916] 2 KB, at 749.
[86]   *ibid.*, at 752 (Low J.).
[87]   [1917] 1 KB 922.
[88]   *ibid.*, at 923–4.

Government has no intention of enforcing the provisions of the Act of 1914 against such refugees.' (Pickford L.J.)[89]

Though Swinfen Eady L.J. was of the opinion that the respondent had failed to establish that he was a political refugee or that he was medically unfit to undertake military service in France, he went on to say that whether or not that was the case, such considerations ought not to affect his judgement.[90] The Court was happy to accept the Attorney-General's assurance that, while safeguards for refugees were no longer present under the 1914 Act, 'the Executive had no intention whatever of taking advantage of their powers over aliens to deport political refugees'.[91] This apparent retreat from *Sarno* and adoption of a *Musgrove/Poll/Cain*-type subservience to absolute discretion, whether in the form of Crown privilege or executive power, is of particular note. The failure by counsel for the respondent to argue *Sarno* in support of their case provides a partial explanation for the retreat (though, in view of Swinfen Eady's comments, it is doubtful whether this would have assisted their cause). Counsel chose instead to raise the question of Crown privilege, or lack of it, an issue which Bankes L.J. rightly declared irrelevant in view of the introduction of legislation. Yet the continued legacy of Crown privilege was, it is suggested, very evident in the *Duke of Château Thierry* decision. As Legomsky notes, '[. . .] despite the lack of express reliance on the prerogative, it remains possible that the court was simply hesitant to adopt an interpretation arguably derogating from the common law.'[92]

Two subsequent cases provide further support for the view that the judiciary was adopting an increasingly restrictive approach: *R. v Chiswick Police Station Superintendent, ex parte Sacksteder*[93], and *R. v Inspector of Leman St Police Station, ex parte Venicoff, R. v Secretary of State for Home Affairs, ex parte Venicoff.*[94] In *Sacksteder*, the Court refused to overturn an order for arrest and detention of an alien. Pickford L.J. declared:

2.12

'I am not prepared to say that in every case where there is an order of detention or imprisonment the Court is entitled to go behind that and see what the motives for making that order were. But I certainly am not inclined to say that in no case can the Court go behind an order which on the face of it is valid ordering detention or custody. If that order is, if I may say so, practically a sham, if the purpose behind it is such as to show that

---

[89] *ibid.*, at 933.
[90] *ibid.*, at 928.
[91] *ibid.*, at 929.
[92] S. Legomsky, *Immigration and the Judiciary – Law and Politics in Britain and America* (Oxford: Clarendon Press, 1987), p. 97.
[93] [1918] 1 KB 578.
[94] [1920] 3 KB 72.

the order is not a genuine or bona fide order, it seems to me that the Court can go behind it.'

Once again, Pickford bowed to Home Office discretion; his hesitant suggestion that the Court might, in certain circumstances, question an order for detention is rather meaningless. As Thornberry wryly notes, 'How can the court discover whether an order is "practically a sham," *i.e.*, discern the "purpose behind it" without first *going behind it?*'[95] In *Venicoff*, the Earl of Reading, who had been involved in the *Sarno* decision, made no reference to his previously articulated premise that the Court was entitled to question an order where there may have been misuse of power. Instead, he confirmed that where a Home Secretary makes a deportation order on the basis of the public good, it was not for the Court to pronounce whether the making of the order was or was not conducive to the public good,[96] nor was the Home Secretary required to hold an inquiry or hear the party concerned prior to issuing the order. He was an executive and not a judicial officer.[97]

There is no doubt that this string of decisions reinforced executive power in the immigration and refugee fields. Though the courts suggested on occasion the possibility of judicial review of the Home Secretary's decisions under the aliens legislation, they seldom acted upon their words. Even where claims to refugee status were made, the judiciary proceeded with caution, unwilling to peer behind the veil of absolute discretion. One explanation for such overt conservatism is that these cases coincided with a period 'in which the British courts were just beginning to develop a more restrained view of their role'.[98] Such restraint was to be long-lasting.

THE INTER-WAR YEARS: 1918–38

Government policy: national restriction continues

2.13   The introduction of stringent alien legislation was understandable on the outbreak of war, but the continuation of similar measures after

---

[95] C. Thornberry, 'Dr. Soblen and the Alien Law of the United Kingdom', (1968) 12 *ICLQ*, p. 457.
[96] [1920] 3 KB 78.
[97] *ibid.*, at 80–81.
[98] S. Legomsky, *Immigration and the Judiciary – Law and Politics in Britain and America* (Oxford: Clarendon Press, 1987), p. 245.

the 1918 cease-fire was less obviously justified. Armistice brought with it peace but also a number of problems, one of which was the question of alien control. Conscious that the Aliens Restriction Act 1914 was just a war-time instrument, a number of MPs were impatient to enact new law. As early as March 1919, the government was being pressed on when a new Bill would be presented.[99] On March 31, 1919, the Home Secretary introduced an Aliens Restriction Bill, the second reading of which took place on April 15, 1919. Unlike its predecessor, the 1919 Bill was subjected to rigorous debate and careful scrutiny. Nevertheless, from the Secretary of State's opening words, the tenor of the Bill became clear:

'There is [. . .] the alien already in our midst, and [. . .] there is the alien who wishes to come into our midst. The two problems are not quite the same. Equally we have to deal with enemy aliens, those who are to-day or have been in the last four or five years, the subjects of enemy States. We have also to deal with aliens who are the subjects of neutral States or of friendly Allied States.'[100]

There was no mention of refugees, other than to assure Members that 'pure Belgian refugees [. . .] are as rapidly as possible being returned to their own country'.[101]

The government clearly regarded the alien question as an enormous burden requiring particular attention. While the 'safety and the safeguards' of the British people were considered of prime importance, the Home Secretary, perhaps pre-empting the demands of the anti-alienists, warned that it would be impossible to 'pass a single section Act of Parliament to say that no alien of any sort or description [should] be brought within our gates.'[102] He suggested, reasonably, that everything that was necessary in war would not be equally necessary in time of peace.[103] Yet this ran counter to the very purpose of the Bill, and subsequently of the Act, namely 'to continue and extend the provisions of the Aliens Restriction Act, 1914.'[104]

Sir Donald Maclean, pleading for the 'great and noble traditions of the past' to be upheld and for the continuation of asylum,[105] Colonel Wedgwood arguing against persecution of the weak,[106] and Captain Ormsby-Gore vilifying the anti-Semitic speeches of some

---

[99] T. Roche, *The Key in the Lock* (London: John Murray, 1969), pp. 89–90.

[100] HC Deb. Vol. 114 (April 15, 1919), cols. 2745–6.

[101] *ibid.*, col. 2747.

[102] *ibid.*, col. 2746.

[103] *ibid.*

[104] Aliens Restriction (Amendment) Act 1919, 9 & 10 Geo. 5, Ch. 92.

[105] HC Deb. Vol. 114 (April 15, 1919), col. 2750.

[106] *ibid.*, col. 2790.

Members,[107] were isolated voices in the debates. The majority seemed swayed by the extravagant and inaccurate assertions of Horatio Bottomley:

> 'We do not want in these days, when clearing up a great world tragedy which has brought us to the brink of bankruptcy and ruin, to indulge in copy-book maxims about the rights of refugees. We have been the dumping ground for the refugees of the world for too long.'[108]

Noting that under the 1905 Act, aliens could come in if they were fleeing from religious or political persecution, Bottomley went on to state, without providing any authority, that the provision had been very much abused.[109] Though he was personally unhappy with the Bill, finding it too limited in scope and describing it as 'unworkable and stupid',[110] it was finally passed in December 1919.

2.14 All previous assurances that the Aliens Restriction Act 1914 would apply only for the duration of the war were swept aside. Section 1 stated categorically that the powers under Section 1(1) of the 1914 Act, prohibiting landing and embarkation, and providing for deportation and residency restrictions, amongst other matters, were to continue in force for the period of one year. These were, in fact, continued on an annual basis in the Schedule to the Expiring Laws Continuance Act until 1971. In accordance with Bottomley's complaints about the lack of a coherent policy, further restrictions were imposed in relation to, *inter alia*: employment, name changes, participation on juries, and acquisition of property by former enemy aliens. Most importantly, the Aliens Act 1905 was repealed and no alternative arrangement for refugees was offered. Refugees and asylum seekers reverted to the status of 'alien' and were no longer viewed as warranting exceptional treatment. There was no recourse to appeal, as no appeals process had been established to replace that provided for by the 1905 Act. It would seem that the display of judicial deference to the Home Secretary's decision-making powers, as indicated by the case-law, had exhorted the government towards a regime which appeared to augment executive discretion and limit the extent of judicial review.

On the passing of the Aliens Restriction (Amendment) Act 1919,[111] a new Aliens Order was made, containing many of the details of the law.[112] The Order ensured that an alien would only be

---

[107] HC Deb. Vol. 120 (October 22, 1919), col. 86.
[108] HC Deb. Vol. 114 (April 15, 1919), col. 2762.
[109] *ibid.*, col. 2763.
[110] *ibid.*, col. 2766.
[111] 9 & 10 Geo. 5, Ch. 92.
[112] Aliens Order 1920, SR & O 1920 No. 448.

permitted to land if he was in a position to support himself and his dependants, or, if proposing to enter employment, was able to produce a permit issued by the Ministry of Labour and National Service.[113] Such permits were, apparently, issued sparingly.[114] Where permission to land was refused, the alien could, with the leave of an immigration officer, be detained at an approved site.[115] The dual effect of Act and Order was to establish, in the words of the former Lord Chancellor Hailsham (or Quentin Hogg, as he then was), 'one of the least liberal and one of the most arbitrary systems of immigration law in the world [. . .]'.[116] At the heart of this illiberal and arbitrary regime stood ministerial discretion. As Laski commented in 1935:

'Upon the conferment of powers so wide, the warning of James Mill seems to me unanswerable. "Whatever," he wrote, "are the reasons for conferring power, those also are the grounds for erecting safeguards against their abuse." I see no way of justifying a discretion which, like this, is subject neither to limitation nor to control. [. . .] I have known political refugees to whom the privilege of living in exile in England has been refused on grounds which no Minister would venture to defend in public. I have known refusals grounded only in a belief that exile from the particular state involved was in itself considered reprehensible. [. . .] I believe, therefore, that it is essential to organize some method of limiting this absolute discretion.'[117]

According to Laski, however, the discretion involved was not the type to lend itself to critical examination by a judicial or administrative tribunal. He seemed to prefer an informal system whereby consultative committees would be set up to advise the Secretary of State on certain decisions. While Laski was undoubtedly right to denounce the arbitrary nature of the aliens legislation, his proposed solution did not go far enough to check potential abuse of power. Laski's model was based on an arrangement that had been agreed between the Jewish Board of Deputies and the Home Office. The Board of Deputies had for some time been pressing for an appeal for aliens refused leave to land and those subject to deportation. Persuaded by

---

[113] *ibid.*, Arts 1(3)(a) and (b).

[114] A. Sherman, *Island Refuge – Britain and Refugees from the Third Reich 1933–39* (London: Paul Elek), p. 273.

[115] Aliens Order 1920, SR & O 1920 No. 448, Art. 3(3).

[116] HC Deb. Vol. 776 (January 22, 1969), col. 504. Quentin Hogg was speaking here of the Aliens Restriction Act 1914 but his comments can be applied equally to the Aliens Restriction Act 1919.

[117] H. Laski, 'Discretionary Power' (February 1935) *Politica* No. 3, p. 274, cited in C. Fraser, *Control of Aliens in the British Commonwealth of Nations* (London: The Hogarth Press, 1940), p. 70.

their arguments in relation to deportation, the then Home Secretary, Sir Herbert Samuel, appointed a Committee in February 1932. Its main function was to consider and advise on deportation cases. In the four years in which it was consulted, the Committee considered 33 cases. In 19 cases it recommended deportation and in the remaining 14 it advised that the aliens be allowed to stay.[118] Though the Committee did not apparently consider itself bound by Home Office policy, the Home Secretary accepted the Committee's advice in every case. However, in 1936, the Home Secretary, following consultation with the Committee Chairman, decided to refer only those cases that were particularly problematic. In the event, no cases were referred to 1939, and the Committee seems to have fallen into abeyance.[119]

German, Austrian and Czech Jews

2.15 During the inter-war period, enforcement of the aliens legislation was variable. Generally, new arrivals had to meet certain conditions to obtain permission to land, though up to 1931 and the onset of economic crisis, it was accepted practice to admit the majority of aliens without the imposition of conditions.[120] From 1931 onwards, the law was enforced more rigidly. Article 1 of the Aliens Order 1920, which required aliens to have a permit from a prospective employer before permission to land could be granted, and which had not been vigorously applied, now provided the greatest bar to landing in the UK. Simpson reports that from 1933 and the commencement of the German exodus, permission to land was granted where an alien agreed *not* to accept employment, paid or unpaid.[121] Permits could be obtained where an employer could show that he had tried and failed to obtain a British subject or alien of long residence.[122] Up to 1938, the Ministry of Labour granted permits after consulting the Home Office regarding aliens not yet in the country, and *vice versa* for aliens already in the UK.[123] From the summer of 1938, the Home Office handled all employment decisions relating to aliens.[124]

---

[118] Home Office, *Report of the Committee on Immigration Appeals* ('the Wilson Report'), August 1967, Cmnd. 3387, pp. 74–5.
[119] *ibid.*
[120] L. London, 'British Immigration Control Procedures and Jewish Refugees 1933–1939' in W. Mosse ed., *Second Chance – Two Centuries of German-speaking Jews in the United Kingdom* (Tübingen: J.C.B. Mohr (Paul Siebeck), 1991), p. 485.
[121] J.H. Simpson, *The Refugee Problem: Report of a Survey* (London: OUP, 1939), p. 278.
[122] *ibid.*
[123] *ibid*, p. 338.
[124] *ibid.*

Employment conditions were not the only consequence of the 1933 exodus. On April 5, 1933, a Cabinet meeting was held to discuss the admission of Jews entering the country from Germany, and a special Committee was set up to deal with the matter: the Cabinet Committee on Aliens Restrictions.[125] The Chairman to the Committee, the Home Secretary, later reported to the Committee that under the Aliens Order, 'Jewish refugees from Germany who [were] unable to satisfy the Immigration Officer as to their means of maintenance would be refused leave to land.'[126] As a consequence, leading representatives of the Anglo-Jewish community agreed to bear all expenses of German refugees in respect of accommodation and maintenance.[127] The only concession that the Cabinet was prepared to make was to try to attract prominent Jews or those of independent means. None of this was done by changing the law. Though the government favoured certain groups of refugees, it did so discreetly. For example, the highly selective approach adopted by the voluntary Academic Assistance Council in assisting established academics was praised by the Home Secretary, as was the emphasis on re-emigration.[128]

Unfortunately for the Anglo-Jewish representatives, their estimates of the numbers of refugees who would reach the UK were much too conservative (3–4,000).[129] In fact, between 1933 and 1938, the UK took some 11,000 refugees.[130] As a result, the Jewish community found itself having to appeal to the public for funds, despite having raised £3,000,000 by 1939.[131] *The Times* newspaper, with the assistance of the former Prime Minister, Stanley Baldwin, chose also to launch an appeal in 1938, raising £500,000 within a few months.[132] Not until the outbreak of the war did the government contribute to

---

[125] B. Wasserstein, 'The British Government and the German Immigration 1933–45', in G. Hirschfeld, ed., *Exile in Great Britain – Refugees from Hitler's Germany* (Leamington Spa: Berg, 1984), p. 66.

[126] Cited in *ibid.*

[127] *ibid.*

[128] L. London, 'Jewish Refugees, Anglo-Jewry and British Government Policy, 1930–1940' in D. Cesarani, ed., *The Making of Modern Anglo-Jewry* (Oxford: Basil Blackwell, 1990), p. 172.

[129] B. Wasserstein, 'The British Government and the German Immigration 1933–45', in G. Hirschfeld, ed., *Exile in Great Britain – Refugees from Hitler's Germany* (Leamington Spa: Berg, 1984), p. 67.

[130] HC Deb. Vol. 341, November 21, 1938, col. 1314.

[131] B. Wasserstein, 'The British Government and the German Immigration 1933–45', in G. Hirschfeld, ed., *Exile in Great Britain – Refugees from Hitler's Germany* (Leamington Spa: Berg, 1984), p. 69.

[132] F. Carsten, 'German Refugees in Great Britain 1933–1945' in G. Hirschfeld, ed., *Exile in Great Britain – Refugees from Hitler's Germany* (Leamington Spa: Berg, 1984), p. 15.

the funds of the Central Council for Jewish Refugees, donating £533,000 in 1940 and £264,000 in 1941.[133]

While the visa system introduced during the First World War was still in existence for certain passengers, the general use of visas was in gradual decline following intergovernmental agreements.[134] From 1927, neither Austrian nor German citizens needed visas to enter the UK. This remained the position until March 1938, and the *Anschluß* between Germany and Austria,[135] by which time the Home Office was reconsidering its visa policy: 'The proper course is to select our immigrants at leisure and in advance, and this means the institution of a visa system, for Germans and Austrians [. . .] The real point is to prevent potential refugees from getting here at all.'[136] Concerned about a possible 'flood' of Austrian and German Jews, the government imposed a visa requirement on May 2, 1938 for all Austrian passport holders and on May 28, for Germans.[137] With a lack of resources, the Aliens Department found itself unable to cope under the pressure, as did the British embassies on the continent. Lengthy delays were the inevitable consequence. Six months after the re-introduction of visas, and in light of the events of *Kristallnacht* in November 1938, the government was once again forced to review its admission policy.[138] Voluntary groups were authorised to submit lists of individuals selected for admission. Working with this information, the Home Office was able to approve the lists using a block visa system, thereby accelerating considerably the whole process.[139] However, approval was given on the understanding that the voluntary groups remained responsible for ensuring that those listed were

---

[133] *ibid.*

[134] L. London, 'British Immigration Control Procedures and Jewish Refugees 1933–1939' in W. Mosse ed., *Second Chance – Two Centuries of German-speaking Jews in the United Kingdom* (Tübingen: J.C.B. Mohr (Paul Siebeck), 1991), pp. 490–1.

[135] The Treaty of Versailles 1919 proscribed the union between Germany and Austria. After the resignation of the Austrian Chancellor in 1938, the Germans were 'invited' to occupy Austria and the union of Germany and Austria (the *Anschluß*) was formally announced on March 13, 1938.

[136] McAlpine, Memorandum, March 1, 1938, PRO HO 213/94 cited in L. London, 'Jewish Refugees, Anglo-Jewry and British Government Policy, 1930–1940' in D. Cesarani, ed., *The Making of Modern Anglo-Jewry* (Oxford: Basil Blackwell, 1990), p. 175.

[137] L. London, 'British Immigration Control Procedures and Jewish Refugees 1933–1939' in W. Mosse ed., *Second Chance – Two Centuries of German-speaking Jews in the United Kingdom* (Tübingen: J.C.B. Mohr (Paul Siebeck), 1991), p. 504.

[138] On the night of November 9, 1938, there was an outbreak of orchestrated violence against Jews in Germany and Austria which became known as *Kristallnacht* because of the amount of glass smashed in Jewish homes and businesses.

[139] L. London, 'British Immigration Control Procedures and Jewish Refugees 1933–1939' in W. Mosse ed., *Second Chance – Two Centuries of German-speaking Jews in the United Kingdom* (Tübingen: J.C.B. Mohr (Paul Siebeck), 1991), p. 506.

suitable subjects for admission and that they would not become a burden on the state.[140] As a result, it is estimated that in excess of 40,000 refugees arrived in Britain in the period between November 1938 and September 1939.[141] The admission of this number of refugees in a relatively short time exposes the penurious nature of the UK's previous policy, which had seen only 13,000 refugees admitted over a five year period.[142]

Under the Munich Agreement of September 1938, Britain and France agreed with Italy and Germany that the Sudeten area of Czechoslovakia would be ceded to Germany with the rest of Czechoslovakia guaranteed freedom from unprovoked aggression. One immediate consequence was the exodus of people from the ceded territory to other parts of Czechoslovakia, as well as Bohemia, Moravia and Slovakia. Although the Agreement made arrangements for the transfer of populations and for the right to elect Czech nationality, some groups – mainly Jews – found that they were not welcome in Czechoslovakia. Comprising three different groups – Sudeten Germans who were anti Nazi, refugees from Germany and Austria in Czechoslovakia, and Jews from the Sudetenland –, Sudeten refugees were subjected to different categorisation, and thus different treatment, by the British authorities. The first group tended to be regarded as political refugees and casualties of Munich, the second group of 'Old Reich' refugees as political or Jewish refugees, and the third as mainly Sudeten Jews, and therefore Czech.[143] Czechoslovakia's reluctance to admit Czech Jews created difficulties for the British authorities. In an attempt to keep the problem contained in the region, Britain offered significant financial assistance to Czechoslovakia, a large proportion of which was aimed at the resettlement of refugees within the Czech territory as well as overseas, but to the exclusion, it was hoped, of the UK.[144] The public reaction was somewhat more sympathetic and, in response to appeals for assistance, the Lord

2.16

---

[140] *ibid.*

[141] HC Deb. Vol. 352, October 12, 1939, col. 538: The Home Secretary stated that 49,500 refugees had arrived from Germany and Austria, and 6,000 from Czechoslovakia. However, in 1943, the number of refugees stated to have been in Britain at the outbreak of war was given as 78,000: see L. London, 'British Immigration Control Procedures and Jewish Refugees 1933–1939' in W. Mosse ed., *Second Chance – Two Centuries of German-speaking Jews in the United Kingdom* (Tübingen: J.C.B. Mohr (Paul Siebeck), 1991), fn. 7.

[142] *ibid.*, p. 507.

[143] L. London, *Whitehall and the Jews 1933–1948 – British Immigration Policy and the Holocaust* (Cambridge: CUP, 2000), pp. 142–168.

[144] See Czechoslovakia (Financial Assistance) Act 1939, February 28, 1939, and Agreements between His Majesty's Government in the United Kingdom, the Government of the French Republic and the Government of the Czecho-slovak Republic, January 27, 1939, Cmd. 5933 (available as schs to the Act). Britain advanced

Mayor of London established a voluntary fund to aid the Czech refugees. Despite public concerns, the British government resisted pressure to admit large number of Czechs: by October 1938, only 350 special visas had been issued, 250 to Sudeten Germans and 100 to 'Old Reich' refugees.[145] London argues that these '"political refugees" were always at the top of British lists. At the bottom were always Jews with no recognised political activism, who were defined as "racial" or "economic" refugees.'[146] She goes on to claim that '[t]he fact that Jews were wanted by neither the Germans nor the Czechs was not seen as sufficient reason to offer them refuge in Britain.'[147] But the government was not alone in its closed-door policy towards Czech Jews; British Jewish organisations were themselves reluctant to take responsibility for refugees from Czechoslovakia, and Sir Herbert Emerson, the director of the Intergovernmental Committee on Refugees ('IGCR') established in 1938,[148] considered non-political Jews to be, in reality, economic migrants and consequently of low priority.[149]

By the time German troops occupied Czechoslovakia in March 1939, Britain had admitted a total of 2,900 people.[150] Germany's actions made the refugee crisis even more critical. For many, the only route out of Czechoslovakia was through Poland, but the Polish government turned back many illegal entrants. The Anglo-Czech Agreement was suspended and the remaining funds temporarily handed over to the British Committee for Refugees from Czechoslovakia ('BCRC') and later to the Czech Refugee Trust Fund ('CRTF'). These voluntary bodies, which were in charge of selecting suitable cases for emigration and admission to the UK, were in fact largely under Home Office control. Britain chose to adopt a policy aimed at preventing the departure of Jews in an effort to resist Germany's attempts at 'ethnic-cleansing'. Political cases were given priority, as were those in Poland. Visas were reintroduced in April 1939 for the holders of Czech passports. The British seemed to regard many of the refugees as unworthy of protection:

£10 million to Czechoslovakia, of which £4 million was a gift disbursed according to arrangements between the governments, and the remaining £6 million was a loan subject to interest.

[145] London, *Whitehall and the Jews 1933–1948 – British Immigration Policy and the Holocaust* (Cambridge: CUP, 2000), p. 148.
[146] *ibid.*
[147] *ibid.*, p. 150.
[148] See Ch. 4.
[149] London, *Whitehall and the Jews 1933–1948 – British Immigration Policy and the Holocaust* (Cambridge: CUP, 2000), p. 152.
[150] *ibid.*

'[. . .] most of the refugees appear to be Jews who are not in any real danger, and some of them are certainly undesirables whom the Poles would be justified in refusing. Their illegal exodus prejudices the position of refugees who *are* in real danger, and if they stayed it should be possible to emigrate them legally later.'[151]

Notwithstanding the restrictions, by May 15, 1939, the BCRC had assumed responsibility for approximately 7,100 people, plus a further 2,000 placed in other countries.[152] From May onwards, the visa policy took effect and selections were made by committee. Similar criteria were applied as for German and Austrian Jews: namely, 'endangerment, contribution to public life and suitability for re-emigration, taking into account such matters as the applicant's age and profession'.[153] Non-political Jews were the inevitable casualties of such a policy. In the eyes of the visa committee, 'most of the refugees were really all economic'.[154]

The British government's tendency to consider Jewish refugees as immigrants, and to apply a cost-benefit analysis to their admission, is not the only factor that may be singled out for criticism in the interwar period. Anglo-Jewry, while obviously keen to assist German and Austrian Jews, gave no guarantees of support for Czech, Polish, Hungarian or stateless Jews.[155] It shared the government's fears about an increase in anti-Semitism if too many Jews were admitted,[156] and endorsed the imposition of visas, particularly in the case of Austrian shopkeepers and small retail traders.[157] Yet the cautious and collaborative approach adopted by Anglo-Jewish representatives may, in the end, have helped assuage the fears of a nervous government. As Louise London argues, the intercessions of such representatives 'managed sufficiently to contain British hostility towards refugees

---

[151] Randall (Foreign Office) to Emerson, April 28, 1939, cited in L. London, *Whitehall and the Jews 1933–1948 – British Immigration Policy and the Holocaust* (Cambridge: CUP, 2000), p. 156.

[152] *ibid.*, p. 161.

[153] *ibid.*, p. 164.

[154] Cited in London, *Whitehall and the Jews 1933–1948 – British Immigration Policy and the Holocaust* (Cambridge: CUP, 2000), p. 164.

[155] L. London, 'Jewish Refugees, Anglo-Jewry and British Government Policy, 1930–1940' in D. Cesarani, ed., *The Making of Modern Anglo-Jewry* (Oxford: Basil Blackwell, 1990), p. 171.

[156] A.J. Sherman, *Island Refuge – Britain and Refugees from the Third Reich 1933–1939* (London: Paul Elek, 1973), pp. 175–76.

[157] L. London, 'Jewish Refugees, Anglo-Jewry and British Government Policy, 1930–1940' in D. Cesarani, ed., *The Making of Modern Anglo-Jewry* (Oxford: Basil Blackwell, 1990), pp. 175–76

from Germany' and, paradoxically, resulted in the admission of many more refugees than Anglo-Jewry had itself expected or desired.[158]

Spanish Republicans in flight

2.17 Refugees from the Spanish Civil War also encountered British resistance. Despite calls for assistance by the Basque President Aguirre to European governments, the UK was once again slow to respond, perhaps out of a distrust of Republicans and their political motivations.[159] Even in the face of popular support for the refugees, and particularly the children, the Home Office procrastinated. By the time a decision was taken to accept a few children, on the understanding that they would one day return to Spain, France had already taken 10,000 refugees.[160] The UK finally received 4,000 Basque children, placing them in special purpose-built camps where they stayed for months.[161] Once again fundraising was undertaken on a voluntary basis, the main protagonists being the Lord Mayor of London and the National Joint Committee for Spanish Relief, established in the House of Commons.[162] Initially, the British were generous in their support and generally sympathetic. In time, however, some minor incidents of unruly behaviour by some of the children resulted in an anti-Basque campaign in the tabloid press.[163] The inevitable consequence was a decline in donations and in sympathy from the indigenous population. Though some may have subsequently romanticised the welcome accorded the Spanish children, a more accurate picture is of a British people who soon tired of their 'guests' and who gradually came to regard them as an unwanted problem.

THE UNITED KINGDOM AND ITS WARTIME REFUGEES: A DUBIOUS LEGACY

2.18 'If the months between [the] Munich [conference] and the outbreak of war can be said to mark a peak of government and public

---

[158] *ibid.*, p. 189.

[159] T. Kushner & K. Knox, *Refugees in an Age of Genocide* (London: Frank Cass, 1999), p. 105.

[160] *ibid.*, p. 107.

[161] For an account of life in the camps, see T. Kushner & K. Knox, *Refugees in an Age of Genocide* (London: Frank Cass, 1999), Ch. 4.

[162] T. Kushner & K. Knox, *Refugees in an Age of Genocide* (London: Frank Cass, 1999), pp. 106 and 109.

[163] *ibid.*, p. 120.

sympathy for the German emigration, the graph of generosity declined to reach a nadir by the summer of 1940.'[164] The formal declaration of war was accompanied by an immediate cessation of visas. The risks of admitting refugees from enemy territory were deemed too great.[165] The usual wartime suspicion of enemy aliens soon emerged as the government announced the establishment of review tribunals and internment camps.[166] Such developments inaugurated a period in British refugee history which some have described as its darkest hour.

Internment of aliens was not unknown. During the First World War, Britain had interned tens of thousands of Germans and Austrians, who were classified as enemy aliens.[167] Prior to the Second World War, the government had seemed opposed to internment.[168] Yet, on the outbreak of hostilities, an immediate reversal occurred when the Home Secretary, Sir John Anderson, informed Parliament of his intention to 'review [. . .] all Germans and Austrians in this country' through the use of one-man tribunals.[169] The tribunals, 112 in total,[170] which were viewed as administrative bodies rather than law courts, divided enemy aliens into three categories: 'A' (to be interned); 'B' (exempt from internment but subject to restrictions); and 'C' (exempt from internment and from restrictions).[171] Initially, during the 'phoney war', few were actually interned (528 by January 1940), and of these only men were held.[172] Following the collapse of the Netherlands, Belgium and France, and heightened fears about the dangers of a 'Fifth Column' in Britain, the public mood shifted towards mass internment.[173] The increasingly hysterical climate was

---

[164] B. Wasserstein, 'The British Government and the German Immigration 1933–45', in G. Hirschfeld, ed., *Exile in Great Britain – Refugees from Hitler's Germany* (Leamington Spa: Berg, 1984), p. 76.

[165] *ibid.*, p. 77 .

[166] *ibid.*

[167] See P. Panayi, 'An Intolerant Act by an Intolerant Society: The Internment of Germans in Britain during the First World War' in D. Cesarani & T. Kushner, eds., *The Internment of Aliens in Twentieth Century Britain* (London: Frank Cass, 1993), pp. 53–75.

[168] B. Wasserstein, *Britain and the Jews of Europe 1939–1945* (Oxford: Clarendon Press, 1979), p. 83.

[169] HC Deb. Vol. 351, September 4, 1939, col. 367.

[170] M. Seyfert, 'His Majesty's Most Loyal Internees' in G. Hirschfeld, ed., *Exile in Great Britain – Refugees from Hitler's Germany* (Leamington Spa: Berg, 1984), p. 166.

[171] B. Wasserstein, *Britain and the Jews of Europe 1939–1945* (Oxford: Clarendon Press, 1979), p. 85.

[172] B. Wasserstein, 'The British Government and the German Immigration 1933–45', in G. Hirschfeld, ed., *Exile in Great Britain – Refugees from Hitler's Germany* (Leamington Spa: Berg, 1984), p. 77.

[173] The 'Fifth Column' is a popular expression describing enemy sympathisers who might assist an invasion.

partly engendered by the press. The *Daily Mail*, for example, urged its readers:

> 'Act! Act! Act! Do It Now! The rounding up of enemy agents must be taken out of the fumbling hands of local tribunals. All refugees from Austria, Germany and Czechoslovakia, men and women alike, should be drafted without delay to a remote part of the country and kept under strict supervision.'[174]

Between April and June 1940, increasing numbers of enemy aliens were rounded up, until, finally, by mid-July 1940, nearly all male refugees (about 20,000), 800 category 'A' and 3,000 category 'B' women, and several hundred children were in detention.[175] Their passports and visas were removed; they were isolated from the world; and some suffered unacceptable living conditions in the camps. Yet the public approved: in a survey conducted in July 1940, 55 per cent of those polled supported internment of all enemy aliens.[176] Nonetheless, there were some who still considered widespread segregation insufficient. Churchill was one such. Reported to have advocated 'collaring the lot!',[177] the Prime Minister now appeared to favour removing all internees from the UK.[178] Such a policy might have been fully implemented had it not been for the sinking of the *Arandora Star* on the way to Canada and the drowning of 146 Germans and 453 Italians.[179] The admission by the government, under pressure, that over 50 of the passengers had claimed to be refugees had a profound and immediate effect on public opinion. By August 1940, only 33 per cent of those interviewed now favoured mass internment.[180] While deportation was no longer considered a viable option by the majority, its past use was strongly defended. In

[174] *Daily Mail*, April 20, 1940, as cited in M. Seyfert, 'His Majesty's Most Loyal Internees' in G. Hirschfeld, ed., *Exile in Great Britain – Refugees from Hitler's Germany* (Leamington Spa: Berg, 1984), p. 168.
[175] F. Lafitte, *The Internment of Aliens* (London: penguin, 1940), pp. 72; 74.
[176] B. Wasserstein, *Britain and the Jews of Europe 1939–1945* (Oxford: Clarendon Press, 1979), p. 94.
[177] P. and L. Gillman, *'Collar the Lot!': How Britain Interned and Deported its Wartime Refugees* (London, 1980).
[178] *ibid.*, p. 133.
[179] B. Wasserstein, *Britain and the Jews of Europe 1939–1945* (Oxford: Clarendon Press, 1979), p. 99. The numbers given as dead vary; one commentator suggests that 175 Germans died and 486 Italians: L. Burletson, 'The State, Internment and Public Criticism in the Second World War' in D. Cesarani & T. Kushner, eds., *The Internment of Aliens in Twentieth Century Britain* (London: Frank Cass, 1993), p. 111.
[180] B. Wasserstein, *Britain and the Jews of Europe 1939–1945* (Oxford: Clarendon Press, 1979), p. 102.

the words of the Duke of Devonshire, transportation had been 'desir-able both to husband our resources of food and to get rid of useless mouths and so forth'.[181] In the months that followed the *Arandora Star* disaster, deportations declined sharply and thousands of internees were released. Such was the celerity of the government's reversal of policy that by August 1941, only 1,300 refugees remained in camps in the UK.[182]

The UK government's policy on internment and deportation of aliens was not only morally questionable, since many were undoubt-edly refugees, but also questionable in law. The power to detain was threefold: first, under art. 18B of the Defence (General Regulations) 1939, the Home Secretary could detain anyone whom he had rea-sonable cause to believe was of hostile origin;[183] second, under art. 12(6) of the Aliens Order 1920, the Home Secretary was entitled to deport aliens under certain circumstances and could, where neces-sary, authorise detention prior to deportation; and, finally, there appeared to be no rule of international law preventing the Secretary of State from interning civilian enemy aliens.[184] Whether *refugees* could be said rightly to have fallen under any of these provisions is doubtful. They were not individuals of hostile origin, nor were they enemy aliens. While some may have been detained prior to deportation, art.12(6) did not justify wide-scale internment without deportation, which certainly occurred.

2.19

In addition to the questionable nature of the Home Secretary's power to intern under national law, it can be argued that internment flew in the face of international law, in spirit if not technically in law. In his polemic on internment in the Second World War, Lafitte argued that the government had clearly violated the spirit of Art. 8 of the 1938 Convention, which granted refugees 'free and ready access to the courts of law' and which ensured that they should 'enjoy [. . .] the same rights and privileges as nationals'.[185] Internees had no right of appeal. Cohn, in a brief article in the *Modern Law Review* in 1941, suggested that the internment of refugees was contrary to Art. 2 of the Convention, the right to move freely and to reside in the country of refuge.[186] What Cohn failed to recognise was that the UK had adopted a reservation to the definition of 'refugee' under the 1938

---

[181] HL Deb. Vol. 117, August 6, 1940, col. 137.
[182] B. Wasserstein, *Britain and the Jews of Europe 1939–1945* (Oxford: Clarendon Press, 1979), p. 108.
[183] S.R. & O. 1939, No. 927.
[184] E.J. Cohn, 'Legal Aspects of Internment', (1941) *Modern Law Review*, pp. 200–203.
[185] F. Lafitte, *The Internment of Aliens* (London: Penguin, 1940), p. 220. For further discussion of the 1938 Convention, see Ch. 4.
[186] E.J. Cohn, 'Legal Aspects of Internment', (1941) *Modern Law Review*, p. 203.

Convention and had ensured that refugees as defined under Art. 1 only included those coming from Germany who, at the date of ratification, no longer enjoyed the protection of the German government.[187] Since the UK ratified the Convention in September 1938, any Jew fleeing Germany after that date was not a refugee in the eyes of the UK government, and, consequently, there could be no breach of the Convention in respect of post-1938 refugees. As Lafitte later notes with regard to the reservation:

> 'The Government thus has as many loopholes as it could wish for to evade almost all the provisions of the Convention so far as almost all refugees are concerned. That it should do so is contrary to the spirit of the Convention and to common decency; but there can be no doubt that it has done so.'[188]

The easing of the deportation and internment provisions coincided with reports reaching Britain of the treatment of Jews in Europe. From June 1942, a number of articles appeared in the British press on the mass execution of Jews in Poland and their deportation to the east.[189] Though regarded initially with some suspicion, by autumn 1942, they could no longer be ignored by the British government. In October 1942, a brief statement in the House of Lords referred to the persecution of the Jews.[190] This was followed on December 17, 1942 by a declaration of eleven Allied governments and the French National Committee that acknowledged 'this bestial policy of cold-blooded extermination' of the Jews by the German authorities.[191] Though public reaction was immediate and cried out for action to ease the plight of the Jews, once more the British government procrastinated. Within Cabinet circles, it was agreed that no more than 2,000 further refugees could be admitted to Britain,[192] that the quota system set out in the White Paper on Palestine in May 1939 continued to apply,[193] and that the solution to the 'Jewish problem' required international co-operation. The consequence was the Bermuda Conference of April 1943,[194] later described by Law, the Minister of State at the Foreign Office and head of the British delegation, as a 'façade

---

[187] See Ch. 4 for further discussion of the 1938 Convention.
[188] F. Lafitte, *The Internment of Aliens* (London: Penguin, 1940), p. 222.
[189] London, *Whitehall and the Jews 1933–1948 – British Immigration Policy and the Holocaust* (Cambridge: CUP, 2000), p. 198.
[190] HL Deb. Vol. 124, October 7, 1942, cols. 577–87.
[191] HC Deb. Vol. 385, December 17, 1942, col. 2083.
[192] B. Wasserstein, *Britain and the Jews of Europe 1939–1945* (Oxford: Clarendon Press, 1979), p. 348.
[193] *Palestine: A Statement of Policy* (London: May, 1939) Cmd. 6019. The White Paper fixed the number of admissions to Palestine from 1939–1944 at 75,000.
[194] See Ch. 4.

for inaction'.[195] The statistical evidence supports this view. Following the conference, the UK introduced three new visa categories – parents of forces' personnel; parents of unaccompanied children; and enemy aliens willing and acceptable to serve in the forces –, but after six months had issued only 52 visas.[196] According to London, '[F]or the rest of the war, the Home Office's position was simple: more Jewish refugees were not wanted. It also steadfastly resisted pressure to offer visas for the United Kingdom as a way of assisting Jews to enter other territory where they would be safe.'[197] Even Palestine was closed to the majority of adults. Of the original 75,000 places proposed by the 1939 White Paper, 29,000 remained and these were held back for children and some accompanying adults.[198]

CONCLUSION

The UK's refugee policy in the inter-war years, whether in relation to Jews or to the Spanish, is open to serious question. The philanthropy which may have been partly in evidence during the First World War had long since disappeared by the 1930s and had been replaced by a new, ungenerous view of 'refugeehood'. Writing in 1939, Sir John Hope Simpson provided a particularly damning assessment of the UK's restrictive stance:

2.20

> 'Great Britain's record in the admission of refugees is not distinguished if it be compared with that of France, Czechoslovakia, or the United States of America. The strictly enforced restrictive and selective policy of immigration which she has pursued since the War – particularly the emphasis placed on the admission only of aliens with economic resources adequate for their re-establishment – has kept the number of admissions to figures that have little significance in the total numbers of post-war refugees. The one possible exception to this generalization, the admission of Jewish refugees from Germany, is the result of the extraordinary effort and generosity of the Jewish community in Great Britain in undertaking unconditional responsibility for their support.'[199]

This from one of the leading researchers of his day into the refugee question. Though others have formulated a more positive view of the

---

[195] Cited in A. Morse, *While Six Million died: A Chronicle of American Apathy* (New York: Random House, 1968), p. 63.

[196] London, *Whitehall and the Jews 1933–1948 – British Immigration Policy and the Holocaust* (Cambridge: CUP, 2000), p. 220–221.

[197] *ibid.*, p. 221.

[198] *ibid.* see for discussion of White Paper Ch. 4., para. 4.6.

[199] J.H. Simpson, *The Refugee Problem: Report of a Survey* (London: OUP, 1939), p. 344.

UK's legacy, even describing it as 'comparatively compassionate',[200] there is no doubt that those refugees who succeeded in gaining entry to British territory did so heavily against the odds.

While one might be able to explain British refugee policy prior to 1942, when the horrors which were being played out on the European stage were not fully apprehended, it is difficult to condone the government's attitude after the Allied Declaration. Wasserstein writes that even 'in the final year of the war, when escape from Europe again became a practicable proposition for a few of the Jewish survivors, the British government resumed its practice of earlier years in seeking to prevent the departure of Jews from Europe'.[201] What explanations are there for such an approach? Wasserstein suggests that the British government was forced, in the face of war, to weigh up its priorities and balance its interests;[202] the Jewish refugees were a low priority. He concludes that there may have been an element of anti-Semitism underpinning the decision-making process, as well as 'collective paranoia' engendered by war.[203] Finally, he rejects the argument that the UK's record, while unimpressive, was better than that of many other states.[204] This assessment strikes a resonant chord. For a country that has sought for decades to proclaim its great tradition of asylum, its wartime refugee policy was undoubtedly problematic. That the catalogue of its failures in this period has been largely wiped from the public and political memory is a sobering reminder of the ability of authorities to manipulate the historical record.

---

[200] A.J. Sherman, *Island Refuge – Britain and Refugees from the Third Reich 1933–1939* (London: Paul Elek, 1973), p. 267.
[201] B. Wasserstein, *Britain and the Jews of Europe 1939–1945* (Oxford: Clarendon Press, 1979), p. 348.
[202] *ibid.*, p. 355.
[203] *ibid.*
[204] *ibid.*, p. 357.

Chapter Three

The Emergence of a National Refugee Law: Asylum Seeker as Immigrant 1945–1993

INTRODUCTION

Despite the materialisation of a human rights-oriented interna- **3.1**
tional refugee law following the Second World War,[1] UK law
appeared to remain largely unaffected. If the period to 1945 had
established anything in relation to asylum law, it was that policy-
makers persisted in regarding refugees as thinly disguised immigrants. Even individuals who were patently fleeing persecution were
described alternatively as immigrants as well as refugees. Much of
the debate surrounding the Jewish question in the Second World
War had been conducted in the context of immigration, whether
to the UK or Palestine. Having recognised in part that it had failed
many Jewish refugees prior to and during the war, one might have
presumed that the UK government would act swiftly to amend its
laws on aliens. This was not to be. There continued to be neither
a distinct asylum regime nor a right of appeal for failed asylum
seekers, and post-war peace did little to alter the legal perception
of refugees as immigrants.

This chapter will discuss some of the key immigration statutes
which affected asylum seekers to the UK – the Commonwealth Acts
of 1962 and 1968, and the Immigration Act 1971 –, and will provide an outline of the asylum process up to the critical year of 1993,
when an asylum-specific law was enacted. In order to show the
impact of UK law and policy on individual asylum seekers, it will
conclude with some concrete examples relating to Ugandan Asians,
Chileans, South East Asians, Tamils, Kurds and refugees from the
former Yugoslavia.

---

[1] See Ch. 4.

POST-WAR POLICY

3.2 The lack of any stated policy on asylum ensured that much of the decision-making process was shrouded in secrecy; only departmental statements to Parliament helped provide a degree of transparency. Any talk of a permanent aliens statute was dismissed in 1949, the Home Office preferring to proceed with the farcical annual continuation of the Aliens Restriction (Amendment) Act 1919.[2] Calls in 1950 for a right of appeal akin to that in the United States were met with a stern rebuttal: 'As to a question of a tribunal or advisory committee, [. . .] it is better to place the responsibility fairly and squarely on the Minister and make him responsible for answering to the House for any action that is taken or not taken.'[3] When the Aliens Order of 1920 was finally replaced in 1953 by a new Aliens Order, there was little change to the system and no mention of important developments in international law, such as the 1951 Convention Relating to the Status of Refugees.[4] Once again, harking back to the terminology of the 1905 Act, the Order classified those persons to whom leave to land would be refused.[5] The Home Secretary was given the power to deport where an alien had been convicted of an offence punishable with imprisonment and where the court had recommended deportation; or where he deemed it to be 'conducive to the public good'.[6] The enormous discretion accorded the Home Secretary since 1919 allowed him to act very much as he saw fit and without any parliamentary control, as was recognised by the Home Department in relation to deportation:

> 'The Aliens Order gives the Secretary of State power to deport at discretion and the entire responsibility rests with him. He takes the decision himself, [. . .] and it has become the practice for the Secretary of State not to discuss the reasons and to ask the House of Commons to trust him.'[7]

Not altogether a helpful approach for those who wished for greater openness in the Aliens Department. Following the European

---

[2] HC Deb. Vol. 469, November 4, 1948–49, cols 800–17.
[3] HC Deb. Vol. 472, March 9, 1950, col. 447.
[4] See Ch. 4 and *passim* for further discussion.
[5] Arts 4 (1) and (2). Aliens subject to refusal included: those unable to support themselves and any dependants; those in search of employment but not in possession of the Ministry of Labour's voucher; those sentenced abroad for extradition crimes; those of unsound mind or mentally defective; and the medically unfit.
[6] Arts 20 and 21.
[7] HC Deb. Vol. 548, February 2, 1956, col. 1209.

Convention on Establishment,[8] the government did, in 1956, alter the arrangements for deportation. Aliens who had been present in the country for more than two years, and whom it was proposed to deport, could make representations to the Chief Magistrate.[9] There were three crucial exceptions: those whom it was proposed to deport on security grounds; those to be deported on a court recommendation; and illegal entrants.[10] This final exception could prove vital in the case of asylum seekers who were not in possession of correct documentation or who were trying to gain entry to the UK in breach of the immigration rules.

On occasion, the Home Department did offer a little more information on its asylum policies. For example, in 1949, the Under-Secretary of State for the Home Department, in answer to a question on political asylum, made the following statement:

'It is still the practice, as always, not to send back to countries where they would be in danger of persecution people in respect of whom my right hon. Friend is satisfied that they are political refugees. [. . .]

We have not been able to accept the view that just because somebody has been a political refugee in his own country we must necessarily always agree to have him here – if, for instance, he is already in France and has no greater claim on us than he has on France. [. . .]

A number of people – largely stowaways – come here direct from countries where they claim to be in danger of persecution. We do not send them back if we are satisfied there is any real ground for that claim, but the House will appreciate that when somebody arrives without any documents whatever, and probably no one except himself is able to tell us how he came to be on the ship, we have to guard against being made fools of by large numbers of people who have not come here because they were persecuted or hold any political views, or had ever been politically active, but simply think that it is the best story to tell.'[11]

This statement could as easily have been made in 2003 as in 1949. It reveals quite clearly that the desire to keep asylum seekers from the doors of the UK is not a recent phenomenon, nor is the concern with

---

[8] The European Convention on Establishment was signed in Paris in December 1955 and instituted some common rules for the treatment accorded to nationals of each member state in the territory of the others.

[9] In line with Art. 3(3) of the Convention which states: 'Nationals of any Contracting Party who have been lawfully residing for more than ten years in the territory of any other Party may only be expelled for reasons of national security or if the other reasons mentioned in para. 1 of this art. are of a particularly serious nature.'

[10] HC Deb. Vol. 668, November 28, 1962, col. 433.

[11] HC Deb. Vol. 469, November 4, 1948–49, cols. 810–11.

undocumented asylum applicants and illegal entrants. It is also rather striking that, while the statement was made only four years after the end of the war, there was no mention of racial or religious persecution and the concentration was on political asylum – reflecting already perhaps the growing tension with the Soviet bloc.

AN UNUSUAL EXCEPTION: HUNGARIANS IN FLIGHT

3.3   Following the UK's signing of the 1951 Convention, the government was at pains to indicate that it was applying, and had always applied, the principles as laid out in the Convention. Thus, in 1954, the Home Secretary proffered the following opinion:

> 'I would point out, with regard to political asylum, that what I stated to be the principle has not only been the principle acted upon in this country throughout the past years, but is enshrined in the latest Convention that deals with the subject; namely, that political asylum is given where the national of a country is in danger in regard to his life and liberty from political persecution, among other forms of persecution, in that country.'[12]

The failure to take any further measures to incorporate the Convention into national law reinforced the rudimentary nature of the extant system, which relied almost totally upon executive discretion, parliamentary goodwill, and the integrity of government ministers. It persisted in such a state for a number of years. Its one saving grace, flexibility, enabled the government, on purely political grounds, to agree to the admission of thousands of Poles following the war (though they were seldom described as refugees),[13] and of over 21,000 Hungarians following the 1956 uprising (notwithstanding the initial intention to admit only 2,500).[14]

The Hungarians proved to be one of the most favourably treated refugee groups in the post-war era. They received massive public sympathy, though a few parliamentary dissenters feared that Communist agents might be lurking amongst their number.[15] The Lord Mayor of London's Appeal, that ever reliable source of refugee funding, raised a staggering £2,500,000,[16] while the government,

---

[12] HC Deb. Vol. 529, July 1, 1954, col. 1508.
[13] T. Kushner & K. Knox, *Refugees in an Age of Genocide* (London: Frank Cass, 1999), p. 240.
[14] *ibid.*, pp. 248 and 245.
[15] HC Deb. Vol. 562, December 21, 1956, col. 238 (Written Answers).
[16] T. Kushner & K. Knox, *Refugees in an Age of Genocide* (London: Frank Cass, 1999), p. 251.

conscious of the popularity of the cause, donated £355,000 towards the transportation and resettlement costs of the refugees.[17] After the rather dismal record of previous decades, the welcome held out to the Hungarians was striking. As Knox states, 'The Hungarian uprising of 1956 [. . .] galvanised a more meaningful rediscovery of asylum'.[18] It was certainly the first notable episode in post-war refugee history in which the new arrivals were considered to be true refugees rather than immigrants. The explanation for this change in perception is largely self-evident, seen in the context of the Cold War. There can be no doubt that the refugee issue had become a political tool in east-west relations; the admission of Hungarians was as much a political statement against Communism as a humanitarian gesture.

DR SOBLEN: A CATALYST FOR CHANGE

Any renewed faith in British asylum policy was soon to be dashed when, in 1962, the Home Office refused entry to one Dr Soblen, giving rise to an infamous case.[19] Dr Soblen was a Lithuanian Jew who had immigrated to the United States in 1940. In 1961, he was convicted of having conspired to provide secret information to Russia and sentenced to life imprisonment. He appealed to the Supreme Court. On rejection of his appeal, Dr Soblen, using his brother's passport, fled to Israel where he was promptly expelled by the Israeli authorities for illegal entry. He was placed on a flight to the US via Athens and London. Between Athens and London he stabbed himself in the stomach and slashed his wrists, thereby forcing the London authorities to hospitalise him. He was, however, served with a notice of refusal to land by the Home Office. Partly recovered, and pre-empting his imminent forced departure, he applied for a writ of *habeas corpus*. He asked to be sent to Czechoslovakia, against the wishes of the US. He claimed political asylum, which was turned down. Pending the outcome of the *habeas corpus* case, he was transferred to Brixton prison. However, his application for *habeas corpus* was also unsuccessful. Since Dr Soblen's offence was non-extraditable, the Home Secretary made a deportation order on the basis that it was conducive to the public good.

In a second *habeas corpus* action challenging the legality of the deportation order, Dr Soblen's counsel claimed that: (1) the Aliens

3.4

---

[17] HC Deb. Vol. 566, March 6, 1957, cols. 342–3.
[18] T. Kushner & K. Knox, *Refugees in an Age of Genocide* (London: Frank Cass, 1999), p. 240.
[19] *R. v Governor of Brixton Prison (Governor), ex parte Soblen* [1962] 3 AER 641.

Order 1953 was *ultra vires* the Aliens Restriction Act 1914 because there was no longer any war prevailing when the Order was made; (2) the deportation order was invalid because it was made for an alien who had been refused leave to land; (3) the deportation order was invalid because the Home Secretary had not heard representations from Dr Soblen; and (4) the deportation order was being used to disguise an illegal extradition under both US and UK extradition laws. Though Dr Soblen failed to persuade either the vacation judge or the Court of Appeal by his arguments, the courts rehearsed the law on aliens, extradition and deportation. In so doing, they made patently clear that the exercise of the Home Secretary's discretion was unchallengeable by the courts, since they could not look into 'the way in which or the grounds on which he has exercised his discretion, provided that it appears that he has purported to exercise those powers under and in accordance with the Aliens Order.'[20] The judgement also agreed that there was no duty on the Home Secretary to hear representations. Yet the most significant part of the Court of Appeal's decision was in respect of point (4): the possible use of deportation as a disguise for extradition.

Lord Denning, in a brief summary of the law of extradition and the Royal Prerogative, decided, arguably incorrectly, that under international law 'any country is entitled to expel an alien if his presence is for any reason obnoxious to it'.[21] Denning went on to add that the question of alien expulsion under Royal Prerogative was in any case irrelevant, having been supplanted by Articles 20 and 21 of the Aliens Order 1953. The issue for Denning was whether the Home Secretary was surrendering the applicant to the US because it had asked for him, or whether the surrender was being made because his presence was not conducive to the public good. In other words, said the Master of the Rolls:

'It is open to these courts to inquire whether the purpose of the Home Secretary was a lawful or an unlawful purpose. Was there a misuse of the power or not? The courts can always go behind the face of the deportation order in order to see whether the powers entrusted by Parliament have been exercised lawfully or no.'[22]

Since the Home Secretary claimed Crown privilege over written communications between the Home Office and the US about the Soblen case, the power of the Court to establish whether the Home Secretary had acted improperly was purely hypothetical; it could not,

---

[20] [1962] 3 AER at 655.
[21] *ibid.*, at 660.
[22] *ibid.*, at 661.

in fact, 'go behind the face' of the order. Furthermore, the Court seemed to be imposing an unreasonable burden of proof upon the applicant, one that he could never hope to meet. Thus, despite Denning's suggestion that the courts held sway over the executive in such cases, the power granted by the Aliens Order to the Home Secretary enabled him to act unfettered, even though his decision was highly suspect. As in the *Duke of Château Thierry* case 55 years earlier, which bound the Court of Appeal and to which it referred, there was a reluctance to recognise that deportation *was* being used as disguised extradition and that scant regard was being paid to the provisions of the Extradition Act 1870, which barred surrender of political offenders, and to the principle of *non-refoulement* as set out in Article 33 of the 1951 Convention.[23]

This absolute power in the hands of one man, the Home Secretary, led to wide criticism: 'It is submitted that [these discretionary powers] are too immense not to be subjected to judicial process. What one may suffer in a time of war or national emergency in the way of arbitrary exclusion, arrest and deportation, one should not permit in other circumstances.'[24] The inability of an individual to make representations was described by one Member of Parliament as 'monstrous' and unjustifiable 'when all over the world there are people caught up in the flotsam and jetsam of world conditions for which they are not responsible but of which they are the inevitable victims'.[25] In the end, attention came to rest not so much on the failure of the British system to uphold the traditional values of individual liberty and natural justice as on the personal tragedy of Dr Soblen who, before the day of his deportation from the UK, took his own life with an overdose of drugs.

COMMONWEALTH IMMIGRANTS ACTS 1962 AND 1968

The significance of the year 1962 was not due to the *Soblen* case alone; **3.5** it also marked the passing of one of the most significant immigration statutes since 1905: the Commonwealth Immigrants Act 1962. Whereas aliens were controlled by legislation passed in the early part of the century, Commonwealth citizens had a right to enter the UK without restriction. Following the end of the Second World War,

---

[23] See, for further discussion, P. O'Higgins, 'Disguised Extradition: The Soblen Case' (1964) 27 *MLR* pp. 521–539; C. Thornberry, 'Is the Non-surrender of Political Offenders Outdated?' (1963) 26 *MLR*, pp. 555–560.

[24] C. Thornberry, 'Dr. Soblen and the Alien Law of the United Kingdom', (1968) 12 *ICLQ*, p. 468.

[25] HC Deb. Vol. 668, November 28, 1962, col. 413.

Commonwealth citizens, particularly from the Caribbean, began to exercise this right and to enter the 'mother country' in increasing numbers. As their numbers grew, so did the protests. There was an uncanny familiarity about the calls for legislation. Though more than 60 years separated the two Acts, the background to the Aliens Act 1905 and the Commonwealth Immigrants Act 1962 was remarkably similar. Anti-alien and anti-immigration agitation revolved around insecurities about employment. Terms such as 'invasion', 'swamp' and 'flood' were used. The shock of seeing 'people of colour' in the early 1960s was matched at the turn of the century by the strangeness of appearance of many of the Jewish migrants.[26] Just as the native occupants of the East End had complained that their area had been taken over and transformed into a slum by the new arrivals, the people of South and West London, Bradford and the West Midlands now repeated the same arguments. Legislation was the inevitable consequence. The sole significant difference was that while the 1962 Act attempted to control immigration from the Commonwealth, no thought was given to the peripheral matter of asylum. The Act simply required those in possession of a Commonwealth passport, who wished to enter the UK for employment, to apply for a work voucher from the Ministry of Labour. The Act also granted for the first time a power of deportation of Commonwealth citizens following a court recommendation. Numerous commentators criticised the new law, some even proposing that a right of asylum be written into the Act, but their calls fell on deaf ears.[27]

Thus with the end of the time-honoured relationship with the Commonwealth came the arrival of permanent immigration control. All citizens, whether of the Commonwealth or UK and Colonies, were now vulnerable, as was revealed by the case of the East African Asians in the late 1960s. Many East African Asians possessed UK passports. When in 1967 President Kenyatta of Kenya started to introduce discriminatory policies against Asians, a number of them exercised their right to enter the UK. By February 1968, it was estimated that 750 Kenyan Asians per day were arriving in the UK. The government panicked and rushed through a second Commonwealth Immigrants Act in under three days – behaving remarkably like the 1914 government when it passed the Aliens Restriction Act of the same year. However, this time there was no war to justify the unusual haste.

---

[26] J.A. Garrard, 'Parallels of Protests: English Reactions to Jewish and Commonwealth Immigration', (1967–68) 9 *Race*, p. 49.

[27] C. Thornberry, *The Stranger at the Gate*, cited in T.W.E. Roche, *The Key in the Lock* (London: John Murray, 1969), p. 217.

The Act ensured that only those holders of a UK and Colonies' passport who had an ancestral link with the UK were now entitled to enter. For others, a quota system of entry vouchers was used. With one swift move, the government breached its implied promise to the non-white members of the colonies that they would continue to have rights of open entry to the UK. At least 200,000 East African Asians were said to be covered by the Act.[28] Many were left stateless, having failed to take Kenyan citizenship; yet more were bounced from country to country as each refused entry. Though the government ultimately had to relent and grant admission to a significant number, its objective of restricting entry was largely achieved.[29] Later, in 1978, when commenting on this period, the UNHCR stated that many of the individuals from the Commonwealth countries who had sought asylum in the UK from 1962 onwards had not been recognised as refugees, though they had been admitted under other rules at the Home Secretary's discretion.[30]

THE IMMIGRATION ACT 1971

Introduction

In 1971, immigration law was completely overhauled by the Immigration Act 1971. Its aim was to consolidate the law relating to the immigration and deportation of aliens and Commonwealth citizens under one statute. One of its major changes was to restrict rights of entry and abode to Commonwealth citizens who had a 'patrial' connection with the UK – that is, a parent or grandparent had been born in the UK. Despite being the major British immigration statute of the twentieth century, it did not expressly cover asylum; it fell to the Immigration Rules[31] to 'legislate' for asylum-related matters, thereby

3.6

---

[28] HC Deb. Vol 759, February 27, 1968, col. 1246.

[29] See, for further discussion, A. Dummett & A. Nicol, *Subjects, Citizens and Others – Nationality and Immigration Law* (London: Weidenfeld & Nicolson, 1990), Ch. 11; P. Shah, *Refugees, Race and the Legal Concept of Asylum in Britain* (London: Cavendish, 2000), Ch. 5; R. Hansen, *Citizenship and Immigration in Post-war Britain* (Oxford: OUP, 2000), Ch. 7.

[30] Select Committee on Race Relations and Immigration, Session 1977–78, 'The Effect of the UK's Membership of the EEC on Race Relations and Immigration', (410–ix), Minutes of Evidence, July 6, 1978, paras 14 and 15, p. 169.

[31] The Immigration Rules are administrative rules formulated by the Home Secretary and laid before Parliament which set out provisions governing entry and stay in the United Kingdom. In the wording of s. 3(2) of the Immigration Act 1971, the Rules set out 'the practice to be followed in the administration of this Act for regulating the entry into and stay in the United Kingdom of persons required by this Act to

creating a system of control that was administrative and largely discretionary. Despite the formal adherence to the 1951 Convention and
1967 Protocol,[32] the UK had incorporated neither into domestic
law[33] and had failed to establish a satisfactory procedure for refugee
determination.[34] The 1973 Immigration Rules, though spelling out
the criteria of Art. 1A(2) (the definition of a refugee under the
1951 Convention) in the very brief paragraph on 'political asylum',
referred to the Convention only in a footnote:

> 'A passenger who does not otherwise qualify for admission should not be
> refused leave to enter if the only country to which he can be removed is
> one to which he is unwilling to go owing to well-founded fear of being
> persecuted for reasons of race, religion, nationality, membership of a
> particular social group or political opinion.*
>
> * The criterion for the grant of asylum is in accordance with Article 1 of
> the Convention relating to the Status of Refugees (Cmd. 9171).'[35]

The provisions of the Convention were factors to be taken into
account but, since they were not incorporated into UK law, they were
not directly enforceable. Though case law referred on occasion to the
Convention, it was not until 1987 that the House of Lords, in
Bugdaycay v Secretary of State for the Home Department ('*Bugdaycay*'), was
asked to deal with issues arising under the 1951 Convention. Lord
Bridge was moved to point this out, noting: 'This is the first time your
Lordships' House has had to consider the Convention.'[36]

---

have leave to enter, including any rules as to the period for which leave is to be given
and the conditions to be attached in different circumstances'. As the major source
of practical and procedural provisions, the Rules play a prime role in determination
of asylum applications. The current Rules are contained in the 'Statement of
Changes in Immigration Rules' laid before Parliament on May 23, 1994, HC 395
(as amended).

[32] See Ch. 4 for discussion of the Convention and Protocol.

[33] Note that although some case-law has suggested that incorporation had taken place
– see *R. v Secretary of State for the Home Department, ex parte Singh (Parminder)*, *The Times*,
June 8, 1987 –, strictly speaking, the Convention was not formally incorporated.
However, the House of Lords in *R. v Secretary of State for the Home Department, ex parte
Sivakumaran* [1988] Imm AR 147, at 148 stated that 'The United Kingdom having
acceded to the Convention and Protocol, their provisions have for all practical
purposes been incorporated into United Kingdom law.'

[34] In line with recommendations of the UNHCR's Executive Committee in
Conclusions of the Executive Committee 1977 No. 8 (XXVII)(d).

[35] Statement of Immigration Rules for Control on Entry of Commonwealth Citizens,
HC 79, January 25, 1973, para. 54. By 1994, there were 26 paragraphs dealing
specifically with asylum: *Statement of Changes in Immigration Rules*, HC 395, May 23,
1994.

[36] [1987] Imm AR 250, at 253.

Procedure

The absence of detailed legislation on asylum seekers was accompa-   **3.7**
nied by a somewhat unsophisticated procedure, which again lacked
transparency. Neither the law nor the Immigration Rules explained
the bureaucracy of the Home Office, and there was difficulty in keeping abreast of Home Office practice, since it could be altered at any
time and without much publicity.[37] By the early 1980s, port and in-
country applications were being handled separately. Anyone making
an asylum claim at a port of entry was interviewed by an immigration officer, who then forwarded a report, unseen by the asylum
seeker, to the Home Office for a final decision.[38] It is worth noting,
however, that in this period the requirement to refer to the Home
Office was not altogether clear. Paragraph 73 of the 1983 Immigration Rules (HC 169)[39] stated that immigration officers were required
to refer to the Home Office any case in which 'special considerations'
arose; that is, 'where the only country to which a person could be
removed [was] one to which he [was] unwilling to go owing to a well-
founded fear of being persecuted for reasons of race, religion, nationality, membership of a particular social group or political opinion'. In
other words, the Rules appeared to suggest that reference was only
necessary where there was no other country to which the asylum
seeker could be sent.[40] By 1990, this deficiency had been addressed
and all asylum claims had to be referred to the Home Office irrespective of whether there was an alternative country to which the
applicant could be removed, or of other grounds for refusing entry.[41]
Since there was, until 1987, no standard questionnaire to be completed by port applicants, there was no guarantee of consistency
between interviews. Lord Bridge, in the case of *In re Musisi*, commented with some surprise on the procedure for interviewing at ports:
'I find it strange that such an important interview as this should be
entrusted to an immigration officer at the port of entry with no
knowledge of conditions in the country of origin of a claimant for
asylum.'[42] In-country claims generally received more expert attention
in that they were considered initially by Home Office officials with
greater experience in refugee matters. Occasionally, police officers

---

[37] Grant & Martin, *Immigration Law & Practice* (London: The Cobden Trust, 1982),
p. 325.
[38] MacDonald & Blake, *Immigration Law and Practice* (London: Butterworths, 1991)
p. 305.
[39] Effective from February 16, 1983.
[40] MacDonald & Blake, *Immigration Law and Practice* (Butterworths, 1991), p. 305.
[41] Effective from May 1, 1990; para. 75.
[42] [1987] Imm AR 250, at 260.

were called upon to interview an asylum seeker, but it was soon noted that the quality of police interviews was poor.[43] Partly in response to pressure from non-governmental organisations representing refugees ('NGOs') and from the courts, and partly in view of the increasing burden imposed on asylum procedures, a more structured approach was slowly established. By 1993, immigration officers in port cases were expected to conduct a brief interview with the asylum seeker in order to complete a now standard form for referral of asylum cases to the Home Office.[44] Normally, applicants were given temporary admission[45] to the UK at this stage, although a percentage were detained.[46] Following this initial interview, and assuming that the Home Office considered the UK the correct country to deal with the claim, an applicant needed to complete a further form: the Political Asylum Questionnaire ('PAQ').[47] All in-country applicants were also required to complete the PAQ and submit it to the Home Office within a certain time limit.[48]

3.8   On rejecting an asylum claim, the Home Office was not required, until the mid-1980s, to provide reasons for rejection of the claim. Again in deference to judicial opinion,[49] secondary legislation was introduced in 1984 requiring the Home Secretary to give reasons for the decision taken: 'any notice given [of any decision which is appeal-able] [. . .] shall include a statement of the reasons for the decision or action to which it relates.'[50] These reasons did not, however, have to

---

[43] Grant & Martin, *Immigration Law & Practice* (London: The Cobden Trust, 1982), p. 329.

[44] Known as the 'pro-forma referral'. Pro-forma referrals were normally completed by the immigration service when applications for asylum were made at ports in order to determine whether an applicant had arrived from a 'safe third country'.

[45] Temporary admission (normally for short periods of up to three months) may be granted to a person liable to be detained, but is not tantamount to leave to enter the UK (Immigration Act 1971, s. 11 and sch. 2). It can therefore be withdrawn at any stage. There may be conditions attached to the grant of TA, such as residence and employment restrictions, and reporting to the police or immigration officers (Immigration Act 1971, sch. 2, para. 21(2)).

[46] See Chs 5–8 for further discussion of the use of detention in asylum.

[47] Now known as the 'Statement of Evidence Form' ('SEF'), the PAQ was divided into four sections:
A: personal, educational, employment details
B: details of spouse, children, and immediate family
C: the basis for the asylum claim
D: miscellaneous details

[48] Originally, the time allowed for in-country applicants was twelve weeks. In 1994, this was reduced to four weeks.

[49] See, for example, *R. v Secretary of State for the Home Department, ex parte Gurmeet Singh* [1987] Imm AR 489, at 498, in which the Divisional Court stated that 'it would be preferable [. . .] that in a case of an application for asylum reasons for the decision to refuse an application are given to an applicant'.

[50] Immigration Appeals (Notices) Regulations 1984, 4(1)(a).

be comprehensive, as noted by Parker L.J., in the case of *R. v Secretary of State for the Home Department, ex parte Swati*: 'What counsel for Mr Swati is in effect seeking is not reasons for the refusal but the reasons for the reasons for the refusal and for that the 1984 regulations do not provide.'[51] However, a practice was instituted by which a 'minded to refuse' letter was sent to the applicant notifying him or her of the Home Office's intention to refuse the asylum claim and offering the applicant an opportunity to comment on the reasons for refusal.

Not all refusals resulted in removal of the applicant. Until 1979, 'asylum' as opposed to refugee status was retained as a separate category in the UK and was 'usually considered more appropriate than refugee recognition for Commonwealth citizens'.[52] The use of secondary status continued nonetheless. Some applicants who failed to meet the refugee criteria were granted, outside the Immigration Rules and on a discretionary basis, 'exceptional leave to remain' ('ELR'). ELR entitled an applicant to stay in the UK but did not carry with it the same rights as refugee status. For example, there was no right to family reunion and the applicant had to have been living in the UK for at least four years before the Home Office would consider a claim for such reunion; seven years' residence was usually required before a settlement application would be entertained. Whereas housing and social benefits were similar to those available to refugees, individuals granted ELR, unlike the refugee, were not entitled to travel documentation.[53] Prior to the Asylum and Immigration Appeals Act 1993, ELR was generally awarded where it would have been 'unreasonable or impracticable' to return the applicant to his or her original country, as in cases where the country of origin was in a continuing state of upheaval.

Appeals

The limitations of the asylum system went beyond the initial stage of refugee determination. Under the Immigration Act 1971, there were limited rights of appeal accorded to asylum applicants; this was partly as a result of the conclusions arrived at by the 'Wilson Committee' set   **3.9**

---

[51] [1986] 1 WLR 477, at 490.
[52] Home Affairs Committee Race Relations and Immigration Sub-Committee, Session 1984–85, 'Refugees', Minutes of Evidence, December 17, 1984, paras 5 and 9, p. 68. All those granted asylum were, in July 1979, recognised as refugees.
[53] See, for an early discussion of ELR, Home Affairs Committee Race Relations and Immigration Sub-Committee, Session 1984–85, 'Refugees', Minutes of Evidence, December 17, 1984, paras 44–47, p. 77.

up in 1967 to examine the whole issue of immigration appeals.[54] The Committee spent very little time on refugee rights but did agree that claims to political asylum 'could be suitably dealt with under the appeal system' proposed – that is, under a general immigration appeals system.[55] It recommended that special arrangements be made to expedite the hearing of appeals where the appellant was seeking political asylum, and recognised that some such appeals would need to be heard in private. Wilson accepted that where an appellant claimed to be a refugee within the competence of the UNHCR, the UK Representative of the High Commissioner should be given notice of the proceedings and have an opportunity to make his or her views known.[56] In line with the recommendations of the Wilson Committee, an immigration appeals system was established,[57] but the appeal rights of asylum seekers remained very limited. However, it was agreed that the UNHCR be advised of appeals by asylum applicants and be treated as a party to an appeal on request.[58] Though this allowed the expertise of the UNHCR to be called upon in certain cases, the value of the UNHCR's presence in such appeals was soon questioned. A Working Party on Appeals against Refusal of Asylum in the UK, established in 1977, expressed its concern 'that the participation of the Office of the UNHCR apparently made little difference to the outcome of the appeal'.[59] Despite this view, the UNHCR continued to play a part in the appeals process. The Working Party also reported its concern that 'appeals by people who are seeking asylum in Britain are dealt with under the same procedure and in the same way as those of immigrants, students or visitors to this country', and that the success rate in refugee appeals was 0 per cent compared with 10–15 per cent in immigration appeals.[60]

The route of appeal was first to an adjudicator (a single judge appointed by the Lord Chancellor) and then to a three-person Immigration Appeal Tribunal ('IAT'); an appeal to the IAT against the decision of the adjudicator was possible on obtaining leave to appeal and only on the grounds that the adjudicator had erred in law or that

---

[54] Report of the Committee on Immigration Appeals ("Wilson Report"), 1967, Cmnd. 3387.

[55] ibid., para. 145.

[56] ibid., recommendation 16, p. 66.

[57] Immigration Appeals Act 1969.

[58] Immigration Appeals (Procedure) Rules 1972, SI 1684, para. 7(3).

[59] Select Committee on Race Relations and Immigration, Session 1977–78, 'The Effect of the UK's Membership of the EEC on Race Relations and Immigration' (410–ix), Minutes of Evidence, July 6, 1978, para. 4, p. 254.

[60] ibid., para. 3.

his or her findings were grossly misdirected.[61] Members of the IAT were also appointed by the Lord Chancellor and did not require legal qualifications, although a lawyer was required to preside at sittings. In the case of deportation, the 1984 Immigration Appeals Procedure Rules provided that leave should be granted where the Tribunal judged that the deportee had a well-founded fear of persecution.[62]

It should be stressed that at no time could an asylum seeker appeal against refusal of asylum or refugee status, and this continues to be the case today. Any appeal may be based on another ground, for example refusal of leave to enter or against deportation, and it is during this appeal that asylum grounds may, in certain circumstances, be raised. This provides for a complicated and at times confusing process. Prior to the 1993 legislation, the asylum seeker's position on appeal depended on his or her immigration status at the time the application was lodged. Where an applicant arrived at a port, without entry clearance or a current visa, applied for asylum and was refused refugee status or exceptional leave to remain, there was no in-country right of appeal before being returned to the originating country.[63] The applicant could, in certain circumstances, contest the decision by seeking judicial review. In judicial review cases, the court would only review the decision-making process, not the merits of the decision, and on three grounds: illegality, irrationality (or *Wednesbury* unreasonableness) and procedural impropriety.[64] In *Bugdaycay v Secretary of State for the Home Department*, Lord Bridge made it clear that 'the resolution of any issue of fact and the exercise of any discretion in relation to an application for asylum as a refugee lie exclusively within the jurisdiction of the Secretary of State subject only to the court's power of review'.[65] He went on to add that within those limitations, the court was 'entitled to subject an administrative decision to [. . .] more rigorous examination, to ensure that it is in no way flawed, according to the gravity of the issue which the decision determines'.[66] Where an asylum seeker was to be removed as an illegal entrant, there was no appeal to an adjudicator and the only recourse was, once again, to seek judicial review (or, very rarely, *habeas corpus*, if detained). In cases of judicial review, leave to apply had first to be sought, and following the decision of *R. v Secretary of State for the Home Department, ex parte Swati* [1986] 1 AER 717, an application for

---

[61] This two-tier system was a remnant of the Immigration Appeals Act 1969 which provided an appeals process for Commonwealth citizens only.

[62] Immigration Appeals (Procedure) Rules 1984, rule 14(2)(a).

[63] Immigration Act 1971, s. 13(3).

[64] This continues to be the applicable test where judicial review is available.

[65] [1987] Imm AR 250, at 263.

[66] *ibid.*

judicial review could normally be made only in asylum cases in which there was a right of appeal on another ground, once the appellate system had been exhausted. The decision of *ex parte Swati* created a significant hurdle in the path of potential judicial review applicants.

3.10   In certain cases, asylum seekers were protected by in-country appeal rights: when challenging either a refusal to enter, where there was entry clearance at the time of the application,[67] or a refusal of leave to remain;[68] when contesting the destination to which the Home Office intended to send an individual;[69] or when contesting deportation.[70] Thus overstayers, who were subject to deportation proceedings, could argue during the deportation hearing that they were Convention refugees and should not be removed;[71] in-country applicants, and new arrivals who were denied entry despite a valid visa or entry clearance, had a right of appeal before removal, and a subsequent appeal against deportation on Convention grounds. The 1983 Immigration Rules (HC 169, para. 165) made it clear that deportation should not take place if it would lead to a breach of the *non-refoulement* principle contained in Article 33 of the 1951 Convention: namely, that 'no Contracting State shall expel or return (*"refouler"*) a refugee in any manner whatsoever to the frontiers of territories where his life or freedom would be threatened on account of his race, religion, nationality, membership of a particular social group or political opinion.' This principle was endorsed when, in the Immigration Act 1988, appeal rights of most overstayers were diminished, but asylum claimants were exempted from the restrictive provisions and were permitted to appeal on the basis that they were refugees.[72]

The lack of an in-country appeal for refused port applicants who had not been granted entry for another purpose did cause concern in

---

[67] Immigration Act 1971, s. 13(3).

[68] *ibid.*, s. 14. This applied so long as the application for extension of leave was made while the asylum seeker had current leave.

[69] *ibid.*, s. 17. This did not, however, allow an asylum seeker to raise asylum as a primary issue, only to challenge the destination and to provide an alternative.

[70] *ibid.*, s. 15.

[71] This came about only after referral of a case to the European Commission of Human Rights. In *R. v IAT, ex parte Muruganandarajah* [1986] Imm AR 382, the Court of Appeal held that where an individual was convicted in a criminal court for overstaying and recommended for deportation under the Immigration Act 1971, s. 3(6), his or her asylum application could not be considered by the court. In contrast to a 'civil deportation' case (Immigration Act 1971, s. 3(5)), the only immigration appeal was against removal directions, not deportation. During the European proceedings, the government suggested that it would, in most cases, allow an appeal against deportation in both 'civil' and 'criminal' deportations: MacDonald & Blake, *Immigration Law & Practice* (London: Butterworths, 1991), p. 313.

[72] Immigration Act 1988, s. 5, and Immigration (Restricted Right of Appeal Against Deportation)(Exemption)(No 2) Order 1988, SI 1988/1203.

the 1980s, particularly among refugee-support groups and practitioners. The linking of the immigration status of the asylum seeker at
the time of the application with his or her appeal rights was considered to have potentially serious consequences. The British Refugee
Council explained its anxiety in 1987:

> '[A]sylum-seekers fall under many different categories [. . .] including
> illegal entrants, overstayers, 'detained pending removal', as well as those
> who have valid permission to be in the UK. Treating asylum-seekers
> differently on the basis of their original immigration status and denying
> all asylum-seekers equal opportunity to present their case run contrary to
> natural justice. All asylum-seekers should have the same right of appeal
> to an independent tribunal, irrespective of their status at the time of
> application.'[73]

The Home Office itself had already acknowledged that there was
'some force in the argument that a right of appeal after removal is of
no benefit to someone who maintains that he will be in danger of persecution in the country to which he is being returned'.[74] Despite such
reservations, the government remained in favour of the status quo,
fearing that the introduction of an in-country right of appeal for all
cases 'would be likely to stimulate a large number of unfounded
applications made only with the aim of securing a right of appeal in
this country and thus gaining entry for those not otherwise qualified
for it'.[75]

BEYOND THE LAW: REFUGEES AND REALITY

The largely administrative regime set up to deal with asylum cases   **3.11**
was quickly put to the test in the years following the passing of the
Immigration Act 1971. Almost as soon as the Act had been passed,
new crises emerged which would challenge the government's
approach to those in need of refuge. With the Ugandan Asians, the
government remained confused as to their status: were they citizens,
immigrants or refugees? With the Chileans and South East Asians,
there was a widespread assumption that they were refugees. Yet in all
three cases, the governments in power were not overly enthusiastic

---

[73] British Refugee Council, *Settling for a Future – Proposals for a British Policy on Refugees*
(1987), p. 8.
[74] Home Affairs Committee – Race Relations and Immigration Sub-Committee,
'Refugees', Session 1984–85, Minutes of Evidence, December 17, 1984, para. 40,
p. 76.
[75] *ibid.*

about admission of large numbers and insisted upon the fulfilment of certain criteria before agreeing to admission. By the 1980s, when asylum applications from a variety of countries were on the rise, the British government resorted increasingly to a negative discourse which perceived the majority of asylum seekers as 'economic migrants' or 'bogus'. With the 1971 regime apparently unable to cope with the strain, the authorities turned once more to legislation.

Ugandan Asians

3.12 On August 4, 1972, President Idi Amin of Uganda issued an expulsion order against all Asians who were subjects of the UK, India, Pakistan or Bangladesh. Since most of the 50,000 individuals who fell under the expulsion order held British passports, it was felt that a large part of the burden would be borne by the UK.[76] The government appealed to other countries to help, while being obliged to permit about 29,000 of the hapless Ugandans to enter.[77] This despite the usual expression of fears by both the national press and some Members of Parliament. Most notable amongst these was Enoch Powell, who agitated against Commonwealth immigration, using the proposed Race Relations Bill to make his now famous speech of an apocalyptic future.[78]

The Ugandan Asians were the first in a succession of asylum seekers from the 1970s to the present day. Significantly, there was one issue on which both the British and many Ugandans agreed: namely, that the Ugandan Asians were not refugees. The British considered them to be immigrants; the Ugandans thought of themselves as British with a right of entry. As one former Ugandan exile, Yasmin Alibhai-Brown, commented in 1995: 'We were not refugees. We were British. This is something that no British politician has properly acknowledged.'[79] From a legal perspective, being British subjects, they could have been described as 'nationals' and would therefore have fallen outside Article 1A(2) of the 1951 Convention as they were not outside their country of nationality.[80] The questionable nature of

---

[76] T. Kushner & K. Knox, *Refugees in an Age of Genocide* (London: Frank Cass, 1999), p. 269.

[77] The exact figure is 28,608: Home Office, *Ugandan Resettlement Board Final* Report (London: HMSO, 1974), p. 7.

[78] 'As I look ahead, I am filled with foreboding. Like the Roman, I seem to see "the River Tiber foaming with much blood".' For full speech, see B. Smithies & P. Fiddick, *Enoch Powell on Immigration* (London: Sphere Books, 1969), p. 43.

[79] Y. Alibhai-Brown, *No Place like Home: An Autobiography* (London: Virago, 1995), p. 185.

[80] I. MacDonald, *Immigration Law & Practice* (London: Butterworths, 1987), p. 271.

their status aside, they were certainly an unusual group in that they had a clear link with Great Britain, whatever their 'patriality'. Subsequent groups in the 1970s and 1980s differed in this respect. Chileans and Indo-Chinese had no colonial claims on a 'mother country' but were seeking asylum in a more traditional, and well-understood, sense.

The UK's policy towards Kenyans and Ugandans was considered by the European Commission of Human Rights in the light of the 1950 European Convention on Human Rights. Twenty-five East African Asians who had been refused entry to the UK complained to the Commission, alleging, *inter alia*, a breach of Art. 3 of the Convention which prohibits torture, inhuman or degrading treatment or punishment.[81] The Commission concluded that the racial discrimination to which the applicants had been publicly subjected through the application of the immigration legislation constituted an interference with human dignity which, in the special circumstances of the case, amounted to 'degrading treatment' for the purposes of Art. 3.[82] The special circumstances discussed by the Commission referred to the fact that the applicants were not aliens under British immigration law but had been denied entry to the UK under the 1968 Act following the 'Africanisation' policies of Kenyatta and subsequently of Amin.

Chileans

Chilean refugees to the UK constituted a relatively small group, about 3,000 at most. Nevertheless, the government, still smarting from the Ugandan crisis, was less than enthusiastic about the prospect of more arrivals. In a letter to the UNHCR, the Foreign Secretary stated: **3.13**

> 'Her Majesty's Government is in no position to accept refugees from Chile while having to turn away Commonwealth citizens. Nevertheless, in view of the humanitarian terms in which your appeal [for resettlement opportunities] has been made, the British Government is willing exceptionally to consider some applications on an individual basis from those who express as their first choice their wish to be resettled in the United Kingdom and who have some ties with the United Kingdom.'[83]

---

[81] See also Ch. 4 for a discussion of this case.
[82] *East African Asians v UK* (1973) 3 EHRR 76, para. 208.
[83] HC Deb. Vol. 864, November 22, 1973, col. 518 (Written Answers).

In addition, fleeing from the Pinochet coup of September 1973, many of the escapees were politically at odds with the then Conservative British government. This perhaps explains the failure to admit any Chileans until the change of government in February 1974 and the promise by the Labour party of a more sympathetic approach to refugee applications from Chile. This did not, however, lead to an acceleration of the asylum procedures overnight. In the first place, following a decree in Chile, all of those wishing to leave had to obtain a visa from their chosen destination. Once again, the grant of visas by the British proved extremely slow. Secondly, the Labour government refused to make any special arrangements to facilitate the entry of Chilean refugees; they were processed through the usual channels as set out in the Immigration Rules. Thus, it is no surprise that in July 1975, only 1,971 of 6,830 applications had been granted;[84] nor is it surprising that the Home Office continued to follow the policy articulated by their Conservative forebears, namely that Chileans with ties in the UK would be favoured, as would those with reliable sponsorship.[85] While some changes were made subsequently to try to improve selection procedures, by mid-1978, the government had lost momentum in its response to the Chilean refugee issue.[86]

The Chilean refugees not only revealed, once again, the shortcomings in the UK's post-war refugee policy but also provided a rare opportunity for the courts to comment on broader issues of refugee law. In *Secretary of State for the Home Department v 'Two citizens of Chile'*, the Immigration Appeal Tribunal verified that the Immigration Appellate Authority was required to decide political asylum appeals in accordance with the Immigration Act 1971 and the Immigration Rules. While the 1951 Convention and the 1948 Universal Declaration of Human Rights were recognised as having some value in assisting in interpretation, the IAT confirmed that they could not overrule national law.[87] Later, in *Secretary of State for the Home Department v X (A Chilean citizen)*,[88] the IAT ruled that an application for asylum could only be considered under the Immigration Rules if the claimant had travelled to the UK and on arrival sought leave to enter as a refugee; an application by a Chilean citizen at the British Embassy in Santiago did not suffice.

---

[84] T. Kushner & K. Knox, *Refugees in an Age of Genocide* (London: Frank Cass, 1999), p. 295.
[85] HC Deb. Vol. 895, July 9, 1975, cols. 173–4 (Written Answers).
[86] T. Kushner & K. Knox, *Refugees in an Age of Genocide* (London: Frank Cass, 1999), p. 296.
[87] [1977] Imm AR 36, at 42.
[88] [1978] Imm AR 73.

South East Asians

In 1975, when US forces were withdrawn from Vietnam, large num-   **3.14**
bers of ethnic Vietnamese from South Vietnam began to flee to the
west. The UK agreed to take any Vietnamese (and later Cambodians
and Laotians) who had connections with the country. In the same
year, only 32 were accepted by the UK, compared with 130,000 taken
by the USA, and 9,500 by France.[89] The following year, 116 were
accepted.[90] This inauspicious admissions record was to be partly but
never completely righted by the UK. One estimate suggests that of
the 1,694,360 people who left South East Asia between 1975 and
1990, the UK accepted only about 18,638, or 1.1 per cent.[91] This is
probably on the low side, since the government estimated in 1984 that
there were 19,000 Vietnamese, Cambodian and Laotian refugees in
the country. Another estimate setting the figure at 22,577 arrivals
between 1975 and 1988 is likely to be more accurate.[92] It is clear that
the majority of the 'Boat People' were admitted to the UK between
1979 (the year of the major exodus by sea and Britain's agreement to
accept an additional quota of 10,000 refugees, all of whom were
selected from Hong Kong) and 1981. Three-quarters of those arriving from 1983 to 1992 were family reunion cases.[93] Whichever admissions figure is accepted as being the most accurate, it is clear that
comparatively small numbers were admitted to the UK. There are a
number of explanations for this. First, as in the case of the Chileans,
the UK required refugees to have a connection with the country prior
to admission; second, there is evidence that most refugees did not
select the UK as their first port of call;[94] third, in contrast to France,
there was no colonial link between country of origin and country of
refuge; fourth, though the UK did carry out some sea rescues of
South East Asian refugees, taking it beyond its 10,000 quota, the
numbers of those rescued at sea were not significant.

---

[89] K. Duke & T. Marshall, *Home Office Research Study No. 142: Vietnamese Refugees since
1982* (London: HMSO, 1995), p. 1.
[90] Home Affairs Committee – Race Relations and Immigration Sub-Committee,
'Refugees', Session 1984–85, Minutes of Evidence, December 17, 1984, para. 2,
p. 88.
[91] T. Kushner & K. Knox, *Refugees in an Age of Genocide* (London: Frank Cass, 1999),
p. 312.
[92] *ibid.*, citing Refugee Council statistics.
[93] K. Duke & T. Marshall, *Home Office Research Study No. 142: Vietnamese Refugees since
1982* (London: HMSO, 1995), p. 7.
[94] 'For many of these refugees the UK was seen as the last resort, having been rejected
by other countries.' K. Duke & T. Marshall, *Home Office Research Study No. 142:
Vietnamese Refugees since 1982* (London: HMSO, 1995), p. 17.

As with the Ugandan Asians, there was some uncertainty as to the true definition of the Indo-Chinese. Were they 'refugees' as defined by the 1951 Convention or were they in reality economic migrants? Those who escaped in 1975, and who feared persecution for their involvement in the former regime, may have been 'Convention refugees'; some of those who followed may have been motivated by broader economic or political reasons, but many who came to the UK were of Chinese origin and faced certain harassment, if not persecution, by the Vietnamese government or the Vietcong police.

3.15   The Vietnamese constituted an important departure in post-war UK asylum policy: they were accepted for asylum prior to their arrival in this country as part of the agreed quota.[95] They were also the last major influx of refugees that required the adoption of a reception and resettlement policy. Drawing on the experience of the Ugandan Asian Resettlement Board, and the Joint Working Group of interested non-governmental agencies which had assisted the Chileans, the government decided to entrust reception and resettlement to the specialist refugee agencies and to provide resources to assist them. Under the programme, Vietnamese were dispersed to all parts of the UK and small clusters of between four and ten families were created in each location. With high unemployment in these areas and a growing sense of isolation, many families soon migrated back to urban centres, and in particular to London.[96] The Home Office admitted failure in its Research and Planning Unit Report on 'Vietnamese Refugees'.[97] In its own evidence to the Sub-Committee on Race Relations and Immigration, the Home Office conceded that:

> 'The need for effective co-ordination, and involvement at all stages of the planning of a refugee programme of staff from all interested Government Departments, particularly the Department of the Education and Science, the Department of the Environment, the Department of the Employment/Manpower Services Commission, and the Department of Health and Social Security, has been amply demonstrated.'[98]

---

[95] K. Duke & T. Marshall, *Home Office Research Study No. 142: Vietnamese Refugees since 1982* (London: HMSO, 1995), p. 2.

[96] See V. Robinson, 'The Vietnamese reception and resettlement programme in the UK', (1985) 6 *Ethnic Groups*, pp. 305–30; V. Robinson, 'British policy towards the settlement patterns of ethnic groups: an empirical evaluation of the Vietnamese programme' in V. Robinson, ed., *The International Refugee Crisis: British and Canadian Responses* (Basingstoke: Macmillan/RSP, 1993).

[97] Jones, *Home Office Research Study No. 13: Vietnamese Refugees* (London: HMSO).

[98] Home Affairs Committee – Race Relations and Immigration Sub-Committee, 'Refugees', Session 1984–85, Minutes of Evidence, December 17, 1984, para. 90, p. 105.

It went on:

'The second major lesson is the extent to which a refugee programme needs to be tailored both to the precise characteristics of the refugees themselves and to the current situation in the host country – especially the existence or absence of established communities of the same ethnic origin, the availability of housing, the ability of local government and other services to respond to special needs, and the economic climate, both for employment and self employment.'[99]

The remaining sections of this chapter, and subsequent chapters, will address the extent to which these wise words, uttered at a time of relatively few asylum applications, were acted upon by successive Conservative and Labour governments when faced with escalating asylum claims.

The 1980s onwards

While the 1970s are, to some extent, distinguished by the arrival of groups of refugees – Ugandans, Chileans, Vietnamese –, the 1980s may be identified as the period in which the pattern of asylum-seeking in the west began to alter and a rise in individual claims became the norm. Within the European Community, the UNHCR recorded a growth from 70,500 claims in 1983 to 290,650 in 1988.[100] Although western European countries reacted with alarm to the growth in numbers and the '"spontaneous arrivals" of asylum-seekers from the "third world"',[101] the statistical evidence indicated that the rise was simply a reflection of the global increase. Europe continued to harbour less than five per cent of the world's refugees and the brunt was, in fact, borne by the poorest countries. Nonetheless the developed countries began to speak of an asylum crisis and academic and NGO commentaries on refugee and asylum issues started to reflect the growing disquiet. Those reaching European Community states were no longer referred to as 'refugees' from the point of arrival but as 'asylum seekers', and later often as 'bogus asylum seekers' as their numbers grew.

Various explanations have been offered for the rise: improved air transport, the well-publicised resettlement of South East Asian refugees in the 1970s, and an increase in global refugee populations (from approximately 10 million to 17 million between 1985 and

3.16

---

[99] *ibid.*, para. 91, p. 105.
[100] UNHCR Regional Office for the European Communities, Brussels, 1991, cited in S. Collinson, *Europe and International Migration* (London: Pinter Publishers for Royal Institute of International Affairs, 1994), p. 19.
[101] *ibid.*, p. 21.

1991).[102] The causes of asylum and refugee flows are undoubtedly complex and no one theory can explain them. The former UN High Commissioner for Refugees, Sadako Ogata, summarised some of the different factors associated with rising numbers of asylum seekers when she argued that:

> '[R]efugees are part of a complex migratory phenomenon in which economic, political, ethnic, environmental and human rights factors contribute to displacement and a lack of national protection. [. . .] With most channels of regular migration to western Europe closed with the exception of family reunification, would-be immigrants tend to use asylum procedures to circumvent immigration controls, bringing the procedures to the verge of collapse.'[103]

The UK was now a country to which primary immigration had ceased. Although it had benefited historically in controlling immigration from its geographical isolation from the rest of the European continent, in the last decades of the twentieth century, it found itself no longer able to rely upon the Channel as a means of deterrence; the new migrants were arriving increasingly by air and claiming asylum. The impact on the statistics for the 1980s is most striking. In 1984, the UK received 2,905 applications for asylum, and in 1985, 4,389. Claims remained under 4,500 until 1989, when a sudden rise of 8,000 on the previous year's figures resulted in a total of 11,640 applications received.[104] As with the rest of Europe, the majority of these cases came from Turkey (2,415), Sri Lanka (1,790), Somalia (1,850) and Uganda (1,235),[105] all countries associated with poor human rights records and civil or political upheaval.

Tamils: changing the law

3.17   With the increase in numbers came the inevitable political reaction. The group to have the greatest influence on asylum law and policy in the 1980s were arguably the Tamils from Sri Lanka. For much of that decade, applications for asylum from Sri Lanka had been consistently high, largely as a result of the discriminatory actions of

---

[102] UNHCR Regional Office for the European Communities, Brussels, 1991, cited in S. Collinson, *Europe and International Migration* (London: Pinter Publishers for Royal Institute of International Affairs, 1994), p. 19.

[103] S. Ogata, 'Refugees and asylum-seekers: a challenge to European immigration policy', in Ogata *et al, Towards a European Immigration Policy* (Brussels: The Philip Morris Institute, 1993), p. 10.

[104] *Home Office Statistical Bulletin, Asylum Statistics UK 1992*, Issue 19/93, July 15, 1993, table 1.3 . These figures exclude dependants.

[105] *ibid.*, table 2.1 . These figures exclude dependants.

the Sinhalese-dominated government. The British press was unsympathetic and associated many of the Tamil asylum seekers with the terrorist organisation 'The Tamil Tigers'. Concerned that the upward trend would continue, and that some of the Tamils were, in fact, economic migrants, the UK's Home Secretary decided in May 1985 to impose a visa restriction against Sri Lanka, which took effect overnight. A somewhat unexpected step in the context of the then immigration practice, especially since Sri Lanka was a Commonwealth country, this was a throwback to pre-war policy and presented a picture of a government panicked into restrictive rule-making.[106] The new visa policy was, however, to become the norm. From this time onwards, in almost every case in which a rise in asylum applications from a specific country was observed, successive Home Secretaries promptly introduced a visa requirement against the country concerned where none previously existed (for example, against Turkey in 1989, Uganda in 1991, the former Yugoslavia in 1992, Sierra Leone and the Ivory Coast in 1994, Kenya in 1996, Slovakia in 1998, Zimbabwe and Algeria in 2003). Nor have governments attempted to hide the real objective behind the visa policy. In 1989, for example, in relation to the newly imposed visa requirement for Turkish citizens, the Home Secretary said:

'A growing number of Turks have claimed asylum in the United Kingdom. Whereas there were only about 60 such applications in 1987, during May alone this year there were about 1,500 [. . .] Unless we take action now the situation is likely to deteriorate through the summer. That is why we have decided to impose a visa requirement on Turkish nationals who wish to enter the UK.'[107]

The expectation that those in flight should obtain a visa before travelling to the UK has been much criticised by refugee organisations. The immediate effect is to hinder the departure of individual asylum seekers from their country of origin since no visa for 'asylum' exists. The serious consequences of such a policy are exacerbated when set alongside the notorious carriers' liability legislation, also introduced as a consequence of the 'Tamil problem'.

On February 13, 1987, 64 Tamils arrived in London on a flight from Sri Lanka. They claimed asylum. 58 of them had entered with either forged visas or none at all, and were consequently detained; six were given temporary admission pending the decision. The Home Office acted with unprecedented celerity and refused the applications

---

[106] See, for further discussion, P. Shah, *Refugees, Race and the Legal Concept of Asylum in Britain* (London: Cavendish, 2000), Ch. 7.

[107] HC Deb. Vol. 154, June 6, 1989, cols. 45–46.

for asylum within four days. During the attempted removal at Heathrow, the Tamils engaged in a now famous protest in which a number of the group tore off their clothing to their underwear and prostrated themselves on the floor. When impelled to enter the aircraft by the police, they continued their demonstration by standing on the seats. As a result of the delay, lawyers representing the group were able to obtain a High Court injunction preventing departure. In a subsequent action, leave was granted to apply for judicial review on the basis that 'the Home Secretary had erred in law, in taking into account the fact that Tamil applicants had used forged visas to arrive in the UK when determining the merits of their asylum claim,' a point which the Home Secretary ultimately conceded.[108]

3.18   In view of the unexpected obstacles placed in the path of its asylum policy by the courts, the government resorted to legislation and announced on March 3, 1987 that a new Bill to fine carriers would be introduced. On May 25, the Immigration (Carriers' Liability) Act 1987 received Royal Assent. It provided for the fining of any carrier (ship or aircraft) to the sum of £1,000 for every undocumented passenger transported, and was given retrospective effect to March 5, 1987 in order to cover the Tamil incident. Once more, the then Home Secretary, Douglas Hurd, made it clear that the motivation behind the new law was the rise in asylum claims. During debate on the Bill, he said: 'The immediate spur to this proposal has been the arrival of over 800 people claiming asylum in the three months up to the end of February.'[109] Carriers' liability legislation introduced a new practice in the immigration field: the transfer of control from the public to the private sector – in this case, from immigration officers to untrained airline personnel. Since its inception, carriers' liability has remained a cornerstone of UK asylum law.[110]

The arrival of the Tamils not only led directly to a change in legislation, it also gave rise to two significant refugee cases: the first before the House of Lords and the second before the European Court of Human Rights. In the UK case, *Secretary of State for the Home Department v Sivakumaran, et al ('Sivakumaran')*, the House of Lords was called upon to consider the crucial question of standard of proof in establishing

---

[108] I. MacDonald, *Immigration Law and Practice* (London: Butterworths, 1987), p. 277; *R. v Secretary of State for the Home Department, ex parte Sivakumaran* (February 24, 1987, unreported).

[109] HC Deb. Vol. 112, March 16, 1987, col. 706.

[110] For a detailed discussion of carriers' liability legislation and its impact in the United Kingdom, see F. Nicholson, 'Implementation of the Immigration (Carriers' Liability) Act 1987: Privatising Immigration Functions at the Expense of International Obligations?' (1997) 46 *International and Comparative Law Quarterly*, pp. 586–634; see also A. Ruff, 'The Immigration (Carriers' Liability) Act 1987: its Implications for Refugees and Airlines' (1989) 1:4 *IJRL*, pp. 481–500.

a 'well-founded fear of persecution' as required under the 1951 Convention.[111] Considering that the first time the House of Lords had
been called upon to discuss the Convention was in February 1987 in
the case of *Bugdaycay*,[112] and that the decision in *Sivakumaran* was
handed down in December 1987, it plays a key role in the development of UK refugee jurisprudence. The case dealt with six Tamils
who had arrived in the UK between February and the end of May
1987 and who had applied unsuccessfully for political asylum. The
crucial question before the courts was the proper interpretation of
Article 1A(2) of the 1951 Convention and the definition of 'refugee'.
In particular, the court was called upon to determine the true meaning of 'well-founded fear' of being persecuted. The Court of Appeal
had found in favour of the asylum applicants and had imposed a
subjective-focused interpretation of 'well-founded fear'. The Master
of the Rolls, Sir John Donaldson, put it thus:

> 'Authority apart, we would accept that "well-founded fear" is demon-
> strated by proving (a) actual fear and (b) good reason for this fear, looking
> at the situation from the point of view of one of reasonable courage
> circumstanced as was the applicant for refugee status. Fear is clearly an
> entirely subjective state experienced by the person who is afraid. The
> adjectival phrase "well-founded" qualifies, but cannot transform, the
> subjective nature of the emotion.'[113]

The House of Lords disagreed, fearing that 'the Court of Appeal's
formulation would accord refugee status to one whose fears, though
genuine, were objectively demonstrated to have been misconceived,
that is to say one who was at no actual risk of persecution for a Convention reason.'[114] Lord Keith went on to say that, in his opinion, 'the
requirement that an applicant's fear of persecution should be well-
founded means that there has to be demonstrated a reasonable
degree of likelihood that he will be persecuted for a Convention reason if returned to his own country.'[115] In other words, an objective
test should be applied but one which remained lower than the normal
civil standard of balance of probabilities. Various alternatives for
'reasonable degree of likelihood' were also offered in the case: 'a reasonable probability', 'a real chance that he will suffer persecution', '
reasonable chance', 'substantial grounds for thinking', or 'serious
possibility'.[116] This test has stood the test of time and remains, in its

---

[111] [1988] Imm AR 147.
[112] [1987] Imm AR 250.
[113] [1987] 3 WLR 1047, at 1052.
[114] [1988] Imm AR 147, at 151.
[115] *ibid.*, at 152.
[116] *ibid.*

varied guises, the internationally agreed lower standard of proof in refugee cases.

The dismissal of the Tamils' judicial review applications resulted in their return to Sri Lanka, from where they were entitled to appeal against the refusal of leave to enter under the immigration provisions.[117] Pending the outcome of the protracted case-law, involving not only appeals by the applicants to the Immigration Appellate Authority, but also counter-actions for judicial review of the IAA's determinations, five of the six original claimants in *Sivakumaran* complained to the European Commission of Human Rights that their removal to Sri Lanka constituted a breach of Arts 3 and 13 of the European Convention on Human Rights.[118] On April 13, 1988, the applications were deemed admissible and on October 30, 1991, the European Court of Human Rights handed down judgement in the case of *Vilvarajah v UK*.[119] Despite the claim by several applicants that they had been maltreated or beaten by Sri Lankan security officers, the Court found that, in fact, there had been no breach of Art. 3:

> 'The evidence before the Court concerning the background of the applicants, as well as the general situation, does not establish that their personal position was any worse than the generality of other members of the Tamil community or other young male Tamils who were returning to their country. Since the situation was still unsettled there existed the possibility that they might be detained and ill-treated as appears to have occurred previously in the cases of some of the applicants. [. . .] A mere possibility of ill-treatment, however, in such circumstances, is not in itself sufficient to give rise to a breach of Article 3. [. . .].'[120]

3.19 In the light of these considerations, the Court held that substantial grounds had not been established for believing that the applicants would be exposed to a real risk of being subjected to inhuman or degrading treatment within the meaning of Art. 3.

With regard to the alleged breach of Art. 13 (the lack of an effective remedy while in the UK), the Court followed its previous judge-

---

[117] Immigration Act 1971, s. 13(3). Note: at this time, the right to appeal to the Immigration Appellate Authority against refusal of an asylum application was dependant on the individual's immigration status at the time the application was made (see above).

[118] UK Treaty Series 38 (1965), Cmnd 2643. Art. 3 states that 'No one shall be subjected to torture or to inhuman or degrading treatment or punishment.' Art. 13 states that 'Everyone whose rights and freedoms as set forth in this Convention are violated shall have an effective remedy before a national authority notwithstanding that the violation has been committed by persons acting in an official capacity.'

[119] (1991) 14 EHRR 248.

[120] *ibid.*, para. 111.

ment in *Soering v UK*[121] and found that the availability of judicial review provided an effective remedy.[122] It referred with approval to the House of Lord's view, as set out in *Bugdaycay*, that '[t]he most fundamental of all human rights is the individual's right to life and when an administrative decision under challenge is said to be one which may put the applicant's life at risk, the basis of the decision must surely call for the most anxious scrutiny.'[123] Despite noted limitations to the powers of the UK courts in judicial review proceedings, the Court was of the opinion that those powers did provide an effective degree of control over the decisions of the administrative authorities in asylum cases and thus satisfied the requirements of Art. 13.[124] The UK government breathed a collective sigh of relief.

The case of the Tamils marked a new phase in British asylum policy. Whereas previous groups – notably, the Hungarians, Chileans and South East Asians – had benefited from resettlement programmes introduced by the government, the Tamils were subjected to quite different treatment. They gave rise to an unease within ministerial circles that the UK would soon be 'flooded' by asylum seekers from the Third World and, as a consequence, the discourse surrounding refugees altered markedly. The Home Secretary, Douglas Hurd, was questioned by a Conservative backbencher in the following terms:

> 'Is he not [. . .] aware that all the Western democracies are having to find other ways to contain the flow of people from Third-world countries who arrive for bogus reasons? Is he not also aware that there is a substantial increase in the forgery, alteration and counterfeiting of passports and other travel documents?'[125]

Thereafter it became the norm to describe asylum seekers as 'manifestly bogus', 'economic migrants' or even 'liars, cheats and queue jumpers', as one MP described the Tamils.[126]

Kurds

Like the Tamils, the Kurds found themselves the victims of discriminatory state policies in the late 1980s. From 1988 onwards, conditions in their countries of origin, Turkey, Iraq, and to some extent Iran, deteriorated to the point where a large number of Kurds chose to flee

3.20

---

[121] (1989) 11 EHRR 439.
[122] (1991)14 EHRR 248, paras 124 & 127.
[123] [1987] Imm AR 250, at 263.
[124] para. 126.
[125] HC Deb. Vol. 111, March 3, 1987, col. 735.
[126] *ibid.*, col. 737.

to western countries, including the UK, rather than remain to face persecution. Of particular significance is the alleged use of chemical weapons by Iraq to massacre thousands of Kurds in the town of Halabjah on March 16, 1988. Of a population of 70,000, it is estimated that over 5,000 died and some 40,000 fled to neighbouring Turkey. Iraq, until the invasion by US and British troops in 2003, continued to take brutal measures against its Kurdish population, while Turkey also stands accused of human rights infringements against the Kurds. The inevitable consequence of such anti-Kurdish policies was an exodus of Kurds from the region from 1989 onwards. The asylum applications received from Turkish citizens for 1989 present a telling picture. While the ethnicity of the Turks is not revealed in Home Office statistics, an assumption can be made that the majority were Kurds. In 1988, 337 claims were recorded for Turkey.[127] By the end of 1989, the figure had risen to 2,415, the highest for any country that year.[128] The welcome handed out to the Kurds was mixed. In June 1989, *The Independent* newspaper reported that 'more than 3,000 Kurds have had to sleep in churches, church halls and makeshift centres while others have been imprisoned.'[129] The government was caught unawares and few preparations had been made for the arrival of the asylum seekers. Moves were made to authorise immigration officers to make checks on board aircraft prior to disembarkation, and to remove any individuals deemed to have no valid claim.[130] As a result, some Kurds, having been prevented from entering the UK, were returned to Istanbul where they were allegedly beaten.[131] Visa restrictions were also imposed and a number were placed in detention, with tragic consequences when two refused Turkish asylum seekers set fire to themselves and one, Siho Iyigüven, subsequently died.[132] The government's hard line on applicants from Turkey was starkly revealed by Home Office Minister Timothy Renton in May 1989. He clearly did not believe that they were persecuted Kurds deserving of special treatment:

> 'Those people have come here without any notice or invitation. In many cases they do not appear to be political refugees by any stretch of the definition. They are in an entirely different situation from the Ugandan Asians or the Vietnamese boat people where reception centres were set up

---

[127] *Home Office Statistical Bulletin, Asylum Statistics UK 1992*, Issue 19/93, July 15, 1993, Table 2.1. These figures exclude dependants.

[128] *ibid.*

[129] *The Independent*, June 26, 1989.

[130] *ibid.*

[131] *ibid.*

[132] See, for further details M. Ashford, *Detained without Trial – A Survey of Immigration Act Detention* (London: JCWI, 1993).

in this country in advance. The Turks are here on a temporary basis until such time as decisions are reached on their applications. The Government have no special responsibility for those people who are not refugees coming here as part of a Government programme.'[133]

It did not help that some 80 applicants had withdrawn their asylum claims. Renton surmised:

'That is not the action of people who fear imminent persecution. We are seeing a gross and transparent abuse of the asylum procedures as a means of obtaining jobs, housing and perhaps social security benefits in the United Kingdom.'[134]

By 1991, the UK government appeared to be supporting a new policy which would ensure that Kurds remained in the Middle Eastern region: the safe haven scheme. A vast population of displaced Kurds gathered in the mountains between Iraq and Turkey leading to a huge international relief effort and the establishment of a safe haven or security zone in northern Iraq. Although the UK government sought to assist the Kurds, such assistance did not comprise formal resettlement in the UK. Instead, countries neighbouring Iraq were expected to assume the responsibility and eventually Turkey yielded, probably as a result of its application to join the European Community, providing areas in which makeshift camps could be established under the auspices of the UN. Very few reached the UK, and where they were successful, they faced the possibility that they would be found to be of Turkish rather than Kurdish ethnicity. This despite the Refugee Council's view that between 1980 and 1993, an estimated 12,500 Turkish Kurds had arrived in the UK.[135] Certainly, Turkey has provided a consistently high number of asylum applicants since the first surge in 1989. The figure has never dropped below 1,400 per annum (excluding dependants), and reached a high of 3,990 in the year 2000.[136] Throughout the 1990s, Turkey held its place in the league table for the top 10 applicant nationalities. Yet cases recognised as refugees have remained surprisingly low, notwithstanding well-documented human rights concerns in relation to Turkey: 460 and 360 were granted asylum in 1992 and 1993 respectively; from 1994 to 1999, the number of Turkish nationals granted

---

[133] HC Deb. Vol. 153, May 26, 1989, cols. 1264–5.
[134] HC Deb. Vol. 153, May 26, 1989, cols. 1268.
[135] Cited in T. Kushner & K. Knox, *Refugees in an Age of Genocide* (London: Frank Cass, 1999), p. 345.
[136] *Home Office Statistical Bulletin, Asylum Statistics UK 1995*, Issue 9/96, May 16, 1996, Table 2.1; *Home Office Statistical Bulletin, Asylum Statistics UK 2000*, Issue 17/01, September 25, 2001, Table 2.1.

asylum did not rise above 90 for any year. The high number of applicants for 2000 was met with a higher acceptance rate (180), although this still is unusually low when compared with some other countries.[137]

3.21   The arrival of Kurdish asylum seekers, and the press coverage they received, helped inform the British public about the realities of the UK's asylum and refugee policy. While the government appeared largely unmoved by the plight of Kurds coming to Britain, the reaction of the public, particularly following the death of Siho Iyigüven, was generally sympathetic. Demonstrations were organised against detention with a modicum of success. The relatively wealthy city of Winchester was the scene of one such effective campaign against detention of asylum seekers in its local prison.[138] In 1993, protests against the breach of human rights against Kurds were held in 20 European cities.[139] The UK government found itself in a difficult position. It did not want to give the impression that it was turning a blind eye to the activities of Kurdish organisations, such as the Marxist Kurdish Workers' Party, or PKK, which advocated violent tactics in its resistance against the Turkish authorities; yet it could not fail to recognise the human rights implications raised by the Kurdish situation. Certainly, there were some within Parliament who advocated a more tolerant attitude towards guerrilla activities where they were employed in the pursuance of a cause perceived to be just. For example, in 1994, Lord Avebury, Chair of the Parliamentary Human Rights Group, wrote to the Foreign Office in the following terms:

> 'To dismiss the PKK as "terrorists", while excusing a government which commits heinous crimes against the whole people, is to see the conflict through the wrong end of a telescope. The fact that Kurds have rebelled against Turkish rule in 1880, 1925, 1938 and 1984 indicates that the PKK are the latest manifestation of a Kurdish will to self-rule, though not necessarily in a separate state.'[140]

In the light of the events of September 11, 2001, and the altered global perspective on terrorism, it is unlikely that quite the same level of understanding would be shown today.

---

[137] *Home Office Statistical Bulletin, Asylum Statistics UK 1995*, Issue 9/96, May 16, 1996, Table 2.1; *Home Office Statistical Bulletin, Asylum Statistics UK 2000*, Issue 17/01, September 25, 2001, Table 2.1.

[138] T. Kushner & K. Knox, *Refugees in an Age of Genocide* (London: Frank Cass, 1999), pp. 347–51.

[139] *ibid.*, p. 351.

[140] Extract printed in *Kurdistan Report* No. 20 (January/February 1995), p. 21, cited in T. Kushner & K. Knox, *Refugees in an Age of Genocide* (London: Frank Cass, 1999), p. 351.

The Former Yugoslavia (1991–1993)

The complex and tragic consequences of the break-up of former **3.22**
Yugoslavia created the next major refugee problem for western
European countries. The calls for independence and rising national-
ism in the region resulted in the worst conflict witnessed in Europe
since the Second World War. Not only were large numbers of people
displaced (estimated between one and three million), but an unsus-
pecting Europe was confronted with a brutality it had thought banished from the region: 'genocide', 'ethnic cleansing' and the use of
rape as a form of persecution. In the face of such barbarity, the UK
government maintained its typical equanimity. Preferring to follow a
co-operative international approach and to provide aid through the
EC and the UN, it did not rush to offer asylum to those fleeing the
fighting in Croatia and later in Bosnia. In July 1992, *The Times* newspaper provided a breakdown of the financial contributions made
towards the Yugoslavian conflict. The EC topped the table with
$71,464,939, followed by the US ($10,000,000) and then Sweden
($5,186,058). The UK's contribution of $2,157,088 placed it after
Switzerland, Denmark and Norway.[141]

Where the UK fell down heavily was in its preparedness to accept
refugees from the former Yugoslavia. The UK stated in July 1992 that
it would accept only about 1,300 despite pressure from Germany and
the UNHCR. Germany, by contrast, had promised to take
200,000.[142] The disparity in the figures was due to the lack of support
by France and the UK for a quota system in dealing with the displaced peoples, since they feared that 'the refugees [would] never
return home'[143] and wanted to encourage people to 'remain as close
as possible to their own homes'.[144] A number of asylum applicants
were also returned to 'safe third countries'. Britain's grudging
response was much criticised in the broadsheets and the government
was accused of 'quibbling over misery'.[145] The then Parliamentary
Under-Secretary, Charles Wardle, responded in a letter to *The Times*
in July 1992, arguing that the UK was the only EC country not to
have a visa regime against any of the republics of the former
Yugoslavia and that 4,000 Yugoslavs had entered the country each

---

[141] I. Murray & A. Le Bor, 'Kohl seeks EC quota to sidestep lenient refugee law', *The Times*, July 30, 1992, p. 10.
[142] A. McGregor & J. Bone, 'Britain refuses to open the door to refugees', *The Times*, July 30, 1992, p. 1.
[143] *Migration News Sheet*, August 1992, p. 4.
[144] C. Moorehead, 'Yugoslav refugees quotas refused', *The Independent*, July 30, 1992
[145] Editorial, *The Times*, July 30, 1992.

month since the beginning of the year (and had not applied for asylum).[146] Wardle went on to claim that only 36 applicants had been returned to third countries, despite the 'vast majority' having arrived from safe third countries. This was evidence, he suggested, of the government's flexibility of policy.[147] Nonetheless, though apparently seldom employed, this practice of deporting asylum seekers from the former Yugoslavia to European countries, such as Germany, which had already accepted so many, did little for the UK's standing in the international community.[148] Bowing to pressure, the government announced in August 1992 that it would adopt a 'flexible approach' to those who wanted to come to the UK from the former Yugoslavia, and that it would relax its policy on safe third country returns: 'If anybody is travelling through another country determined to reach this country then we shall treat their application sympathetically,' said Charles Wardle.[149] The so-called new flexibility was revealed in November 1992 when the Home Secretary, Kenneth Clarke, declared to the House of Commons:

> 'We have informed the UNHCR that we are ready to receive in the first instance 150 former detainees and their dependants, probably making 600 in all. At the same time, I announced the imposition of visas on certain nationals of the former Yugoslavia, making it clear that such action was needed to enable us to target our humanitarian assistance where it was most needed.'[150]

3.23   It is remarkable that the UK government believed this to be an important concession. First, the numbers were paltry in the context of the prevailing crisis; second, it was made clear that any protection provided would be temporary; and third, there was a major price to pay: the imposition of visa restrictions. Within a fortnight, the agreed number to be accepted had risen to 1,000 (about 4,000 with dependants), but the problem of visa control remained very real. The assumption that Bosnians, for example, could obtain a visa with ease was simply unrealistic: there was no consulate in Sarajevo; nor were the full range of services available in Zagreb, as the Foreign Office admitted.[151] The grant of temporary protection became a favoured option by all European countries, not just the UK, in respect of migrants from the former Yugoslavia. The UNHCR was forced to

---

[146] Letters, *The Independent*, August 13, 1992.
[147] *ibid.*
[148] H. Mills, 'International outrage at deportations', *The Independent*, August 13, 1992.
[149] R. Oakley, 'Britain eases rules on refugees', *The Times*, August 13, 1992.
[150] HC Deb. Vol. 214, November 17, 1992, col. 141.
[151] 'Have no visas, can't travel', *The Guardian*, November 6, 1992.

acquiesce in the policy, despite reservations.[152] As in the case of the Iraqi Kurds, it was also expected that use would be made of six safe zones established by the UN Security Council in April and May 1993. Their designation as 'safe' proved to be a misnomer.[153]

As the Yugoslavian crisis worsened, a Bill was presented to Parliament to change the UK's asylum law in 1991 and then again in 1992.[154] Prompted largely by the government's concern over rising 'bogus' asylum claims, the Bill's appearance during the Yugoslavian crisis was not coincidental.[155] The acknowledged fear was of 'receiving uncontrolled numbers of citizens of former Yugoslavia', and this appeared to dictate completely the UK's asylum policy in this period.[156] The true consequences of the UK government's anxiety are exposed by statistics. In February 1993, the UNHCR reported that since the beginning of the conflict, the UK had accepted 4,400 asylum applicants compared with Denmark (7,000), the Netherlands (7,000), Hungary (40,000), Sweden (62,000), Austria (73,000), Switzerland (80,000), and Germany (250,000). Only France was less generous with 4,200.[157] For a country such as the UK, so openly proud of its asylum record, the handling of the case of the former Yugoslavia is testament to the sharp division which exists between rhetoric and reality. Perhaps the best summation of the confusion at the heart of the UK's asylum policy was provided by the then Home Secretary, Kenneth Clarke, during the second reading of the Asylum and Immigration Appeals Bill, when he said:

'Common sense should tell us that we cannot allow anyone to settle here simply because they come from a country in part of whose territory there is civil war or political strife.'[158]

---

[152] J. Fitzpatrick, 'Temporary protection of refugees: Elements of a formalized regime', (April 2000) 94 *American Journal of International Law*, p. 286. See, also, G. Goodwin-Gill, *The Refugee in International Law* (Oxford: Clarendon Press, 1996), pp. 199–202; J. Hathaway & A. Neve. 'Making international refugee law relevant again: A proposal for collectivized and solution-oriented protection' (1997) 10 *Harvard Human Rights Journal*, pp. 115–211.

[153] Sixth Periodic Report on the Situation of Human Rights in the Territory of the Former Yugoslavia, submitted by Tadeusz Mazowiecki, February 21, 1994, UN Doc. E/CN.4/1994/110, para. 296: In the French: 'Dans une large mesure, ces zones n'ont été des "zones de sécurité" que sur le papier.'.

[154] See, for further discussion of the Asylum and Immigration Appeals Bill 1992, D. Stevens, 'Re-introduction of the United Kingdom Asylum Bill', (1993) 5:1 *IJRL*, pp. 91–100.

[155] HC Deb, Vol. 213, November 2, 1992, col. 22.

[156] M. Linton, 'Clarke "slams door" on war refugees', *The Guardian*, November 6, 1992.

[157] *Migration News Sheet*, February 1993, p. 7.

[158] HC Deb, Vol. 213, November 2, 1992, col. 22.

Then later:

'There is a strong and compassionate feeling that we must help people who
have been driven from their homes by warfare and when, for example, the
United Nations High Commissioner for Refugees has said that they must
find refuge outside their former country. We wish to help those people.'[159]

The contradiction between the two statements was not remarked
upon. The government clearly assumed that the circle could be
squared by the use of law. The extent to which it succeeded is the
subject of Part 2 of this book.

CONCLUSION

3.24 The post-war period provides ample evidence of the inter-connection
in UK law of immigration and asylum. For almost 90 years, the
Aliens Act 1905 remained the only statute to legislate for political and
religious asylum. Its early decline left a void in UK law which successive governments saw fit to leave unfilled. Even the events prior to and
during the Second World War, which caused the authorities of the
day some embarrassment, did not spur subsequent governments into
action; nor did the development of human rights law and of international refugee law. The latter, while providing an important framework for refugee protection, failed to persuade the UK to incorporate
the 1951 Convention and 1967 Protocol into its national law. Instead,
the UK's international law obligations were referred to, almost in
passing, in the administrative instrument, the Immigration Rules.
One explanation for the failure to construct an effective and independent asylum regime in the post-war period was the initial Cold
War concentration on east-west refugee flows, such as the Hungarians
to the UK.[160] Changing political, economic and social conditions in
third world countries coincided with the end of the Cold War; many
industrialised countries found their asylum systems unable to cope
with the new arrivals from the south. The UK, amongst others, was
forced to re-evaluate its asylum regime.[161]
There is no doubt that changing migration flows and the increasing ability of the individual to move between continents in the 1980s
altered the UK's view of asylum for the foreseeable future. While it
was able to cope with the limited refugee crises connected with the

---

[159] HC Deb, Vol. 213, November 2, 1992, col. 25.
[160] C. Keely, 'How Nation-States Create and Respond to Refugee Flows', (1996) 30:4
International Migration Review, p. 1057.
[161] *ibid.*

Ugandans, Chileans, and South East Asians – with varying degrees of success –, the now familiar panic about 'numbers' only became evident in the early 1980s and can be dated from the arrival of the Tamils. At the same time, the lexicon relating to asylum and refugees began to change quite markedly. Politicians increasingly spoke of 'economic migrants' when talking of asylum seekers; asylum seekers were either 'bogus' or 'genuine', and to be genuine one had to fall within the narrow confines of the 1951 Convention. Little sympathy was expressed for those fleeing poverty, civil war, or natural disaster, and no explanation of the true complexity of the migration issue was provided for the wider public. The debate was stifled as asylum seekers were categorised simplistically as either 'good' or 'bad'.

Chapter Four

The Refugee as Subject of International Law

INTRODUCTION

The development of UK refugee and asylum law can only be fully **4.1**
understood within the context of international law. The emergence of
international refugee and asylum law has not, however, been clear-
cut. Since much is owed by the contemporary framework to pre-war
antecedents, a discussion of the historical background is called for.
The first part of this chapter deals with the attempts by the League of
Nations to provide an international framework for refugee protection
in the inter-war period. It examines the handling by the international
community and the UK of the refugee crisis created by the anti-
Jewish policies implemented by Nazi Germany. The chapter goes on
to review developments post-1945, and considers in particular the key
instruments to emerge in the history of refugee protection: the 1951
Convention Relating to the Status of Refugees, the 1967 Protocol,[1]
and the 1950 Statute of the UN High Commissioner for Refugees
('UNHCR'). While the protection of refugees is clearly a major focus
of the discussion, the chapter also deals with the more difficult question of asylum seekers. In this regard, the various attempts to introduce an asylum convention are addressed, as well as state practice in
relation to the norm of customary international law: *non-refoulement*.
The analysis concludes with an assessment of the 1950 European
Convention on Human Rights, which offers an alternative and
increasingly effective vehicle for protection of asylum seekers and
refugees alike.

---

[1] 189 *UNTS* 150; 606 *UNTS* 267. Entered into force on April 22, 1954 and October
4, 1967 respectively.

THE EMERGENCE OF INTERNATIONAL COOPERATION: THE
NANSEN YEARS

4.2   One of the most significant developments of the inter-war period was
the emergence of the refugee as a subject of international politics and
law. Despite hopes to the contrary, the numbers of asylum seekers did
not diminish in the decades following the First World War. Once
again, Russian refugees figured prominently in the statistics, number-
ing more than one million in the immediate post-war period.[2] The
Balkans, a notorious hotbed of violent political dispute, remained a
consistent source of refugees well into the 1920s. By the 1930s, the
shadow of fascism had been cast across Europe, bringing with it
Jewish refugees from Hitler's Germany, Republican exiles from
Franco's Spain, and a trickle of refugees from Italy.[3] The issue facing
many western states was how best to handle these recurrent crises.
Two options lay open to them: to continue to receive or refuse
refugees independently of one another and according to their
national restrictions, or to try to develop a coherent and cooperative
international system which treated the issue as a global problem. The
international community, in the guise of the League of Nations,
decided to experiment with the latter course.

   Skran, in her excellent study of refugees in the inter-war period,
identifies a number of factors, unique to the twentieth century, which
led to the quest for an international solution: the movement of millions, rather than thousands, of people; a changing political and
social arena in which the developments within one country had the
potential to have far-reaching, cross-border effects; the rapid global
development of immigration controls which made it difficult for
refugees to find asylum; and increased governmental support for
social welfare resulting in some reluctance to take on financial obligations for non-citizens, including refugees.[4] The most notable development in this period was the seemingly uniform introduction of
restrictive immigration measures across Europe and the Americas.[5]
The United Kingdom, with its Aliens Restriction (Amendment) Act
1919 and consequent Orders, was no exception.

---

[2] C. Skran, *Refugees in Inter-War Europe – The Emergence of a Regime* (New York: Clarendon
Press, 1998), p. 32.

[3] *ibid.*, Ch. 2.

[4] *ibid.*, pp. 13–14.

[5] The United States, Latin America, most of Europe, and even Canada, known for its
generally lenient policies, imposed immigration restrictions. Only France, in the early
1920s, appeared to encourage immigration, but this ceased by 1926 with emerging
employment problems: C. Skran, *Refugees in Inter-War Europe – The Emergence of a
Regime* (New York: Clarendon Press, 1998), pp. 22–25.

It now seems evident that states were forced into action. On the one hand, many preferred to ignore the refugees, while on the other they recognised that some action needed to be taken. In February 1921, Gustave Ador, President of the International Committee of the Red Cross, wrote of his deep concern for the 800,000 impoverished refugees strewn across Europe, and called upon the League of Nations to appoint a 'General Commissioner for the Russian Refugees'.[6] His challenge was accepted and, in September 1921, Dr Fridtjof Nansen was appointed as League High Commissioner for Russian Refugees. A committed and energetic individual, Dr Nansen achieved much in the nine years of his 'reign', particularly in view of his limited resources[7] and governmental insistence that aid be temporary and applicable to Russian refugees alone.[8] First, and most importantly, he secured identity certificates (the 'Nansen passports') for Russians in 1922 and for Armenians in 1924, and persuaded 51 governments to recognise them.[9] These enabled refugees to travel across state borders but were not legally binding. Dr Nansen managed in addition to assume responsibility for Assyrian, Assyro-Chaldean and Turkish refugees, amongst others, in 1928.[10] He persuaded governments to assist destitute refugees; he extracted funds from states (the British government, for example, after considerable procrastination, supplied £20,000 for assistance to Russians);[11] he negotiated repatriation agreements (successful in the case of the Balkans, but unsuccessful in relation to Russia); and he participated in a division of functions in 1925 between the High Commissioner, responsible to the Council of the League, and the Refugee Service, incorporated as part of the International Labour Organisation ('ILO').

THE POST-NANSEN ERA AND INCREASING RESTRICTIONISM

Dr Nansen's untimely death in 1930 was a significant blow to the refugee world, but the one consolation was the establishment of an

4.3

---

[6] *ibid.*, p. 84.

[7] In 1922, for example, the only financial provision was £4,000 and this was provided for administrative expenses: J.H. Simpson, *The Refugee Problem: Report of a Survey* (London: OUP, 1939), p. 200.

[8] G.Loescher, *Beyond Charity – International Co-operation and the Global Refugee Crisis* (Oxford: OUP, 1993), p. 37.

[9] *ibid.*

[10] J. Hathaway, 'The Evolution of Refugee Status in International Law: 1920–1950', (1994) 33 *International Comparative Law Quarterly*, pp. 354–7.

[11] J.H. Simpson, *The Refugee Problem: Report of a Survey* (London: OUP, 1939), p. 201; C. Skran, *Refugees in Inter-War Europe – The Emergence of a Regime* (New York: Clarendon Press, 1998), pp. 186–7.

independent Nansen International Office for Refugees. The Nansen Office, an autonomous organisation under the direction of the League of Nations, had a humanitarian remit for an eight-year period, and was composed of a Governing Body, headed by a President, and a Managing Committee.[12] The League retained the political and legal protection of refugees, and the position of High Commissioner disappeared.[13] One of the new Office's main contributions to the legal protection of refugees was in the preparation of an intergovernmental conference and draft Convention in 1933. In many respects, the final Convention Relating to the International Status of Refugees was a consolidating document.[14] It recognised the previous Arrangements reached with regard to Russian and Armenian refugees,[15] and to Assyrian, Assyro-Chaldean and Turkish refugees;[16] it improved the Nansen certificate system;[17] it granted refugees access to the courts of law of the Contracting Parties, as well as guaranteeing them rights and privileges equivalent to those enjoyed by the nationals of the country in which they resided;[18] it eased labour restrictions against certain categories of refugees,[19] applied the most favourable treatment accorded to foreign nationals with regard to welfare and relief,[20] and ensured that refugees would benefit from the same educational facilities as those provided to other foreigners;[21] and, finally, in a critical provision, it protected refugees against expulsion from or non-admittance to the country which had authorised their stay (except for reasons of national security or

---

[12] J.H. Simpson, *The Refugee Problem: Report of a Survey* (London: OUP, 1939), pp. 209–10.

[13] *ibid.*, p. 85.

[14] Convention Relating to the International Status of Refugees, Geneva, October 28, 1933 (Document C.650 M.311 1933). See J.H. Simpson, *The Refugee Problem: Report of a Survey* (London: OUP, 1939), Appendix VII for copy of Convention, reservations and dates of ratification.

[15] Arrangement relating to the issue of identity certificates to Russian and Armenian refugees, May 12, 1926. The Arrangement defined the term 'refugee' as: 'Any person of Russian origin (respectively, Armenian origin, formerly a subject of the Ottoman Empire) who does not enjoy, or who no longer enjoys, the protection of the Government of the Union of Soviet Socialist Republics (respectively, of the Government of the Turkish Republic) and who has not acquired another nationality.'

[16] Arrangement concerning the extension to other categories of refugees of certain measures taken in favour of Russian and Armenian refugees, June 30, 1928.

[17] Ch. II, Art. 2.

[18] Ch. III, Art. 6.

[19] Ch. IV, Art. 7. It was, admittedly, rather difficult to comply with all of the requirements necessary for suspension of labour restrictions. The refugee had to show that he/she was: domiciled or regularly resident in the host country; resident for no less than three years; married to a national with one or more children possessing the host country's nationality; and an ex-combatant of the Great War (Ch. IV, Art. 7(2)).

[20] Ch. VI, Arts 9–11.

[21] Ch. VII, Art. 12.

public order) – the first ever mention of '*refoulement*' in international refugee law.[22]

The Convention also encouraged the establishment in each Contracting State of a refugee committee or committees.[23] This came into force in 1935, following ratification by Bulgaria and Norway. A number of countries, including the US, were reluctant to accede, believing that they already offered refugees the majority of rights provided for in the Convention.[24] The United Kingdom did sign the Convention, but not until October 1936, later than most. It also adopted a substantial number of reservations to the provisions, thereby undermining the effectiveness of the instrument. Perhaps the most significant were the reservations in relation to the definition of 'refugee' as set out in Art. 1 and the rejection of the principle of *non-refoulement* in Art. 3(2). The UK stated that it regarded the Convention as 'applicable only to Russian, Armenian and assimilated refugees who *at the date of the present accession* no longer enjoy the protection of their country of origin' (emphasis added), thereby ensuring that the UK's obligations would not extend to any refugees who might arise in the future.[25] It went further and rejected outright the undertaking in Art. 3(2) 'not to refuse entry to refugees at the frontiers of their countries of origin' – the only country to do so. Some commentators have suggested that the UK's hard line on *non-refoulement* was due to an incorrect translation of '*refouler*' as 'to refuse entry', whereas the correct meaning is 'to send back'.[26]

1933 was the year that witnessed the signing of the Refugee Convention and the year in which Hitler's National Socialist German Workers' Party came to power in Germany. Within months, anti-Jewish laws were being introduced in Germany, leading to an exodus of 37,000 persons in 1933, 80 per cent of whom it is estimated were Jewish.[27] Whereas post-1918 labour shortages had led some

4.4

---

[22] Ch. II, Art. 3 (in part):

> 'Each of the Contracting Parties undertakes not to remove or keep from his territory by application of police measures, such as expulsions or non-admittance at the frontier (*refoulement*), refugees who have been authorised to reside there regularly, unless the said measures are dictated by reasons of national security or public order. He undertakes (*sic*) in any case not to refuse entry to refugees at the frontiers of their countries of origin.'

[23] Ch. X, Art. 15.

[24] L. Holborn, 'The Legal Status of Political Refugees, 1920–1938', (1938) 32:2 *AJIL*, p. 690.

[25] See HMSO, *Treaty Series* No. 4 (1937) Convention Relating to the International Status of Refugees, October 28, 1933, Cmd. 5347 for English translation.

[26] R. Beck, 'Britain and the 1933 Refugee Convention: National or State Sovereignty?' (1999) 11:4 *IJRL*, p. 621, and see, also, A. Grahl-Madsen, *The Status of Refugees in International Law* Vol. II (The Netherlands: A.W. Sijthoff-Leiden, 1972), pp. 98–9.

[27] T. Sjöberg, *The Powers and the Persecuted – The Refugee Problem and the Intergovernmental Committee on Refugees* (Sweden: Lund University Press, 1991), p. 29.

European countries, in particular France, to welcome asylum seekers, the economic climate of the early 1930s was no longer conducive to an open-door policy.[28] Faced with this problem, the League of Nations agreed once more to the appointment of a High Commissioner for Refugees coming from Germany, and of a Governing Body, consisting of representatives of about fifteen governments, which would assist the High Commissioner.[29] Significantly, both offices were kept separate from the League. The first incumbent of the High Commissioner's post, James McDonald, fought hard against the introduction of restrictive immigration laws and sought to encourage the reception of refugees.[30] He was only partly successful. During his period of office, 1933–35, most countries tightened their immigration policies. The British government, for example, having already enacted stringent aliens legislation, stated in April 1933 that the Aliens Order 1920 would continue to apply to refugees and that permission to land would only be granted if they were able to satisfy Immigration Officers that they could maintain themselves.[31] The High Commissioner was further hampered in his efforts by the lack of financial support provided. At the outset, he was given a small loan of 25,000 Swiss francs (about £1,200–£1,400), which he was required to repay.[32] As a consequence, McDonald was forced to spend a significant proportion of his time raising money from private sources, thereby deflecting him from his original remit. It is estimated that he managed to obtain donations in the region of £1,500,000, a remarkable achievement.[33]

By 1935, and the passing of the Nuremberg Laws,[34] it was clear that Jews no longer had a future in Germany.[35] McDonald issued ominous warnings to the British and Americans about an impending refugee crisis and called for action to be taken. Sir Eric Phipps, the British Ambassador in Berlin, admitted in early December 1935 that

---

[28] T. Sjöberg, *The Powers and the Persecuted – The Refugee Problem and the Intergovernmental Committee on Refugees* (Sweden: Lund University Press, 1991), p. 29.

[29] J.H. Simpson, *The Refugee Problem: Report of a Survey* (London: OUP, 1939), p. 216; Holborn, 'The Legal Status of Political Refugees, 1920–1938', (1938) 32:2 *AJIL*, p. 692.

[30] James McDonald, an American former academic, was appointed in October 1933.

[31] B. Wasserstein, 'The British Government and the German Immigration 1933–45', in . Hirschfeld, ed., *Exile in Great Britain – Refugees from Hitler's Germany* (Leamington Spa: Berg, 1984), p. 66.

[32] HL Deb. Vol. 95, February 6, 1935, col. 821.

[33] *ibid.*

[34] The Nuremberg laws were two racial laws, the first of which deprived those not of German or related blood of German citizenship, and the second of which made marriage or extra-marital relations between Germans and Jews illegal.

[35] T. Sjöberg, *The Powers and the Persecuted – The Refugee Problem and the Intergovernmental Committee on Refugees* (Sweden: Lund University Press, 1991), p. 29.

'the position of the Jews is becoming so desperate as to make it more apparent every day that [. . .] the present Nazi policy threatens the Jewish population in the Reich with extermination.'[36] The politicians of the day chose, however, to ignore his message, deciding that the best course of action was 'to wait and see'. Sherman offers one explanation for their inexorability:

'Phipps rejected the notion that a catastrophic exodus of Jews was to be feared, on the purely practical grounds that no country except Palestine – and even Palestine only to a limited extent – was willing to accept Jewish immigrants without sufficient capital.'[37]

Sherman's view is supported in part by comments made during a parliamentary debate on German refugees held in February 1935. There, a number of Lords, including Lord Cecil, the Chairman of the High Commissioner's Governing Body, made impassioned pleas for greater assistance to be afforded the High Commissioner and for the League of Nations to address the refugee problem with some urgency. Speaking on behalf of the British government, the Under-Secretary of State for War, Lord Strathcona, replied:

'I [cannot] refrain from reminding your Lordships that, sympathetic as the Government is on this question and sympathetic as we must all be in so serious a matter as this, we have at certain times, especially in times like these, to have regard to the conditions of employment and unemployment in this country in dealing with these matters.'[38]

Once more, the interests of Britain came first. It is noteworthy that, at the time of the debate, there were only about 2,500 German refugees in Britain.[39]

McDonald, having grown increasingly tired of governmental **4.5** resistance to his calls for action and to his dire warnings about Hitler's extermination plans, resigned dramatically in late December 1935. His 3,000–word letter of resignation was given wide publicity in national newspapers and, for a short time, drew the world's attention to the plight of German Jews. In it, he declared:

'When domestic policies threaten the demoralization and exile of hundreds of thousands of human beings, considerations of diplomatic correctness must yield to those of common humanity. I should be recreant

---

[36] Cited in A.J. Sherman, *Island Refuge – Britain and Refugees from the Third Reich 1933–1939* (London: Paul Elek, 1973), p. 63
[37] *ibid.*
[38] HL Deb. Vol. 95, February 6, 1935, col. 842.
[39] HL Deb. Vol. 95, February 6, 1935, col. 827.

if I did not call attention to the actual situation, and plead that world opinion, acting through the League and its Member States and other countries, move to avert the existing and impending tragedies.'[40]

In addition to his personal frustration with the members of the League, McDonald also highlighted the difficulties confronting a High Commissioner whose office was separated from the League.[41] The Council paid heed to some of McDonald's suggestions and appointed a temporary High Commissioner, Sir Neill Malcolm, who would report directly to the League and whose remit was exclusively the political and legal status of refugees coming from Germany, and not the domestic politics of that country. Malcolm secured an Arrangement in 1936 on the legal status of refugees coming from Germany, which, in February 1938, was converted into a new Convention.[42] The Convention was extended to Austrian refugees by protocol in September 1939.[43] One of the most important aspects of the 1938 Convention was the inclusion once again of a *non-refoulement* provision in Art. 5:

'2.   Without prejudice to the measures which may be taken within any territory, refugees who have been authorised to reside therein may not be subjected by the authorities to measures of expulsion or reconduction unless such measures are dictated by reasons of national security or public order.

3.(a)   The High Contracting Parties undertake not to reconduct refugees to German territory unless they have been warned and have refused, without just cause, to make the necessary arrangements to proceed to another territory or to take advantage of the arrangements made for them with that object.

   (b)   In such case, the travel document may be cancelled or withdrawn.'

While this was a highly significant provision, endorsing the introduction in the 1933 Convention of a *non-refoulement* principle, its

---

[40] J. McDonald, *Letter of Resignation*, *The Times*, December 30, 1935, p. 6, point 17.

[41] *ibid.*, point 4.

[42] The Convention concerning the Status of Refugees coming from Germany, UK *Treaty Series* No 8 (1939), Cmd. 5929. 'Refugees coming from Germany' were defined in Art. 1 as:

'(a)   Persons possessing or having possessed German nationality and not possessing any other nationality who are proved not to enjoy, in law or in fact, the protection of the German Government;

(b)   Stateless persons not covered by previous Conventions or Agreements who have left German territory after being established therein and who are proved not to enjoy, in law or in fact, the protection of the German Government.'

[43] League of Nations, Document C.258 M.176.1939. XII.

actual impact was rather limited.[44] Few countries signed the Convention,[45] and the UK entered a number of reservations that heavily undermined the effectiveness of the Convention. It insisted, as it had in 1933, on a time limit for German refugees (only those so defined at the time of ratification would be considered) and exempted from *non-refoulement* those refugees who were the subject of extradition proceedings in the UK, or who were on a temporary visit to the UK.

By 1938, Malcolm could claim to have assisted 5,000 refugees from Germany through his personal intervention.[46] However, he could not afford to be complacent. Following the *Anschluß* with Austria on March 12, 1938, the refugee situation once again deteriorated. Neither the High Commissioner nor the Nansen International Office appeared able to cope. President Roosevelt, alarmed by reports of the desperate attempts of Austrian Jews to escape across the border to neighbouring countries, immediately called the governments of France, Belgium, the Netherlands, Denmark, Sweden, Norway, Switzerland, Italy and the American Republics to a conference to address the issue of 'facilitating the emigration from Austria and presumably from Germany of political refugees'.[47] By May, the High Commission's competence was extended to cover refugees coming from Austria and over thirty countries had agreed to attend the conference. The first meeting was held on July 6, 1938 in Evian, France.

THE EVIAN CONFERENCE 1938 AND BEYOND: A WORLD IN CRISIS

To the outside observer, the Evian Conference promised much. It seemed a genuine attempt to address the many issues surrounding the exodus of German and Austrian refugees. Unknown at the time were the limitations placed upon the negotiations even before they had commenced. Firstly, the UK, concerned that the Conference would become a vehicle for discussion about Palestine, entered into secret negotiations with Washington prior to the meeting to ensure that invitations would be sent only to countries of immigration, that the Conference would deal only with refugees and not those threatened with

4.6

---

[44] C. Skran, *Refugees in Inter-War Europe – The Emergence of a Regime* (New York: Clarendon Press, 1998), p. 137.

[45] *ibid.*

[46] J.H. Simpson, *The Refugee Problem: Report of a Survey* (London: OUP, 1939), p. 218.

[47] *Foreign Relations of the United States – 1938* Vol. I (Washington: 1955), pp. 740–41, cited in S. Adler-Rudel, 'The Evian Conference on the Refugee Question', 1968, *Leo Baeck Institute Year Book* p. 236.

persecution, and that Palestine would remain off the agenda.[48]
Despite these early attempts by the UK to dictate the direction taken
by the Conference, it became clear during the first addresses that
there were considerable differences between the British and American
delegations. For the Americans, the ultimate objective was 'to establish an organisation which would concern itself with all refugees
wherever governmental intolerance [. . .] created a refugee problem',
since the refugee problem was 'no longer one of purely private concern' but 'a problem for intergovernmental action'.[49] They recognised, however, that attention would be focused for the time being on
refugees coming from Germany and Austria. The British delegate,
Lord Winterton, stressed, by contrast, that while the UK considered
the problem to be 'mainly a humanitarian one' and while 'it [had]
been the policy of successive British Governments to offer asylum to
persons who, for political, racial or religious reasons, have had to
leave their own countries', '[f]or economic and social reasons, the traditional policy of granting asylum [could] only be applied within narrow limits'.[50] There was no mention of a revitalised role for an
international refugee organisation or of Palestine. Only on the last
day did Lord Winterton refer to Palestine. His response to suggestions
that the 'Gates of Palestine' be thrown open to Jewish immigration
was unequivocal: 'I should like to say, as emphatically as I can, that I
regard any such proposition as wholly untenable.'[51] The reason for
such intransigence became clear in 1939, when the UK government
published its White Paper, *Palestine: A Statement of Policy*, which acceded
to Arab wishes that Jewish migration to Palestine be kept to a minimum. A quota was imposed allowing for a maximum of 75,000 Jews
to enter the country over a period of five years.

Though there was much talk at the Conference of the deep concern over the refugee problem, the outcome cannot be described as a
great success. The respective governments promised to increase
reception of refugees 'within the framework of existing immigration
laws and practices'; private organisations volunteered proposals for a
solution; and an independent Intergovernmental Committee on
Refugees ('IGCR') was established with its seat in London. The Committee, consisting of representatives from all of the countries that had
attended the Conference, held its first meeting on August 3, 1938. It
immediately entered into negotiations with the German government

---

[48] S. Adler-Rudel, 'The Evian Conference on the Refugee Question', (1968) *Leo Baeck Institute Year Book* p. 237.
[49] *ibid.*, p. 243.
[50] *ibid.*, p. 244.
[51] *ibid.*, p. 245.

to try to reach an agreement regarding the 'orderly emigration' of Jewish refugees whereby they were permitted to take money and belongings with them.[52] While they deliberated, Nazi Germany annexed the Sudetenland and Czechoslovakia, with dire consequences for Jews in these countries.[53] Sir Herbert Emerson, recently appointed as the League's High Commissioner for Refugees, was also appointed Director of the IGCR in early 1939, thereby enhancing its status considerably. However, the agreement with Germany that 400,000 Jews would be permitted to emigrate never saw fruition.[54] The US grew increasingly impatient with the IGCR and, within a year of the Committee's creation, the US was considering amalgamating it with refugee organisations of the League, reversing its previous policy that the new refugee body should be permanent and autonomous.[55] The IGCR was partly saved by the outbreak of war in September 1939, when the refugee question was no longer considered a matter of priority and the IGCR was maintained in a 'shadowy limbo existence' until 1943.[56]

On December 11, 1942, *The Manchester Guardian* reported that a **4.7** note on Jewish persecution had been presented by the Polish government in London to the governments of the United Nations, describing the 'new methods of mass slaughter' and 'the ghastly slaughter of the Warsaw Ghetto'. The press report went on:

'The Polish Government asks that the United Nations shall take effective measures to help the Jews not only of Poland but of the whole of Europe, three to four millions of whom are in peril of ruthless extermination.' [. . .]

The situation obviously calls for something more than a reaffirmation of principles or a condemnation of the indescribable deeds being done in fulfilment of a predetermined policy.'[57]

Six days later, on December 17, the Allied Powers finally made public in a joint declaration the fact of Nazi extermination plans and atrocities against the Jews. In the case of the UK, the Secretary of

---

[52] L. Holborn, 'The Legal Status of Political Refugees, 1920–1938', (1938) 32:2 *AJIL*, p. 701.
[53] S. Adler-Rudel, 'The Evian Conference on the Refugee Question', (1968) *Leo Baeck Institute Year Book* p. 260.
[54] T. Sjöberg, *The Powers and the Persecuted – The Refugee Problem and the Intergovernmental Committee on Refugees* (Sweden: Lund University Press, 1991), p. 229.
[55] *ibid.*, p. 230.
[56] B. Wasserstein, *Britain and the Jews of Europe 1939–1945* (Oxford: Clarendon Press/IJA, 1979), p. 9.
[57] *The Manchester Guardian* 'The German massacres of Jews in Poland, December 11, 1942: http://www.guardiancentury.co.uk/1940–1949/Story/0,,127573,00.html.

State for Foreign Affairs, Anthony Eden, made this announcement in the House of Commons:

'[. . .] the German authorities, not content with denying to persons of Jewish race in all the territories over which their barbarous rule has been extended the most elementary rights, are now carrying into effect Hitler's oft-repeated intention to exterminate the Jewish people in Europe.'[58]

Having set out in detail the facts as known at the time, the joint declaration ended by affirming the 'solemn resolution' of the United Nations governments 'to ensure that those responsible for these crimes [should] not escape retribution, and to press on with the practical measures to this end'.[59] The response was immediate. The public called for radical steps to be taken and the British and American governments came under increasing pressure to act.[60] Various plans for rescue of the refugees were announced, but few were realised.[61] Finally, after much discussion between Washington and London, a conference was convened in Bermuda in April 1943. Like Evian, it was, in fact, a most disappointing meeting. Before it even met, the Foreign Office was of the view that 'It [was] time that the idea of "measures of rescue" [. . .] [was] shown up as illusory'.[62] Marrus describes the Bermuda Conference thus:

'The Americans put no pressure on the British over the White Paper quotas for Palestine; the British did not ask the United States to raise its own immigration ceilings. Jewish representatives and inquisitive reporters were kept at bay, and discussions were held in private. No report of the proceedings was ever published. The conference rejected suggestions for negotiations with the Germans or the dispatch of food and assistance to the Jews of Europe. The delegates determined flatly that "no shipping from the United Nations sources could be made available for the transport of refugees from Europe." Although fulsome in praise of what the British and Americans had already done for refugees, the conference report indicated no new prospects for resettlement. The conference did recommend the revival of the dormant Intergovernmental Committee on Refuges (IGCR) with urgent new tasks. The IGCR [. . .] was to try to obtain neutral ships to move refugees and to secure new places of refuge.'[63]

---

[58] HC Deb. Vol. 385, December 17, 1942, col. 2083.
[59] ibid.
[60] B. Wasserstein, *Britain and the Jews of Europe 1939–1945* (Oxford: Clarendon Press/IJA, 1979), pp. 176–9.
[61] M. Marrus, *The Unwanted – European Refugees in the Twentieth Century* (New York: OUP, 1985), p. 283.
[62] Randall minute, April 16, 1943, PRO FO 371/36658, cited in B. Wasserstein, *Britain and the Jews of Europe 1939–1945* (Oxford: Clarendon Press/IJA, 1979), p. 189.
[63] M. Marrus, *The Unwanted – European Refugees in the Twentieth Century* (New York: OUP, 1985), p. 285.

Thus success, it seemed, was reliant upon the Intergovernmental   **4.8**
Committee and 'the degree of life and authority which [could] be
injected into [it], and upon the speed with which the machinery of
the Committee [could] be set in motion [. . .]'.[64] The Conference
called for the reorganisation of the IGCR and an extension of its
mandate, although the British criticised the American habit of making 'frequent references to that body as if it were a kind of *deus ex
machina*, to be produced on the stage whenever any apparently insol-
uble questions of finance, shipping, or politics confronted us'.[65] While
the British remained sceptical about the IGCR's resurrection, and
favoured the creation of a new organisation,[66] Emerson was recalled
as Director and a meeting was arranged for August 1943, with representatives from the UK, USA, Argentina, Brazil, the Netherlands,
and the French National Committee present.[67] It was agreed that the
UK and USA would underwrite the expenses of the IGCR, and that
membership would be extended to the USSR as well.[68] The IGCR's
mandate would cover:

> 'all persons, wherever they may be, who, as a result of events in Europe,
> have had to leave, or may have to leave, their countries of residence
> because of the danger to their lives or liberties on account of their race,
> religion or political beliefs.'[69]

The decision to move away from the group-based assessment of
refugees was an unprecedented step and, for the first time in history,
created a definition of 'refugee' that was all-inclusive. This generalised definition would influence post-War discussions on refugee
protection and later would be encapsulated in the 1951 Convention relating to the Status of Refugees. However, at the time,
notwithstanding all the well-meaning intentions, the Committee
failed to make a real impact on the refugee crisis, arguably bar one
exception: financial support of a Jewish relief and rescue operation

---

[64] Morning conference, April 23, 1943, Long, Box 202, pp. 4–4a, cited in L. London,
Whitehall and the Jews 1933–1948 – British Immigration Policy and the Holocaust
(Cambridge: CUP, 2000), p. 215.

[65] UK delegates to Eden, June 28, 1943, PRO PREM 4/51/3, cited in B. Wasserstein,
Britain and the Jews of Europe 1939–1945 (Oxford: Clarendon Press/IJA, 1979), p. 199.

[66] T. Sjöberg, *The Powers and the Persecuted – The Refugee Problem and the Intergovernmental
Committee on Refugees* (Sweden: Lund University Press, 1991), p.166.

[67] B. Wasserstein, *Britain and the Jews of Europe 1939–1945* (Oxford: Clarendon
Press/IJA, 1979), p. 217.

[68] *ibid.*

[69] Minutes of the Fourth Plenary session of the IGCR, August 15–17, 1944, AJ43–23,
Archives Nationales, cited in T. Sjöberg, *The Powers and the Persecuted – The Refugee
Problem and the Intergovernmental Committee on Refugees* (Sweden: Lund University Press,
1991), p. 146.

in Romania.[70] Sjöberg, in his illuminating study of the IGCR, concludes that:

> 'an essential cause of its failure seems [. . .] to have been that the organ-
> ization was neither created nor sustained with refugee relief as the pri-
> mary goal in mind, despite all the official humanitarian rhetoric.
> Instead, the important aim appears to have been to let IGCR serve as
> a means of deflecting awkward pressure for more active assistance to
> refugees, above all on the two dominant member-states – the United
> States and Britain.'[71]

POST-WAR DEVELOPMENTS: FROM TEMPORARY TO
PERMANENT PROTECTION

IGCR, UNRRA and the IRO

4.9   Following the War, a new climate of hope emerged – hope that international cooperation would once again pave the way for a future of
peace and security.[72] A further conference, convened in the spring of
1945, resulted in the signing of the United Nations Charter in June
1945 and the Universal Declaration of Human Rights in 1948.
Mindful of the huge displacement of people that had occurred as a
result of the war, states recognised that immediate action on refugees
was called for. The United Nations Relief and Rehabilitation Administration ('UNRRA'), which had been established in November 1943,
assumed responsibility for material assistance to and repatriation of
displaced persons. Only after hostilities ceased did the true scale of
the problem become evident.[73] Europe was devastated – an estimated
21 to 30 million non-Germans were displaced or were refugees.[74]
UNRRA differed from the IGCR in that its main interest was displaced persons rather than refugees, and it was concerned with maintenance and repatriation, rather than maintenance and resettlement,

---

[70] B. Wasserstein, *Britain and the Jews of Europe 1939–1945* (Oxford: Clarendon
Press/IJA, 1979), p. 219.

[71] T. Sjöberg, *The Powers and the Persecuted – The Refugee Problem and the Intergovernmental
Committee on Refugees* (Sweden: Lund University Press, 1991), p. 236.

[72] K. Salomon, *Refugees in the Cold War – Toward a New International Refugee Regime in the
Early Postwar Era* (Lund: Lund University Press, 1991), p. 47.

[73] By May 1945, it was believed that the War had created in excess of 40 million
refugees: M. Proudfoot, *European Refugees 1939–52 – A Study in Forced Population Movement* (London: Faber & Faber, 1956), p. 32.

[74] K. Salomon, *Refugees in the Cold War – Toward a New International Refugee Regime in the
Early Postwar Era* (Sweden: Lund University Press, 1991), p. 48.

which fell to the IGCR.[75] In addition, UNRRA was an American-supported body. It had its seat in Washington and was financed largely by the US (of over $3.6 billion, the US contributed in excess of $2.8 billion).[76] Refugee protection became part of its domain in August 1945, when a resolution was enacted extending aid to 'other persons who have been obliged to leave their country or place of origin or former residence'.[77] It was the Washington office which pushed for a generous interpretation to include political dissidents as well as post-war political refugees, much to the disquiet of the UK government:

> 'As [the US] directive now stands, any inhabitant of a liberated area who wishes to leave his country for economic reasons qualifies for UNRRA care on what appears to us the purely fortuitous circumstance of internal displacement.'[78]

With the involvement of three bodies in refugee and displacement problems, the IGCR, the office of the High Commissioner for Refugees, and UNRRA, it was not long before the need for consolidation and greater clarity was recognised. The decision by Member Governments that the refugee problem came under the jurisdiction of the United Nations (as stipulated in Art. 1, para. 3 of the Charter) also helped focus their collective minds on the prospect of a more permanent solution. The first session of the General Assembly in February 1946 delegated the task to the Economic and Social Council. Its recommendation that a new agency, the International Refugee Organisation ('IRO'), be established was accepted by the General Assembly in December 1946, despite opposition from the eastern bloc.[79] In July 1947, the IRO assumed the dual functions of

---

[75] T. Sjöberg, *The Powers and the Persecuted – The Refugee Problem and the Intergovernmental Committee on Refugees* (Sweden: Lund University Press, 1991), p. 153.

[76] K. Salomon, *Refugees in the Cold War – Toward a New International Refugee Regime in the Early Postwar Era* (Sweden: Lund University Press, 1991), p. 48.

[77] (1945) UNRRA Journal 152 for the text of Resolution 17, cited in J. Hathaway, 'The Evolution of Refugee Status in International Law: 1920–1950', (1994) 33 *International Comparative Law Quarterly*, p. 373.

[78] UNRRA Outgoing Cable No 1675 (February 9, 1946), cited in J. Hathaway, 'The Evolution of Refugee Status in International Law: 1920–1950', (1994) 33 *International Comparative Law Quarterly*, p. 373.

[79] G. Loescher, *Beyond Charity – International Co-operation and the Global Refugee Crisis* (Oxford: OUP, 1993), p. 50. The eastern bloc favoured the retention of UNRRA because it channelled aid to their territories and because its mandate was relatively limited. The USSR also considered anyone who refused repatriation to be a criminal or traitor.

the IGCR and UNRRA.[80] Its main functions relating to refugees were identification, registration and classification, care and assistance, legal and political protection, transport, and re-settlement and re-establishment.[81] It adopted a broader, individualised definition of 'refugee', again contrary to the wishes of the USSR. Included within the definition was any person who had left or was outside his country of nationality or former habitual residence and who belonged to one of the following categories: victims of Nazi, Fascist, or quisling regimes; Spanish Republicans and other victims of the Falangist regime on Spain; Jews from Austria and Germany who were victims of Nazi persecution and who were not firmly resettled in those countries; and refugees so-defined prior to the Second World War for reasons of race, religion, nationality or political opinion. Also included were those who were outside their country of nationality or former habitual residence and who, in the wake of the war, were unable or unwilling to avail themselves of the protection of their country of nationality or former nationality; and unaccompanied children who were war orphans and were outside their country of origin. Displaced persons were separately defined, and criminals, quislings and traitors were specifically excluded.[82] During its lifetime, 1947–52, the IRO is said to have resettled successfully over one million refugees and saved hundreds of thousands from starvation.[83] By December 31, 1951, the UK had accepted 86,000 individuals for resettlement. The US took 329,000, Australia 182,000, Israel 132,000, and Canada 123,000. The rest were scattered around the world or had not yet been resettled.[84] The IRO was finally dissolved on March 1, 1952.

4.10   By the late 1940s, there was a growing recognition that, despite the remarkable achievements of the IRO (it resettled the majority of refugees handed over by UNRRA within a year),[85] the problem of refugees was not just a Second World War phenomenon. The onset

---

[80] For a detailed study of the IRO, see L. Holborn, *The International Refugee Organisation: A Specialized Agency of the United Nations – Its History and Work 1946–1952* (London: OUP, 1956).

[81] 1946 Constitution of the International Refugee Organisation, Article 2(1) available on *http://www.yale.edu/lawweb/avalon/decade/decad053.htm*

[82] For the full definitions of 'refugee' and 'displaced person', contained in Part 1, Sections A and B of Annex I to the IRO Constitution, see G. J. Van Heuven Goedhart, 'The Problem of Refugees' (1953) 1 *Académie de Droit International Recueil des Cours*, pp. 275–6.

[83] *ibid.*, p. 277.

[84] See, for table of statistics, J. Vernant, *The Refugee in the Post-War World* (London: Allen & Unwin, 1953), p. 38.

[85] G. Loescher, *Beyond Charity – International Co-operation and the Global Refugee Crisis* (Oxford: OUP, 1993), p. 52.

of the Cold War was giving rise to new refugee problems almost as serious as those generated between 1939 and 1945, and a more comprehensive solution was urgently called for.[86] Refugee protection was by now developing along two lines: the establishment of an agency charge with the practical tasks of protection and assistance, and the creation of an international legal framework setting out the definition of, and obligations towards, refugees.[87] Although states balked at the idea of financing yet another refugee protection organisation – the IRO, in its five-year life-span, had cost nearly $430 million – , discussions were held under the auspices of the United Nations concerning the creation of a new refugee organisation.[88] The US pushed for a temporary body while European states, particularly France and Belgium, wanted a strong, well-resourced and permanent organisation.[89] The UK sided with the US, particularly on the issue of finance, since, from the time the IGCR's mandate was extended, it had been concerned about the cost implications of refugee protection.[90] By the time agreement was reached in 1950, it had been decided that the new body would be called the UN High Commissioner for Refugees ('UNHCR'), that it would have only temporary authority for three years and that its budget would be very modest ($300,000).[91] This was a clear financial underestimation: in 1952, just over $716,000 was spent on the administration expenses of running the UNHCR's Office.[92]

The UNHCR Statute

The Statute of the UNHCR was agreed by General Assembly Resolution on December 14, 1950. Its drafting had not been without difficulty. One of the most contentious issues related to the scope of the High Commissioner's mandate. States were in the process of negotiating a Convention relating to the status of refugees which would provide its own definition of 'refugee'. The question confronting the drafters of the UNHCR's Statute was the extent to which the

4.11

---

[86] *ibid.*, p. 53.
[87] G. J. Van Heuven Goedhart, 'The Problem of Refugees' (1953) 1 *Académie de Droit International Recueil des Cours*, p. 283.
[88] J. Vernant, *The Refugee in the Post-War World*, (London: Allen & Unwin, 1953), p. 37.
[89] G.Loescher, *Beyond Charity – International Co-operation and the Global Refugee Crisis* (Oxford: OUP, 1993), p. 56.
[90] K. Salomon, *Refugees in the Cold War – Toward a New International Refugee Regime in the Early Postwar Era* (Lund: Lund University Press, 1991), pp. 252–3.
[91] D. Gallagher, 'The Evolution of the International Refugee System', (1989) 23:3 *International Migration Review*, p. 580.
[92] J. Vernant, *The Refugee in the Post-War World*, (London: Allen & Unwin, 1953), p. 39.

definitions provided for by the Statute and by the Convention should equate.[93] Holborn, in her comprehensive account of the work of the UNHCR from 1951 to 1972, discusses the tortuous nature of the debate on this issue. The two available options were: (i) the traditional approach, according to which refugees were defined by specified categories, and (ii) the universal approach, according to which the characteristics of refugees would be specified in the instrument.[94] A number of states were very concerned not to include future refugee groups. Interestingly, the UK delegation proposed that the universal approach should be incorporated in the Statute, if not the Convention, since it considered that the definition could be different in the two documents.[95] The final outcome was one of compromise. Both Statute and Convention included a similar definition, which sets a cut-off date of January 1, 1951.[96]

While the Statute contained a second, broader definition that omitted the time limit,[97] the Convention relied solely upon the time-limited version. It also provided for a geographical limitation under which states could elect to restrict the application of the Convention to events occurring in Europe.[98] In 1967, sixteen years after adoption of the Convention, a Protocol was agreed amending the Convention and deleting the time limit contained therein.[99] It is possible to accede to the 1967 Protocol alone (or, for that matter, to the 1951 Convention), but this is an unlikely option for states to pursue. If such a course is taken, there is no possibility of applying a geographical limitation.[100] States which were already party to the Convention on acceding to the Protocol, and which had made a declaration adopting a geographical limitation could continue to apply such a limitation if they chose not to extend the definition to include 'events occurring elsewhere'.[101] States which now follow the recommended route, and accede simultaneously to the 1951 Convention and 1967 Protocol, must make a formal declaration regarding the geographical application under Art. 1B(1) of the Convention. As of September 30, 2002, only four countries were maintaining the geographical limitation: Congo, Madagascar, Monaco and Turkey.

---

[93] See, generally, L. Holborn, *Refugees: A Problem of our Time – The Work of the UNHCR 1951–1972*, Volume 1 (New Jersey: The Scarecrow Press, 1975), pp. 73–84.

[94] *ibid.*, pp. 76–77.

[95] *ibid.*, p. 81.

[96] para. 6A(ii) of the 1950 Statute of the Office of the UNHCR; Art. 1A(2) of the 1951 Convention relating to the Status of Refugees.

[97] para. 6B.

[98] Art. 1B.

[99] 606 *UNTS* 267, Art. 1(2).

[100] Art. 1(3).

[101] Art. 1(3), 1967 Protocol, and Art. 1B(2), 1951 Convention.

The connection between the Statute and the Convention extends beyond the refugee definition. For the first time in the history of refugee law, a formal connection was established between the organisation established to provide protection for refugees, the UNHCR, and the instrument of international refugee law, the 1951 Geneva Convention. Art. 35 to the Convention provides:

> 'The Contracting States undertake to co-operate with the Office of the United Nations High Commissioner for Refugees, or any other agency of the United Nations which may succeed it, in the exercise of its functions, and shall in particular facilitate its duty of supervising the application of the provisions of this Convention.'

Similarly, the High Commissioner is called upon to promote the conclusion and ratification of international conventions for the protection of refugees and to supervise their application.[102]

The UNHCR's mandate

While the 1950 Statute provides the all-important refugee definition   **4.12**
with which the High Commissioner is expected to work, it also sets out the mandate for the UNHCR. It is stated quite clearly that the UNHCR's mandate shall be one of protection and is non-political:

> '1.   The United Nations High Commissioner for Refugees, acting under the authority of the General Assembly, shall assume the function of providing international protection, under the auspices of the United Nations, to refugees who fall within the scope of the present Statute and of seeking permanent solutions for the problem of refugees by assisting Governments and, subject to the approval of the Governments concerned, private organizations to facilitate the voluntary repatriation of such refugees, or their assimilation within new communities.
>
> 2.   The work of the High Commissioner shall be of an entirely non-political character; it shall be humanitarian and social and shall relate, as a rule, to groups and categories of refugees.'[103]

The provision of international protection and search for permanent solutions are at the heart of the UNHCR's activities. The mandate has remained the same, but the UNHCR, for the last 50 years, has had to alter its activities to keep abreast of changing global

---

[102]   para. 8(a), 1950 Statute.
[103]   para. 1.

problems. The numbers of people being assisted by the UNHCR have increased massively. In the aftermath of the Second World War, it was charged with resettling 400,000 refugees; by 1996, it was assisting some 26 million.[104] It has been transformed from an office of 33 staff, handling a budget of $300,000, into a huge enterprise of 5,000 employees with a budget of over $1 billion.[105] Over the years, the UNHCR has inevitably been drawn into activities which some consider to be outside its original mandate – in particular: those internally displaced within their own countries, the victims of war and human rights infringements, and asylum seekers whose status has not been finally determined. The UNHCR is clear that assistance afforded to such groups is consistent with its original mandate and its obligation under paragraph 9 of the Statute to 'engage in such additional activities, including repatriation and resettlement, as the General Assembly may determine [. . .]'.[106] And the General Assembly has been happy to oblige, agreeing that international protection should be accorded to a broad range of people in need of assistance, not just 'refugees'.[107] Despite this, there have been voices suggesting that, in recent years, the UNHCR has lost sight of its *raison d'être* and should reaffirm its humanitarian component.[108] It certainly struggled in the 1980s and 90s to remain true to its non-political character when forced to work in highly politicised situations, such as the former Yugoslavia. It has also extended its protection function to countries of origin, an action that, for some, has introduced 'an element of instability in the international protection regime'.[109] There is an argument that the image of the UNHCR has become tarnished over the years as it strives and sometimes fails to cope with the causes

---

[104] UNHCR, *The State of the World's Refugees – Fifty Years of Humanitarian Action* (Oxford: OUP, 2000), p. 3.

[105] *ibid.* p. 3.

[106] *ibid.*

[107] See, *e.g.*, GA Resolution 1388(XIV), November 20, 1959 (authorisation to use 'good offices' in transmission of contributions to assist non-Convention refugees); GA Resolution 1673(XI), December 18, 1961 (UNHCR to pursue activities on behalf of refugees within mandate 'or those for whom he extends his good offices'); GA Resolution 2039(XX), December 7, 1965 (abandons distinction between Convention and good offices refugees and calls upon UNHCR to pursue his efforts with a view to ensuring an adequate international protection of refugees and to providing satisfactory permanent solutions to the problems affecting the various groups of refugees within his competence); finally, GA Resolution 3445(XXX), December 9, 1975 reaffirmed 'the eminently humanitarian character of the activities of the High Commissioner for the benefit of refugees and displaced persons'.

[108] See, *e.g.*, I. Jackson, 'Ensuring that the exercise of UNHCR's traditional functions is maintained and reinforced in the 21st century', (2000) 12:4 *IJRL*, pp. 589–96.

[109] A. Johnsson, 'UNHCR's protection role continually evolving' (1993) 92 *Refugees*, pp. 15–16.

and consequences of global catastrophes. However, calls for a rewrite of the UNHCR's statute to reflect the realities of population displacement, due to generalised violence rather than individualised persecution have thus far gone unmet.[110]

The 1951 Convention: providing refugee protection

The Convention was established with the main aim of defining a   **4.13** refugee. According to Article 1A(2), a Convention refugee is a person who:

'As a result of events occurring before 1 January 1951 and owing to well-founded fear of being persecuted for reasons of race, religion, nationality, membership of a particular social group or political opinion, is outside the country of his nationality and is unable or, owing to such fear, is unwilling to avail himself of the protection of that country; or who, not having a nationality and being outside the country of his former habitual residence as a result of such events, is unable or, owing to such fear, is unwilling to return to it.'

The key factors are, therefore, that an individual: (i) is outside his or her country of origin; (ii) is unable or unwilling to avail himself or herself of the protection of the country of origin, or to return there; (iii) is unable or unwilling to do so because of a well-founded fear of persecution; and (iv) fears the persecution for reasons of race, religion, nationality, membership of a particular social group, or political opinion.[111] The Convention also provides minimum standards of protection to refugees in 46 Articles and one Schedule. The provisions are divided between the following Chapters: General; Juridical Status; Gainful Employment; Welfare; Administrative Measures; Executory and Transitory Provisions; and Final Clauses. There is an expectation that Contracting States will treat refugees in the same manner as other aliens in their territory.

Excluded from the protection of the Convention are those who are recognised as having the same rights and obligations as nationals by the country in which they are resident,[112] and those who have:

---

[110] G. Goodwin-Gill, 'Asylum: The law and politics of change' (1995) 7:1 *IJRL*, p. 12.
[111] G. Goodwin-Gill, *The Refugee in International Law* (Oxford: Clarendon Press, 1996), pp. 20–21.
[112] Art. 1E.

(a)   committed a crime against peace, a war crime, or a crime
       against humanity, as defined in the international instruments
       drawn up to make provision in respect of such crimes;

(b)   committed a serious non-political crime outside the country of
       refuge prior to their admission to that country as a refugee;

(c)   been guilty of acts contrary to the purposes and principles of the
       United Nations.[113]

If an individual falls into one of these categories, he or she cannot
be declared a refugee. There are circumstances, however, which will
result in refugee status and the Convention ceasing to apply. These
are:

(a)   voluntarily returning to the country of nationality, voluntarily
       re-acquiring a lost nationality, or acquiring a new nationality and
       enjoying the protection of the country of that new nationality;[114]

(b)   voluntary re-establishment in a country which was left due to
       fear of persecution;[115]

(c)   that the circumstances giving rise to refugee status have ceased
       to exist.[116]

4.14   Alongside the definition of a refugee, the most important provision is that relating to *non-refoulement*. This principle, which was
established in the 1933 Convention, was once more included to provide the core of refugee protection: the right not to be returned. Art.
33 states that:

'1.   No Contracting State shall expel or return (*"refouler"*) a refugee in
       any manner whatsoever to the frontiers of territories where his life
       or freedom would be threatened on account of his race, religion,
       nationality, membership of a particular social group or political
       opinion.

2.   The benefit of the present provision may not, however, be claimed by
       a refugee whom there are reasonable grounds for regarding as a
       danger to the security of the country in which he is, or who, having
       been convicted by a final judgement of a particularly serious crime,
       constitutes a danger to the community of that country.'

---

[113] Art. 1F.
[114] Arts 1C(1)-(3).
[115] Art. 1C(4).
[116] Arts 1C(5)&(6).

The drafters of the Convention deemed this provision to be of such importance that no reservation could be entered against it by any Contracting State.[117] It imposed an obligation upon the receiving state to ensure the safety of a refugee, in particular not to return him or her to a country in which life or freedom would be threatened. Thus, where a receiving country is not in a position to accept a refugee, it must not return that individual to the country of origin. The impact of Art. 33 is discussed below.

Arts 32 and 31 are also of significance. Art. 32 prohibits expulsion of a refugee lawfully in the territory of a Contracting State save on the grounds of national security or public order. Art. 31 states that refugees should not be punished if they gain entry to a country through illegal means, provided they come from a territory where their life is threatened and they present themselves without delay to the authorities. This provision proved of particular importance in the 1990s, and more recently, when increasing numbers of applicants were found to be entering northern states illegally.[118]

Though bound by the Convention and Protocol, states maintained their sovereign right to control entry to their territory, and were free to develop their own refugee-determination procedures, so long as they adhered to the principles outlined. The Convention and Protocol did not seek to protect *asylum seekers* as a separately defined group nor to establish minimum criteria for asylum procedures. All that states have to assist them in their interpretation of the Convention are the UNHCR's own *Handbook on Procedures and Criteria for Determining Refugee Status*, a useful but non-binding document, and the conclusions, recommendations and reports of the Executive Committee of the Programme of the UNHCR ('Excom'). The conclusions in particular are a valuable source of guidance for states and lawyers alike, and cover a broad range of issues of concern to the UNHCR from international protection to refugee children and women.[119] Since UNHCR guidelines and recommendations do not bind states, it has fallen to municipal jurisprudence to interpret the 1951 Convention and 1967 Protocol. While this has inevitably led to judicial discrepancies between states, in the last decade there have been real attempts to develop a uniform approach to interpretation of the Convention. This has been assisted by the creation of the International Association of Refugee Law Judges, a forum for refugee law judges to exchange good practice and ideas, as well as the UNHCR's Global

4.15

---

[117] Art. 42 forbids reservations against Arts 1, 3, 4, 16(1), 33, 36 to 46 inclusive.
[118] See Chs 6 and 7.
[119] They are available on *www.unhcr.ch*

Consultations, which took place in 2001, and which have led to the publication of a number of guidelines on key issues.[120]

One of the earliest criticisms of the Convention was its focus on civil and political rights in its definition of persecution to the exclusion of social and economic rights.[121] More recently, attention has been focused on the 'ethno-centric' bias of the Convention and its consequent inadequacy for the future.[122] There is no doubt that the Convention bears the imprint of the political climate at the time of drafting and reflects the divide that was deepening between the western and eastern blocs. Hathaway puts it thus: 'By mandating protection for those whose (Western inspired) civil and political rights are jeopardized, without at the same time protecting persons whose (socialist inspired) socio-economic rights are at risk, the Convention adopted an incomplete and politically partisan human rights rationale.'[123]

Convention in crisis

4.16   Criticisms of the UNHCR's expanded mandate and ability to cope aside, the 1951 Convention has itself, in the last decade, come under attack. The UK proved particularly vocal on this issue. In June 2000, at a meeting in Lisbon of EU ministers, the then Home Secretary, Jack Straw, called for an overhaul of the 1951 Convention, describing it as outdated. He pointed to the 'essential contradiction' at the heart of the Convention: its failure to oblige any country to admit an individual in order to have his or her case assessed, with the result that 'genuine' refugees are frequently forced to enter illegally before lodging a claim.[124] Straw proposed a new scheme whereby EU countries would refuse asylum claims by individuals coming from an agreed list of 'safe countries'. Some six months later, in a speech to the Institute for Public Policy Research, he announced that 'The Convention is no longer working as the framers intended. The environment in which it is applied today is one that has changed almost out of recognition from that which obtained in 1951. The numbers of asylum seekers have vastly increased.'[125] Claiming that the UK was taking the lead in

---

[120] Available on *www.unhcr.ch*. See Ch. 8 for discussion of some of the issues in the UK context.

[121] See J. Hathaway, *The Law of Refugee Status* (Canada: Butterworths, 1991), pp. 6–10.

[122] S. Juss, 'Toward a morally legitimate reform of refugee law: the uses of cultural jurisprudence', (1998) 11 *Harvard Human Rights Journal*, p. 336.

[123] J. Hathaway, *The Law of Refugee Status* (Canada: Butterworths, 1991), p. 8.

[124] K. Lee, 'British Home Secretary campaigns to overturn Geneva Convention on asylum', *World Socialist Web Site*, June 23, 2000.

[125] Jack Straw, 'An effective protection regime for the twenty-first century', Speech to IPPR, February 6, 2001.

driving forward European action in this area, he proposed collective
action by the international community. His three suggestions were: (i)
to help improve conditions in the regions of origin; (ii) to ease the
access of genuine refugees to the protection regimes of western states;
and (iii) to dissuade those who are not refugees from seeking to benefit unjustly from the terms of the 1951 Convention. Similar proposals are now beginning to receive serious consideration at the EU
level.[126]

Partly in response to dissatisfaction with the 1951 Convention, and
partly to celebrate its fiftieth anniversary, the UNHCR initiated, in
December 2000, the Global Consultations on International Protection. The stated purpose was 'to provoke both reflection and action
to revitalize the 1951 Convention framework and to equip States better to address the challenges in a spirit of dialogue and cooperation'.[127] The Consultations were organised into three 'tracks'. The
first track sought to strengthen the commitment of states to respect
the centrality of the 1951 Convention and its 1967 Protocol in the
international refugee protection system. The second track provided a
forum to take stock of developments in refugee law and to examine a
number of emerging issues. This was done through a series of expert
discussions on specific aspects of the interpretation of the Convention and Protocol. The third track was structured around a number
of protection policy matters, including issues not adequately covered
by the 1951 Convention, with discussions being held within the
UNHCR's Executive Committee.[128] Finally, regional meetings were
also held in a number of countries.

The Consultations resulted in a range of useful documents: new
UNHCR Guidelines,[129] Summary Conclusions from expert meetings,[130] and perhaps most significantly, an Agenda for Protection.[131]
The Agenda for Protection is the product of the consultative process
and attempts to reflect a cross-section of concerns and recommendations of states, intergovernmental organisations and NGOs, as well as

---

[126] See Ch. 9.
[127] Executive Committee of the HC's programme, *Agenda for Protection Addendum*,
A/AC.96/965/Add. 1, June 26, 2002.
[128] See Global Consultations website on *www.unhcr.ch*
[129] At the time of writing: Cessation of refugee status under Art. 1C(5) and (6),
HCR/GIP/03/03, February 10, 2003; Gender-related persecution within the
context of Art. 1A(2)/1967 Protocol, HCR/GIP/02/01, May 7, 2002; Membership of a particular social group within the context of Art. 1A(2)/1967 Protocol,
HCR/GIP/02/02, May 7, 2002.
[130] On cessation and exclusion, *non-refoulement*, supervisory responsibility, gender-
related persecution, particular social group, internal flight alternative, illegal entry,
and family unity.
[131] A/AC.96/965/Add. 1, June 26, 2002.

of refugees.[132] On December 12–13, 2001, at the end of the Global Consultations process, states party to the 1951 Convention and/or 1967 Protocol adopted a Declaration recognising the enduring importance of the Convention and Protocol in the protection of refugees and the provision of rights and minimum standards of treatment.[133] It acknowledged 'the continuing relevance and resilience of this international regime of rights and principles, including at its core the principle of *non-refoulement*, whose applicability is embedded in customary international law'.[134] Para. 1 of the Declaration reaffirms the commitment of signatory states to implement their obligations under the Convention and/or Protocol 'fully and effectively in accordance with the object and purpose of these instruments'. Though the Declaration calls on states to strengthen asylum and to ensure the integrity of the asylum institution, through, for example, the careful application of Arts 1F and 33(2),[135] the commitment expressed in the document towards the 1951 Convention is clearly at odds with the continuing disquiet voiced by some members of the UK government and opposition alike.

4.17   Nonetheless, the Agenda for Protection proposes various activities to reinforce international protection of asylum seekers and refugees. Its suggested programme of action has six goals:

1.   Strengthening implementation of the 1951 Convention and 1967 Protocol;

2.   Protecting refugees within broader migration movements;

3.   Sharing burdens and responsibilities more equitably and increasing the ability to receive and protect refugees;

4.   Addressing security-related concerns more effectively;

5.   Redoubling the search for durable solutions; and

6.   Meeting the protection needs of refugee women and refugee children.[136]

4.18   While the Agenda incorporates a lengthy list of goals to be attained by the UNHCR, states and NGOs, in September 2002, the High Commissioner, Ruud Lubbers, went one stage further and called for the development of 'tools of protection', in the form of multilateral

---

[132] A/AC.96/965/Add. 1, June 26, 2002, p. 1.
[133] Preamble, para. 2.
[134] Preamble, para. 4.
[135] paras 6 and 7.
[136] A/AC.96/965/Add. 1, June 26, 2002, p. 5.

'special agreements', to complement the 1951 Convention. These he termed 'Convention Plus'. He was careful to stress that Convention Plus is not about rewriting the Convention but about building upon it.[137] So far the UNHCR has identified a number of areas as possible subjects for Convention Plus agreements: mass influx; burden-sharing; promotion of self-reliance and reintegration of refugees in countries with large populations of refugees, in refugee-hosting communities, and in countries of origin; multilateral commitments for resettlement; and the role of countries of origin, transit and destination in creating irregular or secondary migration.[138] This is a novel departure and is at an early stage in conceptual development (though some may regard it as a simple restatement of the UNHCR's current policy).

The above initiatives are clearly a positive attempt to address many of the pressing issues in relation to forced migration and, consequently, have been embraced by states and NGOs alike. For example, in a recent document produced by the European Commission, reference is made to the UNHCR's Agenda for Protection and Convention Plus, giving rise to the hope that the Global Consultations will make a real impact on formulating EU asylum and refugee protection regimes in the twenty-first century.[139] However, a note of caution should be expressed. It would be all too easy for states to implement potentially damaging initiatives under the guise of the Agenda for Protection. The UK's recent proposals for all asylum claims made in an EU state to be handled by transit processing centres based outside the EU, as well as the return of people to 'safe havens' in the regions from which they have come, are cases in point.[140] This attempt to shift the responsibility for handling asylum seekers and refugees to countries arguably less suited for such a purpose seems to run counter to the very essence of the UNHCR's vision for the future of refugee protection.

Regional refugee instruments

While refugees continued to be protected by a wide range of inter-national instruments and declarations,[141] asylum seekers became, in   **4.19**

---

[137] UNHCR, 'Convention Plus Questions and Answers', May 20, 2003, para. 2.
[138] ibid., para. 4.
[139] Communication from the Commission 'Towards more accessible, equitable and managed asylum systems', COM(2003) 315 final, June 3, 2003.
[140] See Ch. 9.
[141] For example: The Hague Agreement relating to Refugee Seaman (1957); The European Agreement on Abolition of Visas for Refugees (1959); The European Convention on Extradition (1957); The OAU Convention Governing the Specific Aspects of Refugee Problems in Africa (1969); Cartagena Declaration (1984).

effect, the victims of a lacuna in international human rights protection; they have the right to seek and enjoy asylum but no more. The definition of refugee has, of itself, imposed certain limitations. The five grounds – race, religion, nationality, membership of a particular social group, or political opinion – may have seemed comprehensive in 1951, but they have, in a sense, been overtaken by time. Anyone fleeing civil war, man-made disaster, or 'act of God' is not strictly covered by the Convention. Today, this seemingly narrow focus excludes hundreds of thousands of people who either become labelled as 'internally displaced', at best, or 'bogus refugees'/ 'economic migrants', at worst. It is for this reason that some areas of the world have produced their own more generous and inclusive definitions of 'refugee'.

Africa

4.20   The conflicts that accompanied the end of the colonial era in Africa led to a succession of massive refugee movements. By 1963, it was clear to the OAU that a regional refugee convention was called for to take account of the specific aspects of the refugee problems encountered in Africa. Thus in 1969, the Organisation of African Unity Convention Governing the Specific Aspects of Refugee Problems in Africa ('OAU Convention') was adopted and contained, *inter alia*, a broadened refugee definition (Art. 1). Art. 8 also confirmed that the Convention should be the effective regional complement in Africa to the 1951 Convention.

After endorsing the definition of refugee contained in the 1951 Convention, the OAU Convention went further and stated that the term 'refugee' should also apply to anyone who,

> 'owing to external aggression, occupation, foreign domination or events seriously disturbing public order in either part or the whole of his country of origin or nationality, is compelled to leave his place of habitual residence in order to seek refuge in another place outside his country of origin or nationality.'

This is a vital addition. It means that persons fleeing civil war, civil disturbances and violence are entitled to claim the status of refugee in states that are parties to the Convention, irrespective of whether of not they have a well-founded fear of persecution.

Latin America

Unlike Africa, Latin America has a long tradition of granting asylum **4.21**
dating back to the late nineteenth century. In the twentieth century,
two of the key texts on the subject have been the 1954 Convention on
Territorial and Diplomatic Asylum and the 1984 Cartagena Declaration on Refugees. This latter instrument is of particular interest since
it recommends that the definition of refugee used in the region
should, in addition to that contained in the 1951 Convention and
1967 Protocol, extend to persons who have fled their country

> 'because their lives, safety or freedom have been threatened by generalised
> violence, foreign aggression, internal conflicts, massive violation of human
> rights or other circumstances which have seriously disturbed public
> order.'[142]

The similarities with the OAU Convention are evident, and
Cartagena explicitly mentions the precedent set by the OAU
Convention, but, unlike its African counterpart, it is not formally
binding on states. Nonetheless, it has been incorporated into the
domestic legislation of a number of Latin American states, and some
of those who have not been prepared to go so far have applied its
principles in practice.

The Middle East

A somewhat forgotten region in terms of refugee law, the Middle East **4.22**
also agreed a Declaration in 1992 on the Protection of Refugees and
Displaced Persons in the Arab World, following a meeting of the
Group of Arab Experts. Once again, the instrument calls for a
broader approach to refugee protection than is provided by UN texts,
recommending that, 'pending the elaboration of an Arab Convention
relating to refugees, Arab States adopt a broad concept of "refugee"
and "displaced person" as well as a minimum standard for their treatment, guided by the provisions of the United Nations instruments
relating to human rights and refugees as well as relevant regional
instruments'.[143] While not specifying the types of situations in which
the Arab states would provide protection, as was the case in the OAU
Convention and in Cartagena, the Arab Declaration does go on to
suggest that:

---

[142] para. III(3).
[143] Art. 6.

'In situations which may not be covered by the 1951 Convention, the 1967 Protocol, or any other relevant instrument in force or United Nations General Assembly resolutions, refugees, asylum seekers and displaced persons shall nevertheless be protected by:

(a)   the humanitarian principles of asylum in Islamic law and Arab values,
(b)   the basic human rights rules, established by international and regional organisations,
(c)   other relevant principles of international law.'[144]

An Arab convention has yet to be agreed.

A right to asylum?

4.23   During the period in which the IRO was providing practical assistance to refugees, the international community, in the guise of the United Nations, was also searching for broader statements of principle. In the flush of what the eminent refugee scholar and adviser, Paul Weis, described as a 'true revolutionary spirit' following the war, the contracting parties saw fit to include a provision on asylum in the 1948 Universal Declaration of Human Rights ('UDHR').[145] Art. 14(1) states: 'Everyone has the right to seek and enjoy asylum from persecution.' Nonetheless, the 'revolutionary spirit' had its limits. Whereas the original draft of Art. 14 (Art. 12) had spoken of a right 'to seek *and be granted* in other countries asylum from persecution' (emphasis added), the final version was much tempered; it simply acknowledged the right of the individual to search for and to enjoy asylum, and failed to impose any concurrent duty upon states to grant asylum. It was in fact the UK delegation which raised strong opposition to the draft proposal: 'No state could accept the responsibilities imposed by Article 12. The United Kingdom had often had occasion to offer asylum to political refugees [. . .] but it [had] not done so under any obligation.'[146] The UK maintained its own right to admit or refuse to admit any person, and would not countenance any principle that seemed to give the United Nations the right to oblige Member States to grant asylum. Furthermore, argued the British delegation, 'the right of asylum was the right of every state to offer refuge and to resist all demands for extradition. This was the meaning of the expression "to enjoy asylum" contained in the

---

[144] Art. 5.
[145] P. Weis, 'The United Nations Declaration on Territorial Asylum', (1969) *Canadian Yearbook of International Law*, p. 116.
[146] Doc. A/C. 3/SR. 121, p. 4 as cited in F. Morgenstern, 'The Right of Asylum', (1949) 26 *BYIL*, p. 336.

amendment.'[147] The wording of Art. 14, as finally agreed, and its dilution by Member Governments, led one renowned international lawyer to describe it as 'artificial to the point of flippancy'.[148] There is certainly some justification for such a view; since Art. 13(2) grants a right to leave and return to one's country, a right to seek asylum as stated may seem somewhat pointless.[149] The limitation on asylum in the Declaration was somewhat mitigated by the inclusion of other provisions of application to the asylum seeker or refugee: the prohibition of torture and cruel, inhuman or degrading treatment (Art. 5); the prohibition of arbitrary arrest, detention and exile (Art. 9); the right to freedom of thought, conscience and religion, and of opinion and expression (Arts 18 and 19).

Attempts to address the limitation imposed on Art. 14 have largely failed. Almost twenty years after the UDHR, the Universal Declaration on Territorial Asylum was adopted by the General Assembly in December 1967; it was remarkably brief (four Articles), rather conservative and, like its counterpart in human rights, it too was non-binding. Its strength therefore lay not so much in its legal force but in its humanitarian message and its statement of principles. In particular, Art. 3(1) of the Asylum Declaration adds a useful dimension to asylum law. Any person who genuinely seeks asylum, including one who is 'struggling against colonialism', should not be 'subjected to measures such as rejection at the frontier or, if he has already entered the territory in which he seeks asylum, expulsion or compulsory return to any State where he may be subjected to persecution'. Art. 3(1) not only repeats the provision against *non-refoulement* contained in the 1951 Convention, but also imposes an obligation on states not to reject 'genuine' asylum seekers.[150] This 'non-rejection' terminology, first used in the 1933 Convention, can be regarded as an important extension of the principle of *non-refoulement*.[151] In the wake of the Universal Declaration on Territorial Asylum, a draft convention on

[147] Doc A/X. 3/SR. 121, p. 5 as cited in F. Morgenstern, 'The Right of Asylum', (1949) 26 *BYIL*, p. 337.

[148] H. Lauterpacht, 'The Universal Declaration of Human Rights', (1948) 25 *British Yearbook of International Law*, p. 374.

[149] The right to leave one's country is connected to the right to seek asylum, but is 'subject to several limitations applied in order to protect different, and in principle legitimate, state interests.': K. Hailbronner, 'Comments on the Right to Leave, Return and Remain' in V. Gowlland-Debbas, ed., *The Problem of Refugees in the Light of Contemporary International Law* Issues (The Netherlands: Martinus Nijhoff, 1996), p. 111. See, also, G. Goodwin-Gill, 'The Right to Leave, the Right to Return and the Question of a Right to Remain', in V. Gowlland-Debbas, ed., pp. 93–108.

[150] A. Grahl-Madsen, *The Status of Refugees in International Law* Vol. II (Netherlands: A.W. Sijthoff-Leiden, 1972), p. 102.

[151] L. Holborn, *Refugees: A Problem of our Time*, Vol. I (Metuchen, N.J.: The Scarecrow Press, 1975), p. 232.

territorial asylum, drawn up in 1972, was considered at a UN Conference in 1977. Prior to the meeting, the UK had already indicated that it considered such a convention unnecessary;[152] in fact, no agreement on a new convention was reached and the Conference was deemed 'a very costly failure'.[153] Though the General Assembly seems at the time to have anticipated that work on an asylum instrument would be continued, no binding international document has in fact emerged.[154]

Filling the asylum gap?: non-refoulement[155]

4.24 International human rights instruments have granted asylum seekers one main right, the right to seek asylum, but asylum seekers on departing their home countries continue to remain extremely vulnerable. Some protection is offered by the 1951 Convention: first, so long as asylum seekers fulfil the criteria of Art. 1A(2) of the Convention, they constitute refugees without the need for a state declaration on their status; second, they ought not to be subjected to *refoulement* under Art. 33. Realistically, though, no northern state will regard an asylum seeker as a mandate[156] or Convention refugee until he or she has passed successfully through refugee-determination procedures. The limited protection of asylum seekers under international law should come as no surprise. The UDHR and the 1951 Convention were both carefully constructed to ensure that state sovereignty in relation to the admission, residence and settlement of *refugees* remained inviolate.[157] The fact that states were unprepared to cede sovereignty in relation to refugees was a clear indication that asylum seekers, in their uncertain status, were likely to be granted few, if any, rights, and certainly no more than those accorded refugees.

In the absence of an asylum-specific convention, it is arguably the *non-refoulement* provision, contained in both the binding 1951 Conven-

---

[152] A. Grahl-Madsen, *Territorial Asylum* (Sweden: Almquist & Wiksell International, 1980), p. 8.

[153] *ibid.*, p. 66.

[154] *ibid.*

[155] For a comprehensive discussion of the principle of *non-refoulement* see E. Lauterpact & D. Bethlehem, opinion for UNHCR on *The Scope and Content of the Principle of Non-Refoulement* available on *http://www.unhcr.ch/cgi-in/texis/vtx/home/opendoc.pdf?tbl=PROTECTION&page=PROTECT&id=3b33574d1*

[156] A mandate refugee is a refugee falling under the auspices of the UNHCR according to the 1950 Statute of the United Nations High Commissioner for Refugees.

[157] See, for a discussion, J. Hathaway, 'A Reconsideration of the Underlying Premise of Refugee Law', (1990) 33:1 *HILJ*, p. 173.

tion and the non-binding Asylum Declaration, which now offers the greatest form of protection to the asylum seeker. In 1995, Hathaway identified three types of state practice which offend against the principle of *non-refoulement*: 'the return of refugees physically present in the territory of the state, the return of refugees at or near the border, and the evolution of arms-length *non entrée* policies', such as visas, carriers' liability legislation, and the safe third country principle.[158] Though the Convention applies to *refugees* and not to 'asylum seekers' as such, some commentators consider that Art. 33 of the Convention 'also applies to *asylum seekers*, at least during an initial period and in appropriate circumstances'.[159] This reaffirms in part the non-constitutive, but declaratory nature of refugee status in that a refugee is a refugee as soon as he or she fulfils the requirements of the Convention, and not when determined as such by a state.[160] The UNHCR Executive Committee has itself been at pains to stress the importance of *non-refoulement* whether or not individuals have been formally recognised as refugees.[161] To require refugee status as a condition of *non-refoulement* would render *non-refoulement* meaningless, since all asylum seekers could be returned to countries of origin without consideration of their claims. While this may place asylum seekers on the same footing as refugees at the point of entry, states have been loath to extend any further Convention rights to asylum seekers until they are determined to be Convention refugees.

The value of the principle of *non-refoulement* to asylum seekers is heightened by the fact that it is now deemed to be a norm of customary international law. In 1986, however, Goodwin-Gill suggested that state practice had broadened the scope of Art. 33, extending *non-refoulement* beyond expulsion and return to include measures such as rejection at the frontier and even extradition.[162] He argued further that customary international law had 'extend[ed] the principle of *non-refoulement* to include displaced persons who [did] not enjoy the protection of the government of their country of origin'.[163] This view is not widely endorsed.[164] Hailbronner, for example, has described as 'the product of wishful thinking' any suggestion that *non-refoulement*

4.25

---

[158] J. Hathaway & J. Dent, *Refugee Rights: Report on a Comparative Survey* (Toronto: York Lanes Press, 1995), p. 5.

[159] G. Goodwin-Gill, *The Refugee in International Law* (New York: OUP, 1996), p. 137.

[160] UNHCR, *Handbook on Procedures and Criteria for Determining Refugee Status* (Geneva, 1992), para. 28.

[161] UNHCR Executive Committee Conclusion No. 6 (1977), para. c.

[162] G. Goodwin-Gill, '*Non-Refoulement* and the New Asylum Seekers', (1986) 26:4 *Virg JIL*, p. 901.

[163] *ibid.*, p. 902.

[164] See, for a discussion of a range of views, G. Goodwin-Gill, *The Refugee in International Law* (New York: OUP, 1996), pp. 134–7.

has become a norm of customary international law, and applicable to "humanitarian" refugees (defined as 'persons fleeing from generalized violence or internal turmoil').[165] Goodwin-Gill has now accepted that his argument in terms of *non-refoulement* 'was not well chosen', and goes on to maintain that the 'impact on State competence of the broader developments relating to human rights and displacement would have been better served by characterizing State responsibilities in terms of a general principle of *refuge*.'[166] While this revised proposal is still open to question, it is some way removed from Hathaway's belief that customary international law has given rise to a 'right to be considered for temporary admission [. . .] *on the basis of a need for protection*.'[167] The 1951 Convention, however, speaks in the main of obligations upon states rather than rights of refugees. Any norm of customary international law is likely to be duty-based rather than rights-based. While one might support a correlative rights system in which all rights entail correlative duties,[168] the reverse is not necessarily true: states may be less willing to endorse a new right from an accepted obligation. Thus, in the case of *non-refoulement*, the obligation not to return refugees to their countries of origin, while possibly giving rise to a right not to be '*refouled*', does not automatically give rise to a right of admission, nor to a right to temporary refuge/protection. The theoretical position aside, the practical effect of *non-refoulement* is that protection of some sort is often afforded, either in the country of asylum or elsewhere, for Convention refugees or for the asylum seeker during the period of asylum determination.

In 2001, as part of the UNHCR's Global Consultations on International Protection, a meeting of experts was held in Cambridge to consider the principle of *non-refoulement*. They were provided with a comprehensive legal opinion by Lauterpacht and Bethlehem[169] and concluded the following: *non-refoulement* is a principle of customary international law.[170] It applies to refugees irrespective of their formal recognition, and to asylum seekers up to the point where their status is finally determined. *Non-refoulement* encompasses any measure attributable to the state that may lead to the return of an asylum seeker or refugee to the frontiers of territories where his life or freedom would

---

[165] K. Hailbronner, '*Non-Refoulement* and "Humanitarian" Refugees: Customary International law or Wishful Legal Thinking?', (1986) 26:4 *Virg JIL*, pp. 858–9.

[166] G. Goodwin-Gill, *The Refugee in International Law* (New York: OUP, 1996), p. 136.

[167] J. Hathaway, *The Law of Refugee Status* (Canada: Butterworths, 1991), p. 26.

[168] See J. Raz, 'Right-based Moralities', in J. Waldron, *Theories of Rights* (Oxford: OUP, 1984), pp. 182–200.

[169] E. Lauterpacht & D. Bethlehem, opinion for UNHCR on *The scope and content of the principle of non-refoulement*, June 20, 2001.

[170] UNHCR, Global Consultations on International Protection, *Summary conclusions – the principle of non-refoulement*, Cambridge, July 9–10, 2001.

be threatened, or where he or she is at risk of persecution, including interception, rejection at the frontier, or indirect *refoulement*. The principle of *non-refoulement* applies in situations of mass influx. The Summary Conclusions ended with a caution that exceptions to *non-refoulement*, contained in Art. 33(2), should be interpreted very restrictively, subject to due process safeguards, and as a measure of last resort. In cases of torture, no exceptions are permitted.

Protection through other instruments

Since 1951, the protection afforded by the Convention has been supplemented by a number of additional human rights instruments, in particular : International Convention on the Elimination of All Forms of Racial Discrimination 1965;[171] International Covenant on Economic, Social and Cultural Rights 1966 ('ICESCR');[172] International Covenant on Civil and Political Rights 1966 ('ICCPR');[173] Convention against Torture and Other Cruel, Inhuman or Degrading Treatment or Punishment 1984 ('CAT');[174] Convention on the Rights of the Child 1989 ('CRC');[175] and European Convention for the Protection of Human Rights and Fundamental Freedoms 1950 ('ECHR').[176] Contracting states were careful not to include in any of these a right to asylum from persecution, although again the draft to the ICCPR, prepared in 1954, did contain such a right. The reason for this omission was the refusal, once more, by states to relinquish their sovereign power to admit and exclude aliens.[177] However, there is some mitigation provided for this restrictive line by a number of instruments.

    4.26

The British made up for their role in the watering down of Art. 14 of the UDHR by proposing Art. 13 to the ICCPR, which protects aliens from expulsion.[178] Arbitrary expulsion of an alien from the

---

[171] Adopted on December 21, 1965 and entered into force on January 4, 1969.

[172] Adopted on December 16, 1966 and entered into force on January 3, 1976.

[173] Adopted on December 16, 1966 and entered into force on March 23, 1976.

[174] Adopted on December 10, 1984 and entered into force on June 26, 1987. See, for further discussion of the Convention, B. Gorlick, 'The Convention and the Committee against Torture: A Complementary Protection regime for Refugees', (1999) 11:3, *IJRL*, pp. 479–495.

[175] Adopted on November 20, 1989 and entered into force on September 2, 1990.

[176] Entered into force on September 3, 1953.

[177] R. Plender, 'International Human Rights Law on Asylum' in *Asylum Law* (London: IARLJ, 1995), p. 42.

[178] *ibid.* Art. 13, ICCPR, states: 'An alien lawfully in the territory of a State Party to the present Covenant may be expelled therefrom only in pursuance of a decision reached in accordance with law and shall, except where compelling reasons of national security otherwise require, be allowed to submit the reasons against his

territory of a Contracting State where he or she is lawfully resident is also prohibited under Protocol 7, Art. 1 to the ECHR (only adopted as late as 1984). Most importantly, Art. 3(1) of the CAT provides for *non-refoulement*:

> 'No State party shall expel, return (*refouler*) or extradite a person to another State where there are substantial grounds for believing that he would be in danger of being subjected to torture.'

While the UK has recognised the competence of the CAT Committee to receive and consider communications by a state party that the UK is not fulfilling its obligations under the Convention (Art. 21), it has not issued a declaration that it recognises the competence of the Committee to receive complaints from individuals (Art. 22).[179] Likewise with the ICCPR, the UK has accepted the competence of the UN Human Rights Committee to receive interstate complaints (Art. 41) but has not ratified the Optional Protocol permitting individual complaints to be made, despite the fact that the majority of other European countries have done so. The only case in which the UK has made a declaration that individuals may lodge a petition is that of the ECHR (Art. 25). The continued refusal of the UK to recognise individual complaints in the case of the ICCPR and CAT clearly undermines the human rights protection afforded individuals by those instruments. Furthermore, the UK government entered a reservation against the CRC, asserting the primacy of executive discretion in immigration control over the principle of the child's best interests as provided by the Convention.[180] In the case of the UK, it is to the ECHR that one must therefore turn for real protection of the individual asylum seeker or refugee beyond the 1951 Convention.

---

    expulsion and to have his case reviewed by, and be represented for the purpose before, the competent authority or a person or persons especially designated by the competent authority.'

[179] For further discussion of CAT decisions, and its possible application to ECHR cases, see N. Blake & R. Husain, *Immigration, Asylum & Human Rights* (Oxford: OUP, 2003), pp. 84–86; see, also, C. Harvey, *Seeking Asylum in the UK: Problems and Prospects* (London: Butterworths, 2000), pp. 35–38.

[180] The reservation states: 'The United Kingdom reserves the right to apply such legislation, in so far as it relates to the entry into, stay in and departure from the United Kingdom of those who do not have the right under the law of the United Kingdom to enter and remain in the United Kingdom, and to the acquisition and possession of citizenship, as it may deem necessary from time to time.'

EUROPEAN CONVENTION ON HUMAN RIGHTS AND ITS
APPLICATION TO ASYLUM[181]

The applicability of the ECHR to asylum seekers is not altogether   **4.27**
apparent since it was established with the peoples of Europe in mind
rather than the 'outsider'. It does not provide explicitly for either
refugees or asylum seekers, and any protection it affords has derived
from judicial interpretation of its fundamental provisions. The case
law of the European Court of Human Rights based in Strasbourg
('ECtHR'), and of the Commission, does not guarantee a right to
enter, reside or remain in a particular country, but decisions on
admission to or expulsion from a state party to the Convention should
be carried out within the framework of the Convention. Those with
potential application to the asylum seeker/refugee are Arts 3 (protection from torture, inhuman and degrading treatment), 5 (right to liberty and security), 8 (respect for private and family life), 13 (the right
to an effective remedy) and 14 (non-discrimination in the application
of the Convention's rights). In extreme cases, Art. 2 (the right to life)
may be engaged. Arts 2–4 of Protocol 4 make specific provision for
freedom of movement and protection from arbitrary expulsion, but
the UK has not ratified this Protocol. In any event, the Protocol does
not detract from or limit the protection afforded by other Convention
rights.

Article 3

For the asylum seeker, the most important provision is arguably Art.   **4.28**
3, which declares that:

> 'No one shall be subjected to torture or to inhuman or degrading treat-
> ment or punishment.'

This has been deemed to be 'one of the fundamental values of the
democratic societies making up the Council of Europe'[182] and contains an absolute guarantee of the rights it protects. Derogation is not
possible in peacetime. It has 'proved a difficult provision to interpret
because of the generality of its text'[183] and, for some, is narrower

---

[181] For an excellent analysis of the ECHR in relation to immigration and asylum in the
UK context, see N. Blake & R. Husain, *Immigration, Asylum & Human Rights* (Oxford:
OUP, 2003).

[182] *Vilvarajah v United Kingdom Series A*, No. 215, (1991) 14 EHRR 248, para. 108.

[183] D. Harris, M. O'Boyle & C. Warbrick, *Law of the European Convention on Human Rights*
(London: Butterworths, 1995), p. 88.

than the 1951 Convention's requirement of a well-founded fear of persecution for reasons of race, religion, nationality, membership of a particular social group, or political opinion. 'Torture', as defined by the ECtHR in its 1978 judgement of *Ireland v UK*, covers 'deliberate inhuman treatment causing very serious and cruel suffering'.[184] 'Inhuman treatment' need not be intended to cause suffering but 'must attain a minimum level of severity',[185] whereas degrading treatment means treatment that debases or grossly humiliates.[186] These thresholds are undoubtedly difficult to meet and restrict the application of Art. 3. However, two important points need to be underlined. First, the concept of persecution has not always covered all forms of inhuman and degrading treatment, and therefore can be regarded as somewhat limited in its own right. Second, though the Art. 3 definitions have lasted for some time, the ECtHR has chosen in its recent interpretation to adopt a creative and expansive approach, which has been of particular assistance to asylum seekers.[187]

In a 1997 decision involving the detention, aggravated rape and severe ill-treatment of a 17 year-old Kurdish girl by the Turkish police, the Court found that 'the accumulation of acts of physical and mental violence inflicted on the applicant and the especially cruel act of rape to which she was subjected amounted to torture in breach of Art. 3 of the Convention'.[188] *Aydin v Turkey* clearly broadened the definition of torture beyond that applied in *Ireland v UK*. This relaxation in the Court's approach is further revealed by *D v United Kingdom*.[189] In this case, the applicant arrived in the UK and was arrested, detained and charged with serious drug offences. In detention, he was found to be suffering from AIDS. He applied for leave to remain in the UK but was refused and steps were taken to remove him. In a petition to the European Commission, it was claimed that his proposed removal to St Kitts would be in breach of Arts 2, 3, 8 and 13. The Court held that the abrupt removal of the medical and counselling services he was receiving in the UK would hasten his death, and that the conditions of adversity which awaited him in St Kitts would further reduce his life expectancy and subject him to acute mental and physical

---

[184] Series A, No. 25, (1978) 2 EHRR 25, para. 167.

[185] *ibid.*

[186] See, for a discussion of inhuman and degrading treatment, A. Fabbricotti, 'The concept of inhuman or degrading treatment in international law and its application in asylum cases' (1998) 10:4 *IJRL*, pp. 637–661.

[187] See, for a detailed but now outdated discussion, T. Einarsen, 'The European Convention on Human Rights and the Notion of an Implied Right to *de facto* Asylum', (1990) 2:3 *IJRL*, pp. 361–389.

[188] *Aydin v Turkey* (1997) 25 EHRR 251, para. 86.

[189] *D v United Kingdom* (1997) 24 EHRR 423.

suffering.[190] While it could not be said that the conditions which would confront him in St Kitts were themselves in breach of Art. 3, the Court felt that 'his removal would expose him to a real risk of dying under most distressing circumstances and would thus amount to inhuman treatment'.[191] Here, then, was a clear preparedness by the Court to look beyond a strict, conservative interpretation of Art. 3 to one that countenanced interference with human dignity as well as torture.[192] Such decisions as *Aydin* and *D v UK* offer reassurance to asylum seekers to Europe who do not fit into the strict confines of the 1951 Convention nor, indeed, of the early definition of 'torture' under Art. 3.

There is no right under the Convention not to be expelled or extra-   **4.29**
dited from a Convention state. The ECtHR has emphasised frequently the right of states to control entry residence and expulsion of aliens. States party to the Convention are free to conclude and carry out extradition agreements. However, there are limits. Refusal of entry and/or expulsion can engage Arts 3 or 14. In entry cases, discrimination is usually the issue at stake; in expulsion, it is the risk of torture and/or inhuman or degrading treatment on return to the country of origin. In *East African Asians v UK*, the Commission held that discrimination based on race could amount to degrading treatment within the meaning of Art. 3 if certain special circumstances applied.[193] Special circumstances were deemed to apply in the case. Firstly, the purpose of the Commonwealth Immigrants Act 1968, in removing the guarantee to East African Asians to enter the UK, was found to be racially discriminatory. Secondly, the destitution faced by these applicants from East Africa and the way in which UK immigration control was conducted in their case – in particular, the manner in which individuals were passed between numerous countries as 'refugees in orbit' – were an affront to human dignity.[194] This last point was taken up by the Commission in the case of *Harabi v Netherlands*:

---

[190] *ibid*, para. 52.

[191] *ibid*, para. 53.

[192] N. Blake, 'Entitlement to Protection: A Human Rights-based Approach to Refugee Protection in the United Kingdom' in F. Nicholson & P. Twomey, eds., *Current Issues of UK Asylum Law and Policy* (Aldershot: Ashgate, 1998), p. 254.

[193] See, for a recent discussion of the case, Lord Lester of Herne Hill, 'Thirty years on: East African Asians case revisited' (2002) Spring *Public Law*, pp. 52–72.

[194] D. Harris, M. O'Boyle & C. Warbrick, *Law of the European Convention on Human Rights* (London: Butterworths, 1995), p. 82; K. Starmer, '*European Human Rights Law – The Human Rights Act 1998 and the European Convention on Human Rights* (London: LAG, 1999), p. 508.

'[. . .] the repeated expulsion of an individual, whose identity was impossible to establish, to a country where his admission is not guaranteed, may raise an issue under Article 3 of the Convention. Such an issue may arise, *a fortiori*, if an alien is over a long period of time deported repeatedly from one country to another without any country taking measures to regularise his situation.'[195]

Asylum seekers will generally claim breach of Art. 3 in relation to deportation, removal or extradition proceedings. Cases raising such matters have given rise to an expanding jurisprudence. In *Soering v United Kingdom*, for example, the Court held that a decision by a Contacting State to extradite a fugitive could raise an issue under Art. 3 if the individual concerned faced a real risk of being subjected to torture or to inhuman or degrading treatment in the country to which he or she was sent.[196] Of course, this means that the conditions in the country requesting the individual need to be assessed. In *Soering*, the applicant faced extradition to Virginia in the USA, where he was accused of murder, in accordance with the UK/USA extradition treaty. He had confessed to the killings and it was likely that he would receive a death sentence. The claim was that returning him to the USA would expose him to the 'death row phenomenon' (waiting in prison for years before execution finally is carried out) and therefore constituted inhuman and degrading treatment or punishment. The Court agreed that Art. 3 was engaged, particularly when account was taken of the delays in appeal and review giving rise to psychological trauma, the age and mental state of the applicant (he was only 18), the length of detention, the extreme conditions which he expected to confront on 'death row', and 'the constant spectre of the execution itself'.[197] The Court subsequently extended the *Soering* principle to cases involving expulsion or deportation as opposed to extradition (see, for example, *Cruz Varas & Others v Sweden*),[198] and clarified further the requirement and assessment of 'real risk' of ill-treatment on return (*Vilvarajah v United Kingdom*). It is insufficient, for example, to show that a conscientious objector will be forced to undertake

---

[195] Application No. 10798/84, reported in 46 D&R 112, p. 116, cited in R. Plender, 'International Human Rights Law on Asylum' in *Asylum Law* (London: IARLJ, 1995), p. 52.

[196] *Soering v United Kingdom* Series A, No. 161, (1989) 11 EHRR 439, para. 91.

[197] Para. 105. Note that the death penalty is not prohibited under Art. 2 but has now been supplemented by Optional Protocol 6 which provides for the abolition of the death penalty. The UK ratified Optional Protocol 6 in January 1999, and this means that an applicant may not be returned to a country in which he or she may face the death penalty.

[198] *Cruz Varas & Others v Sweden* Series A, No. 201, (1992) 14 EHRR 1.

military service, or that an individual will face criminal proceedings and even a lengthy prison sentence if returned.[199] As *Vilvarajah* confirms:

> 'In its *Cruz Varas* judgment [. . .] the Court held that expulsion by a Contracting State of an asylum seeker may give rise to an issue under Article 3, and hence engage the responsibility of that State under the Convention, where substantial grounds have been shown for believing that the person concerned faced a real risk of being subjected to torture or to inhuman or degrading treatment or punishment in the country to which he was returned.'[200]

In 1997, in the significant decision of *Chahal v United Kingdom*,[201] the Court reconfirmed the absolute nature of Art. 3 when rejecting the proposed deportation of an individual allegedly involved in terrorist activities in his home country. Mr Chahal was an Indian Sikh who entered the UK illegally in 1971 but who had been granted indefinite leave to remain. He visited the Punjab during a period of political violence in the 1980s. On return to the UK, he became a leading figure in the Sikh community and an activist against the Indian government. In 1990, the Home Secretary decided that Mr Chahal should be deported, on the grounds that his presence was contrary to the public good for reasons of national security and the international fight against terrorism. He applied for asylum but was refused. He was detained and challenged the refusal of asylum, the deportation order and the detention by means of judicial review, before a special advisory panel (because of the national security elements, there was no right of appeal against deportation). The UK's arguments that refusal of asylum and deportation on the grounds of national security were justified and could not be appealed (though judicial review was available) failed to hold sway. With this decision, the ECtHR added an extra layer of protection for asylum seekers who might conceivably fall under the exception to *non-refoulement* provided by Art. 33(2),[202] or within the exclusion clauses to the Convention contained

4.30

---

[199] K. Starmer, '*European Human Rights Law – The Human Rights Act 1998 and the European Convention on Human Rights* (London: LAG, 1999), p. 510.

[200] para. 103.

[201] *Chahal v United Kingdom* (1997) 23 EHRR 413.

[202] Art. 33(2) states: 'The benefit of the present provision may not, however, be claimed by a refugee whom there are reasonable grounds for regarding as a danger to the security of the country in which he is, or who, having been convicted by a final judgement of a particularly serious crime, constitutes a danger to the community of that country.'

in Art. 1(F).[203] Even in national security cases, the actions of the applicant are largely irrelevant. There is no room for balancing the risk of ill-treatment against the reasons for expulsion in determining whether a state's responsibility under Art. 3 is engaged:

> 'Article 3 enshrines one of the most fundamental values of democratic society [. . .]. The Court is well aware of the immense difficulties faced by States in modern times in protecting their communities from terrorist violence. However, even in these circumstances, the Convention prohibits in absolute terms torture or inhuman or degrading treatment or punishment, irrespective of the victim's conduct. [. . .] Article 3 makes no provision for exceptions and no derogation from it is permissible under Article 15 even in the event of a public emergency threatening the life of the nation [. . .].

> The prohibition provided by Article 3 against ill-treatment is equally absolute in expulsion cases. [. . .] the activities of the individual in question, however undesirable or dangerous, cannot be a material consideration. The protection afforded by Article 3 is thus wider than that provided by Articles 32 and 33 of the United Nations 1951 Convention on the Status of Refugees [. . .].'[204]

The definition of 'inhuman or degrading treatment' is becoming increasingly important as states, including the UK, attempt to withdraw support from asylum seekers.[205] The issue at stake here is whether denial of support constitutes 'treatment' for the purposes of Art. 3 and whether, of itself, it amounts to inhuman or degrading treatment. The ECtHR has made it clear in the past that failure by the state to provide shelter does not of itself equate to inhuman or degrading treatment, even where the applicant was evicted from temporary accommodation and lived on the streets with a chest infection and asthmatic condition.[206] The type of treatment required to fall within Art. 3 has been recently clarified in *Pretty v UK*:

---

[203] Art. 1(F) states that: 'The provisions of this Convention shall not apply to any person with respect to whom there are serious reasons for considering that:

(a) he has committed a crime against peace, a war crime, or a crime against humanity [. . .];

(b) he has committed a serious non-political crime outside the country of refuge prior to admission to that country as a refugee;

(c) he has been guilty of acts contrary to the purposes and principles of the United Nations.'

[204] paras 79; 80.
[205] See Chs 5–8.
[206] *O'Rourke v UK* (39022/97, June 23, 2001, Admissibility Decision, Unreported). See *The Queen on the Application of Q & Others v SSHD* [2003] EWCA Civ 364, paras 54; 59.

'[. . .] the Court's case law refers to "ill-treatment" that attains a minimum level of severity and involves actual bodily injury or intense physical or mental suffering. Where treatment humiliates or debases an individual showing lack of respect for, or diminishing, his or her human dignity or arouses feelings of fear, anguish or inferiority capable of breaking an individual's moral and physical resistance, it may be characterised as degrading and also fall within the prohibition of Article 3. The suffering which flows from naturally occurring illness, physical or mental, may be covered by Article 3, where it is, or risks being exacerbated by treatment, whether flowing from conditions of detention, expulsion or other measures, for which the authorities can be held responsible.'[207]

The United Kingdom's Court of Appeal held recently that where someone applies for asylum in a condition capable of engaging Art. 3, as described in *Pretty*, the Secretary of State will be obliged to provide support.[208] However, the Court did not consider that the real risk that an individual asylum seeker would be reduced to a state of degradation of itself engaged Art. 3.[209]   **4.31**

A final case of note is that of *T.I. v UK*.[210] Here, the applicant, a Sri Lankan Tamil, having been refused asylum in Germany, travelled to the UK where he again claimed asylum. Germany accepted responsibility for the applicant under the terms of the Dublin Convention and the Secretary of State issued a certificate under the safe third country provisions of the then law (s. 2 of the Asylum and Immigration Act 1996) without examining the substance of the asylum claim.[211] Directions were issued to remove the applicant to Germany. Having failed in his appeals to the UK courts, the applicant took his case to the ECtHR. In an important statement of principle, the Court held that indirect removal to an intermediary state, which was also a Contracting State, did not affect the responsibility of the UK to ensure that the applicant was not, as a result of the decision to expel, exposed to treatment contrary to Art. 3.[212] Nor could the UK rely automatically on the arrangements made in the Dublin Convention concerning the allocation of responsibility between European Union states for deciding asylum claims.[213] While there was no suggestion that the applicant would be maltreated in Germany, his removal to Germany was 'one link in a possible chain of events which might result in his return to Sri Lanka where it [was] alleged that he would

---

[207] (2002) 35 EHRR 1, para. 52.
[208] *The Queen on the Application of Q & Others v SSHD* [2003] EWCA Civ 364, para. 62.
[209] *ibid.*, para. 63.
[210] Application No. 43844/98; [2000] INLR 211.
[211] See Chs 5 and 9.
[212] [2000] INLR 211, at 228F.
[213] *ibid.*, and see Ch. 9 for discussion of the Dublin Convention.

face the real risk of [treatment contrary to Art. 3]'.[214] On the facts, and following assurances from the German government concerning its domestic law and practice, the ECtHR was persuaded that there was no real risk that Germany would return the applicant to Sri Lanka in breach of Art. 3, but the point had been made.[215] This decision has particular significance for UK asylum law, which has, over the years, introduced various mechanisms by which the Home Secretary may return asylum claimants to safe third countries without substantive consideration of their claims.[216] In addition, as the UNHCR noted after the judgement was handed down, the Court also made it clear that removal of asylum seekers from a Council of Europe Member State to a country where they could face ill-treatment was in breach of the ECHR, regardless of whether the ill-treatment emanated from the state or from non-state agents.[217]

Article 3 (ECHR) versus Article 33 (1951 Geneva Convention)

4.32   In 1986, Hailbronner, in an article dealing with *non-refoulement*, suggested that it was 'not clear whether Article 3 of the European Convention on Human Rights may embrace a right of temporary refuge when rejection at the frontier would amount to inhuman treatment'.[218] He went on to argue that 'since the arguments applicable in cases of deportation or extradition apply equally to non-rejection at the frontier', it was safe to assume that the European Commission would interpret Art. 3 as giving a right of entry or residence when there was no other protection available.[219] Such an interpretation would indeed be far-reaching. It would broaden protection well beyond that anticipated for *refugees* under the 1951 Convention, since it would imply not only a principle of *non-refoulement* for asylum seekers who do not constitute Convention refugees, but also a *right* of entry; it might also lead to longer-term residence for Art. 3 applicants than for refugees. Unlike the 1951 Convention, which allows for cessation of refugee status if there has been a fundamental change of circumstances, *inter alia*, in the country of origin,[220] or for *refoulement*

---

[214]   [2000] INLR 211, at 228E.

[215]   *ibid.*, at 231B and 231G.

[216]   See Chs 5, 7 and 8 for further discussion. See, also, I. Macdonald & F. Webber, *Macdonald's Immigration Law & Practice* (London: Butterworths, 2001), para. 12.156.

[217]   Cited in (2000) 12:2 *IJRL*, p. 275.

[218]   K. Hailbronner, '*Non-Refoulement* and "Humanitarian" Refugees: Customary International law or Wishful Legal Thinking?', (1986) 26:4 *Virg JIL*, p. 893.

[219]   *ibid.*

[220]   Art. 1C(5).

where a refugee has become a danger to the security of the country of refuge or has committed a 'particularly serious crime',[221] there is no mention of temporary protection or cessation in the ECHR. As Hathaway has noted, 'The [1951] Convention conceives of refugee status as a transitory phenomenon, which expires when a refugee can either reclaim the protection of her own state or has secured an alternative form of enduring protection.'[222] This is not true of the ECHR. Goodwin-Gill argues that individual refugee status, as perceived by the 1951 Convention/1967 Protocol, 'may properly give rise to a presumption or expectation that asylum in the sense of a local, lasting solution will be forthcoming',[223] though he goes on to recognise that, in relation to the concept of 'temporary protection',[224] 'the political and legal reality is that states generally have not undertaken, and foreseeably will not undertake, an obligation to grant asylum in the sense of a lasting solution.'[225] Thus while temporary protection (in the sense of a limited solution) is foreseen by the 1951 Convention, it is not envisaged by the ECHR.[226] As the ECtHR stated unambiguously in *Chahal* (quoted above) and in *Ahmed v Austria*: 'The protection afforded by Art. 3 is wider than that provided by Art. 33 of the United Nations 1951 Convention on the Status of Refugees.'[227] Consequently, a refugee who lost his refugee status under Art. 33(2) of the Convention and was subject to *refoulement* could not be deported on account of Art. 3.

---

[221] Art. 33(2).

[222] J. Hathaway, *The Law of Refugee Status* (Canada: Butterworths, 1991), p. 189.

[223] G. Goodwin-Gill, *The Refugee in International Law* (New York: OUP, 1996), p. 197.

[224] 'Temporary protection' refers here to recent state practice in Europe whereby temporary protection is afforded to asylum seekers, without processing their claims. The expectation is that once the reason for their flight has been removed, they will return to their countries of origin. The UNHCR has identified a number of advantages to temporary protection:

(1)   it provides immediate security to a large number of people;

(2)   it relieves states of the need to examine thousands of individual asylum applications;

(3)   it has led states to acknowledge a broader humanitarian obligation to provide a safe haven for victims of war;

(4)   it has helped to reassert the principle of international burden sharing.

(*The State of the World's Refugees 1997–98 – A Humanitarian Agenda* (Oxford: OUP, 1997), pp. 209–10).

[225] G. Goodwin-Gill, *The Refugee in International Law* (New York: OUP, 1996), pp. 201–2.

[226] In practice, however, cessation under the 1951 Convention would be unlikely since many states grant permanent residence to refugees after a certain period of time.

[227] *Ahmed v Austria* (1996) 24 EHRR 278, para. 41.

4.33   Two additional points throw further light on the broadening application of Art. 3. Whereas the 1951 Convention has been interpreted to apply to persecution by state authorities or to 'serious discriminatory or other offensive acts committed by the local populace' where they are tolerated by the authorities or against which the authorities are unable to offer effective protection,[228] *D v United Kingdom* clarified that Art. 3 of the ECHR has no such limitation.[229] The source of the threat of exposure to inhuman or degrading treatment or punishment does not need to be the state in circumstances where the state is unable to remove the threat (as in *HLR v France*, where the applicant argued that if returned to Columbia he would be exposed to the risk of reprisals from drug traffickers).[230] It applies whether or not there has been state involvement, and can extend to a situation where the risk of a breach of Art. 3 arises out of the lack of state authority.[231] Furthermore, it should also be noted that, in contrast again to the 1951 Convention, Art. 3 remains unrestricted by the Convention grounds of race, religion, nationality, membership of a particular social group, or political opinion.

Formerly, there was one cloud overshadowing the generally optimistic analysis of the ECHR's potential in the international protection of asylum: Contracting States had not always submitted to the Commission's will. Following the application made to the European Commission in the case of *Cruz Varas*, the Commission called upon Sweden to suspend its expulsion of the applicant. Sweden ignored the request. Despite a reminder that states failing to comply with the Commission's 'indication' assumed 'the risk of being found in breach of Article 3', the Court was unable to impose a duty upon states to abide by interim measures.[232] It could only warn that any breach of Art. 3 under these circumstances would have to be seen as aggravated. The worry was, of course, that, as a result of this decision, other states might also have been willing to ignore the Commission's rulings and to live with the risk of being guilty of an 'aggravated' breach of Art. 3. Since November 1998, the system in Europe has changed. The Commission was abolished by Protocol 11 and a new structure and court established.[233] Unfortunately, the Chamber, which

---

[228] UNHCR, *Handbook on Procedures and Criteria for Determining Refugee Status* (Geneva, 1992), para. 65.

[229] (1997) 24 EHRR 423, para. 49.

[230] (1998) 26 EHRR 29.

[231] *Ahmed v Austria* (1996) 24 EHRR 278, paras 44–47.

[232] *Cruz Varas & Others v Sweden* Series A, No. 201 (1991) 14 EHRR 1, para. 103.

[233] The new procedure involves a three-part Court of Human Rights: a Committee of three judges; a Chamber of seven judges; and a Grand Chamber of 17 judges. The Committee decides on admissibility. If admissible, the case passes on to the Chamber which also considers the question of admissibility and goes on to look at the

now hears the majority of cases for determination of admissibility, was not granted an express power to issue mandatory interim orders, although it can indicate that interim measures be adopted 'in the interests of the parties or of the proper conduct of the proceedings before it'.[234]

Article 2

Article 2(1) states: **4.34**

> 'Everyone's right to life shall be protected by law. No one shall be deprived of his life intentionally save in the execution of a sentence of a court following his conviction of a crime for which this penalty is provided by law.'

In *D v UK*, the applicant raised the right to life under Art. 2, but in light of findings under Art. 3 the ECtHR did not find it necessary to examine the complaint under that provision. Given the fundamental character of the right to life, state responsibility may be engaged where expulsion puts an individual's life at risk. However, death must be an almost certain consequence of return, and this may be too high a threshold in many cases. As has been seen, the one exception is the death penalty (*Soering v UK*), but the supplementation of Art. 2 by Optional Protocol 6 (the abolition of the death penalty in peacetime) does enhance the protection provided by the ECHR.

Article 5

Article 5, which grants a right to liberty and security of person, has obvious implications for asylum seekers in relation to detention. It does not grant a right of admission to or residence in a Contracting State. Rather, issues arise in relation to whether an individual has been detained as 'prescribed by law' and with a view to deportation or extradition, which is permitted (Art. 5(1)(f)):

4.35

---

merits of the case, if appropriate. Where no settlement is forthcoming between the parties, the Chamber issues a judgement. The Grand Chamber only considers matters of importance referred to it within three months of the Chamber's judgement.

[234] Rules of Court, Rule 39(1); see, also, for further discussion of the new system A. Mowbray, 'The composition and operation of the new European Court of Human Rights' (1999) *Public Law*, p. 219.

'Everyone has the right to liberty and security of person. No one shall be deprived of his liberty save in the following cases and in accordance with the procedure prescribed by law:

(f)   the lawful arrest or detention of a person to prevent his effecting an unauthorised entry into the country or of a person against whom action is being taken with a view to deportation or extradition.'

The ECHR also requires that there is a procedure in place whereby the detainee can quickly challenge before a court the lawfulness of his or her detention (Art. 5(4)).[235]

Two decisions raising Art. 5 issues have been of particular interest in the asylum field: *Amuur v France*[236] and *Chahal v United Kingdom*.[237] *Amuur* dealt with four Somali asylum seekers who arrived from Syria at Orly airport in Paris. They were refused entry but applied for asylum and were kept in detention in a hotel near the airport. They applied to the *juge* for an order that their detention was unlawful, but before the *juge* heard the case, they were returned to Syria on refusal of their political asylum claim by the Minister of the Interior. The main question for the Court in *Amuur* was whether deprivation of liberty had occurred for the purposes of Art. 5. The Court set out certain principles:

'In order to ascertain whether a deprivation of liberty has complied with the principle of compatibility with domestic law, it [. . .] falls to the Court to assess not only the legislation in force in the field under consideration, but also the quality of the other legal rules applicable to the persons concerned. Quality in this sense implies that where a national law authorises deprivation of liberty – especially in respect of a foreign asylum-seeker – it must be sufficiently accessible and precise, in order to avoid all risks of arbitrariness. These characteristics are of fundamental importance with regard to asylum-seekers at airports, particularly in view of the need to reconcile the protection of fundamental rights with the requirements of States' immigration policies.'[238]

Though the Court was referring in this case to the holding of aliens in transit zones in international airports, there are much wider implications of the decision for asylum seekers generally, in particular the need for accessible legal, humanitarian and social assistance.[239] In

---

[235] 'Everyone who is deprived of his liberty by arrest or detention shall be entitled to take proceedings by which the lawfulness of his detention shall be decided speedily by a court and his release ordered if the detention is not lawful.'
[236] (1996) EHRR 533.
[237] (1996) EHRR 413. See above for facts.
[238] (1996) EHRR 533, para. 50.
[239] *ibid.*, para. 53. The Court found a breach of Art. 5(1).

view of the length of the detention – 20 days – and the restriction suffered, the Court concluded that the applicants' treatment constituted
deprivation of liberty under Art. 5. Deprivation of liberty under Art.
5(1)(f) is only permissible where deportation or extradition proceedings are in progress, and they must be prosecuted with due diligence.
The Court also stressed that those in detention should be afforded an
opportunity to have the conditions and length of time of their detention reviewed and that the domestic law should provide for legal,
humanitarian and social assistance to allow detained asylum seekers
to take steps to challenge detention.[240]

The issue of access to legal processes was also examined in the
Chahal decision. While the Court found no breach of Art. 5(1) –
domestic procedures had been conducted with due diligence – [241],
nor of Art. 5(1)(f) – Mr Chahal's detention was lawful under national
law, was effected 'in accordance with a procedure prescribed by law',
and was not arbitrary – [242], there were concerns about Art. 5(4). This
decision is somewhat surprising in view of the fact that Mr Chahal
was confined for six years by the time the judgement was heard, he
was not entitled to legal representation before the advisory panel, the
proceedings were not public, he was not informed of the reasons for
his deportation, and the panel's advice to the Home Secretary was
not binding and was not disclosed.[243] Though the Court found no
breach of Art. 5(1), it did hold that neither the proceedings for *habeas
corpus* or judicial review of the decision to detain Mr Chahal, nor the
advisory panel procedure, satisfied the requirements of Art. 5(4).[244]
The advisory panel suffered from various procedural inadequacies
and could not be considered a 'court' for the purposes of 5(4). Art.
5(4) had therefore been violated. As a result of the Court's judgment,
the UK passed the Special Immigration Appeals Commission Act
1997, establishing a Special Immigration Appeals Commission to
hear appeals where asylum is refused on account of Art. 1(F) of the
1951 Convention.[245]

---

[240] *ibid.*
[241] (1996) EHRR 413, para. 117.
[242] *ibid.*, para. 119.
[243] *ibid.*, para. 130.
[244] *ibid.*, para. 132.
[245] See Ch. 5 for further discussion of the Special Immigration Appeals Commission
Act 1997 and Ch. 8 for cases connected with the Act.

Article 8

4.36 Article 8(1) states:

> 'Everybody has the right to respect for his private and family life, his home and his correspondence.'

Article 8(2) prohibits public authorities from interfering with this right except where: (i) the grounds for interference are in accordance with law; (ii) they are necessary in a democratic society;[246] and (iii) they pursue a legitimate aim, such as the interests of national security, public safety or the economic well-being of the country, the prevention of disorder or crime, the protection of health and morals, and the protection of the rights and freedoms of others.

Family life is defined quite broadly and covers many close relationships. A 'lawful and genuine marriage' gives rise to family life,[247] but Art. 8(1) can cover other apparently less legitimate relationships. The Court decided in 1979 that Art. 8 makes no distinction between the 'legitimate' and the 'illegitimate' family.[248] The establishment of family life is a question of fact 'depending upon the real existence in practice of close personal ties'.[249]

Art. 8 is a very general right and does not deal explicitly with immigration. However, the Court confirmed that asylum and immigration procedures must be exercised in accordance with the principles of the ECHR and that Art. 8 did apply in the immigration context.[250] This must always be balanced against the right of states to control entry of aliens. Deportation or removal is permitted and the exclusion by a state of family members does not in itself breach the obligations imposed by the Convention. The case of *Abdulaziz, Cabales and Balkandali v UK*, which concerned the refusal by the UK to allow the foreign husbands of the applicants to join them in the UK, made this clear:

> 'The duty imposed by Article 8 [. . .] cannot be considered as extending to a general obligation on the part of a Contracting State to respect the choice by married couples of the country of their matrimonial residence and to accept the non-national spouses for settlement in that country. In the present case, the applicants have not shown that there were obstacles

---

[246] In other words, they are 'justified by a pressing social need and, in particular, proportionate to the legitimate aim pursued': *Beldjoudi v France* (1992) 14 EHRR 81, para. 74.
[247] *Abdulaziz, Cabales and Balkandali v UK* (1985) 7 EHRR 471, para. 62.
[248] *Marckx v Belgium* (1979) 2 EHRR 330, para. 31.
[249] *K v UK* [1986] 50 DR 199, at 207.
[250] *Abdulaziz, Cabales and Balkandali v UK* (1985) 7 EHRR 471, paras 59–60.

to establishing family life in their own or their husbands' home countries or that there were special reasons why that could not be expected of them.'[251]

Thus for an infringement of Art. 8 to exist, the applicant needs to show that it is impossible to establish family life elsewhere on the exclusion of a family member. Obstacles to the establishment of family life in another country would include language barriers, place of past residence, ability to adapt to living abroad, relationships with other family members, cultural, religious and social practices, and health, employment or family issues.[252] In the asylum context, Art. 8 is likely to be raised following a decision to deport, and, in serious cases, will be pleaded alongside Art. 3. A number of cases dealing with deportation have reached the ECtHR in recent years. Though not dealing with asylum seekers or refugees, their principles have a wider impact and may apply to asylum cases.

These cases are also of interest in that they have revealed a surprising lack of certainty amongst the judges about the correct approach to be adopted. In most cases, the applicant was to be deported because he had committed a criminal offence in the European country in which he was resident. In the one case in which a crime was not involved, and where the applicant was to be deported having failed to obtain a residence permit, the Court held that balancing the competing interests of 'legitimate aim' with 'necessity in a democratic society' did not justify interfering with Art. 8 rights.[253] This despite the government arguing that deportation was required to protect the economic well-being of the country. In the remaining cases, all involving crimes of varying severity, the Court was clearly engaged in weighing a number of factors: interference with family life; length of time spent in respondent country; seriousness of crime(s) committed; links with country to which return was to be made; special circumstances of the applicant; and languages spoken.[254] In the majority of cases, the Court held that deportation would interfere with Art. 8 rights – even where the applicant had

4.37

---

[251] *ibid.*, para. 68.

[252] I. Macdonald & F. Webber, *Macdonald's Immigration Law & Practice* (London: Butterworths, 2001), paras 8.58–8.60.

[253] *Berrehab v Netherlands* (1989) 11 EHRR 322, paras 28–29.

[254] See *Moustaquim v Belgium* (1991) 13 EHRR 802; *Beldjoudi v France* (1992) 14 EHRR 801; *Nasri v France* (1996) 21 EHRR 458; *C v Belgium* Judgement of August 7, 1996; *Boughanemi v France* (1996) 22 EHRR 228; *Boujlifa v France* (122/1996/741/940) Judgement of October 21, 1997; *El Boujaidi v France* 30 EHRR 223; *Bouchelkia v France* (1998) 25 EHRR 686; *Mehemi v France* Judgement of September 26, 1997.

been convicted of gang rape (*Nasri v France*).[255] In that case, the Court was persuaded by the 'accumulation of special circumstances':

'In view of this accumulation of special circumstances, notably his situation as a deaf and dumb person, capable of achieving a minimum psychological and social equilibrium only within his family, the majority of whose members are French nationals with no close ties with Algeria, the decision to deport the applicant, if executed, would not be proportionate to the legitimate aim pursued. It would infringe the right to respect for family life and therefore constitute a breach of Article 8.'[256]

This is perhaps an exceptional case, since the severity of the crime committed does tend to give rise to a finding that Art. 8 would not be breached by deportation.[257] Interestingly, these are later cases in the Court's jurisprudence. One commentator has argued that the main focus of the 1997 cases was on family life, whereas earlier cases had considered social ties and the establishment of a private life in more detail.[258] Some of the judges were aware that some confusion might be caused by the differing outcomes in these Art. 8 cases, and have commented accordingly. Judge Martens in the *Boughanemi* case could not have expressed his disquiet more clearly when he said:

'The majority's case-by-case approach is a lottery for national authorities and a source of embarrassment for the Court. A source of embarrassment since it obliges the Court to make well-nigh impossible comparisons between the merits of the case before it and those which it has already decided. It is – to say the least – far from easy to compare the cases of *Moustaquim v Belgium* [. . .], *Beldjoudi v. France* [. . .], *Nasri v France* [. . .] and *Boughanemi v France*. Should one just make a comparison based on the number of convictions and the severity of sentences or should one also take into account personal circumstances? The majority has, obviously, opted for the latter approach and has felt able to make the comparison [. . .], but – with due respect – I cannot help feeling that the outcome is necessarily tainted with arbitrariness.'[259]

Judge Martens has also advanced the 'integrated alien' doctrine, which suggests that aliens who are integrated within a society, either through having been born and bred in a state or through long

---

[255] *Nasri v France* (1996) 21 EHRR 458.

[256] para. 46.

[257] See, for example, *C v Belgium* Judgement of August 7, 1996; *Boujlifa v France* (122/1996/741/940) Judgement of October 21, 1997; *El Boujaidi v France* 30 EHRR 223; *Bouchelkia v France* (1998) 25 EHRR 686.

[258] A. Sherlock, 'Deportation of aliens and art. 8 ECHR' (1998) *E.L. Rev*, 23 Supp HRs, pp. 62–75.

[259] para. 4, Dissenting opinion of Judge Martens.

residence, should be treated no differently from nationals.[260] This approach is now receiving more support from the Court.

In the relatively recent decision of *Bensaid v UK*, the applicant, on a visit to Algeria, was discovered to have entered into a marriage of convenience while in the UK. On his return to the UK, he was refused entry and was threatened with removal to Algeria. His judicial review of the Home Secretary's decision was unsuccessful and he applied to Strasbourg, claiming that he was schizophrenic and that removal to Algeria would deprive him of essential medical treatment as well as sever his close ties with the UK. Articles 3, 8 and 13 were invoked. The ECtHR held that there was no violation of Art. 3. He did not meet the high threshold set by the Article, nor did he disclose the exceptional circumstances of *D v UK*, where the applicant was in the final stages of a terminal illness and had no prospect of medical care or family support on expulsion to St Kitts.[261] It was recognised that treatment which does not breach Art. 3 may still breach Art. 8 in its private life aspect where there are sufficiently adverse effects on moral and physical integrity.[262] Furthermore, it was held that mental health must be regarded as a crucial part of private life associated with moral integrity.[263] Nonetheless, the Court did not feel that Bensaid's moral integrity would be substantially affected 'to a degree falling within the scope of Article 8', nor that his health would be damaged.[264] This notwithstanding his residence in the UK for the previous eleven years and his establishment of relationships there.[265] Interference with his private life through removal fell within Art. 8(2); in other words, the right to control immigration was a valid ground for derogating from Art. 8 rights in this case.[266]

Finally, it has been suggested by lawyers that the system of cashless support for asylum seekers, which was introduced in 1999 in the UK, may raise issues regarding the right to respect for private life, and that the 'summary eviction of asylum seekers from the only accommodation they have following rejection of an asylum appeal may constitute unjustifiable interference with the right to respect for "home" if they have been in occupation for a reasonable period and may need to remain in the country (to seek judicial review, or for medical or other

4.38

---

[260] See Judge Martens' concurring opinion in *Beldjoudi v France* (1992) 14 EHRR 801.
[261] (2001) 33 EHRR 205, para. 40.
[262] para. 46.
[263] para. 47.
[264] para. 48.
[265] *ibid.*
[266] See *R. (Ullah) v Special Adjudicator; Do v SSHD* [2002] EWCA Civ 1856; [2003] INLR 74, para. 46.

special reasons)'.[267] Recently, a UK court held that 'if a denial of support to an asylum seeker impacts sufficiently on the asylum seeker's private and family life, which extends to the individual's physical and mental integrity and autonomy, [. . .], the Secretary of State will be in breach of the negative obligation imposed by Article 8, unless he can justify his conduct under Article 8(2).'[268] Nonetheless, while the court considered that Art. 8 was capable of being engaged, it concluded that it added little to Art. 3.[269]

CONCLUSION

4.39   For refugee law, the real significance of the first half of the twentieth century lies not so much in the restrictionism of the UK's national rules, as in the growing involvement of international law. The record of the inter-war years in relation to refugees was variable. The fear of immigration, in a time of economic depression and impending war, was clearly a key factor in controlling the direction in which international refugee law developed. While a significant advance was made in placing the issue on the political agenda, leading members of the League of Nations lacked any real will to find a permanent and durable solution. Despite this, acceptance of a legal definition of refugees incorporated in an instrument of international law, the convention, was a fundamental development. Both the 1933 and 1938 Conventions can now be considered as milestones in terms of refugee protection. They helped to define the refugee, though admittedly in fairly narrow terms, and made provision for basic principles regarding refugee protection. Though the impact of the Conventions was not as real as might have been hoped, by 1945, the message had been disseminated that refugees were an important subject warranting international intervention and humanitarian treatment.

Following the cessation of hostilities, the international community had an opportunity to consider once more the question of refugee protection in the light of an emerging human rights paradigm in the international law context. The UK was keen to participate in international discussions on refugees and to declare its sympathy for refugees, evidenced by its accession to the 1951 Convention, as well as the 1967 Protocol. With the range of rights granted to refugees, and the development of norms of customary international

---

[267] I. Macdonald & F. Webber, *Macdonald's Immigration Law & Practice* (London: Butterworths, 2001), para. 8.65.
[268] *The Queen on the Application of Q & Others v SSHD* [2003] EWCA Civ 364, para. 64.
[269] *ibid.*, para. 119(ix).

law in relation to some of their provisions, the 1951 Convention and accompanying Protocol remain the bulwark of international refugee protection. Notwithstanding recent criticisms of the work of the UNHCR and attempts to undermine the 1951 Convention, the Global Consultations held in 2001 indicate continuing support for the current system of refugee protection, not only by NGOs and experts working in the field, but also by signatory states. More recently, the regional instrument of the ECHR is proving an increasingly valuable tool in the protection of the rights of asylum seekers and refugees.

The UK's own record in relation to the Convention is arguably disappointing, having failed to incorporate it into its municipal law.[270] From a UK perspective, the years 1945 to 1993 provide an instructive study of two contrasting approaches to the role of law in the asylum field: on the one hand, international law attempted to establish clear and generous principles of protection for refugees; on the other, the UK, while refusing to incorporate leading instruments, continued to treat asylum law as a branch of general immigration law, proceeding for almost fifty years with a haphazard and piecemeal system of control. As will be discussed in Chapter 5, it was only in 1993, with the advent of the Asylum and Immigration Appeals Act, that an attempt was made finally to legislate specifically on the issue of asylum and to accord *primacy* to the 1951 Convention. While such statutory acknowledgement of the Convention was long overdue, the continued hesitation to seek full incorporation is telling. It is also arguably at odds with the introduction of the Human Rights Act 1998 and the consequential development of UK jurisprudence on ECHR rights.[271]

---

[270] See Ch. 5 for further discussion on this point.
[271] See N. Blake & R. Husain, *Immigration, Asylum & Human Rights* (Oxford: OUP, 2003).

Chapter Five

UK Asylum Law in the 1990s and Beyond: An Overview

INTRODUCTION

Despite the major contribution made by international law in the pro-   **5.1**
tection of refugees, municipal law continues to play a leading role in
the process of refugee determination. Post-war international refugee
law laid down the ground rules for protection, but contracting states
retained their sovereign right to decide whom to admit to their territory, as well as the freedom to implement their own refugee determination process. It is therefore the national law that sets out the
procedures for, *inter alia*, admission of asylum seekers, assessing
refugee cases, rights of appeal, detention, deportation and removal.
While such procedures must operate within the framework created by
international law, they are generally dependent on the policies of the
national government for their detail. Thus states are free to adopt
whichever system for refugee determination they deem appropriate
and, beyond the European Union, there has been little attempt to
develop minimum guarantees for procedural criteria.[1]

The United Kingdom, alongside other industrialised countries,
asserted its right in 1993 to devise its own asylum determination procedures by introducing detailed legislation. This was the first of four
Acts. The concern of the present chapter will be to provide an
overview of legislation in the last decade: the Asylum and Immigration Appeals Act 1993, the Asylum and Immigration Act 1996, the
Immigration and Asylum Act 1999, and the Nationality, Immigration
and Asylum Act 2002. Brief consideration will also be given to the
Special Immigration Appeals Commission Act 1997 and the Anti-
terrorism, Crime and Security Act 2001. This and subsequent

---

[1] Though the UNHCR's Handbook, Ex Com Conclusions, and Global Consultations
have provided valuable guidance on the collective approaches to a variety of key
issues in refugee law.

chapters will seek to show how, through the progressive hardening of asylum law, the asylum seeker has been subjected to a policy of deterrence, and on occasion of exclusion, either by the introduction of specific restrictive measures targeted at the asylum seeker, or by the categorisation of the asylum seeker as *de facto* refugee, economic migrant, bogus refugee, or even quasi-criminal.[2]

5.2   ACT ONE: THE ASYLUM AND IMMIGRATION APPEALS
ACT 1993

Background

5.3   Throughout the 1980s and early 1990s, western Europe witnessed a sharp rise in asylum applications.[3] It became clear that a change was taking place in the pattern of migration. The influx of groups of refugees (such as the South East Asians) was gradually replaced by individually-based applications from an expanding range of countries. According to the UNHCR, the increase in numbers was due in the main to people fleeing 'war, generalized violence and chaos in their home countries', but there was also 'the undeniable abuse of the asylum channel by growing numbers of people who [were] trying to enter the labour market rather than escape persecution'.[4] In the United Kingdom, 11,640 applications were received in 1989, almost a threefold increase on those of the previous year.[5] By 1991, the figure reached 44,840.[6] In addition, a large backlog of undecided cases

---

[2] A *de facto* refugee is a person who either does not meet the Convention criteria but is permitted to remain in the country of asylum on humanitarian grounds, or does meet the criteria but is not formally recognised as a Convention refugee. N.B. refugee status is declaratory in nature *i.e.* a refugee 'does not become a refugee because of recognition, but is recognized because he is a refugee': UNHCR, *Handbook on Procedures and Criteria for Determining Refugee Status* (Geneva, 1992), para. 28.

[3] In 1985, a total of 157,280 asylum applications were received in EU Member States; by December 31, 2002, this figure had risen to 373,891 (excluding Italy). A high was reached in 1992, with 673,947 applications lodged: UNHCR, *Asylum Applications in Industrialized Countries 1980–1999* (Geneva: UNHCR, November 2001), table II.2; UNHCR, *Asylum Applications in Industrialized Countries: Levels and Trends, 2000–2002* (Geneva: UNHCR, March 2003), table 2.

[4] UNHCR, *The State of the World's Refugees* (New York: Penguin, 1993), p. 36.

[5] Home Office, *Statistical Bulletin Asylum Statistics 1992* (Government Statistical Service, 15 July 1992), table 1.2.

[6] Home Office, *Statistical Bulletin Asylum Statistics 1995* (Government Statistical Service, May 16, 1996), table 1.2. This figure excludes dependants and information on applications from overseas. With dependants, the total number of applications for 1991 was 73,400.

was building up. This 'relentless rise'[7] would alone have constituted sufficient grounds for legislative intervention; additional impetus was provided by discussions which had, for some time, been taking place in secret intergovernmental meetings at the European Union level. From the occasional leaked memorandum, it became evident that EU ministers, sharing a common disquiet over the rising number of asylum applications in their countries, were considering developing a co-ordinated asylum policy, the basic thrust of which appeared to be deterrence and restriction.[8]

The first indication in the UK that a more restrictive line was to be adopted came in July 1991, when the Conservative Home Secretary, Kenneth Baker, publicised the government's intention to introduce new statutory controls on asylum. The resulting Asylum Bill[9] and accompanying changes to the Immigration Rules were severely criticised by refugee-support groups, the UNHCR, the Law Society and the Bar Council, as were additional proposals to abolish legal aid for all immigration cases. The Bill, unable to complete its passage through Parliament prior to the 1992 general election, failed to become law. Undeterred, the new Conservative government under John Major introduced a second Bill in October 1992: the Asylum and Immigration Appeals Bill.[10] Announced as a package of measures to address the growing number of asylum applications, a large proportion of which the government considered abusive, and to introduce 'a better system for making prompt and fair decisions',[11] the new Bill, associated Immigration Rules and Appeals Procedure Rules opened the way for radical change.

Overview of the 1993 Act

When the Act finally received Royal Assent in July 1993, it heralded a new departure in asylum policy in the UK. Its major proposals were to:

5.4

- provide a definition of a claim for asylum;[12]

- ensure primacy of the 1951 Convention;[13]

---

[7] UNHCR, *The State of the World's Refugees* (New York: Penguin, 1993), p. 2.
[8] See Ch. 9.
[9] HMSO, Bill 1, Session 1991/92. See, for further discussion, D. Stevens, 'Race relations and the changing face of United Kingdom asylum policy' (1992) 26:1&2 *Patterns of Prejudice*, pp. 96–102.
[10] HMSO, Bill 69, Session 1992/93. For further discussion, see D. Stevens, 'Reintroduction of the United Kingdom Asylum Bill', (1993) 5:1 *IJRL*, pp. 91–100.
[11] HC Deb Vol. 213, November 2, 1992, col. 22.
[12] s. 1
[13] s. 2.

- empower immigration officers, amongst others, to fingerprint asylum applicants and their dependants;[14]

- limit the duty of local authorities to house asylum seekers;[15]

- grant asylum seekers a right to remain in-country pending appeals;[16]

- curtail leave to enter and stay of in-country applicants;[17]

- permit the detention of applicants awaiting deportation following curtailment of leave;[18]

- grant a right of appeal in all cases;[19]

- create a 'fast track' or accelerated appeals system for claims held to be 'without foundation';[20]

- extend carriers' liability legislation to transit passengers.[21]

The recommendation by the House of Lords that a statutory advisory panel be established to assist unaccompanied asylum seekers under the age of 18 was rejected by the House of Commons on the grounds that the cost of providing an adviser for every unaccompanied child was too great.[22]

The 1993 Act saw the first real implementation in UK refugee policy of a legal framework devoted to asylum cases. The asylum seeker clearly benefited from some of the measures, not least the statute granting 'primacy' to the 1951 Convention. Though urged to incorporate all relevant international human rights instruments into UK law, in particular the 1950 European Convention on Human Rights, the 1966 International Covenant on Civil and Political Rights, the 1984 UN Convention Against Torture, and the 1989 UN Convention on the Rights of the Child,[23] the government resisted. Although an in-country right of appeal was introduced in asylum cases, the majority of the provisions were arguably restrictive in tenor. Issues of especial concern included: fingerprinting of all asylum claimants, including children; the withdrawal of local authority responsibility to

---

[14] s. 3.
[15] ss. 4 and 5.
[16] s. 6
[17] s. 7.
[18] s. 7.
[19] s. 8.
[20] s. 8 and sch. 2, para. 5.
[21] s. 12.
[22] See, for example, Baroness David, HL Deb Vol. 541, January 26, 1993, col. 1182.
[23] HC Standing Committee A, November 10, 1992.

house certain categories of asylum seekers; and, of greatest import, the creation of a 'fast track' appeals system for claims deemed to be 'without foundation'.

Appeals

The 1993 Act recognised the need for an in-country right of oral appeal against refusal of an asylum claim, removing the requirement in certain cases for the appellant to appeal from abroad. This was certainly a most significant change to the legislation; for the first time, nearly all asylum seekers were granted an in-country right of appeal to a special adjudicator.[24] However, it is important to note that, as previously, the appeal remained classified 'according to the nature of the decision and not separately as an appeal against a refusal of asylum'.[25] In other words, there was no free-standing appeal against a failed asylum claim. The right of appeal was opened up from the IAT to the Court of Appeal, an option that was not available prior to 1993.[26] The uniform right of appeal for asylum seekers was subject now to a two-tier appeals system: the 'fast' and the 'standard' track. The 'fast track' applied only to those cases deemed to be 'without foundation', that is, those cases which did not call into question the UK's obligations under the 1951 Convention, or were considered 'frivolous or vexatious'.[27] The majority of 'without foundation' cases were subsequently found to be cases falling within the 'safe third country rule'.[28] Though the main countries to which the UK returns

5.5

---

[24] There were three main exceptions: where national security was a ground for refusal; where an individual had previously been refused asylum; and where ELR, rather than refugee status was granted: see Macdonald & Blake, *Macdonald's Immigration Law and Practice* (London: Butterworths, 1995), para. 12.105.

[25] D. Jackson, *Immigration Law and Practice* (London: Sweet & Maxwell, 1999), p. 809, and see Ch. 3 for discussion of the position under the Immigration Act 1971.

[26] Asylum and Immigration Appeals Act 1993, s. 9. This provision was aimed at reducing judicial review of IAT decisions: Following the case of *R. v Secretary of State for the Home Department, ex parte Swati* [1986] 1 AER 717, which restricted applications for leave for judicial review to those cases in which the appellate system had been exhausted, unless there were exceptional circumstances, the number of applications for leave to seek judicial review in asylum cases fell rapidly: in 1986, there were 305 applications; in 1987, there were 85. See Sunkin, Bridges, Mészáros, *Judicial Review in Perspective* (London: The Public Law Project, 1993).

[27] Asylum and Immigration Appeals Act 1993, sch. 2, para. 5(3).

[28] According to the Immigration Rules, a safe third country is one to which an asylum applicant can be sent on account of the fact he or she is not a national or citizen of the country, that his or her life or liberty would not be threatened, and that the government of the country concerned would not contravene its Convention obligations. The country of origin is viewed as the first country, the country in which the

asylum seekers are in the EU, the application of this so-called 'rule' has led to widespread condemnation in view of the risk of *refoulement* by the third country.[29] A number of cases in the 1990s challenged the Home Secretary's decision to return asylum seekers to a third country, and met with a fair degree of success.

The UK approach has to be placed in its European context. Since 1990, and the signing of the Convention Determining the State Responsible for Examining Applications for Asylum Lodged in One of the Member States of the European Community ('the Dublin Convention'), EU Member States have attempted to resolve the problem of shuttling asylum seekers between countries ('refugees in orbit') by enforcing the 'first country of asylum' concept. This principle supports the view that asylum seekers should apply for asylum in the first safe country they reach after fleeing their country of origin. While less contentious than the safe third country rule, it does bar the asylum seeker from choosing a preferred final destination. It should be noted, however, that this interpretation of 'first country of asylum' differs from that of the UNHCR. The UNHCR stresses, instead, that a '"first country of asylum" is a country where a person has already been granted some legal status allowing him/her to remain in the territory either as an asylum seeker or as a refugee, with all the guarantees which international standards attach to such status. A country where the person could have found protection is not a first country of asylum in this sense.'[30]

The time limits imposed in the 1993 Act in 'without foundation' cases were very tight.[31] On being personally served with the Secretary

---

claim is lodged is the second, and the country through which the applicant travelled, and in which the asylum application should have been lodged, is the third country: Statement of Changes in Immigration Rules, HC 395, para. 345.

[29] See S. Lavenex, *Safe Third Countries – Extending EU Asylum and Immigration Policies to Central and Eastern Europe* (Hungary: CEU Press, 1999); N.A Abell, 'The compatability of readmission agreements with the1951 Convention relating to the status of refugees' (1999) 11:1 *IJRL*, pp. 60–83; Amnesty International, *Playing Human Pinball: Home Office Practice in 'Safe Third Country' Asylum Cases* (London: AI British Section, June 1995); A. Achermann & M. Gattiker, 'Safe third countries: European developments' (1995) 7:1 *IJRL*, pp. 19–38; K. Hailbronner, 'The concept of "safe country" and expeditious asylum procedures: A western European perspective' (1993) 5:1 *IJRL*, pp. 31–65.

[30] UNHCR, Background paper No. 2, 'The application of the "safe third country" notion and its impact on the management of flows and on the protection of refugees' (Geneva: UNHCR, May 2001), and see, also ,UNHCR Ex. Com. Conclusion, 'Problem of refugees and asylum-seekers who move in an irregular manner from a country in which they had already found protection' (No. 58 (XL) – 1989); UNHCR Ex. Com. Conclusion, 'Refugees Without an Asylum Country' (No. 15 (XXX) – 1979).

[31] See Asylum Appeals (Procedure) Rules 1993, SI 1993/1661.

of State's decision that a case was 'without foundation', the asylum seeker had two days in which to lodge his or her appeal. On receipt of the notice of appeal, the special adjudicator had three days in which to fix the date, time and place of the hearing, and was expected to have decided the appeal within seven days of receipt. There was no further right of appeal against the decision of the special adjudicator where he or she concurred with the decision of the Home Secretary.[32] While allowing more time for applicants to prepare their papers, the standard procedure was also designed to ensure that the whole process was completed within a tightly specified time-frame. Applicants had 10 days in which to lodge their appeals from the date of the decision, and the special adjudicator was granted 42 days in which to determine the appeal.

ACT TWO: THE ASYLUM AND IMMIGRATION ACT 1996

Background

Though only two years had passed since the introduction of the first statute focusing on asylum seekers, the Major government announced further proposals for change in the latter part of 1995. Two principal factors accounted for the haste in revisiting such recent legislation. In the first place, statistical evidence proved to the government's satisfaction that the 1993 Act had not been as successful as anticipated in deterring asylum seekers from applying to the UK, nor in clearing the backlog; according to the Home Office, applications continued to rise unabated. In line with its promise to monitor the effectiveness of the 1993 Act, the government, through the Home Office and Lord Chancellor's Department, commissioned the accountancy firm KPMG Peat Marwick ('KPMG') to carry out a survey of the 'difficulties experienced in operating the Asylum Appeals (Procedure) Rules 1993'.[33] Though the researchers for the report used a relatively small sample (214 cases), and their terms of reference related to asylum appeals alone, the report concluded by suggesting that further primary and/or secondary legislation might be necessary.[34]

The second explanation for this early review of legislation was the perceived political value in the issues of immigration and asylum.

5.6

---

[32] Asylum and Immigration Appeals Act 1993, sch. 2, para. 5(5), (unamended).

[33] KPMG Peat Marwick, *Review of Asylum Appeals Procedure Final Report* (London: KPMG Peat Marwick, December 1994), para. 1, p. 4.

[34] For further information, see D. Stevens, 'The Asylum and Immigration Act 1996: Erosion of the Right to seek Asylum' (1998) 61 *Modern Law Review*, pp. 207–222.

The announcement at the Conservative Party's annual conference in October 1995 by the Home Secretary, Michael Howard, that the government intended to introduce new asylum laws was enthusiastically applauded by delegates. Following the speech by the Secretary of State for Social Security, Peter Lilley, who pledged to restrict the rights of asylum seekers to receive state benefits, the Home Secretary's proposed tightening of asylum legislation was considered by many non-Conservatives to be a cynical ploy in the run-up to the general election of 1997. Attention was drawn to the first Asylum Bill, which had been announced six months prior to the 1992 general election. The Conservative Party believed that a strong line on immigration was an election winner, prominent members of the party having admitted as much: a former head of research in Conservative Central Office stated that immigration had been raised successfully in 1992 and again in the 1994 Euro-elections campaign. Immigration, he conceded, 'played particularly well in the tabloids and still has the potential to hurt'.[35] The Joint Council for the Welfare of Immigrants ('JCWI') was scathing in its attack on the political dimension to the 1995 Bill, describing it as 'the most extreme vote-oriented immigration legislation since the 1960s'.[36]

Overview of the 1996 Act[37]

5.7 Despite considerable objections to the Bill and to accompanying changes in social security legislation, it received Royal Assent in July 1996 as the Asylum and Immigration Act 1996. The new Act amended some of the provisions of the Asylum and Immigration Appeals Act 1993, but did not abolish it. Its main provisions were:

- the extension of the 'fast track' procedure to a wider number of asylum claims;[38]

- the power to designate countries in which it appeared to the Secretary of State that there was 'in general no serious risk of persecution';[39]

---

[35] Nick Cohen, 'Fortress Britain', *The Independent on Sunday*, October 29, 1995.

[36] Alan Travis, 'Asylum Bill lists benefits cuts', *The Guardian*, November 30, 1995.

[37] See, for further discussion, D. Stevens, 'The Asylum and Immigration Act 1996: Erosion of the right to seek asylum' (1998) 61 *Modern Law Review*, pp. 207–222; L. Leigh & C. Beyani, *Blackstone's Guide to the Asylum and immigration Act 1996* (London: Blackstone Press, 1996); M. Supperstone & D. O'Dempsey, *Supperstone & O'Dempsey on Immigration and Asylum* (London: FT Law & Tax, 1996), Chs. 25 & 26.

[38] s. 1, amending Asylum and Immigration Appeals Act 1993, sch. 2, para. 5.

[39] sch. 2, para. 5, as amended.

- the statutory endorsement of the Secretary of State's right to remove an applicant to a 'safe third country';[40]

- the abolition of an in-country right of appeal and the limitation of grounds of appeal in some 'safe third country' cases;[41]

- a new offence of facilitating for gain the entry into the UK of asylum seekers;[42]

- increased powers of search and arrest in suspected cases of: illegal entry; obtaining leave to enter or remain by deception; failing to observe a condition of leave; or overstaying;[43]

- a new power to fine employers up to £5,000 for employing people not granted leave to enter or remain, or without 'valid and subsisting' leave, or with a condition of leave preventing them from taking up employment;[44]

- the right granted to the Secretary of State to withdraw entitlement to housing accommodation and assistance;[45]

- the removal of entitlement to child benefit of 'persons subject to immigration control';[46]

- the power to remove by secondary legislation social security benefits for certain asylum seekers.[47]

The result of the 1996 Act was a more complicated set of rules with a stronger emphasis on deterrence and speed of process.

'White list' and appeals

One of the Act's most contentious innovations was the power granted   **5.8**
to the Secretary of State to designate so-called 'safe countries' in which there was considered to be 'in general no serious risk of persecution'.[48] This became known as the 'white list'. The provision allowed the Home Secretary to 'create a rebuttable presumption

---

[40] s. 2.
[41] s. 3.
[42] s. 5.
[43] s. 7.
[44] s. 8.
[45] s. 9.
[46] s. 10.
[47] s. 11.
[48] Asylum and Immigration Act 1993, sch. 2, para. 5(5), as amended by Asylum and Immigration Act 1996, s. 1.

against the application' for asylum,[49] if not a blanket ban. In addition, white-listed applicants were 'fast-tracked' through the appeals process. The new procedure rules specified two days' notice of appeal where the applicant was in detention and personally served with the refusal, and seven days for remaining cases.[50] Once more, there was only one level of appeal – the adjudicator.

The accelerated appeals provisions were not restricted to 'white list' cases. In fact, the majority of asylum applicants were now covered by the 'fast track' process. The only asylum seekers to escape 'fast tracking' under section 1 of the 1996 Act were those who established either fear of persecution for a 1951 Convention ground, or reasonable likelihood of having been tortured in the country to which they were to be returned.[51]

Having introduced a general in-country right of appeal in 1993, the government proceeded to reverse this in the 1996 Act. 'Safe third country' applications, which had constituted the majority of 'without foundation' cases, were denied an in-country appeal under the new rules. In addition, the 1996 Act removed an in-country right of appeal in the case of EU member states or those designated by order, such as the USA, Canada, Norway and Switzerland.[52] Applicants were required to lodge their appeals within 28 days from the safe country to which they were sent, assuming they had not in the meantime been passed on to another country.[53] An appeal could be made to a special adjudicator to set aside a certificate on the grounds that the conditions for the certificate were not fulfilled. However, this was unlikely to succeed. Consequently, judicial review of the decision to certify was the only alternative.[54]

Housing and social security benefits

5.9 The 1993 Act imposed the first restrictions on access to housing for asylum seekers. It excluded asylum seekers from eligibility for housing assistance under the homelessness legislation where they were classified as having accommodation, 'however temporary', in the UK.[55] The Asylum and Immigration Act 1996 proceeded to impose further

---

[49] Ann Widdecombe, HC Standing Committee D, January 16, 1996, col.158.
[50] Asylum Appeals (Procedure) Rules 1996, r. 5.
[51] Asylum and Immigration Appeals Act 1993, sch. 2, para. 5(5), as amended by Asylum and Immigration Act 1996, s. 1.
[52] Asylum and Immigration Act 1996, ss. 2(3) and 3(2).
[53] ss. 2 and 3; Asylum Appeals (Procedure) Rules 1996, r. 5(5).
[54] ss. 2(2) and 3(1).
[55] Asylum and Immigration Appeals Act 1993, s. 4(1).

limitations on asylum seekers, extending its reach not only to housing but to social security. Benefits – income support (90 per cent), housing benefit and council tax benefit – were made available only to those who claimed asylum on arrival or who were the subject of a 'state of upheaval' declaration. A state of upheaval declaration was made when a specified country was 'subject to such a fundamental change in circumstances that [the Secretary of State] would not normally order the return of a person to that country'.[56] In order to qualify for benefits under such a declaration, an individual had to claim asylum within three months of the declaration. Any other asylum seeker was excluded from entitlement to welfare benefits, as were all appellants against a refusal decision by the Home Secretary. Whereas prior to the enforcement of the 1996 Act, all asylum seekers were eligible for child benefit,[57] the Act withdrew this right.[58] In relation to housing, the same restrictions were imposed on asylum seekers as those for benefits. Asylum seekers who claimed asylum on arrival or within three months of a state of upheaval declaration were eligible for housing under the homelessness legislation.[59] Housing and benefits were therefore linked: eligibility for one assumed eligibility for the other.

Criminal offences and employers' liability

The accentuation by the 1996 legislation of the restrictive aspects of the 1993 Act was also evident in the increasing use of criminal sanctions. Section 3 of the Asylum and Immigration Appeals Act 1993 had introduced a power to fingerprint asylum applicants; ss. 4–7 of the 1996 Act created two new criminal offences of knowingly assisting asylum seekers for gain to enter the UK, and knowingly helping someone to obtain leave to remain in the UK through deception.

5.10

---

[56] See, for example, Council Tax Benefit (General) Regulations 1992, SI 1992/1814, r. 4A, as amended by Social Security (Persons from Abroad) Miscellaneous Amendments Regulations 1996, SI 1996/30. The first state of upheaval declaration was made in relation to Zaire on May 16, 1997 and lasted until August 15, 1997; the second was made in relation to Sierra Leone on July 1, 1997 and lasted until September 30, 1997.

[57] Subject to a six-month presence test.

[58] See Asylum and Immigration Act 1996, s.10. Under the Child Benefit (General) Amendment (No. 2) Regulations 1996, benefit was not payable to a person 'whose right to reside or remain in Great Britain is subject to a limitation or condition', excepting refugees and those granted exceptional leave to remain.

[59] On housing, see Asylum and Immigration Act 1996, s.9; Housing Act 1996, ss. 175 and 186; Housing Accommodation and Homelessness (Persons Subject to Immigration Control) Order 1996.

(The assistance of illegal entrants to gain entry to the UK was already an offence.)[60] In addition, penalties associated with immigration offences were increased,[61] and the powers to search and arrest of the police and immigration officers were strengthened.[62]

The final major initiative undertaken by the Asylum and Immigration Act 1996, in s. 8, was to make it a criminal offence for any employer to employ an individual who was subject to immigration control and who required leave to enter or remain, or who was prevented from taking up employment due to a condition attached to his or her entry or admission.[63] To avoid liability for the penalty (£5,000 maximum), an employer needed to prove that, prior to the commencement of the employment, the employee produced a document of a type specified by the Home Office, and that the employer kept or copied the document.[64]

ACT THREE: THE IMMIGRATION AND ASYLUM ACT 1999

Background

5.11   On April 13, 1997, weeks before the general election, the Labour shadow Home Secretary, Jack Straw, declared to *The Sunday Times* that he would repeal most of the 1996 Act if elected, close the 'white list' of countries, refuse to implement s. 8 of the Act on employers' liability, and ensure that asylum applicants who were refused benefits were not left destitute.[65] This apparently generous stance stood in marked contrast to that of the opposition leader, Tony Blair, who had, the previous month, assured *The Sun* readers that a Labour government would not only retain a restrictive policy on immigration, but would outdo the Conservatives' record in this area. Stating that he had no intention of scrapping Tory immigration laws, he continued: 'Under this government, thousands of people every year settled in Britain illegally. We are determined to clamp down on this.'[66]

In light of the Labour Party's vociferous opposition to the 1993 and 1996 Acts, and the assurances of many Labour MPs that a Labour

---

[60] Immigration Act 1971, s. 25(1).

[61] s. 6.

[62] s. 7.

[63] s. 8.

[64] Immigration (Restriction on Employment) Order 1996, SI 1996/3225; Asylum and Immigration Act 1996, s. 8(2).

[65] S. Grey & M. Prescott, 'Straw signals U-turn to ditch tough Tory immigration laws', *The Sunday Times*, April 13, 1997.

[66] *ibid.*

government would dilute the harsher aspects of the legislation, hopes were high among refugee-support groups in the wake of the election. Their expectations were to be put on hold when, in August 1997, the new government announced a comprehensive study of the asylum process, involving wide consultation with government departments, local authorities and groups representing asylum seekers and refugees.[67] The review of the asylum regime became incorporated into the government's general Comprehensive Spending Review. In the meantime, the Asylum and Immigration Act 1996 continued to be enforced in its entirety, including s. 8 on employers' liability, which had been specifically earmarked by Jack Straw as ripe for repeal.

In July 1998, the Home Office published its White Paper, *Fairer, Faster and Firmer – A Modern Approach to Immigration and Asylum*.[68] Together with two further consultation papers on the control of unscrupulous immigration advisers (January 1998) and the review of asylum and immigration appeals (July 1998), the White Paper was described by the Home Secretary, Jack Straw, as 'the most wide-ranging review of immigration and asylum for decades'.[69] The proposals were said to provide a 'long-term strategy', capable of tackling the failings of the asylum system and of addressing the challenges facing immigration control in the years ahead. Repeating what had now become a ministerial mantra on asylum issues, the White Paper spoke of the government's commitment to develop a 'fairer, faster and firmer' approach in the interests of all.[70]

While clearly disappointed with large sections of the White Paper, refugee-support groups did express guarded approval of some of the measures. These included the immediate grant of settlement ('indefinite leave to remain') to over 10,000 asylum seekers waiting for a first decision on their claims since before July 1, 1993, and the grant of ELR to approximately 20,000 people who claimed asylum between July 1, 1993 and December 31, 1995 and who were also awaiting a first decision. Two further important concessions were made: the reduction from seven to four years of the settlement application waiting period in ELR cases, and the grant to refugees of indefinite leave to remain with immediate effect. **5.12**

Finally, the government completed its review in 1999 and published a new Bill entitled Immigration and Asylum. Both its 1993 and 1996

---

[67] Home Office Press Release, 'Immigration minister outlines asylum study', August 21, 1997.

[68] Cm. 4018.

[69] Home Office Press Release, 'Fairer, faster, firmer – Immigration control for the future', July 27, 1998.

[70] Home Office White Paper, *Fairer, Faster and Firmer – A Modern Approach to Immigration and Asylum*, Cm. 4018, July 1998, Preface.

predecessors had a marked effect on asylum in the UK. Described by turns as unduly harsh and restrictive, devoid of the humanitarianism that should accompany asylum claims, or in breach of the UK's obligations under international law, they created controversy and met with criticism. The key question now was whether the Immigration and Asylum Bill would reverse the restrictive trend. To counter anticipated criticism, the government took the rather unusual step of calling on the services of a Special Standing Committee. Although the time taken for passing the Bill was lengthened as a result, the Bill was subjected to detailed scrutiny. The Special Committee's reports provided useful insights to the UK's asylum and refugee law and policy and set the Bill in its social, legal and political context.[71]

By the time the Bill received Royal Assent on November 11, 1999, it had stretched to 170 sections and 16 schedules. A large proportion of the Act was reliant upon secondary legislation for enforcement, the details of which were to be introduced at a later date and, consequently, were not subject to debate. This unsatisfactory state of affairs meant that at the time the Act was promulgated, its true effect remained unknown to politicians and practitioners alike and only emerged in the months and years since the passing of the Act.[72]

Overview of the 1999 Act[73]

5.13 The intervention of the Special Standing Committee, and the lively parliamentary debates on the Bill, gave rise to numerous amendments during Committee and Report stages in both Houses, the majority of which were instigated by the government. In substance, though, the Act reflected the major provisions of the Bill. It provided ten Parts, and covered all aspects of asylum law.[74] Some of the more important components were:

---

[71] The Special Standing Committee held 25 sittings between March 2, 1999 and May 18, 1999. The Reports are available on *www.publications.parliament.uk/pa/cm199899/cmstand/special/special.htm*

[72] An up-to-date list of secondary legislation is available on the Immigration and Nationality Directorate's web-site: *www.ind.homeoffice.gov.uk/default.asp?PageId=353*

[73] For further discussion of the 1999 Act, see D. Stevens, 'The Immigration and Asylum Act 1999: A missed opportunity?' (2001) 64:3 *Modern Law Review*, pp. 413–438; Current Law Statutes Annotated, Immigration and Asylum Act 1999, c. 33 (London: Sweet & Maxwell); Macdonald & Webber, *Macdonald's Immigration Law and Practice* (London: Butterworths, 2001), Ch. 12.

[74] These were: General Immigration; Carriers' Liability; Bail; Appeals; Immigration Advisers and Immigration Service Providers; Support for Asylum Seekers; Power to Arrest, Search and Fingerprint; Detention Centres and Detained Person; Registrar's Certificates; Miscellaneous and Supplemental.

- the replacement of previous rights of appeal in asylum cases, and the introduction of a 'one-stop appeal' procedure;[75]

- the introduction of a new Human Rights Act 1998 appeal;[76]

- the introduction of statutory bail hearings for detainees, and a presumption in favour of bail;[77]

- the continued, though reformed, use of detention for asylum seekers;[78]

- the introduction of numerous proposals to strengthen immigration controls before, on and after entry to the UK, including the power of immigration officers to enter and search premises, arrest without warrant, and use of reasonable force;[79]

- the expansion of the criminalising of the use of deception to obtain leave to enter or remain, or to avoid enforcement action;[80]

- the creation of a new penalty for carrying clandestine entrants, enabling the government to fine those responsible and to detain their vehicles, ships or aircraft;[81]

- the retention of section 8 of the Asylum and Immigration Act 1996;

- the withdrawal of all remaining rights to social security benefits, the amendment of the National Assistance Act 1948 and homelessness legislation (removing responsibility for the support of destitute or homeless asylum seekers from local authorities);

- the introduction of 'support in kind' in place of the 1996 maintenance provisions;[82]

- the imposition of a duty on marriage registrars to report 'suspicious marriages'.[83]

Since the passing of the Nationality, Immigration and Appeals Act 2002, some of the provisions of the 1999 Act have been repealed,

---

[75] ss. 69–73 and s. 74.
[76] s. 65.
[77] ss. 44–54.
[78] ss. 147–159.
[79] ss. 128–146.
[80] s. 28.
[81] s. 32.
[82] ss. 94–127.
[83] s. 24.

some have been amended and some remain unchanged.[84] The discussion below does not take account of subsequent changes; these will be highlighted in the section on the 2002 Act.

Appeals

5.14   The scheme for asylum appeals remained the same as under the 1993 Act: the appeal (set out in s. 69) was against the immigration decision which arose from a refusal of asylum, namely: the refusal of leave to enter and the issue of removal directions;[85] the refusal to vary leave and requirement to depart;[86] a deportation order;[87] or the issue of removal directions against an illegal entrant.[88] No one could bring an appeal under s. 69 unless he or she had lodged an asylum claim,[89] and the ground for appeal in these cases was that removal would be contrary to the 1951 Convention. Section 15 protected asylum claimants from removal or deportation pending the decision by the Home Secretary on the claim, reflecting a similar provision in the 1996 Act (s. 6). One exception to this prohibition, however, was safe third country removals (see below). As previously, any appeal was to an adjudicator, and then, in certain cases, to the IAT and the Court of Appeal.[90]

The practice of certification of cases, developed and extended in the 1993 and 1996 Acts, was maintained in the 1999 Act. However, the controversial 'white list' was removed by the 1999 Act, and the list of certifiable claims was set out in sch. 4, para. 9. Unless there was a reasonable likelihood that an appellant had been tortured in a country to which he was to be sent,[91] the following circumstances would lead to certification:

---

[84] See Appendix A for details of repeals and amendments of sections referred to in this chapter.

[85] s. 69(1). Removal directions originally applied to illegal entrants and did not carry a right of appeal. The Immigration and Asylum Act 1999, s. 10 extended summary removal to overstayers. Asylum claimants were generally protected from removal (s. 15) unless they were returned to 'safe third countries' (ss. 11 & 12).

[86] s. 69(2).

[87] s. 69(4). A deportation order is an order requiring an individual to leave the UK and preventing him or her from entering (Immigration Act 1971, s. 5(1)).

[88] s. 69(5).

[89] s. 70(7). Note that an appeal could only be brought under s. 69 if a claim for asylum was made *before* the decision or action was taken against which he or she was appealing: *e.g.* the refusal of leave to enter.

[90] The term 'special adjudicator' was replaced by 'adjudicator'.

[91] sch. 4, para. 9(7).

- failure to produce a passport on request without reasonable explanation;[92]

- production of an invalid passport without admission;[93]

- failure to show fear of persecution for a 1951 Convention ground;[94]

- a fear of persecution is shown but it is manifestly unfounded or the circumstances giving rise to the fear no longer subsist;[95]

- the claim is made following refusal of leave to enter, recommendation or decision to deport, or notification of removal;[96]

- the claim is manifestly fraudulent or the evidence adduced in its support is manifestly false;[97]

- the claim is frivolous or vexatious.[98]

If on appeal an adjudicator agreed with the Home Secretary's certification, there was no further appeal to the IAT. The 1999 Act and accompanying Appeals Rules extended the time limits for appealing and provided a uniform time limit for all cases.[99] The dual procedures for standard and fast-tracked cases were thus removed, although a distinction still existed between in-country and out-of-country appeals. For in-country appellants, notice of appeal had to be given no later than ten days after notice of the decision was received;[100] out-of-country appeals had 28 days following departure in which to lodge an appeal.[101] Appellants who were already out-of-country also had 28 days from the date on which they received the refusal in which to appeal.[102] These time scales were much more realistic than those provided under the 1993 Act.

5.15

In a bold move, the Act also introduced a completely novel appeal right: it was now open to an asylum seeker to argue that an authority had, 'in taking any decision [. . .] relating to that person's entitlement to enter or remain in the United Kingdom acted in breach of his [or her] human rights' (that is, by acting or failing to act in a way which

---

[92] sch. 4, para. 9(3)(a).
[93] sch. 4, para. 9(3)(b).
[94] sch. 4, para. 9(4)(a).
[95] sch. 4, para. 9(4)(b).
[96] sch. 4, para. 9(6)(a).
[97] sch. 4, para. 9(6)(b).
[98] sch. 4, para. 9(6)(c).
[99] Immigration and Asylum Appeals (Procedure) Rules 2000, SI 2000/2333.
[100] r. 6(1).
[101] r. 6(2).
[102] r. 6(2)(b).

is made unlawful by s. 6(1) of the Human Rights Act 1998).[103] For the purposes of the appeal, an 'authority' included the Secretary of State, an immigration officer, or an entry clearance officer. The important aspect of this new appeal was that it was either wholly free-standing[104] or could be attached to another asylum/immigration appeal.[105] However, the rights associated with a human rights appeal could be curtailed, for example, by the Home Secretary certifying that an allegation of breach of human rights was 'manifestly unfounded',[106] or, where an appeal had already been heard, that such a claim should have been raised earlier and that the purpose of the claim was to delay removal from the UK.[107] The latter determined the appeal once and for all, and, in safe third country cases, the former resulted in removal before an appeal was heard (see below).[108]

Safe third country appeals

5.16   An exception to the above framework was provided in the case of safe third country cases. As has been described, the 1996 Act removed an in-country right of appeal for safe third country cases because the majority of 'without foundation' certifications, as defined under the 1993 Act, were found to be safe third country.[109] Dissatisfied with these changes, the government introduced, rather late in the day, further amendments in the 1999 Act on safe third country cases. Sections 11 and 12 replaced s. 2 of the 1996 Act and altered the rules on certification of such cases. Whereas previously the Home Secretary was required to certify that certain conditions applied (that the returnee was not a national or citizen of the country to which he was to be sent; that his life and liberty would not be threatened for a Convention reason; and that the government of that country would not *refoule* him),[110] the new provisions imposed no such onerous obligations. Instead, where EU Member States were involved, the Home Secretary had to certify that the state to which the applicant was to be sent had accepted responsibility for handling the claim under the 'standing arrangements' (in other words, according to the Dublin

---

[103] s. 6(1) states that: 'It is unlawful for a public authority to act in away which is incompatible with a Convention right.'
[104] s. 65(1).
[105] s. 65(3).
[106] s. 72(2)(a).
[107] s. 73(2).
[108] ss. 72(2)(a) and 73(3).
[109] Asylum and Immigration Act 1996, s. 2.
[110] *ibid.*, s. 2(2).

Convention), and that the applicant was not a national or citizen of
that state.[111] Removal then followed, so long as the certificate had
not been set aside on human rights grounds (under s. 65). There was
therefore a presumption of safety for those countries that had signed
up to the Dublin Convention, a presumption that was arguably misplaced. Section 12 dealt with removal to an EU Member State but
not under the standing arrangements, or to a country which the Secretary of State designated by order, or to one which fell into neither
of these categories.[112] In the second instance, the usual suspects were
listed: Canada, Norway, Switzerland and the USA.[113] Section 12
removals were slightly less stringent than those of s. 11 in that certification could only take place if the 'old' conditions applied: that the
returnee was not a national or citizen of the country to which he was
to be sent; that his life and liberty would not be threatened for a
Convention reason; and that the government of that country would
not *refoule* him.[114] There was therefore more chance of a successful
challenge to certification in such cases.

The appeal rights associated with third country cases also had a
limiting effect. It was open to an applicant to appeal to an adjudicator against a certificate but only on the grounds that the conditions on
which the certificate was based were not satisfied when issued, or had
since ceased to be satisfied.[115] The likelihood of succeeding on such
an appeal was remote for s. 11 cases involving EU Member States.
Furthermore, the Act ensured that a challenge to a certificate could
only be made out-of-country for Member States and designated
countries.[116] By contrast, return to a non-Member State or non-
designated country did earn an in-country appeal right.[117]

Since an in-country appeal was out of the question where return
was to a Member State, and since appealing against the certificate
was very unlikely to succeed, one was left with the impression that a
challenge to removal in such circumstances was almost hypothetical.
However, there was one further route of appeal, open to applicants in
all removal cases: the s. 65 human rights appeal. Here, a possible
human rights argument was that the state to which the individual
was to be sent was likely to *refoule* him or her and that this would
therefore constitute a breach of Art. 3 of the ECHR. It should be
noted, however, that this in-country appeal would be lost if the

---

[111] s. 11(2)(a).
[112] ss. 12(1)(a),(b) and 12(4).
[113] The Asylum (Designated Third Countries) Order 2000, SI 2000/2245.
[114] s. 12(7).
[115] s. 71(2).
[116] *ibid.*
[117] *ibid.*

Secretary of State certified that the allegation of breach of human rights was itself manifestly unfounded.[118] Of course, this still left open a challenge to the certification of 'manifestly unfounded' by way of judicial review, leaving one to conclude that if the legislation was an attempt to close off judicial review, it was unlikely to be an overwhelming success.

One-stop appeals

5.17 One further significant addition to the appeals process in asylum cases was the introduction of a 'one-stop appeal'. The government had been frustrated by the multiplicity of appeals available under the previous regime and which could be used by an individual to delay departure. Under the Immigration Act 1971 and the Asylum and Immigration Appeals Act 1993, 'it was possible for an applicant to enjoy an appeal under the rules (*e.g.* a student appeal), then a deportation appeal for overstaying, and finally an appeal against a refusal to revoke a deportation order, on asylum grounds.'[119] Following failure at all these stages, a member of the principal applicant's family could then apply for asylum, with further appeals, thereby delaying departure of the whole family yet again.[120] To prevent exploitation of the system, the Act provided for the issue of a one-stop notice in certain circumstances. The notice required that all additional grounds for remaining in the UK were clearly stated.[121] Failure to do so barred consideration on appeal, unless they were asylum, human rights, or discrimination grounds, or the Home Secretary considered that the applicant had a reasonable excuse for omission, or was not aware of the ground at the time.[122] Even if asylum were claimed after the statement had been sent, it was still open to the Secretary of State to certify that the purpose of the claim was to delay removal from the UK and there was no other legitimate reason for making the claim.[123] The consequence of such certification was that no appeal could then be made under s. 69. Human rights or discrimination issues could still be raised though, as no certification applied to these.

---

[118] s. 72(2)(a).

[119] Macdonald & Webber, *Macdonald's Immigration Law and Practice* (London: Butterworths, 2001), para. 18.109.

[120] *ibid.*, para. 18.108.

[121] See Immigration and Asylum Appeals (One-Stop Procedure) Regulations 2000, SI 2000/2244.

[122] Immigration and Asylum Act 1999, s. 76(2)(b), s. 76(3)(a) (as amended by the Race Relations (Amendment) Act 2000, sch. 2, para. 38) and s. 76(3)(b).

[123] Immigration and Asylum Act 1999, s. 76(5).

Detention and bail

The detention of asylum seekers has long been in practice. The wide **5.18** and somewhat unchecked power to detain was originally granted by the Immigration Act 1971.[124] A decision to detain is often taken by an immigration officer, although asylum applicants may also be detained following directions to remove them or when they apply for asylum once deportation action is commenced.[125] Instructions on detention criteria have been issued to immigration personnel and are also described in the Immigration and Nationality Directorate's Asylum Policy Instructions, which are now publicly available:[126]

'Detention is only used when there is no alternative and there are good grounds for believing that the person will not keep in touch voluntarily. When deciding whether or not to detain someone factors such as whether there is a sponsor, satisfactory evidence of ID and past immigration history, and whether detention accommodation is available should be considered.'[127]

According to the Immigration Service Instructions on Detention of December 1991, 'the policy remains to grant temporary admission/release wherever possible'.[128] Numerous criteria are listed setting out the factors to be taken into consideration in determining whether detention is appropriate.[129] The 1999 Act continued the policy of detention and placed the then detention system on a statutory footing. Part VIII of the Act provided for the management and operation of detention centres, clarified the responsibilities of detainee custody officers, and allowed for the distribution of rules on the regulation and management of detention centres, now published as the Detention Centre Rules 2001.[130]

The issue of detention raises the associated question of release. The rules regarding release and bail arise from the Immigration Act

---

[124] Immigration Act 1971, sch. 2, para.16.

[125] Asylum Policy Instructions, 'Deciding Claims – Handling Claims – Detention', para. 4.1.

[126] See Immigration Service Instructions, December 3, 1991 and September 20, 1994 available in *Butterworths Immigration Law Service*, Vol. I; Asylum Policy Instructions available at *www.ind.homeoffice.gov.uk/default.asp?PageId=711*

[127] Asylum Policy Instructions, 'Deciding Claims – Handling Claims – Detention', para. 4.1.

[128] See, for copy, *Butterworths Immigration Law Service* D[971].

[129] See Immigration Service Instruction on Detention, December 3, 1991; Immigration Service Instruction on Detention, September 20, 1994 and Immigration Directorate's Instructions, Section C, Chapter 31, Section 1 Detention Annexe A, January 1997, available in *Butterworths Immigration Law Service* D[977–979].

[130] SI 2001/238.

1971, sch. 2, and have been amended over the years by the Asylum and Immigration Act 1996 and the Immigration and Asylum Act 1999. A detainee is entitled to apply for bail from the Chief Immigration Officer, a police inspector (or higher), or an adjudicator, and bail may be granted as long as seven days have elapsed and a recognisance is entered into.[131] Past operational guidelines indicated that a figure of between £2,000 and £5,000 per surety would normally be appropriate.[132] The guidelines also set out a list of factors to be taken into consideration in assessing the acceptability of any surety.[133]

The Immigration and Asylum Act 1999 incorporated a fundamental amendment to the previous bail provisions: the introduction of a statutory *right* to bail through two routine bail hearings, the first to take place no later than the tenth day following detention, and the second no later than the thirty-eighth day.[134] Certain exceptions applied, such as deportation cases on the recommendation of a court.[135] Furthermore, a completely new presumption in favour of bail was included which required the court to release the detained person on bail unless it was satisfied that the detainee would: fail to comply with the conditions of bail or any recognizance; commit an imprisonable offence while on bail; be likely to cause danger to public health; or be a serious threat to public order.[136] Further exceptions also applied under the Act and could be introduced at a later date by the Secretary of State.[137] Unfortunately, while this comprehensive scheme was provided for by statute, its implementation was dependent on secondary legislation, which was not forthcoming. As will be seen, the government indicated its intention to renege on its obligations under the 1999 Act when it announced in a new White Paper in February 2002 that Part III, on bail, was to be repealed. This was subsequently carried through in the Nationality, Immigration and Asylum Act 2002.[138]

Carriers' liability and clandestine entrants

5.19   Alongside detention, carriers' liability has also become a mainstay of UK immigration policy. Introduced in 1987 under the Immigration

---

[131]   Immigration Act 1971, sch. 2, para. 22.
[132]   *Immigration Nationality Directorate Operational Enforcement Manual*, December 21, 2000, para. 39.5.1.
[133]   *ibid.*, 39.5.2.
[134]   ss. 44(7)(b)(i) and (ii).
[135]   s. 44(3)(b), and see, generally, s. 44(3).
[136]   s. 46
[137]   ss. 46(3) and 46(8).
[138]   s. 68, and see below.

(Carriers' Liability) Act to cover ships and aircraft,[139] carriers' liability was extended by secondary legislation in 1998 to include passenger trains from Belgium.[140] The 1999 Act, though repealing the
1987 statute, replaced its core with a number of new ss. (40–42) and
brought road passenger vehicles within its power. The definition of
road passenger vehicles was intended to cover commercial vehicles
only and excluded taxis.[141] The same sanctions applied under the
1999 Act as under earlier (amended) legislation. Thus any owner of a
ship, aircraft, or road passenger vehicle, or the operator of a train,
would face a charge of £2,000 for each passenger who arrived in the
UK without the requisite documentation.[142] The new provisions went
one stage further than previously and empowered senior officers to
detain transporters pending payment of any charge.[143]

Carriers faced a heavy onus to establish that all passengers were
carrying the correct documentation. There were, however, a number
of defences: if a document was produced on embarkation, the Secretary of State could only sanction the carrier where it was 'reasonably
apparent' that the document was false.[144] Further defences provide
that owners and train operators be exempted from charges if they
could show that under the law of the country of embarkation they
were not permitted to require production of the required documents;
that there were in place satisfactory arrangements to ensure that passengers who did not have the correct documentation were not carried; that all practicable steps were taken to establish that passengers
had the required documentation, and, where they did not, that they
did not reach the UK.[145]

In addition to these amendments, Part II of the 1999 Act introduced a completely new civil penalty for those responsible for the
transport of 'clandestine entrants' to the UK.[146] Whereas the 1987
Act and the related provisions of the 1999 Act focused on the carriage
of undocumented passengers, the new provision, in s. 32, was
concerned with the growing problem of clandestine asylum seekers.
A clandestine entrant is defined as someone who: arrives in the UK

---

[139] Ch. 3.
[140] Channel Tunnel (Carriers' Liability) Order 1998, SI 1998/1015.
[141] See s. 40(11).
[142] ss. 40(1) and (2).
[143] s. 42.
[144] See ss. 40(4) and (6) and *R. v Secretary of State for the Home Department, ex parte Hoverspeed* [1999] INLR 591, at 601, where it was held, in relation to the 1987 Act, that
'it is for the carrier in the first instance to establish that a purported travel document
was produced to him and, if that burden is discharged, that the Secretary of State
can only then charge if he proves the document's falsity to have been reasonably
apparent'.
[145] s. 40(5).
[146] s. 32.

concealed in a vehicle, ship or aircraft; passes or tries to pass through immigration control concealed in a vehicle; or arrives in the UK on a ship or aircraft, having embarked outside the UK while concealed therein. The concealed individual must also either claim or intend to claim asylum in the UK, or evade or attempt to evade immigration control.[147] Any 'responsible person', that is an owner or captain of a ship or aircraft, or the owner, hirer or driver of a vehicle, in which a clandestine was found, was liable to a penalty of £2,000 per clandestine.[148] As under s. 40, a senior officer was entitled to detain any vehicle or craft where he or she considered that there was a significant risk that the penalty would not be paid within the required time.[149] The only defences which the carrier could raise were that he or she, or an employee, was (i) acting under duress,[150] or (ii) that he or she did not know and had no reason to suspect that a clandestine entrant might be concealed in the transporter; that an effective system for preventing the carriage of clandestines was in operation; and that the system was operated properly on the occasion in question.[151] To assist operators, the government produced Codes of Practice for vehicular and rail transport.[152]

Employers' liability

5.20   Section 8 of the Asylum and Immigration Act 1996 introduced a new criminal offence for employers who employed persons subject to immigration control who were not entitled to work in the UK. Until recently, some asylum seekers did have permission to find employment. This concession, which had existed since 1986, was ended in July 2002.

According to the Home Office, the historical concession had become 'increasingly irrelevant' in view of the fact that the majority of asylum seekers receive an initial decision within six months. Instead, £1 million was to be invested in 'a substantial programme of "summer activities" for asylum seekers' and the rules on voluntary work undertaken by asylum seekers were to be reviewed.[153]

---

[147] s. 32(1).
[148] s. 32(2).
[149] s. 36(1) and (2).
[150] s. 34(2).
[151] s. 34(3).
[152] Carriers' Liability (Clandestine Entrants)(Code of Practice) Order 2000, SI 2000/684; Carriers' Liability (Clandestine Entrants)(Code of Practice for Rail Freight) Order 2001, SI 2001/312.
[153] Home Office Press Release, 'Faster asylum decisions – historical employment concession ended', July 23, 2002.

The only concrete change to the legislation made by the Immigration and Asylum Act 1999 was an amendment to s. 8 requiring the Secretary of State to publish a Code of Practice for employers. This was agreed by the government in order to assuage fears that employers might discriminate on racial grounds as a result of the law. The Code was finally published on May 2, 2001, and is available in full on the IND website.[154]

Sham marriages

One of the more unusual aspects of the 1999 Act was the statutory introduction of a new duty on marriage registrars to report so-called 'suspicious' or 'sham' marriages. While registrars were already required to report such marriages, the Act brought the existing procedure onto a statutory footing. A 'sham marriage' is defined as a marriage '(a) entered into 'between a person ('A') who is neither a British citizen nor a national of an EEA state other than the United Kingdom and another person (whether or not such a citizen or such a national); and (b) entered into by A for the purpose of avoiding the effect of one or more provisions of United Kingdom immigration law or the immigration rules.'[155]   **5.21**

Beyond this definition, there is no explanation of how a registrar is expected to recognise a sham marriage. It was suggested by some that an implicit requirement for a sham marriage is that the parties do not intend to live together as man and wife.[156] The White Paper described a 'bogus marriage' as 'one arranged for the sole purpose of evading statutory immigration controls'.[157] Any marriage found to be sham would prevent the party concerned from obtaining a right to enter or remain.

Criminal offences

One of the key features of the 1999 Act was its focus on criminal activity in the immigration and asylum fields. The first area of consideration involves the activities of the individual asylum seeker. Since 1971, and the Immigration Act of that year, it has been an offence   **5.22**

---

[154] For the full Code, go to *www.ind.homeoffice.gov.uk/default.asp?PageId=1366*
[155] s. 24(5).
[156] MacDonald & Webber, *Macdonald's Immigration Law & Practice* (London: Butterworths, 2001), para. 11.46.
[157] Home Office White Paper, *Fairer, Faster and Firmer – A Modern Approach to Immigration and Asylum*, Cm. 4018, July 1998, para. 11.4.

'knowingly' to enter the UK in breach of a deportation order or without authority.[158] Such an offence may be described as 'illegal entry'. In 1996, a further offence was added – the use of deception to obtain leave to enter or remain.[159] The 1999 Act replaced this 1996 section with a new, expanded version:

'A person who is not a British citizen is guilty of an offence if, by means which include deception by him –

(a) he obtains or seeks to obtain leave to enter or remain in the United Kingdom; or
(b) he secures or seeks to secure the avoidance, postponement or revocation of enforcement action against him.'[160]

It is clear from the wording of this offence that the government was seeking to tackle what it perceived as a growing problem of fraudulent asylum claims. It is wide enough to cover the submission of false evidence in support of an application and the failure to admit that false documentation has been presented to an immigration officer. The possible sanctions for the offence have also been increased. They include, on summary conviction, imprisonment for up to six months and/or a fine up to the statutory maximum, or imprisonment for up to two years and/or a fine, for conviction on indictment.[161]

5.23   The second area of concern for the government related to the activities of the so-called immigration racketeers. As in the case of illegal entry, the Immigration Act 1971 already contained a prohibition against assisting any person to enter the UK where there was reasonable cause to believe that the person concerned was an illegal entrant (s. 25(1)). Various amendments have been made to s. 25(1), including an important change by the Asylum and Immigration Act 1996: facilitating the entry into the UK of anyone whom one knows, or has reasonable cause to believe, is an asylum seeker.[162] The use of deception in facilitating entry is also covered.[163] The legislation targets those who profit by bringing individuals into the UK who apply for asylum. It is not intended to be used in the prosecution of 'anything done to assist an asylum claimant by a person in the course of his employment by a *bona fide* organisation, if the purposes of that

---

[158] Immigration Act 1971, s. 24(1)(a).
[159] Asylum and Immigration Act 1996, s. 4, inserting s. 24(1)(aa) in the Immigration Act 1971.
[160] Immigration and Asylum Act 1999, s. 28, inserting s. 24A(1) in the Immigration Act 1971.
[161] The current maximum fine is £5,000.
[162] Immigration Act 1971, s. 25(1)(b).
[163] *ibid.*, s. 25(1)(c).

organisation include assistance to persons in the position of the asylum claimant'.[164] Nor is it intended to prohibit help being provided to those in detention or on temporary admission.[165] For the purposes of this section, 'asylum seeker' is given a broader definition to include not only those who should not be removed from the UK in accordance with the obligations under the 1951 Convention, but also those who are protected by the ECHR.[166] In recognition of the seriousness with which the government regarded the above offences, the 1999 Act raised the maximum term of imprisonment from seven to ten years. The possible sanctions were changed to read: a fine up to the prescribed maximum and/or imprisonment for up to six months on summary conviction, or, for conviction on indictment, a fine and/or imprisonment for up to ten years.[167]

Increased powers for immigration officers

While immigration officers have always possessed powers to assist their enforcement of the law, the 1999 Act augmented the range of those powers and brought them into line with those of the police.[168] Thus immigration officers can now enter and search premises with or without a warrant; they may arrest individuals for breach of certain immigration laws; and they are entitled to use reasonable force where executing a warrant.[169] This expansion of powers has also engaged the Police and Criminal Evidence Act 1984 ('PACE') and the protection of some aspects of the PACE Codes of Practice therefore applies.[170]

    The power of immigration officers to fingerprint asylum applicants was included in the Asylum and Immigration Appeals Act 1993 and is endorsed by ss. 141–143 of the 1999 Act. Simply stated, authorised persons (immigration officers, police, prison officers, *inter alia*) are empowered to fingerprint all asylum seekers, including

5.24

---

[164] Immigration and Asylum Act 1999, s. 29(3), amending s. 25(1A) in the Immigration Act 1971.

[165] Immigration and Asylum Act 1999, s. 29(3), amending s. 25(1C) in the Immigration Act 1971.

[166] *ibid.*

[167] Immigration Act 1971, s. 25(1).

[168] ss. 128–139.

[169] ss. 128–132; 134–135; 141; 146, and see ss. 137, 138 and 140 for safegu~ search warrants.

[170] See Immigration (PACE Codes of Practice) Direction 2000, February ˊ Immigration (PACE Codes of Practice No 2 and Amendment) Dˊ November 19, 2000.

dependants.[171] Children under sixteen may only be fingerprinted in the presence of a parent, guardian, or other adult responsible for the child in question.[172]

Accommodation and social security

5.25   While previous legislation witnessed the gradual erosion of welfare provision for asylum seekers, the Immigration and Asylum Act 1999 provided a complete restructuring of the system.[173] From April 3, 2000, when the Social Security (Immigration and Asylum) Consequential Amendments Regulations 2000 came into force,[174] non-contributory social security benefits were ended for 'persons subject to immigration control', including asylum seekers.[175] A 51–year old Act, the National Assistance Act 1948, which had been used by the judiciary to provide protection for potentially destitute asylum seekers refused local authority housing,[176] was specifically excluded.[177] A new mechanism for support was introduced by the Act, the National Asylum Support Service ('NASS'), whereby certain asylum claimants were provided with support and accommodation, or support only.[178] The Secretary of State was under no duty to provide support but was simply empowered to do so.[179] Where an asylum seeker applied for support and appeared to be 'destitute' or 'likely to become destitute' within the prescribed period,[180] he or she *might* be entitled to receive support.[181] If, however, an asylum

---

[171] s. 141.

[172] s. 141(3).

[173] See, for a discussion of the welfare implications of the 1999 Act, P. Billings, 'Alienating asylum seekers: Welfare support in the Immigration and Asylum Act 1999' (2002) 2, *Journal of social Security Law*, pp. 115–144; S. Willman, S. Knafler & S. Pierce, *A Guide to Legal and Welfare Rights – Support for Asylum Seekers* (London: Legal Action Group, 2001).

[174] SI 2000/636.

[175] s. 115. The benefits covered are: income support; income-based jobseeker's allowance; attendance allowance; invalid care allowance; severe disablement allowance; disability living allowance; working families tax credit; disabled person's tax credit; child benefit; housing benefit; council tax benefit; and social fund payments. Note that asylum seekers are not excluded from claiming contributory benefits – such as job seeker's allowance, incapacity benefit, and maternity allowance – but are unlikely to have contributed sufficiently to qualify.

[176] See *R. v Hammersmith and Fulham LBC, ex parte M*; *R. v Lambeth LBC, ex parte P and X*; *R. v Westminster CC, ex parte A* [1997] 1 CCLR 69.

[177] s. 116.

[178] See Pt VI and schs. 8 & 10; Asylum Support Regulations 2000, 2000/704; Asylum Support Appeals (Procedure) Rules 2000, 2000/541.

[179] s. 95(1).

[180] See s. 95(3), and the Asylum Support Regulations 2000, 2000/704, regs. 7 & 10(6). Originally, 14 days; later extended to 28 days.

[181] s. 95(1).

seeker with dependent children applied and was found to be destitute within the meaning of s. 95(3), the Secretary of State was *required* to provide support as local authority assistance for children and their families was specifically excluded.[182]

NASS, based in the Home Office's Immigration and Nationality Directorate, determined the eligibility of an asylum seeker for support by considering his or her actual or potential resources. Support was arranged by NASS through contracts with private, public and voluntary bodies. It covered accommodation adequate for the needs of the supported person, essential living needs, non-legal expenses incurred in connection with the asylum claim, expenses incurred to attend bail proceedings, and any other support for exceptional circumstances.[183] Under the 1999 Act, it normally took the form of accommodation, if required, vouchers, exchangeable in certain shops, and some cash (originally £10 per person per week).[184] In addition, asylum seekers were entitled to free treatment under the National Health Service and were able to receive free medicines and other services as long as they held an exemption certificate (HC2). Children of asylum seekers were entitled to be treated in the same way as British children and had a right to education.

The amount received in vouchers was dependent on the status of **5.26** the individual. For example, in early 2003, a single person aged 25 or over was entitled to £38.26 per week; a couple to £60.03 per week; and a child under 16 to £38.50.[185] As for the accommodation offered, it was the purpose of the Act to disperse asylum seekers around the country in an attempt to address the problems faced by London and Kent due to a concentration of asylum seekers. Accommodation was offered on a no-choice basis and any preference of the asylum seeker as to the locality of his or her accommodation was not taken into account.[186] The original aim of dispersal was to send asylum seekers to cluster areas outside the South East where their language was spoken, but this has proved almost impossible to achieve.[187] Where an

---

[182] ss. 122(2)–(6).

[183] s. 96.

[184] Note that on October 29, 2001, the Home Secretary announced that he intended to phase out vouchers by autumn 2002: Home Office Press Release, 'Radical reform unveiled for more robust asylum system', October 29, 2001. As from April 8, 2002, the system was replaced by cash support, and from September 23, 2002, applicants were transferred from receipt book to Application Registration Card ('ARC') payments.

[185] Asylum Support (Amendment)(No 2) Regulations 2003, SI 2003/755. Current levels are available on the NASS website: *www.ind.homeoffice.gov.uk/*

[186] s. 97(2)(a).

[187] *Report of the Operational Reviews of the Voucher and Dispersal Schemes of the National Asylum Support Service*, October 29, 2001, para. 3.2.2.

asylum claim was withdrawn, refused, or granted, entitlement to support ceased. An asylum seeker then had 14 days in which to find alternative means of support.[188] Refugees or those with ELR[189] became eligible to apply for welfare benefits and for housing under the Housing Act 1996.

An asylum seeker refused support or accommodation could appeal. A new appeals mechanism was established under s. 103 and sch. 10 to the Act. The asylum support adjudicator was granted jurisdiction to hear appeals against the refusal or cessation of support by the Home Secretary, but not against the type or level of support. In contrast to the traditional immigration adjudicators, these new adjudicators were appointed by the Home Secretary, and questions have therefore been raised about their impartiality.[190] The rules governing the appeals process in support cases were contained in the Asylum Support (Appeals) Procedure Rules 2000.[191] The main focus of the procedure was speed,[192] and there was only one level of appeal: to the adjudicator. Since the inception of the Asylum Support Appeals system, the number of appeals made has been on the rise. Between April and December 2000, only 139 appeals were received;[193] in 2001, a total of 1,342 appeals were lodged, and in 2002, 3,845 were received.[194]

THE FINAL ACT? THE NATIONALITY, IMMIGRATION AND
ASYLUM ACT 2002

Background

5.27   In view of the extensive changes to UK immigration and asylum law introduced by the 1999 Act, it was somewhat surprising when, on February 7, 2002, the government published yet another document

---

[188] Asylum Support Regulations 2000, 2000/704, reg. 2(2).

[189] As of April 1, 2003, ELR ceased to exist and was replaced by Humanitarian Protection and Discretionary Leave: APU Notice 01/2003, 'Humanitarian protection and discretionary leave'.

[190] See, *e.g.*, S. Willman, S. Knafler & S. Pierce, *A Guide to Legal and Welfare Rights – Support for Asylum Seekers* (London: Legal Action Group, 2001), para. 3.140 querying whether there were implications under the Human Rights Act 1998, Art. 6(1).

[191] SI 2000/541.

[192] See s. 104(3): appeals should be brought and disposed of 'with the minimum of delay'.

[193] S. Willman, S. Knafler & S. Pierce, *A Guide to Legal and Welfare Rights – Support for Asylum Seekers* (London: Legal Action Group, 2001), para. 3.141.

[194] See ASA website for statistical and other useful information: *www.asylum-support-adjudicators.org.uk/about/index.shtml*.

setting out its revised vision for the future of asylum policy in the UK: *Secure Borders, Safe Haven – Integration with Diversity in Modern Britain*.[195] This White Paper was described by the Secretary of State, David Blunkett, as 'offering an holistic and comprehensive approach to nationality, managed immigration and asylum that recognises the interrelationship of each element in the system'.[196] Chapter 4, of eight, is specifically devoted to 'Asylum', while a number of other chapters contain proposals relevant to asylum law and policy: 'Tackling Fraud – People Trafficking, Illegal Entry and Illegal Working' (Ch. 5), 'Border Controls' (Ch. 6), and 'Marriage/Family Visits and War Criminals' (Ch. 7).

Once more, the suggested changes on asylum were wide-ranging and touched on all stages of the asylum process. The key reforms were described as follows:

- 'Preparing a resettlement programme to establish gateways for those most in need of protection to come here legally.

- Introducing a managed system of induction, accommodation, reporting and removal centres to secure a seamless asylum process.

- Introducing an Application Registration Card to provide more secure and certain evidence of identity and nationality.

- Phasing out voucher support.

- Better assisting Unaccompanied Asylum Seeking Children and sharing support for these children across a wider number of local authorities while sifting out adults posing as children.

- Streamlining our appeals system to minimise delay and cut down barriers to removal.

- Increasing the number of removals of people who have no claim to stay here.

- Enhancing refugee integration through our Refugee Integration Programme and labour market measures.'[197]

In addition, the White Paper promised to strengthen the law against people traffickers and smugglers,[198] develop new initiatives and improve technologies to control borders,[199] and strengthen the

---

[195] Cm 5387.
[196] HC Deb. Vol. 379, February 7, 2002, col. 1027.
[197] para. 4.15.
[198] paras 5.22–5.30.
[199] paras 6.4–6.22.

194

CHAPTER FIVE

ability to deal with suspected and convicted war criminals.[200] It acknowledged for the first time that alternative routes of migration needed to be established, partly in order to counter an increase in illegal smuggling and the use of the asylum process as an avenue to immigration, but also in recognition of the benefits brought to the UK by economic migration. Thus it advocated the adoption of a Highly Skilled Migrants Programme, the option for postgraduates to switch into employment, and the extension of the seasonal workers' scheme. The White Paper also proposed improving naturalisation procedures and opening up appeals once more for all asylum cases from the adjudicator to the IAT. In contrast to previous discussion documents on the same subjects, many aspects of the 2002 White Paper were cautiously welcomed by NGOs.[201] Notwithstanding the guarded reception, there were, as expected, a number of areas of concern: the insufficiently radical reform of migration policy; the extension of discriminatory border controls; and, in the field of asylum, the establishment of induction, accommodation, reporting and removal centres, the repeal of the automatic bail hearings provided for by the 1999 Act, and the limitation of appeals against refusals.[202]

On April 12, 2002, the new Bill was published and introduced in the House of Commons. The Home Office heralded its arrival as follows:

'The Nationality, Immigration and Asylum Bill sets out a comprehensive range of provisions to deliver an efficient and robust immigration system. It would improve the security of UK immigration controls, crack down on those who try to abuse them, and build the confidence necessary to head off threats to good race relations and strong social cohesion.'[203]

5.28   The Home Secretary was bullish in his presentation of the Bill to Parliament, accusing both colleagues and opponents of misinterpreting its measures and complaining that he had hoped for greater unanimity.[204] He had some cause for concern; only four months after the Second Reading, a critical report on the Bill was published by the

---

[200] para. 7.21.

[201] See, for example, Refugee Council, *Response to Secure Borders, Safe Haven: Integration with Diversity in Modern Britain*, February 2002; Immigration Advisory Service, *IAS response to the White Paper "Secure Borders, Safe Haven: Integration with Diversity in Modern Britain"*, March 22, 2002.

[202] JCWI, *JCWI's Initial Response to the White Paper Secure Borders, Safe Haven: Integration with Diversity in Modern Britain*, February 2002.

[203] Home Office Press Release, 'Trust and confidence in our nationality, immigration and asylum system – Bill published', April 12, 2002.

[204] HC Deb. Vol. 384, April 24, 2002, col. 341.

Joint Committee on Human Rights.[205] The original measures were subject to considerable revision. Employing the same tactics as in 1999, the government introduced a range of amendments during the various Parliamentary stages, some so late in the process that they failed to be subjected to adequate debate and scrutiny. The impetus to amend the Bill was due in part to the Home Secretary's harsher stance on asylum, which became increasingly evident as the year progressed. For example, in early October, towards the end of the Bill's lifespan, David Blunkett suddenly announced that a new 'white list' would be introduced to prevent people from the ten EU accession states from being granted asylum. He also declared that the presumption of support for in-country applicants would be ended and that asylum seekers would have to claim asylum at the earliest opportunity.[206] In an interview with BBC Radio 4's Today programme, he said:

> 'The message has got out that if you get here and you claim asylum, then we'll support you. . . . Well, that's absolutely crazy. We'd have to be absolutely mad to say "come here, have a holiday and we'll pick up the tab".'[207]

Both Houses fought a number of battles in an attempt to wring concessions from the government. There was a modicum of success when peers inflicted three defeats on the government. They rejected plans to: (i) deport refugees who commit a 'serious crime' and who are sentenced to at least two years (ten years was proposed instead); (ii) establish accommodation centres with capacity for 750 asylum seekers (250 was set as the limit); and (iii) educate children of asylum seekers in accommodation centres rather than in local schools. A Tory-Liberal Democrat alliance in the Commons also opposed locating accommodation centres in rural areas. While the government managed to overturn most of the Lords' amendments on the Bill's return to the Commons, it did concede on the location of centres, mainly because parliamentary time was running out, and agreed that an independent monitor of accommodation centres would assess, on an annual basis, the suitability of location.[208] On account of the government's large majority, there was little more the opposition could do other than tamper around the edges of the Bill and protest repeatedly about the extremely late tabling of major clauses.[209]

---

[205] Joint Committee on Human Rights, *Nationality, Immigration and Asylum Bill,* Seventeenth Report, Session 2001–02, June 17, 2002, HL 132/ HC 961.

[206] Refugee Council Press Release, October 7, 2002.

[207] bbc.co.uk/1/hi/ok_politics2304613.stm

[208] HC Deb. Vol. 392, November 7, 2002, col. 456.

[209] P. Wintour, 'Refugee bill pulled apart in Lords', *The Guardian*, October 10, 2002.

When the 2002 Act was finally passed, it proved, like its predecessor, to be remarkably long, stretching to 164 sections and nine schedules. The government also repeated its previous practice of deferring the detail of a number of provisions to secondary legislation, thereby avoiding unwelcome parliamentary scrutiny. This summary of the main provisions impacting on asylum takes account of relevant secondary legislation where published.

Overview of the 2002 Act[210]

5.29 The Act is divided into eight parts.[211] In relation to asylum and refugee law, the main changes are as follows:

- new developments in relation to nationality;[212]

- the establishment of accommodation centres;[213]

- removal of support where an asylum seeker or dependant commits a listed offence;[214]

- removal of support-only option contained in the 1999 Act;[215]

- right to refuse support and accommodation where asylum claim is not made 'as soon as reasonably practicable';[216]

- power to introduce secondary legislation to withhold NASS support from in-country asylum applicants in certain circumstances;[217]

---

[210] For a detailed discussion of the Act, see Current Law Statutes Annotated, Nationality Immigration and Asylum Act 2002, c. 41 (London: Sweet & Maxwell); See, also, Nationality, Immigration and Asylum Act 2002, Explanatory Notes; Refugee Council, 'The Nationality, Immigration and Asylum Act 2002: changes to the asylum system in the UK', December 2002; Legal Action, 'Recent developments in immigration law', March 2003; May 2003; June 2003; R. McKee, 'Within the meaning of the Act: Notes and queries on the Nationality, Immigration and Asylum Act 2002', (2003) 17:1 *IANL*, pp. 8–18; J. Farbey, 'Joined-up government or loss of judicial powers? Part 5 Of the Nationality, Immigration and Asylum Act 2002' (2003) 17:1 *IANL*, pp. 36–40.

[211] These are: Nationality; Accommodation Centres; Other Support and Assistance; Detention and Removal; Immigration and Asylum Appeals; Immigration Procedure; Offences; General.

[212] Pt 1.

[213] s. 16

[214] s. 26.

[215] s. 43.

[216] s. 55 and sch. 3.

[217] s. 57.

- immigration officer powers granted to the Secretary of State to detain in certain circumstances;[218]

- repeal of Part III of 1999 Act on statutory bail;[219]

- power to require an asylum seeker to reside in an induction centre for up to 14 days;[220]

- a refugee or asylum seeker sentenced to two years imprisonment or convicted of a specified offence loses protection of Article 33 of the 1951 Convention;[221]

- extension of section 11 of the 1999 Act's 'standing arrangements' to include bilateral agreements;[222]

- repeal of Part IV of the 1999 Act on appeals and replacement with new appeal rights;[223]

- new penalties for carriers in 'authority to carry scheme';[224]

- right to obtain physical data such as imprints of the iris;[225]

- new offence of trafficking in prostitution;[226]

- new powers of entry and search.[227]

The provisions of the Act are slowly coming into force with the publication of commencement orders and the introduction of secondary legislation. While, at the time of writing, it is too early to comment upon the full impact of the new statute, by September 2003 a number of very important parts of the Act were in force, including appeals,[228] and a highly significant Court of Appeal case on the question of refusal of support under s. 55 had already been heard: *The Queen on the Application of 'Q' & Others v SSHD.*[229] This overview will consider the changes in the order in which they appear in the Act and will indicate the extent to which they amend or repeal earlier legislation.

---

[218] s. 62.
[219] s. 68.
[220] s. 70.
[221] s. 72.
[222] s. 80.
[223] Pt 5.
[224] s. 124
[225] s. 126.
[226] s. 145.
[227] ss. 153–154.
[228] See The Immigration and Asylum Appeals (Procedure) Rules, SI 200?
[229] [2003] EWCA Civ 364, and see Ch. 8.

Nationality

5.30 Clearly, Part 1 on nationality, which amends the British Nationality
Act 1981, is aimed mainly at those applying for British citizenship.
While it imposes a requirement to pass an English language test, to
have 'sufficient knowledge about life in the UK', and to undergo a citizenship ceremony with oath of allegiance and pledge,[230] it also
allows the Secretary of State to deprive someone of citizenship where
he or she 'has done anything seriously prejudicial to the vital interests
of the UK or British overseas territory'.[231] The Home Secretary used
his new powers in April 2003 when he served the controversial cleric
Sheikh Abu Hamza with notice that his British citizenship was to be
withdrawn. Abu Hamza appealed to the Special Immigration
Appeals Commission.[232]

Accommodation Centres

5.31 The whole issue of accommodation centres received considerable
attention during the Bill's progress through Committee and both
Houses of Parliament. Section 16 finally granted a power to the Secretary of State to set up centres with full-board accommodation,
access to health care, education, interpreters, and legal advice, plus
anything else the Home Secretary decides ought to be provided
for 'proper occupation' or 'maintaining good order'.[233] Residence
restrictions and reporting requirements may be imposed through
regulations and an individual asylum seeker shall normally remain in
an accommodation centre for a maximum period of six months,
extendable to nine months if agreed with the asylum seeker, or if the
Secretary of State thinks it is appropriate in the circumstances.[234]

---

[230] ss. 1; 3 and sch. 1. The pledge is: 'I will give my loyalty to the UK and respect its
rights and freedoms. I will uphold its democratic values. I will observe its laws
faithfully and fulfil my duties and obligations as a British citizen.'
[231] s. 4, amending s. 40 of the British Nationality Act 1981.
[232] See new s. 40A(2) to the British Nationality Act 1981, as inserted by s. 4 of the 2002
Act. See, also, s. 2B of the Special Immigration Appeals Commission 1997 Act, as
also inserted by s. 4 of the 2002 Act, which provides that a person may appeal against
a decision by the Secretary of State to make an order depriving him of a British citizenship status, where he is not entitled to appeal to an adjudicator or the IAT by
reason of a certificate by the Home Secretary's that he relied upon information
which should not be made public. For a brief discussion of appeals to the Special
Immigration Appeals Commission, see below on the Special Immigration Appeals
Commission Act 1987 and the Anti-terrorism, Crime and Security Act 2001.
[233] s. 29.
[234] ss. 25(1) and (2).

Asylum seekers and their dependants may be placed in accommodation centres if they are destitute or likely to become destitute within a prescribed period.[235] This provision is akin to support provisions of s. 95 of the 1999 Act, and therefore, once the first accommodation centres are open, the Home Secretary will have two options for those deemed to be destitute or likely to become destitute: transfer to a centre, or dispersal through NASS.[236] For the purposes of this part of the Act, 'asylum seeker' is defined as someone who is at least 18 years old, is in the UK, has claimed asylum at a designated place, has the claim recorded but undecided, and who has claimed that removal from the UK would be contrary to the 1951 Convention/1967 Protocol, or Art. 3 of the ECHR.[237] Similar to the definition in the 1999 Act, a destitute does not have and cannot obtain adequate accommodation, food and other essential items.[238] It is expected that the new definition will be applied in the same way as the old, despite the slight differences. The final noteworthy point in this part of the Act is that the Secretary of State may stop providing temporary support or accommodation for a destitute asylum seeker in an accommodation centre if he or she, or a dependant, commits a listed offence.[239]

Other support and assistance

The Act also provides the Secretary of State with the power to remove the support-only option contained in s. 96 of the Immigration and Asylum Act 1999.[240] This allowed asylum seekers to find their own accommodation and claim support for food and other essential items.[241] Once the regulations are in place, asylum seekers will be expected to have both accommodation and essential living needs provided by the state. Amendments are made to the important ss. 94 and 95 of the 1999 Act: the definition of 'destitute asylum seeker'. These are in general relatively minor changes and mirror the definitions provided elsewhere.[242]

5.32

---

[235] s. 17.
[236] s. 22.
[237] s. 18.
[238] s. 19(1).
[239] s. 26 and see, also, s. 35 for offences.
[240] s. 43.
[241] This is the new definition substituted in s. 96(1)(b), 1999 by s. 45, 2002.
[242] Thus an 'asylum seeker' is someone of at least 18 years who is in the UK, has claimed asylum at a place designated by the Secretary of State, and whose claim has been recorded but not determined. To be found to be 'destitute', an asylum seeker must not have and must be unable to obtain adequate accommodation, food and other essential items: ss. 44(2) and 44(6), inserting new s. 95(2) and (3), 1999.

The Act clarifies the position regarding children. Where an application is received from a destitute asylum seeker with a child, the Secretary of State is under a duty to provide support for the child as part of the asylum seeker's household.[243] Regarding unaccompanied children under 18 applying for asylum, the position remains the same: they are supported by the local authority under ss. 17 (children in need) or 20 (power to take children into care) of the Children Act 1989. Under s. 48, local authorities may be reimbursed by the government for any support given to unaccompanied asylum-seeking children.

Prior to the 2002 Act, there existed a power to support those with temporary admission, released from detention, or on bail. While some asylum seekers fell within these categories, the Act extends the power to include *all* failed asylum seekers. However, NASS policy is to apply this provision only to exceptional cases, such as where a rejected asylum seeker cannot be removed from the country immediately due to illness or late pregnancy. In these so-called 'hard cases', the Secretary of State is empowered to provide 'facilities for the accommodation of a person' and any dependant (i.e. full-board accommodation outside London, but no cash).[244]

In summary then, the Secretary of State now has a choice of the form of support he can offer – either under s. 17 of the 2002 Act or under s. 95 of the 1999 Act –, and he can take into account administrative, personal or other factors in arriving at a decision.[245]

Withholding, withdrawing and refusing support

5.33   Sections 54, 55 and 57 of the Act have proved to be some of the most contentious. Section 54 introduces sch. 3, which ensures that support and community care are not available to certain categories of people, including: failed asylum seekers who do not cooperate with removal directions, persons unlawfully present in the UK, those with refugee status abroad, and EEA nationals.[246] Where a family loses support under these provisions, children under 18 will remain eligible and could be taken into care.[247] Allowance is made, however, for families with children to be provided with accommodation until their

---

[243] s. 47, inserting new s. 122, 1999. The previous s. 122 did not mention children.
[244] s. 49.
[245] s. 51, and see HC Deb. Vol. 386, June 12, 2002, col. 917.
[246] sch. 3, paras. 1 and 4–7.
[247] sch. 3, para. 2.

journey home.[248] Associated secondary legislation came into force in January 2003.[249] The chief aim of s. 54 was not necessarily to deter asylum seekers but 'to ensure that [specified] individuals could not move to the UK for the sole or main purpose of accessing residential accommodation and other services in preference to similar services in the EEA country of origin.'[250]

Section 55, on the other hand, permits the Secretary of State and local authorities to refuse support where the Secretary of State is not satisfied that 'the claim was made as soon as reasonably practicable after the person's arrival in the United Kingdom'.[251] Introduced as a very late amendment to the Bill, the intention behind this provision was to ensure that people applied for asylum as quickly as possible. In the words of Lord Filkin, 'There is clearly an issue about whether people [illegally in the UK] should be supported by the state while they make an asylum claim which, on all the evidence, appears to be substantially late.'[252] It refers only to asylum seekers, not dependants, though s. 55(5) ensures that the Secretary of State can provide support to avoid a breach of the ECHR, or to children and their families.[253] This provision is remarkably similar to that provided by the Asylum and Immigration Act 1996 and Social Security (Persons from Abroad) Miscellaneous Amendments Regulations 1996,[254] which required that an asylum seeker claimed 'on arrival' in order to be eligible for benefits under the previous system.[255] Section 55, which came into force on January 8, 2003, specifically excludes a right of appeal to an asylum support adjudicator and therefore the only remedy is by way of judicial review.[256] The government immediately adopted a tough approach. It seemed that the interpretation of 'as soon as reasonably practicable' was in fact 'immediately on arrival'. A significant number of single asylum seekers and couples without children were deprived of support and, as a result, a high profile and successful challenge to refusal of support was lodged, claiming breach

---

[248] sch. 3, para. 9.

[249] The Withholding and Withdrawal of Support (Travel Assistance and Temporary Accommodation) Regulations 2002, SI 2002/3078.

[250] Department of Health, A Note of Clarification, 'Section 54 of the Nationality, Immigration and Asylum Act 2002 and community care and other social services for adults from the EEA living in the UK'.

[251] s. 55(1).

[252] HL Deb. Vol. 639, October 24, 2002, col. 1470.

[253] ss. 55(5)(a)–(c).

[254] SI 1996/30.

[255] See above.

[256] s. 55(10); Nationality, Immigration and Asylum Act 2002 (Commencement No. 1) Order 2002, SI 2002/2811.

of Arts 3, 6 and 8 of the ECHR : *R. (Q and Others) v Secretary of State for the Home Department.*[257]

Section 57 additionally amends para. 12(c), sch. 8 to the Immigration and Asylum Act 1999 (Provision of Support: Regulations) to read that the Secretary of State can introduce support regulations that 'provide for an application not to be entertained where the Secretary of State is not satisfied that the information provided is complete or accurate or that the applicant is co-operating with the authorities'. Discussion of this late change was not as comprehensive as it might have been due to the attention given to s. 55. Nonetheless, a second report on the Bill by the Joint Committee on Human Rights dealt with the clause and concluded that there were a number of human rights as well as legal problems associated with it.[258]

Detention and bail

5.34   Part 4 of the Act deals with detention and removal powers. Under the 1999 Act, the Secretary of State assumed some of the powers that had previously been the preserve of immigration officers (for example, the examination of passengers on arrival and setting removal directions).[259] In the new Act, the Secretary of State's powers are further extended with regard to detention. Under sch. 3 of the Immigration Act 1971, the Secretary of State already possesses the power to detain or release someone against whom deportation action is taken. He can also grant temporary admission to an asylum seeker applying at a port, but cannot detain such a person.[260] Section 62 changes this and empowers the Secretary of State to detain (i) pending a decision to set removal directions and pending removal; and (ii) where the Secretary of State is empowered to examine a person or give or refuse leave to enter the UK, pending certain circumstances.[261] The test to be employed by the Secretary of State is that he 'has reasonable grounds to suspect that he may make a decision'.[262]

---

[257] February 19, 2003. The Court of Appeal decision was promulgated on March 18, 2003. See Ch. 8 for discussion of this case.

[258] Joint Committee on Human Rights, *Nationality, Immigration and Asylum Bill: Further Report*, Twenty-third Report, Session 2001–02, October 23, 2002, HL 176/HC 1255, paras 21–29.

[259] R. McKee, 'Within the meaning of the Act: Notes and queries on the Nationality, Immigration and Asylum Act 2002', (2003) 17:1 *IANL*, p. 9.

[260] Nationality, Immigration and Asylum Act 2002, Explanatory Notes, s. 62.

[261] ss. 62(1) and (2). The circumstances are: the examination; the decision to give or refuse leave; or the decision to give directions, or removal of such a person.

[262] s. 62(10).

Whereas previously someone could be detained pending removal, the new provision only requires the Secretary of State to suspect, albeit reasonably, that he will make a decision before effecting detention – a significant change to the erstwhile position.

Section 66 puts in place the change in nomenclature of detention centres to removal centres, as promised by the White Paper. More significantly, s. 68 repeals Part III of the Immigration and Asylum Act 1999, which introduced a system of routine bail hearings and a presumption in favour of bail, but was never implemented.[263] It also transfers to the Secretary of State powers to grant bail under sch. 2, para. 16 to the Immigration Act 1971 (*i.e.* after the eighth day of detention; prior to this, the power continues to be exercised by the chief immigration officer or higher). In a more positive amendment, s. 69 enables the Secretary of State to pay reasonable travel expenses for asylum seekers who are required to travel in order to comply with reporting restrictions.

Alongside accommodation centres, the government also introduced 'induction centres' in which to process asylum seekers and their dependants. Section 70 explains the workings of such a system. It authorises that an asylum seeker and any dependant may be required to reside at a specified location (which is at or near a 'programme of induction') for a period of up to 14 days.[264] The purpose of such a residence restriction is to provide every new asylum seeker with information on the asylum process in the UK; the legislation specifically does not mention the availability of education, health care, or legal advice. Also, the definition of 'asylum seeker' is the same as that of s. 18 to the 2002 Act, but excludes s. 18(1)(a), which states that an asylum seeker must be at least 18 years old. In other words, unaccompanied children who apply for asylum will be placed in induction centres alongside adults.

The Act goes on to provide that asylum seekers with existing leave to enter or remain at the time of their application may have reporting and residence restrictions imposed on them.[265] This alters the position that has existed for over thirty years. Furthermore, failure to comply with such restrictions gives rise to liability to detention under sch. 2, para. 16 of the Immigration Act 1971.

---

[263] s. 68(6)
[264] s. 70(1).
[265] s. 71.

Removal

5.35   The first point to stress is that there is statutory protection against
removal in asylum cases while a claim or appeal is pending, though
preparatory action may be taken.[266]

In a somewhat unusual move, but one reflecting the current climate,
the government legislated that an asylum seeker or refugee convicted
of an offence and sentenced to at least two years' imprisonment is presumed to have been convicted of a particularly serious crime and is a
danger to the community.[267] This presumption is rebuttable. Attempts
in debate to increase the sentence to ten years for the definition of 'a
particularly serious crime' failed. A similar presumption may be raised
on conviction for any offence irrespective of the sentence if specified
as such by order. Both these presumptions result in loss of protection
under Art. 33(2) of the 1951 Convention and the person may be
removed. An appeal can be made against the Secretary of State's certificate that a presumption applies, but the IAA or Special Immigration Appeals Commission 'must begin the substantive deliberation on
the appeal by considering the certificate'.[268] In other words, it will be
very difficult to overturn the certificate.

The second noteworthy amendment on removals relates to s. 11 of
the Immigration and Asylum Act 1999. This provision, discussed
above, allows the Secretary of State to return applicants to countries
participating in the 'standing arrangements' (that is, the Dublin
Convention). It is, consequently, an exception to s. 77, which bars
removals pending consideration of an asylum claim. Section 80 of
the 2002 Act, in inserting a new s. 11 to the 1999 Act, extends the certification procedure to include bilateral agreements on asylum returns
between Member States.[269] It repeats the assumption that a Member
State is to be regarded as a place where life and liberty are not threatened for a Convention reason, and from where a person will not be
refouled. Thus there is once more a statutory presumption of safety
that will be difficult to overturn on appeal. In any case, the appeal is
non-suspensive, unless a human rights claim has been made, but this
can again be sidestepped by the Secretary of State certifying that the
human rights claim is 'clearly unfounded' under s. 93(2)(b).[270] In
safe third country removals, then, the asylum seeker continues to be
forced down the route of judicial review of the Secretary of State's
certification of 'clearly unfounded'.

---

[266] ss. 77 and 78.
[267] s. 72.
[268] s. 72(10).
[269] s. 80(5).
[270] ss. 80(3) and (4).

Appeals

The all-important appeals chapter of the Act (Part 5), which came **5.36**
into force on April 1, 2003, has brought in some radical amendments.[271] Firstly, the whole of Part IV of the 1999 Act is repealed.[272]
However, for the purposes of practitioners, the appeal rights contained in three previous Acts – 1971, 1993 and 1999 – will continue
to apply to decisions pre-dating April 1, 2003. Secondly, section 82,
setting out general rights of appeal, differs considerably from previous legislation in that there is one right of appeal against any of the
listed 'immigration decisions'.[273] The 1999 Act specified the rights of
appeal in a number of sections; s. 82 provides an exhaustive list.[274]
As has been the case since the passing of the Immigration Act
1971, there is no separate appeal against the refusal of asylum;
rather, the appeal is against the decision to remove. An asylum
seeker can, however, appeal against rejection of an asylum claim where he
or she has been granted 'humanitarian protection' in excess of one
year.[275] The appeal must be on the basis that removal of the appellant from the UK would breach the UK's obligations under the 1951
Convention.[276]

Section 82 should be read alongside s. 84, as the latter lists the
grounds of appeal. In the case of asylum, the likely ground will be
s. 84(1)(g), which states that 'removal of the appellant from the United
Kingdom in consequence of the immigration decision would breach
the United Kingdom's obligations under the Refugee Convention or
would be unlawful under s. 6 of the Human Rights Act 1998 as being
incompatible with the appellant's Convention rights'.

Yet again, time limits have been changed. These are spelled out in
The Immigration and Asylum Appeals (Procedure) Rules 2003,
which bring the appeals provisions of the Act into force.[277] For those
in the UK, notice of appeal must be given within five days of service

---

[271] See, also, The Immigration and Asylum Appeals (Procedure) Rules 2003, SI
2003/652 (L.16); specifically on Pt 5: J. Farbey, 'Joined-up government or loss of
judicial powers? Pt 5 Of the Nationality, Immigration and Asylum Act 2002' (2003)
17:1 *IANL*, pp. 36–40.

[272] s. 114.

[273] Nationality, Immigration and Asylum Act 2002, Explanatory Notes, s. 82.

[274] Current Law Statutes Annotated, Nationality, Immigration and Asylum Act 2002,
c. 41 (London: Sweet & Maxwell), s. 82.

[275] s. 83.

[276] s. 84(3).

[277] SI 2003/652 (L. 16). See, also, The Immigration and Asylum Appeals (Fast Track
Procedure) Rules 2003, SI 2003/801 (L. 21), which applies to appellants in
detention at Harmondsworth Immigration Removal Centre, in the first instance.

of the IND's decision, if in detention, and within ten days for all other cases. If a person is outside the UK, and was in the UK when the decision was taken, but cannot appeal while in the UK due to the provisions of the 2002 Act, he or she has 28 days in which to appeal following departure. All other appellants based outside the UK have 28 days following service with notice of the IND's decision.[278] The same time limits apply to the same categories of appellants in the case of permission to appeal to the IAT.[279] The reduction in the time limit for appealing in detained cases was criticised by the Immigration Law Practitioners' Association ('ILPA'). It argued that 'the speed of the decision-making process for detained persons undermines their ability to get competent and effective legal advice, prepare and present their application in an informed and proper fashion and get representation for an appeal'.[280] Furthermore, it was 'wholly wrong to assume that detained cases are inherently less meritorious than others'.[281]

A significant aspect to the 1999 Act was the launch of the 'one-stop' appeals process, under which all grounds of appeal were considered in the same appeal. This is retained by the present Act but has been revised to clarify what was a very complicated procedure: 'An appeal under s. 82(1) against a decision shall be treated by the adjudicator as including an appeal against any decision in respect of which the appellant has a right of appeal under s. 82(1).'[282] This wording could be interpreted to mean that the adjudicator must consider all appeals, where a right exists, whether or not the appellant has exercised those rights.[283] Where an applicant has been served with the 'one-stop warning' and asked to state additional grounds as to why he or she should be permitted to remain in the UK,[284] the adjudicator is required to consider any matter raised in the statement which constitutes a ground of appeal under s. 84(1), irrespective of whether this has been put forward by the appellant or whether the statement is made after the appeal commences.[285]

---

[278] The Immigration and Asylum Appeals (Procedure) Rules 2003, SI 2003/652 (L. 16), r. 6.

[279] r. 16.

[280] ILPA, 'ILPA's response to LCD consultation paper CPL 01/03 on Immigration and Asylum Appeals (Procedure) Rules 2003', February 10, 2003, pp. 1–2.

[281] *ibid.*, p. 2.

[282] s. 85(1).

[283] R. McKee, 'Within the meaning of the Act: Notes and queries on the Nationality, Immigration and Asylum Act 2002', (2003) 17:1 *IANL*, p. 12.

[284] s. 120, mirroring s. 74, 1999 but much simplified. This section is aimed at preventing applicants from raising additional grounds later in the process and delaying departure.

[285] ss. 85(2) and (3).

Significantly, the 2002 Act incorporates a presumption against in-country appeals in s. 92. It states that an in-country appeal only applies to those decisions spelled out in the section.[286] If the appellant has made asylum or human rights claims, then he or she is entitled to an in-country appeal[287] (unless the Secretary of State has certified, under s. 94(2), that the claim is 'clearly unfounded'). In effect, s. 94 gives the Secretary of State the power to prevent appeals from being heard in-country and will force many appellants abroad, which will undoubtedly hamper their chances of mounting a successful appeal. The certification that a claim is 'clearly unfounded' is, nevertheless, subject to judicial review.

5.37

Section 94(2) is therefore critical to the asylum appeals process. It replaces the previous grounds for certification set out in sch. 4, para. 9 to the 1999 Act and substitutes the term 'manifestly unfounded' with 'clearly unfounded'. With repeal of para. 9 comes the removal of the special protection accorded to survivors of torture contained therein. The reason for the use of 'clearly' in place of 'manifestly', which has been employed for some considerable time, is not altogether apparent, but did raise queries from lawyers anxious about its implications. Was a different test to be employed? Apparently not, if one accepts statements made during debate on the Bill. Lord Falconer, speaking on behalf of the government during the Committee stage in the House of Lords, engaged in some semantic finessing:

> 'It is the view of parliamentary counsel that "clearly" and "manifestly" mean the same. It is a view to which we accord the greatest respect. I confirm that we will not argue that "clearly" means anything different from "manifestly". [. . .] It is the view of parliamentary counsel that "clearly" is a clearer word than "manifestly", a view that I share. Our commitment to treat "clearly" as "manifestly" is unswerving.'[288]

Consequently, it will be possible to apply previous case-law on 'manifestly unfounded' claims to the new provision. Finally, as an apparent sop to the many critics of these proposals on certification, the government offered to appoint a monitor to report annually to the Secretary of State on the use of s. 94(2).[289]

Alongside the general discretion of the Home Secretary to certify a claim (s. 94(2)), there is also a duty to do so if certain conditions apply, namely that the claimant is entitled to reside in one of the ten

---

[286] ss. 92(2)–(4).
[287] s. 92(4).
[288] HL Deb. Vol. 638, July 23, 2002, col. 342.
[289] s. 111.

listed accession countries that will join the EU in May 2004.[290] The
Home Secretary has also been granted a power to add (and remove)
new states to this original list if he is satisfied that there is, in the state
in question, no *serious* risk of persecution and that removal to the state
will not breach the ECHR.[291]

In February 2003, seven countries were added to the list: Albania,
Bulgaria, Jamaica, Macedonia, Moldova, Romania, and Serbia-
Montenegro.[292] The list was again extended in June 2003 with the
inclusion of Bangladesh, Bolivia, Brazil, Ecuador, South Africa, Sri
Lanka and Ukraine.[293] It is worth emphasising that this 'new' provi-
sion has striking parallels with the 'white list' of the Asylum and
Immigration Act 1996, which was widely condemned by Labour in
opposition.

5.38   Where the Secretary of State certifies that it is proposed to remove
an asylum or human rights claimant to a country of which he or she
is *not* a national or citizen, and it is believed that the claimant's human
rights will not be breached, there is no in-country right of appeal.[294]
To prevent appeals against designation of country, the Act states that
the country specified 'is to be regarded as' a place where a person's
life and liberty will not be threatened for a 1951 Convention ground,
and which also will not *refoule* him or her.[295] This wording harks back
to that of the 1999 Act (ss. 11(1) and (7)) and the 1996 Act (s. 2(2)),
and it has been suggested that the case-law relating to those earlier
provisions will be pertinent to the interpretation of s. 94(8).[296] While
specification of the country might not be reviewable, it may be possible to challenge the Secretary of State's belief that the person's rights
under the ECHR will not be breached in the country in question.[297]

The final amendment warranting particular comment is that of
s. 101. This section implements three radical changes. First, it reduces
the jurisdiction of the IAT to consideration of points of law only, not
fact.[298] Second, it withdraws the right of a party to seek judicial

---

[290] s. 94(4). The tens countries listed are: Cyprus, the Czech Republic, Estonia,
Hungary, Latvia, Lithuania, Malta, Poland, Slovakia and Slovenia.

[291] s. 94(5).

[292] Home Office Press Release, 'Driving forward asylum reform: further measures to
cut abuse', February 6, 2003; The Asylum (Designated States) Order 2003, SI
2003/970.

[293] Home Office Press Release, 'Safe country list expanded to cut asylum abuse', June
17, 2003.

[294] s. 94(7).

[295] s. 94(8).

[296] Current Law Statutes Annotated, Nationality, Immigration and Asylum Act 2002,
c. 41 (London: Sweet & Maxwell), s. 94.

[297] R. McKee, 'Within the meaning of the Act: Notes and queries on the Nationality,
Immigration and Asylum Act 2002', (2003) 17:1 *IANL*, p. 14.

[298] s. 101(1).

review of an IAT decision that rejects leave to appeal to the IAT.[299] Instead, a party to an application to the Tribunal for 'permission' to appeal (no longer 'leave') may apply to the High Court for a review of the Tribunal's decision 'on the ground that the Tribunal made an error in law'.[300] In other words, this is a statutory review, to be carried out by a sole judge who will arrive at a decision on the basis of the written submissions only and whose decision will be final.[301] As may be expected, this revision of the law was condemned in the strongest terms by both practitioners and NGOs. The third change is more positive. The 1999 regime prevented appellants in certified cases from appealing to the IAT; s. 101 makes no exception for certified cases and, with the repeal of sch. 4, para. 9 of the 1999 Act, all appellants in asylum cases will now be able to apply for permission to appeal to the Tribunal against an adjudicator's decision.

Carriers' liability and clandestine entrants

The 2002 Act has introduced some further amendments to the carri-   **5.39**
ers' liability scheme first pioneered in 1987 and subsequently enhanced in 1999. The first innovation is brought about by s.124: the Authority to Carry ('ATC') scheme. The Secretary of State will draft regulations to effect the provision, but its principal aim is to require carriers to obtain authority in advance to carry passengers. Failure to do so will result in a penalty. At the time of writing, the regulations were not available but, according to the Explanatory Notes to the Act, it is envisaged that carriers will be required to check details of passengers travelling to the UK against information held on a Home Office database in order 'to confirm that they pose no known immigration or security risk and to confirm that their documents are in order'.[302]

Section 125 brings sch. 8 to the 2002 Act into force. Schedule 8 amends various sections of the 1999 Act on carriers' liability, as well as inserting completely new sections into that Act.[303] Section 32, on the penalty to be imposed for carrying clandestine entrants, is revised following the Court of Appeal judgement in *International Transport Roth*

---

[299] See, also, The Civil Procedure (Amendment) Rules 2003 SI 2003/364.
[300] s. 101(2).
[301] s. 101(3). See, for further discussion, 'J. Luqmani, 'Statutory review under the Nationality, Immigration and Asylum Act 2002, (May 2003) *Legal Action*, p. 24.
[302] Nationality, Immigration and Asylum Act 2002, Explanatory Notes, s. 124.
[303] For a useful discussion of the changes, see IND, *Civil penalty – regulatory impact assessment*; IND, *Civil penalty – Level of Penalty: Code of Practice*, both available on IND website: *www.ind.homeoffice.gov.uk*

Gmbh & Others v Secretary of State for the Home Department.[304] There the Court declared the civil penalty regime incompatible with the ECHR, and was particularly critical of the fixed nature and severity of the penalty imposed.[305] Consequently, s. 32 changes the penalty from fixed to variable, with an individual maximum penalty of £2,000 per clandestine entrant for each responsible person, up to a total of £4,000 per clandestine.[306] Owners and hirers of vehicles will now be jointly liable with the driver.[307] A new statutory right of appeal against the imposition of a penalty has been brought in.[308] Both liability to and the level of the penalty can be challenged. The current power to detain a vehicle where there is a risk that a fine will not be paid is maintained, but an additional power is included to permit detention of a transporter where a person who has been issued with a penalty notice still uses the transporter in the course of business.[309] However, the court has been empowered to release a detained vehicle if a penalty notice was not issued or it simply considers it right to do so.[310]

A new s. 40 is inserted in the 1999 Act. This relates to the charge in respect of passengers arriving in the UK without proper documents, as opposed to clandestine entrants. Ship and aircraft owners continue to be liable to a charge of £2,000 per undocumented traveller; train operators may become liable if the Secretary of State decides to apply the section by order; owners and operators of road passenger vehicles will no longer be liable. Once more, a right of appeal against any such charge is available.[311]

Finally, the Act makes provision for the introduction of future regulations requiring an immigration application to be accompanied by specified information on external physical characteristics of the applicant, such as imprints of the iris; these are, apparently, more reliable than fingerprints.[312] The Home Secretary may choose also to operate a scheme that allows people voluntarily to provide data.[313]

---

[304] [2002] 3 WLR 344.
[305] See Ch. 8 for further comment.
[306] See amended s. 32(3) and The Carriers' Liability Regulations 2002, SI 2002/2817; The Carriers' Liability (Clandestine Entrants) (Level of Penalty: Code of Practice) Order 2002.
[307] Amended s. 32(4).
[308] s. 35A.
[309] s. 36A.
[310] s. 37(3A).
[311] s. 40B
[312] s. 126.
[313] s. 127.

Criminal offences

The last issue to be discussed on the new Act is that of offences. Once   **5.40**
more, the government deemed it necessary to tamper with the prevailing provisions on 'assisting unlawful immigration'. As has been
discussed earlier, prior to 2002, it was already an offence under
amended s. 25(1) to the Immigration Act 1971 to secure or facilitate
the entry to the UK of an illegal entrant or, if done for gain, of an
asylum seeker. It was also an offence to assist a person to obtain leave
to remain through deception. Both carried a maximum penalty of 10
years imprisonment and/or unlimited fine. Section 25(2) prohibited
the harbouring of an illegal entrant, an overstayer, or anyone breach-
ing a condition of leave. Breach of s. 25(2) could result in six months
in prison and/or a fine of £5,000. Section 143 repeals the whole of
s. 25, replacing it with four new ss.: 25, 25A, 25B and 25C. The
changes are as follows. It is now an offence to:

- assist unlawful entry to an EU Member State, not just the UK;[314]

- help an asylum seeker to enter the UK where this is done for gain
  (this is a repetition of the current s. 25(1)(b), 1971, which was
  added by the 1996 Act);[315]

- assist entry to the UK of an EU citizen in breach of a deportation
  or exclusion order.[316]

The maximum sanction for these offences is 14 years imprisonment and/or a fine, where convicted on indictment, or six months
imprisonment and/or a fine, on summary conviction.[317] Courts are
empowered, as they were prior to the Act, to order the forfeiture of
ships, aircraft and vehicles where the owner, hirer or driver is convicted on indictment of an offence under ss. 25, 25A or 25B.[318]
While revision of s. 25 is clearly very significant, the Act has also
attempted to tackle a growing problem and one which all parties to
the asylum debate would wish to see addressed: traffic in prostitution.
A new offence has therefore been created: according to s. 145(1), a
person commits a criminal offence where 'he arranges or facili-
tates the arrival in the United Kingdom of an individual (the "passenger") and (a) he intends to exercise control over prostitution by the

---

[314] New s. 25, Immigration Act 1971.
[315] New s. 25A, Immigration Act 1971.
[316] New s. 25B, Immigration Act 1971.
[317] New ss. 25(6), 25A(4), and 25B(4), Immigration Act 1971.
[318] New s. 25C, Immigration Act 1971.

passenger in the United Kingdom or elsewhere, or (b) he believes that another person is likely to exercise control [. . .].' It is also an offence for a person to arrange travel in the UK if he or she believes that the passenger has been brought to the UK for the purposes of prostitution, and it is intended to control the passenger in prostitution anywhere in the world.[319] A person 'exercises control over prostitution by another if for the purposes of gain he exercises control, direction or influence over the prostitute's movements in a way which shows he is aiding, abetting or compelling the prostitution'.[320] This is a summary or indictable offence, with a maximum sentence, on indictment, of 14 years' imprisonment, and/or unlimited fine.[321] The offence has extraterritorial effect where committed by a British citizen, amongst others.[322]

Increased powers for immigration officers

5.41   It is clear from the overview of the 1990s that increased enforcement and investigatory powers were a recurrent theme of the legislation. The 2002 Act is certainly no exception. Alongside adjusting the provisions on assisting entry, the Act also amends s. 8 to the Asylum and Immigration Act 1996 on employer's liability. The erstwhile defence available to employers – that they had taken copies of a specified document belonging to the employee – is replaced. Instead, employers will need to prove that they complied with any relevant order by the Secretary of State (yet to be published), which could include the copying of specified documents.[323] Enforcement of s. 8 of the 1996 Act has been further strengthened by the grant of a completely new power of arrest by warrant to immigration officers where there are 'reasonable grounds for suspecting' that a person has committed an offence under s. 8 (as well as s. 24(1)(d) of the Immigration Act 1971 – failure to comply with a requirement to report to, attend or submit to a medical examination).[324] Police officers already possess such a power.

Three further powers are added to the Immigration Act 1971: ss. 28CA, 28FA and 28FB. The first gives immigration officers and police officers the power to enter and search business premises without a warrant, and to arrest anyone suspected of having committed a

---

[319] s. 145(2).
[320] s. 145(4).
[321] s 145(5).
[322] s. 146.
[323] s. 147.
[324] s. 152, inserting new s. 28AA in the Immigration Act 1971.

specified immigration offence. The second grants immigration officers and police officers the power to search premises for personnel records without a warrant where a person has been arrested or it is believed is liable to arrest for a specified offence.[325] Furthermore, the search should only take place if the immigration or police officer suspects that there are employee records on the premises that will be of 'substantial value' in the investigation of an immigration employment offence or of fraud in the provision of support to an asylum seeker.[326] The last new power allows immigration officers to enter and search business premises with warrant where the officer believes that an employer has provided inaccurate or incomplete information under s. 134 of the 2002 Act (i.e. compulsory disclosure of information on the Home Secretary's request). The belief or suspicion held must, in all cases, be 'reasonable'.

It seems that, with this supplementation of enforcement powers, immigration officers are now on an equal footing with the police. Where they believe an individual to be in breach of immigration conditions, they can now enter and search homes and business premises, seize material, search individuals, use reasonable force, and detain on suspicion.

SPECIAL IMMIGRATION APPEALS COMMISSION ACT 1997

In *Chahal v United Kingdom*,[327] the European Court of Human Rights criticised the UK practice in national security or political cases of forwarding appeals against exclusion to an advisory panel of 'three wise men'. Mr Chahal was not entitled to legal representation before the advisory panel, the proceedings were not public, he was not informed of the reasons for his deportation, and the panel's advice to the Home Secretary was not binding and was not disclosed.[328] The ECtHR therefore found the advisory panel not to be a court within the meaning of Art. 5(4). MacDonald and Webber put it thus: 'The Court deprecated the use of the shibboleth of 'national security' by the executive to attempt to free itself from effective control by the domestic courts and commended the arrangements in Canada which "both accommodate legitimate security concerns [. . .] and yet accord the individual a substantial measure of protection"'.[329]

5.42

---

[325] Breach of ss. 24(1), 24A(1) or sch. 2, para. 17, Immigration Act 1971.
[326] New s. 28FA, Immigration Act 1971.
[327] (1996) 23 EHRR 413, and see Ch. 4.
[328] para. 130.
[329] Macdonald & Webber, *Macdonald's Immigration Law and Practice* (London: Butterworths, 2001), para. 18.186; (1996) 23 EHRR 413, para. 130.

In response to the ECtHR's uncompromising criticism, the UK government introduced the Special Immigration Appeals Commission Act 1997 to deal with the distinct problem of national security and political cases. The Act sets up a body known as the Special Immigration Appeals Commission ('SIAC'),[330] which consists of 'such number of members appointed by the Lord Chancellor as he may determine',[331] and which hears appeals against exclusion on national security and political grounds in almost all cases.[332] The Immigration and Asylum Act 1999 barred a person from appealing under s. 69 in public interest cases or where there were 1951 Convention issues under Art. 1F – that is, the commission of war crimes, serious non-political crimes, and crimes or acts contrary to the purposes and principles of the UN.[333] For example, where the reason for refusal of asylum was that the applicant was a person to whom the 1951 Convention did not apply by reason of Art. 1F to the Convention, and where the Secretary of State certified that the disclosure of material on which the refusal was based was not in the interests of national security, the applicant was specifically excluded from appealing under s. 69(3) of the Immigration and Asylum Act 1999.[334] Section 97 of the Nationality, Immigration and Asylum Act 2002 repeats this prohibition where the Secretary of State certifies that a decision was taken on national security or public interest grounds, or on account of certain information. While there is no appeal to the IAA or courts, there is the possibility of an appeal to SIAC under s. 2 of the 1997 Act, which has been substituted by sch. 7 to the 2002 Act. This now provides that a person may appeal to the Commission against a decision to reject an asylum claim, where he is prevented from appealing to an adjudicator or the IAT because the Secretary of State has certified that the decision was taken on national security or other public interest grounds.[335]

---

[330] s.1.

[331] Special Immigration Appeals Commission Act 1997, sch. 1, para. 1(1).

[332] See Immigration and Asylum Act 1999, ss. 60(9), 62(4), 64(1)-(2) and 70(1)-(6). The one exception is set out in s. 2(2) to the 1997 Act: an appeal against refusal of entry clearance on 'conducive grounds' (that is conducive to the public good) where the appellant does not rely on an enforceable Community right, or a family connection.

[333] ss. 70(1)–(6)

[334] s. 70(4).

[335] See, also, The Special Immigration Appeals Commission (Procedure) Rules 2003, SI 2003/1034.

ANTI-TERRORISM, CRIME AND SECURITY ACT 2001[336]

On December 13, 2001, a month after the publication of the Bill of   **5.43**
the same name, the Anti-terrorism, Crime and Security Act 2001
received Royal Assent. Rushed through Parliament in the wake of the
events of September 11, 2001, the Act introduced a number of
highly controversial provisions, despite widespread criticism. While it
covers a range of issues relating to terrorism and security, one part
refers specifically to 'Immigration and Asylum' (Part 4). Implications
for asylum seekers are therefore serious, particularly during a period
of heightened anxiety about international terrorism.

Part 4 on Immigration and Asylum runs from ss. 21–36. It deals
with the problem of the 'suspected international terrorist' and
increases the powers of the Home Secretary to deport, remove and
detain. Under s. 21, the Home Secretary may issue a certificate if
he reasonably believes that a person's presence in the UK is a risk
to national security, and suspects that the person is a terrorist. A
'terrorist' 'means a person who:

'(a) is or has been concerned in the commission, preparation or
       instigation of acts of international terrorism,
 (b) is a member of or belongs to an international terrorist group, or
 (c) has links with an international terrorist group.'[337]

'Terrorism' has been given the same meaning as in section 1 of the
Terrorism Act 2000:

'1.   In this Act [Terrorism Act 2000] 'terrorism' means the use or
        threat of action where:

 (a)   the action falls within subsection (2);
 (b)   the use or threat is designed to influence the government or to
        intimidate the public or a section of the public; and
 (c)   the use or threat is made for the purpose of advancing a political,
        religious, or ideological cause.

---

[336] See, for discussions of the Bill, Joint Committee on Human Rights, Second Report,
      Session 2001–02, November 16, 2001, HC 372/HL 37; Home Affairs Committee,
      First Report, Session 2001–02, November 15, 2001, HC 351. For information on
      the Act, see Liberty, 'Anti-terrorism Legislation in the UK', (London: Liberty,
      2002); Amnesty International, 'Rights denied: the UK's response to September 11,
      2001', (AI (UK), September 2002; AI Index: EUR 45/016/2002); H. Fenwick,
      'The Anti–Terrorism, Crime and Security Act 2001: A Proportionate Response
      to September 11?' (2002) 65:5 *Modern Law Review*, pp. 724–762; D. Bonner,
      'Managing terrorism while respecting human rights? European aspects of the
      Anti-terrorism Crime and Security Act 2001' (2002) 8:4 *European Public Law*, pp.
      497–524; A. Tomkins, 'Legislating against terror: the Anti-terrorism, Crime and
      Security Act 2001', (2002) Summer *Public Law*, pp. 205–220.
[337] s. 21(2).

2.   Action falls within this sub-section if it:

(a)   involves serious violence against a person;
(b)   involves serious damage to property;
(c)   endangers a person's life, other than that of the person committing the action;
(d)   creates a serious risk to the health or safety of the public or a section of the public; or
(e)   is designed seriously to interfere with or seriously to disrupt an electronic system.'

5.44   Suspected international terrorists may be refused leave to enter or remain, deported or removed (s. 22), as well as detained (s. 23). Actual removal from the UK can be prevented if it will incur a breach of international law or is impossible. However, s. 22(1) provides that a removal order can be made in such circumstances, even where it cannot be executed. In this case, the suspect is likely to be detained. Detention of a 'certified' suspected terrorist may be for an indefinite period if an individual cannot be deported or extradited due, once more, to a point of international law (for example, a breach of Art. 3 of the ECHR might occur as a result of deportation) or a 'practical consideration'.[338] Applications for bail are catered for but may only be made to the Special Immigration Appeals Commission.[339] Likewise, a suspected international terrorist may appeal to the Commission against his or her certification by the Home Secretary.[340] A limited appeal right exists for appeals from the Commission to the Court of Appeal, but only on points of law. The Commission is required to review a s. 21 certificate after the expiry of six months in the first instance, and then every three months thereafter.[341] There is a sunset clause allowing for the expiration of ss. 21–23 after 15 months, but they can be renewed by the Home Secretary for a period not exceeding one year.[342] In any event, ss. 21–23 are due to expire definitively on November 10, 2006.[343]

Section 23, on detention of suspected international terrorists, caused some disquiet during debate on the Bill. S. 23(1) provides:

'A suspected international terrorist may be detained under a provision specified [. . .] despite the fact that his removal or departure from the United Kingdom is prevented (whether temporarily or indefinitely) by (a) a point of law which wholly or partly relates to an international agreement, or (b) a practical consideration.'

---

[338] s. 23(1).
[339] s. 24.
[340] s. 25.
[341] s. 26.
[342] s. 29.
[343] s. 29(7).

The provisions specified in s. 23(1) relate to the detention of persons liable to examination or removal (sch. 2, para. 16, Immigration Act 1971), and detention pending deportation (sch. 3, para. 2, Immigration Act 1971). By February 2003, the Home Secretary had detained fifteen foreign nationals under s. 23, of whom two had voluntarily departed.[344]

In order to permit detention, which is unlawful under Art. 5(1)(f) of the ECHR since it is only permitted where 'action is being taken with a view to deportation',[345] the government had to derogate from the said Art., a right which is conferred by Art. 15(1) of the Convention in times of war or public emergency.[346] Such derogation is now contained in the Human Rights Act 1998 (Amendment No. 2) Order 2001 and, according to the government, allows for detention in those cases where, 'notwithstanding a continuing intention to remove or deport a person who is being detained, it is not possible to say that "action is being taken with a view to deportation" within the meaning of Art. 5(1)(f) as interpreted by the Court in the *Chahal* case'. However, it is the view of a number of commentators that, despite the government's confident assertion that its action was appropriate in the post- September 11, 2001 circumstances, the derogation on this occasion was unlawful.[347]

5.45 Lord Carlile of Berriew was appointed to carry out an independent review of the operation of ss. 21–23 of the 2001 Act.[348] His first report, published in March 2003, was generally positive. The Secretary of State was found to have certified persons as international terrorists only in appropriate cases, and had exercised his independent judgement in each case, 'giving due regard to advice from officials'.[349] Lord Carlile's three main suggestions were: (i) the removal of the word 'links' in s. 21; (ii) the update of SIAC's procedural rules; and (iii) the provision of separate facilities 'more suitable to the special circumstances of executive detention of persons who have not been

---

[344] Joint Committee on Human Rights, *Continuance in force of ss. 21–23 of the Anti-terrorism, Crime and Security Act 2001*, Session 2002–03, February 26, 2003, HL 59/HC 462, para. 10.

[345] *Chahal v United Kingdom* (1996) 23 EHRR 413, para. 112.

[346] Art. 15(1): 'In time of war or public emergency threatening the life of the nation any High Contracting Party may take measures derogating from its obligations under this Convention to the extent strictly required by the exigencies of the situation, provided that such measures are not inconsistent with its obligations under international law.'

[347] For a valuable discussion of the issues at stake, see Joint Committee on Human Rights, *Continuance in force of ss. 21–23 of the Anti-terrorism, Crime and Security Act 2001*, Session 2002–03, February 26, 2003, HL 59/HC 462.

[348] See s. 28.

[349] Lord Carlile of Berriew QC, Antiterrorism, Crime and Security Act 2001, Pt IV Section 28 Review, March 12, 2003, p. 36.

charged with any offences'.[350] The Joint Committee on Human Rights, which also reported on the continuance in force of ss. 21–23, was less sanguine. It raised a number of concerns, including the unsatisfactory procedure used in relation to the derogation order, the delay in commencing hearings in respect of appeals before SIAC, and the use of 'closed' evidence before SIAC, which inevitably disadvantages detainees and places a fair trial at risk.[351]

In the refugee context, in any asylum appeal before the Commission, s. 33 grants the Secretary of State a power to certify that an appellant is not entitled to protection against *refoulement* provided by Art. 33(1) of the 1951 Convention because either Art. 1F or Art. 33(2) applies to the appellant, and the removal of the appellant from the UK would be conducive to the public good.[352] Importantly, the appellant is prevented from questioning the decision by the Secretary of State to certify.[353] If such a certificate is issued by the Home Secretary, the Commission must first consider the statements in the certificate and, if it agrees with those statements, it must dismiss such part of the asylum appeal as amounts to a claim for asylum.[354] In other words, the exclusion clauses are applied *before* any consideration is given to inclusion, an issue which has recently received a degree of academic commentary.[355]

Section 34, like s. 33, is a radical measure. It removes any duty on a decision-maker to balance the seriousness of the applicant's conduct against the alleged fear of persecution arising from the threat of removal. In other words, no proportionality test is applied. According to s. 34, where Arts 1F or 33(2) of the 1951 Convention are held to apply, no consideration need be given to the gravity of:

'(a)   events or fear by virtue of which Article 1A would or might apply to a person if Article 1F did not apply, or

(b)   a threat by reason of which Article 33(1) would or might apply to a person if Article 33(2) did not apply.'

---

[350] Lord Carlile of Berriew QC, Antiterrorism, Crime and Security Act 2001, Pt IV Section 28 Review, March 12, 2003, p. 36.

[351] Joint Committee on Human Rights, *Continuance in force of sections 21–23 of the Antiterrorism, Crime and Security Act 2001*, Session 2002–03, February 26, 2003, HL 59/HC 462, pp. 20–21.

[352] s. 33(1).

[353] s. 33(8).

[354] ss. 33(3) and (4).

[355] See, *e.g.*, H. Storey, 'More questions than answers: the exclusion clauses in the light of September 11' presented at IARLJ/ILPA Seminar, London, March 4, 2002 (in author's possession); EU Commission Working Document – *The Relationship between safeguarding internal security and complying with international protection obligations and instruments* (COM(2001) 743 final, December 5, 2001, para. 1.4.3.2; J. Hathaway & C. Harvey, 'Framing refugee protection in the new world disorder' (2001) 34 *Cornell Int'l L. J.*, pp. 257–319.

CONCLUSION

The legislative changes undertaken in the 1990s were a clear response **5.46** to the pressures brought to bear on the post-war asylum regime by increasing applications from Africa and Asia, and latterly from Europe. During the Cold War, refugees from Communist countries were considered acceptable and even to be encouraged. However, the changing nature of asylum applications in the mid- to late 1980s and early 1990s gave rise to a panicked response and a misguided belief in the power of legislation to reduce numbers and deter asylum seekers. The passing of four statutes in nine years is arguably testament to the failure of such an approach. The question now being posed is whether this four-Act 'drama' has reached its *denouement*. It seems unlikely. Only six months after passing the 2002 Act, a huge and complex piece of legislation, the Home Secretary declared that he was considering further legislative measures to tackle:

- 'the continuing problem of asylum applicants lodging groundless appeals to frustrate the process and delay removal' by the introduction of a single-tier appeal [by amalgamating adjudicators with the IAT];

- 'the problem of asylum seekers deliberately destroying or disposing of their documents in order to make fraudulent claims and prevent removal'; and

- the 'abuse of the legal aid system'.[356]

This announcement was all the more surprising as it was made concurrently with a Home Office report that asylum applications had fallen by one third, and followed evidence given by the Minister of Immigration, Beverley Hughes, to the Home Affairs Select Committee on May 8, 2003, that there were no specific proposals for further legislation.[357] Perhaps the government is rightly cautious in light of the statistical record, which reveals that though the 1993 and 1996 Acts were followed immediately by a drop in asylum claims, the fall was unsustained.

The present dilemma for any government is how to identify and remove swiftly the 'undeserving' without jeopardising the right to seek asylum of the so-called 'genuine'. The remaining chapters of this book will consider the extent to which the rights of refugees

---

[356] Home Office Press Release, 'Asylum applications down by a third', May 22, 2003.
[357] Home Affairs Select Committee, 'Asylum Applications', Oral Evidence, Beverley Hughes, May 8, 2003.

may have been sacrificed in the name of increasing deterrence and exclusion, as the UK government struggles to find a solution to the seemingly intractable 'asylum problem': increasing and multiple applications, human smuggling, illegal entry and working, failure to remove rejected claimants, and growing public disenchantment with government policy.

Chapter Six

Exclusion and Deterrence through Home Office Policy: From Arrival to Decision

INTRODUCTION

While statutory law provides the regulatory framework to control **6.1** asylum in the UK, it is to Home Office policy that one must turn to understand the true impact of legislation on asylum seekers. As noted in earlier chapters, Home Office policy in the immigration and asylum fields has always been difficult to monitor. At first, this was due to lack of information. Now, with greater transparency and the creation of the Immigration and Nationality Directorate ('IND') website, there is a surfeit of detail available. Constant changes to policy make it difficult for the non-practitioner to keep abreast of developments. This is particularly true of the asylum field, which has received extensive political, media and legislative attention in the past decade.

Chapters 6 and 7 will examine Home Office policies in the light of recent asylum law, tracing their impact on the asylum seeker at various stages of his or her journey to the UK: pre-arrival, the application process, pending the decision, the determination criteria, and post-decision. The aims of the analysis are threefold: first, it will detail the mechanisms employed to deter and exclude asylum seekers; second, it will reveal the failure of current UK asylum law and policy to distinguish between the 'bogus' and 'genuine' asylum seeker; and finally, it will seek to assess the impact of Home Office policy on asylum in the UK.

CONTEXT

6.2   In 1997, the non-governmental organisations JUSTICE, ILPA and ARC[1] published a report entitled *Providing Protection – Towards Fair and Effective Asylum Procedures*, in which they suggested that:

> '[. . .] a sustainable first-instance decision-making process [. . .] should be a transparent, well-informed procedure where the decision-maker has access to all the information required, can examine the applicant and his or her representative directly on any matters at issue, and where any errors of fact or interpretation can be corrected as early as possible. Any refusals should be supported by reasoned decisions, setting out the facts and issues which are accepted and rejected, and by any evidence relied on in reaching the decision.'[2]

The Report went on to criticise the appellate system, arguing that it suffered from structural and conceptual weaknesses, inadequate administrative infrastructure, lack of adjudicator training, and poor decision-making.[3] Since then, the UK asylum regime has come under wholesale attack from political commentators: 'Asylum seekers push Blunkett £1bn over budget';[4] 'Asylum-seekers vanish and hope for the best';[5] 'Hague attacks Labour's asylum policies';[6] 'Number of asylum seekers reaches record';[7] 'Welcome to the asylum: A year-long investigation into how Britain's immigration system is in the grip of madness'.[8]

In light of such condemnation, the government sought in the Immigration and Asylum Act 1999 and Nationality, Immigration and Asylum Act 2002 to address the underlying problems with the UK

---

[1] JUSTICE is a legal human rights organisation that aims to improve British justice through law reform and policy work, publications and casework. ILPA is the Immigration Law Practitioners' Association and is the UK's professional association of immigration lawyers, academics and advisers. ARC is the Asylum Rights Campaign and was established in 1991 to ensure that refugees in the UK were treated fairly and humanely.

[2] *Providing Protection – Towards Fair and Effective Asylum Procedures* (London: JUSTICE/ILPA/ARC, 1997), p. 38.

[3] *ibid.*, pp. 50–1. For earlier criticism, see A. Harvey, *'The Risks of Getting it Wrong': the Asylum and Immigration Bill Session 1995–96 and the Determination of Special Adjudicators* (London: ARC, 1996). See, also, M. Henderson, *Best Practice Guide to Asylum Appeals* (London: ILPA, 1997); Asylum Aid, *'No Reason at All' – Home Office Decisions on Asylum Claims* (London: Asylum Aid, 1995); Asylum Aid, *'Still No Reason at All' – Home Office Decisions on Asylum Claims* (London: Asylum Aid, 1999).

[4] F. Elliott, *The Sunday Telegraph*, June 2, 2002.

[5] D. Kennedy, *The Times*, May 31, 2002.

[6] *The Guardian*, May 18, 2001.

[7] J. Burns, *Financial Times*, January 25, 2001.

[8] *Daily Mail*, September 4, 2001.

asylum system. However, its motives for legislating were clearly at odds with the concerns of the NGOs. For example, during parliamentary debates on both Acts, government ministers indicated that removal of various 'pull factors' was high priority. These were repeatedly identified as: the generous system of support, the prospect of permanent settlement, the delay in the determination process, and the failure to remove.[9] In 1999, the Minister of State in the House of Lords, Lord Falconer, declared that if the government did 'not respond effectively to the systematic abuse of the asylum system, [. . .], the genuine asylum seekers [would] become lost in a system that [would] be completely overloaded'.[10] These fears have given rise to a range of 'tough' measures, including the withdrawal of benefits, greater enforcement powers, the creation of accommodation and removal centres, the reduction of in-country appeal rights and tight time limits for appeal. Yet refugee-support groups disagree about the significance of 'pull factors' and are convinced that the government's unrelenting determination to rid the system of 'abuse' has resulted in poor legislation, ineffective policy, and questionable first instance decision-making.

REACHING THE UNITED KINGDOM

Visas and carriers' liability

The first and most obvious way to exclude asylum seekers from the UK is to prevent their arrival. This policy is, of course, not new. As has been seen, it was employed, prior to the Second World War, when the use of visas had very serious consequences for many Jews attempting to escape Germany. Since the 1930s, visas have remained a key component of UK immigration policy. With the introduction of carriers' liability legislation in 1987, they have assumed even greater significance in relation to asylum policy, particularly as their use has been on the rise since 1985.[11] As there is no visa for asylum seekers,

6.3

---

[9] HC Special Standing Committee, March 22, 1999, Mr Jack Straw. For a comprehensive list, see Home Affairs Select Committee, 'Border Controls', First Report, Session 2000–01, January 23, 2001, HC 163, paras 10 and 409. See, for a contrasting view of reasons for migration to the UK, V. Robinson & J. Segrott, *Understanding the Decision-Making of Asylum Seekers*, Home Office Research Study 243, (London: Home Office RDSD, July 2002).

[10] HL Deb. Vol. 605, October 18, 1999, col. 774.

[11] See, for a wider discussion, A. Cruz, *Carriers Liability in the Member States of the European Union* (Brussels: Churches Commission for Migrants in Europe, 1994); E. Feller, 'Carrier Sanctions and International Law', (1989) 1 *IJRL*, 48.

and those forced to leave their country are unlikely to obtain standard visas, it has been conceded that the 1987 Act, coupled with visa restrictions, may 'pose substantial obstacles in the path of many refugees wishing to come to this country'.[12] The UNHCR has been more forthright in its condemnation: 'The problem with such immigration controls is that while they may be directed at non-refugee groups or abusers of the asylum process, they work indiscriminately to also hinder the access by refugees to status determination procedures and the rights and protection these persons enjoy.'[13]

Despite such protestations, the UK has continued to enhance its pre-entry controls. Under the 1993 Act, carriers' liability was extended to transit passengers.[14] Later, the new Labour government announced that the Immigration (Carriers' Liability) Act 1987 would be extended to cover the Channel Tunnel Rail Company, overseers of trains crossing to and from the continent, and called for the strengthening of the 1987 Act in its 1998 White Paper: *Fairer, Faster and Firmer – A Modern Approach to Immigration and Asylum*. Though it claimed that the Act was an 'important and effective deterrent', carriers have been consistently remiss in payment of their fines. By way of example, it was reported in Parliament in 1995 that fines of £80.2 million had been incurred, of which £46.11 million had been paid, while £16.29 million were being pursued in debt recovery actions.[15] The antagonism caused by fining has forced the government to propose a 'partnership with carriers to help them with their responsibilities'.[16] What this entails is not entirely apparent. The 1998 White Paper went on to endorse another Conservative initiative. In 1993, the Immigration Service placed an 'Airline Liaison Officer' ('ALO') in New Delhi to assist airlines operating from India, Bangladesh and Sri Lanka in the detection of fraudulent documentation, and to work with the immigration services and police in those countries. Between 1996 and 1997, the number was increased to five (New Delhi, Dhaka, Colombo, Accra and Nairobi), and then, in 1998, to 20, so successful

---

[12] *R. v Secretary of State for the Home Department, ex parte Yassine* [1990] Imm AR 354, at 359–60; see, also, Amnesty International British Section, *UK, A Duty Dodged: the Government's Evasion of its Obligations under the 1951 UN Convention on Refugees* (London: AI, October 1991), p. 5.

[13] UNHCR, Note on International Protection: UN Doc. A/AC.96/728 (August 2, 1989), cited in Amnesty International British Section, *United Kingdom – A Duty Dodged: The Government's Evasion of its Obligations under the 1951 UN Convention on Refugees* (London: AI, October 1991).

[14] Asylum and Immigration Appeals Act 1993, s. 12.

[15] HC Deb. Vol. 263 Pt 2, Written Answers, July 18, 1995, col 1034.

[16] Home Office, *Fairer, Faster and Firmer – A Modern Approach to Immigration and Asylum*, Cm 4018 (London: The Stationery Office, 1998), para. 5.13.

did they prove.[17] Evidence of their success was recently provided when it was claimed that 'during 2001, 22,515 inadequately documented passengers en route to the UK and elsewhere were denied boarding by carriers at ALO locations'.[18]

In the latest White Paper, *Secure Borders, Safe Haven – Integration with Diversity in Modern Britain*, the government reaffirmed that 'visa regimes remain an effective tool in the control of those seeking to come to the UK',[19] but failed to acknowledge their inability to discriminate between the 'genuine' and the 'bogus'. In a significant new development, the White Paper, arguing that 'visa regimes are not always appropriate', proposed the adoption of pre-clearance schemes.[20] These allow British immigration officers based at airports abroad to carry out checks on passengers seeking to fly to the UK. Such a scheme had been introduced at Prague airport, with the prime aim of addressing the problem of large numbers of 'inadmissible Czech citizens arriving in the UK, many of which applied for asylum'.[21] The White Paper failed to mention that the Prague pre-clearance scheme was, in fact, targeted at the Roma 'who are perceived as serial abusers of the asylum system', and that the only alternative would have been the introduction of visas for all Czech nationals.[22] The conclusion that the Roma are 'bogus' as a category ignores the expectation laid down in the 1951 Convention that each applicant's circumstances should be individually examined. It also pays no heed to persuasive evidence that the Czech Roma, while perhaps not suffering persecution as defined by the Convention, face discrimination and are subjected often to racially motivated attacks.[23] The Prague scheme was challenged recently before the UK courts and declared legal by the Court of Appeal.[24]

---

[17] *ibid.*, para. 5.20; and see Home Affairs Select Committee, 'Border Controls' and 'Border Controls: Minutes of Evidence and Appendices', First Report, Session 2000–01, January 23, 2001, HC 163–I and II.

[18] Home Office, *Secure Borders, Safe Haven – Integration with Diversity in Modern Britain*, Cm 5387 (London: The Stationery Office, 2002), para. 6.5.

[19] *ibid.*, para. 6.6.

[20] *ibid.*, para. 6.8.

[21] *ibid.*, para. 6.8.

[22] K. Connolly, 'The rights of Roma', *The Guardian*, August 1, 2001.

[23] See D. Stevens, 'The migration of the Romanian Roma to the UK: a contextual study' (2003) 4 *European Journal of Migration and Law*; D. Stevens, 'Roma asylum applicants in the UK: 'scroungers' or 'scapegoats'?' in Joanne van Selm, *et al*, eds., *The Refugee Convention at 50: a View from Forced Migration Studies* (USA: Lexington Books, 2003), pp. 145–60; OSCE High Commissioner for National Minorities, *Report on the Situation of Roma and Sinti in the OSCE area*, April 2000, available on *www.osce.org/hcnm/documents/reports/roma/report_roma_sinti_2000.pdf*

[24] *European Roma Rights Centre & Others v The Immigration Officer at Prague Airport; Secretary of State for the Home Department* [2003] EWCA Civ 666, and see Ch. 8 for further discussion.

6.4   A version of the pre-clearance scheme was introduced by the
Nationality, Immigration and Asylum Act 2002 in the form of an
'Authority to Carry' requirement. Carriers, as opposed to immigration officers, will be obliged to obtain authority in advance before permitting passengers to journey to the UK.[25] Failure to do so will result
in a penalty, the amount of which has yet to be determined by secondary legislation. This additional bureaucratic burden is not welcomed by the transport sector, which feels it has borne the financial
brunt of the government's failure to control its borders. For example,
in February 2002, Eurotunnel claimed to have invested £6 million in
measures aimed at preventing asylum seekers from entering the
UK.[26] Latterly, its main battle has been fought against the notorious
Red Cross asylum camp at Sangatte, near Calais, from which scores
of people tried to enter the UK illegally. Eurotunnel sought twice,
and failed, to have Sangatte closed by the French courts.[27] Finally,
agreement was reached between the British and French governments,
and Sangatte ceased its activities at the end of December 2002.[28]

The 2002 Act also continues the work undertaken in earlier legislation.[29] Thus ship and aircraft owners are still liable to fines of
£2,000 per undocumented traveller.[30] The civil penalty, introduced
by the Immigration and Asylum Act 1999, is also maintained, though
in amended form following the unfavourable decision of *International
Transport Roth GmbH and Others v Secretary of State for the Home Department*.[31] While the government was forced to change the penalty from
a fixed to a variable charge, and to set a maximum fine for each clandestine entrant,[32] it did so willingly, claiming that the civil penalty
regime has 'significantly contributed towards a major reduction in the
number of clandestine entrants entering the UK in road vehicles and
freight wagons'.[33] The power to detain transporters still applies and is
perceived as a useful complement to the penalty.

The discovery of 9,326 clandestines at Dover in 2001 represented
a fall of 27 per cent on the previous year, a statistic used to justify the

---

[25] Nationality, Immigration and Asylum Act 2002, s. 124.
[26] A. Travis, 'Blunkett drops Eurotunnel fines', *The Guardian*, February 5, 2002.
[27] See, *e.g.*, J. Henley, 'Shutdown of French centre blocked by French', *The Guardian*, September 12, 2001.
[28] A. Travis, 'Britain to accept 1,200 migrants in Sangatte deal', *The Guardian*, December 3, 2002.
[29] For a useful and in-depth discussion of the issues raised by pre-2002 controls, see Home Affairs Select Committee, 'Border Controls', First Report, Session 2000–01, January 23, 2001, HC 163.
[30] New s. 40, Immigration and Asylum Act 1999.
[31] [2002] 3 WLR 344, and see Chs 5 and 8 for further discussion.
[32] £2,000 per clandestine per carrier; combined maximum of £4,000 per clandestine.
[33] IND, 'Fact sheet – Asylum Policy', available on *www.ind.homeoffice.gov.uk/default.asp? PageId=3659*

maintenance of the civil penalty regime.[34] The Home Office has also argued that the civil penalty acts as an incentive for carriers to prevent their transporters from being used by clandestines to enter the UK. Without it, it is contended, a 'key plank of the government's policy on controlling illegal entry' would be undermined and 'any increase in clandestine entry [would] have significant consequences for the taxpayer'.[35] This provides little comfort to carriers who have long opposed the adoption of sanctions and civil penalties and do not see it as their role to enforce UK immigration policy. There is an alternative explanation for the drop in numbers of clandestine entrants apprehended: it is possible that those attempting to enter the UK are simply becoming more successful in evading immigration controls.

The Home Office recently published the results of major research on the impact of asylum policies in Europe from 1990 to 2000.[36] Though the study concluded that 'causal links between policies and impacts were tenuous' and that 'direct measures – i.e. pre-entry – *appeared* to have the greatest impact on the number of asylum claimants' (emphasis added),[37] the Home Office quickly issued a press notice entitled 'Border controls most effective way of reducing asylum claims'.[38] There it was made very clear that the government regarded the research as fully endorsing its policy of increased pre-entry measures and border controls.

Trafficking and smuggling[39]

The government has been forced yet again to turn to legislation to tackle a relatively new phenomenon: the trafficking and smuggling of human beings. In this context, trafficking refers to the transport of individuals to another country in order to exploit them for prostitution or forced labour. Smuggling, by contrast, relates to the carriage of people across borders in breach of immigration controls. Most   **6.5**

---

[34] *ibid.*

[35] IND, *Civil penalty – Regulatory impact assessment*, available on *www.ind.homeoffice.gov.uk/default.asp?pageid=2963*

[36] R. Zetter *et al*, *An Assessment of the Impact of Asylum Policies in Europe 1990–2000*, Home Office Research Study 259 (London: Home Office RDSD, June 2003).

[37] *ibid.*, p. 122.

[38] Home Office Press Release, June 23, 2003.

[39] There are a number of reports on trafficking and smuggling. See UNICEF, *End Child Exploitation: Stop the Traffic!* (London: UNICEF, July 2003), J. Morrison, *The Trafficking and Smuggling of Refugees: The End Game in European Asylum Policy?* (Geneva: UNHCR, July 2000), J. Morrison, *The Cost of Survival: The Trafficking of Refugees to the UK* (London: The Refugee Council, July 1998).

western governments suspect that trafficking and smuggling are now endemic and provide a major source of income for organised crime: 'World-wide, migrant smuggling and trafficking is now worth between $12 billion (IOM estimate) and $30 billion (US sources). [. . .] Profits are approaching drug smuggling levels and with lower criminal penalties if caught, there are few disincentives.'[40] Traffickers and smugglers are universally condemned, and those who employ their services are not always regarded as victims. The Home Office argues that carriers' liability legislation is being undermined 'by racketeers and organised crime exploiting and facilitating economic migration by people *who are not entitled to enter the UK*' (emphasis added).[41] From this statement, it is clear that those who turn to smugglers for assistance are not looked upon as asylum seekers but as people intent on evading immigration control. Such an interpretation arguably arises from the long-term association of 'asylum seeker' with 'economic migrant', and the negative press of the last decade. Yet, in reality, the reasons for migration are manifold, as are the methods employed to gain entry to another country.

The law has long targeted immigration offences. Over time, s. 25(1) to the Immigration Act 1971 has been strengthened. As noted in Chapter 5, prior to 2002, people were prohibited from helping an illegal entrant, or an asylum seeker, to enter the UK, for gain. The maximum penalty for this offence was 10 years imprisonment and/or an unlimited fine, and a court had the right to order the forfeiture of any ship, aircraft or vehicle used in the commission of the offence. The measures adopted in the 1999 Act to deal with the growth in the smuggling industry did not prove as successful as the authorities anticipated. The numbers of people charged and convicted under ss. 25(1)(a) and (b) of the Immigration Act 1971 were relatively low. In the year 2000, 210 were proceeded against, 148 were found guilty and 149 were sentenced to custody.[42] Consequently, the 2002 Act introduced some quite radical amendments: the replacement of s. 25 with four new ss.: 25, 25A, 25B and 25C.[43] It is now an offence to assist unlawful entry to any EU Member State, not just the UK,[44] and to assist entry to the UK of an EU citizen in breach of a

---

[40] Home Affairs Select Committee, 'Border Controls', First Report, Session 2000–01, January 23, 2001, Home Office Evidence, Appendix 1, para. 9.2.

[41] Home Office, *Fairer, Faster and Firmer – A Modern Approach to Immigration and Asylum*, Cm 4018 (London: The Stationery Office, 1998), para. 5.15.

[42] HC Deb. Vol. 380, Written Answers, February 27, 2002, cols. 1384W-1386W. The numbers sentenced to custody exceed those found guilty as they include those committed for sentence from the magistrates courts in the previous year.

[43] s. 143.

[44] New s. 25, Immigration Act 1971.

deportation or exclusion order.[45] New s. 25A replaces s. 25(1)(b) to the 1971 Act with reference to the offence of assisting an asylum seeker to enter the UK, where done for gain. The maximum penalty for all these offences has been raised to 14 years in prison, and may include a fine. Courts continue to have the power to detain vehicles, ships or aircraft if used in connection with the offence.[46] The legislation appears now to cover all possible immigration offences and ministers are hopeful they will help arrest the rise in smuggling.

A macabre illustration of the law's failure to deter smugglers **6.6** occurred in June 2000, when 58 asphyxiated bodies were discovered in the back of a refrigerated lorry that arrived at Dover on an overnight ferry. They proved to be the Chinese victims of a smuggling racket organised by the notorious Snakehead gangs.[47] Instantly, the then Minister for Immigration, Barbara Roche, called for a Europe-wide plan to 'beat people smugglers' through the improved sharing of information on fingerprinting, photographs and intelligence, and full utilisation of Europol.[48] Mrs Roche supported plans to bring national laws closer together and proposed the imposition of tougher sanctions on traffickers. In an important change of policy, she added that western states 'need to find ways to meet legitimate desires to migrate, be ready to think imaginatively about how migration can meet the emerging social and economic needs', and that they could not allow their migration policies to be 'randomly dictated by racketeers and facilitators'.[49] While reiterating the long-standing policy of increased sanction and surveillance, Mrs Roche's willingness to broaden the debate was an important admission that the issue of migration was more complex than previously declared and that a purely restrictive line was not working.

The government's new approach became apparent on publication of the 2002 White Paper. There it announced the establishment of new 'rational and credible routes' of migration to enable men and women to live and work in the UK. Amongst the proposals were new provisions for postgraduate students to switch into employment; consideration of ways to meet the demand for short-term casual labour; and review of the Working Holidaymaker Scheme. In January 2002, the Home Office introduced the Highly Skilled Migrant Programme, which allows individuals with 'exceptional

---

[45] New s. 25B, Immigration Act 1971.
[46] New s. 25C, Immigration Act 1971.
[47] N. Hopkins, J. Vasagar, P. Kelso & A. Osborn, 'Grim find of 58 bodies in lorry exposes smugglers' evil trade', *The Guardian*, June 20, 2000.
[48] Home Office News Release, 'Together Europe can beat people smugglers – Roche', July 21, 2000.
[49] *ibid.*

personal skills and experience' to work in the UK.[50] Initially run as a pilot for twelve months, it aimed to service the needs of the UK employment market and economy. In January 2003, it was declared a success and extended indefinitely.[51] In addition, a Seasonal Agricultural Workers' Scheme has also been implemented, allowing overseas nationals to enter the UK and work in the agricultural industry to meet its demand for seasonal labour. The quota for 2003 was 25,000. The government clearly considers that such alternatives will help reduce the numbers resorting to illegal methods of entry, but, realistically, the impact is unlikely to be significant.

Following a comprehensive review of the law on sex offences in July 2000,[52] the White Paper proposed two new laws to deal with trafficking for sexual and labour exploitation. The concern about labour exploitation relates to the movement of people from one location to another for the purposes of exploiting their labour and usually with the use of force, fraud or coercion.[53] The White Paper referred to the establishment of a multi-agency task force chaired by the National Crime Squad to tackle smuggling and trafficking, and also recognised the need for greater co-operation with EU members in targeting immigration crime. Following the EU Tampere summit, there has been some progress on this issue – for example, agreement on a Framework Decision on Strengthening of the Penal Framework to Prevent the Facilitation of Unauthorised Entry, Transit and Residence, and associated Directive.[54]

Taking account of the urgent need for action, the Nationality, Immigration and Asylum Act 2002 created a new offence of trafficking people to and from the UK for the purpose of controlling them in prostitution.[55] It carries a maximum sentence, on indictment, of 14 years imprisonment and/or a fine, or, on summary conviction, imprisonment for six months and/or a fine. The Act did not prohibit labour exploitation and therefore fell short of the White Paper's expectations. Nonetheless, in October 2002, just months before the passing of the 2002 Act, it was announced in Parliament that the government intended to legislate further against trafficking for the purposes of both labour and sexual exploitation as soon as time permitted, and before July 2004, in line with the EU Framework

[50] See 'Notice to Customers, Highly Skilled Migrant Programme (HSMP)', on IND website: *www.ind.homeoffice.gov.uk/default.asp?PageID=2754*.
[51] For information on HSMP, see IND website.
[52] Home Office, *Setting the Boundaries – Reforming the Law on Sex Offences*, July 2000.
[53] Home Office, *Secure Borders, Safe Haven – Integration with Diversity in Modern Britain*, Cm 5387 (London: The Stationery Office, 2002), para. 5.29.
[54] OJ 2002 L328/1; 2002/90/EC; OJ 2002 L328/17. See, also, Ch. 9 for further discussion of the EU dimension.
[55] s. 145, and see Ch. 5.

Decision.[56] The Sexual Offences Bill 2003 proposes new, more comprehensive offences of trafficking for sexual exploitation 'to replace the stop-gap offence introduced by the Nationality, Immigration and Asylum Act 2002 of Trafficking in Prostitution'.[57]

The imposition of such stringent measures in relation to smuggling   **6.7** and trafficking is quite understandable in view of the line promulgated in some quarters that the UK is losing control of its borders.[58] With few legal routes of entry to the UK, there is little alternative open to refugees but to resort to smugglers. As much has been admitted by government ministers. In answer to a question in January 2002 as to whether there were any legal means by which an individual could enter this country to claim asylum, Lord Rooker replied: 'I think that the short answer [. . .] is no.'[59] Once people are forced into the hands of human smugglers and traffickers, the potential for disasters such as the case of the 58 Chinese is increased. The Institute of Race Relations calculated that 742 people had died trying to access the EU area between January and July 2003.[60] Those who survive have limited protection:

> 'Victims of trafficking may find themselves at risk of serious harm when traffickers are arrested, particularly if they co-operate with any prosecution and subsequently have to return to their countries of origin.
>
> Victims of trafficking need support and reflection period [*sic*] before they decide whether to co-operate with a criminal investigation (the government defeated amendments [to the 2002 Bill] proposing this).'[61]

In a disturbing development, a report by UNICEF has provided evidence of a rapidly increasing problem of the traffic of children to the UK for sexual exploitation, domestic service, or benefit fraud.[62] As indicated, UK law currently prohibits trafficking for commercial sexual exploitation,[63] but child rights' campaigners are demanding further legislation to criminalise trafficking for *any* purpose. They

---

[56] HL Deb. Vol. 640, October 30, 2002, col. 189.

[57] Home Office Press Release, 'More help for victims of sex trafficking', March 10, 2003.

[58] For example, the right-wing tabloid press, and Migration Watch, a voluntary and independent body that examines the arguments for and against migration and lobbies for changes in policy.

[59] HL Deb. Vol. 630, January 23, 2002, col. 1462.

[60] L. Fekete, *Death at the Border – Who is to Blame?* (London: IRR, 2003).

[61] Refugee Council Briefing, *The Nationality, Immigration and Asylum Act 2002: Changes to the Asylum System in the UK*, (London: Refugee Council, December 2002), p. 25.

[62] UNICEF, *End Child Exploitation: Stop the Traffic!* London: UNICEF, July 2003), and see UNICEF website on the issue: *www.endchildexploitation.org.uk/index.asp*

[63] See Nationality, Immigration and Asylum Act 2002, s. 145; Sexual Offences Bill 2003.

have also called for the provision of safe house accommodation for children rescued from their minders. (In March 2003, it was announced that safe houses would be provided for women on a six-month pilot.)[64] Although the numbers exploited in this way are uncertain, it is estimated that 1.2 million children per year are trafficked globally, with a possible 250 sent to the UK every month.[65] Some of these children are instructed to apply for asylum on reaching the UK, before disappearing into an unknown life. A lucky few might escape and claim asylum in their own right.

ARRIVAL IN THE UNITED KINGDOM

The Application process[66]

6.8 The Home Office's determination criteria are set out in the Immigration Rules and the IND's Asylum Policy Instructions ('APIs'), and provide the key to first-instance decision-making.[67] To be considered in the UK, an individual must either claim asylum on arrival at a port, or, if already in the country, apply in person or in writing to the Immigration and Nationality Directorate of the Home Office, based in Croydon. In-country applications can also be submitted at a Public Enquiry Office in Belfast, Glasgow, Liverpool or Birmingham. The post-1993 Rules placed the burden of applying for asylum squarely on the shoulders of the applicant.[68] Once an individual claims asylum, the procedure for assessing the application is immediately triggered. This normally entails screening, preferably by a member of the Asylum Screening Unit ('ASU'), during which personal details are recorded, fingerprints and photographs taken, and the route to the UK noted. A second, substantive interview should follow at a later date. The claim is then considered and finally determined. In both port and in-country cases, it is the Secretary of State, through Home Office decision-makers, who is required to make the decision

---

[64] Home Office Press Release, 'More help for victims of sex trafficking', March 10, 2003.
[65] BBC 2, Newsnight report, July 29, 2003.
[66] For useful discussion of the application process, see JCWI, *Immigration, Nationality & Asylum Law Handbook* (London: JCWI, 2002); ILPA, *Making an Asylum Application – A Best Practice Guide* (London: ILPA, May 2002). See, also, ILPA updates for frequent changes on this topic.
[67] HC 395, paras 327–352.
[68] Statement of Changes in Immigration Rules, HC 395, para. 328 states that: 'Every asylum application made by a person at a port or airport in the United Kingdom will be referred by the Immigration Officer for determination by the Secretary of State in accordance with these Rules.'

in accordance with the UK's obligations under the 1951 Convention.[69] In 1998, the Integrated Casework Directorate ('ICD') was set up in the IND. In the new arrangement, each case management unit dealt with the full range of immigration and asylum casework. Previously, asylum cases were assigned to specialist teams that were often responsible for only one country's casework. However, the Home Office at the time stressed that the specialist expertise of the IND staff would be preserved and cases would be allocated to staff with the necessary knowledge and skills.[70] In 2003, the structure was again modified and the ICD was replaced with three main directorates – Asylum Support and Casework, Managed Migration, and Operations (i.e. the Immigration Service).[71] In the Asylum Directorate, there are around 33 case-working units, each of which concentrates on certain countries, thereby maintaining some degree of specialisation in the system, but also allowing for greater flexibility.[72] Despite these changes, quality of decision-making continues to be heavily criticised by asylum law practitioners.[73]

Port applicants

6.9 It is evident that the interview plays a fundamental part in any asylum seeker's application, since it is the interview that provides the IND with the requisite information for a decision. In port cases, a screening interview is usually conducted to determine details about the claimant and to check whether he or she is a candidate for, detention, temporary admission, 'safe third country' removal or for Oakington Reception Centre (which fast tracks cases). Most port applicants are issued with a Statement of Evidence Form ('SEF') to be completed and returned to the IND.[74] Though a long and complex document, forming the basis of the asylum claim, it must be completed in English and returned within ten working days (28 days for minors). If the SEF is not returned in time, the application can be determined on the information available to the decision-maker. Once the Home Office has considered the SEF, the

---

[69] HC 395, para. 328.

[70] Home Office, *Information about the Integrated Casework Directorate*.

[71] The Asylum Directorate is responsible for NASS, casework and appeals. See ILPA Information for Members, June 2003.

[72] Home Affairs Select Committee, 'Asylum Applications', Uncorrected Oral Evidence, Ken Sutton, May 8, 2003.

[73] See Ch. 7 for further discussion of decision-making.

[74] This was originally known as the Political Asylum Questionnaire and has undergone a number of transformations over the years. SEF was introduced in the year 2000. There are a variety of forms, depending on the circumstances of the applicant.

applicant should be called for substantive interview at Croydon, Leeds or Liverpool.

Immigration officers at ports should not be making substantive decisions about asylum cases. However, in 1999, ILPA issued the results of research conducted on asylum interviews held at ports.[75] It made worrying reading. Tensions clearly existed between legal advisers and immigration officers, whose attitude to some asylum applicants was highly questionable. For example, in one interview with the researcher, a chief immigration officer at Gatwick commented: 'The claims we see that are genuine shine out like a beacon because of the detail and because they have a genuine air of plausibility [. . .] but the overwhelming majority are not genuine.'[76] Given the tendency to proceed with the substantive interview as soon as possible after receipt of a claim, few applicants were legally represented at their interviews. There was a disquieting uncertainty as to the purpose of the substantive interview, not only between adviser and interviewer, but also between the Immigration Service and the ASU, and even on the part of individual immigration officers. The report noted that 'inexplicably, in-country and port applicants are given substantially different explanations about the purpose and conduct of the interview'.[77]

The IND's leaflet to in-country applicants explained that the purpose of the interview was to establish full details of the claim; it acknowledged that the applicant might need to talk about events which were 'painful and embarrassing'; it reassured the interviewee that any information divulged would be treated in confidence.[78] By contrast, the Immigration Service, representing immigration officers, produced a leaflet that offered little explanation as to the purpose of the interview and little reassurance as to confidentiality. It was felt that immigration officers' confusion about the purpose of the substantive interview had led some to test the *credibility* of the applicant during the interview rather than simply obtain information. As a consequence, damaging details might have been forwarded to the IND, gleaned from applicants who were tired, emotional, confused, unrepresented, and who did not realise the significance of the interview. The evidence provided by ILPA's hard-hitting report supported JUSTICE'S earlier contention that: 'The gap between decision-maker and interviewer is a fertile ground for misrepresentation and error.'[79]

---

[75] H. Crawley, *Breaking Down the Barriers – A Report on the Conduct of Asylum Interviews at Ports* (London: ILPA, 1999).

[76] *ibid.*, para. 3.80.

[77] *ibid.*, para. 5.6.

[78] *ibid.*, para. 5.6, and see accompanying text from IND's Asylum Directorate's 'Asylum Applications a brief guide to procedures in the UK'.

[79] *Providing Protection – Towards Fair and Effective Asylum Procedures* (London: JUSTICE ILPA/ARC, July 1997), p. 39.

It would appear from information provided by practitioners that such misrepresentation and error continue to mar the asylum process.

In-country applicants

Applicants who apply in writing will be invited to attend an interview at the ASU.[80] Many in-country cases appear in person at the ASU, where they are screened on arrival. It transpired in early 2002 that a new screening questionnaire, with four 'levels' of scrutiny, was introduced for some in-country claimants, and for port applicants.[81] The first and second levels cover basic screening questions, and brief questions on the basis of the claim. It is at this stage that the SEF is normally issued.[82] If there are doubts about the applicant's identity or nationality, the third level is engaged, comprising an open-ended interview. Level four consists of an interview at a police station where it is suspected that the claimant has committed an immigration offence.[83] Once applicants are screened, their details are placed on an Application Registration Card ('ARC'), a biometric smart card, indicating that they have entered the asylum process.[84] This allows an applicant to access the support service and also helps prevent fraud. If an applicant has leave to remain in the UK when the claim is made, then he or she ought not to be detained. However, the IND will arrange for detention or referral to Oakington for some applicants, and therefore in-country applicants do not necessarily escape detention.

The fingerprinting of port and in-country applicants, introduced in the 1990s in asylum cases, is assuming a new significance. As indicated, fingerprints are normally taken by immigration officers at ports or by officials in the ASU. Police officers, prison officers and employees of detention centres are also empowered to take fingerprints,[85] and reasonable force can be used.[86] Children under 16 may be fingerprinted in the presence of a responsible adult. The APIs note that it is not current policy to fingerprint children under five.[87] All

6.10

---

[80] JCWI, *Immigration, Nationality & Asylum Law Handbook* (London: JCWI, 2002), p. 169.

[81] *ibid.*

[82] See below.

[83] JCWI, *Immigration, Nationality & Asylum Law Handbook* (London: JCWI, 2002), p. 180.

[84] ARC replaced the Standard Acknowledgement Letter ('SAL') as from January 2002 and is being gradually phased in. It is the size of a credit card and contains all the applicant's personal details, a photograph, and a fingerprint.

[85] Home Office, Asylum Policy Instructions, 'Miscellaneous guidance for caseworkers – Fingerprinting', para. 1.

[86] Immigration and Asylum Act 1999, ss. 141–142.

[87] Home Office, Asylum Policy Instructions, 'Miscellaneous guidance for caseworkers – Fingerprinting', para. 1.

fingerprints are retained at the Immigration Fingerprint Bureau and no longer need be destroyed on resolution of an asylum claim, a power granted by the Anti-terrorism, Crime and Security Act 2001.[88] They will normally be held for ten years.[89]

As of January 2003, and the launch of the EU-wide database, EURODAC, fingerprints are cross-checked against records held by European Member States to establish if applicants have lodged claims elsewhere.[90] While fingerprint technology already plays a large part in the UK in the drive to cut fraud and prevent abuse of the immigration and asylum system, EURODAC is regarded by the government as 'a valuable resource to tackle multiple asylum applications and deter asylum shopping'.[91]

The substantive interview

6.11   The substantive interview, whether for port or in-country applicants, is usually held to enable the asylum seeker to describe their experiences and explain the basis of their claim. It may take place on the same day as the claim is made or, more usually, at a later date, once the SEF has been returned. If the interview takes place on the day of the claim, the SEF is completed during the interview. Although an applicant can bring a legal representative to the interview, there is no legal right to representation and an interview will not normally be delayed simply because the representative is not present. An interpreter is provided free of charge if required.

While it is understandable that port applicants might have difficulty obtaining legal representation, particularly where immigration officers refuse to wait for advisers to arrive before commencing a substantive interview, the lack of legal representation at in-country interviews is less acceptable. For some time, legal representatives were advised to attend interviews held by the ASU to ensure that nothing of substance was raised.[92] However, in August 1999, the Lord Chancellor announced new arrangements on funding for representation before the Immigration Appellate Authority.[93] While details of the arrangements related to exclusive contracting and to a merits test

---

[88] s. 36.

[89] Home Office, Asylum Policy Instructions, 'Miscellaneous guidance for caseworkers – Fingerprinting', para. 2.3.

[90] See Ch. 9 for further details.

[91] Home Office Press Release, 'EU asylum fingerprint database begins operating today', January 15, 2003.

[92] JCWI, *Immigration, Nationality & Refugee Law – A User's Guide* (London: JCWI, 1999), p. 106.

[93] For details of the arrangement, see November 1999, *Legal Action*, pp. 10–12.

for representation at appeal, the end of (the then) Legal Aid payments for those accompanying asylum applicants to the ASU was also announced.[94] The Legal Aid Board (now The Legal Services Commission ('LSC')) appeared to have agreed the removal of funding for screening interviews on assurances from the Home Office that they would not be turned into substantive interviews in relation to asylum applications.[95] The IND also confirmed that, in relation to screening at ports, representatives would not be admitted to any part of the screening process.[96] At the time, practitioners complained that inappropriate questions were still being asked of applicants in screening interviews.[97] It now seems that the new four-level screening is raising further concerns, particularly in relation to level two, where details of the grounds of the claim might be discussed without the presence of a legal representative.[98] The LSC does not sanction funding for attendance at a screening interview, other than for minors.[99]

First instance decision-making procedures

As is widely acknowledged, the asylum process – from claim to decision – ought to be conducted quickly, but should always ensure high standards of fairness.[100] One of the major impediments to achieving high standards in the UK has been the delay in handling applications, leading to growing backlogs. The 1998 White Paper confirmed that the backlog stood at 'over 50,000 cases awaiting decision and over 20,000 queuing for an appeal hearing'.[101] By the end of January 2000, the backlog had reached a record 103,495 applications.[102] The White Paper noted further that 'the key to restoring effectiveness to our asylum system and to tackling abuse is swifter determination of

6.12

---

[94] *Immigration Supplement of the Exclusive Contracting on Legal Advice and Assistance for Civil Matters and Certificated Legal Aid in Family/Matrimonial Matters*, r. 10.

[95] See Letter from Legal Aid Board to ILPA – September 29, 1999, ILPA Information for Members, October 1999.

[96] See Letter from IND to Legal Aid Board – July 20, 1999, ILPA Information for Members, October 1999.

[97] Letter from ILPA to Legal Aid Board – November 3, 1999, ILPA Information for Members, November 1999.

[98] JCWI, *Immigration, Nationality & Asylum Law Handbook* (London: JCWI, 2002), p. 180.

[99] ILPA, *Making an Asylum Application – A Best Practice Guide* (London: ILPA, May 2002), p. 60.

[100] See Ex. Com. Report, 28th Session 1977, and UNHCR *Handbook*, para. 192 for basic procedural requirements.

[101] Home Office, *Fairer, Faster and Firmer – A Modern Approach to Immigration and Asylum*, Cm 4018 (London: The Stationery Office, 1998), para. 8.7.

[102] Home Office, *Asylum Statistics: December 2000 United Kingdom*.

applications and appeals'.[103] Such a conclusion is not new. The declared aim of the 1993 Act was to process asylum cases with speed. Yet within a year of that Act coming into force, the Home Office had already formed the view that asylum determination continued to be too slow. Consequently, a number of changes were made to asylum procedures over the intervening years. The current system, based on SEF, has been in place since the year 2000.

The reliance on SEF maintains the focus on speed. The original time period for completion of the form was 14 days, but this was reduced to ten to bring it into line with the submission time for the 'one-stop statement', introduced by the 1999 Act and subsequent secondary legislation.[104] A failure to return the SEF within the specified time can lead to a refusal for non-compliance.[105] Understandably, there was considerable objection to the time scales from practitioners and refugee-support groups, who regarded ten (and even 14) days as insufficient time adequately to complete the form. Many applicants would be unable to find a representative to assist with completing the SEF, a problem exacerbated by changes in funding of representatives and increased dispersal of asylum seekers around the country.[106] Despite the refusal for non-compliance of a considerable number of cases, the government held firm, believing that this timeframe was reasonable.

The Home Office has over the years run a number of pilots in which the SEF is not used, known as the 'SEFless procedure', to establish the impact it makes on decision-making.[107] In these cases, following the interview, applicants are given five days in which to provide further representations before an initial decision is made. In in-country cases, applicants are screened as usual in the ASU on the day of their application. They are then provided with a date for their interview two weeks after their screening. The decision on the application is generally made after day 25. The Home Office considers that the introduction of more SEFless procedures will enable it to 'work faster, more flexibly and efficiently'.[108] Critics believe, however, that the five-day limit imposes an unnecessary burden on legal representatives and asylum seekers in their attempt to collate additional information in support of the case. It is further claimed that these

---

[103] Home Office, *Fairer, Faster and Firmer – A Modern Approach to Immigration and Asylum*, Cm 4018 (London: The Stationery Office, 1998), para. 8.7.

[104] I. McDonald & F. Webber, *Macdonald's Immigration Law and Practice* (London: Butterworths, 2001), para. 12.108, fn. 9.

[105] HC 395, para. 340.

[106] Letter from ILPA to Chris Hudson, IND, ILPA Information for Members – March 28, 2000. See Ch. 5 and below for discussion on dispersal.

[107] See IND letter to ILPA, ILPA Information for Members, October 10, 2001.

[108] IND letter to ILPA, ILPA Information for Members, March 26, 2001.

time limits can damage fair decision-making, since certain material, such as medical evidence of torture, might be very difficult to obtain within five days.[109] In other words, it is the refugee who is likely to suffer most from these provisions.

Legal representation

While the accelerated application procedures may cause difficulties for asylum seekers, the fundamental changes to legal aid and the regulation of immigration advisers also present their own problems. One of the stated aims of the Immigration and Asylum Act 1999 was to clamp down on unscrupulous immigration advisers who were exploiting clients for financial gain.[110] Part V of the Act introduced a new system of regulation of immigration advisers and representatives and established an Immigration Services Commissioner whose duty was to promote good practice.[111] Only a 'qualified person', as defined by the Act, is entitled to provide immigration advice or services; breach of this provision is a criminal offence and carries a maximum penalty of two years in prison and a fine.[112] Part of the definition of a 'qualified person' involves registration with the Commissioner. An Office of the Immigration Services Commissioner has now been established and has published 'The Commissioner's Rules' and Code of Standards, which together control the conduct and fee charging of immigration advisers.[113] The Act also created the Immigration Services Tribunal to hear appeals against certain decisions of the Commissioner.[114]

Of greater significance, from the viewpoint of the asylum seeker, has been the fundamental shake-up of the provision of legal services and of financial assistance for legal fees. The Community Legal Service ('CLS') replaced the old civil scheme of Legal Aid from April 2000. The CLS's aim is 'to improve access, for the public, to quality information, advice and legal services through local networks of services supported by co-ordinated funding and based on an assessment of local needs'.[115] Those wishing to be part of the CLS network and

6.13

---

[109] The Refugee Council Briefing Paper, *Indefinite Leave to Remain, Exceptional Leave to Remain, Refugee Status: What the Government's New Proposals Mean* (London: The Refugee Council, September 1998).

[110] See The Lord Chancellor's Advisory Committee on Legal Education and Conduct, *Improving the Quality of Immigration Advice and Representation – A Report,* July 1998, which preceded the 1999 Act.

[111] s. 83(3).

[112] ss. 84 and 91.

[113] For further information, see the OISC website: *www.oisc.org.uk/home.stm*

[114] s. 87, and see IST's website: *www.immigrationservicestribunal.gov.uk/*

[115] See LSC website: *www.legalservices.gov.uk/*

to provide immigration services and advice need to obtain a 'Quality Mark' from the LSC; this will only be granted if they demonstrate they meet the standard required for the type of service being delivered. The three Quality Mark standards are: Information; General Help; and Specialist Help. CLS funding is available for legal help, controlled legal representation (appeals before the adjudicator and IAT), and legal representation (cases before the High Court, Court of Appeal, and House of Lords). Eligibility for financial assistance is strictly controlled in order to prevent hopeless cases from being undertaken by advisers, and applies to those with little or no means.[116] Many LSC-franchised firms have not survived the new climate and have lost their contracts, or have handed them back to the LSC.

For thirty years, there has been a power, laid down in statute, for the Home Secretary to make a grant to a voluntary organisation that provides immigration or asylum advice and assistance. Under the 2002 Act, the power is spelled out in s. 110. It states that the Secretary of State may make a grant to a voluntary organisation that provides 'advice or assistance to persons who have a right of appeal under Part 5 [Immigration and Asylum Appeals]' and 'other services for the welfare of those persons'.[117] Two organisations that have benefited in the past from the Home Office grant are the Immigration Advisory Service ('IAS') and the Refugee Legal Centre ('RLC'). However, a recent decision by the government to transfer the Home Office funding to the LSC will have a serious operational impact on the IAS and RLC and will end their ability to offer completely free legal advice and representation beyond the LSC.

In June 2003, a consultation paper was published by the Lord Chancellor's Department proposing major modifications to the funding of immigration and asylum work. Noting that legal aid costs of advice and representation in immigration and asylum cases (including judicial reviews) have risen from £81.3 million in 2000–2001 to £127.9 million in 2001–2002 and £174.2 million in 2002–2003, the paper makes a number of suggestions: the introduction of a maximum limit for advice under Legal Help – in the case of asylum, five hours' work –, maximum fees for representatives' and interpreters' costs at the adjudicator stage, and a separate maximum when applying for permission to appeal to the IAT.[118] Needless to say, a five-hour

---

[116] See, for further detail, JCWI, *Immigration, Nationality & Asylum Law Handbook* (London: JCWI, 2002), Ch. 3.

[117] s. 110; formerly, Immigration and Asylum Act 1999, s. 81.

[118] Lord Chancellor's Department Consultation Paper, *Proposed Changes to Publicly Funded Immigration and Asylum Work*, June 2003, paras 24 and 32.

cut-off for Legal Help is very severe and will, undoubtedly, be opposed by practitioners.

The likely consequences of all these developments are that all cases will need to meet the LSC's eligibility criteria, there will be no alternative option for free legal advice, and there will be fewer competent advisers (currently, there are 617 contracted suppliers) willing to take on immigration and asylum work.[119] This cannot be helpful for either asylum seekers or the asylum system as a whole.

AWAITING THE DECISION

Induction, accommodation and detention

Immigration officers have two main options open to them when an asylum seeker arrives at a port: to grant temporary admission, or to detain. In the past, as an alternative to detention, the majority of asylum seekers were granted temporary admission, which is usually subject to certain restrictions, such as residence, reporting and employment.[120] The power to detain under the Immigration Act 1971 is a formidable instrument in the hands of the Immigration Service and Home Secretary, and is therefore unlikely to be repealed. Administrative detention is, nonetheless, a highly controversial subject.   **6.14**

Asylum seekers can be detained in a variety of facilities: specialised detention centres, reception centres, police stations, prisons,[121] and even ships. The first reception centre was opened in March 2000 at a former army barracks in Oakington, Cambridgeshire. The centre has 400 beds, catering for single men and women, as well as families, and provides accommodation for up to ten days. The RLC and the IAS provide legal advice and representation, and are present during the SEF interviews. Once all information is received, including further representations, a decision is made. If refused, an applicant has two days in which to appeal. At this point the asylum applicants are either dispersed to suitable accommodation (under the support and dispersal system), granted temporary admission, or taken into further detention.

---

[119] *ibid.*

[120] Immigration Act 1971, sch. 2, paras 21(1) and (2).

[121] The government announced in its 2002 White Paper that the routine use of prison accommodation for immigration detainees ended mid-January 2002. A small number of individuals, including asylum seekers, would continue to be held in prison for reasons of security: Home Office, *Secure Borders, Safe Haven – Integration with Diversity in Modern Britain*, Cm 5387 (London: The Stationery Office, 2002), paras 4.78–9.

The method of case selection for Oakington is telling. Initially, Oakington was intended for port applicants whose claims the Home Office considered could be handled quickly – i.e. 'manifestly unfounded' cases. It soon became clear that in-country applicants were also being transferred to Oakington. At first, applicants from Eastern Europe (Poland, the Czech Republic, Estonia and Romania) were targeted. Subsequently, a number of other countries were added to the list (for example, Ghana, Slovakia, China and Lithuania). In effect, the Home Office, by identifying such countries, created an informal 'white list' of perceived safe countries, following repeal of the actual 'white list' provision contained in the Asylum and Immigration Act 1996. The policy changed yet again when all cases deemed 'straightforward' were directed to Oakington.[122] Subsequent to the 2002 Act, only those countries from which claims were presumed to be unfounded (EU accession and other designated states)[123] were being handled at Oakington.

Oakington's facilities have generally been commended. Two years after opening, it was favourably reviewed by HM Inspectorate of Prisons:

> 'Oakington was essentially a place of safety providing a high standard of custodial care. The needs and dignity of detainees were respected by Centre staff, except for the splitting of families during and after detention, and within the limits of a fast and inflexible process. Unlike at other Centres, there was access to on-site case information and legal representation, though there could be more structured activities, particularly for juveniles, and incentives to take part, in order to ease the tension associated with the serious business of the Centre. Arrangements for those leaving the Centre needed improvement.'[124]

6.15   In her first reports on immigration removal centres, the new Chief Inspector of Prisons, Anne Owers, again endorsed this largely positive account in April 2003.[125] However, the Oakington process has not completely escaped criticism. In recent judicial review proceedings, in the case of *R. v Secretary of State for the Home Department, ex parte Saadi et al*,[126] Collins J., while finding detention to be lawful under domestic law, considered the detention of the claimants in Oakington

---

[122] S. Maguire, IAS London Conference 'Dispersing Asylum Seekers – Punitive or Practical?, June 22, 2000.

[123] See Nationality, Immigration and Asylum Act 2002, s. 94 and Ch. 5.

[124] HM Inspectorate of Prisons, *An Inspection of Oakington Reception Centre*, March 2002, available on *www.ind.homeoffice.gov.uk/filestore/Oakington%20master%20April%201st%20final.pdf*

[125] Available on Chief Inspector of Prisons website: *www.homeoffice.gov.uk/justice/prisons/inspprisons/*

[126] [2001] EWHC Admin 470.

to be in breach of Art. 5(1)(f) of the ECHR. Compensation to thousands of ex-Oakington detainees loomed as a prospect. To the government's relief, his decision was overturned on appeal before the Court of Appeal and House of Lords.[127] The arrangements made at Oakington were accepted by the higher courts as providing reasonable conditions, both for individuals and families, and the period of detention was not regarded as excessive. In fact, detention under the Oakington procedure was deemed 'proportionate and reasonable'.[128]

While the government insists that there is a presumption in favour of temporary admission or release,[129] the numbers of people held in detention have increased over the years. Children are not excluded. At the end of 1998, there were approximately 741 asylum seekers held in detention;[130] by December 2001, this number had reached 1,055 (68 per cent of the total detained).[131] Of the asylum detainees, 89 per cent were male and 23 per cent had been in detention for four months or more.[132] Home Office ministers frequently assert that the number detained constitutes a very small percentage of the total number of asylum seekers: 'At any one time, only about 1.5 per cent of those liable to detention under immigration powers are actually detained.'[133] For those few held, detention can be a traumatic experience, particularly where incarceration is long-term. In the case of asylum seekers, liability to detention only arises in certain circumstances: for example, application at a port, cases pending deportation, or involving illegal entrants and those refused leave to enter.[134] The number of those who are liable to be detained is therefore proportionately lower; one figure suggests that 60 per cent of all asylum applicants fall into this category.[135] For 2001, this would mean that about 42,800 asylum seekers were liable to detention (there were 71,365 applications, excluding dependants), and that, consequently, the proportion actually detained was nearer 3 per cent, not 1.5 per cent. When account is also taken of those sent to Oakington Reception Centre, the figure rises. Approximately 9,125 cases were received

---

[127] [2001] 4 All ER 961, CA; [2002] INLR 523, HL. See ch. 8 for further discussion of this case.

[128] [2002] INLR 523, para. 47.

[129] Home Office, *Fairer, Faster and Firmer – A Modern Approach to Immigration and Asylum*, Cm 4018 (London: The Stationery Office, 1998), para. 12.3.

[130] Home Office, *Asylum Statistics United Kingdom 2000*, table 9.1.

[131] This figure excludes Oakington. See Home Office, *Asylum Statistics United Kingdom 2001*, July 31, 2002, table 9.1.

[132] Home Office, *Asylum Statistics United Kingdom 2001*, July 31, 2002, table 9.1.

[133] Home Office, *Fairer, Faster and Firmer – A Modern Approach to Immigration and Asylum*, Cm 4018 (London: The Stationery Office, 2002), para. 12.1.

[134] Immigration Act 1971, sch. 2, para. 16.

[135] N.S. Ghaleigh, *Immigration Detention and Human Rights: Deserving the Name of Democracy* (London: ARC), p. iv.

at Oakington during 2001.[136] Again, of those liable to detention in 2001, the proportion detained for more than 24 hours was about 24 per cent, much higher than the relatively insignificant statistics cited by government. The figures for 2002 indicate a drop in the numbers of asylum seekers held in detention: excluding Oakington, there were 755 asylum detainees as at December 28, 2002. Of these, 33 per cent had been held in detention for less than one month, 17 per cent for between one and three months, 18 per cent for between two and four months, and 32 per cent for four months or more.[137] Over the year, Oakington processed 8,595 cases, excluding dependants.[138]

6.16   While the statistics on detention indicate a decline, recent changes are likely to reverse this trend. In the 2002 White Paper, the government stated that 'although the main focus of detention will be on removals, there will continue to be a need to detain some people at other stages of the process'.[139] The White Paper proposed a complex new regime involving induction, reception, accommodation, and removal centres (the renamed detention centres), and this has now been effected in the Nationality, Immigration and Asylum Act 2002. The government has described induction centres as 'the first stage in achieving a holistic approach to the handling of asylum seekers' applications'.[140] In the induction centres, asylum seekers will be provided with full-board accommodation and with information on the UK procedures and support arrangements; they will be expected to remain there for up to 14 days. Once they have been processed, applicants will be granted temporary admission (and moved to an agreed address), transferred to an accommodation centre, or dispersed to accommodation around the UK if seeking support from the National Asylum Support Service. The first induction centre was opened in January 2002 in Dover and has been declared a success.[141] The Minister for Immigration is looking to create a national network of induction centres, though she was forced in April 2003 to withdraw from two potential sites, due to local objections.[142] By March 2003,

---

[136] Home Office, *Asylum Statistics United Kingdom 2001*, July 31, 2002, table 10.1. Oakington has capacity to handle 250 applicants each week, up to a maximum of 13,000 in a year.

[137] Home Office, *Asylum Statistics: 4th Quarter 2002 United Kingdom*, p. 8; tables 10–13.

[138] *ibid.*, p. 8; Home Office, *Asylum Statistics: 3rd Quarter 2002 United Kingdom*, p. 10; Home Office, *Asylum Statistics: 2nd Quarter 2002 United Kingdom*, p. 10; Home Office, *Asylum Statistics: 1st Quarter 2002 United Kingdom*, p. 10.

[139] Home Office, *Secure Borders, Safe Haven – Integration with Diversity in Modern Britain*, Cm 5387 (London: The Stationery Office, 2002), para. 4.76.

[140] *ibid.*

[141] Home Office Press Release, 'Dover induction centre opens', January 22, 2002; Home Office Press Release, 'Induction centres – way forward', April 7, 2003.

[142] *ibid.*

concrete offers of only 685 bed spaces had been received from local authorities; the government needs a total of about 3,500 throughout the country.[143]

The proposed accommodation centres are a significant new development.[144] The initial intention was to provide 3,000 bed spaces (four centres of 750 people each) on a trial basis. Following extensive deliberation in both Houses of Parliament on the relevant provision in the Nationality, Immigration and Asylum Bill, it was agreed that one centre would be trialed on a smaller basis (about 400) and would be for single men only.[145] The Minister for Immigration promised that the Home Office would work with the Refugee Centre on its alternative 'cluster-based' proposal (smaller centres of 250 each, or centres of 600 but housing people in hostels of 50–100). The centres will provide full-board accommodation, health care, education, interpretation, access to legal advice, plus anything else considered necessary for 'proper occupation' or 'maintaining good order'.[146] The government introduced a late amendment which confirms that a resident would normally remain in an accommodation centre for a maximum of six months (on the assumption that decisions and appeals would be completed within this time). This period may be extended to nine months on agreement with the asylum seeker, or if the Home Secretary deems it appropriate.[147]

The White Paper and subsequent press releases stressed that accommodation centres would not be secure facilities and that people would be free to come and go.[148] Residential restrictions may, however, apply. The initial sites selected were: the Defence Storage and Distribution Centre (Bicester, Oxfordshire), RAF Newton (Nottinghamshire), and QinetiQ Pershore (Throckmorton Airfield, Worcestershire). Further sites are being evaluated and the common factor for selection seems to be their isolation from neighbouring towns, though, in debate, the Minister for Immigration conceded that the Home Office would consider smaller centres in urban areas. Public reaction to site selection was not favourable. Villagers in Throckmorton were particularly aggrieved, since this had been an area chosen for disposal of

6.17

---

[143] HC Deb., March 3, 2003, col. 658.

[144] For an independent review of the proposals, see New Policy Institute, *Asylum City* (London: The Asylum Coalition, September 2002).

[145] HC Deb. Vol. 392, November 5, 2002, col. 150.

[146] s. 29.

[147] ss. 25(1) and (2).

[148] Home Office, *Secure Borders, Safe Haven – Integration with Diversity in Modern Britain*, Cm 5387 (London: The Stationery Office, 2002), para. 4.36; Home Office Press Release, 'First sites chosen for trial asylum seeker accommodation centres', May 14, 2002.

100,000 carcasses during the foot and mouth crisis.[149] The Chief Executive of the Immigration Advisory Service, Keith Best, observed: '[. . .] when you put large numbers in rural locations it is a recipe for racial tensions and will fan the flames of the Right wing'.[150] Throckmorton Airfield was dropped as a possible location just prior to the passing of the Act, though the government remains committed to siting two 750–place centres at Bicester and Newton.[151] A smaller site, to house 400 single men, has been identified at HMS Daedalus in Gosport.[152]

While it is clear that the decision to create accommodation centres is due in part to the criticism attracted by detention centres over the years, the government still considers that asylum seekers should be separated as far as possible from the host population. The Home Secretary, David Blunkett, stated on Radio 4's Today Programme that children of asylum seekers would be educated in accommodation centres to stop them 'swamping' local schools.[153] The use of the term 'swamping' caused a minor furore and Blunkett was challenged in the House of Commons about his use of such an 'emotive term'. 'I did not use deliberately emotive language', he responded. 'I'm not withdrawing, by the way, the language that I used because it was intended in a very balanced interview – simply to indicate that there is a major problem for some schools and some GP practices in some limited parts of our country.'[154] The former Shadow Home Secretary, Ann Widdecombe, had previously proposed similar accommodation centres, but with the important difference that her centres were to be secure and therefore akin to detention centres. It remains the view of some on the Conservative benches that Labour's proposals are doomed to fail for lack of security. If they do prove effective, it is suggested that the government will look to create 15 centres with a capacity to process 22,000 asylum seekers per year.[155]

Alongside accommodation centres, the plans for 'removal centres' add a further dimension to the new regime. In 2001, 9,285 failed asylum seekers were removed, an increase of 3 per cent on the previous

---

[149] P. Johnston, 'Fury over huge asylum centres near villages,' *The Daily Telegraph*, May 15, 2002.

[150] *ibid.*

[151] HC Deb. v. 392, November 5, 2002, col. 151; Home Office Press Release, 'Next steps in asylum seeker accommodation trial', February 11, 2003.

[152] Home Office Press Release, 'Accommodation centres for asylum seekers', May 2, 2003.

[153] M. White & A. Travis, 'Blunkett defends 'swamping' remark', *The Guardian*, April 25, 2002.

[154] *ibid.*

[155] A. Travis, 'Minister stirs row over plans for 15 new centres', *The Guardian*, May 15, 2002.

year (8,980 removals).[156] Considering that 87,990 asylum claims were rejected in 2001, there needs to be a dramatic increase in removals for the government to regain public support for its asylum policy.[157] The relatively low levels of removals, and the suggestion that many of those refused simply 'disappear' into the population, have provided ammunition for political point scoring. Negative media coverage has also increased pressure on the government to prove that rejected asylum seekers are removed. Following a riot and the burning down of a substantial part of Yarl's Wood detention centre in February 2002, the Home Secretary spoke of tougher policies on removals: 'I intend to press ahead with expanding the number of places in secure removal centres to 4,000', he said. 'There will be no uncertainty, no misunderstanding.'[158]

In truth, the former detention centres have simply been renamed 'removal centres'.[159] This change in nomenclature has been described as a 'blatant political sleight-of-hand' and a cosmetic exercise perpetrated 'to placate the more prejudiced part of the public'.[160] Certainly, it appears unlikely that a name change and an increase in detention spaces will achieve the government's objective. Unless constant track is kept of all asylum seekers from arrival to refusal, there will always be a substantial number who will disappear when their appeal rights are exhausted and the next step is removal. The only way of preventing this is to detain applicants from the moment of arrival until the point of departure. Until recently, no one in Labour advocated such a policy, though it was proposed by the Conservatives under the leadership of William Hague. Hague promised that: 'The Conservative government will detain all new applicants for asylum, whether port applicants or in-country applicants, in reception centres until their cases have been determined.'[161] He was forced to back down due to the cost involved, and suggested instead that those from approved safe third countries would be detained in the first instance.[162] In March 2003, the Home Office quietly announced a

---

[156] Home Office, *Asylum Statistics United Kingdom 2001*, July 31, 2002, table 11.1. Parliamentary Under-Secretary for the Home Department, Angela Eagle, admitted in Standing Committee on the Nationality, Immigration and Asylum Bill that 30,000 removals per year was very ambitious: HC Standing Committee E, Tuesday May 14, 2002, col. 251.

[157] Home Office, *Asylum Statistics 4th Quarter 2002 United Kingdom*, table 2.

[158] 'Clampdown on asylum removals', *The Guardian*, February 25, 2002.

[159] s. 66.

[160] K. Best, Chief Executive, Immigration Advisory Service, Introductory speech presented at IAS conference 'Immigration & Asylum policy: What are the White Paper objectives?', February 27, 2002.

[161] P. Wintour, 'Tories retreat on asylum detentions', *The Guardian*, November 29, 2000.

[162] *ibid.*

new pilot scheme to fast track certain asylum claims from arrival to removal. Up to 90 asylum seekers, again with 'straightforward' claims, will be detained throughout the asylum process in Harmondsworth Removal Centre, and unfounded claimants will be removed from the UK within a month.[163] If successful, the scheme will be extended. The first group of detainees came mainly from Pakistan, Nigeria and Turkey.[164]

Much is riding on this pilot. In July 2002, David Blunkett announced a target of 30,000 removals per year; two months later, the government conceded that this was, as most suspected, unrealistic – removals had only just reached 1,000 a month.[165] The final figure for removals in 2002 was 10,410 principal applicants; while a 12 per cent increase on 2001, it was still a far cry from the above objective.[166] There is broad agreement that, if the system is to regain credibility, these figures will need to improve dramatically.

Bail

6.18   While administrative detention has been widely criticised, the issue of bail has received relatively little attention, despite its obvious significance. The process for applying for bail has been described in earlier chapters. There it was noted that suspected criminals were better protected than detainees under the Immigration Act 1971, who did not have an automatic right to a bail hearing. Whereas Part III of the Immigration and Asylum Act 1999 created a system for bail hearings, and incorporated a presumption in favour of bail,[167] it was never brought into force. Section 68 to the Nationality and Immigration Act 2002 repeals Part III of the 1999 Act. In a conference held by the Immigration Advisory Service in February 2002 to discuss the White Paper proposals, the IND Deputy Director General of Policy, Peter Wrench, stated that while the IND were aware of 'some concern that most of Part III of the 1999 Act will be repealed [. . .] existing bail arrangements enabling detainees to apply for bail will remain in place.'[168] The Home Office would 'continue to ensure that asylum seekers and others who are detained have effective opportunities to

---

[163] Home Office Press Release, 'New fast track pilot for asylum claims', March 18, 2003.

[164] ILPA meeting with the Home Office Appeals Group – May 15, 2003, ILPA Information for Members, June 2003.

[165] A. Travis, 'Expulsion target dropped'. *The Guardian*, July 16, 2002.

[166] Home Office, *Asylum Statistics: 4th Quarter 2000 United Kingdom*, p. 5.

[167] See Ch. 5.

[168] Peter Wrench, Speech presented at IAS conference 'Immigration & Asylum policy: What are the White Paper objectives?', February 27, 2002.

seek bail'.[169] This may be of little comfort for those in detention. In the case of children, amendments to the 2002 Bill were proposed, which sought either to prevent children being held in detention, or to limit their confinement to ten days. The government opposed both, and the amendments failed.

It is not altogether clear why the government reneged on its previous promises concerning bail, which were widely commended by practitioners in the field. The two most obvious explanations are: (i) the cost involved in instituting a system of automatic bail hearings; and (ii) the fear that bail would frustrate the process of detention and removal, thereby undermining the government's objectives of tighter security and deterrence. The Parliamentary Under-Secretary for the Home Department, Angela Eagle, admitted that 'The trouble with automatic bail hearings is their inflexibility and the sheer numbers of hearings that would be imposed on a system already experiencing increases.'[170] It is still surprising that the government only became aware of the implications for the appellate authorities of Part III after passing the 1999 Act. One would have expected such arguments to have been rehearsed during the lengthy debates and consultation process on the Bill.

The support of asylum seekers

Most asylum seekers will, at some point in the determination process, seek support from the state. The problem of providing such support has proved one of the most intractable. As numbers of applications have risen almost year on year,[171] governments of right and left have concluded that the UK is targeted by asylum seekers for its generous social security provision. In 1995, the Secretary of State for Social Security announced that 'Britain should be a safe haven, not a soft touch'.[172] As a result, the 1996 Act included numerous amendments to the support arrangements for asylum seekers.[173] Its basic aim was to limit certain benefits[174] and housing to those who applied

6.19

---

[169] Peter Wrench, Speech presented at IAS conference 'Immigration & Asylum policy: What are the White Paper objectives?', February 27, 2002.

[170] HC Standing Committee E, Tuesday May 14, 2002, cols. 257–8.

[171] There was a fall in 2001 (71,365) on the figures for 2000 (80,315), but a rise again in 2002 (85,865). A downward trend in applications was announced in May 2003: Home Office Press Release, 'Asylum applications down by a third – Home Secretary welcomes significant progress', May 22, 2003.

[172] 'Lilley to curb benefits for asylum seekers', *The Independent*, October 12, 1995.

[173] See Ch. 5, and Asylum and Immigration Act 1996, s. 11; sch. 1; Social Security (Persons from Abroad) Miscellaneous Amendments Regulations 1996, SI 1996/30.

[174] Income support, income-based jobseeker's allowance, housing benefit, and council tax benefit.

immediately on arrival at port, or those who claimed within three months of a 'state of upheaval' declaration.[175] The government did not define the meaning of 'on arrival' and the words fell to be interpreted by the Social Security Appeals Tribunal. Other benefits[176] required claimants to be resident in the UK. With no right to reside, asylum seekers were excluded. Entitlement to child benefit was also withdrawn from asylum seekers (i.e. persons 'subject to immigration control').[177] Those with refugee status or ELR were eligible for support.

In opposition, Labour had been highly critical of Conservative plans to restrict benefit entitlement, as observed by Shadow Home Secretary, Jack Straw:

> 'How typical of the Government that, instead of seeking to cut delays, they cut people's benefit. Under the proposals, there will be no benefit: not for those in severe hardship or ill-health; nothing for babies, infants or children; not a penny for pregnant women; none for victims of torture.'[178]

Yet, on election to government, Labour pursued a more radical line than any of its Conservative predecessors. Despite recognising that cash-based support was administratively convenient and comparatively low in cost,[179] the new government decided to withdraw all rights to social security benefits for asylum seekers, to amend the National Assistance Act 1948 (which provided a loophole for destitute asylum seekers to obtain local authority assistance for warmth, food and shelter),[180] and to remove any outstanding obligations on the part of local authorities to house homeless asylum seekers. In their place, a support-based system was introduced, substituting benefits with support in kind (accommodation and vouchers), and providing each person with £10 per week in cash.[181] The National Asylum Support Service was established within the Home Office to manage the voucher system and disperse asylum seekers to 'cluster areas' in the UK. To qualify for NASS support, an asylum seeker had to be 'destitute' within the meaning of s. 95(3) to the 1999 Act.[182] One of the aims of NASS dispersal was to ensure that asylum seekers were kept

---

[175] Asylum and Immigration Act 1996, s. 11.
[176] Family credit, disability working allowance, attendance allowance, disability living allowance, invalid care allowance, severe disablement allowance.
[177] Asylum and Immigration Act 1996, s. 10.
[178] HC Deb. Vol. 268, December 11, 1995, cols. 720–1.
[179] Jane Fiddick, *Immigration and Asylum*, Research Paper 99/16 (London: Home Affairs Section of House of Commons Library, February 19, 1999), p. 56.
[180] *R. v Hammersmith and Fulham LBC, ex parte M*, [1997] 1 CCLR 69, and see Ch. 8.
[181] See Ch. 5 for further details.
[182] Now amended by the 2002 Act. See Ch. 5 for details.

away from London and the South East, to which they tended to gravitate. Vouchers could be exchanged for food and basic necessities at designated shops, but shops were prohibited from giving change.

The reasons for Labour's apparent change of heart require some explanation. The government suddenly suggested that cash was, in fact, a pull-factor and had been the cause of a dramatic rise in asylum applications.[183] This despite a lack of evidence to support such a contention.[184] The original plan was to provide no cash but, when faced with a backbench revolt, the government caved in and offered a cash payment of £10 per week per person to placate rebel Labour MPs; its tactic worked, though seven did still defy the Whip and voted against the government's proposals. Unexpectedly, the Conservatives abstained, revealing something of the uncertainty that surrounds the question of asylum support.

Dispersal

While many NGOs considered the government's measures an improvement, there were still some concerns: the potential for stigmatisation on use of vouchers; inadequate dispersal arrangements; the use of poor accommodation; and dispersal to inappropriate areas. In June 2000, the Audit Commission published a comprehensive report on the plans for implementation of the dispersal system under the Immigration and Asylum Act 1999, and listed 25 recommendations.[185] These included: **6.20**

- the Home Office should ensure that government policy on asylum seekers and refugees was better co-ordinated nationally;

- the Home Office, and the Departments of Education and Health, should ensure that resources were available to meet the reasonable costs of statutory services for new dispersal areas;

- NASS should analyse the comparative costs of services to asylum seekers around the country.[186]

---

[183] HC Deb. Vol. 326, February 22, 1999, col. 46.
[184] See Refugee Council, *Briefing on the Immigration and Asylum Act 1999* (London: The Refugee Council, 2000), p. 11. See, also, V. Robinson & J. Segrott, *Understanding the Decision-Making of Asylum Seekers*, Home Office Research Study 243, (London: Home Office RDSD, July 2002), which established that welfare benefits and housing were not a major factor in seeking asylum in the UK.
[185] The Audit Commission, *Another Country – Implementing Dispersal under the Immigration and Asylum Act 1999* (London: The Audit Commission, June 2000), pp. 93–95.
[186] The Audit Commission News Release, 'Improvements needed in managing the dispersal of asylum seekers', June 1, 2000.

In addition, local authorities and regional consortia were urged to:

- work together to review services for asylum seekers, establishing clear lines of responsibility;

- take steps to make local services more accessible;

- identify the needs and profile of all asylum seekers within their area;

- develop positive public relations strategies to promote consistent messages in their area.[187]

Once dispersal commenced, however, accounts soon emerged of poor practice, disorganised local authorities, and dispersal to extremely unsuitable parts of the country. Perhaps the most notorious case of ill-conceived dispersal was organised by Glasgow City Council, which accommodated more than 2,000 asylum seekers in one of the city's most deprived estates – Sighthill. In August 2001, tensions between local youths and young Kurdish asylum seekers reached a peak, resulting in a fatal stabbing.[188] This incident helped publicise one of the worst aspects of the system: the 'dumping' of asylum seekers in rundown and unsuitable properties.[189] Research conducted by Shelter into the housing of asylum seekers established that some 26 per cent of the dwellings visited were unfit for human habitation, 86 per cent were unfit for the number of actual or intended occupants, and over 80 per cent of the houses in multiple occupation were exposed to unacceptable risks of fire.[190] By any measure, these findings were extremely worrying, and put paid to popular perceptions that asylum seekers were placed in comfortable accommodation. It also became clear that local residents were not being notified of the arrival of asylum seekers in their areas. The consequence was growing disenchantment with the system and an increase in racial tension.

6.21   Some of the problems associated with dispersal were finally acknowledged by the government in October 2001, when it published a review of the voucher and dispersal policies. In relation to dispersal, the report identified a continued need for improvement. It called on the authorities to address the following range of concerns:

---

[187] The Audit Commission News Release, 'Improvements needed in managing the dispersal of asylum seekers', June 1, 2000.

[188] G. Harris, 'Protesting Kurds taunted by mob, *The Guardian*, August 7, 2001.

[189] D. McGrory, 'Dejected refugees end up with bed, breakfast and broken windows', *The Times*, August 8, 2001.

[190] D. Garvie, *Far From Home – The Housing of Asylum Seekers in Private Rented Accommodation* (London: Shelter, 2001), p. 7.

- the impact of dispersal of large numbers of asylum seekers on local communities, including increased racial tensions and burdens on local services;

- the nature and condition of accommodation, in particular the use of private landlords and sub-contractors, and the monitoring of accommodation standards;

- the problems caused by dispersal when the local authority is not consulted or notified, including difficulties with social integration and access to public services.[191]

Almost two years on, little had changed. Robinson, in the first book to examine the UK's dispersal policy, argues that it is not only expensive and inefficient, but is largely driven by the fears of a white electorate.[192] Calling for an informed national debate on the issue, he suggests that 'compulsory dispersal has led to a denial of the basic human right of asylum seekers and refugees to choose where they live' and that 'the government must question the rationale for its policy and decide whom it is intended to serve'.[193] In January 2003, the Minister for Immigration commissioned a further review to advise on how NASS could be improved. When the report was finally completed in July 2003, the Home Office refused to release it in full, publishing only the recommendations. This gave rise to speculation that its conclusions were very critical.[194] Simon Hughes, Shadow Home Secretary for the Liberal Democrats, protested: 'To withhold a supposedly independent review on a subject of major public interest raises huge suspicions. If the Home Office has any commitment to open government it should publish this document now.'[195] Certainly, the recommendations indicated that serious problems with the system still persisted. According to the report, NASS needed:

- 'to have its purpose, aims and role clarified and reaffirmed by Ministers';

- 'urgently to improve its operational performance and standards of customer care. It needs to get better at working with its partners

---

[191] *Report of The Operational Reviews of The Voucher and Dispersal Schemes of The National Asylum Support Service*, p. 6, available on: *http://194.203.40.90/filestore/voucher%20 review.pdf*

[192] A. Travis, 'Asylum seeker dispersal 'a waste of money'', July 30, 2003. See R. Andersson, S. Musterd & V. Robinson, *Spreading the 'Burden'?: A Review of Policies to Disperse Asylum-Seekers and Refugees* (London: The Policy Press, 2003).

[193] *ibid.*

[194] A. Travis, 'Asylum service criticised – Minister demands action plan after damning report', *The Guardian*, July 16, 2003.

[195] *ibid.*

and stakeholders, and much slicker at sorting out basic processing errors especially when these affect individual asylum seekers and damage the reputation of the organisation';

- 'a period of stability to enable it to get on top of the job'.[196]

The Minister remained unabashed by the criticism, arguing that urgent action had already been taken and NASS was showing signs of improvement. The senior management team had been strengthened and regional offices had been established across the country. She went on: 'But there is much more still to do. I am determined that this review should not simply be a paper exercise and have asked NASS for an action plan to set out how it intends to take forward the other recommendations of the review.'[197] In the meantime, asylum seekers cannot be guaranteed a fair and efficient support system.[198]

Vouchers

6.22   The switch from cash benefits to vouchers came into effect in April 2000. Within months, the government revealed its intention to review the operation of the scheme in order to identify any problems and to propose changes where necessary. This suggests that it was aware from their inception that vouchers might prove unviable, as had always been argued by NGOs. On October 29, 2001, the review of the voucher and dispersal schemes was published. It concluded that there was restricted availability of accurate and up-to-date information for asylum seekers in a language they could understand. The number of post offices where vouchers could be collected was limited, and few retailers accepted vouchers. Furthermore, participating shops often failed to operate the voucher scheme correctly. There was clear evidence that vouchers stigmatised their users, and the whole scheme was vulnerable to fraud. Finally, administrative and operational difficulties resulted in a poor service by NASS to asylum seekers.[199] With this report in mind, the Home Secretary made an announcement on asylum, migration and citizenship to the House of

---

[196] Home Office Press Release, 'Independent review into the operations of the National Asylum Support Service, July 17, 2003.

[197] A. Travis, 'Asylum service criticised – Minister demands action plan after damning report', *The Guardian*, July 16, 2003.

[198] See R. Dunstan, *Distant Voices: CAB clients' Experience of Continuing Problems with the NASS* (London: CAB, October 2002).

[199] *Report of The Operational Reviews of The Voucher and Dispersal Schemes of the National Asylum Support Service*, pp. 4; 7, available on: http://194.203.40.90/filestore/voucher%20 review.pdf

Commons.[200] In his speech, he stated that it was the government's intention 'to phase out the current system of support and dispersal'.[201] In the meantime, the value of voucher support was to be up-rated and the cash allowance increased from £10 to £14, until the whole voucher system was superseded by autumn 2002.[202]

While every indication pointed to the withdrawal of vouchers in the latter part of 2002,[203] the government changed its mind yet again and issued a statutory instrument amending the former regulations, with effect from April 8, 2002.[204] There it stated that vouchers would be redeemable for cash (previously redeemable for goods, services and cash) and that the amounts granted would be increased.[205] They equated to 70 per cent of income support for adults and 100 per cent for children. This was a major amendment and allowed asylum seekers supported by NASS to receive their subsistence support in vouchers which they could exchange for cash at post offices. Though this was welcomed by NGOs, the Refugee Council was disappointed that the total amount for adults was still only 70 per cent of income support, and that there continued to be serious delays in processing vouchers.[206] A study of evidence collated from forty organisations working with asylum seekers in England and Scotland revealed that 'asylum-seekers have barely enough money to buy food of a quantity and quality to maintain an adequate diet, and often experience poor health and hunger'.[207] In addition, they frequently did not receive the support to which they were entitled, or received it too late.[208]

The issue of vouchers provides a fine example of the confusion at the heart of much of the UK's asylum policy. Following its brief experiment with cashless-vouchers, the government conducted an unexpected volte-face and reverted to the pre-1999 cash-based

[200] HC Deb. Vol. 373, October 29, 2001, cols. 627–648; Home Office Press Release, 'Radical reform unveiled for more robust asylum system', October 29, 2001.

[201] ibid., col. 628.

[202] ibid., Home Office Press Release, 'Radical reform unveiled for more robust asylum system', October 29, 2001.

[203] See, also, Home Office, Secure Borders, Safe Haven – Integration with Diversity in Modern Britain, Cm 5387 (London: The Stationery Office, 2002), para. 4.52.

[204] Asylum Support (Amendment) Regulations 2002, No. 2002/472, amending Asylum Support Regulations 2000, No. 2000/704.

[205] The Asylum Support (Amendment) Regulations 2002, No. 2002/472, Reg. 4. Current levels of support are provided in The Asylum Support (Amendment)(No. 2) Regulations 2003, SI 2003/755: qualifying couple £60.03; single person 25 or over £38.26; child under 16 £38.50.

[206] The Refugee Council, 'The National Asylum Support Service (NASS)' available on: www.refugeecouncil.org.uk/infocentre/entit/sentit001.htm

[207] Oxfam & Refugee Council, Poverty and Asylum in the UK (London: Oxfam/Refugee Council, 2002), p. 4.

[208] ibid., p. 5.

position (albeit using vouchers), despite arguing a few years earlier that cash constituted a pull-factor. No satisfactory explanation for this policy reversal has been provided and it must therefore be concluded that either the current Home Secretary no longer believes cash to be an attraction, or he considers the disadvantages outweigh the advantages. A range of restrictive measures incorporated in the Nationality, Immigration and Asylum Act 2002 soon dashed any expectation that this revision of the vouchers scheme presaged a more lenient policy on support.

Sections 54 and 55, Nationality, Immigration and Asylum Act 2002

6.23   As noted earlier, two of the most stringent measures of the 2002 Act are ss. 54 and 55. Introduced only a month before the Act was passed, s. 54 removes support and community care from certain categories of people, including failed asylum seekers who do no cooperate with removal directions.[209] Where a family loses support under these provisions, children under 18 will remain eligible and could be taken into care.[210] Allowance is made, however, for families with children to be provided with accommodation until their journey home.[211] The chief aim of s. 54 was stated to be 'to ensure that [specified] individuals could not move to the UK for the sole or main purpose of accessing residential accommodation and other services in preference to similar services in the EEA country of origin.'[212]

Section 55, on the other hand, permits the Secretary of State and local authorities to refuse support where the Secretary of State is not satisfied that 'the claim was made as soon as reasonably practicable after the person's arrival in the United Kingdom'.[213] In contrast to s. 54, this provision is intended to deter claimants by ensuring that people apply for asylum as soon after their arrival as possible. It covers only childless asylum seekers and specifically excludes a right of appeal to an asylum support adjudicator.[214] From the day it came into force, January 8, 2003, s. 55 was applied aggressively: the words 'as soon as reasonably practicable' were at once interpreted to mean

---

[209] sch. 3, paras 1 and 4–7.

[210] sch. 3, para. 2.

[211] sch. 3, para. 9.

[212] Department of Health, A Note of Clarification, 'S. 54 of the Nationality, Immigration and Asylum Act 2002 and community care and other social services for adults from the EEA living in the UK'.

[213] s. 55(1).

[214] s. 55(10); Nationality, Immigration and Asylum Act 2002 (Commencement No. 1) Order 2002, SI 2002/2811.

'immediately on arrival'. In a statement explaining the introduction of the provisions, Beverley Hughes said:

> 'It is a reasonable expectation that desperate people fleeing for their lives will claim asylum as soon as they can and we will continue to support these people in the same way we do now. However, we are determined to tackle abuse and these measures send a clear signal across the world that the asylum system must be used for its proper purpose. It is not acceptable for people to claim asylum after being in the UK for weeks or months working illegally, simply as a way of staying on at the taxpayer's expense and delaying removal.'[215]

Support was refused to many claimants. The inevitable outcome was litigation. On March 18, 2003, the Court of Appeal upheld the judgement of Collins J. in the High Court in *R. (Q and Others) v Secretary of State for the Home Department*, finding that the system assessing asylum seekers for support under s. 55 was unfair and the assessment process flawed.[216] Urgent changes were called for. It was not unlawful for the Secretary of State to decline support unless and until it was clear that charitable or other support had not been provided and the individual was incapable of fending for him- or herself.[217] Nonetheless, Art. 3 of the ECHR could be engaged where the asylum seeker's condition was so severe that it passed the threshold described in *Pretty v UK*.[218]

Days after the High Court's decision, the Home Secretary railed against the judiciary: 'If public policy can always be overridden by individual challenge through the courts, then democracy itself is under threat.'[219] He acknowledged that there was a balance between the rights of parliament to bring about change and the role of the judiciary in protecting people from abuse of power. However, he argued that this balance had not been achieved in first instance judgements as they were frequently overturned on appeal.[220] The Home Secretary was forced to modify his position following the Court of Appeal's endorsement of much of Collins' J. judgement and its call for revision of the s. 55 process. In what *The Guardian* called an 'unusual display of humility', the Home Secretary accepted

6.24

---

[215] Home Office Press Release, 'New measures to cut asylum abuse come into force', January 8, 2003.

[216] [2003] EWHC 195 Admin; [2003] EWCA Civ 364, paras. 85–86, 94, 98–99. See Ch. 8 for discussion of this case.

[217] [2003] EWCA Civ 364, para. 63.

[218] [2003] EWCA Civ 364, para. 62. *Pretty v UK* (2002) 35 EHHR 1, and see Ch. 4.

[219] R. Sylvester, 'Blunkett accuses judges of damaging democracy', *The Telegraph*, February 21, 2003.

[220] *ibid.*

the decision and thanked the judges for finding in his favour on the crucial points of law (i.e. in relation to Art. 3).[221]

The changes introduced by the Home Office in the light of *Q & Others* were soon put to the test in late July 2003 with another application for judicial review challenging refusals of asylum support.[222] Once more, the High Court condemned the impact of s. 55 on the applicants. As a result of the provision, three asylum seekers – a Somalian, Malaysian and Ethiopian – had been forced to sleep rough and beg for food. All three were malnourished. They had been reduced to a condition verging on the degree of severity described in *Pretty*. This, said the judge, was a breach of Art. 3. Though he indicated he would appeal against the decision, the Home Secretary may be forced to think again. A battle is about to be waged between the judiciary and the Home Secretary on the human rights of asylum seekers in the context of the government's obligations to provide support for the destitute.

Unaccompanied children[223]

6.25 Details of unaccompanied children (under 18) are passed by the Home Office, ostensibly within 24 hours of the claim being lodged, to a special unit within the Refugee Council: The Children's Panel of Advisers. The Panel offers short-term advice and assistance. Unaccompanied children are not supported by NASS. They, like British children, are the responsibility of local authority social services departments under the Children Act 1989. Under s. 17 of the 1989 Act, the local authority is charged with a duty to assess children in need and to provide them with an appropriate range and level of

---

[221] A. Travis, 'Appeal court upholds asylum ruling', *The Guardian*, March 19, 2003; Home Office Press Release, 'Court of Appeal ruling', March 18, 2033.

[222] *R. v Secretary of State for the Home Department, ex parte S, D & T*, [2003] EWHC 1941 (Admin), July 31, 2003.

[223] See, for further discussion of unaccompanied children, A. Hunter, 'Between the domestic and the international: The role of the European Union in providing protection for unaccompanied refugee children in the United Kingdom' (2001) 3 *European Journal of Migration and Law*, pp. 383–410; E. Nykänen, 'Protecting children? The European Convention on Human Rights and child asylum seekers' (2001) 3 *European Journal of Migration and Law*, pp. 315–345; The Children's Society/Refugee Council/Save the Children, *A Case for Change: How Refugee Children in England are Missing Out*, April 2002; BAAF/Refugee Council, *Where are the Children?*, June 2001; S. Kidane, *Food, Shelter and Half a Chance* (London: BAAF, 2001); S. Russell, *Most Vulnerable of All* (London: Amnesty International, 1999); L. Williamson, 'A safe haven?: The development of British policy concerning unaccompanied refugee children 1933–93' (1995) 14:1 *Immigrants and Minorities*, pp. 47–66.

services.[224] A child in need is defined as someone who 'is unlikely to achieve or maintain, or have the opportunity of achieving or maintaining, a reasonable standard of health or development without the provision of services by a local authority'.[225] Section 20 obliges the local authority to provide accommodation to children in need if they require it. The wishes of the child regarding provision of accommodation should be taken into account as far as possible.[226] However, under s. 20, social services departments have discretion on what is provided for children between 16 and 17 years old. As a result, their treatment has varied considerably between local authorities. Some children have been placed in hostels and have been well supported; others have been sent to bed and breakfast establishments and largely ignored.[227] For those reaching 18, there is a risk of dispersal around the country by NASS. The position is now improving on account of the Children (Leaving Care) Act 2000, and each case will be considered on its merits. It has also been agreed that NASS will not disperse those who reach 18 before a final decision is made on their asylum claim, 'if they have been previously accommodated by the local authority under s. 20 of the Children Act 1989 and qualify as 'former relevant children' under s. 23c of the Children (Leaving Care) Act 2000'.[228]

Employment and employers' liability

Research suggests that, while awaiting the decision on their claim,   **6.26**
most asylum seekers would prefer to work.[229] From 1986 to 2002, they were permitted to do so after six months had passed, and following application to the Home Office (it was not an automatic entitlement). To the surprise of many, in the summer of 2002, the Minister for Immigration announced the end of the historical employment concession.[230] Describing the concession as 'increasingly irrelevant', Beverley Hughes maintained that 'The vast majority – around 80 per cent – of asylum seekers receive a decision within six

---

[224] Children Act 1989, s. 17(1).

[225] *ibid.*, s. 17(10).

[226] *ibid.*, s. 20(6).

[227] Refugee Council, 'Support arrangements for 16 to 17 year old unaccompanied asylum seeking children', June 2000.

[228] Home Office, 'Unaccompanied asylum-seeking children information note', July 2002, para. 17.2

[229] See V. Robinson & J. Segrott, *Understanding the Decision-Making of Asylum Seekers*, Home Office Research Study 243, (London: Home Office RDSD, July 2002), p. 53.

[230] Home Office Press Release, 'Faster asylum decisions –historical employment concession ended', July 23, 2002.

months, and we are working to improve that further. An increasingly small number of people, therefore, are entitled to apply for the concession and I have decided to abolish it.'[231] This was clearly not the main reason, as soon became apparent in the press release: 'Pull factors are, of course, highly complex, but we believe that there is an incorrect perception that all asylum seekers are allowed to work while their case is considered. I want to make absolutely clear that is not the case.'[232] This conclusion was arguably a distorted reading of the Home Office's own research study into the motivations of asylum seekers who come to the UK, published in the same month as the Minister's announcement. There it was stated that 'many respondents did not expect to work immediately upon arrival in the UK', though they did believe they would be permitted to find work once they had adjusted to life in the UK.[233] It would seem, then, that the prohibition of work is a deterrent measure. There are two unfortunate consequences: the restriction can give an ill-informed public the impression that asylum seekers do not want to work and come to the UK simply to 'scrounge' off the 'generous benefits system'; it can also create tension and unease in local populations when groups of bored young foreign men congregate in city and town centres with little to occupy them.

Successive governments have also introduced legislation targeted at employers to ensure that they did not engage certain people who are subject to immigration control and are precluded from taking up employment.[234] Thus clandestine entrants, those with temporary admission, overstayers, or anyone who needs Home Office permission to work are prevented from so doing. To achieve this, the section uses a non-public official, the employer, to police illegal activity.[235] Until recently, it was a defence for an employer to prove he or she had checked and retained a copy of specified documentation of any person employed.[236] The 2002 Act replaces the defence in s. 8(2) to the 1996 Act with order-making powers under which the Secretary of State can spell out the requisite steps to be taken by an employer before engaging an employee.[237] These are likely to include copying and retaining documents, but allow the Home Secretary to impose

---

[231] Home Office Press Release, 'Faster asylum decisions –historical employment concession ended', July 23, 2002.

[232] *ibid.*

[233] V. Robinson & J. Segrott, *Understanding the Decision-Making of Asylum Seekers*, Home Office Research Study 243, (London: Home Office RDSD, July 2002), p. 53.

[234] Asylum and Immigration Act 1996, s. 8(1) (as amended).

[235] See, in addition, Ch. 5.

[236] The full list is contained in the Code of Practice which is available on: *www.ind.homeoffice.gov.uk/default.asp?pageid=17*

[237] s.147.

more demanding obligations on employers. Employers continue to be under a statutory duty to avoid racial discrimination in their recruitment practices, as explained in a government-issued Code of Practice. The Code only came into force in May 2001, some time after the implementation of the original employers' liability provision, as it became increasingly evident that employers might use ethnicity as an indicator of an individual's legality, and avoid employing those who appear foreign rather than risk criminal prosecution.

Employment raises a further issue: the acknowledged need for more skilled and unskilled workers, particularly in the face of an ageing population and a demographic decline in Europe.[238] Though population decline has been an issue at EU level for some time, it is only recently that UK ministers have addressed this, obliquely, in the form of 'managed migration'.[239] In the UK, this necessitates opening the legal routes of entry. Managed migration is beginning to be regarded as a new approach to the 'asylum crisis' but, in its present form, it is fairly limited and unlikely to resolve the underlying reasons for migration or the problems relating to demographic decline in the UK. It is, nonetheless, a start and thus to be welcomed.[240]

CONCLUSION

This chapter has discussed ways in which Home Office policy, via a range of pre- and post-arrival measures, seeks to deter and exclude asylum seekers.[241] There has been a tendency to categorise asylum   **6.27**

---

[238] This has been recognised for some time. The accession of the 12 candidate countries would hasten the demographic decline rather than reverse it, due to a dramatic and continuing decline in childbirth in these countries: see 'Demographic consequences for the EU of the accession of twelve candidate countries', *Statistics in Focus – Population and Social Conditions*, Theme 3 –12/2001 (Eurostat).

[239] See, *e.g.*, Barbara Roche MP, former Immigration Minister, 'UK migration in a global economy', speech delivered at Institute for Public Policy Research Conference, London, September 11, 2000, available on *www.homeoffice.gov.uk/ipprspch.htm*

[240] See Ch. 9 for UK's recent proposals on transit processing centres and regionalisation of the asylum issue. For a recent discussion of managing migration in Europe, see T. Veenkamp, T. Bentley & A. Buonfino, *People Flow: Managing Migration in a New European Commonwealth* (London: Demos, 2003); S. Castles, H. Crawley & S. Loughna, *States of Conflict: Causes and Patterns of Forced Migration to the EU and Policy Responses* (London: IPPR, 2003); R. Haque *et al*, *Migrants in the UK: their characteristics and labour market outcomes and impacts*, RDS Occasional Paper No. 82 (London: Home Office, December 2002).

[241] For research on the actual effects of Home Office policies, see R. Zetter *et al*, *An Assessment of the Impact of Asylum Policies in Europe 1990–2000*, Home Office Research Study 259 (London: Home Office RDSD, June 2003).

seekers – tacitly by the government, explicitly in the tabloid press – as 'bogus refugees', 'scroungers', 'economic migrants', even 'criminals' and 'terrorists'. Seldom a day passes at present when 'asylum' does not receive media coverage. On July 23, 2003, 'BBC Asylum Day' saw a whole series of programmes dedicated to the issue. There is constant talk of fraudulent claims, illegal entrants playing the system, 'floods' of asylum seekers, the trafficking and smuggling of asylum seekers by ruthless gangs, the ineffective removals system, and the financial burden of asylum on the UK taxpayer. Little wonder, then, that a beleaguered government promises greater restriction and turns to the law for assistance.

The 2002 White Paper, *Safe Borders, Secure Havens*, seemed to herald a new departure, with a recognition by the government that the asylum issue could only be resolved within the wider context of changing patterns of global migration:

> 'One of the issues which troubles the public most in relation to nationality and immigration is a belief that entry into this country and residence here is subject to abuse. The amount of column inches devoted to those trying to reach our shores through clandestine routes illustrates that the issue of asylum outweighs the much broader debate about migration, nationality and integration.

> This White Paper intends to refocus the agenda onto the wider issues of migration: on the global reality of increasing international mobility, how we can harness the benefits of this movement for all concerned (sending and receiving countries), and how we can foster a greater sense of community and social integration at home.'[242]

Prudent words, but the extent to which their message is being translated into concrete policy is still open to question. By any measure, the Nationality, Immigration and Asylum Act 2002 cannot be described as reorienting the debate away from asylum abuse; on the contrary, it is clear from ministerial statements that this is still very much the focus of government policy. Though David Blunkett has admitted that 'the real issue is whether we are going to face up to the need for properly managed migration',[243] any proposals he might have on this score are lost amidst the anxiety surrounding asylum. In the current climate, in which persecution is seldom mentioned, there is a danger that the rights of the 'genuine' refugee will be increasingly sidelined.

---

[242] Home Office, *Secure Borders, Safe Haven – Integration with Diversity in Modern Britain*, Cm 5387 (London: The Stationery Office, 2002), paras 1.1 –1.2.

[243] 'Blunkett attacks BBC asylum day', BBC News, July 24, 2003.

Chapter Seven

Exclusion and deterrence through Home Office policy: from decision to removal

INTRODUCTION

This chapter continues the examination of Home Office policy and **7.1** focuses on the most significant part of the asylum process: the assessment and determination of the claim. The aim of the chapter is not to provide detailed coverage of refugee case-law but to offer an insight into the workings of the Home Office. Particular regard is paid, therefore, to the IND's Asylum Policy Instructions ('APIs'), which provide caseworkers with the basic tools to reach a decision. These, like the Immigration Rules, are a 'living instrument', subject to change at any time. The version referred to here is that of March 2003, which takes account of the Nationality, Immigration and Asylum Act 2003. Previously unavailable to the public, the APIs are now accessible on the IND web-site.[1]

The chapter considers the Home Office's interpretation of Art. 1A(2) to the 1951 Convention and its use of credibility criteria, the 'safe third country rule', certification and 'white listing' of cases, and *de facto* status. Statistical information on applications, decisions and appeals is examined, as is the quality of decision-making in the UK and the particular problem of removals.

ASSESSMENT OF THE CLAIM

International obligations

All asylum claims must be assessed according to the UK's obligations **7.2** under international law. This is clearly articulated in the APIs:

---

[1] Available on: *www.ind.homeoffice.gov.uk/default.asp?PageId=711*

'Applications for asylum in the United Kingdom are considered in accordance with the UK's obligations under the 1951 United Nation's Convention Relating to the Status of Refugees and the 1967 Protocol. [. . .]

A person who fulfils the criteria set out in the 1951 Convention or 1967 Protocol is a refugee. [. . .]

The UK will grant asylum to any applicant if:

i)   they satisfy the criteria set out in the 1951 Convention or 1967 Protocol; and
ii)   they are in the UK or have arrived at a port of entry; and
iii) refusing the application would result in their refoulement contrary to our obligations under the 1951 Convention; and
iv)   they do not fall to be excluded from protection under the Convention.'[2]

Clearly, therefore, the definition of a refugee and the restriction against *refoulement* provided for by the 1951 Convention are critical to the Home Office's consideration of any asylum application. Thus the definition of a refugee applied by the Home Office is a person who:

'[. . .] owing to well-founded fear of persecution for reasons of race, religion, nationality, membership of a particular social group or political opinion, is outside the country of his or her nationality and is unable or, owing to such fear, is unwilling to avail himself or herself of the protection of that country; or who not having a nationality and being outside the country of his or her former habitual residence [. . .], is unable or, owing to such fear, is unwilling to return to it'.[3]

---

[2] Home Office, Asylum Policy Instructions, 'Deciding Claims – Assessing the Claim – Pt 1', para. 3, and see Statement of Changes in Immigration Rules, HC 395, para. 334:

'An asylum applicant will be granted asylum in the United Kingdom if the Secretary of State is satisfied that:

(i)   he is in the United Kingdom or has arrived at a port of entry in the United Kingdom; and
(ii)   he is a refugee, as defined by the Convention and Protocol; and
(iii) refusing his application would result in his being required to go (whether immediately or after the time limited by an existing leave to enter or remain) in breach of the Convention and Protocol, to a country in which his life or freedom would be threatened on account of his race, religion, nationality, political opinion or membership of a particular social group.'

[3] 1951 UN Convention Relating to the Status of Refugees, Art. 1A(2).

In order to assess whether an applicant meets the above inclusion criteria, Home Office instructions direct the caseworker to consider seven main questions:

'1) Has the applicant expressed a fear of return to their home country or country of nationality?
2) What is the harm feared?
3) Is the harm related to one or more of the five Convention grounds?
4) Who are the agents of persecution and is effective state protection available in response to their actions?
5) Is the fear well-founded?
6) Is the fear well-founded as to the whole of the country of origin?
7) Is the applicant excluded from international protection by operation of the exclusion clauses of the Convention?'[4]

To assist them further, caseworkers are also provided with a check-list of additional points. How a caseworker is advised to answer these questions is discussed below.

Refugee definition

'Outside country of nationality'

One of the first, and easiest, facts for the caseworker to determine is whether an applicant is outside his or her country of nationality. A complication may arise where a claimant has dual nationality, and is able to turn to one of the countries of nationality for protection. In this case, refugee status will be refused by the Home Office under paras 334 and 336 of the Immigration Rules;[5] as long as one country is free from persecution, there is no breach of the *non-refoulement* provision if the claimant is returned to that country.[6] Before the UK grants refugee status, an asylum seeker who is state-less, and has no nationality, needs to establish that he or she is outside the country of former habitual residence, and that the fear of perse-cution relates to that country rather than the country of original nationality.[7] The removal or deportation of stateless persons can be problematic as the country of former residence may refuse entry, and

7.3

---

[4] Home Office, Asylum Policy Instructions, 'Deciding Claims – Assessing the Claim Pt 1', para. 3.
[5] See fn. 2 above for r. 334.
[6] Home Office, Asylum Policy Instructions, 'Deciding Claims – Assessing the Claim Pt 1', para. 6.1.
[7] *ibid.*, para. 6.2.

caseworkers are instructed to take this into account and to seek further advice before issuing a refusal.

'Well-founded fear'

7.4 The most difficult part of the refugee definition to establish is 'well-founded fear of persecution'. The other elements – being outside the country of origin, nationality, or habitual residence, and an unwillingness to return – are essentially questions of fact.[8] Yet despite its importance, no standard test for determination has been provided. Normal principles of treaty interpretation therefore apply: a treaty 'shall be interpreted in good faith in accordance with the ordinary meaning to be given to the terms of the treaty in the context and in the light of its object and purpose'.[9] Recourse may be had to the *travaux préparatoires* of the 1951 Convention, or to 'supplementary means of interpretation', but only where the meaning of the treaty is 'ambiguous or obscure; or [. . .] leads to a result which is manifestly absurd or unreasonable'.[10] As described in Chapter 4, in order to assist Contracting States in their understanding of the criteria for refugee status determination, the UNHCR issued a *Handbook on Procedures and Criteria for Determining Refugee Status*. Though only a source of guidance for government officials, the *Handbook* inevitably carries some weight. There, the concept of 'well-founded fear of persecution' has been interpreted as requiring both a subjective and an objective assessment:

> 'To the element of fear – a state of mind and a subjective condition – is added the qualification "well-founded". This implies that it is not only the frame of mind of the person concerned that determines his refugee status, but that this frame of mind must be supported by an objective situation. The term "well-founded fear" therefore contains a subjective and an objective element, and in determining whether well-founded fear exists, both elements must be taken into consideration.'[11]

This view of Art. 1A(2) of the Convention has given rise to much debate. Some, such as Grahl-Madsen, the renowned refugee lawyer, appear to agree, but are dismissive of the need to prove 'fear':

---

[8] P. Weis ed., *The Refugee Convention 1951, The Travaux Preparatoires analysed, with a commentary by Dr Paul Weis* (Cambridge: Cambridge University Press, 1995), Introduction by C. Beyani, p.xv.

[9] Vienna Convention on the Law of Treaties 1969, Art. 31(1).

[10] *ibid.*, Art. 32.

[11] UNHCR, *Handbook on Procedures and Criteria for Determining Refugee Status* (Geneva, 1992) para. 38.

'"Fear" is, generally speaking, a subjective condition, a state of mind. [. . .] The adjective "well-founded" suggests that it is not the frame of mind of the person concerned which is decisive for his claim to refugeehood, but that this claim should be measured with a more objective yardstick. [. . .] In fact, [. . .] the frame of mind of the individual hardly matters at all. Every person claiming [. . .] to be a refugee has "fear" ("well-founded" or otherwise) of being persecuted in the sense of the present provision [. . .].'[12]

Other commentators, notably Hathaway, are more critical of the **7.5** need for a subjective element. In his celebrated work, *The Law of Refugee Status*, Hathaway suggests that 'it is not accurate to speak of the Convention definition as "containing both a subjective and an objective element": it is rather an objective test to be administered in the context of present or prospective risk for the claimant'.[13] His dislike of a subjective test is founded, partly, on the belief that refugee status may be denied on account of 'negative inferences tending to show an absence of subjective fear'.[14] Removal of the two-pronged approach should, in theory, eliminate an unnecessary hurdle in the asylum seeker's path.

The lack of a clear standard for determination has forced individual Contracting States to interpret for themselves the meaning of 'well-founded fear of persecution'. In *R. v SSHD, ex parte Gurmeet Singh & Others*, the High Court, referring to the UNHCR's *Handbook*, held that 'A well-founded fear involves both a subjective element and an objective element. The individual whose status is under consideration must in fact have the fear and that fear must be one which from an objective standpoint would be regarded as well-founded.'[15] This continues to be the approach of the courts and the Home Office. In the APIs, it is stated: 'In assessing whether an applicant's fear is well-founded, the caseworker must be satisfied both that (i) the applicant has a subjective fear of persecution, and (ii) that objectively there are reasonable grounds for believing that the persecution feared may in fact materialise in the applicant's country of origin.'[16] However, the Instructions do not discuss the definition of 'fear', nor do they make further reference to the subjective element, preferring to focus on the objective limb of the test, and, in particular, on the House of Lords ground-breaking decision in *Secretary of State for the Home Department v*

---

[12] A. Grahl-Madsen, *The Status of Refugees in International Law* Vol. II (The Netherlands: A.W. Sijthoff-Leiden, 1972), pp. 173–4.

[13] J. Hathaway, *The Law of Refugee Status* (Toronto: Butterworths, 1991), p. 69.

[14] *ibid.*, p. 75.

[15] [1987] Imm AR 489, at 495.

[16] Home Office, Asylum Policy Instructions, 'Deciding Claims – Assessing the Claim Pt 1', para. 7.

Sivakumaran.[17] The Home Office's approach seems to correspond with that of the IAT in *Asuming*:

'[. . .] although logically the establishment of fear may precede any consideration of whether it is well founded fear, establishing that it is well founded will almost always show the existence of fear.'[18]

And further, in *Ali*:

'[. . .] it may be inadvisable to place too much weight upon the subjective element of the refugee definition in order to avoid different treatment of persons similarly placed, and in order to avoid penalising the courageous'.[19]

Sivakumaran is one of the most significant cases in UK asylum law. There, the Court held that 'the requirement that the applicant's fear of persecution should be well-founded means that there has to be demonstrated a reasonable degree of likelihood that he will be persecuted for a Convention reason if returned to his own country'.[20] In assessing the meaning of 'reasonable degree of likelihood', Lord Keith paid heed to Lord Diplock's words in *R. v Governor of Pentonville Prison, ex parte Fernandez*, where the expressions 'a reasonable chance', 'substantial grounds for thinking', and 'a serious possibility' were all deemed appropriate.[21]

It is worth noting that, while the *Sivakumaran* test of reasonable likelihood is adopted in the APIs, the most recent version, in contrast to its predecessor, does not, in fact, refer to the case by name. The phrase 'reasonable likelihood' is actually described as 'vague', and no further clarification is provided. The APIs stress, nonetheless, that 'The aim is to identify the genuine refugee as quickly as possible. When applying the test of reasonable likelihood, if the considerations are finely balanced, the benefit of the doubt should always be given to the applicant.'[22] Caseworkers are advised to consider 'at the date that they are making their decision' whether there is a reasonable likelihood of the applicant being persecuted in their country of origin, and this point is emphasised in the Instructions.[23] Special mention is

---

[17] [1988] Imm AR 148.

[18] (11530), November 11, 1994, cited in M. Symes, *Caselaw on the Refugee Convention – The United Kingdom's Interpretation in the light of the International Authorities* (London: Refugee Legal Centre, 2000), p. 42.

[19] (17300), June 19, 1998, cited in M. Symes, *ibid.*

[20] [1988] Imm AR 147, at 152.

[21] [1971] 1 WLR 987. (*Ex parte Fernandez* was concerned with the interpretation of a provision of the Fugitive Offenders Act 1967.)

[22] Home Office, Asylum Policy Instructions, 'Deciding Claims – Assessing the Claim Pt 1', para. 3.

[23] *ibid.*, para. 7.2.

made of 'past events' and of the key judgement: *Karanakaran v Secretary of State for the Home Department.*[24] According to the APIs, the Court of Appeal in *Karanakaran* held that: 'the proper approach to looking at evidence of past events is **not** to look at the matter in terms of standard of proof: generally a decision-maker will be able to conclude that he accepts evidence as true or rejects it as untrue and he or she is entitled to proceed on that basis'.[25] This is a very simplistic interpretation of *Karanakaran*, since the Court stressed the need for the decision-maker to weigh up all the evidence before arriving at its decision and not to dismiss information summarily.[26] This point is not highlighted sufficiently in the APIs.

'Persecution'

According to the Home Office, 'there is no universally accepted definition of "persecution" for the purposes of the Convention'.[27] Caseworkers are instructed to infer that 'a threat to life or freedom on account of race, religion, nationality, political opinion or membership of a particular social group is always persecution', and that serious violations of human rights would also constitute persecution.[28] They are referred for guidance to paras 51–60 of the UNHCR *Handbook.*[29] These repeat the same point, but also advise that whether other prejudicial acts or threats would amount to persecution depends on the circumstances of the case.[30]

The APIs go on to mention that 'persecution may be said to involve the continuous or systematic failure of the state to offer protection to someone suffering a threat to life or freedom on account of race, religion, nationality, political opinion or membership of a particular social group'.[31] Interestingly, earlier APIs made direct reference to Hathaway's widely accepted definition of persecution: 'persecution is most appropriately defined as the sustained or systemic failure of state protection in relation to one of the core entitlements which has

7.6

---

[24] [2000] INLR 122.
[25] Home Office, Asylum Policy Instructions, 'Deciding Claims – Assessing the Claim Pt 1', para. 7.3.
[26] See Ch. 8 for a discussion of this case.
[27] Home Office, Asylum Policy Instructions, 'Deciding Claims – Assessing the Claim Pt 1', para. 8.
[28] *ibid.*
[29] *ibid.*
[30] para. 52.
[31] Home Office, Asylum Policy Instructions, 'Deciding Claims – Assessing the Claim Pt 1', para. 8.1.

been recognised by the international community'.[32] This has been removed and replaced by a blander and more generalised description of human rights breaches in the context of persecution. While this reference to human rights infringements is crucial, the Home Office is careful to point out that not all human rights breaches amount to persecution within the meaning of the 1951 Convention, and that judgement is needed in each individual case, taking all relevant circumstances into account.[33] The main requirement is that the actions suffered or feared must be sufficiently serious, by their nature or repetition, and should constitute a basic attack on fundamental human rights.[34] Thus unjustifiable attacks on life and limb are covered, as are slavery, torture, cruel, inhuman or degrading punishment or treatment (including: unjustifiable killing or maiming, or physical or psychological torture, rape, and other serious sexual violence).[35]

7.7   The *Handbook* addresses, in particular, the difficult issue of discrimination (or other measures not in themselves amounting to persecution) and suggests that 'the various elements involved may, if taken together, produce an effect on the mind of the applicant that can reasonably justify a claim to well-founded fear of persecution on "cumulative grounds"'.[36] However, the UNHCR does state that only in certain circumstances will discrimination amount to persecution. 'This would be so if measures of discrimination lead to consequences of a substantially prejudicial nature for the person concerned, *e.g.* serious restrictions on his right to earn his livelihood, his right to practise his religion, or his access to normally available educational facilities.'[37] The Home Office lists certain acts of discrimination or ill-treatment that might amount to persecution. These are violations of the right to:

- freedom of thought, conscience and religion;

- freedom from arbitrary arrest and detention;

- freedom of expression, assembly and association;

- privacy;

- access to public employment without discrimination;

---

[32] J.C. Hathaway, *The Law of Refugee Status* (Canada: Butterworths, 1991), p. 112.
[33] Home Office, Asylum Policy Instructions, 'Deciding Claims – Assessing the Claim Pt 1', para. 8.1.
[34] *ibid.*
[35] *ibid.*, para. 8.2.
[36] para. 53.
[37] para. 54.

- access to normally available services such as: food, clothing, housing, medical care, social security, education, right to work, or a combination of such measures assessed cumulatively;

- equal protection of the law.[38]

In accordance with the advice given in the *Handbook*, any violations of rights need to be applied in a discriminatory manner and have serious consequences. They should amount to persistent and serious ill-treatment without just cause, be of a substantially prejudicial nature and strike at a significant part of an individual's or group's existence so as to make the individual's life intolerable if he or she were to return to the country in which persecution is likely.[39]

In relation to prosecution, the Home Office's line follows that of the UNHCR: persecution must be distinguished from punishment or prosecution,[40] and persons fleeing from prosecution or punishment for an offence are not normally refugees.[41] The one exception is a situation where prosecution involves victimisation in its application by the authorities, or where the punishment meted out is so cruel, inhuman or degrading that it constitutes persecution.[42]

An issue that has proved particularly problematic is that of persecution by non-state agents. As the *Handbook* rightly indicates, persecution is normally related to action by the authorities of a country. However, there may be occasions where the agents of persecution are groups within the country other than the authorities. Once again, the Home Office instructions adopt the UNHCR's approach and, while acknowledging that no government can offer a guarantee of absolute protection, accept that seriously discriminatory or other offensive acts committed by the local populace may be considered persecution where knowingly tolerated by the authorities, or where the authorities refuse, or prove unable, to offer effective protection.[43] The caseworker is called upon to consider 'whether or not the applicant has sought the protection of the authorities, any outcome of doing so or the reason for not doing so'.[44]

---

[38] Home Office, Asylum Policy Instructions, 'Deciding Claims – Assessing the Claim Pt 1', para. 8.3.
[39] *ibid.*
[40] See paras 56–60.
[41] Home Office, Asylum Policy Instructions, 'Deciding Claims – Assessing the Claim Pt 1', para. 8.6.
[42] *ibid.*
[43] Home Office, Asylum Policy Instructions, 'Deciding Claims – Assessing the Claim Pt 1', para. 8.5, and see UNHCR *Handbook*, para. 65.
[44] *ibid.*

7.8   Guidance on this matter is provided by the House of Lords decision of *Horvath v Secretary of State for the Home Department*.[45] The APIs
state that, in the case of *Horvath*, the House of Lords looked at the
failure of a state to protect an individual against non-state agents of
persecution, and that their findings were as follows:

> '*The definition of persecution*: Mr Horvath argued that persecution is simply
> severe ill treatment for a Convention reason. The [Home] Department's
> argument, accepted by the House of Lords, was that persecution for the
> purposes of the 1951 Convention involves not only unjustifiable severe ill
> treatment but also a failure by the state to make protection available.
>
> *The meaning of the words "unwilling to avail himself of protection"*: Here Mr
> Horvath argued that under the 1951 Convention a refugee may be a "per-
> son unwilling to avail himself of the protection" of his country of nation-
> ality where he fears persecution by non-state agents, notwithstanding the
> state's protection. The Department argued that the individual must show
> that protection with which the state is required to provide him is not
> available or that he has a well founded belief that he will be persecuted
> for availing himself of it. The majority of the House of Lords accepted
> the Department's argument that the individual's fear can only be well
> founded if it is a fear of being persecuted for availing himself of the state's
> protection.'[46]

In determining whether there is sufficient protection against persecution, the Home Office follows the decision in *Horvath* and determines whether the country of origin has in place a system of criminal
law that punishes attacks by non-state agents, and whether there is a
reasonable willingness to enforce the law. Significantly, the Home
Office also stresses that, in accordance with *Horvath*, the whole risk of
persecution need not be eliminated and, consequently, there does not
need to be a guarantee of complete protection in the home state.[47]

Convention grounds

7.9   While the proof of persecution is obviously crucial to refugee determination, there must also be a causal connection with one of the five
Convention grounds: race, religion, nationality, membership of a particular social group, or political opinion. The Home Office will not
grant refugee status merely because someone belongs to a particular

---

[45] [2000] INLR 239, and see Ch. 8.
[46] Home Office, Asylum Policy Instructions, 'Deciding Claims – Assessing the Claim
Pt 1', para. 8.5.
[47] *ibid.*

race, religion, nationality or social group, or holds a certain political opinion; the applicant must show that there is a well-founded fear of persecution on account of that reason.[48]

'Race'

In relation to its assessment of race, religion, and nationality, the Home Office follows the guidance provided by the UNHCR *Handbook*. Thus race is taken as covering a wide range of ethnic groups that are referred to as 'races'. It also covers 'membership of a specific social group of common descent forming a minority within a larger population'.[49] The *Handbook* advises that discrimination on racial grounds will frequently amount to persecution for the purposes of the Convention where, as a result of the discrimination, 'a person's human dignity is affected to such an extent as to be incompatible with the most elementary and inalienable human rights, or where the disregard of racial barriers is subject to serious consequences'.[50]

7.10

'Religion'

Persecution for religious reasons may assume various forms: prohibition of membership of a religious community, of worship in private or in public, of religious instruction, or serious measures of discrimination imposed on persons because they practise their religion or belong to a particular religious community.[51] The APIs warn that 'mere membership of a particular religious community will normally not be enough to substantiate a claim to refugee status'.[52] Of course, there are exceptions and caseworkers are instructed to 'consider the individual circumstances of each case in the context of the country information', as well as seek further guidance from the *Handbook*. This is the extent of the Home Office information provided on the subject of persecution for reasons of religion.

7.11

---

[48] *ibid.*, para. 9.
[49] *ibid.*, and UNHCR *Handbook*, para. 68.
[50] UNHCR *Handbook*, para. 69.
[51] Home Office, Asylum Policy Instructions, 'Deciding Claims – Assessing the Claim Pt 2', para. 9.2, and UNHCR *Handbook*, para. 72.
[52] Home Office, Asylum Policy Instructions, 'Deciding Claims – Assessing the Claim Pt 2', para. 9.2.

'Nationality'

7.12 Yet again, with regard to nationality, the Home Office advice is a basic reworking of the guidance provided by the *Handbook*: '[T]he term nationality does not only refer to citizenship but also to membership of an ethnic or linguistic group and may occasionally overlap with the term race. Persecution for reasons of nationality may consist of adverse attitudes and measures against a national (ethnic or linguistic) minority and in certain circumstances the fact of belonging to such a minority may in itself give rise to a well-founded fear of persecution. A persecuted nationality does not necessarily have to be a minority.'[53]

'Membership of a particular social group'

7.13 In assessing membership of a particular social group, caseworkers are pointed to the extremely significant case of *Islam v Secretary of State for the Home Department; R. v Immigration Appeal Tribunal & Another, ex parte Shah*,[54] and to the UNHCR *Handbook*, paras 77–79.[55] The Home Office's interpretation of *Islam and Shah* is as follows:

'i) Members of a social group have to have in common an immutable characteristic which is either beyond the power of an individual to change, or is so fundamental to their identity or conscience that it ought not to be required to be changed.

ii) Whilst social group must exist independently of persecution, discrimination against the group could be taken into account in identifying it as a social group, **i.e. discrimination against the group could be a factor contributing to the identity of a social group.**'[56]

The Instructions suggest that in light of the case, groups which share an immutable characteristic (including women and homosexuals, or other persons defined by their sexual orientation) may constitute a social group, if they are subjected to persecution in their society because they are members of that group.[57] Much will depend on the circumstances of the asylum application under consideration, but in

---

[53] Home Office, Asylum Policy Instructions, 'Deciding Claims – Assessing the Claim Pt 2', para. 9.3.
[54] [1999] INLR 144, HL.
[55] Home Office, Asylum Policy Instructions, 'Deciding Claims – Assessing the Claim Pt 2', para. 9.4.
[56] *ibid.*
[57] *ibid.*

all cases, the applicant will need to establish (a) well-founded fear of persecution, (b) that the authorities are unable or unwilling to offer protection, and (c) persecution is *because of* their membership of a particular social group. While the previous APIs commented on the *Islam and Shah* decision, this has been removed and the advice now given is too concise.[58] Thus the particular significance of *Islam and Shah* for women is, unfortunately, not highlighted.[59] Furthermore, it is striking that the Home Office, unlike the Immigration Appellate Authority, has not issued detailed guidelines on handling claims involving women and gender issues.[60]

'Political opinion'

Inexplicably, earlier versions of the APIs did not discuss the ground   **7.14**
of political opinion, but this has now been rectified. According to the current information, an asylum seeker who simply holds a political opinion different from that of his or her government will not succeed. There must also be fear of persecution for holding such an opinion.[61] In other words, causation is, again, crucial. This is in contrast to the *Handbook*, which states that 'While the definition speaks of persecution "for reasons of political opinion" it may not always be possible to establish a causal link between the opinion expressed and the related measures suffered or feared by the applicant.'[62] The caseworker needs to determine whether 'sooner or later' the applicant's political opinions will find expression and come to the state's attention, and whether the state's response is likely to be persecution. That said, it must be remembered that persecution for reasons of a political opinion can arise where a political opinion is *imputed* to an individual, and this fundamental point is accepted by the Home Office. The Instructions are quite comprehensive and urge decision-makers 'not to underestimate or overlook the political dimension of an individual's experience of persecution even though an individual may not regard

---

[58] See Ch. 8 for further discussion of the case.
[59] For which, see Ch. 8. See, on the issue of refugee women, N. Kelly, 'The Convention refugee definition and gender-based persecution: A decade's progress' (2001) 13:4 IJRL, 559–568; H. Crawley, '*Refugees and Gender: Law and Process* (Bristol: Jordans, 2001); H. Crawley, *Women as Asylum Seekers* (London: ILPA, 1997).
[60] Immigration Appellate Authority, *Asylum Gender Guidelines*, November 2000, available on: *www.iaa.gov.uk/gender.pdf*
[61] Home Office, Asylum Policy Instructions, 'Deciding Claims – Assessing the Claim Pt 2', para. 9.5.
[62] para. 81.

themselves as making a political statement'.[63] In fact, an individual may not actually claim persecution for holding a political opinion, and it is down to the caseworker to recognise this. Prosecution, in contrast to persecution, for a politically motivated act is acceptable if it complies with the law of the country concerned, irrespective of whether the applicant fears such prosecution. The one exception is where the sanctions involved following prosecution are deemed excessive or arbitrary.

An important part of the Home Office's interpretation of political opinion is the recognition that political activity need not involve direct action such as demonstrating publicly against the government; rather, it is accepted that more benign activities such as 'hiding people, passing messages or providing community services, food, clothing and medical care' can be an expression of a political opinion.[64] Since gender is not of itself a ground of persecution under Art. 1A(2), women often need to base their claims either on 'membership of a particular social group' (per *Islam and Shah*) or on 'political opinion'. The inclusion of indirect action in the interpretation of the political opinion ground is therefore imperative. The APIs state further:

'A woman who opposes institutionalised discrimination against women or expresses views of independence from the social or cultural norms of society may sustain or fear harm because of her actual political opinion or a political opinion that has been imputed to her. She is perceived within the established political/social structure as expressing politically antagonistic views through her actions or failure to act. If a woman resists gender oppression, her resistance is political.'[65]

Internal flight and civil war situations

7.15   An asylum seeker to the UK will not be granted refugee status if he or she could reasonably be expected to find effective protection within a different area of his or her own country.[66] The assumption is that such a person is not in need of international protection. This option has become known as 'internal flight' or 'internal relocation'. Though the APIs refer to the House of Lords judgement *R. (Yogathas and Thangarasa) v Secretary of State for the Home Department*, which expressed

---

[63] Home Office, Asylum Policy Instructions, 'Deciding Claims – Assessing the Claim Pt 2', para. 9.5.
[64] *ibid.*
[65] *ibid.*
[66] Home Office, Asylum Policy Instructions, 'Additional Considerations – Internal Flight', para. 1.

a preference for 'internal relocation' rather than 'internal flight',[67] the APIs persist with use of the term 'internal flight'.

Where an application raised internal relocation issues, the case-worker needs to address a number of questions to determine whether it is an option:

- 'Is there a part of the country in which the applicant would not have a well-founded fear of persecution?
- Is it **reasonable** to expect the applicant to live in that part of the country?'[68]

Particular emphasis is placed on the case of *R. v Secretary of State for the Home Department & Immigration Appeal Tribunal, ex parte Robinson,* in which the Court of Appeal set out certain factors to be considered when assessing the feasibility of relocation by an applicant.[69] The Home Office has summarised these as follows:

'i)   Is the safe part of the country reasonably accessible? (Financial, logistical and any other good reasons need to be taken into account.)
ii)   Would the applicant/appellant be required to encounter great physical danger in travelling to or staying in another part of the country?
v)   Would they be required to undergo undue hardship in travelling or staying there?
vi)   Does the quality of the internal protection meet basic norms of civil, political and socioeconomic human rights?'[70]

The key factor in a caseworker's determination of the internal relocation alternative is the issue of reasonableness. Attention is drawn once more to the decision of *Karanakaran*, a case on internal relocation, which is summarised as having established that a decision-maker must 'take into account the cumulative effect of a whole range of disparate considerations'.[71] The caseworker must show that there is some form of government and infrastructure in the alternative area.[72] While the absence of close family ties in the identified safe area will be an important part of the assessment, this will not prevent the Home Office refusing asylum and requiring return. Other factors for

---

[67]   [2002] INLR 620, para. 6.
[68]   Home Office, Asylum Policy Instructions, 'Additional Considerations – Internal Flight', para. 2.1.
[69]   [1997] Imm AR 568.
[70]   Home Office, Asylum Policy Instructions, 'Additional Considerations – Internal Flight', para. 2.1.
[71]   *ibid.*
[72]   *ibid.*

consideration are separation from family, loss of livelihood, and comparative living conditions in the separate parts of the country concerned.[73] Ultimately, following *Robinson* and *Karanakaran*, the claimant must establish that relocation is *unduly harsh*, which is a stringent test.[74] Where it is decided that it is not reasonable to expect an applicant to live in another part of his or her country of origin, the Home Office will grant asylum rather than humanitarian protection or discretionary leave. Finally, the updated APIs note that if a caseworker considers that there might be a breach of Art. 3 of the ECHR in returning an applicant, he or she should apply the same reasoning to the human rights claim as to the asylum claim when considering internal relocation. Citing the IAT case of *Secretary of State for the Home Department v AE and FE*,[75] the Instructions specify that 'where IR is in issue the Refugee Convention and the European Convention on Human Rights will march together'.[76]

In the case of civil war, where law and order have broken down and there are clashes between rival clans or sub clans (as in Somalia), the Home Office adopts a fairly tough line. It does not consider a state of civil war to give rise to an automatic right to refugee status, unless the applicant can show that he or she is 'at risk of adverse treatment over and above the risk to life and liberty which occurs during civil war'.[77] While this is clearly the Home Office's reading of the case *R. v Secretary of State for the Home Department, ex parte Adan*,[78] it is surprising that there is no further assistance provided to caseworkers on civil war situations in view of the high-level judicial discussion of this issue (for which, see Chapter 8). Applications from Somalia are consistently high, leaving one to wonder whether the Home Office's cursory explanation of civil war is in some way related to this fact.

Exclusion clauses

7.16 The exclusion clauses of the 1951 Convention, contained in ss. D, E and F of Art. 1, provide for the exclusion of persons from refugee status who otherwise have the characteristics of refugees. Such

---

[73] Home Office, Asylum Policy Instructions, 'Additional Considerations – Internal Flight', para. 2.1.

[74] *ibid.*, para. 2.2.

[75] [2002] UKIAT 05237 Starred.

[76] Home Office, Asylum Policy Instructions, 'Additional Considerations – Internal Flight', para. 4.

[77] Asylum Policy Instructions, 'Deciding Claims – Assessing the Claim Part 1', para. 6.5.

[78] [1998] INLR 325.

persons fall into three groups: those receiving UN protection or assistance (Art. 1D); those who are not considered to be in need of international protection (Art. 1E); and those who fall within a listed category of persons not considered to be deserving of international protection (Art. 1F).[79] UK decision-makers are instructed to refuse asylum to anyone falling under the exclusion clauses, but discretionary leave may be granted in its place. In practice, Arts 1D and 1E are rarely employed. Art. 1D applies to the United Nations Relief and Works Agency for Palestinian Refugees (UNRWA), operating in the Middle East, while persons with refuge elsewhere, and therefore not in need of international protection, will be refused under Art. 1E.[80] Rather oddly, earlier instructions suggested that no case in Art. 1E would arise in the UK; this statement has now been removed.

By contrast, there is a real possibility that Art. 1F will be applied to refuse refugee status, particularly following the bombing of the World Trade Centre on September 11, 2001, and the heightened anxiety surrounding the issue of terrorism. The current guidance states that many asylum applicants claim to have committed violent acts for political reasons (for example, some Kurdish asylum seekers would fall into this category). In such cases, the decision-maker is instructed to assess first whether the claim falls within the inclusion criteria of Art. 1A(2), and then whether the actions of the applicant invoke the exclusion clause or not. Where an individual has been recognised as a refugee, but is convicted of a particularly serious crime within the UK, it is open to the Home Office to consider returning the refugee to his country of origin, if there are reasonable grounds for regarding him or her as a danger to the security of the UK (Art. 33(2) – the exception to *non-refoulement*). However, it should be noted that the UK would, in such circumstances, still be required to adhere to its obligations under international human rights law, in particular Art. 3 of the ECHR.[81]

Despite the guidance, Art. 1F has been reportedly underused, even in cases involving Serbian and Angolan soldiers. However, there are no statistics on the use of exclusion clauses and this makes assessment difficult. It is anticipated that the Home Office will be more likely to exclude on the basis of Art. 33(2) rather than on 1F, since Art. 33(2) applies to refugees settled in the UK. In the current political climate, changes will inevitably emerge, and the UK is looking to other

---

[79] UNHCR *Handbook*, para. 140. For wording of Arts 1F and 33(2), see Ch. 4.
[80] Asylum Policy Instructions, 'Deciding Claims – Assessing the Claim – Pt 3', para. 12.3.
[81] *ibid.*, para. 12.4, and see humanitarian protection and discretionary leave.

countries, in particular Canada and Australia, to learn about their application of the exclusion clauses. At the time of writing, the APIs had not been updated to reflect shifting attitudes towards politically or religiously motivated violence, though a specific instruction on Art. 1F is due.

Cessation clauses

7.17   Alongside exclusion clauses, the caseworker should also consider whether any of the cessation clauses apply, though these are omitted in the APIs. The cessation clauses come into effect after an individual has been determined a refugee and are not part of the original assessment, as is the case with the exclusion clauses. They are contained in Art. 1C of the Convention.[82] Articles 1C(1) to (4) deal with personal changes in the circumstances of the refugee, while (5) and (6) are based on changes in the country where persecution is feared. The purpose of the cessation clauses is to absolve the country of refuge of responsibility for an individual who ceases to be a refugee. In such a case, international protection is no longer necessary or justified.[83] Since the cessation clauses are 'negative in character' and 'exhaustively enumerated', the UNHCR calls upon countries to interpret the cessation clauses restrictively and to refrain from adducing other reasons 'by way of analogy to justify the withdrawal of refugee status'.[84]

Credibility

7.18   In reaching a decision on an asylum seeker's claim, caseworkers will not only examine whether the applicant meets the requirements of the 1951 Convention but will also assess his or her credibility. This will entail considering evidence of immigration history, general country information,[85] and any other additional factors. The Home Office's own criteria will also be heavily drawn upon. These are

---

[82] For the cessation requirements, see Ch. 4.

[83] UNHCR *Handbook*, para. 111.

[84] *ibid.*, para. 116.

[85] The Country Information and Policy Unit of the Home Office (CIPU) gathers and collates country information for use by caseworkers. It focuses on 35 countries that generate the largest number of applications in the UK. In compiling the assessments, researchers make use of a wide range of sources, including UNHCR, Amnesty International, the Foreign and Commonwealth Office, and Reuters news database. Despite this apparently comprehensive approach, there are frequent accusations by asylum seeker representatives that Home Office country assessments are outdated or inaccurate.

contained in the non-statutory Immigration Rules, paras 340 to 344.[86] These five paragraphs are arguably the key to the whole UK determination process. Known as the 'credibility criteria', they explain the circumstances in which the Home Office deem an applicant to be lacking in credibility, and therefore subject to refusal. They are also repeated in slightly different wording in the APIs.[87] In summary, an asylum seeker's case may be damaged if he or she:

- fails without reasonable explanation to make a prompt and full disclosure of material facts;[88]

- fails without reasonable explanation to apply forthwith on arrival in the UK;[89]

- makes an application after refusal to enter, following a recommendation for deportation, or following notification of a decision to deport or remove;[90]

- adduces manifestly false evidence in support of an application, or has otherwise made false representations;[91]

- fails to produce a passport on arrival in the UK, or produces a false passport and fails to inform the immigration officer of that fact;[92]

- without reasonable explanation destroys, damages, or disposes of any passport, document, or ticket relevant to the claim;[93]

- has undertaken any activities in the UK which are inconsistent with previous beliefs and behaviour and which are calculated to create or substantially enhance his/her claim to refugee status;[94]

- has lodged concurrent applications for asylum in the United Kingdom or in another country.[95]

In addition, the Secretary of State is permitted to take into account some further factors when deciding whether or not to refuse an application:

---

[86] Statement of Changes in the Immigration Rules HC 395 (as amended).
[87] Asylum Policy Instructions, 'Deciding Claims – Assessing the Claim – Pt 3', para. 11.1.
[88] para. 340.
[89] para. 341(i).
[90] para. 341(ii).
[91] para. 341(iii).
[92] para. 341(iv).
[93] para. 341(v).
[94] para. 341(vi).
[95] para. 341(vii).

- the actions of anyone acting as an agent for the asylum applicant;[96]

- the identification of part of the country from which the applicant claims to be a refugee in which he would not have a well-founded fear of persecution, and to which it would be reasonable to expect the applicant to go;[97]

- the applicant's inclusion in a group whose claims are clearly not related to the criteria for refugee status in the Convention and Protocol.[98]

These credibility and other criteria have been widely criticised. For example, the UNHCR has suggested:

'It is not advisable to list [. . .] the factors which should be given consideration in assessing an asylum-seeker's credibility. Evaluation of credibility is a process which involves the consideration of many complex factors, both objective and subjective, which are impossible to enumerate. Since all these may be equally important, singling out any of these factors will, by necessity, be incomplete and arbitrary.'[99]

7.19   This advice seems largely to have been ignored in the UK, and credibility has, in the past decade, played an increasingly important role in asylum refusals. Assessing credibility is bound to be an immensely difficult task, and there is a risk that the listed criteria may be applied to the letter, allowing little room for the 'benefit of doubt'. However, the APIs do provide a note of caution in advising caseworkers that 'question marks over an applicant's credibility do not negate their claim to asylum'.[100] So, for example, where an applicant has destroyed his or her passport or other documentation relevant to the claim, the applicant should be asked for an explanation. The Instructions remind decision-makers that 'genuine asylum seekers sometimes have no alternative but to travel on forged travel documents which may subsequently have to be returned to an agent'.[101] It is important that applicants should be given an opportunity to explain any apparent discrepancies and reasons for any change in their accounts.[102] Untrue statements in themselves are not a reason for

---

[96] para. 342.

[97] para. 343.

[98] para. 344.

[99] Cited in JCWI, *Immigration, Nationality and Refugee Handbook – A User's Guide* (London: JCWI, 1999), p. 101.

[100] Asylum Policy Instructions, 'Deciding Claims – Assessing the Claim – Pt 3', para. 11.

[101] *ibid.*, para. 11.1.

[102] *ibid.*

refusal and the case should be considered in light of all evidence.[103] That said, many practitioners doubt that Home Office employees approach refugee determination with such an open mind.

Research on memory and the psychiatric health of refugees is drawing attention to the risks associated with use of credibility criteria. [104] Various studies suggest that those suffering from genuinely traumatic events may have difficulty in recalling them.[105] There may also be inconsistencies in recall. Furthermore, refugees are at increased risk of post-traumatic stress disorder and depression, which may affect their behaviour and their willingness to talk to immigration officials. These failings are likely to affect their credibility. Yet one psychology-based analysis revealed that while interviewers *believe* that those who lie are less consistent than truth-tellers, there was in fact no difference in consistency between liars and truth-tellers. More importantly, the interviewer can actually cause certain behaviour in an interviewee, which may then result in his or her being deemed not credible.[106] It is unlikely that Home Office interviewing officers are sufficiently equipped to handle traumatised people. It is, of course, the refugee who is likely to suffer when found not to be credible.[107]

Section 31 of the Immigration and Asylum Act 1999

Following a significant decision of the High Court in 1999, *R. v Uxbridge Magistrates' Court and Another, ex parte Adimi* ('*Adimi*') on the use of false documentation by asylum seekers,[108] in which Home Office policy on the application of Art. 31 of the 1951 Convention was severely criticised, a number of changes were made to UK law via   **7.20**

---

[103] *ibid.*

[104] See, for example S.W. Turner *et al*, 'Mental health of Kosovan Albanian refugees in the UK' (2003) 182 *British Journal of Psychiatry*, pp. 444–448.

[105] Professor Chris Brewin, 'Memory and PTSD', speaking at BMA Conference, *Recent Research into Memory and its Relevance to Asylum Seekers*, London, March 18, 2003.

[106] Professor Ray Bull, 'Research and development on enhancing victim/witness recall', speaking at BMA Conference, *Recent Research into Memory and its Relevance to Asylum Seekers*, London, March 18, 2003.

[107] Professor Ray Bull of the Department of Psychology, University of Portsmouth, advocates a seven-phase approach to interviewing: great and establish rapport; explain aims of interview; initiate a free report; questioning; varied and extensive retrieval; summary; close: Professor Ray Bull, 'Research and development on enhancing victim/witness recall', speaking at BMA Conference, *Recent Research into Memory and its Relevance to Asylum Seekers*, London, March 18, 2003

[108] [1999] INLR 490, and see Ch. 8.

s. 31 to the 1999 Act.[109] This provides a statutory defence for refugees charged with obtaining, possessing or using false documents:

> 'It is a defence for a refugee charged with an offence to which this section applies to show that, having come to the United Kingdom directly from a country where his life or freedom was threatened (within the meaning of the Refugee Convention), he –
>
> (a) presented himself to the authorities in the United Kingdom without delay;
> (b) showed good cause for his illegal entry or presence; and
> (c) made a claim for asylum as soon as was reasonably practicable after his arrival in the United Kingdom.'[110]

Where the refugee stops in another country outside the UK, the defence applies only if it is unreasonable to expect protection to be given in that country.[111] As the APIs note, s. 31 is more restrictive than the *Adimi* judgement, but, since it represents Parliament's interpretation of Art. 31, it takes priority over the earlier decision of *Adimi*.[112] The main point is that *refugees* only can rely on the defence; those refused asylum but granted humanitarian protection or discretionary leave are not protected by the provision.[113] This contrasts with the view held by the UNHCR. In a four-page commentary on the API covering s. 31, the UNHCR argues that 'the protection of s. 31 is presumptively applicable to asylum seekers until a final negative decision on their claim to international protection has been reached'.[114] It also points out that Art. 31 is applicable to all offences committed as a result of illegal entry or presence, not just the few listed in s. 31.[115] The Home Office also expects people to claim asylum without delay (*i.e.* generally within a couple of days) in order to benefit from s. 31.[116] The UNHCR calls for this criterion to be interpreted flexibly. A more generous construction is applied to the requirement in s. 31(2) that asylum seekers who stop in another country should claim asylum there. The Instructions recognise that asylum seekers in transit

---

[109] Art. 31 concerns the imposition of penalties on refugees on account of their illegal entry or presence – see Ch. 4.

[110] s. 31(1).

[111] s. 31(2).

[112] Asylum Policy Instructions, 'Miscellaneous guidance for caseworkers – Art. 31 of the 1951 Convention and s. 31 of the Immigration and Asylum Act 1999, para. 3.

[113] *ibid.*

[114] UNHCR, 'Comments on October 2002 Home Office Policy Instruction (API) on s. 31 of the Asylum and Immigration Act 1999 (*sic*) and Art. 31 of the 1951 Convention relating to the Status of Refugees', March 3, 2003, p. 2.

[115] *ibid.*

[116] Asylum Policy Instructions, 'Miscellaneous guidance for caseworkers – Art. 31 of the 1951 Convention and s. 31 of the Immigration and Asylum Act 1999, para. 7.

through a third country might not be able to lodge an application with immigration officials. 'Under these circumstances, and taking into account all the information available, it may be considered reasonable for the defence of s. 31 to apply.'[117] Despite this concession, the UNHCR lists a whole range of reasons why a refugee 'could not reasonably have expected to be given protection' in a particular country, which are not specified in the API.

Safe third country cases

As indicated in Chapter 6, one of the functions of screening is to determine whether an asylum seeker has arrived from a safe third country. If this is established, an asylum claim can be refused without substantive consideration and the claimant removed. A specialist unit exists in the Immigration Service to handle such cases – the Third Country Unit ('TCU'). The statutory law relating to safe third country cases, and the appeal rights associated with them, were set out in Chapter 5. There it was described how ss. 11 and 12 to the Immigration and Asylum Act 1999 replaced the previous provisions of the 1993 and 1996 Acts on third country cases and set up an alternative regime for four categories of cases: removal of an asylum applicant under standing arrangements with EU Member States (*i.e.* the Dublin Convention),[118] removal to a Member State outside the standing arrangements,[119] removal to a state designated by the Secretary of State,[120] and removal to a country which is neither designated nor a Member State.[121] The 2002 Act amended s. 11 to include in the definition of 'standing arrangements' bilateral agreements on asylum returns between EU Member States.[122] The presumption in ss. 11 and 12 is that the countries concerned will comply with their obligations under the 1951 Convention and not *refoule* any applicant. One of the main problems with safe third country removals for asylum seekers in the UK has been the restriction on appeal rights. Appeals are non-suspensive and can only be lodged from abroad: that is, removal will take place unless an applicant can successfully argue that

7.21

---

[117] *ibid.*, para. 8.
[118] s. 11. The EU Member States concerned are Austria, Belgium, Denmark, Finland, France, Germany, Greece, Ireland, Italy, Luxembourg, Netherlands, Portugal, Spain, Sweden and the UK. Since, April 1, 2001, Norway and Iceland have also been applying the Dublin Convention procedures. See Ch. 9 for further information on the Dublin Convention.
[119] s. 12(1)(a).
[120] s. 12(1)(b).
[121] s. 12(4).
[122] See Ch. 5.

there will be a breach of human rights and the Secretary of State does not determine such a claim to be 'clearly unfounded'.[123] The Immigration Rules help to clarify the workings of ss. 11 and 12:

'(1) In a case where the Secretary of State is satisfied that the conditions set out in either section 11(2) or 12(7) of the Immigration and Asylum Act 1999 are fulfilled, he will normally refuse the asylum application and issue a certificate under section 11 or section 12 of the Immigration and Asylum Act 1999 (as the case may be) without substantive consideration of the applicant's claim to refugee status.'[124]

7.22   The bulk of the APIs on third country cases explain the legal position. However, a useful summary of the IND's practice is also provided:

'In all cases where there is material evidence of the responsibility of one of the Member States for consideration of the application the papers should be referred only to TCU. These cases are referred to as "definite runners". ICD [Integrated Casework Directorate] caseworkers should only receive these cases if the third country action has failed. Where there is no material evidence of the responsibility of a particular Member State TCU will make preliminary inquiries with one or more Member States in order to determine responsibility under the Dublin Convention. These cases are simultaneously referred to TCU and ICD as "concurrent third country cases" so that a substantive decision can be made if the TCU enquiries do not result in a Dublin Convention decision. TCU must be consulted before any substantive action is taken on a concurrent case.'[125]

The Instructions also note that where a return to a non-EU country is planned, the TCU must be satisfied that an applicant either had an opportunity at the border or within the territory of a safe third country to make contact with the country's authorities in order to seek protection, or that there is other clear evidence of the applicant's admissibility to a safe third country.[126]

Under the Dublin Convention ('Dublin I'), one of the basic criteria is that the state where the applicant first entered the EU is responsible for assessing the asylum claim. At the time of signing, it therefore seemed that there was a cast-iron case for British immigration to remove to a neighbouring country any asylum seeker who had

---

[123] See Nationality, Immigration and Asylum Act 2002, s. 93(2)(b).
[124] para. 345.
[125] Asylum Policy Instructions, 'Refusals without substantive consideration – Third country cases' – para. 2.
[126] *ibid.*, para. 3.

crossed Europe by land to reach the UK. This proved wholly erroneous. The systematic destruction of personal documents by asylum seekers made it almost impossible to track their exact routes. A stark illustration of how the Convention failed the UK is provided by the Sangatte asylum camp. The Immigration Service was unable to return the majority of those who entered the UK via Sangatte, as France refused to assume responsibility for *sans papiers,* arguing that they must have first accessed another EU country. As a consequence, the renegotiation of Dublin II was, for some time, a key objective of the British government. Many commentators remain unconvinced, however, that it will operate more effectively than its predecessor.[127] Even the Conservatives, who signed up to Dublin I, have proposed that the UK should reinstate the pre-1990 bilateral agreement with France, since, on their calculation, this would facilitate the return of approximately 30,000 asylum applicants across the Channel.[128] This must be wishful thinking. France is highly unlikely to agree to an arrangement that will impose a heavier burden on its asylum system. What is more, the lengthy wrangle over the closure of Sangatte is testament to France's past reluctance to assist the UK authorities, though, with greater co-operation between the two on security at French ports, this may now be changing.

Certification and white lists

The law relating to certification and white lists has been discussed in some detail in Chapter 5. However, on account of the crucial place of certification in the asylum determination process, it warrants further mention. As noted earlier, UK governments have, since the 1993 Act, certified certain cases as 'without foundation', 'manifestly unfounded' or 'clearly unfounded'. By and large, certification has led to accelerated appeal procedures as well as limited appeal rights. Initially, the majority of 'without foundation' certificates were issued for safe third country cases, a fact which prompted Amnesty International to describe the regulations as a cynical attempt by the government to pass the responsibility for asylum determination to a neighbouring country.[129] Later, the list of certifiable cases subject to the 'fast tracking' procedures was greatly extended. Although it seemed to cover most possibilities, the 1996 Act went a step further and introduced a completely new provision under the accelerated

7.23

---

[127] See Ch. 9 for further discussion of the Dublin Convention.
[128] HC Deb. Vol. 379, February 4, 2002. col. 606.
[129] Amnesty International, *UK – Passing the Buck: Deficient Home Office Practice in 'Safe Third Country' Cases* (London: Amnesty International, 1993).

appeals section: the designated countries provision, more commonly known as the 'white list', for which there was a presumption of safety.[130] Consequently, in order to succeed in their asylum claims, applicants from these countries were forced to rebut the presumption, an undertaking many practitioners considered nigh impossible.

The first designations by the Secretary of State created consternation since they included countries in which human rights infringements were on recent record. Of the list – Bulgaria, Cyprus, Ghana, India, Pakistan, Poland and Romania –,[131] India and Pakistan were singled out in an Amnesty International report as having raised serious human rights concerns.[132] In addition, at the time, the maltreatment of the Roma in Romania, Poland, the Czech Republic and Slovakia was just coming to light. The fact that 1996 witnessed the onset of systematic migration of Roma to the west provided one explanation for the designation of a number of eastern European countries. Following the repeal of the 1996 white list provision, some NGOs accused the Asylum Policy Unit of maintaining a covert list:

'According to the Home Office there are currently no designated safe countries of origin, but it would be true to say that in practice the designated safe countries (previously known as the 'white list') does operate in the determination of asylum applications via the fast-tracking system.'[133]

The changes implemented in the 2002 Act have substantially altered the position regarding certification. Certification under the 1999 Act ceased on April 1, 2003 and the new provisions of the 2002 Act took effect. Once more, there is a list of countries for which a presumption of safety applies. To date, 24 countries have been designated 'safe' under ss. 94(4) and (5). When questioned recently about the inclusion of the Czech Republic and Slovakia on the list, countries in which the Roma continue to suffer discrimination, if not persecution, and about the way in which the presumption would operate, the Minister for Immigration replied:

'Within the context of that presumption, [. . .] each case is examined on its merits, and certainly it is possible for somebody to establish a Convention reason within the system itself; it is not a system in which the presumption is applied in a way that makes it impossible for somebody who

---

[130] s.1, inserting sch. 2, para. 5(2) in the Asylum and Immigration Appeals Act 1993.
[131] Asylum (Designated Country of Destination and Designated Safe Third Countries) Order 1996, SI 1996/2671.
[132] Amnesty International, *Slamming the Door – The Demolition of the Right to Asylum in the UK* (London: Amnesty International, 1996), p. 29.
[133] Refugee Council Briefing, *Claiming Asylum in the UK*, January 2002, p. 6.

is being persecuted to establish that they have reached the Convention threshold.'[134]

This is remarkably similar to Ann Widdecombe's response as Home Secretary to the same question in 1996.[135] In addition, the EU accession countries on the list were all, according to the current Minister, making substantial progress in relation to human rights in order to meet the targets set for EU membership.[136] Even so, recent research on the Roma is considerably less sanguine about the treatment of Roma in eastern Europe.[137]

In tandem with designation, there is also a power to certify a claim as clearly unfounded under s. 94(2). The Home Office clarified in June 2003 that while a clearly unfounded claim made by a resident of a designated state *must* be certified, it was *discretionary* whether a clearly unfounded claim made by a resident of a non-designated state would be certified.[138] From June 8, 2003, a managed roll-out of case-by-case certification under s. 94(2) commenced.[139] How the Home Office will implement this discretionary power is yet to be determined, but the consequences for the asylum seeker are potentially very serious, as certified claimants have no right of appeal while in the UK. The Minister herself conceded that there was a need in certification cases, which were not country specific, to 'proceed very cautiously indeed' and to build up some case-law on the issue.[140]

Unaccompanied children

In 2001, 3,469 unaccompanied children claimed asylum in the UK; this represented a 27 per cent increase on the year 2000.[141] A whole API is dedicated to children, though, at the time of writing, this was being revised and was unavailable for consultation. The comments here are therefore based on information which is in the public   **7.24**

---

[134] Home Affairs Select Committee, 'Asylum Applications', Uncorrected Oral Evidence, Beverley Hughes, Session 2003–04, May 8, 2003, Q. 66.

[135] HC Standing Committee D, January 16, 1996, col. 158.

[136] Home Affairs Select Committee, 'Asylum Applications', Uncorrected Oral Evidence, Beverley Hughes, Session 2003–04, May 8, 2003, Q. 66.

[137] See D. Stevens, 'The migration of the Romanian Roma to the UK: a contextual study' (2003) 5; 4 *European Journal of Migration and Law.*

[138] Letter from IND to S. Meah, IAS – June 17, 2003, ILPA Information for Members, June 2003.

[139] *ibid.*

[140] Home Affairs Select Committee, 'Asylum Removals', Oral Evidence, Beverley Hughes, Session 2003–04, March 4, 2003, Qs. 631–2.

[141] Home Office, *Asylum Statistics United Kingdom 2001* (London: Home Office RDSD, July 2002), table 2.3. There were no figures at time of writing for 2002.

domain, but which may soon be replaced. A child is defined by para.
349 of the Immigration Rules as 'a person who is under 18 years of
age, or who, in the absence of documentary evidence establishing
age, appears to be under that age'. To be regarded as an unaccompanied child asylum seeker, the individual must also apply for asylum
in his or her right and be without adult family members or guardians
in the UK.[142] Unaccompanied children are to be accorded particular
priority and care in view of their potential vulnerability.[143] Interviews,
though rarely necessary, must be conducted in the presence of a
guardian or other adult who has taken responsibility for the child.[144]
The credibility criteria are equally relevant to children, though caseworkers are advised to apply 'the benefit of the doubt' more liberally.

Within 24 hours of an asylum claim being lodged by an unaccompanied child, details are forwarded to the Refugee Council's Children's Advisory Panel, which will provide advice and support. As
noted in Chapter 6, such children are the responsibility of the local
authorities under the Children Act 1989, and will not be subject to
dispersal by NASS. According to the Home Office, unaccompanied
children are only detained in the most exceptional circumstances.[145]
Increasingly, the Home Office disputes the age of applicants. An asylum seeker who claims to be a child, but whose appearance strongly
suggests an adult, will be treated as an adult and offered NASS support where appropriate, until medical or documentary evidence
establishes the correct age.[146] The IND information admits that 'the
medical determination of age is an inexact science and the margin of
error can be substantial, sometimes by as much as five years either
side'.[147] It is more inclined, therefore, to accept an assessment by
social services departments, where this differs from its own.[148]

Children who fail to obtain asylum and who have no human rights
claim are subject to removal. However, this will only be effected
where the Home Office is satisfied that adequate reception and care
arrangements are in place in the country of return.[149] In the past,
where this could not be guaranteed, the IND was prepared to grant
a period of exceptional leave to remain: children under 14 years
received four years' ELR and were then entitled to apply for settlement (indefinite leave to remain ('ILR')); children between 14 and 17

---

[142] paras 349–352.
[143] para. 350.
[144] para. 352.
[145] Home Office Information Note, 'Unaccompanied asylum seeking children', July
2002, para. 7.1.
[146] ibid., para. 6.1.
[147] ibid., para. 6.3.
[148] ibid., para. 6.2.
[149] ibid., para. 8.3.

years were granted leave to remain until their eigtheenth birthday, after which they were expected to leave the country, so long as satisfactory arrangements for return could be made.[150] The removal of ELR (for which see below) has altered the position, but the new leave arrangements are uncertain. The APIs simply confirm that where an unaccompanied child qualifies for discretionary leave 'on more than one ground (i.e. on the ground of inadequate reception arrangements and also under another ground) they should be granted such leave on the basis of the ground that provides the longer period of stay'.[151] It is hoped that the forthcoming API on children will add much needed clarity.

THE DECISION

Current Home Office information indicates that there are four **7.25** possible decisions that can be taken on an asylum claim:

- grant of asylum;
- refusal of asylum, but grant of humanitarian protection;
- refusal of asylum, but grant of discretionary leave;
- refusal of asylum.[152]

To understand the shifting patterns in Home Office decision-making and the actual impact of legislation on asylum applications lodged in the UK, consideration must be given to statistical data on asylum.[153]

'Lies, damned lies and statistics': applications, decisions, and removals in the UK

The early years: 1989–1996

1989 was the first year to see a marked rise in applications: with **7.26** almost a three-fold increase on the previous year, claims reached

---

[150] *ibid.*, paras 8.3(i) and (ii).

[151] See below for discussion on discretionary leave and humanitarian protection; Home Office, Asylum Policy Instructions, 'Post refusal decision – discretionary leave', para. 2.4.

[152] Asylum Policy Instructions, 'Deciding Claims – Assessing the Claim – Pt 3', para. 14.

[153] All statistics exclude dependants unless otherwise stated.

11,640.[154] This was to be the start of what the government would come to regard as a crisis in asylum applications. By 1991, there were 44,840 claims, the dramatic upsurge due, in the main, to increasing arrivals from Africa. While there was a fallback in 1992 (24,605), robust action was deemed necessary to arrest the upward trend. The Asylum and Immigration Appeals Act 1993 was therefore implemented with the clear aims of dealing expeditiously with claims and deterring the 'bogus'. The Home Office was also becoming acutely aware of a growing backlog of cases (at December 31, 1992, there were some 49,100 asylum applications outstanding).[155] At the time, there was concern among refugee campaigners that the refusal rate would increase and, concomitantly, the numbers of applicants granted ELR would fall.

This forecast was soon proved accurate. In the first six months of 1993, prior to the passing of the Act, 17,585 asylum cases were decided by the Home Office: 64 per cent of applicants were granted either asylum or ELR (7 per cent Convention status (1,285), and 57 per cent ELR (10,075)); the remaining 35 per cent (6,230) were refused.[156] The effects of the Act on Home Office decision-making seemed immediate. In the second half of the year, of 5,815 decisions, only 23 per cent were granted asylum or ELR (5 per cent Convention status (315), and 18 per cent ELR (1,050)), and 77 per cent (4,460) were rejected.[157] Final figures for 1994 confirmed a downward trend: of the total 20,990 decisions taken in 1994, 825 (4 per cent) were recognised as refugees, 3,660 (17 per cent) were granted ELR, and 16,500 (79 per cent) were refused.[158] These statistics should be set against the rise in the number of asylum applications in 1994 to 32,800 (excluding dependants), an increase of over 10,000 in one year.[159] By any measure, this information revealed a dramatic turn-around in the use of ELR and a huge increase in the refusal rate.

By 1995, applications to the UK had again reached a worrying level: 43,965 in 1995, though this fell back to 29,640 in 1996.[160] Arguably, the reduction may be attributed to the introduction of the

---

[154] Home Office, *Asylum Statistics United Kingdom 1997* (London: Home Office RDSD, May 1998), table 1.2.

[155] Home Office, *Asylum Statistics United Kingdom 1992* (London: Home Office RDSD, July 1993), para. 21.

[156] Home Office, *Asylum Statistics United Kingdom 1993* (London: Home Office RDSD, July 1994), table 1.4.

[157] *ibid.*

[158] Home Office, *Asylum Statistics 1994* (London: Home Office RDSD, June 1995), table 1.3; the total figure has been rounded to the nearest five.

[159] There were 22,400 applications (excluding dependants) in 1993.

[160] Home Office, *Asylum Statistics United Kingdom 1997* (London: Home Office RDSD, May 1998), table 1.2.

1996 Act and the partial removal of social security benefits. The Home Office itself has admitted that a 15 per cent drop of in-country applications between 1995 and 1997 'was probably as a result of the amendments made to DSS benefit entitlement and also the imposition of visa regimes'.[161] However, claims had once again risen to 32,500 by the end of 1997,[162] and to a record 46,015 by 1998.[163] Any impact on applications from either the 1993 or 1996 Act was patently short-term. In order to appreciate the full picture, it is necessary to examine applicants' countries of origin. Part of the explanation for the rise lay in an increase in claims from the former Yugoslavia (rising from 1,030 in 1996 to 2,260 in 1997) and from China (rising from 820 in 1996 to 1,945 in 1997);[164] Somali applications in 1997 remained high at 2,730, constituting 8 per cent of the total and the main applicant nationality. It appeared that the continuing high rate of refusals was making few inroads into the problem: of the 38,960 decisions taken in 1996, 2,240 (6 per cent) were recognised as refugees, 5,055 (13 per cent) were granted ELR, and 31,670 (81 per cent) were refused.[165]

Labour pains: 1997-present

The apparent reluctance to grant asylum in the early to mid-1990s was attributed to a 'culture of disbelief' in the IND.[166] The new Labour Minister for Immigration, Mike O'Brien, interviewed in November 1998, was anxious to stress that Labour was encouraging a more sympathetic approach in the Home Office: '[Caseworkers] were working under a political agenda under the previous government, and are now working under another agenda. We have increased the recognition rate from 6 per cent to 16 per cent.'[167] Certainly, refugee recognition rates did increase from 11 per cent in 1997 to 17 per cent in 1998; ELR rose from 9 per cent in 1997 to 12 per cent in 1998, but refusals remained high (80 per cent and 71 per cent

7.27

---

[161] *ibid.*, para. 3.

[162] *ibid.*, table 1.1.

[163] Home Office, *Asylum Statistics United Kingdom 1999* (London: Home Office RDSD, October 2000), table 1.2.

[164] Home Office, *Asylum Statistics United Kingdom 1997* (London: Home Office RDSD, May 1998), table 1.2.

[165] *ibid.*, table 1.3. These figures exclude dependants; the total is rounded to the nearest five.

[166] See, *e.g.*, JUSTICE *et al, Providing Protection – Towards Fair and Effective Asylum Procedures* (London: JUSTICE/ILPA/ARC, July 1997), p. 41.

[167] The Refugee Council, *In Exile*, November 1998, p.4.

respectively).[168] In addition, the 1999 statutory changes were accompanied by measures to speed up Home Office decision-making. Changes in interview procedures were part of the picture; the Minister also demanded that decisions on refugee status be made within two months and appeals be completed within four months thereafter.[169] (By May 2003, the average time to process a claim, including appeals, was five months, 78 per cent of cases being decided by the IND within two months.)[170] He admitted that the onus was upon the Home Office to keep to the time limits and that, to achieve this, £120 million was to be invested in the IND from April 1999.[171] The government also proceeded with a new computer system for the IND (originally contracted by the previous Conservative government), moved the IND to new premises in Croydon, and established the Integrated Casework Directorate. However, arrangements for the move (necessitating shifting 2,000 staff and 14 miles of files), and installation of a Siemens computer system (described by Mike O'Brien as 'short term pain for long term gain'), soon descended into the realms of farce. A rumour circulated that rats had eaten a number of files languishing in the basement of the former offices. The computer system, which was to change the IND to a paperless office, failed to be delivered.

In the meantime, some 1,200 experienced caseworkers had been laid off in preparation for computerisation.[172] With the rapid rise in asylum claims in 1999, largely as a result of the break-up of the former Yugoslavia, the Home Office was unable to cope. By the end of 1999, a huge total of applications for the UK had been reached (71,160), but with a correspondingly low rate of decisions (33,720 in total).[173] By December 31, 1999, over two years after Labour had come to power, and in the year of its comprehensive statute on immigration and asylum, 119,200 applications were awaiting a first decision.[174] This despite the introduction of a backlog clearance scheme in 1999.[175] The system was in serious crisis.

---

[168] Home Office, *Asylum Statistics United Kingdom 1999* (London: Home Office RDSD, October 2000), table 1.3.

[169] Mike O'Brien, speaking at Immigration Advisory Service Conference, *Fairer? Or Fundamentally Flawed?*, March 4, 1999.

[170] Home Affairs Select Committee, 'Asylum Applications', Uncorrected Oral Evidence, Beverley Hughes, Session 2003–04, May 8, 2003, Q. 5; *ibid.*, Bill Jeffrey, Q. 22.

[171] Mike O'Brien, speaking at Immigration Advisory Service Conference, *Fairer? Or Fundamentally Flawed?*, March 4, 1999.

[172] Home Affairs Select Committee, 'Asylum Applications', Uncorrected Oral Evidence, Beverley Hughes, Session 2003–04, May 8, 2003, Q. 17.

[173] Home Office, *Asylum Statistics United Kingdom 2001* (London: Home Office RDSD, July 2002), table 1.1.

[174] *ibid.*

[175] See below under ELR.

1999 was consequently an extremely embarrassing time for a gov-   **7.28**
ernment that had promised so much in terms of addressing the asylum issue and clearing the backlog of cases. In desperation, the Home
Office was forced to recruit 400 new caseworkers in 2000,[176] though
the IND's Director General conceded that it would take a great deal
of time to solve the problems.[177] By the end of 2000, though 80,315
applications had been lodged and 88,600 claims were still outstanding, 109,205 decisions had been taken.[178] The statistics for 2001 were
even more encouraging from a Home Office perspective: there were
71,365 applications, an incredible 119,015 decisions, and 38,800
claims outstanding.[179] In 2002, 85,865 applications were received,
and 82,715 decisions made; this left a backlog of 40,800 by the end
of the year.[180] The Home Office recently announced that there was a
33 per cent decline in quarterly applications for the first three months
of 2003, and that the monthly rate in March 2003 was down 49 per
cent to 4,565, compared with 8,900 in October 2002.[181] While these
figures are clear testament to an immense initiative on the part of the
IND to expedite decision-making and to clear the backlog, commentators warn that speed does not equate to quality; there is concern,
therefore, that the decisions may be substandard and that, as a result,
the pressure will simply transfer to the appellate level. The fixation
with numbers by the government also fails to recognise 'the close cor-
relation between countries in upheaval and the countries producing
the highest numbers of asylum applications'.[182]

Of the decisions taken in 2000, 9.5 per cent were granted refugee
status, while 10.5 per cent were granted ELR, and 69 per cent refused
(under the backlog clearance exercise, 9.5 per cent were granted ELR
or asylum, and 1 per cent refused).[183] By the end of 2001, the figures
had altered once more, with only 9 per cent obtaining refugee status,
17 per cent ELR, and 74 per cent refused.[184] For 2002, refugee grants

---

[176] Home Affairs Select Committee, 'Border Controls', First Report, Session 2000–01,
January 23, 2001, HC 163, para. 54.
[177] *ibid.*
[178] Home Office, *Asylum Statistics United Kingdom 2001* (London: Home Office RDSD,
July 2002), table 1.1.
[179] Home Office, *Asylum Statistics: 4th Quarter 2002 United Kingdom* (London: Home Office
RDSD) table 1.
[180] *ibid.*
[181] Home Office Press Release, 'Asylum applications down by a third – Home
Secretary welcomes significant progress', May 22, 2003.
[182] ILPA Submission to Home Affairs Select Committee enquiry into 'Asylum
Applications', March 25, 2003, p. 1.
[183] Based on figures in Home Office, *Asylum Statistics United Kingdom 2001* (London:
Home Office RDSD, July 2002), table 1.3.
[184] Home Office, *Asylum Statistics: 4th Quarter 2002 United Kingdom* (London: Home Office
RDSD) table 1.

remained relatively static at 10 per cent, while ELR was, again, on the rise (24 per cent of the total), and refusals accounted for 66 per cent of all decisions.[185] The information on refusals is now split into three categories: following full consideration, on safe third country grounds, and on non-compliance grounds. Non-compliance may be invoked where there has been:

- failure to attend the screening interview;

- failure to return or late return of the Statement of Evidence Form;

- failure to attend or late attendance at an asylum interview.[186]

7.29   Non-compliance refusals account for between 32 per cent (in 2000) and 22 per cent (in 2002) and are therefore quite significant. The justification for such refusals lies in para. 340 of the Immigration Rules, which states that 'a failure, without reasonable explanation, to make a prompt and full disclosure of material facts, either orally or in writing, or otherwise to assist the Secretary of State in establishing the facts of the case may lead to refusal of an asylum application.' A list of examples is then provided. Nonetheless, the power is discretionary and failure to comply will not always result in refusal.[187] The APIs add that though para. 340 provides the means of refusing asylum, it is to para. 336 that one must turn for the actual power to refuse.[188]

Of all the refusal grounds, failure to return the SEF on time met with the greatest opposition. On its introduction, the Home Office proved intransigent, sticking rigidly to the ten-day limit. While this boosted the refusal rates, it was regarded as much too inflexible.[189] There was also confusion over an apparent 'five-day grace' period, which it later transpired was an internal time-limit to enable the SEF to find its way to the appropriate caseworker in the IND.[190] Eventually, the Home Office agreed that an application could be made to extend the ten-day limit, which would be considered on its merits, discretion being exercised only in 'the most exceptional

---

[185] Home Office, *Asylum Statistics: 4th Quarter 2002 United Kingdom* (London: Home Office RDSD) table 1.

[186] Home Office, Asylum Policy Instructions, 'Refusals without substantive consideration – Non-compliance', para. 1.1.

[187] *ibid.*, para. 2.

[188] para. 336: 'An application which does not meet the criteria set out in para. 334 will be refused.'

[189] See Letter from ILPA to IND – March 28, 2000, ILPA Information for Members, April 2000.

[190] See Letter from ILPA to Barbara Roche – October 24, 2000, ILPA Information for Members, November 2000.

circumstances'.[191] An extension will not be granted to allow an applicant to obtain legal advice on completion of the form.[192]

The reason for the rise in use of ELR is not entirely clear; it could represent, as argued by the Minister for Immigration, 'a generous granting of exceptional leave to remain when an asylum claim was felt not to be met'.[193] An alternative explanation is that the UK has hardened its criteria for granting refugee status, and decision-makers have been forced to make greater use of ELR on account of the inhumane conditions that prevail in many countries. Certainly, the number of grants of ELR for Iraqis and Afghans has been very high, reaching 12,840 of a total 19,965 in 2002. Somalis, too, have always accounted for a high proportion of ELR grants, with the exception of a sudden dip between 1998 and 1999.

One gauge of the quality of Home Office decisions is the number **7.30** of successful appeals. In assessing the figures, it should be noted that only a proportion of those refused asylum go on to appeal, and that they are therefore only a partial indicator of the quality of initial decisions. Interestingly, in 1999, 27 per cent of the total determinations by *adjudicators* were allowed (5,280 of 19,460), whereas in 2001, this figure dropped to 19 per cent (8,155), while the number of cases heard was much higher (43,415).[194] By the close of 2002, a worrying 22 per cent of cases determined were allowed (13,875 of 64,405).[195] These figures do not take account of appeals before the IAT. However, here the proportion succeeding is very small: in 1994, only 4 per cent were allowed, while 70 per cent were remitted to adjudicators for further consideration (but only 270 appeals were heard).[196] In 2000, 31 per cent of appeals determined (815 of 2,635) were allowed, with 8 per cent remissions, and in 2001, of 3,190 determinations, 15 per cent were allowed and 45 per cent remitted.[197] The statistical information on the IAT is difficult to analyse, as it is unclear from the figures which party has been successful on appeal. According to the Home Office, the majority (70 per cent) of appeals brought by

---

[191] Home Office, Asylum Policy Instructions, 'Refusals without substantive consideration – Non-compliance', para. 4.

[192] *ibid.*, para. 4.

[193] Home Affairs Select Committee, 'Asylum Applications', Uncorrected Oral Evidence, Beverley Hughes, May 8, 2003, Q. 7.

[194] Home Office, *Asylum Statistics United Kingdom 2001* (London: Home Office RDSD, July 2002), table 7.1.

[195] Home Office, *Asylum Statistics: 4ᵗʰ Quarter 2002 United Kingdom* (London: Home Office RDSD) table 5.

[196] Home Office, *Asylum Statistics United Kingdom 2001* (London: Home Office RDSD, July 2002), table 7.2.

[197] *ibid.*, table 7.3.

appellants were dismissed.[198] (At the time of writing, figures for the IAT were not available for 2002.)

What is certain is that appeals, like applications, are on the rise: 74,365 were lodged with the Home Office in 2001, 47,905 of which were prepared for hearing and passed to the IAA.[199] In 2002, an estimated 49,500 appeals were received by the Home Office and 64,125 prepared for the IAA.[200] This compares with 28,935 in 2000. Obviously, with the dramatic increase in decision-making by the Home Office, appeals will also rise. However, the rate of success at the adjudicator stage is relatively consistent at around 20 per cent. Like the Home Office before it, the IAA is now confronting a huge administrative burden with its own backlog. Consequently, the Home Secretary, together with the Lord Chancellor's Department, announced an injection of resources into the IAA to tackle the problem. Funding for the IAA was increased by £50 million for the period 2000–2003, extra adjudicators were recruited (there are currently 423 part-time and 169 full-time adjudicators), a new IAT President was appointed, and different working practices instituted.[201] As a result, by May 2003, in its quest to clear 65 per cent of all asylum cases through both appellate tiers within four months,[202] the IAA was reportedly handling 6,000 appeals per month.[203]

Exceptional leave to remain

7.31 As indicated, a failed claim does not automatically result in the return of an applicant. Many applicants are granted a *de facto* status, such as exceptional leave to remain, and permitted to stay; some simply disappear without trace. However, with effect from April 1, 2003, the longstanding option of 'exceptional leave to remain' was scrapped by the Minister for Immigration, Beverley Hughes, and replaced by two new categories: 'humanitarian protection' and 'discretionary leave'.[204] The Minister made the change because she believed that the

---

[198] Home Office, *Asylum Statistics United Kingdom 2001* (London: Home Office RDSD, July 2002), para. 21.

[199] *ibid.*, para. 19.

[200] Home Office, *Asylum Statistics: 4ᵗʰ Quarter 2002 United Kingdom* (London: Home Office RDSD) table 5.

[201] See *The Court Service Plan 2000–2003 – Tribunals*, available on: *www.courtservice.gov.uk/about_us/our_performance/csp2/tribunals.htm*

[202] Home Office, *Asylum Statistics: 1ˢᵗ Quarter 2003 United Kingdom* (London: Home Office RDSD), p. 4.

[203] Home Affairs Select Committee, 'Asylum Applications', Uncorrected Oral Evidence, Beverley Hughes, Session 2003–04, 8 May 2003, Q. 93.

[204] Home Office APU Notice, 'Humanitarian protection and discretionary leave', April 1, 2003.

use of ELR encouraged abuse and acted as a pull factor. She suggested that economic migrants applied for asylum believing they would be granted ELR when their asylum claim failed.[205] Admittedly, as seen, there was a marked rise in ELR grants in 2002: ELR accounted for 24 per cent of the total decisions taken, a rise of 7 per cent on the previous year.[206]

From the Minister's comments, and her talk in November 2002 of 'significantly tightening the basis on which leave is granted',[207] one might assume that the criteria for ELR were excessively lenient. In the past, ELR was granted to many claims which, if not falling strictly within the definition of the 1951 Convention, did require compassion on humanitarian grounds. Early policy on ELR was described to the 1984 Home Affairs Sub-Committee on Race Relations and Immigration: ELR could be granted 'to individuals in the light of the particular circumstances of their cases, and on a more general basis to nationals of certain countries which are experiencing particular disruption, whose return against their will it is judged to be unreasonable to enforce'.[208] The Asylum and Immigration Appeals Act 1993 signalled a general hardening of attitude. Although it was assumed that ELR had only ever been granted on humanitarian grounds, comments from the Home Office post-1993 suggested otherwise. The Home Office's statistical bulletin for 1993 noted, for example, that grants of ELR had been *confined* to those cases where there were 'compassionate grounds'.[209] This implied that before 1993, ELR had been granted for other unspecified reasons, as well as on compassionate grounds. Although the Minister for Immigration stated that information on ELR was 'not readily available',[210] there was evidence that prior to the 1993 Act, Home Office practice was to grant ELR for substantial delay in decision-making. This seems reasonable, as delay could constitute humanitarian grounds where excessive, or where applicants are accompanied by children and have established a base in this country.

Earlier instructions set out the specific criteria for grant of exceptional leave to remain (or enter):   **7.32**

---

[205] Home Office Press Release, 'Home Office publishes latest asylum statistics', November 29, 2002.

[206] Home Office, *Asylum Statistics: 1ˢᵗ Quarter 2003 United Kingdom* (London: Home Office RDSD), table 1.

[207] Home Office Press Release, 'Home Office publishes latest asylum statistics', November 29, 2002.

[208] Home Affairs Sub-Committee on Race Relations and Immigration, Minutes, Memorandum submitted by Home Office, December 17, 1984, para. 44.

[209] Home Office, *Asylum Statistics 1993* (London: Home Office RDSD July 1993), p. 6.

[210] HC Deb Vol. 247, Written Answers, July 19, 1994, col. 164.

'Where the 1951 UN Convention requirements are not met in the individual case but return to the country of origin would result in the applicant being subjected to torture or other cruel, inhuman or degrading treatment, or where the removal would result in an unjustifiable break up of family life. For example:

- Where there are **substantial** grounds for believing that someone will suffer a serious and wholly disproportionate punishment for a criminal offence *e.g.* execution for draft evasion.
- Where there is **credible** medical evidence that return, due to the medical facilities in the country concerned, would reduce the applicant's life expectancy and subject him to acute physical and mental suffering, in circumstances where the UK can be regarded as having assumed responsibility for his care. In cases of doubt, a second opinion should be sought from a credible source.
- Where the applicant does not satisfy the criteria for refugee status but there are compassionate or humanitarian reasons which merit not requiring the person to return to their country of origin or habitual residence.
- Where ministers have agreed that, for humanitarian reasons, a general country policy will apply. These countries are reviewed by ministers at appropriate intervals [. . .]

In addition, exceptional leave **may** be granted in cases where a decision has **not** been taken seven years after the application was made.'[211]

These requirements do not seem excessively lenient; a judgement is required as to whether an applicant falls within one of the categories and there is certainly no automatic entitlement to ELR. However, ELR has been employed in other circumstances. In 1999, the government announced a backlog clearance policy, and under this scheme, any asylum applications still undecided on July 27, 1998 were eligible for the special administrative exercise (except where the applicant was subject to enforcement action, or his or her presence was not considered conducive to the public good). Cases were resolved as follows:

- where the asylum claim was made before July 1, 1993, indefinite leave to remain was normally granted due to the significant delay;
- where the application was made between July 1, 1993 and December 31, 1995, and asylum was refused, four years' ELR were granted if the delay and compassionate circumstances, such as family and community ties, warranted such a decision;

---

[211] Previous instructions now withdrawn: Home Office, *Asylum Policy Instructions*, Ch. 5, s.1(2.1).

- post-January 1, 1996 applications were considered under normal procedures.[212]

Here, ELR was used exceptionally to help address a seemingly intractable problem: the escalating backlog.

Without doubt, ELR has held an important place in the asylum regime. Not only did it protect the vulnerable from removal, it gave rise to eligibility for settlement. Prior to 1999, ELR was granted for 12 months initially, and then for two consecutive periods of three years each, before consideration could be given to settlement. In 1999, the Labour government changed the policy and reduced the waiting time for eligibility for settlement to four years.[213] However, the policy on family reunion for those granted ELR remained unchanged: family members could only qualify to join an individual with ELR after four years, unless there were 'compelling compassionate circumstances' warranting earlier entry clearance. This occurred, for example, where separation was resulting in significant hardship, or a parent, who was solely responsible for children, died or became seriously ill. This contrasts with refugee status, where admission of family members would normally be agreed with immediate effect.

Humanitarian protection

Though removal of ELR is undoubtedly a major step, some still regard its replacement with 'humanitarian protection' ('HP') or 'discretionary leave' ('DL') as no more than an exercise in semantics or, in the words of the Refugee Council, 'pure spin'.[214] However, the recently amended APIs have set out in some detail the basis on which humanitarian protection and discretionary leave will be granted. With reference to HP, it is stated that: **7.33**

- 'Humanitarian Protection is leave granted to a person who would, if removed, face in the country of return a serious risk to life or person arising from:
  death penalty;
  unlawful killing; or
  torture or inhuman or degrading treatment or punishment

---

[212] 'New measures for dealing with asylum claims (Asylum and Appeals Policy Directorate Letter, April 1999)' available in *Briefing Butterworths Immigration Law Service*, 2B[14].

[213] *ibid.*

[214] *www.bbc.co.uk/radio4/news/wato/topstory.shtml*

- If a person's removal would breach the ECHR they may be granted either Humanitarian Protection or Discretionary Leave depending on the circumstances of the case [. . .]
- In assessing whether a person qualifies for Humanitarian Protection the principles of internal flight/relocation and sufficiency of state protection should be applied. [. . .]
- Those granted Humanitarian Protection will have access to public funds and will be entitled to work.'[215]

It seems that the principles used to determine refugee status are to be applied equally to HP. Thus the standard of proof required is a 'reasonable degree of likelihood' or 'real risk'.[216] This means that if removed, there must be a real risk of: the death penalty; unlawful killing by the state, or by non-state agents where there is insufficient state protection (this includes a war/conflict situation); or torture, inhuman or degrading treatment (*i.e.* contrary to Art. 3 of the ECHR). Critically, the *Horvath* 'sufficiency of protection' test and the *Robinson* criteria for 'internal relocation' are germane to HP, thereby extending their use beyond asylum.[217] With regard to Art. 3, the APIs go on to clarify that there are a variety of circumstances in which a person whose asylum claim has failed might be granted HP:

- 'The treatment feared amounts to persecution but is not for one of the five Convention reasons.
- The treatment or punishment is in the narrow category of actions which are of a severity and nature to amount to Article 3 treatment but not to amount to persecution – for example, where the actions feared do not have a sufficiently systemic character to amount to persecution. As the Tribunal noted in *Kacaj*, few cases are likely to fit this description.'[218]

---

[215] Home Office, Asylum Policy Instructions, 'Post refusal decision – humanitarian protection', para. 1.

[216] *ibid.*, para. 2.1

[217] *ibid.*, paras 3.1 and 3.2. See, also, Ch. 8.

[218] Home Office, Asylum Policy Instructions, 'Post refusal decision – humanitarian protection', para. 2.4. In the starred decision *Secretary of State for the Home Department v Klodiana Kacaj; Klodiana Kacaj v Secretary of State for the Home Department* [2001] INLR 354, para. 19, the IAT said: 'We recognise the possibility that Article 3 could be violated by actions which did not have a sufficiently systemic character to amount to persecution, although we doubt that this refinement would be likely to be determinative in any but a very small minority of cases. But apart from this and a case where conduct amounting to persecution but not for a Convention reason was established, we find it difficult to envisage a sensible possibility that a breach of Article 3 could be established where an asylum claim failed.' See, also, *R. v IAT, ex parte Hari Dhima* [2002] INLR 243.

However, HP will not be available where removal would be in **7.34** breach of Art. 3 due to the applicant's medical condition (because there is no need for international protection); in these circumstances, DL is an option, though the threshold is extremely high.[219] Interestingly, the APIs entertain the very rare possibility that conditions in a country might be so deplorable that removal could lead to a breach of Art. 3. The examples given are: 'absence of water, food or basic shelter'.[220] Here, discretionary leave as opposed to humanitarian protection would be granted. It is striking that s. 55 of the 2002 Act has spawned a number of cases before UK courts in which asylum seekers claim breach of Art. 3 *in the* UK on similar grounds of destitution.

The exclusion criteria provided by Art. 1F(a) and (c) of the 1951 Convention apply equally to humanitarian protection.[221] In addition, those deemed a threat to national security may be excluded, as may those convicted of a 'serious crime' in the UK (denoting a custodial sentence of at least 12 months, or a crime falling within Art. 1F(b)), or those whose character, conduct or associations are deemed inappropriate. People who fail to be granted asylum because they are excluded under Art. 1F or 33(2), but argue that their removal to the country of return would engage Art. 3, are not eligible for HP.[222] Discretionary leave is, however, an option.

A person qualifying for HP will generally be granted leave for three years, and will be able to apply for settlement after expiry of this period, if the circumstances giving rise to the need for protection persist.[223] Once ILR is obtained, family members qualify for reunion.[224] As was the case with ELR, an application to join a family member with HP, prior to the expiry of the three-year period, will be granted where there are 'compelling compassionate circumstances'.[225]

Discretionary leave

Like its partner humanitarian protection, discretionary leave is to be **7.35** applied sparingly. It is only an option if both asylum and HP have been rejected and the case falls within the narrow criteria specified in the Instructions. These are:

---

[219] Home Office, Asylum Policy Instructions, 'Post refusal decision – humanitarian protection', para. 2.4, and see below.
[220] *ibid.*
[221] *ibid.* para. 2.5.
[222] *ibid.*, para. 2.4.
[223] *ibid.*, para. 1.
[224] Home Office, Asylum Policy Instructions, 'Family – family reunion', para. 3.3.
[225] *ibid.*

i.   cases where removal would involve a direct breach of Art. 8 of the ECHR (right to respect for private and family life);

ii. claims based on torture, inhuman or degrading treatment, but HP has been turned down, either because the case fell within the exclusion criteria, or the claim was based on a person's medical condition or severe humanitarian conditions in the country of return; the threshold here is very high;[226]

iii. cases involving unaccompanied children who have been turned down for asylum and HP, but cannot be returned to their country of origin due to inadequate reception arrangements;[227]

iv. exceptionally, any other 'compelling' case;[228]

v.   claims based on the death penalty or unlawful killing which would have qualified for HP, but fall within the exclusion criteria.[229]

The inclusion of medical cases under (ii) is evidently an attempt by the government to address the growing perception that asylum seekers are targeting the UK for free NHS treatment.[230] A particular concern for the Home Office in recent years has been an increase in HIV/AIDS cases where asylum claimants resist return to their country of origin on account of their medical condition. The APIs spell out the IND's position quite clearly, stating that the UK's obligations under Art. 3 are only engaged where:

- 'The United Kingdom can be regarded as having assumed responsibility for the individual's care;
- There is credible evidence that return, due to complete absence of medical treatment in the country concerned, would significantly reduce the applicant's life expectancy; and
- Return would subject them to acute physical and mental suffering.'[231]

7.36   This is a repetition of previous policy. For some time, the Home Office has been applying a restrictive interpretation. It has, on occasion, been supported in its view by case-law. For example, in *R. v*

---

[226] Home Office, Asylum Policy Instructions, 'Post refusal decision – discretionary leave', para. 2.3.

[227] *ibid.*, para. 2.4.

[228] *ibid.*, para. 2.5.

[229] *ibid.*, para. 2.6.

[230] G. Hinsliff, 'Britain slams the door on foreign NHS cheats', *The Observer*, February 9, 2003.

[231] Home Office, Asylum Policy Instructions, 'Post refusal decision – discretionary leave', para. 2.6.

Secretary of State for the Home Department, ex parte Kasasa, the Court of Appeal was in full agreement with the Home Office, and refused to adopt a rule that 'any country which did not have a health service which was available free to all people within its bounds, would be a place to which it would be inhuman and degrading to send someone'.[232] However, the Home Office recognises that 'Cases will continue to require careful individual consideration of their particular circumstances'.[233]

The same exclusion criteria pertaining to HP are also relevant to DL. However, part of the rationale for DL is that it is available to people who fall within the exclusion criteria for asylum or HP, but who cannot be removed due to Art. 3. They will, instead, be granted DL for a limited period.[234] This reasoning does not apply to Art. 8, which, unlike Art. 3, is not an absolute right. If granted DL, the period of leave is dependent on the underlying ground. Thus Art. 8 cases should be granted two years; Art. 3 cases three years; unaccompanied children three years or leave until 18, whichever is the shorter; other compelling cases three years; and exclusion from HP six months.[235] There is discretion to grant shorter periods of leave, depending on the individual circumstances.[236] In addition, cases falling within (i)–(iv) of the above list, which are also subject to exclusion, may only obtain six months leave.[237] In other words, where the exclusion criteria apply to an asylum claim, the best that can be hoped for is six months' discretionary leave.

Those granted DL 'will have access to public funds and will be entitled to work'.[238] They may also be considered for ILR after six continuous years of DL, unless falling within the exclusion clauses, in which case the period is 10 continuous years (not counting any time in prison).[239] Again, family members are eligible to come to the UK once their relative has been granted ILR, i.e. after six years. There is no right of appeal against HP or DL because they exist outside the Immigration Rules.[240]

---

[232] Unreported (February 16, 2000). Cited in N. Blake & R. Husain, *Immigration, Asylum and Human Rights* (Oxford: OUP, 2003), paras 2.124–2.134.

[233] Home Office, Immigration Directorates' Instructions, 'Medical', Ch. 1, s. 8, para. 3.4.

[234] Home Office, Asylum Policy Instructions, 'Post refusal decision – discretionary leave', para. 2.7.

[235] *ibid.*, para. 5.1.

[236] *ibid.*, para. 5.3.

[237] *ibid.*, para. 5.2.

[238] *ibid.*, para. 1.

[239] *ibid.*, para. 8.

[240] See *ibid.*, para. 9; Home Office, Asylum Policy Instructions, 'Post refusal decision – humanitarian protection', para. 10.

While there are many similarities between ELR and HP/DL, there has, without doubt, been a considerable tightening up of the criteria for leave beyond asylum, and it is anticipated that there will be therefore a dramatic downward adjustment to the numbers granted *de facto* status in the future.

THE HUMAN RIGHTS ACT 1998 AND THE LINK WITH ASYLUM

7.37 In an essential chapter on the ECHR, the APIs inform caseworkers about the significance of the Convention in asylum cases. Compared with the Instructions generally, there is relatively detailed discussion of some case-law. It is not, however, comprehensive and many significant cases, such as *Pretty v UK*, do not get a mention. Caseworkers are charged with the tasks of identifying human rights issues, even where these are not cited by the claimant, and of assessing whether removal might impinge on the UK's obligations under the ECHR.[241] Interestingly, the APIs suggest that the rights likely to be raised are those contained in Arts 2, 3, 8 and 14.[242] There is no mention of Art. 5 (in relation to detention), which is an odd omission. With respect to Art. 3 breaches, the notes advise that there can be a direct or indirect breach. For indirect breaches, there must be 'substantial grounds for believing that there is a real risk that a person might, after expulsion to another State, be tortured there or subjected to inhuman or degrading treatment or punishment'.[243] The standard of proof is the same as that for asylum: to a reasonable degree of likelihood.[244] The advice given to decision-makers, in line with the IAT case of *Kacaj*, is that treatment not amounting to persecution under the 1951 Convention will 'rarely be sufficiently severe to pass the threshold for establishing an Article 3 claim'.[245] The APIs also apply part of the decision of *R. v Special Adjudicator, ex parte Ullah; Do v Secretary of State for the Home Department* (on appeal to the House of Lords)[246] to Home Office policy:

'Where the European Convention is invoked on the sole ground of the treatment to which an alien, refused the right to enter or remain, is likely

---

[241] Home Office, Asylum Policy Instructions, 'Post refusal decision – European Convention on Human Rights', para. 4.1.

[242] *ibid.*, para. 3.

[243] *ibid.*, para. 5.1.

[244] *ibid.*, para. 5.3.

[245] *ibid.*, para. 7.2; *Secretary of State for the Home Department v Klodiana Kacaj; Klodiana Kacaj v Secretary of State for the Home Department* [2001] INLR 354, para. 19.

[246] [2003] INLR 74.

to be subjected by the receiving State, and that treatment is not sufficiently severe to engage Art. 3, the English court is not required to recognise that any other Article of the European Convention is, or may be, engaged.'[247]

Thus a claim of indirect breach of any article other than Art. 3 will fail unless the treatment in the country of return is so severe as to amount to a breach of Art. 3.[248] To restrict further the application of the ECHR, the tests of 'sufficiency of protection' and 'internal relocation' are applied equally to ECHR cases.

QUALITY OF DECISION-MAKING

The foregoing discussion has concentrated on the Home Office approach to asylum determination. This section will examine in greater detail the critical issue of quality. For some time, many commentators outside the IND (applicants, community groups, legal representatives, experts involved in training departmental staff, and those involved at the appeals stage) have criticised the standard of refugee determination.[249] In their 1997 report on UK asylum procedures, in which the Home Office's decision-making was seriously questioned, JUSTICE *et al* commented:

7.38

'It is widely believed that the decision-making process operates to a high threshold test, governed by a "culture of disbelief", where any inconsistencies or evidential gaps will result in negative findings of credibility. Nor is the decision-making process transparent and properly reasoned. Refusal decisions may rely on unpublished notes and guidance; they may contain untested assertions; they are often inadequately reasoned, and do not clarify the facts and issues in dispute.'[250]

Admittedly, this comment was made in relation to the pre-Labour regime. However, in 1999, a different NGO, Asylum Aid, published an informative examination of Home Office decisions on asylum claims, entitled *Still No Reason at All*.[251] Its conclusions make stark reading, alleging in summary that:

---

[247] [2003] INLR 74, para. 64.

[248] Home Office, Asylum Policy Instructions, 'Post refusal decision – European Convention on Human Rights', para. 5.1.

[249] *Providing Protection – Towards Fair and Effective Asylum Procedures* (London: JUSTICE/ILPA/ARC, 1997), p. 38.

[250] *ibid.*

[251] Asylum Aid, *Still No Reason At All – Home Office Decisions on Asylum Claims* (London: Asylum Aid, May 1999).

- 'Medical evidence often corroborating horrific physical abuse is frequently dismissed. [. . .]
- Many asylum seekers are refused asylum because evidence and proof of their persecution is demanded of them to a high standard which is not only impossible to obtain in circumstances of flight, but contrary to international law.
- Any attempt is made to discredit the applicant. [. . .]
- Current procedures of conducting interviews are inappropriate as a method of ascertaining the facts and are inadequate for detecting victims of torture. [. . .]
- Refusals of asylum are frequently based on inaccurate or incomplete country information. [. . .]'[252]

These accusations were rejected by the then Minister for Immigration, who maintained that the UK met its international and human rights obligations on asylum claims, that country assessments were under review, interviewers were trained and closely monitored, interviews were primarily a fact-finding exercise, and that the quality of decision-making was not poor, as evidenced by the low numbers of appeals allowed by adjudicators.[253] True, in 1998, adjudicators allowed only 9 per cent of appeals, but this would rise to 27 per cent by the end of 1999.[254] What the Minister failed to acknowledge was that success on appeal was heavily dependent on the quality of the representative, if any. Nor did the statistics at the time show the success rate before the IAT.

7.39   The Home Office's drive to clear the backlog, and the speed with which this has been done, is of concern. As noted earlier, by the end of 2000, there were 88,600 applications outstanding; by the end of 2001, there were only 38,800.[255] This remarkable turnaround reflects the heavy investment in the IND, in terms of both finances and human resources. But it should not be forgotten that the IND lost many of its more experienced caseworkers in 1999, and the new appointees have only been *in situ* since 2000 at the earliest. It would be remarkable if the standard of refugee determination did not suffer as a consequence.

One supposed marker of quality is success on appeals. This has remained fairly static at around the 20 per cent mark, though the statistics for the first quarter in 2003 show a drop to 17 per cent, sug-

---

[252] Asylum Aid, *Still No Reason at All – Home Office Decisions on Asylum Claims* (London: Asylum Aid, May 1999), p. 1.

[253] *ibid.*, p. 75.

[254] Home Office, *Asylum Statistics United Kingdom 1999* (London: Home Office RDSD, October 2000), table 8.1.

[255] Home Office, *Asylum Statistics United Kingdom 2001* (London: Home Office RDSD, July 2002) table 1.1.

gesting little improvement in Home Office decisions.[256] The message of practitioners in the field has remained consistent over the years. They argue that it frequently falls to the adjudicator to assess the case properly. As the ILPA representative informed the Home Affairs Select Committee in February 2003,

> '[. . .] the experience of our members is that the quality of initial decision-making is poor [. . .]. I think the reason why initial decision-making may be poor is lack of training and the quality of persons who engage in that initial decision-making. [. . .] a lack of up-to-date and accurate information adds to poor quality decision-making.'[257]

There is widespread concern about the nature of country of origin information, which plays such a critical part in decision-making. The general consensus is that it is often out-of-date, which obviously affects the decision and may prompt an appeal.[258] What is more, it is less than satisfactory that the decision-maker, the Home Office, relies on its own country information in support of its case: the Canadian model, in which there is an independent documentary centre, is much preferred. With this in mind, the Nationality, Immigration and Asylum Act 2002 has created an Advisory Panel on Country Information. It will be composed of between 10 and 20 individuals whose job it is to advise the Home Secretary about the content of country information.[259] Though he is not obliged to follow the panel's recommendations, this new departure should improve the quality of information upon which asylum determinations are based.

There is also concern that poor decision-making acts as a 'pull factor'. For example, Professor Goodwin-Gill, giving evidence to the Home Affairs Select Committee in January 2001, stated:

> 'I have no doubt in my own mind that those that come without reason or refugee-related reasons would [. . .] be deterred by a process that reached defensible decisions quickly.'[260]

While ministers frequently accept that delay can constitute a pull-factor, they tend to sidestep the issue of poor decision-making as an   **7.40**

---

[256] Home Office, *Asylum Statistics: 1st Quarter 2003 United Kingdom* (London: Home Office RDSD, 2003), table 5.

[257] Home Affairs Select Committee, 'Asylum Removals', Session 2003–04, March 4, 2003, Qs. 381 and 384.

[258] *ibid.*, Q. 388.

[259] s.142.

[260] Home Affairs Select Committee, 'Border Controls', First Report, Session 2000–01, January 23, 2001, HC 163, Q. 293.

attraction, preferring to argue that 80 per cent success on appeal is
evidence of good decision-making. For example, Jack Straw, speaking
to the same Committee, said:

> 'If you look at any other area of decision-making in the public service,
> eight out of ten of the original decisions to be confirmed on appeal for
> independent judicial figures show a very high quality of original decision-
> making [. . .].'[261]

More recently, internal and external quality assurance processes
have been instituted in the Home Office. The aim of the first is to
find 80 per cent of decisions to be 'fully effective or better' from a random sampling of asylum grants and refusals.[262] The second, also a
random review, is conducted by Treasury solicitors, and has the same
objective. Although the sampling is unsystematic, the intention is that
every caseworker will have his or her decisions reviewed at some
point.[263] The results of these audits will provide valuable data on the
thorny issue of quality. For the time being, however, it cannot be
stated with any conviction that decisions have improved markedly
since the JUSTICE report in 1997.

REMOVALS

7.41   It was stated above that not all refused applicants leave the country,
due to an ineffective (though improving) removals policy; this failing
has long been the focus of attack by the press and political opponents.
In the year 2000, 8,980 principal applicants were removed; in 2001,
this had risen to 9,285.[264] These figures included those departing voluntarily after enforcement action had been initiated against them,
and those partaking of the Voluntary Assisted Returns Programme,
which is run by the International Organisation for Migration ('IOM')
and has been operational since February 1999.[265] Jack Straw, as
Home Secretary, vowed in a rash moment to remove 30,000 failed

---

[261] Home Affairs Select Committee, 'Border Controls', First Report, Session 2000–01,
January 23, 2001, HC 163, Q 426.
[262] Home Affairs Select Committee, 'Asylum Applications, Uncorrected Oral Evidence, Beverley Hughes, Session 2003–04, May 8, 2003, Q 26.
[263] *ibid.*
[264] Home Office, *Asylum Statistics United Kingdom 2001* (London: Home Office RDSD,
May 2002, table 11.1.
[265] See Home Office, *The Voluntary Assisted Returns Programme: an Evaluation*, Findings
175, July 2002; for further information about the activities of the IOM, see its
website on: *www.iom.int/en/news/main_press_brief_notes.shtml*

asylum seekers by the end of 2001.[266] Even as Straw uttered these words, Home Office officials were back-tracking, admitting that it would be difficult on humanitarian grounds to return applicants from Iraq and Iran.[267] Within two months, the new Home Secretary, David Blunkett, issued a statement saying that the pledge of 30,000 removals per year had been overly ambitious. Despite this, the target remained in the 2002 Public Service Agreement Annual Report.[268] The Home Office has not published a revised target, and is now reluctant to do so, stating simply that: 'The [removal] target will be met if the proportion of refused asylum seekers (including dependants) removed in the target year (2005–06) is greater than those removed in the baseline year (2002–03).'[269] Not much of a commitment, some would argue. The Home Affairs Select Committee, which looked into removals and reported in April 2003, was scathing in its criticism of the government's target setting on asylum:

'We deprecate the setting of wholly unrealistic targets which serve only to arouse false expectations and which can only prove demoralising for all concerned. We are at a loss to understand the basis for the belief that a target of 30,000 removals a year was achievable, and ministerial pronouncements on the subject are obscure. It is surely not too much to expect that, if it is thought necessary to set targets for removals, they should be rational and achievable.'[270]

Most commentators in the asylum field now agree that effecting removal of failed asylum seekers is crucial for the credibility of the system.[271] As the Refugee Council itself has stated, 'the overall integrity of the asylum process relies on the ability ultimately to remove those found not to be in need of protection'.[272] The preference is for people to choose to return to their countries voluntarily, with the assistance of the IOM. The numbers participating in the programme have not been encouraging, totalling only 1,196 in the year 2002.[273] Enforced removal, or deportation in limited

---

[266] 'Straw targets 30,000 would-be asylum seekers', *The Guardian*, April 25, 2001.
[267] ibid.
[268] Home Affairs Select Committee, 'Asylum Removals', Session 2003–04, March 4, 2003, para. 28.
[269] Home Office, *SR2002 Public Service Agreement Technical Notes* (London: Home Office, March 2003), p. 20, available on: *www.homeoffice.gov.uk/docs/sr2002psa_tn.pdf*
[270] Home Affairs Select Committee, 'Asylum Removals', Session 2003–04, March 4, 2003, para. 32.
[271] ibid., para. 8.
[272] ibid.
[273] ibid., para. 45.

circumstances,[274] is the only alternative. Not only can this prove costly for the government, often involving chartering special aircraft, but it is also traumatic for all concerned, especially when children are involved.[275] There have been a number of disturbing accounts of enforced removals in Europe in which people have been bound, gagged and even injected with sedatives. Some have died of asphyxiation.[276]

Current statistical information indicates that 10,410 principal applicants were removed in 2002, and that in the first quarter of 2003, 2,620 were removed; this is the highest number on record and denotes some progress on removals, albeit gradual.[277]

CONCLUSION

7.42 The lessons to be learned from Home Office policy in the last decade are quite clear. Suffering until recently from under-resourcing, low morale and inadequate training and supervision, the IND struggled to meet the growing challenge of increased asylum applications. The result was an asylum system brought close to collapse. Repeated legislation failed to rectify the situation and even created further difficulties. The government now recognises the need for further investment in the IND. Increased funding and recruitment, better case management and the new audit system are already welcome developments. There are also signs that fewer cases are succeeding on appeal, and this may indicate some improvement in Home Office decision-making, though it is still too early to measure this with any precision. At the appellate level, the IAA has also benefited from investment and is making inroads into the appeals backlog.

Notwithstanding these various advances, the system continues to be beset with problems. While the APIs provide a useful basis for decision-making, they are by no means comprehensive. There is a general lack of reference to case-law, and, where key cases are cited,

---

[274] Deportation is used for those whose removal from the UK is deemed 'conducive to the public good', or who have been convicted of a criminal offence and recommended for deportation by the court, or who are family members of the person to be deported: Immigration Act 1971 ss. 3(5)(a), 3(5)(b), and 3(6).

[275] See, for example, the case of the Ahmadi family removed to Germany in August 2002: R. Prasad, 'Fight goes on as Afghan family is deported', *The Guardian*, August 15, 2002.

[276] See, *e.g.*, L. Fekete, 'Analysis: Deaths during forced deportation', Institute of Race Relations, January 3, 2000, available on: *www.irr.org.uk/2003/january/ak000003.html*

[277] Home Office, *Asylum Statistics: 1st Quarter 2003 United Kingdom* (London: Home Office RDSD), p. 5.

the discussion tends to be far too limited. This despite a recent 'major review' of the instructions. It is essential that caseworkers be well-trained, motivated and committed to their work, in order to accumulate the requisite experience in refugee status determination. Only then can the UK move to a position where practitioners have confidence in the quality of decisions. A further area crying out for improvement is that of removals. It is widely accepted that failed asylum seekers should be removed both effectively and humanely. At present, this is not happening to a sufficient degree. The issue of removals is one of the most difficult confronting the present government. Given the high public profile of asylum, how it is handled will prove a significant factor in the final assessment of Labour's record in government.

Chapter Eight

The Role of the Courts in the Protection of Asylum Seekers

INTRODUCTION

The courts' role in the development of asylum law during the twen- **8.1**
tieth century was briefly discussed in earlier chapters. As noted, prior
to 1993, asylum and immigration were inextricably linked. No statute
on asylum existed and there was no free-standing right of appeal in
asylum cases. Asylum seekers could only challenge removal on the
basis of the 1951 Convention where appealing against another immigration decision, such as a refusal to enter or a deportation order.
Judicial review of decisions of government ministers, the Immigration Service, or the IAT was also an option in certain circumstances,
and has played a key role in the shaping of UK asylum law.

In 1993, the passing of the Asylum and Immigration Appeals Act
markedly altered the legal landscape. The introduction of an appeals
framework for asylum cases, whereby appeals could lie to an adjudicator,[1] and thereon, with leave, to the IAT and higher courts, opened
up an avenue for increased judicial involvement in asylum matters.
Subsequent legislation in 1996, 1999 and 2002 maintained the basic
asylum appeals framework, though various changes were introduced
limiting appeal rights in certain cases. Judicial review remains available where appeal rights have been exhausted, and continues to be an
important arm of protection for the asylum seeker fighting removal
from the UK.

This chapter will consider the 'ebb and flow' of judicial decision-
making in asylum law from the latter part of the twentieth century to
the present. It will focus on the post-1993 environment, assessing the
extent to which the courts and IAT have helped protect asylum seekers and refugees, or contributed to their exclusion.[2] Beginning with a

---

[1] The term 'special' was dropped in the 1999 Act.
[2] In the year 2000, the President of the IAT, Collins J., introduced a system of starring
key cases. Although the decisions of the IAT are not binding, there is an expectation

brief comment on judicial review within the asylum appeals process, the chapter will examine a number of key cases. In an attempt to establish whether the judiciary remains unduly deferential to the executive, or whether it is increasingly prepared to challenge the government in this sensitive area, cases are divided into two groups: those indicative of judicial activism and those exhibiting restraint.

JUDICIAL REVIEW IN THE CONTEXT OF IMMIGRATION AND ASYLUM

8.2   The three grounds of judicial review – illegality, irrationality and procedural impropriety – were famously described by Lord Diplock in *Council of Civil Service Unions v Minister for the Civil Service.*[3] Since it is often difficult to establish that an immigration or asylum decision is illegal or procedurally improper, migrants and asylum seekers have relied largely on the other ground of challenge, that of irrationality, or unreasonableness. This has met with varying degrees of success. As is well known, 'irrationality', now normally referred to as '*Wednesbury* unreasonableness', is based on the judgement of Lord Greene in *Associated Picture Houses Ltd v Wednesbury Corporation.*[4] Most immigration decisions are subject to judicial review but, for much of the twentieth century, *Wednesbury* notwithstanding, the courts have been manifestly reluctant to interfere with the decisions of immigration authorities.[5] One can cite many examples to support this contention, one of the most notable being that of *Zamir v Secretary of State for the Home Department*, a 1980 House of Lords decision.[6] There, Lord Wilberforce stressed repeatedly the limit of the Court's powers in reviewing the decision of an immigration officer or the Secretary of State: 'I conclude therefore that the decision to remove the appellant, and his consequent detention, can only be attacked if it can be shown that there were no grounds upon which the Secretary of State, through his

---

that starred decisions will be followed by all panels, avoiding earlier problems of conflict that arose between differently constituted Tribunals. Since starred panels are legally constituted, this change has aided greater consistency and enhanced asylum and refugee jurisprudence in the UK. A number of starred decisions have already proved significant.

[3] [1985] AC 374, at 410.

[4] [1948] 1 KB 223.

[5] See, *e.g.*, S. Legomsky, *Immigration and the Judiciary* (Oxford: Clarendon Press, 1987), pp. 105–6; C. Vincenzi, 'Aliens and the Judicial Review of Immigration Law' (1985) *Public Law*, p. 93; see, also, N. Blake & R. Husain, *Immigration, Asylum & Human Rights* (Oxford: OUP, 2003), paras 5.145–5.262.

[6] [1980] AC 930.

officers, could have acted, or that no reasonable person could have decided, as he did.'[7] The effect of other cases, such as *R. v Secretary of State, ex parte Khawaja*,[8] which appeared to increase the courts' power to review deportation decisions in relation to illegal entrants, was short-lived. Within only four years of *Khawaja*, Lord Bridge had decided that his own opinion in the case was, after all, mistaken and that a more restrictive line was preferable.[9] In a famous asylum case of the 1960s, *R. v Governor of Brixton Prison (Governor), ex parte Soblen*, discussed in Chapter 3, Lord Denning, sitting in the Court of Appeal, seemed prepared to scrutinise a decision of the Home Secretary where deportation was involved:[10]

'It is open to these courts to inquire whether the purpose of the Home Secretary was a lawful or an unlawful purpose. Was there a misuse of the power or not? The courts can always go behind the face of the deportation order in order to see whether the powers entrusted by Parliament have been exercised lawfully or no.'[11]

As noted, however, the Home Secretary claimed Crown privilege over communications between the Home Office and the USA, and it was therefore impossible for the Court to establish the true reason for surrendering Soblen to the USA. Despite Denning's threat of intervention, the reality was that the Home Secretary could act unfettered, whatever his motives. As in the *Duke of Château Thierry* case 55 years earlier,[12] there was a reluctance to recognise that, even in asylum cases, deportation might be used as disguised extradition, and that scant regard was paid to the provisions of the Extradition Act 1870 or to the principle of *non-refoulement* as set out in Art. 33 of the 1951 Convention.[13]

Whether the apparent judicial deference in immigration and asylum cases is in line with the general trend in administrative law is open to question. From the 1960s onwards, administrative law succeeded in breaking away from what Wade described as the 'deep gloom' of the mid-twentieth century, when courts 'showed little stomach for [. . .] imposing law upon government',[14] to reach a position

8.3

---

[7] [1980] AC 930, at 949E.
[8] [1984] AC 74.
[9] *R. v IAT, ex parte Patel* [1988] 2 WLR 1165.
[10] [1962] 3 AER 641.
[11] *ibid.*, at 661.
[12] See Ch. 2.
[13] See, for further discussion, P. O'Higgins, 'Disguised Extradition: The Soblen Case' (1964) 27 *MLR* 521; C. Thornberry, 'Is the Non-surrender of Political Offenders Outdated?' (1963) 26 *MLR* 555.
[14] Wade and Forsyth, *Administrative Law* (Oxford; Clarendon Press, 7th edition, 1994), pp. 17–19.

today, to quote the last Lord Chancellor, in which 'judicial activism in the development of a mature system of public law is likely to count as the century's single greatest judicial achievement.'[15] While the expansion of judicial review has, for some time, been underway in the UK, and is well documented by public lawyers,[16] it has not been a rapid process. The decision of *Wednesbury* has cast a long shadow. However, academics and judges have recently begun to grapple with a new question: to what extent are the principles of judicial review, and in particular '*Wednesbury* unreasonableness', to be reformulated or relaxed in cases involving fundamental rights.

Interestingly, the case that is regarded by many as having sparked a revision in judicial review is the House of Lords decision of 1987, dealing with refugee law: *Bugdaycay v Secretary of State for the Home Department*.[17] There Lord Bridge stated that the courts must

> ' [. . .] be entitled to subject an administrative decision to the more rigorous examination, to ensure that it is in no way flawed, according to the gravity of the issue which the decision determines. The most fundamental of all human rights is the individual's right to life and when an administrative decision under challenge is said to be one which may put the applicant's life at risk, the basis of the decision must surely call for the most anxious scrutiny.'[18]

This was hailed as an 'unequivocal recognition of the need for stricter scrutiny of administrative discretion where fundamental human rights are at stake, and of the need to protect those rights'.[19] Its potential for the development of public law was thought to be great.[20]

This loosening of the *Wednesbury* unreasonableness test, sometimes referred to as 'sub-*Wednesbury*', has been discussed in a number of cases that followed *Bugdaycay*. One of the most important is *Brind v Secretary of State for the Home Department*,[21] which builds on the decision in *Bugdaycay*. With regard to restriction by the Secretary of State of the right to freedom of expression, Lord Bridge held that the court was 'entitled to start from the premise that any restriction of the right to freedom of expression requires to be justified and that nothing less

---

[15] Lord Irvine of Lairg, 'Activism and Restraint: Human Rights and the Interpretative Process' (1999) 4 *EHRLR*, p. 351.

[16] See, *e.g.*, P. Craig, *Administrative Law* (Sweet & Maxwell, 4th edition, 1999), Ch. 17.

[17] [1987] Imm AR 250.

[18] *ibid.*, at 263.

[19] J. Jowell & A Lester, 'Beyond *Wednesbury*: Substantive Principles of Administrative Law', (1987) *Public Law*, p. 368.

[20] *ibid.*

[21] [1991] 1 AC 696.

than an important competing public interest will be sufficient to justify it'.[22] Some commentators have made overstated claims about the
impact of Lord Bridge's words. Norris, for example, is of the view
that they suggest that 'judges are not limited to ensuring that the
decision-maker took into account all relevant matters, including the
interference with human rights resulting from the decision', and that
'the court is also entitled to pass judgement on whether the competing public interest is "important" enough'.[23] However, a number of
judges have been less persuaded that *Brind* introduces a notion of
'sub-Wednesbury' to judicial review, and in particular to human
rights cases. Thus in *R. v Secretary of State for the Environment, ex parte
National and Local Government Officers Association* ('*NALGO*'), the judge,
after examining the *Brind* judgement, stated that, with the exception
of Lord Templeman's speech, he had 'not been able to extract from
the other speeches any real support for the view that the latitude to be
given to a Minister is to be confined within tighter limits when his
decision impinges on fundamental human rights'.[24]

The most recent Lord Chancellor, writing extra-judicially, agreed   **8.4**
with this view that the *Wednesbury* threshold of unreasonableness is
not lowered in fundamental rights cases.[25] He went further and
argued that where courts adopt a more interventionist role to protect
and uphold the rule of law, as well as fundamental rights, they are
straying far beyond the limits laid down in *Brind* and are leading
judges into dangerous territory.[26] Nonetheless, a glimmer of hope was
provided for human rights lawyers, when, in *R. v Ministry of Defence, ex
parte Smith*, Sir Thomas Bingham MR said:

> 'Mr David Pannick, who represented three of the appellants, and whose
> arguments were adopted by the fourth, submitted that the court should
> adopt the following approach to the issue of irrationality:
>
> > "The court may not interfere with the exercise of an administrative dis-
> > cretion on substantive grounds save where the court is satisfied that the
> > decision is unreasonable in the sense that it is beyond the range of
> > responses open to a reasonable decision-maker. But in judging whether
> > the decision-maker has exceeded this margin of appreciation the human

---

[22] *ibid.*, at 748–9.

[23] M. Norris, '*Ex parte Smith*: irrationality and human rights' (1996) *Public Law* 590,
596.

[24] *R. v Secretary of State for the Environment, ex parte National and Local Government Officers
Association* [1993] Admin LR 785.

[25] Lord Irvine of Lairg, 'Judges and Decision-makers: The Theory and Practice of
Wednesbury Review' (1996) *Public Law*, p. 64.

[26] *ibid.*, p. 65.

rights context is important. The more substantial the interference with human rights, the more the court will require by way of justification before it is satisfied that the decision is reasonable in the sense outlined above."

This submission is in my judgment an accurate distillation of the principles laid down by the House of Lords in *Reg. v Secretary of State for the Home Dept, Ex parte Bugdaycay* [. . .] and *Reg. v Secretary of State for the Home Dept, Ex parte Brind* [. . .].'[27]

The *Smith* test was approved and taken forward in subsequent cases.[28]

8.5   The introduction of the Human Rights Act 1998 has cast a different light on judicial review. Not only does it bring into play the ECHR principle of 'margin of appreciation';[29] it also entails a reassessment of the doctrine of 'proportionality'. In their excellent study, *Immigration, Asylum & Human Rights*, Blake and Husain discuss the impact of the 1998 Act on judicial review. They suggest that it is not appropriate to 'read across' from the ECHR margin of appreciation into an equivalent domestic doctrine; rather, what is called for is 'due deference', or 'margin of discretion', to allow for the greater level of scrutiny deemed essential in domestic cases.[30] The degree of scrutiny to be applied has been assessed in the context of proportionality, and, in 1999, in *de Freitas v Permanent Secretary of Ministry of Agriculture, Fisheries, Lands and Housing*, the Privy Council helpfully set out the basic requirements:

'In determining whether a limitation (by an act, rule or decision) is arbitrary or excessive, the court should ask itself:

"whether: (i) the legislative objective is sufficiently important to justify limiting a fundamental right; (ii) the measures designed to meet the legislative objective are rationally connected to it; and (iii) the means used to impair the right or freedom are no more than is necessary to accomplish the objective." '[31]

---

[27] [1996] 2 WLR 305, at 336C-F.

[28] N. Blake & R. Husain, *Immigration, Asylum & Human Rights* (Oxford: OUP, 2003), paras 5.153–5.156.

[29] The ECtHR 'accords to domestic courts a margin of appreciation, which recognises that national institutions are in principle better placed than an international court to evaluate local needs and conditions': *Brown v Stott* [2001] 2 WLR 817, at 842. How wide or narrow the margin exercised is dependent on the subject, and Article, under consideration.

[30] N. Blake & R. Husain, *Immigration, Asylum & Human Rights* (Oxford: OUP, 2003), paras 5.203 and 5.205.

[31] *de Freitas v Permanent Secretary of Ministry of Agriculture, Fisheries, Lands and Housing* [1999] 1 AC 69, at 80.

Lord Steyn, speaking in the highly influential judgement of *R. v Secretary of State for the Home Department, ex parte Daly*, explored the meaning of the proportionality criteria adopted in *de Freitas* and their impact on review:

'Clearly, these criteria are more precise and more sophisticated than the traditional grounds of review. What is the difference for the disposal of concrete cases? [. . .] The starting point is that there is an overlap between the traditional grounds of review and the approach of proportionality. Most cases would be decided in the same way whichever approach is adopted. But the intensity of review is somewhat greater under the proportionality approach. [. . .] I would mention three concrete differences without suggesting that my statement is exhaustive. First, the doctrine of proportionality may require the reviewing court to assess the balance which the decision maker has struck, not merely whether it is within the range of rational or reasonable decisions. Secondly, the proportionality test may go further than the traditional grounds of review inasmuch as it may require attention to be directed to the relative weight accorded to interests and considerations. Thirdly, even the heightened scrutiny test developed in *R. v Ministry of Defence, Ex p Smith* [1996] QB 517, 554 is not necessarily appropriate to the protection of human rights.'[32]

With this in mind, Blake and Husain argue that the doctrine of proportionality requires, when applied in the domestic law context, 'the application of a structured and schematic test, with an emphasis on the decision-maker providing a justification once an interference is made out'.[33] It is their contention that:

'While the *ex parte Smith* test requires justification where there is an interference with human rights, with a variable threshold commensurate with the importance of the right interfered with, the nature of that justification is left unstructured, and there are question marks as to the intensity of the review afforded by the *ex parte Smith* test [. . .]. Proportionality is certainly apt to require more from a decision-maker than *Wednesbury*. The ultimate question is 'is the decision justified?' rather than 'is it reasonable?''[34]

Thus it would seem that, in relation to human rights challenges under s. 6 of the Human Rights Act 1998, *Wednesbury* has been superseded by a more stringent level of review, albeit dependent upon the nature of the decision under challenge.[35]

---

[32] [2001] 2 AC 532, para. 27.
[33] N. Blake & R. Husain, *Immigration, Asylum & Human Rights* (Oxford: OUP, 2003), para. 5.197.
[34] *ibid.*
[35] *ibid.*, para. 5.262.

JUDICIAL REVIEW AND STATUTORY APPEALS POST 1993

8.6 With the passing of four asylum statutes, the introduction of an asylum appeal for all claimants, and the opening up of the higher courts to appeals on questions of law, there is now ample opportunity for judicial intervention beyond judicial review. As noted in Chapter 5, the Nationality, Immigration and Asylum Act 2002 sets out the current position on appeals. Section 82 provides a general right of appeal to an adjudicator against a specified 'immigration decision'. Once more, there is no separate appeal against the refusal of asylum; rather, the appeal is against the decision to remove. Section 84 lists the grounds of appeal. In the case of asylum, the most likely ground will be 'that removal of the appellant from the United Kingdom in consequence of the immigration decision would breach the United Kingdom's obligations under the Refugee Convention or would be unlawful under s. 6 of the Human Rights Act 1998 as being incompatible with the appellant's Convention rights'.[36]

In light of the many legislative changes, the use of judicial review was expected to wane post 1993. This, however, proved not to be the case. The 2001 edition of *Macdonald's Immigration Law and Practice* lists numerous circumstances in which judicial review is the only route by which to challenge a decision, thereby revealing its continuing importance in the field.[37] Frequently, where the government has turned to primary legislation to close off extended appeal rights, such as in the certified asylum cases, applications for judicial review have simply been lodged earlier in the process. In the year 2001, there were 2,210 applications for leave to move for judicial review in asylum cases, of which 290 were granted.[38] At the same time, 380 judicial review cases were heard, of which 260 were allowed, 60 dismissed and 60 withdrawn.[39]

In June 2003, the Public Law Project published the results of research on the impact of the Human Rights Act 1998 on judicial review. A summary of the report stated: 'The largest case category was immigration/asylum, with 850 cases issued in a three month period. In this category, 53 per cent of cases cited the HRA, a rate which was slightly above average. Of those immigration/asylum cases citing the HRA, Art. 3 was cited in 74 per cent of cases, and

---

[36] s. 84(1)(g).
[37] Macdonald & Webber (eds.), *Macdonald's Immigration Law & Practice* (London: Butterworths, 2001), para. 18.198.
[38] Home Office, *Asylum Statistics United Kingdom 2001*, July 31, 2002, table 7.3.
[39] *ibid.*, table 7.1.

Art. 8 was raised in 43 per cent of cases.'[40] This
burden on the High Court, and recent case-law sugge
judicial moves afoot to restrict the use of the E
cases.[41]

INCREASING JUDICIAL ACTIVISM AND THE PROTECTION OF ASYLUM SEEKERS

As already observed, *Bugdaycay* was seen by some as a turning point
in the application of judicial review where human rights were concerned. It was also a critical case in terms of refugee law, since Lord
Bridge stressed that decisions, such as those on asylum, which put
the applicant's life at risk, call for 'the most anxious scrutiny'. From
these words, one might expect that the area of asylum is ripe for
judicial activism.[42] Is there evidence to suggest, then, as some have,
that the courts are rapidly developing a jurisprudence of fundamental rights in asylum cases, and that a progressive, human rights
approach is now emerging? In recent years, the courts have had to
contend with a range of difficult issues: the correct definition of persecution; whether women from Pakistan, who are victims of domestic violence, are 'refugees' for the purposes of the 1951 Convention;
whether certain countries are 'safe' for return of asylum seekers; the
appropriate treatment of asylum seekers travelling on false documents; the correct standard of proof in asylum cases, the impact on
refugee status of the 'internal flight/relocation alternative'; the role
of non-state agents; whether detention of asylum seekers is lawful;
and the implications for asylum seekers of national security provisions. In view of the extent and complexity of the issues before
them, the judges have had ample opportunity to reveal a progressive, rights-based approach, and they have, on occasion, responded
well to the challenge. The present chapter will now examine a number of key cases that can rightly be claimed to have advanced the
protection of asylum seekers.

8.7

---

[40] See The Public Law Project, *The Impact of the Human Rights Act on Judicial Review*:
www.publiclawproject.org.uk/judrevreport.html

[41] See, *e.g.*, *AE & FE v Secretary of State for the Home Department* [2003] EWCA Civ 1032.

[42] In recent years, immigration and asylum cases have been largely responsible for the
rise in judicial review applications: see L. Bridges *et al*, 'Regulating the Judicial
Review Case Load', (2000) *Public Law*, p. 651.

The meaning of persecution

.6   As might be expected, the judges have been instrumental in clarifying the difficult but vital issue of the meaning of 'persecution' in Art. 1A(2) of the 1951 Convention. As noted in Chapter 7, Hathaway defines persecution as the 'sustained or systemic violation of basic human rights demonstrative of a failure of state protection'.[43] He identifies four categories of rights deemed to be basic and inalienable.[44] In his opinion, 'The types of harm to be protected against include the breach of any right within the first category, a discriminatory or non-emergency abrogation of a right within the second category, or the failure to implement a right within the third category which is either discriminatory or not grounded in the absolute lack of resources.'[45] The courts and Tribunal have increasingly turned to academic texts on refugee law, and in particular to Hathaway's work, for guidance on the core principles. Lord Lloyd, for example, described the views of academics as of greater importance than those of judicial authorities, since it is academics who provide the best hope of reaching international consensus on the meaning of the Convention.[46] Hathaway's broad approach appealed not only to the IAT in 1997 in *Gashi and Nikshiqi v Secretary of State for the Home Department*,[47] but was also endorsed by Simon Brown L.J. in the Court of Appeal

---

[43] J. Hathaway, *The Law of Refugee Status* (Canada: Butterworths, 1991), pp. 104–5.

[44] *ibid.*, pp. 109–12. First level: (no derogation possible) freedom from arbitrary deprivation of life; protection against torture or cruel, inhuman, or degrading punishment or treatment, freedom from slavery, the prohibition on criminal prosecution for *ex post facto* offences; the right to recognition as a person in law; and freedom of thought, conscience, and religion. Second level: (derogation possible in times of 'public emergency which threatens the life of the nation and the existence of which is officially proclaimed') freedom from arbitrary arrest or detention; the right to equal protection for all, including children and minorities; the right in criminal proceedings to a fair and public hearing and to be presumed innocent unless guilt is proven; the protection of personal and family privacy and integrity; the right to internal movement and choice of residence; the freedom to leave and return to one's country; liberty of opinion, expression, assembly, and association; the right to form and join trade unions; and the ability to partake in government, access public employment without discrimination, and vote in periodic and genuine elections. Third level: (states required to take progressive steps to realise in a non-discriminatory way) right to work, including just and favourable conditions of employment, remuneration, and rest; entitlement to food, clothing, housing, medical care, social security, and basic education; protection of the family, particularly children and mothers; and the freedom to engage and benefit from cultural, scientific, literary and artistic expression. Fourth level: (uncodified) for example, right to own and be free from arbitrary deprivation of property; and the right to be protected against unemployment.

[45] *ibid.*, p. 112.

[46] *R. v Secretary of State for the Home Department, ex parte Adan* [1998] INLR 325, at 332D.

[47] [1997] INLR 96.

in *R. v IAT, ex parte Sandralingham and Another; R. v IAT and Another, ex parte Rajendrakumar*,[48] and again in the Court of Appeal in *Adan v Secretary of State for the Home Department*.[49] It is now cited on a regular basis. Furthermore, the IAT refers specifically to Hathaway's approach in its Asylum Gender Guidelines when discussing the definition of persecution.

The acceptance of a human rights approach to the 1951 Convention should be seen in a positive light. It moves the interpretation of persecution, a crucial part of refugee determination, away from the dictionary definition into a human rights framework, where refugee law should be situated. As Macdonald and Webber note, the sole disadvantage of linking the definition of persecution to core human rights is 'if the asylum seeker cannot establish the existence of the core right, there will be no persecution'.[50] This aside, the adoption of the human rights approach provides evidence, if such is needed, of the courts' growing belief that the Convention must be treated as a 'living instrument' and that it should be used creatively to deal with circumstances not envisaged at the time of drafting. However, there is still some support for the proposition that 'persecution' be given its ordinary dictionary meaning (see, for example, *Kagema v Secretary of State for the Home Department*[51] and *Horvath v Secretary of State for the Home Department*), which leads to some tension between the two approaches.

Standard of proof

One of the most important issues in refugee determination is the relevant standard of proof. The leading case on the standard of proof is that of *Secretary of State for the Home Department v Sivakumaran*.[52] A 1998 House of Lords judgment, *Sivakumaran* proved an early exemplar of judicial sensitivity to the difficulties faced by the asylum seeker in establishing refugee status, and the need to adopt an inclusive approach. The decision by Lord Keith of Kinkell that an applicant, in establishing well-founded fear of persecution, had to demonstrate a lower standard of proof than the normal civil standard of balance of probabilities, namely 'a reasonable degree of likelihood that he will be persecuted for a Convention reason if returned to his own country', was a bold and generous move.[53]

8.9

---

[48] [1996] Imm AR 97.
[49] [1997] Imm AR 251.
[50] Macdonald & Webber eds., *Macdonald's Immigration Law & Practice* (London: Butterworths, 2001), para. 12.46.
[51] [1997] Imm AR 137.
[52] [1988] Imm AR 147.
[53] *ibid.*, at 152.

Sivakumaran has now been accepted globally as setting the standard of proof required in asylum cases. However, in 1994, in the IAT case of *Koyazia Kaja v Secretary of State for the Home Department*,[54] the Tribunal considered whether the lower standard of proof provided for in *Sivakumaran* applied to both the assessment of events occurring in the past and to the possibility of future persecution. While the majority view was that 'the assessment of whether a claim to asylum is well-founded is based on the evidence as a whole (going to past, present and future)' and should be determined according to the criterion of reasonable degree of likelihood, the minority opinion judged that the *Sivakumaran* standard applied only to the possibility of events occurring in the future; past events, it was suggested, should be assessed according to the balance of probabilities. Though appearing to clarify the position on the issue of standard of proof, *Kaja* gave rise, in fact, to a number of problems in its application. In the wake of the decision, certain adjudicators refused to apply *Kaja*, or decided to adjourn cases because they doubted its validity. This led an irritated IAT to express astonishment that adjudicators, by purposely acting contrary to *Kaja*, were inviting the granting of leave to appeal.[55]

It took some time before a decision of a higher court finally settled the matter: *Karanakaran v Secretary of State for the Home Department*.[56] In this key case, an opportunity arose for the Court of Appeal to revisit some of the issues relating to the standard of proof. It supported the views of the IAT in *Kaja*, stating that an asylum claim should not be assessed as a two-stage process (i.e. findings on past and present facts, and assessment of future risk), but should be decided on the evidence as a whole. The Court went on to restate the essential meaning of *Kaja*, which it regarded as having been wrongly interpreted:

'What they [the IAT panel in *Kaja*] decided was that when assessing future risk decision-makers may have to take into account a whole bundle of disparate pieces of evidence:

(1)   evidence they are certain about;
(2)   evidence they think is probably true;
(3)   evidence to which they are willing to attach some credence, even if they could not go so far as to say it is probably true;
(4)   evidence to which they are not willing to attach any credence at all.

The effect of *Kaja* is that the decision-maker is not bound to exclude category (3) evidence as he/she would be if deciding issues that arise in civil litigation.'[57]

---

[54] [1995] Imm AR 1.
[55] *Asuming v Secretary of State for the Home Department* (11530), November 11, 1994.
[56] [2000] INLR 122.
[57] *ibid.*, at 133E-G.

Applying the restated version of *Kaja* means that the decision-maker should not exclude any matters from consideration when assessing the future, unless they can be safely discarded because there is no real doubt that they did not in fact occur (or are not occurring at present).[58] Thus there is no different standard of proof to be applied to past events. Rather, a balancing exercise of all relevant factors should be conducted. This would necessarily give greater weight to some of the evidence in order to arrive at a 'well-rounded' decision, following a fair evaluation of all the material and Convention issues raised in the appeal. As Sedley L.J. stated, 'everything capable of having a bearing has to be given the weight, great or little, due to it. [. . .] The facts, so far as they can be established, are signposts on the road to a conclusion on the issues; they are not themselves conclusions.'[59] In arriving at this view, the Court of Appeal paid particular attention to a range of international cases, and above all to a number from Australia. In a helpful summation, Sedley L.J. stressed the principles of natural justice in which decision-makers are necessarily engaged when struggling with matters of evidence and refugee status:

8.10

> 'The question whether an applicant for asylum is within the protection of the 1951 Convention is not a head-to-head litigation issue. Testing a claim ordinarily involves no choice between two conflicting accounts but an evaluation of the intrinsic and extrinsic credibility, and ultimately the significance, of the applicant's case. It is conducted initially by a departmental officer and then, if challenged, by one or more tribunals which, though empowered by statute and bound to observe the principles of justice, are not courts of law. Their role is best regarded as an extension of the initial decision-making process [. . .]. Such decision-makers, on classic principles of public law, are required to take everything material into account. Their sources of information will frequently go well beyond the testimony of the applicant and include in-country reports, expert testimony and – sometimes – specialised knowledge of their own (which must of course be disclosed) [. . .]. What the decision-makers ultimately make of the material is a matter for their own conscientious judgment, so long as the procedure by which they approach and entertain it is lawful and fair and provided their decision logically addresses the Convention issues.'[60]

Internal flight/relocation alternative

The case of *Karanakaran*, in addition to dealing with the question of evidential assessment, was concerned with the so-called 'internal

8.11

---

[58] *ibid.*, at 144F.
[59] *ibid.*, at 155A-B.
[60] *ibid.*, at 154F-H and 155A-B.

flight' or 'internal relocation' alternative. Refugee status is surrogate international protection. A person who is a refugee claims the protection of the international community because his or her own country cannot or will not provide protection. However, refugees can only rely on the surrogate protection of another country if they establish a lack of protection from their own country.[61] It is from this principle that the notion of 'internal relocation' arises, since a person who is not prepared to go to less dangerous parts of his or her country may find it more difficult to prove a lack of protection.[62] Sedley L.J. stated in *Karanakaran*:

> '[. . .] in most cases, [. . .], it is in relation to the asylum-seeker's ability or willingness to avail himself of his home State's protection that the question of internal relocation arises. Because, however, unwillingness is explicitly related to the driving fear, it predicates a different set of considerations from inability, which may be indicated or contraindicated by a much wider range of factors.'[63]

The Court of Appeal decision of *R. v Secretary of State for the Home Department & Immigration Appeal Tribunal, ex parte Robinson* addressed the specific issue of reasonableness of relocation.[64] There, Woolf L.J. stated:

> 'Where it appears that persecution is confined to a specific part of a country's territory the decision-maker should ask: can the claimant find effective protection in another part of his own territory to which he or she may reasonably be expected to move? [. . .] We consider the test suggested by Linden JA – "would it be unduly harsh to expect this person to move to another less hostile part of the country?" – to be a particularly helpful one. [. . .] The use of the words "unduly harsh" fairly reflects that what is in issue is whether a person claiming asylum can reasonably be expected to move to a particular part of the country.'[65]

In determining whether it would be reasonable to expect someone to relocate internally,

> 'a decision-maker would have to consider all the circumstances of the case, against the backcloth that the issue is whether the claimant is entitled to the status of refugee. Various tests have been suggested. For example, (a) if as a practical matter (whether for financial, logistical or other good reason) the "safe" part of the country is not reasonably accessible; (b) if the

---

[61] *Florianowicz* (15333), July 31, 1997.
[62] *ibid.*
[63] [2000] INLR 122, at 149C.
[64] [1997] INLR 182.
[65] *ibid.*, para. 29.

claimant is required to encounter great physical danger in travelling there
or staying there; (c) if he or she is required to undergo undue hardship in
travelling there or staying there; (d) if the quality of the internal protection
fails to meet basic norms of civil political and socio-economic human
rights. So far as the last of these considerations is concerned, the preamble
to the Convention shows that the contracting parties were concerned to
uphold the principle that human beings should enjoy fundamental rights
and freedoms without discrimination.'[66]

In accordance with *Karanakaran*,[67] all relevant factors needed to be
considered to determine whether it would be unduly harsh to return
an applicant to his or her country of origin.

The *Robinson* decision is encouraging. Once more it shows a Court
of Appeal prepared to take account of international jurisprudence in
the asylum field before reaching its decision. Its conclusions can
therefore be described as fair and measured, and in accordance with
the general principles of refugee protection, namely that the surrogacy principle applies and that international protection should only
be afforded where an originating state cannot or will not provide protection. However, having set down the criteria for internal relocation,
the Court was unable to control how they were ultimately to be
applied by the decision-maker.

Gender and the law[68]

Perhaps the courts' brightest moment in recent years is to be found in   **8.12**
the 1999 decision of *Islam v Secretary of State for the Home Department; R.
v IAT, ex parte Shah*.[69] Here the appellants, both Pakistani women, had
suffered domestic violence and were at risk of being accused of adul-
tery, with all its consequences, if returned to Pakistan. As gender does
not of itself constitute a ground for persecution under the 1951 Convention, the House of Lords was called upon to adopt an innovative
line of reasoning to provide protection to the women. By a 4:1 majority (Lord Millet dissenting), the Court held that both appellants had a
well-founded fear of persecution by reason of their membership of a
particular social group, within the meaning of the 1951 Convention.
This overturned the judgement of the Court of Appeal which found
the women to have a well-founded fear of persecution, but not to be
a particular social group. What is fascinating about this case is the

---

[66] *ibid.*, para. 18.
[67] See above under Standard of Proof.
[68] For a detailed discussion of the problems associated with women seeking asylum, see
    H. Crawley, *Refugees and Gender – Law and Process* (London: Jordans, 2001).
[69] [1999] INLR 144.

expansive approach adopted by a number of the House of Lords judges. Firstly, and somewhat unusually, special reference was made to the human rights premise underlying the 1951 Convention, as set out in its preamble, and to the concept of discrimination, which Lord Hoffman described as being central to an understanding of the Convention; secondly, recourse was made once more to a line of international cases which had considered the requirements of 'particular social group', and notably whether a degree of 'cohesiveness' was necessary amongst members of a group. Cohesiveness, or interdependence or co-operation, refers here to a connection between members of the group. The court decided that cohesion was not an essential characteristic of a social group, nor did it matter that the 1951 Convention had failed to consider the persecution of women *as* women. According to Lord Hoffman, the framers of the Convention had used a general ground based on social group 'to include whatever groups might be regarded as coming within the anti-discriminatory objectives of the Convention'.[70] The court went on to state that there could only be a particular social group if it exists independently of the persecution.[71] In other words, the group cannot be defined by the persecution.[72] Ultimately, the particular social group was deemed to be very wide: 'women in Pakistan'. This indicated that the Law Lords were prepared to adopt a broad and inclusive interpretation of the 1951 Convention if the circumstances so demanded.

In November 2000, the IAA issued some *Asylum Gender Guidelines* to assist adjudicators and the IAT in 'fully considering all aspects of asylum seekers' claims to international protection under UK law'.[73] Arising from guidance published by the Refugee Women's Legal Group in 1998,[74] the IAA's guidelines note that women may not benefit equitably from the protection of the 1951 Convention for two reasons: (i) because the jurisprudence has not, to date, fully considered the specific issues raised by women's asylum claims and/or has tended to consider them within a framework of male experiences; and (ii) because the procedural and evidential requirements of the domestic asylum determination process are not equally accessible to both women and men.[75]

The Guidelines seek, therefore, to address these problems in three particular ways:

---

[70] [1999] INLR at 162B.

[71] *ibid.*, at 151C.

[72] *ibid.*, at 168E.

[73] Available on *www.iaa.gov.uk/GenInfo/IAA-Gender.htm*

[74] See RWLG website: *www.rwlg.org.uk*

[75] para. 1.1.

- 'Jurisprudence – to ensure that women's asylum claims are fully considered under the Refugee Convention so that jurisprudence properly reflects the experience of both female and male refugees.
- Procedures – to ensure that the asylum determination process is accessible to both women and men and that the procedures used do not prejudice women asylum seekers or make it more difficult for them to present their asylum claims.
- Evidential Requirements – to ensure that the judiciary are aware of the particular evidential problems which may be faced by women asylum seekers and that appropriate steps are taken to overcome them.'[76]

These guidelines are clearly significant. In addition to bringing the UK into line with Canada, Australia and the USA, they have helped compensate for the lack of detailed guidance on women and gender issues in the Home Office.

Safe third countries

The generous spirit witnessed in the *Shah* and *Islam* decision is evident in other asylum cases, and some have made a significant impact on government policy and Home Office practice. For example, in July 1999, in *R. v Secretary of State for the Home Department, ex parte Lul Adan, Sivyampalan Subaskaran & Hamid Aitseguer*,[77] the Court of Appeal considered three combined cases in which the Home Secretary had decided to remove two of the applicants to Germany and one to France, under safe third country provisions. The asylum applicants sought judicial review of the Home Secretary's decision on the grounds that neither France nor Germany interpreted the 1951 Convention correctly, since they did not recognise that persecution from a 'non-state agent' gave rise to a well-founded fear. This approach, known as the 'accountability theory', may be contrasted with the 'protection theory' applied by the majority of states. In applying the protection theory, English courts 'recognise persecution by non-State agents [. . .] in any case where the State is unwilling or unable to provide protection against it, [. . .] whether or not there exist competent or effective governmental or state authorities in the country in question'.[78] The Court held that the Secretary of State was required to examine the practice in the third country to establish if it was consistent with the 1951 Convention's true interpretation, and whether, even if consistent, it still gave rise to the possibility of

8.13

---

[76] para. 1.8.
[77] [1999] INLR 362.
[78] *ibid.*, at 377.

refoulement. The Court judged the accountability theory applied by France and Germany to be at variance with the 1951 Convention's true meaning and the Secretary of State's certificates to have been unlawfully issued.

In December 2000, the House of Lords upheld the decision in *Lul Adan.* Referring to the decision in *Adan v Secretary of State for the Home Department,*[79] the court held that the conclusion reached in that case was correct, namely that in the UK the proper construction of the 1951 Convention requires the acceptance of the protection theory.[80] In *Lul Adan,* the House of Lords confirmed that, in its view, the Secretary of State had 'wrongly proceeded on the twin assumption that there is a band of permissible meanings of Art 1A(2) and that the practice hitherto adopted in Germany and France falls within the permissible range'.[81] Consequently, he had materially misdirected himself and his decisions were quashed. This strong endorsement of majority state practice by the English judiciary was an important step in the development of an international jurisprudence on refugee law, leading to enhanced certainty and consistency in decision-making.

In the final analysis, the impact made by *Lul Adan* was theoretical rather than actual, since the government pre-empted the judgement by introducing ss. 11 and 12 in the Immigration and Asylum Act 1999. It will be recalled that s. 11 replaced s. 2 of the Asylum and Immigration Act 1996. Where the Secretary of State proposes to return an applicant to a Member State under the standing arrangements (*i.e.* under the Dublin Convention), he no longer needs to certify that State to be 'safe'. (S. 12, which concerns removals in other cases, still requires such certification.). The new certification requirements under s. 11 simply oblige the Secretary of State to confirm that the Member State, to which the applicant is to be returned, accepts responsibility for the asylum application, and that he does not believe the applicant to be a national or citizen of that State. The effect of this statutory amendment is to circumvent the obligations imposed in the *Lul Adan* decision.

False documents

8.14   The issue of illegal entry and false documentation provides a further example in which judicial contributions led to a change in legislation. In a notable and much cited House of Lords decision of the early

---

[79] [1998] INLR 325.
[80] *R. v Secretary of State for the Home Department, ex parte Lul Adan and Aitseguer* [2001] INLR 44, at 63D (Lord Hutton).
[81] *ibid.,* at 60B.

1990s, *R. v Naillie; R. v Kanesarajah*,[82] Lord Slynn found that the two respondents, who had helped a number of individuals to enter the UK with forged documentation, had not committed the offence of facilitating illegal entry contrary to s. 25(1) of the Immigration Act 1971. He reached this conclusion because the individuals concerned claimed asylum on arrival and did not rely on the false documents to gain entry or try to deceive the immigration officers. Disembarkation without a passport or in possession of forged documents did not constitute illegal entry. Since the applicants were not illegal entrants, Naillie and Kanesarajah had not facilitated their illegal entry under s. 25. While Lord Slynn recognised the desirability of ending the trafficking in people and documents to gain entry into the UK, the critical feature of the case was that none of the travellers sought to deceive the immigration officers or enter clandestinely. A very different outcome might have ensued, suggested Lord Slynn, where a person sought asylum by relying on forged documents, or relied initially on forged documents, but when challenged, changed tack and claimed asylum. This last point of Lord Slynn's seems to underplay the importance of Art. 31(1) of the 1951 Convention, which calls on Contracting States not to impose penalties, on account of their illegal entry or presence, on refugees who come directly from a territory where their life or freedom was threatened, provided they present themselves without delay to the authorities and show good cause for their illegal entry. This point was addressed in the next case.

In July 1999, the Queen's Bench Division handed down a notable judgement in *R. v Uxbridge Magistrates' Court and Another ex parte Adimi; R. v Crown Prosecution Service, R v Secretary of State for the Home Department ex parte Sorani; R. v Secretary of State for the Home Department and Another ex parte Kaziu*.[83] In this combined case, the three applicants, all asylum seekers, had been charged with offences relating to the possession of false passports and other documents used to travel to the UK. Adimi had travelled to the UK via Italy and France, while Sorani and Kaziu were transiting through the UK on their way to Canada. After addressing the facts of the case, Simon Brown L.J. opened by denouncing current Home Office policy, stating that 'until these challenges were brought, no arm of State, neither the Secretary of State, the DPP, nor anyone else, had apparently given the least thought to the UK's obligations arising under Art 31'.[84] He summed up the position as follows:

---

[82] [1993] AC 674; [1993] Imm AR 462.
[83] [1999] INLR 490.
[84] *ibid.*, at 495D.

'That Art 31 extends not merely to those ultimately accorded refugee status but also to those claiming asylum in good faith (presumptive refugees) is not in doubt. Nor is it disputed that Art 31's protection can apply equally to those using false documents as to those (characteristically the refugees of earlier times) who enter a country clandestinely. There are, however, within the text of the Article certain expressed limitations upon its scope and these clearly require consideration. To enjoy protection the refugee must:

(a)   have come directly from the country of his persecution,
(b)   present himself to the authorities without delay, and
(c)   show good cause for his illegal entry or presence.'[85]

Simon Brown L.J. proceeded to interpret the requirement to 'come directly' rather generously, accepting that there was 'some element of choice [. . .] open to refugees as to where they may properly claim asylum',[86] and that a short stop-over in another country *en route* to the intended country of sanctuary cannot forfeit the protection of the Article. The authorities needed to consider the length of stay in the intermediate country, the reasons for delaying there (even a substantial delay in an unsafe third country would be reasonable were the time spent trying to acquire the means of travelling on), and whether or not the refugee sought or found protection, *de jure* or *de facto*, from persecution.[87] Significantly, he accepted that 'refugees generally had become entitled to the benefit of Art. 31 in accordance with the developing doctrine of legitimate expectations'.[88] In a highly critical turn of phrase, he found that all three applicants should have been exempt from penalty and advised the Crown to alter its approach to the prosecution of refugees for travelling on false passports, and to honour the requisite provision of the Convention.[89] The government heeded the warning and introduced an amendment to the Immigration and Asylum Bill to take account of the case (now, conveniently, s. 31 to the 1999 Act).

Social Security

8.15   In 1996, in *R. v Secretary of State for Social Security, ex parte Joint Council for the Welfare of Immigrants; R. v Secretary of State for Social Security, ex parte*

---

[85] [1999] INLR at 496F.

[86] *ibid.*, at 497B.

[87] *ibid.*, at 497C.

[88] *ibid.*, at 505B. However, see below for a revision of this view by Simon Brown L.J. in *European Roma Rights Centre v Immigration Officer at Prague Airport; SSHD* [2003] EWCA Civ 666.

[89] [1999] INLR 490, at 506H.

B,[90] Simon Brown L.J. famously condemned the introduction of regulations to remove benefits from certain asylum seekers:

'I regard the Regulations as so uncompromisingly draconian in effect that they must be ultra vires. [. . .] Parliament cannot have intended a significant number of genuine asylum seekers to be impaled on the horns of so intolerable a dilemma: the need either to abandon their claims to refugee status or alternatively to maintain them as best they could but in a state of utter destitution. Primary legislation alone could [. . .] achieve that sorry state of affairs.'[91]

The government responded immediately to Simon Brown's L.J. words, not quite as he might have intended: an emergency amendment was made to the Asylum and Immigration Bill, then passing through Parliament, and the removal of benefit entitlements was, indeed, sanctioned by primary legislation.[92]

A second case decided in 1996 provided further evidence of the preparedness of the judiciary to intervene where social security was concerned. In *R. v Hammersmith and Fulham LBC, ex parte M*, Collins J. held that a destitute asylum seeker who had no money and who lacked the means by which to support him or herself might be 'in need of care and attention' within the meaning of s. 21(1)(a) of the National Assistance Act 1948.[93] As a consequence, a duty fell upon local authorities to provide shelter, warmth and food to applicants under the 1948 Act. The judge deemed it impossible that Parliament intended that an asylum seeker lawfully in the UK should be left destitute, starving and at risk of grave illness, and even death, because he could find no one to provide him with the bare essentials for life. The Court of Appeal endorsed the judgement of Collins J. that application of s. 21(1)(a) could be extended to asylum seekers alongside the elderly, sick and disabled.

One commentator has suggested that the judgements of *ex parte JCWI* and *ex parte M* are 'the high watermark of judicial activism in administrative law prior to the Human Rights Act 1998'.[94] Certainly, reference is made in these cases to the fundamental needs of asylum

---

[90] [1996] 4 All ER 385.

[91] *ibid.*, at 402a-c.

[92] See Ch. 5.

[93] *The Times Law Reports*, October 10, 1996. s. 21(1)(a) specifies that 'a local authority may with approval of the Secretary of State, and to such extent as he may direct, make arrangements for providing: (a) residential accommodation for persons aged 18 or over who by reason of age, illness, disability or any other circumstances are in need of care and attention which is not otherwise available to them'.

[94] P. Billings, 'Alienating Asylum Seekers: Welfare Support in the Immigration and Asylum Act 1999', (2002) 9 *Journal of Social Security Law*, p. 125.

seekers and to the rights protected by both the 1951 Convention and the ECHR.[95] They provide further confirmation that certain judges were inclined in the pre-Human Rights Act era to favour an inclusive approach, at least to social security provision, and sought wherever possible to protect the rights of asylum seekers and refugees against perceived abuse of ministerial power.

8.16 However, the courts' approach to the question of support of asylum seekers was tested once more in 2003. In a very high profile case, *R. (Q & Others) v Secretary of State for the Home Department*, the legality of the government's most recent initiative – the refusal of support under s. 55 of the Nationality, Immigration and Asylum Act 2002 – was challenged.[96] Q and five others applied for judicial review, alleging that the Secretary of State's decision that their asylum claims were not made 'as soon as reasonably practicable' was unlawful, and that their human rights had been breached because the effect of the refusal was to deprive them of shelter and food. Collins J., in a lengthy judgement tracing the history of social security provision for asylum seekers, found in their favour. The decision-making process in each case was flawed. There had been:

> '[. . .] a failure initially to investigate the circumstances in which entry was achieved sufficiently and, when there has been reconsideration, the approach has been coloured by an assumption that a failure to claim at the port will itself be justification. The individual's reasons for not claiming must be considered and that means at least asking about the pressures on him, what he was told and what his beliefs were.'[97]

This even included taking into account what the asylum seeker might have been told by a facilitator. Having determined that the process was unacceptable, Collins J. went on to consider the human rights dimension. Parliament, he agreed, had, via s. 55(1), removed the common law of humanity, stated in 1803 by Lord Ellenborough to be 'anterior to all positive laws' and obliging us 'to afford [poor foreigners] relief, to save them from starving'.[98] There was no duty to support asylum seekers who did not claim as soon as reasonably practical, unless there was a breach of their human rights (s. 55(5)). It seemed apparent to Collins J. that:

---

[95] P. Billings, 'Alienating Asylum Seekers: Welfare Support in the Immigration and Asylum Act 1999', (2002) 9 *Journal of Social Security Law*, p. 125.

[96] [2003] EWHC 195 Admin, High Court; [2003] EWCA Civ 364, CA; see, also, Chs 5 and 6 for discussion of s. 55.

[97] [2003] EWHC 195 Admin, High Court, para. 56.

[98] *ibid.*, para. 59, citing *R. v Inhabitants of Eastbourne* (1803) 4 East 103.

'[. . .] if a State puts into effect a measure which results in treatment which can properly be described as inhuman or degrading or which interferes with a person's private life by adversely affecting his mental or physical health to a sufficiently serious extent, Art. 3 or 8(1) will be violated. It is not necessary to wait until damage of a sufficient severity occurs provided there is a real risk that it will occur.

It will not automatically breach Article 3 or Article 8 to refuse someone who is destitute. It must be established that there is a real risk that destitution leading to injury to health will occur. This means that questions should be asked to establish whether there is indeed a realistic chance that there will be a source of support.'[99]

He went on: 'I am satisfied that there will normally be a real risk that to leave someone destitute will violate Article 3 and 8(1). I am not persuaded that charity offers a real chance of providing support.'[100] In addition, there was also breach of Art. 6. '[J]udicial review could not be an adequate remedy unless the facts were properly investigated by the decision maker and adequate reasons were given. Only then could the whole process be regarded as compliant with Article 6.'[101] Since the issue in the case turned on whether the Secretary of State was satisfied that the claim was made as soon as reasonably practicable, the Court would not resolve the facts, but could only consider whether the decision was lawful on the usual grounds.[102] Collins J. was satisfied, therefore, that there was in each case a breach of Art. 6, though fuller investigation and fuller reasons might mean that judicial review was adequate.[103] The Secretary of State appealed to the Court of Appeal.

The Court of Appeal agreed that the system assessing asylum **8.17** seekers was unfair. While the burden was on the applicant to prove that he or she claimed asylum as soon as reasonably practicable, the purpose of the initial interview with the claimant needed to be explained more clearly.[104] The interview needed to be changed: a standard form questionnaire was insufficient; a more flexible approach and greater interviewing skills were called for.[105] More seriously, the fact that the decision-maker was not ordinarily the interviewer was a major defect, as was the inability of the applicant to

---

[99] *ibid.*, paras 70 and 71.
[100] *ibid.*, para. 72.
[101] *ibid.*, para. 85.
[102] *ibid.*, para. 85.
[103] *ibid.*, para. 86.
[104] [2003] EWCA Civ 364, CA, paras 82 and 83.
[105] *ibid.*, para. 90.

explain any matter relied on against him or her.[106] Regarding human
rights breaches, the Court of Appeal did not go as far as Collins J.,
but it was still critical. Lord Phillips MR concluded that the regime
imposed on asylum seekers denied support by reason of s. 55(1)
constitutes 'treatment' within the meaning of Art. 3.[107] But he did not
agree with Collins J. that the fact that there is a real risk that an asylum seeker will be reduced to a state of degradation of itself engages
Art. 3.[108] While '[s]ome who apply for asylum may already be in a
condition which verges on the degree of severity capable of engaging
Article 3 described in *Pretty*, [. . .] [i]t is not unlawful for the Secretary
of State to decline support unless and until it is clear that charitable
support has not been provided and the individual is incapable of
fending for himself'.[109] Furthermore, the Court did not deem it necessary to consider Art. 8 at any length since, on the facts of the case,
it was 'easier to envisage the risk of infringement of Article 3 rights
rather than of Article 8 rights'.[110] That said, it accepted that if the
denial of support impacted sufficiently on the asylum seeker's private
and family life, including on his or her physical and mental integrity
and autonomy, there would be a breach of Art. 8 (unless justified
under Art. 8(2)).[111] Finally, so far as Art. 6 was concerned, the Court
agreed with Collins J.:

> 'The Strasbourg jurisprudence establishes that where the initial decision as
> to civil rights is taken by a person or persons who cannot be described as
> "an independent and impartial tribunal", the fact that the decision is sub-
> ject to judicial review can satisfy Article 6. At the end of the day, however,
> the process as a whole must be capable of fairly determining the civil rights
> that are in play. The inadequacies of the procedure, [. . .], rendered it
> impossible for the officials of the Secretary of State to make an informed
> determination of matters central to the asylum-seekers' civil rights. The
> consequence of this is that the court conducting the judicial review was
> equally unable to do so. All that the court could do was to quash the
> decisions. In these circumstances Collins J. held that the requirements of
> Article 6 were not satisfied. We agree with his conclusion.'[112]

The beleaguered Secretary of State, after thanking the Court for
its decision, noted that the procedural flaws identified by both the
High Court and the Court of Appeal were being rectified. Despite

---

[106] [2003] EWCA Civ 364, CA, paras 98 and 99.
[107] *ibid.*, para. 56.
[108] *ibid.*, para. 63.
[109] *ibid.*, paras 62 and 63.
[110] *ibid.*, para. 64.
[111] *ibid.*
[112] *ibid.*, para. 116.

this, only months later, a second application for judicial review again challenged three decisions of the Home Secretary made under s. 55(1). The grounds of challenge centred on the timing of the applications under s. 55(1), and on breach of Art. 3 of the ECHR. On this occasion, Maurice Kay J. found that the conclusion reached by the Secretary of State that 'D' had made his application 'as soon as reasonably practicable' was not rational or based on a fair procedure; the decisions regarding 'S' and 'T' were justifiable.[113] However, the human rights aspects still needed to be addressed. All three applicants were in a very distressed state: 'S' was forced to beg for food, and suffered from psychological disturbance and significant weight loss; 'D' had also begged for food, was sleeping rough, and felt weak, hungry, frightened and depressed; 'T' had 'lived' at Heathrow, where he found it difficult to sleep due to noise and light and was unable to bathe or wash his clothes; he developed a cough and a problem with one eye, and began to feel increasingly demoralised and humiliated. According to Maurice Kay J., the refusal or withdrawal of support was debasing and showed a lack of respect for human dignity, and the condition of the applicants in all three cases verged on the degree of severity described in *Pretty v UK*.[114] Article 3 had been breached.

This decision was clearly a major blow to the government, though the Minister for Immigration offered the most favourable interpretation: 'I am pleased that the Court has upheld the initial decision to refuse support in two of the three cases. I also welcome the finding that it is not inevitable that anyone refused asylum support will then be able to later claim support under article 3 of the European Convention on Human Rights. However, we are concerned at the finding that article 3 was breached in these cases and are therefore seeking to appeal to the Court of Appeal on this point.'[115] No doubt, the issue of asylum seeker support will continue to provide a battleground for judiciary and executive.

Detention

An issue of great concern in the asylum field, and one which has perhaps received more media coverage than any other, particularly following the destruction by fire of Yarl's Wood Detention Centre in February 2002, is that of detention.[116] It has also been the subject of

8.18

---

[113] [2003] EWHC 1941 (Admin), para.19.
[114] (2002) 35 EHRR 1, para. 52, and see Ch. 4.
[115] Home Office Press Release, 'High court judgement on asylum support', July 31, 2003.
[116] See Ch. 6 for discussion of detention.

a somewhat controversial judgement: *R. v Secretary of State for the Home Department, ex parte Saadi et al.*[117] Sitting in the Administrative Court, Collins J. was called upon to decide the legality of the detention of four Iraqi Kurds who had arrived in the UK in December 2000 and who claimed asylum. They were detained at Oakington Reception Centre during the processing of their asylum claims. Following refusal, they were released, but applied for judicial review of the decisions to detain them, contending that their detention was in breach of UK municipal law as well as the ECHR. As far as domestic law was concerned, Collins J. concluded that the Immigration Act 1971[118] entitled the Secretary of State to detain the claimants if he thought it reasonably necessary in order to deal with their cases expeditiously.[119] The application of Art. 5 of the ECHR was a different matter. The question before the judge was whether Art. 5(1)(f) of the ECHR permitted Dr Saadi's detention.[120] Any deprivation of liberty under Art. 5(1)(f) is only permissible so long as deportation proceedings are due. According to Collins J., it was clear that 'the detention of a person seeking entry and falling within the first part of Art. 5(1)(f) must be to prevent that person effecting an unauthorised entry'.[121] Thus detention could not be justified on the grounds that it might speed up the process of determination of applications, nor could it be justified on the basis that it might deter others from seeking to enter by making false claims for asylum. In a noteworthy statement, the judge continued:

'Once it is accepted that an applicant has made a proper application for asylum and there is no risk that he will abscond or otherwise misbehave, it is impossible to see how it could reasonably be said that he needs to be detained to prevent his effecting an unauthorised entry. He is doing all that he should to ensure that he can make an authorised entry. If his application is refused, further consideration may be given to whether he should be

---

[117] [2001] EWHC Admin 670.

[118] sch. 2, paras 16(1) and (2).

[119] Immigration Act 1971, sch. 2, para. 16(1) states: 'A person who may be required to submit to examination [. . .] may be detained under the authority of an immigration officer pending his examination and pending a decision to give or refuse him leave to enter.' Para. 16(2) (as substituted by the Immigration and Asylum Act 1999) states: 'If there are reasonable grounds for suspecting that a person is someone in respect of whom directions may be given [. . .], that person may be detained under the authority of an immigration officer pending – (a) a decision whether or not to give such directions; (b) his removal in pursuance of such directions.'

[120] Art. 5(1): 'Everyone has the right to liberty and security of person. No one shall be deprived of his liberty save in the following cases and in accordance with a procedure prescribed by law [. . .]
(f) the lawful arrest or detention of a person to prevent his effecting an unauthorised entry into the country or of a person against whom action is being taken with a view to deportation or extradition.'

[121] [2001] EWHC Admin 670, para. 29.

detained under the second part of Article 5(1)(f), but the fact that all these claimants were then granted temporary admission underlines the reality that there was considered to be no danger of any of them effecting an unauthorised entry.'[122]

Nor did the judge consider that it was possible to regard a person who arrives and seeks leave to enter as someone 'against whom action is being taken with a view to deportation', as specified in the second part of Art. 5(1)(f). Consequently, it was 'wholly artificial to regard the detention as within the second part of Art. 5(1)(f)'.[123] It was not possible to justify the detention, and it was accordingly judged unlawful.

The impact of the judgement was instant. The press reported that it could result in the payment of compensation to asylum seekers of up to £110m and that the Home Secretary 'reacted with dismay' and described it as 'deeply disturbing'.[124] He was said to be privately angry with the 'human rights lobby' for seeking to undermine the Oakington Reception Centre, a centre which he considered to be one of the best in the world.[125] An immediate appeal was lodged, the government employing the services of the Attorney General, Lord Goldsmith, and a leading QC in the field, David Pannick, as well as a leading junior, Michael Fordham. It was clear that it had no intention of losing before the Court of Appeal, and did ultimately succeed (see below).

Carriers' liability and civil penalties

In *International Transport Roth Gmbh & Others v Secretary of State for the Home Department*,[126] the Court of Appeal had an opportunity to examine in detail provisions on clandestine entrants introduced by Part II of the Immigration and Asylum Act 1999 ('the civil penalty'), and to assess their compatibility with the ECHR, *inter alia*. In a notable but convoluted decision, and with a dissenting judgement from Laws L.J., the Court found that the so-called civil penalty scheme was, in fact, to be regarded as criminal rather than civil for the purposes of Art. 6 of the ECHR. The scale and inflexibility of the penalty, which could not be mitigated and which was not open to determination by an independent tribunal, made the scheme unfair and in breach of Art. 6. Furthermore, the scheme imposed an excessive burden on the

8.19

---

[122] *ibid.*
[123] *ibid.*, para. 32.
[124] R. Ford, 'Blunkett despair at £110m asylum ruling', *The Times*, September 8, 2001.
[125] *ibid.*
[126] [2002] 3 WLR 344.

carriers, which was disproportionate to the objective to be achieved, and was in breach of Art. 1 of the First Protocol. It was felt that, while the reversal of burden of proof invoked by the penalty (the carrier was forced to disprove dishonesty and negligence) did not of itself breach Art. 6, in combination with the vehicle detention provisions and the inflexibility of the substantial financial penalties, the scheme placed an immense burden on carriers.[127] More worryingly for Parker L.J., the Secretary of State was in danger of being a judge in his own cause.[128]

Though these are the conclusions reached by the majority, the individual judgements vary considerably and do not make easy reading. Judicial differences aside, there is recognition that this is possibly a case of 'high constitutional importance'. As Simon Brown L.J. observes, it 'raises questions as to the degree of deference owed by the courts to the legislature and executive in the means used to achieve social goals'.[129] Parker L.J. comments that 'given that the importance of the social issues raised in the instant case is recognised and acknowledged on all sides, Parliament's discretionary area of judgment in the instant case should in my judgment, be regarded as being as wide as possible'.[130] Yet, for both, the scheme was 'quite simply, unfair to carriers'[131] and warranted intervention by the courts. The bedrock of the right to a fair trial enshrined in Art. 6 was in danger of being eroded.[132]

From the carriers' perspective, this was clearly a positive decision (though they lost their claim that the scheme constituted an unjust restriction on the movement of goods and services across the borders of EU states and was in breach of the EC Treaty). For asylum and immigration law as a whole, *Roth* might be regarded as an illustration of diminishing judicial deference. However, even in the context of the Human Rights Act 1998, judges are very conscious of limits to their power. As counsel for the Roth claimants pointed out, were the Court to create a fresh scheme purportedly under s. 3 of the Act (which requires primary and secondary legislation to be read and given effect in a way which is compatible with ECHR rights),[133] then it would

---

[127] [2002] 3 WLR 344, para. 46.

[128] *ibid.*, para. 157.

[129] *ibid.*, para. 54.

[130] *ibid.*, para. 139.

[131] *ibid.*, para. 54.

[132] *ibid.*, para. 139.

[133] s. 3(1): 'So far as it is possible to do so, primary legislation and subordinate legislation must be read and given effect in a way which is compatible with the Convention rights.'

indeed be failing to show judicial deference owed to Parliament as legislators.[134] Naturally, the Court was not prepared to go this far.

The government reacted to the Court's finding that there was breach of Art. 6 and Art. 1 of the First Protocol by amending the civil penalty provisions and introducing a flexible fining scheme.[135]

JUDICIAL RESTRAINT IN THE FIELD OF ASYLUM

All of the aforementioned decisions may be described rightly as land-marks. They provide evidence that some members of the judiciary are willing to challenge government and Home Office policy. At times, the judgements are phrased in what might be termed the language of 'rights'; at times, they reveal a conscious effort to apply a broad and generous interpretation to the 1951 Convention. But this is not the whole story. Certain areas of asylum law have resulted in more restrictive decisions by the judiciary, particularly in the higher courts. Some have raised concerns that the UK is falling out of line with judicial thinking in other jurisdictions reputed to have a progressive approach to refugee jurisprudence. The issue of support aside, there are a number of recent cases that may be described as limiting the protection afforded asylum seekers within the UK.

8.20

Non-state agents of persecution and the test for protection

In 1998, in *R. v Secretary of State for the Home Department, ex parte Adan*,[136] the House of Lords considered two pressing questions: (i) did applicants have to show a *current* (as opposed to historic) fear of persecution to fall within the 1951 Convention? and (ii) what was the extent of the protection offered by the Convention to asylum claimants from a civil war situation? The case dealt with a Somali national who had fled his home country and claimed asylum on the basis of persecution arising from inter-clan violence. The Secretary of State refused asylum but granted exceptional leave to remain. The claimant successfully appealed to the Special Adjudicator, but the Tribunal allowed the Secretary of State's appeal against this decision. It was accepted that the claimant had fled as a result of well-founded fear of persecution, and that Somalia remained riven by clan- and

8.21

---

[134] [2002] 3 WLR 344, para. 66.
[135] Nationality, Immigration and Asylum Act 2002, s. 125 and sch. 8.
[136] [1998] INLR 325.

sub-clan-based ethnic conflict involving widespread killing, torture, rape and pillage. The claimant then appealed to the Court of Appeal,[137] and was again successful. With Simon Brown L.J. forging the way, the Court offered a generous interpretation of the Convention. First, it decided that an applicant need not show a current fear and that a purely historical fear would suffice. Second, Simon Brown L.J. was of the view that an applicant coming from a civil war could fall within the Convention, even if he or she was at no greater risk in the civil war for reasons of clan membership than any other person. The Secretary of State appealed to the House of Lords.

Lord Lloyd, giving the leading judgement in the House of Lords, disagreed on both counts. Though historical fear remained relevant to establishing current fear, an applicant must show a *current* well-founded fear of persecution.[138] In addition, an applicant has to prove the need for protection against current or future persecution. Thus Lord Lloyd divided the requirements of Art. 1A(2) into two components: establishment of current fear, and establishment of the need for protection.[139] Of equal importance, and with considerable consequences for those fleeing civil war, a person coming from a civil war situation has to show a fear of persecution 'over and above the ordinary risks of civil warfare', in other words, a 'differential impact' must be established.[140] This means that an asylum seeker coming from a civil war situation needs to prove that he or she is at greater risk of ill-treatment than other members of his or her clan, even if the war is being fought on religious or racial grounds.[141] This despite Simon Brown's L.J. view that 'in reality virtually all civil wars will by their very nature be convention-based (the opposing factions divided by issues of race, politics or the like)',[142] and the acceptance that in *Adan* there was 'widespread clan- and sub-clan-based killing and torture'. Lord Lloyd concluded that this was irrelevant so long as the civil war persisted. Once it was over, and order was restored, there was no longer the prospect of people from both sides claiming to be refugees; but, if the vanquished were ill-treated by the victors, they could then claim asylum.

The bizarre conclusion was consequently reached whereby 'exactly the same risk for exactly the same reason [would] be insufficient to

---

[137] For a discussion of the Court of Appeal case, see G. Goodwin-Gill, 'The Margin of interpretation: Different or disparate?' (1999) *IJRL* 11:4, pp.730–37.

[138] [1998] INLR 325, at 333C.

[139] *ibid.*, at 331B-E.

[140] *ibid.*, at 336C.

[141] *ibid.*, at 334C-D, 336G.

[142] *Adan v Secretary of State for the Home Department* [1997] Imm AR 251.

establish refugee status on one day, yet sufficient the next'.[143] Human rights infringements during a civil war seemed, therefore, at least for Lord Lloyd, to be largely outside the domain of the Convention.

This highly restrictive approach was mitigated somewhat by His Lordship's talk of adopting a broad linguistic approach. He accepted that where a state 'is unable to afford protection against factions within the State, then the qualifications for refugee status are complete'.[144] In addition, he suggested that a claim for refugee status need not always be individualised, and that such a claim might be upheld if based on membership of a group which is subject to oppression. This is a welcome admission. Adan's misfortune was to come from a country in civil war.

Arguably, one of the more restrictive decisions of recent times is **8.22** that of *Milan Horvath v Secretary of State for the Home Department*, a second House of Lords judgement dealing with persecution by non-state agents.[145] Decided in July 2000, it concerned the alleged persecution by 'skinheads' of a Roma national from Slovakia. In this case, the Court faced three questions: '(1) does the word "persecution" denote merely sufficiently severe ill-treatment, or does it denote sufficiently severe ill-treatment against which the State fails to afford protection? (2) is a person "unwilling to avail himself of the protection" of the country of his nationality where he is unwilling to do so because of his fear of persecution by non-state agents despite the state's protection against those agents' activities, or must his fear be a fear of being persecuted there for availing himself of the state's protection? (3) what is the test for determining whether there is sufficient protection against persecution in the person's country of origin [. . .]?'[146]

The IAT found that while Horvath had a well-founded fear of violence by skinheads, this did not amount to persecution because he had not shown that he was unable, or through fear of persecution, unwilling to avail himself of the protection of the state.[147] The majority in the House of Lords took a somewhat different view. The Convention was, they said, reliant upon the principle of surrogacy: that is, a person who no longer has the benefit of protection for a Convention reason in his or her own country can turn for protection to the international community, but only where the home country was unable or unwilling to discharge its duty to protect its own nationals.[148] The surrogacy principle was part and parcel of the definition

---

[143] *Butterworths Immigration Law Service,* 2E 573.
[144] [1998] INLR 325, at 331D.
[145] [2000] INLR 239.
[146] *ibid.,* at 242H-243A.
[147] *ibid.,* at 242B.
[148] *ibid.,* at 243E.

of refugee, said the Court. When applied to the issue of non-state
persecution, an applicant had to show that the persecution he or she
feared consisted of acts of violence or ill-treatment against which the
state was unwilling or unable to provide protection.[149] Therefore, the
ability to provide, or availability of, state protection was itself part of
the definition of persecution. In the words of Lord Hope:

> 'I would hold therefore that, in the context of an allegation of persecution
> by non-State agents, the word "persecution" implies a failure by the State
> to make protection available against the ill-treatment or violence which the
> person suffers at the hands of his persecutors. In a case where the allega-
> tion is of persecution by the State or its own agents the problem does not,
> of course, arise. There is a clear case for surrogate protection by the inter-
> national community. But in the case of an allegation of persecution by
> non-State agents the failure of the State to provide the protection is nev-
> ertheless an essential element. It provides the bridge between persecution
> by the State and persecution by non-State agents which is necessary in the
> interests of the consistency of the whole scheme.'[150]

The IAT had been entitled to hold, on the evidence before it, that
there was sufficient state protection in Slovakia for Roma against
attacks by thugs. It would also seem that however severe the threats to
life due to a Convention reason, and however well-founded the fear,
refugee status did not necessarily follow. According to the House of
Lords:[151]

> 'The applicant may have a well-founded fear of threats to his life due to
> famine or civil war or of isolated acts of violence or ill-treatment for a
> Convention reason which may be perpetrated against him. But the risk,
> however severe, and the fear, however well-founded, do not entitle him to
> the status of a refugee. The Convention has a more limited objective, the
> limits of which are identified by the list of Convention reasons and by the
> principle of surrogacy.'[152]

The Court went on to address the question of sufficiency of protection. A state cannot, it suggested, be expected to provide complete
protection against 'isolated and random attacks'. The standard was
not to eliminate *all risk* but was a practical standard, taking proper
account of the duty that the state owed to all its nationals.[153] In the
words of Lord Clyde:

---

[149] [2000] INLR at 248D.
[150] *ibid.*, at 246C-D.
[151] *ibid.*, at 248C-E.
[152] *ibid.*, at 248E.
[153] *ibid.*, at 249C.

'There must be in place a system of domestic protection and machinery for the detection, prosecution and punishment of actings contrary to the purposes which the Convention requires to have protected. More importantly there must be an ability and a readiness to operate that machinery.'[154]

And later:

'The sufficiency of State protection is not measured by the existence of a real risk of an abuse of rights but by the availability of a system for the protection of the citizen and a reasonable willingness by the State to operate it.'[155]

This decision is arguably rather artificial. There is much to suggest **8.23** that it was constructed in order to ensure that the UK did not breach its obligations under the 1951 Convention by returning a Rom to a country in which he was likely to face possible persecution (as per Stuart-Smith L.J. in the Court of Appeal). Lord Lloyd had proposed a two-pronged approach to Art. 1A(2) dealing with the issues of well-founded fear and protection separately. If the Court had followed this approach, it might have found that Horvath had a well-founded fear of persecution, but that Slovakia was able to provide him with protection. This could have led to the uncomfortable outcome that an individual was returned to his country of origin, albeit that he had a well-founded fear of persecution. By finding that state protection was part of the definition of persecution (a 'holistic approach' to the definition based on the principle of surrogacy),[156] the House of Lords was able to circumvent this problem. No well-founded fear of persecution existed because there was no failure by Slovakia to provide protection, and the ability to provide protection was a vital part of the definition of well-founded fear.

In human rights terms, this must be unsatisfactory. It is highly likely that the discrimination faced by the Roma constitutes at least degrading treatment for the purposes of Art. 3 of the ECHR, and that returning an individual to a state in which he or she would suffer such treatment would be in breach of this Article.[157] Lord Clyde's view that the sufficiency of state protection is not measured by the existence of a real risk of an abuse of rights, but by the availability of a system for the protection of the citizen and a reasonable willingness by the state to operate it, is of concern. *Horvath* did not engender

---

[154] *ibid.*, at 259G.
[155] *ibid.*, at 265G.
[156] *ibid.*, at 249F.
[157] See Refugee Legal Centre, *Legal Bulletin No. 76* for a discussion of the possible actions under the ECHR.

confidence that the judiciary would always place asylum law in its wider human rights context. As the New Zealand judge, Haines QC, commented:

> '[. . .] the English position is that an individual can be returned to his or her country of origin notwithstanding the fact that the person holds a well-founded fear of persecution for a Convention reason.

> With the greatest of respect, this interpretation of the United Nations Convention Relating to the Status of Refugees 1951 and Protocol of 1967 is at odds with the fundamental obligation of *non-refoulement*.'[158]

Persecution, standard of proof, sufficiency of protection and the ECHR

8.24   As discussed above, human rights norms have helped clarify the meaning of persecution as well as other key elements of the definition of refugee.[159] For their part, refugee law principles have assisted the interpretation of the ECHR. This is particularly true for *Horvath*. In the starred decision of *Kacaj v Secretary of State for the Home Department*, the IAT confronted the following questions: (i) what is the correct standard of proof to be applied to claims under the ECHR? (ii) does the ECHR apply to actions of non-state agents? (iii) does any article of the ECHR other than Art. 3 have "extra-territorial" effect?[160] In assessing the risk under Art. 3, the IAT stated:

> 'The link with the Refugee Convention is obvious. Persecution will normally involve the violation of a person's human rights and a finding that there is a real risk of persecution would be likely to involve a finding that there is a real risk of a breach of the European Convention on Human Rights [. . .]. Since the approach under each Convention is whether the risk of future ill-treatment will amount to a breach of an individual's human rights, a difference of approach would be surprising.'[161]

The Tribunal confirmed that the standard of proof was the same for ECHR cases as for an asylum appeal, namely that the applicant must establish that there is a real risk that his or her rights under Art. 3 will be breached.[162] Furthermore, the sufficiency of protection test

---

[158] *Refugee Appeal No 71427/99*, [2000] INLR 608, paras 62–63.
[159] N. Blake & R. Husain, *Immigration, Asylum & Human Rights* (Oxford: OUP, 2003), para. 2.84
        [N]LR 354.
        [pa]ra. 10.
        [pa]ra. 39

adopted in *Horvath* applied equally to prospective breaches of Art. 3: where a claim is that Art. 3 rights will be breached by non-state agents, it must be shown that the state is unwilling or unable to offer the necessary protection.[163] Finally, all articles of the ECHR (save perhaps Art. 2) had extra-territorial effect.[164] *Kacaj* was reversed on appeal to the Court of Appeal, but only on the facts; no comment was made on the IAT's analysis of the law.[165]

Some regard the *Kacaj* decision as a clear message that the Human Rights Act 1998 is 'unlikely to have a marked positive impact on asylum seekers and would-be immigrants'.[166] Following the IAT's reasoning, an applicant could establish a real risk of breach of Art. 3 if removed from the UK, but so long as the country of return had in place 'a system of criminal law which makes violent attacks by the persecutors punishable and a reasonable willingness to enforce that law on the part of the law enforcement agencies' (*per* Lord Hope in *Horvath*), this would be sufficient to remove the reality of risk.[167] '[T]hat the system might break down because of incompetence or venality of individual officers' was generally not to be regarded as establishing unwillingness or inability to provide protection.[168] What is more, the Tribunal failed to mention the continued applicability of *Sivakumaran* on the correct standard of proof in asylum cases. This was noted with disapproval[169] in a subsequent IAT case, *Hussain Abdullah Ahmed v Secretary of State for the Home Department*, in which it was stated that:

> '[. . .] the focus of the Tribunal in *Kacaj* on the "real risk" may create a thought that the *Sivakumaran* principle itself is to be qualified. [. . .] The indication that the adjective "real" excludes a "mere possibility" is entirely consistent with *Sivakumaran*. However, there are some aspects of the Tribunal's analysis which may cause some to overlook that the consequence of *Kacaj* is the applicability of *Sivakumaran* rather than any qualification of it. [. . .] According to [*Sivakumaran*] the risk to be established is entirely dictated by the degree of likelihood required to establish it. And it may be that "serious possibility" is a more direct way of putting it than other variations.'[170]

---

[163] *ibid.*
[164] *ibid.*
[165] [2002] EWCA Civ 314.
[166] Refugee Legal Centre, *Legal Bulletin No.97*, p. 4.
[167] [2001] INLR 354, para. 21.
[168] *ibid.*
[169] The IAT must follow an earlier starred decision 'unless it is satisfied that the decision is clearly wrong': *Sepet & Bulbul v Secretary of Sate for the Home Department* [2001] INLR 376, para. 99.
[170] CC-11473–01, March 25, 2002, paras 35–37.

8.25   However, *Kacaj* has been approved by the Administrative Court in
R. (Dhima) v IAT.[171] In assessing the applicability of the *Horvath* test to
ECHR claims, Auld L.J. referred to the human rights test arising from
Soering v UK, which is consistently applied by the ECtHR:

> 'Are there substantial grounds for believing that the person's expulsion
> will expose him to a real risk of suffering torture and/or inhuman or
> degrading treatment?'

He went on to add: 'The words "real risk" in that formulation
mean much the same as the term "real and substantial risk" in the
asylum test, but here the test is not expressly qualified, as in the latter,
by any consideration of State protection.'[172] The IAT in *Kacaj* had
been right to equate the *Horvath* test with that applicable to human
rights claims, and the sufficiency of protection test was therefore just
as relevant to the 1951 Convention in respect of non-state agents as
it was to Art. 3.[173]

In December 2002, in a conjoined case, *R (Ullah) v A Special Adjudicator; Do v Secretary of State for the Home Department*, the Court of Appeal
handed down yet another noteworthy decision.[174] While addressing
the particular facts of each case, the Court sought to answer a broad
question: 'To what extent does the HRA 1998 inhibit the UK from
expelling asylum-seekers who fall short of demonstrating a well-
founded fear of persecution?'[175] This entailed a discussion of ECHR
jurisprudence, in particular *Soering v UK* and *Chahal v UK*.[176] *Soering*
had suggested that the offer of a safe haven to a fugitive could undermine the foundation of extradition, and was therefore a factor to be
taken into account in interpreting the notion of inhuman and
degrading treatment or punishment in extradition cases.[177] *Chahal*, in
contrast, claimed that *Soering* should not be read as giving 'any room
for balancing the risk of ill-treatment against the reasons for expulsion in determining whether a State's responsibility under Article 3 is
engaged'.[178] The Court in *Ullah and Do* found it hard to reconcile
these different views of the ECtHR.[179] It was clear, however, that 'the
underlying rationale for the application of the European Convention
to the act of expulsion is that it is an affront to fundamental human-

---

[171] [2002] INLR 243.
[172] [2002] INLR 243, para. 21.
[173] *ibid.*, para. 36.
[174] [2003] INLR 74.
[175] *ibid.*, para. 1.
[176] (1989) 11 EHRR 439; (1997) 23 EHRR 413; see, also, Ch. 4.
[177] para. 89.
[178] (1997) 23 EHRR 413, para. 81.
[179] [2003] INLR 74, para. 38.

itarian principles to remove an individual to a country where there is a real risk of serious ill-treatment, even though such ill-treatment may not satisfy the criteria of persecution under the Refugee Convention'.[180] Admittedly, the application of Art. 3 in expulsion cases was an extension of the principle of territoriality expressed in Art. 1 (Contracting States are required to secure ECHR rights and freedoms for everyone 'within their jurisdiction'), but this was acceptable because the ECHR was a 'living instrument'.[181] However, the Court drew a line with Art. 3; the extension did not apply to Art. 9 (freedom of thought, conscience and religion), with which the case was concerned, or to any other ECHR Article, where interference with the right fell short of ill-treatment under Art. 3.[182] In the Court's view, Art. 8 had only been successfully invoked where removal or refusal of entry had impacted on the enjoyment of family life of those already *within* the jurisdiction.[183] Consideration given by the ECtHR to Art. 8 as a bar to removal in *Bensaid v UK* was dismissed as an exception.[184] One explanation given for this restrictive approach, at least as far as Art. 9 was concerned, was that an extension of the extra-territorial application of the ECHR 'would open the door to claims to enter this country by a potentially very large new category of asylum-seeker.'[185] This was not a step to be taken by the Court, but was an issue to be determined by the executive or Parliament.[186]

There is no doubt that the usefulness of the ECHR for failed asylum seekers has been severely limited by this decision. Unless treatment in the country of return is sufficiently severe to engage Art. 3, it appears that the courts will not recognise that any other Article of the ECHR is engaged.[187]

Safe third countries

For many years, members of the judiciary challenged the Home Office's application of the third country principle and refused to accept that certain EU Member States were 'safe', ultimately prompting a change in legislation (see *Lul Adan* above). More recently, however, the higher courts have been reluctant to interfere with the will of Parliament, as expressed by statute, and have accepted that the Home

8.26

---

[180] *ibid.*, para. 39.
[181] *ibid.*, para. 47.
[182] *ibid.*, paras 63 and 64.
[183] *ibid.*, para. 47.
[184] *ibid.*, paras 45–47. See Ch. 4 for discussion of the case.
[185] *ibid.*, para. 62.
[186] *ibid.*
[187] *ibid.*

Secretary's current certification powers are, in certain circumstances, unchallengeable. A recent House of Lords case, *R. (Yogathas and Thangarasa) v Secretary of State for the Home Department*, was eagerly awaited by practitioners, who hoped that it would help clarify some issues relating to third country cases.[188]

The two appellants, both Sri Lankan Tamils, arrived in the UK from Germany and claimed asylum on the grounds that they feared persecution by non-state agents in Sri Lanka. Yogathas was refused asylum in Germany, while Thangarasa had been granted asylum there, but, in 1999, was informed that it was safe to return to Sri Lanka. Yogathas' case was certified by the Secretary of State under s. 2(2)(c) to the Asylum and Immigration Act 1996, and Thangarasa's removal was ordered under s. 11(2) to the Immigration and Asylum Act 1999, in accordance with the 'standing arrangements' between Member States. Thangarasa claimed a right of appeal on human rights grounds under s. 65 of the 1999 Act, but the Secretary of State certified this claim as 'manifestly unfounded' under s. 72(2)(a). By way of judicial review, Yogathas challenged the safety of Germany in view of its approach to non-state agents under the 'accountability theory', while Thangarasa challenged the Secretary of State's certification of his case as manifestly unfounded on the same basis.

The House of Lords dismissed the appeals. There was a reminder that the Secretary of State must give adequate consideration to an applicant's claim that his human rights had been breached, and that any certification that the claim is manifestly unfounded was subject to rigorous examination – or 'the most anxious scrutiny' – by the High Court.[189] Nonetheless, the Court held that the Home Secretary had discharged his duty concerning both appellants. Though Germany applied the 'accountability theory' to persecution by non-state actors, he was right to conclude that there was no real risk that the German authorities would send the appellant back to Sri Lanka in breach of the 1951 Convention. Not only had the Home Secretary considered the case of *TI v United Kingdom* in arriving at this conclusion,[190] he had also based his decision on inquiries into the actual practice adopted by Germany in relation to removals.[191] The information before him confirmed that the German authorities automatically considered whether internal relocation was a viable alternative, and therefore, 'as a matter of practical reality', they would not return the appellants in breach of the 1951 Convention.[192] Furthermore, there was no case in

---

[188] [2002] INLR 620.
[189] [2002] INLR 620, para. 74.
[190] [2000] INLR 21, and see Ch. 4.
[191] [2002] INLR 620, paras 47 and 48.
[192] *ibid.*, para. 47.

which the ECtHR had found Germany to be in violation of Art. 3 in respect of the deportation of a rejected asylum seeker, and this satisfied the Court that Art. 3 rights were not at risk of being violated on return to Germany.[193] This judgement departs quite markedly from that of *Lul Adan*, which did not find the German 'accountability theory' to be acceptable. However, according to Lord Hutton, the House of Lords in *Lul Adan* had not considered the question of protection under German domestic law, 'which would, in its practical operation, provide the same safeguards as those provided by the Convention'.[194] *Yogathas and Thangarasa* has effectively quelled any remaining doubts about the safety of Germany for the return of asylum seekers.

Internal flight/relocation alternative

The appellants in *Yogathas and Thangarasa* also failed to persuade the Court that a stricter test applied by Germany to the issue of internal relocation should have a bearing on the decision. In the case, Lord Scott stated: **8.27**

> 'The question whether an asylum applicant is excluded from refugee status because of his unwillingness to avail himself of the protection of his country by relocating in some other part of that country is not a question of interpretation of the European Convention. It requires a judgement as to the reasonableness in all the circumstances of the unwillingness. In different countries, all being signatories to the Convention, different weight may be attached to different elements of the social and economic circumstances pertaining in the area of relocation. The fact that country A applies a stricter test than country B does not mean that one country is acting otherwise than in compliance with the Convention. [. . .] A country's approach to internal relocation may be more liberal than is strictly required for compliance with the Convention. It is arguable that the UK approach is of that character.'[195]

This is quite unsatisfactory. There has been an attempt over the years to develop some consistency between countries on the determination of refugee status, including internal relocation;[196] this decision

---

[193] *ibid.*, para. 56.
[194] *ibid.*, para. 66.
[195] *ibid.*, para. 115.
[196] See, for example, J. Hathaway, 'International refugee law: the Michigan guidelines on the internal protection alternative' (1999) 21 *Mich. J. Int'l L.*, p. 131–140. See, also, UNHCR, *Guidelines on International Protection: 'Internal Flight or Relocation Alternative' within the Context of Article 1A(2) of the 1951 Convention and/or 1967 Protocol relating to the Status of Refugees*, July 23, 2003.

clearly does not assist that objective, and raises the question whether the internal relocation alternative should be abandoned.

In July 2003, the Court of Appeal had an opportunity to resolve any residual uncertainty about internal relocation. *AE & FE v Secretary of State for the Home Department* effectively ended the use of internal relocation as far as the 1951 Convention was concerned.[197] Tracing the history of the principle through case-law, academic commentary and UNHCR contributions, the Court arrived at a definitive statement on its interpretation. The 'unduly harsh' test suggested in *Robinson* was summarised as:

'the means of determining whether an asylum seeker is "unable to avail himself of" the country of his nationality. The protection in question is not simply protection against persecution. It is a level of protection that secures, for the person relocating, those benefits which Member States have agreed to secure for refugees under Articles 2 to 30 of the Refugee Convention.'[198]

There was, stated Lord Phillips MR, confusion in UK case-law as to the test to be applied.[199] He found difficult in identifying the extent to which earlier decisions constituted rulings on the refugee status of asylum seekers as opposed to 'the applications of wider humanitarian considerations'.[200] Hathaway was wrong to argue that 'In situations where, for example, financial, logistical, or other barriers prevent the claimant from reaching internal safety; where the quality of internal protection fails to meet basic norms of civil, political, and socio-economic human rights; or where internal safety is otherwise illusory or unpredictable, state accountability for the harm is established and refugee status is appropriately recognized.'[201] Rather, in the Court's view, 'The failure to provide (as opposed to a discriminatory denial of) the "basic norms of civil, political, and socio-economic human rights" does not constitute persecution under the Refugee Convention.'[202] If a state chooses not to return an asylum seeker to a country where these rights are not enjoyed, it does so on the basis of 'humanity', or, if it be the case, the obligations of the ECHR, but not the obligations of the 1951 Convention.[203]

8.28   Referring to *Yogathas and Thangarasa*, Lord Phillips admitted that it was 'not easy to reconcile Lord Scott's observations [cited above] with

---

[197] [2003] EWCA Civ 1032.
[198] *ibid.*, para. 16.
[199] *ibid.*, para. 25.
[200] *ibid.*, para. 28.
[201] *ibid.*
[202] *ibid.*, para. 38.
[203] *ibid.*

the proposition that the test of internal location is one that goes to refugee status under the Convention', but he believed that Lord Scott's analysis of the position *in practice* was correct.[204] However, the Court was not happy with the extension of the 'unduly harsh' test to include factors beyond those relevant to refugee status.[205] Citing the decision of the IAT in *AE & FE*, apparently with approval, the Court seemed to suggest that, for internal relocation to be regarded as unduly harsh, any breach of fundamental rights must be serious.[206] If this threshold is not met, a claimant might be permitted to remain in the UK on human rights grounds, or for humanitarian reasons, but not on the basis of the 1951 Convention.[207]

In effect, the Court of Appeal applied the same test to internal relocation as required for refugee status determination, and has thereby created an obstacle for asylum seekers that many will find impossible to surmount. They will be forced, as a result, to employ the internal relocation argument in human rights claims, if at all, placing a heavy onus on the ECHR. More worryingly, the Court's whole approach to the 1951 Convention was very narrow. It seemed unduly concerned with the original drafters' intentions behind Art. 1A(2) of the Convention, rather than recognising that it is a 'living instrument' which should be interpreted in the light of current conditions. Its notion that the level of protection to be afforded people relocating is that provided by Arts 2–30 of the Convention is not reflected in the latest UNHCR guidelines on the issue.[208] Though these appeared a week after delivery of the judgement, it is very unlikely that they would have influenced it. The attack on the opinions of Hathaway (and of Goodwin-Gill) was surprising, but it was also, arguably, not well made. The focus by the Court on *discriminatory* denial of basic human rights failed to distinguish between the different levels of rights as identified by Hathaway.[209] To argue that '[t]he failure to provide [. . .] "the basic norms of civil, political, and socio-economic human rights' does not constitute persecution under the Refugee Convention' fails to take account of Hathaway's persuasive proposition that breach of any first level right amounts to persecution.[210]

---

[204] *ibid.*, para. 64.

[205] *ibid.*

[206] *ibid.*, para. 65.

[207] *ibid.*, para. 67.

[208] UNHCR, *Guidelines on International Protection: 'Internal Flight or Relocation Alternative' within the Context of Article 1A(2) of the 1951 Convention and/or 1967 Protocol relating to the Status of Refugees,* July 23, 2003.

[209] See fn. 44.

[210] J. Hathaway, *The Law of Refugee Status* (Canada: Butterworths, 1991), p. 112.

ns J., in the case of *R. v Secretary of State for the Home parte Saadi et al*, produced a strikingly anti-detention above),[211] the Court of Appeal and House of Lords we...... ain, to prove themselves more conservative. In a unanimous reversal of the High Court judgement, the Court of Appeal considered that it was impossible to condemn as irrational the policy of subjecting to a short period of detention asylum seekers whose applications appeared susceptible to rapid conclusion. Detention in the circumstances of the case was a 'measure of last resort' and, consequently, interference with any Art. 5 rights was not disproportionate or unlawful. The claimants argued before the House of Lords that the exceptions to the right to liberty in Art. 5 of the ECHR should be construed narrowly. In addition, though para. (1)(f) did not use the word 'necessary', detention had to be necessary to achieve the objective.[212] Recalling Collins' J. words, counsel for the applicants suggested that once a proper application for asylum was lodged, and there was no risk that an asylum seeker would abscond or misbehave, it was impossible to see how detention was necessary to prevent the asylum seeker effecting an unauthorised entry (one of the limbs of Art. 5(1)(f)). Lord Slynn disagreed. In his view, until the state had authorised entry, the entry was unauthorised. Consequently, the state had power to detain without violating Art. 5 until the application had been considered and the entry authorised.[213] Furthermore, detention to determine whether an asylum claimant should be granted asylum was permitted by Art. 5(1)(f), and there was no requirement to show that detention was *necessary* for that purpose.[214] This limited justification was as much as the Court was prepared to offer on the issue of unauthorised entry. Thus, the action taken against Dr Saadi was deemed 'to prevent [a person] effecting an unauthorised entry into the country' within the meaning of Art. 5(1)(f), was perfectly legal, and, what is more, was also proportionate.[215] In a concluding statement, resonant with political overtones, Lord Slynn stated:

> 'It is regrettable that anyone should be deprived of his liberty other than pursuant to the order of a court but there are situations where such a course is justified. In a situation like the present with huge numbers and difficult decisions involved, with the risk of long delays to applicants seek-

---

[211] [2001] EWHC Admin 470.
[212] [2002] INLR 523, para. 28.
[213] *ibid.*, para. 35.
[214] *ibid.*, para. 36.
[215] *ibid.*, paras 43 and 47.

ing to come, a balancing exercise has to be performed. Getting a speedy decision is in the interests not only of the applicants but of those increasingly in the queue. Accepting as I do that the arrangements made at Oakington provide reasonable conditions, both for individuals and families and that the period taken is not in any sense excessive, I consider that the balance is in favour of recognising that detention under the Oakington procedure is proportionate and reasonable. Far from being arbitrary, it seems to me that the Secretary of State has done all that he could be expected to do to palliate the deprivation of liberty of the many applicants for asylum here.'[216]

This decision was to be expected in light of the ECtHR's long history of granting a wide margin of appreciation to contracting states in the fields of immigration and asylum. The Court has not been inclined, in general, to hinder the effective implementation of immigration and asylum policies through a rigid application of the right to liberty contained in Art. 5.

Carriers' liability, visas and pre-entry clearance

Legislation sanctioning carriers who transport undocumented or clandestine passengers has been a growing feature of UK asylum law since the introduction of the Immigration (Carriers' Liability) Act 1987. It is therefore to be expected that it is now a subject for examination by the courts. An instructive jurisprudence has emerged. Though they recognise that carriers' sanctions may prevent asylum seekers from travelling to the UK, the courts accept that the legislation is an expression of Parliamentary will. Thus in an early decision on carriers' liability, *R. v Secretary of State for the Home Department, ex parte Yassine & Others*,[217] the judge did not think it was appropriate to express any views on the applicants' submission that carriers' liability legislation was in breach of the UK's international obligations.[218] Instead, he proceeded to consider the validity of directions to remove the applicants to Brazil, a country for which they possessed visitor visas, but to which they had no intention of travelling, having claimed asylum while transiting through the UK.

A more illuminating case on carriers' liability legislation is that of *R. v Secretary of State for the Home Department, ex parte Hoverspeed*.[219] Here the applicant challenged the 1987 Act by way of judicial review, raising a number of technical arguments on EC law. In the course of the

8.30

---

[216] *ibid.*, para. 47.
[217] [1990] Imm AR 354.
[218] *ibid.*, at 359.
[219] [1999] INLR 591.

judgement, Simon Brown L.J. commented on the implications for asylum seekers of the Act. Referring to *ex parte Yassine*, and its recognition that 'even genuine asylum-seekers may need to resort to false documents to reach this country so as to make their claim for refugee status',[220] he went on to add that the Home Secretary was not under the least obligation to facilitate their arrival in the first place. In fact, since there were no means by which the carrier could distinguish the 'genuine' from the 'bogus' asylum seeker, the 1987 Act was designed to impede their arrival.[221] The Act was not in breach of international law. The judge simply noted that there was an undoubted tension between the UK's obligation to asylum-seekers under the 1951 Convention on the one hand, and its entitlement to impede their arrival on the other.[222]

In the more recent case of *European Roma Rights Centre & Others v The Immigration Officer at Prague Airport; Secretary of State for the Home Department* (*'ERRC'*), the Court of Appeal endorsed the restrictive approach of *Hoverspeed*.[223] The case concerned the adoption of a pre-entry clearance scheme introduced at Prague Airport in July 2001. British immigration officers based at the airport refused the appellants, all Roma, permission to travel to the UK. Five of the six were intending to apply for asylum and consequently were unable to do so due to their inability to reach the UK. Much of the legal argument before the Court revolved around the UK's obligations under Arts 31 and 33 of the 1951 Convention, and whether there was an obligation not to impede someone from reaching another country in order to apply for asylum. Simon Brown L.J. was not persuaded by either Counsel for the applicants or for the intervener (the UNHCR) that a state could not impede the flow of asylum seekers to its shores.[224] Consequently, he held, again, that the Home Secretary was under no obligation to assist the arrival of asylum seekers and that he was entitled to take steps to prevent their arrival, notwithstanding the obvious implications for the effectiveness of the 1951 Convention.[225] The judge added that he considered the pre-entry scheme to be less iniquitous than visa controls.[226]

On a second but vitally important question, the justiciability of the Convention, the case provides clear evidence of a retrenchment by the judiciary. In an earlier case, *R. v Secretary of State for the Home Depart-*

---

[220] [1999] INLR 591, at 599E.
[221] *ibid.*, at 599F.
[222] *ibid.*, at 600A.
[223] [2003] EWCA Civ 666.
[224] *ibid.*, para. 47.
[225] *ibid.*, para. 43.
[226] *ibid.*, para. 49.

ment, ex parte Ahmed & Patel, Lord Woolf, in the Court of Appeal, suggested, *obiter*, that entry into a treaty by the UK could give rise to a legitimate expectation that the Secretary of State would comply with the obligations under the treaty, on which the public in general was entitled to rely.[227] In *Adimi* (see above), Simon Brown L.J. referred to Lord Woolf's comments and accepted the argument that refugees had become entitled to the benefit of Art. 31 in accordance with the developing doctrine of legitimate expectations.[228] However, in the present Roma case, he decided to reverse his opinion, as given in *Adimi*, stating:

> '[. . .] I now recognise that the views I expressed in the Divisional Court in *Adimi* [. . .] are to be regarded as at best superficial, and that the conclusion I reached there, with regard to the legitimate expectations of asylum seekers to the benefits of article 31, is suspect.'[229]

Laws L.J. went further, arguing that 'The proposition that the act of ratifying a treaty could *without more* give rise to enforceable legitimate expectations seems to me to amount, pragmatically, to a means of incorporating the substance of obligations undertaken on the international plane into our domestic law without the authority of Parliament.'[230] It is unlikely that the House of Lords will disagree. Any hope, then, that an expanded concept of legitimate expectations might pave the way for greater protection of asylum seekers and refugees must surely be dashed.

National security

Chapters 4 and 5 briefly discussed the influential ECtHR case, *Chahal v United Kingdom*,[231] which dealt with the issue of national security. They also referred to the statute that arose from the judgement – the Special Immigration Appeals Commission Act 1997. It will be recalled that exclusion on national security or political grounds is explicitly covered under the Act. In an important non-asylum decision in May 2000, *Secretary of State for the Home Department v Shafiq Ur Rehman*, the Court of Appeal considered the approach of the Special Immigration Appeals Commission to an appeal by Rehman against the Secretary of State's decision ordering deportation conducive to

8.31

---

[227] [1998] INLR 570, at 583G.
[228] [1999] INLR 490, at 505B.
[229] [2003] EWCA Civ 666, para. 51.
[230] *ibid.*, para. 101.
[231] (1997) 23 EHRR 413.

the public good for reasons of national security.[232] SIAC formed the view that a person could only offend against national security if he or she engaged in, promoted or encouraged violent activity targeted at the UK, its system of government, or its people. This included activities that were directed from the UK and were intended to over-throw or destabilise a foreign government, if that government was likely to take reprisals for these activities against the UK, thereby affecting the security of the UK or of its nationals.[233] Actions against the interests of a foreign state might not be sufficient.

The Court of Appeal held that members of SIAC were right to assume that it was their responsibility to determine questions of fact and law.[234] This was the inevitable conclusion to be drawn from the power given to SIAC by Parliament to review the Secretary of State's exercise of discretion.[235] However, it had been inappropriate for SIAC to apply a standard of proof of 'high civil balance of proba-bilities' to issues of fact. On appeal, the House of Lords upheld the Court of Appeal's judgement on the requisite standard of proof, adding that:

'The Secretary of State, in deciding whether it is conducive to the public good that a person should be deported, is entitled to have regard to all the information in his possession about the actual and potential activities and the connections of the person concerned. He is entitled to have regard to the precautionary and preventative principles rather than to wait until directly harmful activities have taken place, the individual in the meantime remaining in this country. In doing so he is not merely finding facts but forming an executive judgement or assessment. There must be material on which proportionately and reasonably he can conclude that there is a real possibility of activities harmful to national security but he does not have to be satisfied, nor on appeal to show, that all the material before him is proved, and his conclusion is justified, to a "high civil degree of probabil-ity". Establishing a degree of probability does not seem relevant to the reaching of a conclusion on whether there should be a deportation for the public good.'[236]

Lord Slynn could not concur with SIAC's examples of the type of action that justified deportation on grounds of national security. In his view, in contemporary world conditions, action against a foreign state may be capable indirectly of affecting the security of the UK.

---

[232] [2000] INLR 531.
[233] See House of Lords judgement, [2002] INLR 92, para. 15.
[234] [2000] IANL 531, para. 42.
[235] *ibid.*
[236] *Secretary of State for the Home Department v Rehman* [2002] INLR 92, para. 22 (Lord Slynn).

Thus, to require the action of Rehman to be capable of resulting *directly* in a threat to national security, as SIAC had suggested, 'limits too tightly the discretion of the executive in deciding how the interests of the State, including not merely military defence but democracy, the legal and constitutional systems of the State need to be protected'.[237] Lord Slynn accepted that there must be a real possibility of an adverse effect on the UK from an individual's actions, but did not accept that it had to be direct or immediate. It was for the Secretary of State to weigh up the possibility of an adverse effect on the UK against the possible injustice to an individual arising from deportation.[238]

Lord Hoffman agreed that, although SIAC had been correct in deciding that, under the 1997 Act, it had full jurisdiction to decide questions of fact and law, it had not made 'sufficient allowance for certain inherent limitations, first, in the powers of the judicial branch of government and secondly, within the judicial function, in the appellate process.'[239] He added that SIAC was 'exercising a judicial function and the exercise of that function must recognise the constitutional boundaries between judicial, executive and legislative power. [. . .] [I]n matters of judgment and evaluation of evidence, [there was a need] to show proper deference to the primary decision maker.'[240] What is meant by 'national security' is a question of construction and therefore a question of law within the jurisdiction of SIAC, subject to appeal.[241] On the other hand, the question of whether something is 'in the interests' of national security is not a question of law. It is a matter of judgment and policy, and consequently not a matter for judicial decision but entrusted to the executive alone.[242]

8.32

This is a fascinating decision. The deference shown by the judiciary to the decision-making arm of the executive is reminiscent of decisions such as *ex parte Duke of Château Thierry* in the early part of the twentieth century, and might, for some, ring alarm bells. The reasons for the strong judicial reiteration of the concept of separation of powers are not hard to fathom. The fact that the judgement was delivered in the wake of the terrorist activities of September 11, 2001 is of itself sufficient explanation. Lord Steyn, for example, points out that, while he arrived at his conclusion, which basically concurred with that of Lord Woolf in the Court of Appeal, by the end of the hearing of the appeal, 'the tragic events of September 11, 2001 in

---

[237] *ibid.*, para. 16.
[238] *ibid.*
[239] *ibid.*, para. 49.
[240] *ibid.*
[241] *ibid.*, para. 50.
[242] *ibid.*

New York reinforce compellingly that no other approach is possible'.[243] For his part, Lord Hoffman adds a postscript that he wrote his judgement some three months before the events in New York and Washington, but that they were a reminder that in matters of national security, 'the cost of failure can be high'.[244] The justification for bowing so completely to ministerial discretion is the subject-matter under consideration: national security and protection of the UK. However, it is vital that the executive remembers the context of this decision and does not read it as a licence to deport.

8.33   In October 2002, in *A & Others v Secretary of State for the Home Department*, the Court of Appeal delivered another judgement in relation to national security, this time with reference to the Anti-terrorism, Crime and Security Act 2001.[245] The facts of the case were as follows: after the 2001 Act had been passed, eleven people were detained under s. 21. Nine went on to appeal to the Special Immigration Appeals Commission on the ground that the 2001 Act and associated Order[246] were discriminatory because they allowed only suspected terrorists who were non-nationals to be detained, when there were equally dangerous British nationals who were not liable to detention. The appellants also argued that the derogation from Art. 5(1) of the ECHR on the grounds of 'public emergency', which the Secretary of State had been forced to issue in order to detain in the first place, was unlawful. It did not, in their view, meet the derogation requirements of Art. 15(1) of the Convention, as the government had failed to establish that there was a 'public emergency', and, even if there were such an emergency, the 2001 Act was disproportionate.[247] It is worth noting that, post September 11, 2001, the UK was the only European country to declare that it was in a state of emergency 'threatening the life of the nation' within the meaning of Art. 15(1). SIAC held that there was a 'state of emergency'. However, it did find that, as the Act and Order only sanctioned the detention of suspected terrorists who were foreign nationals, they were discriminatory and therefore breached Art. 14. The Secretary of State appealed.

The Court of Appeal agreed with SIAC that there was a public emergency threatening the life of the nation, that the measures taken by the UK were strictly those required by the exigencies of the

---

[243] [2002] INLR 92, para. 29.

[244] *ibid.*, para. 62.

[245] [2003] 1 All ER 816.

[246] The Human Rights Act 1998 (Designated Derogation) Order 2001, SI 2001/3644.

[247] Art. 15(1): 'In time of war or other public emergency threatening the life of the nation any High Contracting Party may take measures derogating from its obligations under this Convention to the extent strictly required by the exigencies of the situation, provided that such measures are not inconsistent with its other obligations under international law.'

situation, and that SIAC had not misunderstood its function nor misdirected itself. However, on the issue of whether the measures taken were consistent with this country's other obligations under international law, the court held that SIAC's conclusions on discrimination were wrong. There were, claimed Lord Justice Brooke, good objective reasons entitling the Home Secretary to make a distinction between nationals and non-nationals. In addition, 'both customary international law and the international treaties by which [the UK] was bound gave [it] the right, in time of war or comparable public emergency, to detain non-nationals on national security grounds without necessarily being obliged to detain its own nationals, too.'[248] Lord Woolf put it thus:

'[. . .] I have come to the conclusion that there are objectively justifiable and relevant grounds which do not involve impermissible discrimination. The grounds are the fact that the aliens who cannot be deported have, unlike nationals, no more right to remain, only a right not to be removed, which means legally that they come into a different class from those who have a right of abode.

The class of aliens is in a different situation because when they can be deported to a country that will not torture them this can happen. It is only the need to protect them from torture that means that for the time being they cannot be removed.

In these circumstances it would be surprising indeed if Article 14, or any international requirement not to discriminate, prevented the Secretary of State taking the restricted action which he thought was necessary.'[249]

8.34 The government is entitled therefore to treat nationals and non-nationals differently. Nationals, who have a right of abode, cannot be detained indefinitely without charge and cannot be deported, whereas non-nationals can be detained pending deportation, and can, of course, be deported, if there are no Art. 3 (ECHR) implications. The only caveat is that deportation should take place within a reasonable time. In light of the judgement, it is now clear that non-nationals who cannot be deported because of a threat to their safety can be detained indefinitely where they have been defined as 'suspected international terrorists' within the meaning of the 2001 Act.

The reaction of the pressure group Liberty, which had acted for the respondents in the appeal, was one of 'embarrassment' and outrage at the court's suggestion that a foreign national could be interned

---

[248] [2003] 1 All ER 816, para. 132.
[249] *ibid.*, paras 47–49.

indefinitely.[250] Intriguingly, only ten days prior to the decision, Lord Woolf, speaking at the British Academy in London, had declared that, under the 'pressures created by the need to protect this country from merciless acts of international terrorists', it was almost 'inevitable that, from time to time, [. . .] Parliament or the government will not strike the correct balance between the rights of society as a whole and the rights of the individual'.[251] It was for the courts, through the vehicle of the Human Rights Act 1998, to act as a longstop, but, noted the Lord Chief Justice:

'Sometimes the judicial role will be unwelcome. If initiatives which are thought to be in the interest of the public are interfered with by the judiciary because of their adverse effect on the human rights of a minority, the judiciary will not be popular. But the temporary unpopularity of the judiciary is a price well worth paying if it ensures that this country remains a democracy committed to the rule of law. A democracy which is therefore well worth defending.'[252]

Everything in this speech pointed towards the Court of Appeal in *A & Others* upholding the decision of SIAC. So convinced was *The Guardian* that, in its leader of October 17, 2002, a week prior to the judgement, it called on its readers to 'stand by for another anti-judge blast by David Blunkett if the appeal, as expected, is rejected by the court of appeal'.[253] How wrong it proved to be.

CONCLUSION

8.35 There is clear evidence that an expansive approach has been adopted in some asylum decisions, and the implementation of the Human Rights Act 1998 has certainly played its part in affording asylum seekers greater protection, particularly in relation to Art. 3 of the ECHR. It cannot yet be said, however, that asylum law has broken free of its traditional predisposition towards judicial deference. World events since September 2001 have resulted in an understandable hardening of attitude where national security is at stake. Furthermore, on many general aspects of refugee law, the current Court of Appeal and

---

[250] 'Judges back anti-terror law', October 25, 2002: *http://news.bbc.co.uk/1/hi/uk/2360319.stm*

[251] See, for a copy of the speech, Lord Woolf, 'Human Rights : Have the Public Benefited?', p. 10, available on *www.britac.ac.uk/pubs/src/_pdf/woolf.pdf*

[252] *ibid.*, pp. 10–11.

[253] 'Excellent judgment – Lord Woolf stands up for human rights', *The Guardian*, October 17, 2002.

House of Lords are handing down decisions which some regard as unnecessarily stringent, *AE & FE* being a recent example.

In witnessing the shifts between generosity and restraint, it is tempting to conclude that the so-called progressive judgements have time and again involved the same individuals (notably, Lord Justices Sedley and Simon Brown and Justice Collins). Any such comparison of members of the judiciary is, of course, an inexact science (Simon Brown's judgement in *ERRC* clearly bucked the trend, as did the decisions of Collins J. in *Kacaj* and *AE & FE*). There are also obvious dangers in adopting this individualistic view of judicial decision-making. The last Lord Chancellor, Lord Irvine, warned that, in relation to the judiciary's constitutional duty to interpret human rights texts, the 'perception of the courts' role should emphatically not be determined by the attitudes of individual judges'.[254] This may be a tall order in such a politically sensitive area as asylum. Until we can draw conclusions on the basis of a fuller corpus of judgements, the contention must be that the 'ebb and flow' of judicial decision-making, far from aiding greater consistency in asylum law, has added to the law's considerable uncertainty.

---

[254] Lord Irvine of Lairg, 'Activism and Restraint: Human Rights and the Interpretative Process' (1999) 4 *EHRLR*, p. 355.

Chapter Nine

European Union Policy on Asylum Seekers: Reasonable or Reactionary?

INTRODUCTION

Since the early 1980s, European Union ('EU')[1] Member States have **9.1** attempted to develop a workable policy on asylum, but progress has been slow. Initially, Member States refrained from introducing binding EC law on asylum, but this changed in the late 1980s with the prioritisation of asylum in the EU's work programme. Though there remains a lack of consensus on some fundamentals, a number of asylum-specific instruments have finally now been agreed. The importance of EC policy in this area should not be underestimated. Its tendency to focus on process rather than protection has heavily influenced municipal law.[2] Where national laws have been amended to adopt restrictive provisions on asylum seekers and migrants, these have often been based on formulae established at the European level. Thus, for example, in the UK, the concepts of 'without foundation' or 'manifestly unfounded' cases clearly owe their existence to intergovernmental discussions between European ministers. The same is true of 'safe third countries' and the use of 'white lists', which featured prominently in UK asylum legislation of the 1990s and in the Nationality, Immigration and Asylum Act 2002.[3] It can therefore be

---

[1] The distinction between EU and EC is as follows: technically, EU should only be used when describing the union of Member States; the term 'EU' should not be used when discussing points of law under the EC Treaty. Some commentators use EC when discussing 'First Pillar', and EU when discussing the 'Third Pillar', to draw a distinction between Community and intergovernmental decision-making.

[2] See, *e.g.*, Resolution 'on manifestly unfounded applications', Ad Hoc Immigration Group, SN 4822/1/92 WGI 1282 of December 2, 1992; Resolution 'on a harmonised approach to questions concerning host third countries', Ad Hoc Immigration Group, SN 4823/92 WGI 1283 of November 19, 1992; Conclusion 'on countries in which there is generally no serious risk of persecution', Ad Hoc Immigration Group, SN 4821/92 WGI 1281 of December 1, 1992.

[3] See Resolution and Conclusion cited above, Asylum and Immigration Act 1996, ss. 1–3, and Nationality, Immigration and Asylum Act 2002, s. 94.

argued that, in contrast to the role played in the realm of human rights, Europe has been the instigator of deterrence rather than a force staying the UK's more restrictive tendencies.

Adopting a chronological approach, the present chapter will trace how Member States have dealt collectively with changing patterns of migration to the EU, from the 1980s to the present. It will focus on the gradual harmonisation of EC asylum law and policy – that is, the progressive introduction of asylum norms and standards in all Member States. Beginning with a brief overview of the reasons to harmonise, the chapter will examine different methods of co-operation, from intergovernmentalism to binding legislation. The major changes implemented by the Treaties of Maastricht and Amsterdam, and by the Tampere European Council, will be considered in some detail. Finally, the chapter will offer an assessment of human rights in the EU context and highlight recent proposals on the future direction of EC asylum law.

THE ROUTE TO 'HARMONISATION'

Why harmonise?

9.2   It is generally agreed that the late 1970s and early 1980s witnessed a change in patterns of migration to western Europe, though the explanations for this are varied. The combination of a Europe-wide recession in the 1970s, the introduction by European states of 'zero immigration' policies, the growing ease of travel and consequent emergence of the 'jet age refugee', and the break-up of the former USSR are all regarded as having played a part in the rise of asylum applications in Europe. The increase proved quite dramatic: in 1975, there were approximately 21,558 applications in nine of the main EC countries, plus Austria.[4] By 1979, this had reached 87,752,[5] and by 1980, 149,037, for the same ten countries.[6] An unprecedented high was reached in 1992, when 673,947 asylum applications were lodged in the 15 EU Member States.[7] Although it was clear by the late 1970s that the position was changing, immigration and asylum continued to

---

[4] UNHCR, *Asylum Applications in Industrialized Countries: 1980–1999* (Geneva: UNHCR, November 2001), table VI.5. The figures cover Austria, Belgium, Denmark, France, Germany, Greece, Italy, the Netherlands, Portugal, and the UK.

[5] *ibid.*

[6] *ibid.*, table I.2.

[7] *ibid.*, table V.10. The 15 member states are: Austria, Belgium, Denmark, Finland, France, Germany, Greece, Ireland, Italy, Luxembourg, the Netherlands, Portugal, Spain, Sweden and the UK.

be regarded as matters for national regulation. The move towards greater integration forced a rethink. The EC objectives of free movement of persons, economic and social development, and a single market without internal borders did not sit comfortably alongside increased immigration and asylum to the EC.

The source of difficulty was, in many senses, the Single European Act 1986 ('SEA'). By inserting Art. 8a in the Treaty establishing the EEC (the 'Treaty of Rome'), it introduced the concept of the internal market as an area 'without internal frontiers', in which the free movement of persons, *inter alia*, was guaranteed; it also provided for the adoption of measures to establish an internal market by December 31, 1992.[8] However, a market free of internal frontiers raised a key question: were some border controls still permissible to counter criminal activity, drug or human smuggling and terrorism? In addressing this, Member States soon realised that a single market without internal frontiers could only function as they intended if external borders were adequately controlled, and that the whole concept was, in effect, at the mercy of the Member State with the weakest external checks.[9]

As attention focused on the erection of a so-called *cordon sanitaire* around western Europe, and asylum became 'increasingly politicized as an alternative route for economic immigration in the EU',[10] the distinction between immigration and asylum became blurred.[11] By the early 1990s, the need for an effective collective stand on asylum was very evident. At the time, the renowned German specialist in refugee law, Hailbronner, gave an uncompromising account of the problems created by lack of co-ordination.

'(i)   [. . .] the detrimental effects of insufficiently coordinated measures to execute asylum polices are multiplied for the Community. Unlawful migration to another country and the disappearance of dismissed applicants for asylum are made easier. [. . .];

(ii)   [. . .] It is irreconcilable with the idea of a single territory, with common legal and economic conditions, if refugees are accepted or dismissed on the basis of different procedures, within the Community;

---

[8] The Single European Act 1986 inserted Art. 8a into the Treaty establishing the European Economic Community 1957; this became Art. 7a in the Treaty establishing the European Community 1992, following amendments made by the Treaty on European Union 1992; it is now Art. 14 in the Treaty establishing the European Community 2002 (consolidated version), following amendments made by the Treaties of Amsterdam 1997 and Nice 2002.

[9] D. O'Keeffe, 'The free movement of persons and the single market' (1992) 17:1 *EL Rev*, p. 8.

[10] J. Huysmans, 'The European Union and the securitization of migration' (2000) 38:5 *Journal of Common Market Studies*, p. 755.

[11] I. Boccardi, *Europe and Refugees – Towards an EU Asylum Policy* (The Hague: Kluwer Law International, 2002), p. 201.

(iii) [. . .] It is only with the harmonization of European asylum laws/pro-
       cedures that undesirable sponge effects and selfish acts without con-
       sideration to neighbouring countries can be prevented. The only
       alternative is a race amongst Western European States for the most
       rigid limitations on immigration. [. . .];

(iv)   National immigration and asylum policies are ineffective. [. . .] The
       main reason for the massive and unfounded pleading for asylum lies
       in the fact that the hope not to be sent back is rarely disappointed.
       Clear guidelines on criteria for giving shelter and the termination of
       stay are essential. [. . .]'[12]

This combination of factors forced EU Member States to explore
European solutions to the asylum issue, rather than rely on the traditional national controls.[13] Considerable faith was placed in a single
concept: harmonisation.

How to harmonise?[14]

9.3 The question of how to harmonise necessarily involves addressing the
issue of what to harmonise. There are three main areas that EU
Member States have concentrated on: designation of the state
responsible for handling an asylum application, the development of
minimum procedural standards, and, vitally, the agreed interpretation of Art. 1A(2) of the 1951 Convention. Though these may appear

---

[12] K. Hailbronner, 'Perspectives of a harmonization of the law of asylum after the
Maastricht summit' (1992) 29:5 *CML Rev*, pp. 921–2.

[13] For an early discussion of the issues, see S. Ogata *et al*, *Towards a European Immigration
Policy* (London: The Philip Morris Institute for Public Policy Research, October
1993)

[14] Much has been written on the gradual development of an EC/EU asylum policy.
See, *e.g.*, I. Boccardi, *Europe and Refugees – Towards and EU Asylum Policy* (The Hague:
Kluwer Law, 2002); E. Guild & C. Harlow eds., *Implementing Amsterdam – Immigration
and Asylum Rights in EC Law* (Oxford: Hart, 2001); K. Hailbronner, *Immigration and
Asylum Law and Policy of the European Union* (The Hague: Kluwer Law International,
1999); P. Shah & C. Doebbler eds., *UK Asylum Law in its European Context* (London:
Platinum & GEMS, 1999); V. Vevstad, *Refugee Protection – A European Challenge*
(Norway: Tano Ashehoug, 1998); C. Harvey, 'The European regulation of asylum:
constructing a model of regional solidarity? (1998) 4:4 *European Public Law*, pp.
561–592; E. Guild & J. Niessen, *The Developing Immigration and Asylum Policies of the EU*
(The Hague: Kluwer Law, 1996); R. Wallace, *Refugees and Asylum: A Community* Per-
spective (London: Butterworths, 1996); D. Joly, *Haven or Hell? Asylum Policies and
Refugees in Europe* London: Macmillan, 1996); The Standing Committee of Experts
in International Immigration, Refugee and Criminal Law, *A New Immigration Law for
Europe? The 1992 London and 1993 Copenhagen Rules on Immigration* (Netherlands:
Nederlands Centrum Buitenlanders, 1993); D. Joly, *Refugees – Asylum in Europe?*
(London: Minority Rights Publications, 1992).

uncontroversial, agreement has been far from straightforward, with a variety of methods explored to reach harmonisation.

Intergovernmentalism

The UK human rights lawyer, Blake QC, wrote recently: 'If the road to hell is paved with good intentions, then the highway to Community harmonisation is littered with the debris of intergovernmental agreements.'[15] The initial co-operation on asylum between Member States occurred entirely at an intergovernmental level. As a result, discussions remained outside the formal decision-making process of the EC, and were not subject to the usual scrutiny by European institutions. Such intergovernmental collaboration was nothing new. It started with the signing in 1967 of the Naples Convention on mutual co-operation between customs authorities.[16] Further judicial and foreign policy co-operation began in 1970, under the auspices of 'European Political Co-operation' ('EPC'), which evolved into the 'Common Foreign and Security Policy' under the SEA.[17] Also in this early period, a number of so-called *ad hoc* groups were established to work on asylum, amongst other matters. The first, and in some senses the most significant, group to emerge from EPC was the TREVI Group. Established in 1976 in Rome, it dealt originally with mechanisms to counter terrorism, but was expanded to include a number of working groups, each charged with a specific area of concern.[18] It soon became clear from TREVI discussions that a new body was called for to deal specifically with immigration, and, consequently, in 1986, an Ad Hoc Group on Immigration was created at the instigation of the UK. It, too, spawned a plethora of sub-groups. Regular

9.4

---

[15] N. Blake, 'The Dublin Convention and Rights of Asylum Seekers in the European Union' in E. Guild & C. Harlow eds., *Implementing Amsterdam – Immigration and Asylum Rights in EC Law* (Oxford: Hart, 2001), p. 95.

[16] T. Bunyan ed., *Key Texts on Justice and Home Affairs in the EU Vol. 1 (1976–1993) From Trevi to Maastricht* (London: Statewatch, 1997), p. 9.

[17] *ibid.*, p. 9; S. Peers, *EU Justice and Home Affairs Law* (London: Longman, 2000), p. 9.

[18] Working Group I dealt with terrorism and assessed threats from within and outside the Community. Working Group II was concerned with police co-operation and the exchange of information on matters such as equipment, computers, training, forensic science and public order. Working Group III was set up in 1985 to deal with serious crime including drugs trafficking. TREVI 1992 was established in April 1989 specifically to consider the 'policing and security implications of the Single European Market' and to improve co-operation to 'compensate for the consequent losses to security and law enforcement' in the Members States. Finally, two new groups also began work at this time within the TREVI framework: the Ad Hoc Group on Europol, and the Ad Hoc Group on Organised Crime: See Statewatch, 'TREVI, Europol and Immigration', January 1993.

meetings took place between immigration ministers of Member States, with the result that, by the time of the Treaty on European Union in 1992, a complex decision-making structure was in existence which seemed impossible to dismantle.

The choice of the intergovernmental mechanism to handle immigration and asylum was telling for a number of reasons. Though decisions were taken in the intergovernmental fora that were fundamental to the creation of an internal market, particularly in relation to free movement of migrants, information between 1976 and 1986 was difficult to come by. Aside from information gleaned from the occasional leaked document, the activities of the intergovernmental meetings were kept very secret. There was no accountability for the decisions taken by ministers and other officials attending the meetings; the Commission was pointedly excluded from some of the discussions, and there was certainly no scrutiny by national or European Parliaments. A democratic deficit was very much in evidence; yet it received little, if any, publicity. This despite the fact that intergovernmentalism was, in fact, 'responding to a Community imperative, that of the creation of the internal market, fixed by an instrument of Community law, Article 8a EEC'.[19] The 'dual system' that had developed, and split competence between Member States working intergovernmentally and the Community, was rightly deemed unsatisfactory by a number of academic commentators.[20]

9.5   With regard to asylum, the intergovernmental approach was particularly problematic. Almost immediately, a connection was made between asylum seeking and criminality. The focus was on control, both at internal and external borders, on establishing a common visa policy, and on ending the abuse of political asylum.[21] The shift towards 'criminalisation' of the asylum seeker was very obvious from the mid-1980s onwards. Under the framework of the Ad Hoc Group on Immigration, a system of sanctions for transport operators bringing in undocumented asylum seekers to the EC was agreed; the same group considered a framework for establishing state responsibility for an asylum request. In 1988, a Co-ordinators' Group on the free movement of persons was established, consisting of senior civil servants from the interior ministries of Member States.[22] Within

---

[19] See e.g., D. O'Keeffe, 'The free movement of persons and the single market' (1992) 17:1 EL Rev, p. 12.

[20] ibid.

[21] See, e.g., Declaration of the Belgian Presidency: Meeting of Justice and Interior Ministers of the European Community, Brussels, April 28, 1987 in T. Bunyan ed., Key Texts on Justice and Home Affairs in the EU Vol. 1 (1976–1993) From Trevi to Maastricht (London: Statewatch, 1997).

[22] S. Peers, EU Justice and Home Affairs Law (London: Longman, 2000), p. 10.

months, the Group produced an important instrument of its own: the so-called 'Palma Document'.[23] Controls on visas and asylum were amongst the many measures that the Document considered necessary. It suggested that:

'[. . .] a set of legal, administrative and technical instruments should be established, as criteria will need to be harmonised on treatment of non-Community citizens. Amongst the legal measures, attention should be given to the following:

the conditions governing entry into the Community of nationals of third countries. This point relates particularly to visa policy, especially:

- establishment of a common list of countries whose citizens are subject to visa requirement;
- establishment of a common list of persons to be refused entry;
- harmonisation of the criteria for granting visas, while allowing for the specific circumstances of certain applicants to be taken into account;
- a European visa;
- grant of asylum and refugee status; a common policy will be based on Member States' obligations pursuant to their accession to the Geneva Convention and the New York Protocol.'[24]

Member States quickly sought to formalise Palma's proposals. In 1989, two draft Conventions were drawn up by the French Presidency of the EC and submitted to the Ad Hoc Group: the first on determining responsibility for asylum applications (which became the Dublin Convention – see below),[25] and the second on crossing of external borders. Running almost in parallel with these discussions were the Schengen initiatives.

Multilateral agreements   9.6

Schengen

While Dublin and Schengen are very similar in many respects, with   9.7
provisions on determining responsibility for asylum applications, the
Schengen framework is more comprehensive. Signed in 1985 by

---

[23] 'Free Movement of persons: A Report to the European Council by the Coordinators' Group (Madrid, June 1989)' available in T. Bunyan ed., *Key Texts on Justice and Home Affairs in the EU Vol. 1 (1976–1993) From Trevi to Maastricht* (London: Statewatch, 1997).
[24] *ibid.*, p. 13.
[25] 'Convention Determining the State Responsible for Examining Applications for Asylum Lodged in One of the Member States of the European Communities, done at Dublin on June 15, 1990.'

France, Germany and the Benelux countries,[26] and implemented in June 1990 by a second Convention,[27] the Schengen *acquis*[28] called for the abolition of internal border controls by signatories. Though the main concern was with internal and external border controls, police and security, a computerised joint information system (the 'Schengen Information System' or 'SIS'), and the transport and movement of goods, a number of articles were set aside for asylum. The whole of Chapter 7 of the Convention deals with 'responsibility for the processing of applications for asylum', and is similar in content to the Dublin Convention.

Schengen proposed that rules on carriers' liability be introduced into national law,[29] and dedicated the whole of Chapter 3 (comprising 16 Articles) to visas. Signatories undertook to introduce laws that forced carriers to assume responsibility for aliens brought into a country, but who were subsequently refused entry. Parties to the Convention also undertook to impose penalties on carriers who transported aliens not in possession of the necessary travel documents by air or sea from a third state to their territories.[30] Despite real concerns amongst commentators, and in the UNHCR, about the compliance of such a policy with the 1951 Convention, the Convention seemed to imply conformity with its specific reference to meeting 'the obligations arising out of [. . .] accession to the Geneva Convention, as amended by the New York Protocol [. . .]'.[31] By the time of the Schengen Convention in 1990, the UK had already introduced national legislation on carriers' sanctions: the Immigration (Carriers' Liability) Act 1987.

Since the original signing of the Agreement in 1985, all 15 EU Member States, bar the UK and Ireland, have joined the Schengen system. The UK has continued to reserve its right to maintain border controls against those seeking entry to its territory.[32] This position has

---

[26] Italy, Spain, Portugal, Greece, Austria, Denmark, Finland and Sweden all later acceded. See, for a useful compilation of all Agreements and the Schengen *acquis*: Council of the EU, *The Schengen acquis integrated into the EU*, (Brussels, May 1999), available on: *ue.eu.int/jai/schengen/SCH.ACQUIS-EN.pdf*

[27] Both Agreements are available in T. Bunyan ed., *Key Texts on Justice and Home Affairs in the EU Vol. 1 (1976–1993) From Trevi to Maastricht* (London: Statewatch, 1997), pp. 109–134.

[28] The Schengen *acquis* refers to the Schengen Agreement 1985, the Convention applying the Schengen Agreement 1990, the Accession Protocols, and the Decisions and Declarations adopted by the Executive Committee.

[29] Art. 26.

[30] Art. 26(2).

[31] *ibid.*

[32] A useful discussion of Schengen in the UK context can be found in House of Lords Select Committee on European Communities, 'Schengen and the UK's Border Controls', Session 1998–99, March 2, 1999, HL 37.

now been formally accepted in a Protocol to the 1997 Treaty of Amsterdam.[33] There is no doubt that the Schengen model acted as a template for future EC proposals; many of its measures have informed recent developments: for example, the European Information System, and a common visa policy. Some have argued, as a result, that the effect of Schengen was to lower the standard of refugee protection in Europe.[34]

Dublin

The Dublin Convention ('Dublin I') was also agreed in 1990.[35] The UK signed it in 1992, but the Convention only entered into force in 1997, following the required ratification by all signatories. In the interim, a system of bilateral readmission agreements between Member States emerged, according to which an asylum seeker could be returned to a state through which he or she had passed. This practice was favoured by the UK, which was eager to remove asylum seekers to safe third countries, in particular France, without consideration of their asylum claims. However, from September 1997, when Dublin I replaced the Schengen *acquis* as the main instrument determining with responsibility for asylum claims, the position altered somewhat. The Convention provides that only one EU Member State will examine an asylum claim (thereby addressing the 'refugee in orbit' phenomenon which was emerging in Europe).[36] Member States can 'opt out' and examine any asylum claim that does not fall within Dublin's guidelines, so long as the asylum seeker concerned has agreed.[37] In addition, a Member State that is not responsible under the Convention may for humanitarian reasons, and on particular family or cultural grounds, choose to examine an application at the request of another Member State, provided that the applicant so desires.[38] Arts

9.8

---

[33] Protocol on the application of certain aspects of Art. 7a of the Treaty establishing the European Community to the United Kingdom and Ireland.

[34] See I. Boccardi, *Europe and Refugees – Towards and EU Asylum Policy* (The Hague: Kluwer Law, 2002), p. 44. See, also, for further discussion of Schengen, K. Hailbronner & C. Thiery, 'Schengen II and Dublin: responsibility for asylum applications in Europe', (1997) 34 *CML Rev*, p. 957.

[35] See, for a discussion of the Convention, A. Hurwitz, 'The 1990 Dublin Convention: A comprehensive assessment' (1999) 11:4 *IJRL*, pp. 646–677.

[36] Arts 3(2) and (3). The refugee in orbit phenomenon described the practice adopted by EU states in the 1980s of bouncing asylum claimants to and fro between countries as each tried to pass on responsibility for asylum determination to another. The Dublin Convention was introduced, in part, to address this problem.

[37] Art. 3(4).

[38] Art. 9.

4 to 8 of the Convention set out the criteria for determining the state responsible for an asylum claim, and apply in the order presented below. These are:

- if the applicant has a member of his or her family who has been recognised as a refugee in an EU Member State, that state is responsible for examining the application;[39]

- if the applicant possesses a valid residence permit, the Member State which issued the permit is responsible for examining the application;[40]

- if the applicant possesses a valid visa, the Member State which issued the visa is usually responsible for examining the application;[41]

- if the applicant possesses a residence permit which has expired less than two years previously, or a visa which has expired less than six months previously, the Member State which issued the permit or visa generally assumes responsibility;[42]

- if it can be proved that an asylum applicant illegally entered a Member State from a third country, that Member State is responsible for examining the application, unless the applicant has been living in another Member State for at least six months prior to lodging an asylum claim, in which case the latter state assumes responsibility;[43]

- if an applicant claims asylum while passing through a Member State, that state is responsible for examining the application;[44]

- where no Member State can be designated responsible according to the above criteria, the first Member State in which the asylum claim is lodged becomes responsible.[45]

Article 11 to the Convention is of great significance. It allows for a Member State in which an application is lodged, but which considers another to be responsible for examining the application, to call upon that other state to take charge of the applicant. There is a time limit of six months from the date the application is lodged, so states must act relatively quickly. Article 15 permits the exchange of information

---

[39] Art. 4.
[40] Art. 5(1).
[41] Art. 5(2). There are three exceptions set out in Arts 5(2)(a)–(c).
[42] Art. 5(4).
[43] Art. 6.
[44] Art. 7(3).
[45] Art. 8.

on asylum seekers in order to help identify the state responsible for determining the asylum application.[46] Finally, it is worth noting that Dublin I permits the return of an asylum seeker to a third state (i.e. a non-EU state) 'in compliance with the provisions of the Geneva Convention, as amended by the New York Protocol'.[47] On its face, this suggests that Member States will not act in contravention of Art. 33 on *non-refoulement*, but, as has been discussed in earlier chapters, since Member States have different approaches to interpretation of the 1951 Convention (for example, on non-state agents), there is no guarantee that asylum seekers have not been returned to countries that many would regard as unsafe.

Dublin I was solely concerned with assigning responsibility for status determination. It did not seek either to define asylum or to provide harmonised interpretation of the 1951 Convention. This continued to be the preserve of individual states. As noted in Ch. 6, Dublin I was not a great success. Determining which state was responsible was often a slow process, leaving many asylum seekers in a state of uncertainty. Few were actually returned to other EU states by the UK, and some might have been passed on to regimes where their applications were not given adequate consideration.[48] Member States soon recognised that new arrangements were imperative, and these finally took form in Dublin II (though Dublin I remains in force: see below).

Visa lists

A common visa list was a long-standing objective of immigration ministers across Europe. As noted above, this was a key requirement of the Palma Document. Schengen, too, contains a complicated set of rules on visas and border controls. They entitle third country nationals to enter the Schengen area if they possess the necessary entry documents, including a visa if required. Chapter 3 and Art. 19 of the Schengen Convention deal with visas. The Convention promotes the idea of a uniform visa for the entire area and allows for travel in the Schengen area for up to three months.[49] Those holding a uniform visa are entitled to move freely within the territories of all the

9.9

---

[46] Art. 15.

[47] Art. 3(5).

[48] See for a discussion on many of the issues relating to the working of the Dublin Convention: House of Lords Select Committee on European Union, 'Asylum Applications – Who Decides?', Session 1998–99, March 19, 2002, HL 100.

[49] Arts 10 and 11.

Contracting Parties.[50] Visas for periods in excess of three months are national visas granted by one of the Contracting Parties under its own legislation.[51]

Negotiation on the visa list proved to be a protracted process, due to divergent political and historical considerations. Schengen states finally agreed three lists: countries requiring a visa; countries exempted from a visa; and countries on which a decision had not yet been reached.[52] The lists drawn up clearly target countries regarded as producing large numbers of asylum seekers or illegal migrants. As in the UK, there is no exception made in the case of asylum, and asylum seekers are required to obtain normal visas. In fact, any country producing large numbers of asylum seekers will find its way on to the list.

'Soft law'

9.10 It is generally assumed that Schengen was a laboratory for the development of an EU-wide asylum policy. It is certainly true that current initiatives owe much to the Schengen *acquis*. Following the 1990 Schengen Convention, the role of EC institutions continued to be minimal, with discussions still confined to intergovernmental fora. However, in 1991, the Commission, seeking to influence decisions from which it was excluded, issued two Communications – on asylum and on immigration –in the hope of contributing to the debate.[53] Harmonisation of asylum policy was now seen as the best means of addressing the growing asylum 'crisis' in a number of Member States, and the European Council's work programme reflected this by prioritising harmonisation of substantive asylum law.[54] Nonetheless, Member States continued to prefer the use of 'soft law'. [55] Thus in 1992, in London, Ministers responsible for immigration adopted three key Resolutions: 'on manifestly unfounded applications for asylum'; 'on a harmonised approach to questions concerning host third

---

[50] Art. 19.
[51] Art. 18.
[52] European Commission, *Background Report the Schengen Agreements*, ISEC/B4/95, March 9, 1995.
[53] Communication 'on Asylum' SEC(91)1857 final, and Communication 'on Immigration' SEC(91)1885 final.
[54] R. Fernhout, 'The harmonised application of the definition of the term "refugee" in the EU' in *Refugee and Asylum Law: Assessing the Scope for Judicial Protection* (Netherlands: Nederlands Centrum Buitenlanders, International Association of Refugee Law Judges, Second Conference, Nijmegen, 1997), p. 155.
[55] 'Soft law' refers to non-binding instruments. These include, *inter alia*, Resolutions, Recommendations, Conclusions, Joint Positions and Joint Actions.

countries'; and 'on certain common guidelines as regards the admission of particularly vulnerable persons from the former Yugoslavia'.[56] The first two covered concepts that the UK adopted with alacrity: the acceleration of manifestly unfounded asylum claims through the asylum system (introduced in the Asylum and Immigration Appeals Act 1993), and the processing of cases from safe third countries. Regarding manifestly unfounded asylum cases, the Resolution required Member States to introduce the concept into their national laws,[57] though the actual fast tracking procedures were left to the discretion of the state.[58] The host third countries Resolution permitted the return of applicants to safe third countries,[59] as well as the use of accelerated procedures in such cases.[60] In a rather bizarre choice of language, the Resolution seems to forbid the examination of asylum cases in safe third country cases: 'if there is a host third country, the application for refugee status may not be examined and the asylum applicant may be sent to that country'.[61] Naturally, the key to the Resolution lies in its definition of 'host third country'. It is described as any country: which does not threaten the life or freedom of the asylum applicant, within the meaning of Art. 33 of the 1951 Convention; which does not expose the applicant to torture, inhuman or degrading treatment; which has already granted protection to the asylum applicant or where the applicant has had opportunity to make contact with the authorities in order to seek their protection; and which will afford the applicant effective protection against *refoulement* within the meaning of the 1951 Convention.[62]

The unusual brevity of the Resolutions, and their obvious attempt to ease the burden on Member States, irrespective of potentially serious consequences for asylum applicants, have given rise to considerable comment.[63] At the same meeting in London, Ministers also agreed a Conclusion on countries in which there is generally no serious risk of persecution, and a Conclusion on people displaced by the

---

[56] Copies of these Resolutions, plus other soft law measures, are available in: E. Guild & J. Niessen, *The Developing Immigration and Asylum Policies of the EU* (The Hague: Kluwer Law, 1996).

[57] para. 1(a).

[58] para. 2.

[59] para. 1(c)

[60] para. 1.

[61] para. 1(c).

[62] para. 2.

[63] See *e.g.*, *A New Immigration Law for Europe? The 1992 and 1993 Copenhagen Rules on Immigration* (The Netherlands: Nederlands Centrum Buitenlanders, 1993); E. Guild & J. Niessen, *The Developing Immigration and Asylum Policies of the EU* (The Hague: Kluwer Law, 1996), pp. 141–176; S. Peers, *Mind the Gap! Ineffective Member State Implementation of EU asylum Measures* (London: ILPA/Refugee Council, May 1998).

conflict in the former Yugoslavia. Once more, the UK government eagerly complied with the first Conclusion's recommendations when, in the Asylum and Immigration Act 1996, it introduced a 'white list'.[64] Further Recommendations[65] and Resolutions[66] were entered into prior to the enforcement of the Treaty on European Union ('TEU' or 'Maastricht Treaty') in November 1993.

The general consensus is that this adoption of 'soft law' provides concrete evidence of the shift towards greater restriction in EU policy-making, and of the distancing of refugee protection from its human rights origins.

Treaty law: Maastricht and beyond

9.11   At the same time as these intergovernmental measures were agreed, discussions were taking place on a new Treaty. One of the questions under consideration was whether asylum should continue to be dealt with intergovernmentally or whether it ought to be transferred to the jurisdiction of the EC. The final format – contained in the TEU and signed in February 1992 – was testament to the reluctance of Member States to relinquish competence in asylum matters. Adopting a 'pillar' structure,[67] it included provisions relating to asylum, in the main, in the Third Pillar on Justice and Home Affairs ('JHA') (Title VI), which remained largely outside the jurisdiction of EU institutions and continued to be run intergovernmentally. Member States regarded asylum policy and immigration policy, *inter alia*, as matters of 'common interest'.[68] Under the Third Pillar, Ministers of Justice and Home Affairs were expected to agree on initiatives put to them by the Commission and by Member States; decision-making had to be unanimous, except on procedural matters or in relation to Conventions, when a two-thirds majority sufficed. The jurisdiction of the Court of Justice ('ECJ') over Title VI was explicitly excluded,

---

[64] See Chs 5 and 7.

[65] 'On expulsion practices to be followed by Member States'; 'on transit for the purposes of expulsion'; and 'on checks on and expulsion of third country nationals residing or working without authorisation in a Member State'.

[66] Resolution 'on the harmonisation of national polices on family reunification'; Resolution 'on certain common guidelines as regards admission of particularly vulnerable groups of persons from the former Yugoslavia'.

[67] The First Pillar covers the European Communities; the Second Pillar deals with co-operation on Foreign and Security policies; and the Third Pillar is Justice and Home Affairs.

[68] Art. K.1. The areas covered include asylum, external borders, immigration, combating drug addiction and fraud, judicial co-operation in civil and criminal matters, customs co-operation, and police co-operation.

although under Art. K3(2)(c), jurisdiction could be granted to the Court in any convention concluded in the areas specified in Art. K.1 (this covered asylum policy). A particularly important provision, in the context of asylum, was the *passerelle* procedure laid down in Art. K.9. This catered for the possible transference of competence in asylum and immigration matters to the Community.[69] Once more, this could only happen with unanimous agreement of the Council on an initiative of the Commission or a Member State. Nonetheless, in a Declaration on asylum attached to the TEU, it was stated that the Council would consider 'as a matter of priority questions concerning Member States' asylum policies, with the aim of adopting, by the beginning of 1993, common action to harmonize aspects of them [. . .]', and that the Council would consider 'by the end of 1993, [. . .] the possibility of applying Art. K.9 to such matters'. Asylum and immigration, it seemed, were privileged areas, thought ripe for transference to EC competence, and for harmonisation.

One issue that did fall to the first pillar, and therefore under the jurisdiction of all EC institutions, was that of visas. Article 100c of the EC Treaty (as amended by the TEU) stated that the Commission could propose, after consultation with the Parliament, a common visa list for third country nationals, and the Council would agree the proposal on the basis of unanimity (except where there was a sudden, threatened inflow of third country nationals, when decisions would be taken by qualified majority).[70] The Commission soon used its new power to propose Council Regulations laying down the uniform format for visas, and listing the third countries whose nationals required a visa to cross external borders. Both were adopted in 1995.[71] However, the Regulation on visas for third country nationals ran into trouble when the Parliament, aggrieved at the Council's rejection of its proposed amendments to the Commission's proposal, as well as to core components (such as a 'positive visa list'), successfully sued the Council before the Court.[72] The Regulation remained in force pending a replacement, which was forthcoming in 1999, though the Council chose once more to ignore the Parliament's amendments.[73]

Unfortunately, any hope that the new structure would clarify the existing set-up was misplaced. On the one hand, much of the framework of Title VI was intergovernmental; on the other, there were elements of 'creeping Communitarisation'.[74] With the introduction of

9.12

---

[69] Under Art. 100c(6).
[70] See also Art. K.9.
[71] Reg. 1683/95, OJ 1995 L 163/1; Reg. 2317/95, OJ 1995 L 234/1.
[72] Case C-392/95 *European Parliament v Council* (visa regulation) [1997] ECR I-3213
[73] Reg.n 574/1999, OJ 1999 L 72/2.
[74] D. O'Keeffe, 'The emergence of a European immigration policy' (1995) 20:1 *EL Rev*, pp. 20–36.

various committees and fora in the decision-making process, the whole framework appeared excessively complicated, and, in some senses, less transparent than in the pre-Maastricht era, though this view is not universally held. The Commission, for example, regarded Title VI as laying down 'clear rules and procedures for co-operation in these new areas, spelling out the respective roles of Member States, the Commission and the European Parliament, and opening up the possibility of engaging the interpretative authority of the Court of Justice'.[75] The TEU, while encouraging co-operation, also suggested that the Council could adopt a number of measures in relation to asylum: Joint Positions, Joint Actions and Conventions.[76] It did not, however, mention Resolutions, Recommendations, Decisions or Conclusions, often, as has been seen, the preferred method of decision-making in the asylum field.[77] Of the list of specified and unspecified measures, conventions alone are binding,[78] and, in those countries with a dualist system (such as the UK), only when given effect under their municipal law. Thus, while the TEU was an apparent attempt to harmonise asylum laws and procedures, the reality was very different. Member States clearly balked at the idea of handing competence over to EC institutions in such a contentious area as asylum, and in the post-Maastricht era, they continued to favour non-binding instruments not listed in the Treaty. In fact, in 1994, the Commission admitted failure when it noted that 'Immigration Ministers have adopted a number of Resolutions, which are not of a legally binding nature', and that 'The present stage of the process could [. . .] best be described as approximation rather than harmonisation of immigration and asylum policies.'[79]

Some important examples in the asylum field of 'creeping Communitarisation', not quite reaching the elevated status of harmonisation, were the Resolution 'on minimum guarantees for asylum procedures'[80] and the Joint Position 'on the harmonised application

---

[75] Communication from the Commission to the Council and the European Parliament 'on Immigration and Asylum Policies', COM(94) 23 final, February 23, 1994, para.18.

[76] Arts K.3(2)(a)–(c).

[77] E. Guild & J. Niessen, *The Developing Immigration and Asylum Policies of the EU* (The Hague: Kluwer Law, 1996), p. 53.

[78] See *R. v Secretary of State for the Home Department, ex parte Adan* [1998] INLR 325, at 332 and 327 for description of the Joint Position 'on the harmonized application of the definition of the term 'refugee' in Art. 1 of the Geneva Convention' as 'guidelines' and 'non-conclusive'. The Joint Position itself states in its preamble that 'it shall not bind the legislative authorities or affect decisions of the judicial authorities of Member States'.

[79] Communication from the Commission to the Council and the European Parliament on Immigration and Asylum Policies, COM(94) 23 final, February 23, 1994, para. 34.

[80] 5585/95 adopted June 20, 1995; OJ 199 C 274/13.

of the definition of the term 'refugee' in Art. 1 of the 1951 Convention'.[81] The first protected the right against *refoulement* in undecided cases,[82] and set out guarantees for the examination of asylum applications,[83] as well as certain rights of asylum seekers during examination, appeal and review procedures.[84] Once more, some of the most important aspects of the Resolution, in terms of its impact on national legislation, were the special provisions that apply to 'manifestly unfounded asylum applications'.[85] In such cases, Member States were allowed to exclude an appeal against a refusal decision if 'an independent body which is distinct from the examining authority has already confirmed the decision'.[86] They could also derogate from the general principle contained in the Resolution that asylum applicants be allowed to remain in the Member State in which the application was lodged or was being examined;[87] in other words, the appeal in manifestly unfounded cases could be non-suspensive. These guidelines were adopted by the UK government in the three Acts of the 1990s, and continued to play a significant role in the most recent national legislation in the area: the Nationality, Immigration and Asylum Act 2002.[88] However, not all Member States have been so compliant. In 1998, a comparative study was undertaken to determine the extent of implementation of the 1995 Resolution 'on minimum guarantees for asylum procedures', and it was established that 'important aspects of procedural protection have not been harmonised effectively'.[89] The differences were extensive and included failure to translate the reasons for rejection, failure to inform third states that an asylum claim has not been examined substantively, and divergences in the use of suspensive appeals and treatment of asylum seekers at the border.[90]

---

[81] 96/196/JHA Joint Position 'on the harmonized application of the definition of the term 'refugee' in Art. 1 of the Geneva Convention', OJ 1996 L 63/2. For a useful list and discussion of the measures introduced in the post-Maastricht period see: R. Wallace, *Refugees and Asylum: a Community Perspective* (London: Butterworths, 1996), Ch. 2.

[82] Pt II(2).

[83] Pt III.

[84] Pt IV.

[85] Pts IV(18)–(22).

[86] Pt IV(19).

[87] Pts IV(12) and (17).

[88] See Chs 5–7 for further discussion.

[89] S. Peers, *Mind the Gap! Ineffective Member State Implementation of EU Asylum Measures* (London: ILPA/Refugee Council, May 1998), p. 16.

[90] *ibid.*, pp. 16–17. See also, S. Peers, *EU Justice and Home Affairs Law* (London: Longman, 2000), pp. 118–19; I. Boccardi, *Europe and Refugees – Towards and EU Asylum Policy* (The Hague: Kluwer Law, 2002), Ch. 3.

9.13   By contrast, the 1996 Joint Position on a definition of 'refugee',
which referred to the word 'harmonised' in its title, seemed a more
successful attempt at convergence – in this case, on interpretation of
the term 'refugee'. Certainly, the Joint Position addressed many critical aspects of refugee status determination: the evidence required for
grant of refugee status; 'persecution' within the meaning of the Art.
1A of the 1951 Convention; origins of persecution; grounds for persecution; relocation within the country of origin; refugees *sur place*;
cessation of refugee status (Art. 1C), and exclusion from protection
(Art. 1F). While adoption of guidelines on these important components might seem a positive step in the move towards harmonisation
of EC refugee law, the Joint Position was still subject to criticism.
Firstly, it was not binding, stating in its preamble that 'it shall not bind
the legislative authorities or affect decisions of the judicial authorities
of the Member States'. This alone could be regarded as undermining
the harmonisation principle. Secondly, the guidelines described 'persecution' as being 'generally the act of a State organ'; persecution by
third parties only fell within the 1951 Convention where it was based
on one of the grounds of Art. 1A, and was 'individual in nature and
[. . .] encouraged or permitted by the authorities'.[91] Where, however,
'the official authorities fail to act, such persecution should give rise to
individual examination of each application for refugee status, *in accordance with national judicial practice*, in the light in particular of whether
or not the failure to act was deliberate. The persons concerned may
be eligible in any event for appropriate forms of protection under
national law (emphasis added)' (para. 5.2). This compromise, proposed by the French, avoided the more generous interpretation supported by the UNHCR that serious discriminatory or other offensive
acts committed by non-state agents could amount to persecution
where a state was unwilling or unable to control them (the 'protection
theory').[92] Article 1A(2) does not refer specifically to action by the
state or a state authority and does not therefore require persecution
to be imputable to the state.

9.14   At the time of drafting of the guidelines, only a few Member
States, France and Germany included, applied the narrower
'accountability theory' as opposed to the 'protection theory' preferred
by the majority; the Joint Position therefore followed the line taken by
the minority of European states.[93] Sweden, clearly unhappy with this

---

[91] para. 5.2.
[92] UNHCR *Handbook*, para. 65.
[93] See Ch. 8 for discussion of UK case law on non-state agents of persecution. The
accountability theory is that a state is not responsible for persecution by non-state
agents unless persecution emanates from the state or can be attributed to the state,
whereas the protection theory holds that failure of effective state protection (state is

position, informed the Council that it considered persecution by third parties to fall within the scope of the 1951 Convention where it was encouraged or permitted by the authorities, and that it could fall under the Convention in cases where the authorities were unable to offer protection.[94] The UNHCR, also concerned about the apparent adoption of the 'accountability theory', declared in a press release that the EU position would 'allow states to avoid recognizing as refugees people persecuted by 'non-state agents' – such as rebel groups or extremist organizations'.[95] Para. 5.2 certainly seemed to do little for the harmonised interpretation of the 1951 Convention.

The Joint Position also supported the application of the 'internal relocation alternative' where persecution was confined to a specific part of a country's territory, and it was reasonable to expect a person to move elsewhere within his or her country.[96] At the time of drafting of the Joint Position, the European Council for Refugees and Exiles ('ECRE') firmly believed that the internal relocation alternative should not be applied, as it could 'only further restrict access of refugees to international protection'; it went on, though, to suggest criteria that should be applied if states insisted upon using the concept.[97] ECRE also adopted the view that persons fleeing from civil war situations should never be automatically denied refugee status.[98]

A further problem identified with the Joint Position was its failure to refer to gender as potential grounds for refugee status. While this approach was in accordance with the 1951 Convention, it did not take account of increasing recognition that women might be persecuted on gender-related grounds.[99] In relation to conscientious objectors, the Joint Position again adopted a more restrictive interpretation

---

unwilling or unable to afford protection against persecution by non-state agents) suffices to warrant international protection under the 1951 Convention: ECRE, *Research Paper on Non-state Agents of Persecution* (London: ECRE, 2000), p. 60, available on *www.ecre.org/research/nsagents.shtml*

[94] Cited in G. Noll & J. Vedsted-Hansen, 'Non-communitarians: Refugee and asylum policies' in P. Alston ed., *The EU and Human Rights* (Oxford: OUP, 1999), p. 379.

[95] UNHCR, 'UNHCR expresses reservation over EU asylum policy, November 27, 1995, cited in ECRE, *Research Paper on Non-state Agents of Persecution* (London: ECRE, 2000), p. 7.

[96] Para. 8. 'Internal flight alternative' is the more familiar term, but some consider 'internal protection alternative' (IPA) or 'internal relocation alternative' (IRA) less misleading: H. Storey, 'From nowhere to somewhere – An evaluation of the UNHCR 2nd track global consultations on international protection', speaking at IARLJ Conference, Wellington, New Zealand, October 22–25, 2002. See, also, *R. (Yogathas and Thangarasa) v Secretary of State for the Home Department* [2002] INLR 620.

[97] ECRE, *Note from ECRE on the harmonisation of the interpretation of Art. 1 of the 1951 Geneva Convention*, June 1995, points 10–11.

[98] *ibid.*, point 15.

[99] See Ch. 8 for discussion of the *Shah* and *Islam* case.

than that provided by the Handbook. The former declared that
refugee status might be granted in cases of punishment for conscientious objection or deliberate absence without leave, and for desertion
on grounds of conscience (if the performance of military duties
would lead to participation in acts excluded by Art. 1F of the 1951
Convention).[100] The Handbook, by contrast, states that 'where [. . .]
the type of military action, with which an individual does not wish to
be associated, is condemned by the international community as contrary to basic rules of human conduct, punishment for desertion or
draft-evasion could [. . .] in itself be regarded as persecution'.[101] This
certainly seems broader than the European measure.[102]

While it is true that the Joint Position has been widely criticised,
there are some who regard it as a rather liberal instrument, not
deserving of its depiction as the lowest common denominator in
asylum law-making.[103]

Yugoslavia – a catalyst

9.15   Perhaps the best example of failed consensus in the asylum field is the
former Yugoslavia. When confronted with an actual refugee crisis,
Member States arguably failed to meet the challenge. Any harmonisation of policy seemed restrictive in tenor: for example, in 1992, Member States imposed a visa requirement against Bosnia-Herzegovina,
thereby revealing their true attitude towards the half million asylum
seekers from the region. While there was general reluctance to grant
refugee status, most arrivals were accorded a secondary status in recognition of the impossibility of return. The greatest burden was felt by
Germany, which received the vast majority of fugitives. For example,
in 1992, it recorded 115,395 applications from the former Yugoslavia,
and 6,197 from Bosnia-Herzegovina.[104] Its total number of asylum
claims for the year was 438,191. Alongside this, the UK's 24,625
claims paled into insignificance (with only 5,635 from the former
Yugoslavia – albeit the highest asylum-producing country for the
UK for the year –, and none from Bosnia-Herzegovina).[105] It was

---

[100] para. 10
[101] para. 171.
[102] R. Fernhout, 'The harmonised application of the definition of the term "refugee" in
the EU' in *Refugee and Asylum Law: Assessing the Scope for Judicial Protection* (Netherlands:
Nederlands Centrum Buitenlanders, International Association of Refugee Law
Judges, Second Conference, Nijmegen, 1997), p. 166.
[103] *ibid.*
[104] UNHCR, *Asylum Applications in Industrialized Countries: 1980–1999* (Geneva:
UNHCR, November 2001), table III.10.
[105] *ibid.*, table III.23.

unsurprising, then, when Germany began to exert pressure on its fellow EU states to accept more asylum seekers, and discussions turned towards burden sharing and 'new practices' with which to deal with the problems created by the break-up of the former Yugoslavia.

In their London meeting in December 1992, Immigration Ministers adopted a Conclusion 'on people displaced by the conflict'.[106] Recognising that 'large scale movements of people outside the former Yugoslavia are likely to encourage the inhumane and illegal practice of ethnic cleansing', Ministers agreed that displaced people should be encouraged to stay 'in the nearest safe areas to their homes'.[107] They further agreed that they would offer protection to nationals of the former Yugoslavia who were within their borders having come 'direct from combat zones', and who were unable to return to their homes as a direct result of the conflict and human rights abuses.[108] The Conclusion also provided for material assistance from EU states towards supporting reception centres in the former Yugoslavia.[109]

Joly has described the EU approach as one of 'internalization', 'containment' and 'temporary protection'.[110] Internalising refugees consisted of holding them in their area of origin in so-called 'safe havens';[111] if this failed, then a policy of containment was adopted whereby refugees were encouraged to stay in the territory of the former Yugoslavia with the provision of material assistance for reception centres. The Conclusion reluctantly agreed to provide temporary protection to those who made it to the territory of an EU Member State. This was supplemented by the Resolution 'on certain guidelines as regards the admission of particularly vulnerable persons from the former Yugoslavia, agreed in June 1993'.[112] As its title suggests, it was aimed at 'particularly vulnerable persons', namely those who had been held in prisoner-of-war or internment camps, the injured or seriously ill, those under direct threat to life or limb, and those who had been subjected to sexual assault. Temporary protection would only be offered where there was no (local) alternative.[113]

---

[106] Available in T. Bunyan ed., *Key Texts on Justice and Home Affairs in the EU Vol. 1 (1976–1993) From Trevi to Maastricht* (London: Statewatch, 1997), pp. 74–5.

[107] Preamble.

[108] para. 4.

[109] *ibid.*

[110] D. Joly, *Haven or Hell? Asylum Policies and Refugees in Europe* London: Macmillan, 1996), p. 75. On the notion of containment, see A. Shacknove, 'From asylum to containment' (1993) 5:4 *IJRL*, pp. 516–533.

[111] For a discussion of safety zones in the Yugoslavian context, see K. Landgren, 'Safety zones and international protection: a dark grey area' (1995) 7:3 *IJRL*, pp. 436–458.

[112] Available in T. Bunyan ed., *Key Texts on Justice and Home Affairs in the EU Vol. 1 (1976–1993) From Trevi to Maastricht* (London: Statewatch, 1997), pp. 76–7.

[113] para. 1.

9.16   While the concept of temporary protection, or at least temporary refuge, is not new,[114] its adoption in the European context was at odds with its previous application.[115] It has long been accepted that, as refugee status is by nature temporary, temporary refuge was an intermediate stage on the way to the preferred goal of a durable solution.[116] The Executive Committee of the UNHCR published two Conclusions, in 1980 and 1981, dealing with the issue and related problems: Temporary Refuge (No. 19 (XXXI) – 1980), and Protection of Asylum-Seekers in Situations of Large-Scale Influx (No. 22 (XXXII) – 1981). In the latter, it stated:

> 'In situations of large-scale influx, asylum seekers should be admitted to the State in which they first seek refuge and if that State is unable to admit them on a durable basis, it should always admit them at least on a temporary basis and provide them with protection according to the principles set out below. They should be admitted without any discrimination as to race, religion, political opinion, nationality, country of origin or physical incapacity.'[117]

Admission on a durable basis is clearly the preferred option, with temporary protection as a fallback. The UNHCR Conclusions go on to stress that the fundamental principle of *non-refoulement* must be 'scrupulously observed'.[118] Notwithstanding the UNHCR's exhortation, it became apparent that, while *refoulement* was in many cases not taking place, temporary refuge was failing to provide a lasting solution.[119] The European model of 'temporary protection' differed from previous incarnations in a number of ways: it was based on eventual return rather than resettlement; it involved admission to a Member State's territory rather than to a camp; and Member States bore the cost of admission.[120] That said, temporary protection on a group

---

[114] See G. Goodwin-Gill, *The Refugee in International Law* (Oxford: Clarendon, 1996, pp.196–199; D. Perluss and J. Hartman, 'Temporary refuge: emergence of a customary norm' (1986) 26:3 *Virginia Journal of International Law*, pp. 552–626.

[115] There are many commentaries on the topic of temporary protection. See *e.g.*, M. Kjaerum, 'Temporary protection in Europe in the 1990s' (1994) 6:3 *IJRL*, pp. 444–456; D. Luca, 'Questioning temporary protection, together with a selected bibliography on temporary refuge/temporary protection' (1994) 6:4 *IJRL*, pp. 535–561; J. Thorburn, 'Transcending boundaries: temporary protection and burden-sharing in Europe' (1995) 7:3 *IJRL*, pp. 459–481; K.Kerber, 'Temporary protection: an assessment of the harmonisation policies of European Union member states' (1997) 9:3 *IJRL*, pp. 453–471.

[116] M. Kjaerum, 'Temporary protection in Europe in the 1990s' (1994) 6:3 *IJRL*, p. 445.

[117] para. II(A)(1).

[118] para. II(A)(1).

[119] See G. Goodwin-Gill, *The Refugee in International Law* (Oxford: Clarendon, 1996), p. 199.

[120] *ibid.*, pp. 199–200.

basis allowed states to sidestep the protracted and often costly asylum determination procedures associated with individual assessment, and to assuage any concerns that refugees would remain indefinitely in host countries.[121]

In 1994, the Commission noted in its Communication 'on asylum and immigration policies' that Member States had adopted their own individual legislative provisions on temporary protection, and that no uniform pattern in the secondary rights of those enjoying temporary protection existed.[122] While welcoming national schemes on temporary protection, the Commission advocated harmonisation and the elaboration of a scheme for temporary protection, with a guarantee of a minimum level of protection to those concerned.[123] In addition, the Commission recognised that some matching of national absorption capacities was called for in emergency situations of mass influx, but it did not go so far as to suggest a formal arrangement of burden sharing.[124] In fact, the Council proceeded in 1995 to adopt a Resolution 'on burden sharing with regard to the admission and residence of displaced persons on a temporary basis',[125] followed, in 1996, by a Decision 'on an alert and emergency procedure for burden sharing with regard to the admission and residence of displaced persons on a temporary basis'.[126] The latter was soon put to the test during the Kosovo crisis, but did not help resolve disagreements regarding refugee quotas.[127] While the two measures may be deemed to 'fall far short of a coherent legal system on displaced persons', they do provide a starting point for greater co-ordination of European policy on the issue of temporary admission and burden sharing.[128]

In 1997, the issue of temporary protection once more came to the fore, when the Commission, using, for the first time, its initiative under the Amsterdam Treaty regarding asylum matters, proposed a Joint Action concerning temporary protection of displaced persons.[129] It failed to win support due largely to the inclusion of a

9.17

---

[121] M. Kjaerum, 'Temporary protection in Europe in the 1990s' (1994) 6:3 *IJRL*, pp. 449–50.

[122] Communication from the Commission to the Council and the European Parliament 'on Immigration and Asylum Policies', February 23, 1994, COM(94) 23 final, paras 24–25.

[123] *ibid.*, para. 93.

[124] *ibid.*, paras 98–99.

[125] OJ 1995 C 262/1.

[126] OJ 1996 L 63/10.

[127] I. Boccardi, *Europe and Refugees – Towards and EU Asylum Policy* (The Hague: Kluwer Law, 2002), p. 114.

[128] K. Kerber, 'Temporary protection: an assessment of the harmonisation policies of EU Member States' (1997) 9:3 *IJRL*, p. 462.

[129] OJ 1997 C 106/13.

scheme for burden sharing, which Member States were still reluctant to countenance.[130] However, the Commission was not to be dissuaded, and several months later, in June 1998, it produced two further draft Joint Actions – the first on temporary protection of displaced persons; the second on 'solidarity' in the admission and residence of beneficiaries of the temporary protection of displaced persons (*i.e.* burden sharing).[131] By ostensibly separating the issue of 'solidarity', or burden sharing, from temporary protection, the Commission hoped that the proposals would be adopted. However, Art. 5 of the temporary protection proposal still promoted solidarity in the application of the temporary protection regime, and cross-referred to the solidarity proposal. Though the draft Joint Actions contained some realistic measures to handle problems of mass influx, such as had occurred in the Kosovo crisis, Member States were unable to agree and presented the picture of a discordant Union to the wider world. The best they could achieve was the adoption of a Joint Action 'on establishing projects and measures to provide practical support in relation to the reception and voluntary repatriation of refugees, displaced persons and asylum seekers, including emergency assistance to persons who have fled as a result of recent events in Kosovo'.[132] Its aim was to improve the conditions in which refugees, displaced persons and asylum seekers were received in Member States and to assist their voluntary repatriation and reintegration in their countries of origin.[133] In the first instance, 15 million Euros were made available for the programme for 1999.[134] The Joint Action only lasted till December 31, 1999,[135] but following the Amsterdam Treaty, further attempts were made to arrive at much needed co-operation on temporary protection and to resolve remaining differences.[136]

---

[130] G. Noll & J. Vedsted-Hansen, 'Non-communitarians: Refugee and asylum policies' in P. Alston ed., *The EU and Human Rights* (Oxford: OUP, 1999), p. 391.

[131] OJ 1998 C 268/13; OJ 1998 C 268/22. For a discussion of the Joint Actions, see H. Lambert, 'Building a European asylum policy under the "First Pillar" of the consolidated Treaty establishing the EC' (1999) 11:2 *IJRL*, pp. 327–337.

[132] OJ 1999 L 114/2.

[133] Art. 1.

[134] Art. 2.

[135] Art. 15.

[136] See below. For a survey of the pre- Amsterdam developments, see K. Kerber, 'Temporary protection in the EU: a chronology' (1999) 14 *Georgetown Immigration Law Journal*, pp. 35–50.

HARMONISATION ACHIEVED?

The Treaty of Amsterdam

Despite the steady drift towards convergence during the late 1980s   **9.18**
and early 1990s, it is quite clear from the above discussion that Title
VI of the TEU failed to harmonise EC asylum policy. Art. K.9 was
not employed to effect real change in the asylum and immigration
fields, either because Member States remained reluctant to commit
themselves seriously to the harmonisation project, or because they
were already aware, by 1996, that revision of the TEU pillar structure was imminent.[137] In the build-up to the Amsterdam Treaty, it
became clear that there was growing support for the transfer of some
of the Third Pillar matters to the First Pillar, and asylum and immigration were at long last seen as suitable subjects for Community
competence.[138] The reasons for this change are manifold: first, as has
been seen, harmonisation, or communitarisation, was a long-standing
objective of EC states, despite their reluctant implementation; second, it was finally recognised that the non-binding measures in the
pre- and post-Maastricht eras had failed to deliver satisfactory solutions to a burgeoning asylum problem – that is, by controlling abuse
and reducing numbers; third, some feared that the Community was
heading towards a 'patchwork of national standards' resulting in the
'contradictory, arbitrary, and unequal treatment of asylum seekers
and other migrants across the EU';[139] fourth, the lack of transparency
and secret decision-making, which had played such a significant role
in the intergovernmental era, had not been sufficiently remedied by
the TEU;[140] and fifth, and perhaps most critical in view of its direct
impact on states themselves, the Yugoslavian crisis had acted as an
impetus to Member States to act in union rather than individually.

---

[137] G. Noll & J. Vedsted-Hansen, 'Non-communitarians: Refugee and asylum policies'
in P. Alston ed., *The EU and Human Rights* (Oxford: OUP, 1999), p. 370.

[138] J. Monar, 'European Union – Justice and Home Affairs: a balance sheet and an
agenda for reform' in G. Edwards and A. Pijpers, eds., *The Politics of the European
Treaty Reform – The 1996 Intergovernmntal Conference and Beyond* (London: Pinter, 1997),
p. 336.

[139] R. Hansen, 'Asylum policy in the EU' (2000) 14 *Georgetown Immigration law Journal*,
p. 795.

[140] G. Noll & J. Vedsted-Hansen, 'Non-communitarians: Refugee and asylum policies'
in P. Alston ed., *The EU and Human Rights* (Oxford: OUP, 1999), p. 372.

Pros and cons of the Amsterdam provisions

9.19   Much has been written on the changes introduced by the Amsterdam Treaty, for very evident reasons.[141] The revision of asylum law was dramatic. The ostensibly simple step of transference from Third to First Pillar brought the whole of EC asylum policy within EC competence. Situated in a new section in the Treaty establishing the European Community (Part III, Title IV), which deals with visas, asylum, immigration and free movement of persons in general (Arts 61–69), asylum was a key component of an area of freedom, security and justice.[142] Two significant new elements are: (i) the consultation of the European Parliament in relation to new measures; and (ii) the role of the ECJ regarding interpretation of Title IV provisions. However, during the transition period of five years from the date of entry into force of the Amsterdam Treaty (1999), certain constraints apply. These include the inability of the ECJ to issue rulings to low level national courts;[143] the ability of Member States alongside the Commission to take initiative in relation to Title IV matters;[144] the requirement of unanimity voting by the Council;[145] and the inability of the Parliament to amend or veto measures, which contrasts with its powers under Art. 251 in relation to other areas of the First Pillar.[146] The prerequisite of unanimous decision-making led some to argue that there was little hope for improvement to asylum policy during the first five years following entry into force of the Treaty.[147] However, this interpretation fails to pay sufficient regard to the Treaty provisions themselves. Art. 63 demands that:

---

[141] See for fuller commentaries: H. Garry, 'Harmonisation of asylum law and policy within the EU: a human rights perspective' (2002) 20:2 *Netherlands Quarterly of Human Rights*, pp. 163–184; E. Guild and C. Harlow eds., *Implementing Amsterdam – Immigration and Asylum Rights in EC* law (Oxford: Hart, 2001); G. Simpson, 'Asylum and Immigration in the EU after the Treaty of Amsterdam (1999) 5:1 *European Public Law*, pp. 91–124; ECRE/ENAR/MPG, *Guarding Standards – Shaping the Agenda* (ECRE/ENAR/MPG, 1999); S. Peers, *The Amsterdam Proposals – The ILPA/MPG Proposed Directives in Immigration and Asylum* (London: ILPA/MPG, 2000).

[142] Art. 61.

[143] Art. 67(2) allows the Council to act unanimously after five years to adapt the provisions relating to the powers of the ECJ. This could bring them into line with their standard powers.

[144] Following the five-year period, the Commission will be given the sole right of initiative on asylum: Art. 67(2).

[145] Except for decisions on visas and the uniform format on visas, which are already subject to qualified majority voting: Art. 67(3).

[146] ECRE/ENAR/MPG, *Guarding Standards – Shaping the Agenda* (ECRE/ENAR/MPG, 1999), p. 2. According to Art. 67(2), the Council will take a unanimous decision on whether the Parliament be given full powers of veto and amendment.

[147] G. Noll & J. Vedsted-Hansen, 'Non-communitarians: Refugee and asylum policies' in P. Alston ed., *The EU and Human Rights* (Oxford: OUP, 1999), p. 371.

'the Council, acting in accordance with the procedure referred to in Article 67, shall, within a period of five years after the entry into force of the Treaty of Amsterdam, adopt:

'(1) measures on asylum, in accordance with the Geneva Convention of July 28, 1951 and the Protocol of January 31, 1967 relating to the status of refugees and other relevant treaties, within the following areas:

    (a) criteria and mechanisms for determining which Member State is responsible for considering an application for asylum submitted by a national of a third country in one of the Member States;

    (b) minimum standards on the reception of asylum seekers in Member States;

    (c) minimum standards with respect to the qualification of nationals of third countries as refugees;

    (d) minimum standards on procedures in Member States for granting or withdrawing refugee status;

(2) measures on refugees and displaced persons within the following areas:

    (a) minimum standards for giving temporary protection to displaced persons from third countries who cannot return to their country of origin and for persons who otherwise need international protection;

    (b) promoting a balance of effort between Member States in receiving and bearing the consequences of receiving refugees and displaced persons.'

The focus on minimum standards raises concerns that, with unanimity voting, there will be a 'race to the bottom', and that restrictionism will triumph over human rights to the detriment of refugee protection. Some of these concerns have been partially allayed by recent proposals before the Council.[148]

Of greater import, perhaps, are the limitations placed on the ECJ.   **9.20**
In non-asylum references from national courts under Art. 234, any court or tribunal can refer a matter to the ECJ for clarification of EC law. Not so in the case of asylum: only courts and tribunals at the final level of appeal are empowered to make such references.[149] This was seen as a worrying development. ECRE puts it thus: '[Article 68] is fairly threatening to the coherence of the legal order in the Community, as it permits lower level courts to interpret Community Law in whatever way they see fit'.[150] Furthermore, according to Art. 234,

---

[148] See below.
[149] Art. 68(1)
[150] ECRE, *Analysis of the Treaty of Amsterdam in so far as it relates to Asylum Policy* (ECRE, November 1997), p. 5.

where a question of interpretation is raised before a court or tribunal of a Member State against whose decisions there is no judicial remedy under national law, that court is required to bring the matter before the ECJ.[151] Inconsistency between Member States will be the inevitable outcome. This obligation does not pertain to questions of interpretation of Title IV. Instead, the court or tribunal (of last instance) 'shall, if it considers that a decision on the question is necessary to enable it to give judgment, request the Court of Justice to give a ruling thereon'.[152] There is one exception to the ECJ's jurisdiction: it may not rule on any measure or decision taken relating to the maintenance of law and order and the safeguarding of internal security.[153] This places the ECJ at odds with the ECtHR, which has ruled on such matters in cases such as *Chahal* and *Ahmed*.[154] Once more, Art. 68 does not help establish consistency of decision-making across the EU, and may ultimately result in differing levels of protection between Member States.

This aside, one of the major impediments to harmonisation, in the sense of uniform application of asylum law, is the Protocol on the position of the UK and Ireland, attached to the Treaty of Amsterdam. This stipulates categorically that these two countries shall not take part in the adoption of measures pursuant to Title IV and are not bound by any such measures or by interpretative decisions promulgated by the ECJ.[155] While they have effectively excluded themselves from the decision-making process, the UK and Ireland retained for themselves the power to 'opt in' within three months of a proposal or initiative being presented to the Council, or following an adoption

---

[151] The Court of Justice shall have jurisdiction to give preliminary rulings concerning:

    (a)   the interpretation of this Treaty;

    (b)   the validity and interpretation of acts of the institutions of the Community and of the ECB;

    (c)   the interpretation of the statutes of bodies established by an act of the Council, where those statutes so provide.

Where such a question is raised before any court or tribunal of a Member State, that court or tribunal may, if it considers that a decision on the question is necessary to enable it to give judgment, request the Court of Justice to give a ruling thereon.

Where any such question is raised in a case pending before a court or tribunal of a Member State against whose decisions there is no judicial remedy under national law, that court or tribunal shall bring the matter before the Court of Justice.

[152] Art. 68.

[153] Art. 68(2).

[154] See Ch. 4. ECRE, *Analysis of the Treaty of Amsterdam in so far as it relates to Asylum Policy* (ECRE, November 1997), p. 5.

[155] Arts 1 and 2.

of a measure by the Council.[156] In addition, the Protocol integrating the Schengen *acquis* into the framework of the European Union confirms that the UK and Ireland are not bound by the Schengen *acquis*, although, again, they are entitled to request participation in some or all of its provisions.[157]

There is one further contentious matter regarding the Treaty of Amsterdam: the Protocol on asylum for nationals of Member States of the European Union. The sole article in this Protocol makes an extraordinary declaration:

'Given the level of protection of fundamental rights and freedoms by the Member States of the European Union, Member States shall be regarded as constituting safe countries of origin in respect of each other for all legal and practical purposes in relation to asylum matters. Accordingly, any application for asylum made by a national of a Member State may be taken into consideration or declared admissible for processing by another Member State only in [certain limited] cases.'[158]

This measure effectively removes the right of EU citizens to claim asylum in another EU state. This is arguably a highly significant amendment to European asylum law, but it passed almost unnoticed. The Protocol owes its existence to Spanish lobbying. It is Spain's attempt at preventing certain Member States, such as Belgium, from examining asylum applications by Basque nationalists in accordance with their constitutional obligations. The measure has rightly been described as extradition in disguise.[159] The UNHCR, too, expressed serious reservations, which were not assuaged by the assurances in the preamble to the Protocol:[160]

'We are very concerned at the EU decision. If the EU applies limitations to the Convention, others can follow and could weaken the universality of the instrument for the international protection of refugees. We do not, therefore, share the position taken in the preamble stating that the protocol respects the Convention.'[161]

---

[156] Arts 3 and 4.

[157] Art. 4.

[158] These are where: (a) the applicant's state of nationality derogates under Art. 15 of the ECHR on national security grounds; (b) the Council considers taking action against or has acted against the applicant's Member State for a serious or persistent breach of principles of human rights; and (c) a Member State should so decide unilaterally in respect of the application of a national of another Member State (in which case the Council must be informed immediately).

[159] S. Peers, *EU Justice and Home Affairs Law* (London: Longman, 2000), p. 129.

[160] Note: these were to the finality and objectives of the 1951 Convention, not to the 1967 Protocol.

[161] UNHCR Press Release, 'UNHCR concerned about restricted access to asylum in Europe', June 20, 1997.

9.21   This unprecedented step by European Member States could certainly be regarded as militating against an important element of the
1951 Convention that guaranteed unqualified access to asylum.[162] It
was mitigated by the fact that Belgium declared that it would continue to carry out an individual examination of any asylum request
made by a national of another Member State.[163] Significantly, even
prior to Amsterdam, the European Parliament had itself called on the
Council 'to establish in a clear and binding manner that every Member State shall consider as clearly unfounded any request for asylum
or for refugee status submitted by a national of another Member
State and shall in any event reject such a request'.[164] While it is
doubted that the Protocol will have much impact, it does highlight,
yet again, the failure of EU Member States to achieve consensus.

It would however be facile to suggest that the new Title brought
with it no positive aspects. The Amsterdam Treaty was regarded by
some as 'a golden opportunity to set legislative standards which will
not only approximate current diverging national asylum laws and
practices but which also reflect existing best practice'.[165] That said,
much depends on the courage of Member States to create a Community asylum law with a high standard of protection, and which
heeds fundamental principles of human rights. In a Declaration to
Art. 63, a commitment was made to establish consultations with the
UNHCR and other relevant international organisations on matters
relating to asylum. While this placed current arrangements on a formal footing, it was not clear whether the term 'international organisations' included non-governmental organisations, or referred solely
to inter-governmental bodies.[166] Concerns over the limitations
imposed on the power of the Parliament aside, it was generally
acknowledged that transparency would be improved by the new
arrangement and that there should be greater democratic accountability.[167] In relation to the ECJ, it was assumed that some role for the
Court was better than none at all. The EC Treaty provided a positive

---

[162] UNHCR Press Release, 'UNHCR concerned about restricted access to asylum in
Europe', June 20, 1997.
[163] Declaration by Belgium 'on the Protocol on asylum for nationals of Member States
of the European Union'.
[164] Resolution 'on the Council Resolution on minimum guarantees for asylum
procedures', OJ 1996 362/270.
[165] ECRE, *The Promise of Protection: Progress towards a European Asylum Policy since Tampere*
(ECRE, November 2001), p. 3.
[166] ECRE, *Analysis of the Treaty of Amsterdam in so far as it relates to Asylum Policy* (ECRE,
November 1997), p. 4.
[167] M. Colvin, 'Human rights and accountability after the Treaty of Amsterdam
(1998) 2 *European Human Rights Law Review*, p. 191.

message on the contentious issue of 'burden sharing',[168] and there was some hope that Art. 63(2)(b) would go part of the way to achieving effective protection of refugees. It was expected that all these factors would help reverse restrictive national legislation introduced by countries, such as Germany, which bore the brunt of the 'burden' in the 1990s.[169] The unanswered question, in the immediate aftermath of the Treaty of Amsterdam, was whether it would succeed in reversing an increasingly restrictive trend in EU asylum and immigration policies.

REINFORCING AMSTERDAM: TAMPERE, LAEKEN, SEVILLE AND THESSALONIKI

Less than a year after the signing of the Treaty of Amsterdam, the **9.22** Austrian Presidency of the EU cast a shadow over developments when it published a contribution to the asylum debate entitled *Strategy Paper on Migration and Asylum Policy*.[170] Though not meant for public consumption, it was leaked to the press in July 1998 and caused a great deal of alarm within the UNHCR and NGOs. Highlighting asylum and migration as a key feature of the Presidency, the paper suggested that political interest was no longer focused on the asylum question and problems of temporary protection, but on general questions of migration, combating smuggling networks and expulsion issues.[171] It appeared to confuse the root causes of refugee movement with other forms of migration, and recommended improved deterrence to solve the problem of increased population movements to the EU territory.[172] One of the more notorious suggestions was a proposal for a new Convention 'supplementing, amending or replacing the Geneva Convention'.[173] The new approach advocated by the paper harked back to the 'beginnings of the development of asylum law when the affording of protection was not seen as a subjective individual right but rather as a political offer on the part of the host

---

[168] Note: some commentators in the field object to the use of this term in view of its negative connotations.

[169] H. Garry, 'Harmonisation of asylum law and policy within the EU: a human rights perspective' (2002) 20:2 *Netherlands Quarterly of Human Rights*, p. 173.

[170] Council of the EU, 9809/98, Brussels, July 1, 1998, available on: *www.proasyl.de/texte/europe/eu-a-o.htm*

[171] para. 14.

[172] paras 15, 29 and 53. ECRE, *Observations by ECRE on the Austrian Presidency of the EU's Strategy Paper on Immigration and Asylum Policy*, September 4, 1998, available on *www.proasyl.de/texte/europe/eu-a-e.htm*

[173] para. 103.

country'.[174] The paper also proposed, rather oddly, that 'in every case
where the border is crossed in other than the appropriate manner the
status quo is first restored – i.e. the individual is put back on the other
side of the border and any procedures are initiated only after that has
been done'.[175] Alongside uncertainty as to how exactly this would
work, this plan clearly ran counter to the principle of *non-refoulement*.
The UNHCR, ECRE and other refugee-support groups reacted
strongly to the Austrian proposals. At the time, the UNHCR
acknowledged that the 1951 Convention might have to be supplemented with other legal instruments in order to address the protection needs of an increasing number of asylum seekers who were not
covered by the Convention. It continued to believe, however, that the
1951 Convention was 'still a perfectly valid and viable legal instrument to address the needs of persons fleeing, *inter alia*, internal armed
conflict, ethnic tensions, civil war or persecution by non-state agents,
provided those needs meet the criteria contained in the refugee
definition in Article 1A of the 1951 Convention'.[176] Faced with
widespread objection, the Austrian Presidency backtracked, revising
the strategy paper and deleting any reference to the replacement or
amendment of the 1951 Convention. ECRE remained unconvinced, and maintained that the paper undermined existing refugee
protection standards.[177]

Within months, EU governments were beginning to distance themselves from the revised paper. By the end of 1998, it was agreed that
a High Level Working Group on Asylum and Migration would be
established and charged with drawing up a list of countries of origin
and transit of asylum seekers and migrants, as well as some action
plans on a 'cross pillar approach' by March 1999.[178] A cross-pillar
approach implied examining migration issues, exerting diplomatic
pressure on countries of origin and their neighbours, and providing
economic aid for the same.[179] The Working Group was expected to
prepare a report in time for the European Summit held in Tampere,
Finland, in October 1999.

[174] para. 102.
[175] para. 92.
[176] UNHCR, *Preliminary Observation by UNHCR on the Austrian Presidency Strategy Paper on Immigration and Asylum Policy* (Brussels, September 9, 1998), available on *www.proasyl.de/texte/europe/eu-a-unh.htm*
[177] ECRE, *Observations by ECRE on the September 1998 Revision of the Austrian Presidency's Strategy Paper on Migration and Asylum Policy*, available on
[178] 'Presidency Migration plan sidelined and resurrected' (November-December 1998) 8:6 *Statewatch*, p. 2.
[179] *ibid.*

Tampere

The Tampere Extraordinary European Council, to give it its full name, was devoted exclusively to building an area of freedom, security and justice in the EU.[180] Asylum and migration policy were matters of priority. In many senses, Tampere was a high point in the development of an EU asylum policy. Most significantly, the European Council stated that its aim was an 'open and secure European Union, fully committed to the obligations of the Geneva Refugee Convention and other human rights instruments, and able to respond to humanitarian needs on the basis of solidarity'.[181] The European Council also reaffirmed the importance which the Union and Member States attached to absolute respect of the right to seek asylum. It agreed to work towards establishing a Common European Asylum System ('CEAS'), based on the full and inclusive application of the Geneva Convention. This meant 'ensuring that nobody is sent back to persecution, i.e. maintaining the principle of *non-refoulement*'.[182] This was a clear signal that attitudes towards asylum had changed fundamentally. No longer were asylum measures introduced simply to reinforce the internal market. They were, as Boccardi notes, 'an independent objective rooted in the new Human Rights dimension of the Union'.[183]

9.23

The Presidency Conclusions of Tampere focused on a number of key elements in the development of a common EU policy: partnership with countries of origin; a CEAS; fair treatment of third country nationals; and management of migration flows. For some, the CEAS was a re-expression of earlier plans, such as the Palma Document. It certainly repeated many of the strategies formulated over the years by Member States, either acting intergovernmentally or within the framework of the EU: notably, a clear and workable determination of the State responsible for the examination of an asylum application, common standards for a fair and efficient asylum procedure, common minimum conditions of reception of asylum seekers, and the approximation of rules on the recognition and content of refugee status.[184] Tampere also urged the Council to step up its efforts to reach agreement on the issue of temporary protection for displaced

---

[180] For an excellent overview of non-governmental and inter-governmental observations on Tampere, see ECRE, *The ECRE Tampere Dossier*, June 2000, available on: *www.ecre.org/policy/research_papers.shtml*

[181] Presidency Conclusions Tampere – October 15 & 16, 1999, SN 200/99, para. 4.

[182] *ibid.*, para. 13.

[183] I. Boccardi, *Europe and Refugees – Towards and EU Asylum Policy* (The Hague: Kluwer Law, 2002), p. 174.

[184] Presidency Conclusions Tampere – October 15 & 16, 1999, SN 200/99, para. 14.

persons on the basis of solidarity between Member States,[185] and to finish its work on the system for identification of asylum seekers (EURODAC).[186] As if these goals were insufficiently exacting, Tampere also called for more efficient management of migration flows, with priority given to the problems of human trafficking and smuggling. Closer co-operation with countries of origin was expected to help prevent illegal migration and to assist with voluntary returns.[187] Finally, the EU recognised at Tampere that a comprehensive approach to migration was needed to address political, human rights and development issues in countries and regions of origin and transit.[188]

Tampere was unique. It called for a combination of measures to prevent illegal migration, to handle asylum fairly and humanely, and to promote return where appropriate. While the Conclusions were undoubtedly positive towards asylum,[189] there were some areas of uncertainty. The Conclusions appeared to recognise the sensitivities of managing migration within a human rights framework. The right to seek asylum was strongly reaffirmed, but there continued to be a close link drawn between migration and asylum, which could lead to conflict.[190] The establishment of a CEAS signalled a desire by Member States to move beyond minimum levels of harmonisation of their asylum laws and policies, but this might be difficult to achieve in view of the undoubted pressures created by human smuggling.[191] Would economic assistance to countries of origin or transit be conditional upon their taking measures counter to the absolute respect for the 'right to seek asylum'?[192] It was certainly an ambitious agenda for the EU, and NGOs across Europe watched closely to ensure that refugee protection did not suffer in the name of immigration control.

Post Tampere

9.24   Tampere can be described unquestionably as the highpoint in the development of EU asylum policy. Yet, for refugees, it did no more

---

[185] Presidency Conclusions Tampere – October 15 & 16, 1999, SN 200/99, para. 16.
[186] *ibid.*, para. 17.
[187] *ibid.*, paras 22–27.
[188] *ibid.*, para. 11.
[189] See *e.g.*, ECRE, *Observations by the ECRE on the Presidency Conclusions of the Tampere European Council*, in ECRE, *The ECRE Tampere Dossier*, June 2000.
[190] Presidency Conclusions Tampere – October 15 & 16, 1999, SN 200/99, para. 10.
[191] UNHCR, *The Tampere Summit Conclusions – UNHCR's Observations*, in ECRE, *The ECRE Tampere Dossier*, June 2000.
[192] *Observations by the ECRE on the Presidency Conclusions of the Tampere European Council*, in ECRE, *The ECRE Tampere Dossier*, June 2000, para. 19.

than promise protection. To what extent, then, has the EU risen to the challenges it set itself? Mindful of history, particularly in the post-Maastricht years when Member States lost the will to implement the necessary concrete measures, the Council charged the Commission at Tampere to maintain a 'scoreboard' charting developments. A full debate assessing progress was arranged for the European Council meeting in December 2001, in Laeken (see below). In the meantime, the Commission published a number of important Communications on asylum and immigration: 'towards a common asylum procedure and a uniform status, valid throughout the Union, for persons granted asylum';[193] 'a Community immigration policy'; [194] and 'on an open method of co-ordination for the Community immigration policy'.[195] The Commission also published two reports on asylum and these provided extremely useful information on the progress of the CEAS, as well as an insight into the Commission's thinking on the subject.[196]

In the two years following Tampere, the Commission, through its Justice and Home Affairs Directorate, has certainly been busy, and has made huge strides towards the establishment of a CEAS, drafting legislation in the areas identified as the 'building blocks' of such a system.[197] It has also worked on the so-called 'flanking measures' that support the key components.

The first stage proposals

By November 2001, just prior to the meeting of the European Council in Laeken the following month, the Commission had framed all the proposals for the first stage of creating a CEAS. In accordance with Tampere, the first stage required the adoption of a number of key measures, including: **9.25**

---

[193] COM(2000) 755 final.

[194] COM(2000) 757 final.

[195] COM(2001) 387 final;

[196] Communication from the Commission to the Council and the European Parliament 'on the common asylum policy, introducing an open co-ordination method (First report by the Commission on the application of Communication COM(2000) 755 final of November 22, 2000)' COM(2001) 710 final; Communication from the Commission to the Council and the European Parliament 'on the common asylum policy and the Agenda for protection (Second Commission report on the implementation of Communication COM(2000) 755 final of November 22, 2000)' COM(2003) 152 final.

[197] ECRE, *The Promise of Protection: Progress towards a European Asylum Policy since Tampere*, November 2001, p. 6.

- a Directive on minimum standards for procedures on granting and withdrawing refugee status;

- a Directive on minimum standards for reception of asylum seekers;

- a Regulation on criteria and mechanisms for determining the state responsible for examining asylum requests (Dublin II);

- a Directive on minimum standards for the qualification and status of third country nationals and stateless persons as refugees or as persons who otherwise need international protection;

- a Directive on subsidiary forms of protection.

The second stage had a long-term objective of a common asylum procedure and a uniform status for those who are granted asylum valid throughout the Union.[198]

Proposal for a Directive on asylum procedures

9.26 In September 2000, the Commission published its proposed Directive on one of the fundamental aspects of a CEAS – minimum standards on procedures. The Directive was to replace the London Resolutions of 1992 and the Council Resolution of 1995 'on minimum guarantees for asylum procedures'. The main aim of the proposed Directive was stated as being the introduction of 'a minimum framework in the European Community on procedures for the determination of refugee status, ensuring that no Member State expels or returns an applicant for asylum in any manner whatsoever to the frontiers of territories where his life or freedom would be threatened on account of his race, religion, nationality, membership of a particular social group or political opinion'.[199] It was intended that the Directive would help Member States 'to operate a quick and simple system that swiftly and correctly processes applications for asylum in accordance with the international obligations and constitutions of the Member States'.[200] This document received widespread attention and scrutiny.[201] Most

---

[198] Presidency Conclusions Tampere – October 15 & 16, 1999, SN 200/99, para. 15. For a fuller discussion of Commission's intentions in this regard, see Communication from the Commission to the Council and the European Parliament 'Towards a common asylum procedure and a uniform status, valid throughout the Union, for persons granted asylum', COM(2000) 755 final.

[199] COM(2002) 326 final/2, Preamble (5).

[200] *ibid.*, Preamble (11).

[201] See *e.g.*, House of Lords Select Committee on European Union, 'Minimum Standards in Asylum Procedures', Session 2000–01, Eleventh Report, March 27, 2001.

organisations and commentators supported the underlying objective of the Proposal, as part of a move towards harmonisation of EU asylum policy that could lead to improved standards for asylum seekers. However, endorsing harmonisation may be a risky strategy; it could be a means by which to opt for the lowest common denominator, which clearly runs counter to the wishes of refugee-support groups. JUSTICE has repeatedly argued that harmonisation should consider three factors: 'the establishment of common standards on the criteria against which claims are decided; the procedures for determining claims; and the form of status granted to those offered protection'.[202] As the then Director of Justice, Anne Owers, said: 'Unless all three march together it is going to be very difficult for countries in Europe to have systems that they can genuinely feel are compatible and are up to the relevant standards.'[203] The Refugee Council and JCWI, in their evidence in 2001 to the House of Lords Select Committee on European Union, felt uncomfortable with considering minimum standards on procedures without having first agreed a basic definition of who is or is not a refugee.[204]

Following discussion of the proposed Directive, a revised version was submitted in 2002,[205] but, once again, it has proved disappointing. The main areas of concern are: **9.27**

- there is no reference to Art. 3, ECHR, as an additional source of protection;

- there is no reference to Art. 3, ECHR, as excluding an asylum application from being 'manifestly unfounded';[206]

- applications are subjected to accelerated procedures if they are 'inadmissible',[207] 'manifestly unfounded';[208] or other

---

[202] *ibid.*, para. 33.
[203] *ibid.*
[204] *ibid.*, paras 33 & 34.
[205] COM (2002) 326 final/2.
[206] *ibid.*
[207] *ibid.*, Art. 25 states: 'Member States may reject a particular application for asylum as inadmissible if:
  a) another Member State, or Norway or Iceland, has acknowledged responsibility for examining the application, according to the criteria and mechanisms for determining which Member State is responsible for considering an application for asylum submitted by a national of a third country or stateless person in one of the Member States;
  b) a country which is not a Member State is considered as a first country of asylum for the applicant, pursuant to Art. 26;
  c) a country which is not a Member State is considered as a safe third country for the applicant, pursuant to Arts 27 and 28;
  d) a country other than the country of origin of the applicant has made an extradition request and that country is either another Member State or a third

cases;[209] these cover an exceptionally broad range of contingencies, many of which are arguably unacceptable;

- the Directive supports the 'safe third country' concept; Member States may designate a country as 'safe' even where an applicant has never been admitted to that country and it could reject such a claim as inadmissible;[210]

- Member States may designate a country as a 'safe country of origin' and any application from such a country will be 'manifestly unfounded and subject to accelerated appeal procedures;[211] the use of the concept of designated safe third countries of origin is highly suspect;[212]

- asylum seekers are not protected from removal from the territory of the Member State in accelerated appeals cases; removal is dependent on national law;[213]

- the grounds for detention of asylum seekers are not listed and detention is left largely to the discretion of the Member State;[214]

- there is no right to seek independent advice on applying for asylum, nor a right to legal representation following a rejection.[215]

---

country which can be considered a safe third country in accordance with the principles set out in Annex I, provided that extradition to this country is legal;
   e)   an indictment by an International Criminal Court has been made.'

[208] COM (2002) 326 final/2., Arts 29 and 32. Art. 29 states: 'Member States may reject an application for asylum as manifestly unfounded if the determining authority has established that:
   a)   the applicant in submitting his application and presenting the facts, has only raised issues that are obviously not relevant to the Geneva Convention;
   b)   the applicant is from a safe country of origin within the meaning of Arts 30 and 31 of this Directive;
   c)   the applicant is prima facie excluded from refugee status by virtue of Council Directive . . ./ . . . [*Proposal for a Council Directive on minimum standards for the qualification and status of third country nationals and stateless persons as refugees or as persons who otherwise need international protection*]'.

[209] *ibid.*, Art. 32. These cover situations where the applicant: has used/made false or misleading information /representations; resubmitted an application with no new facts; is making a claim to prevent removal; fails to comply with Directive's obligations; is an illegal entrant who fails to contact authorities expeditiously; or is a threat to national security.

[210] *ibid.*, Arts 28(1)(b) and 25(c).

[211] *ibid.*, Arts 29–31.

[212] See discussion of 'white list' in Asylum and Immigration Act 1996, Chs 5 and 7.

[213] COM(2002) 326 final/2, Art. 40(1).

[214] *ibid.*, Art. 17.

[215] *ibid.*, Art. 9.

These are major deficiencies and suggest that the proposed Directive will fall far short of the high aspirations spelled out in the Commission's 2000 Communication on asylum. By August 31, 2003, agreement on the Directive still had not been reached, and further discussions were scheduled for the end of the year.

Directive on minimum standards for the reception of asylum seekers

Proposed by the Commission in April 2001, the Directive laying down **9.28** minimum standards for the reception of asylum seekers was adopted on January 27, 2003.[216] The UK has opted in. Once more, the original Directive was subject to discussion and amendment. For example, the House of Lords Select Committee on the European Union undertook a comprehensive review of the original proposal, calling on a number of expert witnesses to give evidence.[217] In addition, in July 2000, the UNHCR published a detailed report on *Reception Standards for Asylum Seekers in the European Union*. This provided a valuable list of recommendations for a minimum level of reception standards.[218]

The Directive can be broadly welcomed. The provisions on access to education and health care (Arts 10 and 15), on identity documents (Art. 6), and on information for asylum seekers on procedures and legal assistance (Art. 5) are certainly to be commended. The section on provisions for persons with special needs, including vulnerable individuals, victims of torture or violence, unaccompanied children, pregnant women and the disabled (Ch. IV) is also a positive advance. However, it could be argued that a large part of the Directive gives too much latitude to Member States to adapt it to their convenience. There are also a number of omissions. One particular area of concern is the failure by EU states to harmonise their different national policies and practices regarding access to employment. Another is the power included in the Directive to reduce or withdraw reception conditions – that is, the full set of measures detailed in the Directive – where an asylum seeker abandons a place of residence without notifying the authorities, does not comply with reporting requirements, has already lodged an application in the same Member State, or conceals financial resources

---

[216] OJ 2003 L 31/18.

[217] House of Lords Select Committee on European Union, 'Minimum standards of reception conditions for asylum seekers', Session 2001–02, Eighth Report, November 27, 2001.

[218] See also Global Consultations of International Protection, *Reception of Asylum Seekers, Including Standards of Treatment, in the Context of Individual Asylum Systems*, 3rd meeting, EC/GC/01/17, September 4, 2001.

(Art. 16). While the importance of setting in place controls is obvious, this could result in destitution of an asylum seeker, thereby violating international human rights law. One can also question whether the requirement of medical screening on public health grounds (Art. 9) is compatible with the right to privacy enshrined in Art. 8, ECHR, and whether restricting asylum seekers to certain areas runs contrary to Protocol 4, ECHR.[219] (The UK has not ratified Protocol 4).

Dublin II

9.29 Universal acceptance that the 1990 Dublin Convention was not working led Member States to consider its replacement or review. In March 2000, the European Commission produced a working paper entitled 'Revisiting the Dublin Convention: developing Community legislation for determining which member state is responsible for considering an application for asylum submitted in one of the member states'.[220] The Commission's working paper and subsequent proposal for a Council Regulation met the obligations imposed by the Treaty of Amsterdam to legislate on this issue.[221]

The new proposals were not particularly well received. ILPA, for example, noted:

'It is very disappointing that the Commission has not taken the opportunity to revise the criteria for determining responsibility and that the proposed Regulation [is] based on the same principles as the Dublin Convention. Whilst it might be considered that the tightening up of mechanisms in the proposed Regulations (*sic*) will lead to the more successful operation of the Regulation than its predecessor, ILPA doubts that to be the case. Not only is the current proposed Regulation unlikely to be successful in terms of reducing multiple applications or secondary movements within the European Union, it lacks the scope to respond to the humanitarian concerns and to address the complex and uncertain situation in which many asylum applicants find themselves.'[222]

---

[219] See, for further discussion, ECRE, *The Promise of Protection: Progress towards a European Asylum Policy since Tampere* (ECRE, November 2001), p. 10.

[220] SEC(2000) 522.

[221] COM(2001) 447 final, July 26, 2001. All documents are available on the website of ECRE: *www.ecre.org*

[222] ILPA's Scoreboard on the Proposal for a Council Regulation establishing the criteria and mechanisms for determining the Member State responsible for examining an asylum application lodged in one of the Member States by a third country national, available on *www.ecre.org/eu_developments/stateresp.shtml*

Despite this, the draft measure finally became law on February 18, 2003 as Regulation 343/2003.[223] It entered into force on February 20, 2003 and applies to asylum applications from August 1, 2003.[224] While the UK and Ireland have opted into the Regulation,[225] Denmark has chosen not to. Dublin I therefore remains in force and applies between Denmark and the Member States.

The determination of the state responsible for examining the application is as follows, and applies in the order listed:

- if the applicant is an unaccompanied minor, the Member State where family are present; in the absence of family, the Member State where the application is lodged;[226]

- if the applicant is an adult, the Member State where he or she has family;[227]

- if the asylum seeker has a family member whose application for asylum has not yet been decided, the Member State that is processing the application;[228]

- if the applicant possesses a valid residence document, the Member State that issued the document;[229]

- if the applicant possesses a valid visa, generally, the Member State that issued the visa;[230]

- if the applicant possesses more than one valid residence document or visa issued by different Member States, responsibility is assumed according to set criteria;[231]

- if the applicant possesses a residence document that has expired less than two years previously, or a visa that has expired less than six months previously, the Member State that issued the document or visa, in the first instance;[232]

---

[223] OJ 2003 L 50/1.
[224] Art. 29.
[225] In accordance with Art. 3 of the Protocol on the position of the UK and Ireland annexed to the Treaty on European Union and to the Treaty establishing the European Community.
[226] Art. 5.
[227] Art. 7.
[228] Art. 8.
[229] Art. 9(1).
[230] Art. 9(2).
[231] Art. 9(3)
[232] Art. 9(4).

- if it can be proved that an asylum applicant illegally entered a Member State from a third country, the Member State so entered, up to 12 months after the illegal entry;[233]

- if an applicant enters a Member State that has waived a visa, that Member State;[234]

- the Member State where an applicant claims asylum in transit;[235]

- where no Member State can be designated according to the above criteria, the first Member State in which the asylum claim is lodged.[236]

9.30   Unfortunately, it appears that the Regulation is based on the same flawed principles as Dublin I, namely that responsibility for examining an asylum application is linked in many cases to responsibility for entry control to the EU.[237] Thus, for example, a Member State that has issued a visa to a third country national will generally be responsible for determining the asylum claim. As ECRE makes clear, such a policy has a number of potentially detrimental outcomes: (i) the new accession states of Central and Eastern Europe and the southern European states will carry the greatest burden of controlling entry; yet they have the least developed structures for asylum in the EU; (ii) the process of identifying the Member State which was first entered is resource intensive; (iii) the approach risks encouraging *refoulement*, since states might try to avoid responsibility for status determination; and (iv) the approach encourages extra-territorial enforcement, such as the expansion of the UK's use of Airline Liaison Officers at selected ports outside the EU.[238] The UNHCR is generally in agreement. It is particularly concerned that 'serious imbalances in the distribution of asylum applicants among Member States' might occur through the entry responsibility approach, and that delays might result in the processing of claims.[239]

---

[233] Art. 10(1).

[234] Art. 11.

[235] Art. 12.

[236] Art. 13.

[237] Comments from the European Council on Refugees and Exiles on the Proposal 'for a Council Regulation establishing the criteria and mechanisms for determining the Member State responsible for examining an asylum application lodged in one of the Member States by a third country national', available on *www.ecre.org/eu_ developments/stateresp.shtml*, p. 1.

[238] *ibid.*, p. 2.

[239] UNHCR's observations on the European Commission's Proposal 'for a Council Regulation establishing the criteria and mechanisms for determining the Member State responsible for examining an asylum application lodged in one of the Member States by a third country national' (COM(2001) 447 final), p. 3, available on *www.ecre.org/eu_developments/stateresp.shtml*

It is true that one of the oddest aspects of Dublin II is that it does very little to resolve the problem of states refusing to accept responsibility, an issue which proved such an irritant for the UK when attempting to apply Dublin I. According to Art. 10 of Dublin II, if an asylum seeker appears in the UK without any documentation, the authorities will still need to prove which Member State was entered. The Regulation sets out criteria for proof (Art. 18), and circumstantial evidence can also be used, but these provisions are unlikely to improve the situation from a UK government perspective. The promise that 'the requested Member State shall acknowledge its responsibility if the circumstantial evidence is coherent, verifiable and sufficiently detailed to establish responsibility' is not wholly convincing. Rather, it is anticipated that unless proof is incontrovertible, no removal under Dublin II will occur.[240] ECRE proposed a simple solution. The State responsible for examining an asylum claim should be determined by two criteria alone:

'(i)   where the asylum applicant has a family member, provided s/he agrees;
(ii)   where the asylum application is lodged'.[241]

ECRE also stressed that 'no system of allocation of responsibility for examining asylum applications can function fairly without harmonisation of substantive laws and their interpretation, and the harmonisation of asylum procedures'.[242] This has not yet materialised.

The Regulation does make some improvements to Dublin I. For example, the definition of 'member of the family' is extended to include an asylum seeker's spouse or unmarried partner in certain circumstances.[243] The Regulation also provides for family reunification for applicants whose family member has applied for asylum, but has not yet received a first decision.[244] In the case of unaccompanied minors, responsibility for the asylum claim will transfer to another Member State if there is a member of the family of the minor legally present in that state, provided that this is in the best

---

[240]   Art. 18(5).
[241]   Comments from the European Council on Refugees and Exiles on the Proposal 'for a Council Regulation establishing the criteria and mechanisms for determining the Member State responsible for examining an asylum application lodged in one of the Member States by a third country national', available on *www.ecre.org/eu_developments/stateresp.shtml*, p. 3.
[242]   *ibid.*, p. 4.
[243]   These are where the legislation or practice of the Member State concerned treats unmarried couples in a way comparable to married couples under its law relating to aliens: Art. 2(i).
[244]   Art. 8.

interest of the minor.[245] Under Art. 20, an asylum seeker will be notified that responsibility for his or her claim rests with another Member State, and that consequently he or she will be transferred to that State. There is a right of appeal against such a decision, but it is non-suspensive.[246]

Dublin I clearly failed in its objective. Dublin II seems not to have solved many of the past problems connected with trying to establish a Member State responsible for asylum determination, and the future does not look promising. As ECRE pessimistically declared: 'just like its predecessor the Dublin Convention is doomed to be ineffective and unworkable'.[247]

Proposal for a Directive on minimum standards for the qualification and status of third country nationals and stateless persons as refugees or as persons who otherwise need international protection

9.31　One of the central features of a CEAS, if not the central feature, is a harmonised view of the criteria for refugee definition. The Commission's Proposal sets out a common interpretation of the criteria for refugee status determination under the 1951 Convention and 1967 Protocol. It also includes criteria for qualification for subsidiary protection status as well as minimum standards of treatment for refugees and beneficiaries of subsidiary protection. Due to its centrality to EU asylum law, the Proposal, which was first presented in September 2001, should have been adopted prior to other first stage Directives; it was, in fact, the last draft to be produced by the Commission.[248] This will undoubtedly affect the adopted Directives, since the critical issue of 'who is a refugee' remains to be determined by the status Directive. At Seville, the Council was asked to approve the Directive by mid-2003 and, in any event, to have it completed by April 2004, in accordance with the Amsterdam Treaty. In the JHA Council held in June 2003, there was still no agreement, and discussions were postponed till October 2003.

---

[245] Art. 6.

[246] Art. 20(1)(e). A suspensive appeal suspends removal from the state's territory pending the outcome of the appeal.

[247] Comments from the European Council on Refugees and Exiles on the Proposal 'for a Council Regulation establishing the criteria and mechanisms for determining the Member State responsible for examining an asylum application lodged in one of the Member States by a third country national', p. 1, available on *www.ecre.org/eu_developments/stateresp.shtml*

[248] COM(2001) 510 final; OJ 2002 C 51/325.

The proposed Directive has a number of very welcome features, and is, in many places, a surprisingly liberal document.[249] It suggests that the cornerstone of the system should be the 'full and inclusive application of the Geneva Convention, complemented by measures offering subsidiary protection to those persons not covered by the Convention but who are nonetheless in need of international protection'.[250] Running to seven chapters, it takes as its starting point the Joint Position of 1996 on the harmonised application of the definition of the term 'refugee' (see above). The Proposal, taking account of criticisms of the Joint Position and of current thinking on interpretation of the 1951 Convention, includes the following provisions:

- the recognition that refugee status is a declaratory act;[251]

- acknowledgement that the UNHCR Handbook provides valuable guidance to Member States;[252]

- past persecution strongly indicates a reasonable possibility of future persecution or harm;[253]

- persecution may emanate from either the state, parties or organisations controlling the state, or *non-state actors* where the state is unwilling to provide effective protection;[254]

- the internal protection alternative is based on reasonableness and must have regard to the circumstances in the relevant part of the country, as well as respect for human rights and the personal circumstances of the applicant;[255]

---

[249] For discussions of the European Commission's Proposal 'for a Council Directive on minimum standards for the qualification and status of third country nationals and stateless persons as refugees or as persons who otherwise need international protection' (COM(2001) 510, see: House of Lords Select Committee on the European Union, 'Defining Refugee Status and those in need of International Protection', Session 2001–02, Twenty-Eighth Report, July 16, 2002; UNHCR's observations, November 2001; ILPA's submission, April 2002; Comments from ECRE, March 2002; JUSTICE comments, July 2002; Amnesty International's Comments, October 2, 2002; ILGA Europe position paper, February 2002.

[250] COM(2001) 510 final, p. 5.

[251] *ibid.*, Preamble, para. 10; this reflects the UNHCR's view: UNHCR *Handbook*, para. 28. See also, A. Grahl-Madsen, *The Status of Refugees in International Law* Vol. 1 (Netherlands: A.W. Sijthoff-Leyden, 1966), p. 34: 'a formal act of recognition has only declaratory, not constitutive, effect'.

[252] COM(2001) 510 final, Preamble, para. 10

[253] *ibid.*, Art. 7(c).

[254] *ibid.*, Art. 9.

[255] *ibid.*, Art. 10(2); Note: the European Parliament amended the term from 'internal protection' to 'internal flight alternative', which is a arguably a retrograde step, despite the UNHCR proposing this amendment.

- particular attention is drawn to the potential vulnerability and unique circumstances of children, and to the possibility of persecution of women through sexual violence or other gender-specific means;[256]

- subsidiary protection status must be granted where an applicant cannot return to his or her country of origin owing to a well-founded fear of being subjected to: torture or inhuman or degrading treatment or punishment; serious violation of a human right; threat to life, safety or freedom due to indiscriminate violence or systematic or generalised violation of human rights.[257]

The NGO Statewatch, which monitors activities in Europe in the justice and home affairs fields, reported in December 2002 that secret discussions were being held in the Council on the Directive.[258] In the original document, sexual orientation, and age or gender were specifically covered in 'the reasons for persecution'.[259] In the most recent version, however, the definition of 'particular social group' does not explicitly refer to age or gender, though sexual orientation is still a determining factor. Instead, a general statement is made that a social group exists where members of that group share an innate characteristic, or a common background which cannot be changed, or a characteristic or belief that is so fundamental to identity or conscience that a person should not be forced to renounce it.[260] The draft chooses to define persecution somewhat narrowly, requiring a risk to an applicant's 'life, freedom or security'. This definition appears to ignore the generally accepted Hathaway approach, namely that 'persecution may be defined as the sustained or systemic violation of basic human rights demonstrative of a failure of state protection'.[261] The draft also provides that 'state' protection might be offered by international organisations and 'stable quasi-state authorities' which control a clearly defined territory, and which can protect individuals from harm in a similar manner to that of an internationally recognised state.[262] This is arguably an alarming suggestion: there is no definition of a 'quasi-state'; international organisations and quasi-states

---

[256] COM(2001) 510 final, Art. 7.

[257] *ibid.*, Art. 15.

[258] Statewatch, 'EU: All refugee status to be temporary and terminated as soon as possible', December 2002.

[259] COM(2001) 510 final, Art. 12. Previously, 'reasons for persecution' was described as 'the nature of persecution', but Art. 12 was amended by the Council Committee of the Permanent Representatives, Room Doc. ASILE 14/02, November 27, 2002.

[260] Council Committee of the Permanent Representatives, Room Doc. ASILE 14/02, November 27, 2002.

[261] J. Hathaway, *The Law of Refugee Status* (Canada: Butterworths, 1991), pp. 104–5.

[262] COM(2001) 510 final, Art. 9(3).

are not subjects under international law to the extent that they are accountable for their actions; and it is unlikely, in any event, that they will be capable of providing suitable protection.

Another recent change introduced by Coreper[263] is in relation to cessation clauses. The new version of the Directive *requires* Member States to revoke refugee status where the refugee ceased to be a refugee in accordance with Art. 13 (cessation of refugee status).[264] This can certainly be regarded as a harsh provision; many countries do not systematically apply the cessation clauses of the 1951 Convention (Art. 1C), since refugees have often settled in the host country and are loath to return, or fear repatriation. What is more, the draft Directive does not incorporate the whole of Art. 1C of the 1951 Convention, which makes exception for refugees who are able to invoke compelling reasons arising out of previous persecution for refusing to return to the country of origin.[265] In relation to subsidiary protection, a similar power to revoke is also included where a person ceased to be eligible for subsidiary protection in accordance with Art. 16 of the directive (cessation of subsidiary protection status).[266] This, too, is unnecessarily restrictive. Finally, draft Art. 14B(4) allows for revocation of refugee status where there are reasonable grounds for regarding a refugee as a danger to the security of the EU state in which he or she is resident, or the refugee has been convicted of a particularly serious crime and constitutes a danger to the community of the Member State concerned. This amendment is clearly intended to deal with fears about terrorism, but it does seem rather excessive, especially as the 1951 Convention does not allow for such revocation and the Directive already includes the exclusion clause of Art. 1F of the Convention.[267]

The inclusion of subsidiary protection status can be considered essential. However, it is of limited duration and does not carry with it comparable rights to refugee status. For example, there is no access to employment associated with subsidiary protection, and there is not the same right to family reunification. Furthermore, it was not included in the draft Directive on minimum procedures, thereby giving rise to the possibility of future inconsistency in Member State practice. The Proposal also takes the somewhat contentious step of excluding EU nationals from the definition of 'refugee'.[268]

These concerns aside, the Directive should play a pivotal role in the future asylum policy of the EU. It is imperative that it is adopted as

9.32

---

[263] Council Committee of the Permanent Representatives.

[264] Art. 14B(1).

[265] Arts 1C(5) and (6).

[266] Art. 17B.

[267] Art. 14(c).

[268] COM(2001) 510 final, Art. 2(c).

soon as possible to provide the central 'building block' around which
so much of asylum policy must revolve. The UK will opt in.

'Flanking' and additional measures

9.33   In addition to the first stage components of the CEAS, a number of
'flanking' and additional measures have been introduced to support
the system.

Temporary protection in the event of a mass influx of displaced persons

9.34   In July 2001, the Council finally adopted a Directive 'on minimum
standards for giving temporary protection in the event of a mass
influx of displaced persons and on measures promoting a balance of
efforts between Member States in receiving such persons and bearing
the consequences thereof'.[269] The UK has opted in. In force since
August 2001, Member States were required to incorporate it into
their national legislation by December 31, 2002. The Directive certainly improves the previous position. It affords a number of rights to
those granted temporary protection, makes provision for groups
deemed especially vulnerable, and guarantees access to the asylum
determination procedures of the relevant Member State. It also seeks
to establish a solidarity mechanism. Though this Directive was the
first of its type passed – all previous drafts having failed to meet with
Council approval –, it still has various weaknesses. ECRE's report on
the progress towards a European asylum policy since Tampere
provides an excellent summary of the main shortcomings of the
Directive:

> 'Even in an emergency situation, visa controls and other restrictions will
> not be lifted to ease access to the EU (other than via an evacuation pro-
> gramme). There is no right of appeal against a refusal of temporary pro-
> tection, no guarantee of freedom of movement (despite the commitment
> at Tampere to a "right to move freely throughout the Union"), and tem-
> porary protection can be withdrawn from a person who applies for asylum
> [. . .].'[270]

---

[269]   Directive 2001/53/EC, OJ L 212/12.
[270]   ECRE, *The Promise of Protection: Progress towards A European Asylum Policy since Tampere*
(ECRE, November 2001), p. 9.

It is also revealing that between the draft and final version of the Directive, the duration of temporary protection was extended from two to three years, suggesting that Member States increasingly view temporary protection as a longer-term solution and a means by which to avoid the grant of full refugee status. There is a distinct possibility that temporary protection will be used in the future to undermine the obligations owed by Member States in respect the 1951 Convention.

Visa list

As was discussed above, a European visa list has been in existence for some time and was one of the first concrete initiatives undertaken by the EC in its quest for harmonisation of asylum and immigration policies. The latest Regulation of March 15, 2001 complies with the requirement in Art. 62(2)(b) of the EC Treaty that the Council adopt rules relating to visas for short stays.[271] The Regulation listed countries whose nationals must have a visa to enter the EU for periods under three months, and those whose nationals are exempted. It has since been amended: first, Romania was removed from the 'black list', and Romanian nationals are now exempted from the visa requirement;[272] second, Ecuador was added to the visa list in March 2003.[273] Needless to say, the UK is not bound by the EU visa lists, preferring to apply its own visa requirements.

9.35

EURODAC

First proposed in 1992 as an essential complement to the Dublin Convention, EURODAC (European Automated Fingerprinting System of Asylum Applicants) was finally adopted in December 2000.[274] Costing 6.5million Euros, the centralised fingerprinting system has now been established in Brussels and was officially launched on January 15, 2003. Its main aim is to prevent multiple asylum applications in the EU. Fingerprints of illegal entrants and of all asylum seekers over the age of 14 must be taken when they apply for asylum. They are then sent to a national access point in each participating

9.36

---

[271] Council Regulation No 539/2001, March 15, 2001; OJ 2001 L 81/1.
[272] Council Regulation No 2414/2001 amending Regulation 539/2001, December 7, 2001; OJ 2001 L 327/1.
[273] Council Regulation No 453/2003, amending Reg. No 539/2001; OJ 2003 L 69/10.
[274] Council Regulation No 2725/2000, concerning the establishment of 'Eurodac' for the comparison of fingerprints for the effective application of the Dublin Convention, OJ 2000 L 316/1.

country, and are transmitted electronically to the central database in Brussels, where they can be stored for up to 10 years. They will be removed from the database if an asylum seeker gains full citizenship. New fingerprints are compared with those already stored on the database.[275] If a match is found, Member States enter into discussions to decide responsibility for the asylum application in accordance with Dublin I. The UK has opted in to EURODAC.

Clearly, such a system could infringe human rights law, especially Art. 8 of the ECHR (the right to respect for private and family life), in view of storage of personal details on a database. This is a developing area of ECHR jurisprudence, but it is likely that obtaining personal details such as fingerprints, and storing them on a database, is permitted under Art. 8(2).[276] Whether or not fingerprinting itself can be justified is debatable. Previous case-law has accepted that fingerprinting could be exempted under Art. 8(2), where the UK government sought to prevent terrorism.[277] In the asylum context, the question is whether the preclusion of multiple applications is in the public interest or will help prevent further crimes, as demanded by the exception provided by Art.8(2). Furthermore, the storage of information on a database for up to 10 years must also be justified as 'necessary in a democratic society', and once more, it is unclear whether the prevention of immigration offences is an adequate reason under Art. 8(2).

Trafficking and smuggling

9.37   Trafficking and smuggling of human beings has been frequently discussed at the EU level, but generally in the context of immigration policy. The EU Tampere Summit set out an agenda for dealing with immigration, and some concrete measures have now emerged – for example, the Framework Decision on Combating Trafficking in Human Beings,[278] a proposed Framework Decision on Combating the Sexual Exploitation of Children and Child Pornography,[279] and

---

[275] Directorate-General Justice and Home Affairs, *Eurodac – The Fingerprint Database to help Asylum Seekers*, No. 22.1, January 2003.

[276] 'There shall be no interference by a public authority with the exercise of this right except such as is in accordance with the law and is necessary in a democratic society in the interests of national security, public safety or the economic well-being of the country, for the prevention of disorder or crime, for the protection of health or morals, or for the protection of the rights and freedoms of others.'

[277] *McVeigh, O'Neill and Evans v UK* (1981) 5 EHRR 71.

[278] 2002/629/JHA, July 19, 2003; OJ 2002 L 203/1.

[279] Council Doc. 10458/01, July 2, 2001.

the Framework Decision on Strengthening of the Penal Framework to Prevent the Facilitation of Unauthorised Entry, Transit and Residence.[280] The last is connected with a Directive defining the facilitation of unauthorised entry, transit and residence, agreed on November 28, 2002.[281] Further co-operation is still needed, though, with source and transit countries. A recent European Commission Communication 'on a common policy on illegal immigration' identified an action plan in six possible areas: visa policy; information exchange, co-operation and co-ordination; border management (with an eye to establishing a European Border Guard); police co-operation; aliens law and criminal law; and return and readmission policy. It is the Commission's view that efficient action in the prevention of and fight against illegal immigration and trafficking in human beings is key to the successful completion of the EU programme on asylum and immigration.[282] Public support for a common asylum regime and for a genuine immigration policy, which is 'in line with Europe's tradition of hospitality and solidarity', is regarded as imperative.[283]

That said, it is possible that these measures do not go far enough. For example, though the Framework Decision on trafficking refers to 'victims', it does not reach the level of protection proposed by the UN protocol 'to prevent, suppress and punish trafficking in persons'.[284] A key problem is what to do with the victims once discovered, and the UN acknowledges that developed countries are reluctant to permit those who are trafficked to remain in their territories, partly for fear of encouraging trafficking and illegal migration. The Framework Decision sidesteps this issue,[285] but it is highly unlikely that the EU will soften its stance in the future.[286]

European Refugee Fund

The European Refugee Fund ('ERF') was created to bring together all the disparate budgets relating to refugees and establishes a single 'pot of money' to: improve reception conditions for asylum-seekers   **9.38**

---

[280] 2002/946/JHA, November 28, 2002; OJ 2002 L 328/1.

[281] 2002/90/EC; OJ 2002 L 328/17.

[282] COM(2001) 672 final, para. 5.

[283] ibid.

[284] See Arts 4–6. The Protocol is to the UN Convention against Transnational Organized Crime 2000.

[285] See Art. 7.

[286] See, also, Commission Communication 'on the development of a common policy on illegal immigration, smuggling and trafficking of human beings, external borders and the return of illegal residents', COM(2003) 323 final.

and streamline eligibility procedures; improve integration of refugees; and promote action to enable refugees, displaced persons and asylum seekers who wish to return to their country of origin to do so in the best possible conditions.[287] The ERF was finally approved in September 2000 and was granted a total budget of 216 million Euros over five years.[288]

On the whole, the ERF is to be commended. As the UNHCR observes, 'the Fund allows for greater coherence in implementing Community policy in the areas eligible for funding, as well as increased predictability and flexibility in allocating resources'.[289] EU states will also be better prepared to address any future situations of mass influx.[290] This can only be good for refugees. One can also praise the provision in the Council Decision establishing the ERF that grants each Member State a fixed amount of the annual allocation of the Fund (Art. 10). The remainder of available resources is then distributed proportionally between Member States according to the number and category of persons who have entered their territories in the previous three years.[291] This should allow for a fairer allocation.

Nonetheless, the ERF does have its weak points. The amount allocated to the fund could be described as inadequate, on account of the size of the EU, and the five-year duration may prove too brief. It is arguable that a fairer system of allocation of funds between Member States would be based on a ratio between numbers of refugees entering the territory and the size of the population.[292] Furthermore, the arrangements for the distribution of remaining resources in Art. 10 favour asylum seekers, those benefiting from temporary protection, and those whose right to temporary protection is being examined in a Member State.[293] Refugees and *de facto* refugees are less privileged. Boccardi contends that this could have been read as a clear warning to Member States not to increase their refugee recognition rates.[294]

---

[287] Proposal 'for Council Decision on European Refugee Fund', IP/99/982 Brussels, December 14, 1999. For further information, see the ERF website: *www.european-refugee-fund.org/*

[288] Council Decision of September 28, 2000, establishing a European Refugee Fund, OJ 2000 L 252/12.

[289] UNHCR observations on the Council Decision creating a European Refugee Fund (September 28, 2000)(following Commission Proposal COM (1999) 686 final), para. 2.

[290] Council Decision of September 28, 2000, establishing a European Refugee Fund, OJ 2000 L 252/12, Art. 6.

[291] Art. 10(2).

[292] See I. Boccardi, *Europe and Refugees – Towards and EU Asylum Policy* (The Hague: Kluwer Law, 2002), p. 183.

[293] Art. 3.

[294] I. Boccardi, *Europe and Refugees – Towards and EU Asylum Policy* (The Hague: Kluwer Law, 2002), p. 184.

This might be an unduly negative interpretation of EU motives. Member States have long kept grants of refugee status down without incentives from the EU, and, in any event, most states invest considerably more on receiving and processing asylums seekers than on refugee integration. They would therefore not regard refugees as a priority area for funding.

Laeken, Seville and Thessaloniki

It is evident that, immediately prior to the meeting of the European Council in Laeken in December 2001, a considerable amount had been achieved in meeting the demands of Amsterdam and Tampere in the asylum field. A number of Directives and Regulations had been adopted, and the Commission had fulfilled its obligations by presenting proposals in all the key areas of the first stage. However, there remained some unresolved issues, and the requirement imposed by Amsterdam of unanimity voting was stalling agreement on some politically sensitive issues.[295] Laeken confirmed that progress had been 'slower and less substantial than expected' and that a new approach was needed.[296] The section of the Presidency Conclusions dealing with a 'true common asylum and immigration policy' only runs to four paragraphs and is essentially a restatement of Tampere. It set a deadline of April 30, 2002 for the Commission to submit amended proposals on asylum procedures, family reunification and the Dublin II Regulation; it also called upon the Council to expedite its proceedings on draft proposals concerning reception standards, the definition of the term 'refugee' and subsidiary protection.[297]

9.39

By the time of the European Council meeting in Seville in June 2002, a subtle change of emphasis was perceptible. There it was stated:

> 'Measures taken in the short and medium term for the joint management of migration flows must strike a fair balance between, on the one hand, a policy for the integration of lawfully resident immigrants and an asylum policy complying with international conventions, principally the 1951 Convention, and on the other, resolute action to combat illegal immigration and trafficking in human beings.'[298]

---

[295] C. Boswell, 'EU immigration and asylum policy: from Tampere to Laeken and beyond' (February 2002) *The Royal Institute of International Affairs*, Briefing Paper New Series No. 30, p. 4.

[296] Presidency Conclusions Laeken – December 14 & 15, 2001, SN 300/1/01 REV 1, para. 38.

[297] *ibid.*, para. 41.

[298] Presidency Conclusions Seville – June 21 & 22, 2002, Brussels October 24, 2002, 13463/02, para. 28.

Illegal immigration and trafficking in human beings were priori-
tised over asylum in the Seville Presidency Conclusions.[299] On the
specific issue of asylum, the European Council once more urged the
adoption of certain measures: Dublin II by December 2002; minimum standards for qualification for refugee status by June 2003; and
common standards for asylum procedures by December 2003.[300] As
has been indicated, the Regulation on Dublin II and the Directive on
reception conditions have now been agreed and adopted, but the rest
remain subject to ongoing discussion.

The third post-Tampere European Council summit was held in
June 2003 in Thessaloniki in Greece. Though the Presidency Conclusions on asylum were again very brief, they were crucial.[301] At a
time when various options for the 'regionalisation of asylum' and for
the creation of 'transit processing centres' outside the EU were being
presented, at the instigation of the UK (see below), the Council called
on the Commission to consider alternative methods of protection for
people seeking to enter the EU area, and to present a report before
June 2004.[302] Critically, it insisted on the participation of the
UNHCR in any discussions, and with the UNHCR to take a leading
role. The Conclusions also stressed the importance of adoption of
outstanding basic legislation by the end of 2003,[303] and reaffirmed
'the importance of a more efficient asylum system within the EU to
identify quickly all persons in need of protection, in the context of
broader migration movements, and developing appropriate EU programmes'.[304] This positive statement was somewhat mitigated by
para. 27, which invited further examination of the ways in which asylum procedures could be made more efficient in order to accelerate
the processing of 'non-international protection-related applications'.

A EUROPEAN CONSTITUTION – WHAT IMPACT ON ASYLUM?

9.40   In accordance with the Declaration on the future of Europe contained in the Treaty of Nice, the Laeken European Council decided
to hold a Convention on the future of the Union. Its inaugural meeting, under the Chairmanship of former President of France, Valéry
Giscard d'Estaing, was held on February 28, 2002. The Convention's

---

[299] Presidency Conclusions Seville – June 21 & 22, 2002, Brussels October 24, 2002,
13463/02, Ch. III.
[300] *ibid.*, para. 37.
[301] Presidency Conclusions Thessaloniki – June 19 & 20, 2003, paras 24–27.
[302] *ibid.*, para. 26.
[303] *ibid.*, para. 24.
[304] *ibid.*, para. 25.

objectives were very broad. In an expanding Europe, it was recognised that the role of the EU must change. It fell to the European Convention to propose ways of adapting and renovating Europe's institutional and political framework, and to set out clear and consensual answers to some basic questions:

- 'How is the division of competence between the Union and the Member States to be organised?

- How can the European institutions' respective tasks be better defined?

- How can the coherence and efficiency of the Union's external action be ensured?

- How can the Union's democratic legitimacy be strengthened?'[305]

The Convention concluded on July 10, 2003 and submitted its report to the European Council together with a draft Treaty establishing a Constitution for Europe.[306] These will form the basis of discussion at the Intergovernmental Conference in 2004.

The drafting of a European Constitution was clearly a mammoth task and one with far-reaching consequences. Working Groups were established to discuss certain key issues. There were eleven in total, and the two most closely associated with asylum and refugee law were Working Group X, on freedom, security and justice, and Working Group II on the Charter and ECHR. Both issued their final reports towards the end of 2002.[307] Working Group X submitted three main recommendations with regard to asylum:

- 'That qualified majority voting and codecision be made applicable in the Treaty for legislation on asylum, refugees and displaced persons;

- That Art. 63(1) and (2) be redrafted in order to create a general legal base enabling the adoption of the measures needed to put in place a common asylum system and a common asylum policy on refugees and displaced persons as set out in Tampere. This legal base should, as in the present Treaty, ensure full respect of the Geneva Convention but enable the Union also to provide further complementary forms of protection not embraced by that Convention;

---

[305] See *european-convention.eu.int/enjeux.asp?lang=EN*
[306] Report from the Presidency of the Convention to the Presidency of the European Council, Brussels July 18, 2003, CONV 851/03.
[307] Available on the European Convention website: *european-convention.eu.int/*

- While acknowledging the responsibilities of the Member States, to enshrine in the Treaty the principle of solidarity and fair sharing and responsibility (including its financial implications) between the Member States, applying as a general principle to the Union's asylum, immigration and border control policies. A specific legal basis should enable the adoption of the detailed policies necessary to give effect to this principle.'[308]

These principles were uncontentious. The UK government strongly endorsed qualified majority voting in relation to asylum, as well as the proposed lifting of the national veto. However, Working Group X also concluded that Europol needed a new wording of tasks and powers, establishing its central role in the framework of police co-operation. It went on to propose the introduction in the long term of an integrated system for the management of external border controls and the creation of a European Border Guard. As noted earlier, this last suggestion corresponded with the Commission's own views.n its turn, Working Group II, which examined fundamental rights in the EU, concluded that the Charter should be incorporated into any constitutional treaty, and that the EU should accede to the ECHR.[309] These two actions, according to the Group, would enhance the protection of fundamental rights of citizens vis-à-vis action at European level, and highlight the moral and ethical commitments of the European Union. Although unstated, a corollary of this would be enhanced protection for third country nationals.

9.41   The final version of the draft Constitution, published on July 18, 2003, did in fact incorporate the Charter and proposed accession to the ECHR.[310] It also extended the jurisdiction of the ECJ to cover Justice and Home Affairs in their entirety, and consequently EC asylum law is included.[311] The specific article on asylum, currently Art. III–167, states:

'1.   The Union shall develop a common policy on asylum and temporary protection with a view to offering appropriate status to any third-country national requiring international protection and ensuring compliance with the principle of *non-refoulement*. This policy must be in accordance with the Geneva Convention of July 28, 1951 and the Protocol of January 31, 1967 relating to the status of refugees and other relevant treaties.

---

[308] The European Convention, *Final Report of Working Group II*, CONV 354/02, October 22, 2002.

[309] The European Convention, *Final Report of Working Group X "Freedom, Security and Justice"*, CONV 426/02, December 2, 2002, p. 4

[310] Title II, Arts 7(1) and (2).

[311] Art. III–274.

2. For this purpose, European laws or framework laws shall lay down measures for a common European asylum system comprising:

(a) a uniform status of asylum for nationals of third countries, valid throughout the Union;

(b) a uniform status of subsidiary protection for nationals of third countries who, without obtaining European asylum, are in need of international protection;

(c) a common system of temporary protection for displaced persons in the event of a massive inflow;

(d) common procedures for the granting and withdrawing of uniform asylum or subsidiary protection status;

(e) criteria and mechanisms for determining which Member State is responsible for considering an application for asylum or subsidiary protection;

(f) standards concerning the conditions for the reception of applicants for asylum or subsidiary protection;

(g) partnership and cooperation with third countries for the purpose of managing inflows of people applying for asylum or subsidiary or temporary protection.

3. In the event of one or more Member States being confronted by an emergency situation characterised by a sudden inflow of nationals of third countries, the Council of Ministers, on a proposal from the Commission, may adopt European regulations or decisions comprising provisional measures for the benefit of the Member State(s) concerned. It shall act after consulting the European Parliament.'

In his declaration accompanying the Convention's report, Giscard d'Estaing expressed his desire that the Constitution be signed in May 2004.

HUMAN RIGHTS AND ASYLUM IN THE EU[312]

The three founding Treaties of the European Communities made no reference to human rights.[313] Consequently, the step taken at Tampere to place asylum policy within its human rights context was significant, even if the Union had expressed, in the past, its commitment to fundamental human rights in general. For example, the 1986 Single European Act referred to the EC working within a human   **9.42**

---

[312] For an excellent analysis of human rights in the EU up to the year 2000, see P. Alston ed., *The EU and Human Rights* (Oxford: OUP, 1999).

[313] Treaty establishing the European Coal and Steel Community 1951; Treaty establishing the European Economic Community 1957; Treaty establishing the European Atomic Energy Community 1957.

rights context in its preamble,[314] and, more specifically, Art. F.2 of the Maastricht Treaty declared: 'The Union shall respect fundamental human rights, as guaranteed by the European Convention for the Protection of Human Rights and Fundamental Freedoms [. . .] and as they result from the constitutional traditions common to the Member States, as general principles of Community Law.' Significantly, from an asylum perspective, Art.K.2(1) guaranteed that matters referred to in Art. K.1 (which included asylum) would be dealt with in compliance with the ECHR, as well as the 1951 Geneva Convention. The consolidated version of the TEU 1997, as amended by the Amsterdam Treaty, repeated the Union's respect for the fundamental rights of the ECHR,[315] and insisted that any state applying for membership of the EU is required to respect the principles set out in Art. 6(1).[316] Article 6(1) states: 'The Union is founded on the principles of liberty, democracy, respect for human rights and fundamental freedoms, and the rule of law, principles which are common to the Member States.' Furthermore, as is well known, despite lacking competence under Treaty law, the ECJ in its early days 'decided to fill a threatening gap in the legal protection of individuals by formulating its own doctrine of the protection of fundamental rights as an unwritten part of the *Community* legal order'.[317] It did so by making use of 'general principles' as a source of law and drew upon a range of human rights instruments including the ECHR.[318] Post Amsterdam, following the amendment made to the pillars, the ECJ now has the power to ensure respect for fundamental rights and freedoms by the European institutions.[319] In relation to asylum and immigration, Art. 63(1) requires that any measures adopted on asylum be in accordance with the 1951 Convention and the 1967 Protocol relating to the status of refugees, and other relevant treaties.

The Charter

9.43   In the same year that Amsterdam came into force, the German EU Presidency proposed that an EU Charter of Fundamental Rights be

---

[314] 'DETERMINED to work together to promote democracy on the basis of the fundamental rights recognized in the constitutions and laws of the Member States, in the Convention for the Protection of Human Rights and Fundamental Freedoms and the European Social Charter, notably freedom, equality and social justice.'

[315] Art. 6(2).

[316] Consolidated version of the TEU, Art. 49.

[317] B. de Witte, 'The past and the future role of the ECJ in the protection of human rights' in P. Alston ed., *The EU and Human Rights* (Oxford: OUP, 1999), p. 863.

[318] See *ibid* for a discussion of the ECJ's creation of a doctrine of fundamental rights.

[319] Consolidated version of the TEU, Art. 46.

established, an idea that was pursued at the Tampere summit in October 1999. This was in response perhaps to the ECJ's ruling in Opinion 2/94 that an amendment to the EC Treaty was needed before the EC as a body could sign the ECHR.[320] Member States failed to make the amendment in either the Treaty of Amsterdam or the Treaty of Nice, preferring, it would seem, to establish a non-binding EU Charter. The text was finally agreed in December 2000.[321] Space does not permit a full discussion of the Charter, though reference should be made to Arts 18 and 19, which address asylum. Article 18 incorporates a 'right to asylum': 'The right to asylum shall be guaranteed with due respect for the rules of the Geneva Convention of July 28, 1951 and the Protocol of January 31, 1967 relating to the status of refugees and in accordance with the Treaty establishing the European Community.' It is noteworthy that Member States chose only to pay 'due respect' to the Convention. Presidency Conclusions from Tampere, Laeken, and Seville all declare a much higher level commitment, using expressions such as 'full and inclusive application of the Geneva Convention'; 'in accordance with the principles of the 1951 Geneva Convention'; and 'complying with international conventions, principally the 1951 Geneva Convention'. According to Peers 'it might be argued that the different wording is justified because the Geneva Convention does not as such set out a right to asylum.'[322] However, it is worth noting that Art. 18 goes further than Art. 14 of the Universal Declaration of Human Rights, which simply guarantees a 'right to seek and to enjoy in other countries asylum from persecution'. Article 19 of the Charter provides protection in the event of removal, expulsion or extradition. It prohibits collective expulsions (Art. 19(1)), and does not allow for the removal of an individual to a State where there is a serious risk that he or she would be subjected to the death penalty, torture or other inhuman or degrading treatment or punishment (Art. 19(2)). In other words, it prohibits *non-refoulement*. Article 19, like its counterpart in the 1951 Convention, is not subject to derogations.

In addition, while the Charter might be centred on the rights of EU citizens, it does incorporate further provisions which, if not asylum-focused, might still enhance the conditions of an asylum seeker or refugee while in a Member State. They include the right to

---

[320] [1996] ECR-I 1759.
[321] OJ 2000 C 364/1. For a discussion of the background to the Charter and its content, see S. Peers, 'Immigration, asylum and the European Union Charter of Fundamental Rights' (2001) 3: 2 *European Journal of Migration and Law*, pp. 141–169; see, also, House of Commons Research Paper 00/32, *Human Rights in the EU: the Charter of Fundamental Rights*, March 20, 2000.
[322] S. Peers, 'Immigration, asylum and the European Union Charter of Fundamental Rights' (2001) 3: 2 *European Journal of Migration and Law*, p. 161.

social security and social assistance;[323] access to preventative health care and medical treatment;[324] for third country nationals authorised to work, equivalent working conditions to those of citizens of the Union;[325] education;[326] and the right of children to 'such protection and care as is necessary for their well-being'.[327] Currently, the Charter is not binding; nonetheless, Rogers argues that it has been 'taking hold in certain quarters by stealth, winning friends and influencing people. It is gathering a momentum of its own, not just in academic circles', and '[i]ts practical effects, both actual and potential, can no longer be ignored.'[328] In the field of asylum law, this is certainly true. Not only does it reinforce the rights-based nature of asylum and migration law,[329] but it also provides a useful new interpretative force. Thus, for example, in *Sepet & Bulbul v Secretary of State for the Home Department*,[330] a UK case involving Turkish nationals of Kurdish origin who were claiming asylum on the basis that, if returned to Turkey, they would be required to perform compulsory military service on pain of imprisonment, reference was made by Lord Bingham in the House of Lords to Art. 10 of the Charter (freedom of thought, conscience and religion).[331] Likewise, the significant case of *R. (Yogathas and Thangarasa) v Secretary of State for the Home Department*,[332] discussed in Chapter 8 and which concerned Tamil asylum seekers who resisted removal to Germany on the grounds that their claim would not be as fully and favourably considered there as in the UK, also referred to the Charter, and specifically to Arts 18 and 19.[333] These national references aside, the Charter has been strongly endorsed before the European Court, both in the opinions of Advocates-General[334] and

---

[323] Art. 34.

[324] Art. 35.

[325] Art. 15.

[326] Art. 14.

[327] Art. 24.

[328] I. Rogers, 'From the Human Rights Act to the Charter: not another human rights instrument to consider', (2002) 3: 3/4 *European Human Rights Law Review*, p. 343.

[329] S. Peers, 'Immigration, asylum and the European Union Charter of Fundamental Rights' (2001) 3: 2 *European Journal of Migration and Law*, p. 167.

[330] [2003] UKHL 15.

[331] *ibid.*, para. 15.

[332] [2002] INLR 620.

[333] *ibid.*, para. 36.

[334] See Advocate-General Tizzano's opinion in Case C-173/99 *Broadcasting, Entertainment, Cinematographic, and Theatre Union (BECTU) v Secretary of State for Trade and Industry*, February 8, 2001, para. 28: 'I think therefore that, in proceedings concerned with the nature and scope of a fundamental right, the relevant statements of the Charter cannot be ignored; in particular, we cannot ignore its clear purpose of serving, where its provisions so allow, as a substantive point of reference for all those involved – Member States, institutions, natural and legal persons – in the Community context.'

by the Court of First Instance itself.[335] Despite its non-binding status, it seems clear, therefore, that the Charter is growing in legal potency at both municipal and EU levels.[336]

In July 2001, the European Parliament recommended that a net- **9.44** work be established consisting of human rights legal experts from each of the Member States. Its remit would be to report annually to the Parliament on the implementation of each of the rights laid down in the EU Charter. The Commission in September 2002 set up such a network and its first report was submitted in March 2003.[337] A substantial document running to 316 pages, it raised numerous concerns relating to refugees and asylum seekers, and highlighted problems in specific Member States. For example, in relation to the UK, it noted that the Nationality, Immigration and Asylum Act 2002 was very restrictive, referring to the introduction of accommodation centres for asylum seekers and their dependants who request support, as well as to the new harsh appeal restrictions for certain certified claims.[338] Reference was also made to concerns of the UN Committee on the Rights of the Child about the ongoing detention of children in the UK.[339] In a second report, dedicated to the matter of anti-terrorism legislation, the group of experts expressed considerable disquiet about anti-terrorist measures adopted by EU Member States since September 11, 2001.[340] As part of its conclusions, the report stated:

'In the United Kingdom, the adoption of the Anti-terrorism, Crime and Security Act 2001 gave rise to a notification of a derogation addressed to the Secretary General of the Council of Europe on the basis of Article 15 of the European Convention of Human Rights, although it is doubtful that the conditions required for the use of this provision are met, or that the detention that the derogation intends to cover is admissible under the derogation that has been notified [. . .]. International law on human rights is not opposed to States taking measures to protect against the terrorist threat [. . .] but the consequences for the guarantee of individual freedoms [must be] limited to a strict minimum. In particular, independent control mechanisms must be provided that can counter possible abuse committed

---

[335] See, *e.g.*, Case T-54/99 *max.mobil Telekommunikation Service GmbH v Commission*, January 30, 2002, para. 48, citing Art. 41(1) of the Charter.

[336] I. Rogers, 'From the Human Rights Act to the Charter: not another human rights instrument to consider', (2002) 3: 3/4 *European Human Rights Law Review*, p. 350.

[337] EU Network of Independent Experts in Fundamental Rights (CFR-CDF) *Report of the Situation of Fundamental Rights in the EU and its Member States in 2002*, March 31, 2003.

[338] *ibid.*, pp. 141 and 152.

[339] *ibid.*, p. 146.

[340] EU Network of Independent Experts in Fundamental Rights (CFR-CDF) *The Balance between Freedom and Security in the Response by the European Union and its Member States to the Terrorist Threats*, March 31, 2003.

by the Executive or criminal prosecution authorities. In addition, restrictions made to individual freedoms in response to the terrorist threat must be limited to what is absolutely necessary. These restrictions were adopted to cope with an immediate threat, but one that is not necessarily permanent, and as such, they should be of a temporary character and be assessed regularly under some kind of mechanism.'[341]

While both reports provided mainly documentary evidence of human rights compliance by Member States, its apparent willingness to judge their performance suggests that, together with future reports, it should prove a valuable source of information on human rights adherence in the EU.

THE FUTURE OF EU ASYLUM POLICY: WHICH WAY FORWARD?

9.45 In a letter to the Greek Presidency of the Council on March 10, 2003, the UK Prime Minister, Tony Blair, proposed some major changes to the processing of asylum claims in the EU.[342] His 'new vision' advocated:

- working to prevent the conditions which cause population movements;

- working to ensure better protection in source regions;

- developing more managed resettlement routes from source regions to Europe;

- raising awareness and acceptance of state responsibility to accept returns;

- considering whether protection in the regions should and could reach a level in which people could be moved from Europe to the protected areas of processing (the so-called 'safe havens' idea);

- considering establishing protected zones in third countries to which those arriving in the EU and claiming asylum could be transferred to have their claims processed (referred to as 'transit processing centres' or 'TPC's').

---

[341] EU Network of Independent Experts in Fundamental Rights (CFR-CDF) *The Balance between Freedom and Security in the Response by the European Union and its Member States to the Terrorist Threats*, March 31, 2003, p. 52.

[342] Available on *www.statewatch.org/news/2003/apr/blair-simitis-asile.pdf*

The last two suggestions prompted considerable press coverage and a number of NGOs issued statements warning against the establishment of complementary processing systems as an alternative to Member States' duties to examine asylum requests of persons arriving spontaneously.[343] There was also considerable doubt about the practicality of transferring responsibility for processing asylum applications to third countries, particularly those bordering the current EU.[344] Amnesty International was clearly very suspicious about the initiative: 'The real goal behind the UK proposal appears to be to reduce the number of spontaneous arrivals in the UK and other EU states by denying access to territory and shifting asylum seekers to zones outside the EU where refugee protection would be weak and unclear.'[345] The UK legal and human rights organisation, JUSTICE, obtained counsels' opinion on the legality of the UK's proposal to establish transit processing centres. This concluded:

'(1)   Automatic removal of asylum seekers to a location outside of the European Union before substantive consideration of their application for asylum would not conform with internationally recognised human rights and refugee protection standards and is likely to be in breach of the United Kingdom's international obligations under the Refugee Convention.

(2)   Removal of asylum seekers to a TPC is likely to give rise to a serious possibility of a breach of the European Convention on Human Rights.'[346]

The publication of the UK's safe havens' proposal coincided with a furore that broke in the British press. The Conservative Party issued various statements urging the UK's withdrawal from relevant international agreements if it proved the only route to a 'fairer and more humane asylum system'.[347] Oliver Letwin, the Shadow Home Secretary, called for a reservation to be entered against Art. 3 of the ECHR, to give the UK the power to deport foreign nationals judged to be a risk to the public.[348] The Conservative Party was also said to be considering 'renegotiation' of the 1951 Convention and 1967 Protocol, as well as Dublin II. Not to be outdone, the Home Secretary, David Blunkett, announced that he had opened discussions with the UN about the UK's obligations under the 1951 Convention, and

---

[343]   ECRE, Statement of the ECRE on the European Council Meeting on March 21 & 22, 2003, March 17, 2003.

[344]   *ibid.*

[345]   A. Travis, 'Amnesty condemns "safe haven" scheme', *The Guardian*, March 28, 2003.

[346]   Available on: *www.justice.org.uk/inthenews/index.html*

[347]   BBC News, 'Tories propose asylum detention', February 5, 2003.

[348]   *ibid.*

that he wanted the Convention revised to reflect the new global situation.[349]

The UK government claimed that there was considerable interest from EU Member States in its 'new vision', and that safe havens and transit processing centres were viable options.[350] Within weeks of making this statement, it was backing down in the face of opposition from Germany and Sweden, amongst others.[351] In June 2003, just prior to the European Council meeting in Greece, the Minister for Immigration, Beverley Hughes, confirmed to the House of Commons that, while there was 'steady progress' with the proposals on safe havens, there were no plans to process asylum seekers on the borders of the EU and that no camps were being built, as had been reported in parts of the press.[352] It seems, then, that, for the time being, the idea of transit processing centres has been put to one side.

9.46   One explanation for the partial failure of the UK's proposals is the involvement of the European Commission. In June 2003, it entered the debate on the future of EU asylum policy by issuing yet another Communication, this time entitled 'towards more accessible, equitable and managed asylum systems'. There it analysed the UK paper, set out the views of the UNHCR and other NGOs, and provided a number of approaches for 'more accessible, equitable and managed asylum systems'.[353] This document needs to be read alongside an earlier Communication on the common asylum policy and an 'agenda for protection', which the Commission presented on March 26, 2003.[354] The Commission's view was that 'there is a crisis in the asylum system [. . .] and a subsequent malaise in public opinion'.[355] It noted the rising abuse of asylum procedures and the use of smuggling practices, a phenomenon that it regarded as 'a real threat to the institution of asylum and more generally for Europe's humanitarian tradition'.[356] The response suggested was structural, but the Commission warned that any new proposals should complement the stage-by-stage approach adopted at Tampere.[357] They should also be underpinned by 10 basic premises, which require the Member States to: respect fully international legal obligations; address root causes of

---

[349] BBC News, 'Asylum "havens" considered by UK, February 5, 2003; BBC News, 'UK discussing UN asylum obligations', February 5, 2003.

[350] Home Affairs Select Committee, 'Asylum Applications', Uncorrected Oral Evidence, Beverley Hughes, Session 2003–04, May 8, 2003, Qs. 103–109.

[351] I. Black, 'EU urged to rethink asylum policies', *The Guardian*, June 18, 2003.

[352] ' "No plans" for asylum camps outside EU', *The Guardian*, June 16, 2003.

[353] COM(2003) 315 final, June 3, 2003.

[354] COM(2003) 152 final, March 26, 2003.

[355] COM(2003) 315 final, June 3, 2003, p. 11.

[356] *ibid.*

[357] *ibid.*

forced migration; allow access to legal immigration channels; combat illegal immigration; develop full partnerships with and between countries of origin, transit, first asylum and destination; improve the quality of decisions in the EU, consolidate protection capacities in the region of origin, and treat protection requests as close as possible to needs (*i.e.* regulate access to the EU by establishing 'protected entry schemes' and resettlement programmes); complement rather than substitute the CEAS; finalise the delayed CEAS directives; ensure enforcement of the UNHCR Agenda for Protection and Convention Plus; and 'respect the current financial perspective'.[358] Finally, with these basic premises in mind, the Commission outlined its new approach:

> 'The overall aim of such a new approach to asylum systems is to better manage asylum-related flows in their European dimension and in regions of origin, resulting in more accessible, equitable and managed asylum systems. These asylum systems should enable persons in need of international protection to access such protection as soon as possible and as closely as possible to their needs, and therewith reducing [*sic*] felt needs and pressures to seek international protection elsewhere.'[359]

This approach is based on three policy objectives: (i) the orderly and managed arrival of persons in need of international protection in the EU from the region of origin; (ii) burden and responsibility sharing within the EU as well as with regions of origin, enabling them to provide effective protection as soon as possible and as closely as possible to the needs of persons requiring international protection; and (iii) the development of an integrated approach to efficient and enforceable asylum decision-making and return procedures.[360] As the Communication itself notes, one of the key legal questions relates to the definition of 'effective protection'.[361] Clearly, this is of considerable importance. Member States have reached agreement that 'protection can be said to be "effective" when, as a minimum, the following conditions are met: physical security, a guarantee against *refoulement*, access to UNHCR asylum procedures or national procedures with sufficient safeguards, where this is required to access effective protection or durable solutions, and social-economic well-being, including, as a minimum, access to primary healthcare and primary education, as well as access to the labour market, or access to means of subsistence sufficient to maintain an adequate standard of

---

[358] *ibid.*, pp. 11–12.
[359] *ibid.*, p. 13.
[360] *ibid.*
[361] *ibid.*, p. 6.

living'.[362] Though the summit at Thessaloniki could not endorse the
Commission's Communication, it did take note of it, and urged the
Commission to explore all possibilities of ensuring 'more orderly and
managed entry in the EU of persons in need of international protection'.[363] Any exploration of ways to provide better protection for
refuges in their region of origin must be carried out in full partnership with countries of origin and on the basis of recommendations
from the UNHCR.[364]

Contrary perhaps to expectations, the UNHCR, which would have
needed to participate in any transit processing centre scheme and
screen asylum applicants, gave the UK's proposal serious consideration. At the time, a spokesman informed the press that the 'UNHCR
is discussing a number of proposals with the UK government, including regional approaches to dealing with asylum claims. These proposals would not, however, be a substitute for a fair and effective
domestic asylum system.'[365] However, it soon issued its own discussion
document in April 2003, and then an updated version in June, entitled 'UNHCR's three-pronged proposal'.[366] The three prongs are:
regional (improved access to solutions in the region of origin); domestic (improved national asylum systems of destination states); and EU
(processing 'manifestly unfounded' cases). The UNHCR has emphatically denied that its 'regional prong' equates to the UK's idea of 'safe
havens' or 'zones of protection'.[367] It is 'primarily concerned with
making more concerted and imaginative efforts to grapple with specific situations in refugees' regions of origin, not with creating some
sort of new geographical or physical entities'.[368] The third prong,
relating to the EU, differs from the idea of transit processing centres
in that economic migrants will be transferred to processing centres
based *within* the EU. This is critical. The UNHCR has suggested that
EU-based processing should be piloted for asylum applicants coming
from designated countries of origin who are primarily economic
migrants using the asylum channel. Upon arrival in the EU, they

---

[362] COM(2003) 315 final, June 3, 2003, p. 6.

[363] Presidency Conclusions Thessaloniki – June 19 & 20, 2003, para. 26.

[364] *ibid.*

[365] A. Travis, 'Blunkett pushes for refugee safe havens', *The Guardian*, March 1, 2003.

[366] Available on www.statewatch.org; see, for a discussion of many of the issues, G.
Noll, 'Visions of the exceptional: Legal and theoretical issues raised by transit
processing centres and protection zones' (2003) 5:3 *European Journal of Migration
and Law*; see, also, G. Loescher & J. Milner, 'The missing link: the need for comprehensive engagement in regions of refugee origin' (2003) 79:3 *International Affairs*,
pp. 583–617.

[367] UNHCR Briefing Note,' UNHCR asylum policy: setting the record straight', June
20, 2003.

[368] *ibid.*

would be transferred immediately to closed reception centres, where their claims would be processed within one month.[369] Those in need of protection would be distributed between EU states; those not would be returned to countries of origin. While admitting that the problem of people entering without identification or with fraudulent documentation would remain unresolved by these proposals, the UNHCR is still persuaded that 'A joint EU-based mechanism, if efficiently managed, should have the effect of (i) deterring abuse of the asylum system, as well as smuggling; (ii) avoiding burden-shifting within Europe; and (iii) building on ongoing burden sharing within the EU.'[370] It would also 'represent an important step towards creating a common asylum system'.[371] This is unlikely to assuage the concerns of the UK, which has seen the numbers of undocumented claimants rise; nor is it likely to help end human smuggling, despite the UNHCR's optimistic prognosis.

CONCLUSION

The road towards a harmonised asylum policy in the EU has been long and hazardous. Having emerged from an era of secrecy into a more open and transparent decision-making process, the EU is now at the threshold of a Common European Asylum Policy. A number of important measures have finally been agreed (Dublin II and the Directive for minimum standards for asylum seekers); others, while not yet implemented, are due for adoption in the near future (the proposed Directives on asylum procedures and refugee status). It is clear from the foregoing discussion that, if harmonisation has been achieved, it is only up to a point. There is evidence to suggest that the objective might now have changed. The British Government, for example, recently referred to 'common or co-ordinated policies', and argued against the concept of 'harmonisation', when discussing the draft Constitution.[372] This could be regarded simply as semantics, but it does suggest that 'harmonisation' – in its true sense of convergence of asylum norms – is now recognised to be impossible, or, in fact, undesirable.

With the implementation of new Directives and Regulations, the agreement of a Charter of Fundamental Rights in the EU, and the

9.47

---

[369] UNHCR Working Paper, 'UNHCR's three-pronged proposal', June 2003, p. 6.

[370] *ibid.*

[371] *ibid.*

[372] Peter Hain, Government Representative on the Convention on the Future of Europe, Report of the Convention's Working Group X on 'freedom, security and justice', European Scrutiny Committee, March 25, 2003.

advent of an EU Constitution, it is clear that the asylum landscape will be subject to change for some time yet. Furthermore, Member States are constantly seeking new solutions to the 'asylum problem', as was so manifestly revealed by the UK government's proposals for a 'new vision for refugees'. EC documentation stresses the importance of adhering to international refugee law and human rights standards; at the same time, some western European countries have called for revision of the 1951 Convention, a degree of regionalisation of the refugee issue, and even the possibility, in extreme cases, of military intervention to deal with forced migration.[373] There is also a sense now that a two-tier system will emerge in the EU, in which asylum seekers who arrive spontaneously will be regarded as unworthy of protection, while those who choose the orderly route of UNHCR quotas or 'protective entry procedures' in countries of origin will be deemed 'genuine'.[374] Though there may not yet be consensus on how EU asylum policy will develop, all are agreed that change is inevitable.

---

[373] '[Our] focus should be on ensuring that forced migration is for a temporary period only [. . .]. [The] international community must take action to resolve conflicts, and human rights abuse and commit to post conflict reconstruction to enable sustainable return. There is no international law permitting such intervention and it is still highly controversial. Nevertheless, refuge flows have been used in the past to justify intervention, for example in Kosovo [. . .]. As a last resort, there needs to be military intervention.' UK government 'restricted policy', draft final report, February 5, 2003, cited in Statewatch News Online, 'Asylum in the EU: the beginning of the end?' available on www.statewatch.orgo

[374] J van der Klaauw, 'Irregular migration and asylum-seeking: Forced marriage or reason for divorce', speaking at University of Leicester Conference, *Irregular Migration and Human Rights*, June 28–29, 2003.

Conclusion

With the uncertainty surrounding so much of current asylum law and policy, it seems a particularly apposite point at which to reflect on the past and its contribution to contemporary problems and proposed solutions. It is clear from the historical overview provided by this book that, through time, the state attempted to 'manage' migration in relation to asylum. Part of the approach was to classify those seeking a safe haven on British soil according to their perceived contribution to the host community. As noted, with such classification came approval or disapproval, inclusion or exclusion. Up to the end of the nineteenth century, 'asylum seekers' assumed many different forms – '*réfugié*', *émigré*, exile, immigrant, to name only a few –, but for much of the twentieth century, they were assigned to two main categories: 'refugees' and 'immigrants'. Such division worked reasonably effectively so long as numbers claiming asylum remained relatively low. However, from the 1980s onwards, a rise in applications proved particularly disruptive, as policy-makers and government ministers struggled to meet a major challenge: the establishment of a just, humane and effective asylum system, which could distinguish properly between the refugee and the economic migrant.

There is a paradox at the heart of current asylum policy. On the one hand, the UK has committed itself to the protection of human rights as never before. The adoption of the Human Rights Act 1998, the signing of the EU Charter, and frequent statements of adherence to the 1951 Convention are all testament to a country dedicated to upholding human rights. On the other hand, as it struggles to take a secure hold on the asylum issue, it has tended increasingly towards exclusion and deterrence, with the introduction of more restrictive rules and criteria that cannot be said with confidence to distinguish between the 'genuine' and the 'bogus'. The commitment in principle to justice and humaneness risks being compromised in practice by a growing element of arbitrariness and restriction. Nor has repeated legislation resulted in greater efficiency. Accusations by NGOs and practitioners of poor first instance decision-making and of a deplorable lack of consistency are commonplace. The Home Office

and Appellate Authority continue under the weight of a huge burden
imposed by numbers, and progress is very slow. Even where decisions
are arrived at quickly, and refugee status is refused, insufficient numbers of failed asylum seekers are removed. Critics and supporters of
government policy alike recognise that the current position is untenable and that public confidence in the asylum system risks being
severely damaged.

   If legislation and greater regulation are not working, what alternatives remain for a beleaguered government? There are some who
continue to advocate further controls, and see improved border
checks and the introduction of national identity cards as the next
step.[1] There are others who contend that the effectiveness of the
asylum system is dependent entirely on the quality of its workforce.
For them, there will be no advance without increased investment in
the Home Office, Immigration Service and Appellate Authority. A
possible 'third way' is open to the UK: the route provided by Europe.
EC harmonisation of asylum policy, or at the very least greater co-
operation, could have some political expediency for the government.
Adoption of European Directives and Regulations might enable it to
draw benefit from a collective EU approach on aspects of asylum law
– and also, *in extremis*, to disclaim responsibility for certain elements of
its policy. But this could be a double-edged sword for the UK: once
the components of refugee status determination and minimum procedures are fixed by EC law, Member States will be unable to lower
the threshold of protection, if they so desire.

   No clear solution is in sight. The UK's proposals to establish transit processing centres outside the EU, and to consider regionalisation
of the asylum issue, signal clearly the government's limited faith in
the currently available options. In some senses, the proposals were
remarkable for their audacity, but they also raise a very serious question: is the UK government reassessing the state's role in the management of migration in relation to asylum? They certainly constitute
the most blatant attempt to date to treat asylum as an extra-territorial
problem, thereby diminishing the role of domestic law. For the time
being, these proposals have not wholly won support from the UK's
European partners, who, though not yet inclined to countenance the
end of spontaneous asylum applications in EU Member States, are
also investigating alternatives in a broader, global context.

   History teaches us that when human beings feel impelled to
migrate, there is little that states can do to prevent it. Exclusion and
deterrence, regulation and control might have some impact, as recent

---

[1] See, for announcement of pilot on identity cards, A. Travis, 'ID cards to be tested in
"a small market town"', *The Guardian*, August 27, 2003.

asylum statistics in the UK suggest,[2] but this may be for a limited period only. In all probability, the pressure will simply shift to another channel, such as increasing resort to false documentation by those who anticipate that they will not be favourably received. Current predictions for the future are that forced migration is likely to increase rather than diminish, even if developed countries were to provide greater financial aid and support to asylum-producing states. The many causes of migration are well-known: persecution, human rights abuse, poverty, famine, civil war, and the simple desire for a better life. Yet there is one relatively untested issue with the potential for a profound impact on human migration: climate change. Evidence is emerging that the predicted global warming and consequent rise in sea levels could result in major movements of people, spurred on either by drought, as in the case of Africa, or by submergence, as in the case of Bangladesh.[3] In such circumstances, the government might be forced yet again to redefine the asylum seeker and to introduce an underused category to UK asylum policy: the 'environmental refugee'.

---

[2] See Home Office, *Asylum Statistics: 2nd Quarter 2003 United Kingdom* (London: Home Office RDSD).

[3] See D. Verschuren, K. Laird and B. Cumming, 'Rainfall and drought in equatorial east Africa during the past 1,100 years', (January 27, 2000) 403: 6769 *Nature*, 410 L. Brown, 'Rising sea level forcing evacuation of island country', *The Earth Policy Institute*, May 13, 2002; see also S. Castles, *Environmental change and forced migration: making sense of the debate* Working Paper No. 70 (Geneva: UNHCR, October 2002)

Appendix A

(This appendix is not intended to be comprehensive and serves only as a guide to sections mentioned in this book.)

Act	Extent of Repeal	Repealing Act	Extent of Amendment	Amending provision
IA 1971	s. 25	2002		
			new s. 25	s. 143, 2002
			new ss. 25A, 25B & 25C	s. 143, 2002
			new ss. 28AA, 28CA, 28FA, 28FB	s. 152, 2002 s. 153, 2002
BNA 1981			s. 40	s. 4, 2002
			new s. 40(A)(2)	s. 4, 2002
I(CL)A 1987	Whole Act	1999		
AIAA 1993	ss. 3–12 sch. 1–2	1999		
AIA 1996	ss. 1–4	1999		
	s. 5	2002		
	s. 7	1999		
	ss. 9–11		s. 8	s. 147, 2002
	sch. 2, para. 1(2)	1999		
	1(3)	1999		
	3	"		
	4(2)	"		
	sch. 3, para.	"		
	1	1999		
	2	"		
	5	"		

Act	Extent of Repeal	Repealing Act	Extent of Amendment	Amending provision
SIACA 1997	s. 2A	2002	new s. 2	sch. 7(20), 2002
	s. 4	"		
	ss. 5(1)(a)&(b)	"		
	s. 5(2) wording	"	new s. 2B	s. 4, 2002
	s. 7(4)	1999		
	s. 7A	2002		
	sch. 2	2002		
	sch. 2, para. 5	1999		
IAA 1999			s. 4	s. 49, 2002
	s. 10(1)(c) wording	2002		
	s. 15	"		
	s. 29	"		
			s. 32	s. 128 & sch. 8, 2002
	s. 33(2)(b) wording	"		
	s. 34 wording	"		
	s. 36(1) wording	"		
	s. 37(3)(c) wording	"		
	ss. 38(1)&(3)	"		
	s. 39	"		
			s. 40	s. 128 & sch. 8, 2002
	s. 42	"		
	s. 43 wording	"		
	s. 44–52	"		
	s. 55	2002		
	ss. 56–81	"		
	ss. 94(5)&(6)	"	s. 94(1)	ss. 44(2)–(3), 2002
			s. 94(3)	s. 44(4), 2002
			ss. 95(2)–(8)	s. 44(6), 2002
	ss. 96(4), (5)&(6)	"	s. 122	s. 47, 2002
			s. 147	s. 66, 2002
	s. 147 wording	"		
	s. 166(4)(e)	"		
	sch. 1 wording	"		
	schs 2–4	"		
	sch. 8(2)&(6)	"		
			sch. 8, para. 12(c)	s. 57, 2002
	sch. 14 various	"		

Select Bibliography

Abell, N.A., 'The compatability of readmission agreements with the 1951
  Convention relating to the status of refugees' (1999) 11:1 *International Journal
  of Refugee Law*, 60
Achermann & Gattiker, 'Safe third countries: European developments' (1995)
  7:1 *International Journal of Refugee Law*, 19
Adler-Rudel, S., 'The Evian Conference on the Refugee Question', *Leo Baeck
  Institute Year Book* 1968, 235
Alibhai-Brown, Y., *No Place like Home: An Autobiography* (London: Virago, 1995)
Alston, P. ed., *The EU and Human Rights* (Oxford: OUP, 1999)
Amnesty International, *Playing Human Pinball: Home Office Practice in 'Safe Third
  Country' Asylum Cases* (London: AI British Section, June 1995)
Amnesty International, *Slamming the Door – The Demolition of the Right to Asylum
  in the UK* (London: Amnesty International, 1996)
Andersson, Musterd & Robinson, *Spreading the 'Burden'?: A Review of Policies to
  Disperse Asylum-Seekers and Refugees* (London: The Policy Press, 2003)
Ashford, M., *Detained without Trial – A Survey of Immigration Act Detention*
  (London: JCWI, 1993)
Asylum Aid, *'No Reason at All' – Home Office Decisions on Asylum Claims* (London:
  Asylum Aid, 1995)
Asylum Aid, *'Still No Reason at All' – Home Office Decisions on Asylum Claims*
  (London: Asylum Aid, 1999)
Audit Commission, *Another Country – Implementing Dispersal under the Immigration
  and Asylum Act 1999* (London: The Audit Commission, June 2000)
Baron, S.W., *A Social and Religious History of the Jews*, vol. XI (Jewish Publica-
  tion Society/Columbia University Press, 1967)
Beck, R., 'Britain and the 1933 Refugee Convention: National or State
  Sovereignty?' (1999) 11:4 *International Journal of Refugee Law*, 621
Billings, P., 'A Comparative Analysis of Administrative and Adjudicative
  Systems for Determining Asylum Claims' (2000) 52:1 *Administrative Law
  Review*, 253
Billings, P., 'Alienating asylum seekers: Welfare support in the Immigration
  and Asylum Act 1999' (2002) 2 *Journal of Social Security Law*, 115
Blake & Husain, *Immigration, Asylum & Human Rights* (Oxford: OUP, 2003)
Boccardi, I., *Europe and Refugees – Towards an EU Asylum Policy* (The Hague:
  Kluwer Law International, 2002)
Bonner, D., 'Managing terrorism while respecting human rights? European
  aspects of the Anti-terrorism Crime and Security Act 2001' (2002) 8:4
  European Public Law, 497
Boswell, C., 'EU immigration and asylum policy: from Tampere to Laeken
  and beyond' (February 2002) *The Royal Institute of International Affairs*, Brief-
  ing Paper New Series No. 30

Bradshaw & Emanual, *Alien Immigration – Should Restrictions be imposed?* (London: Isbister & Co., 1904)

Bramwell, A ed., *Refugees in the Age of Total War* (London: Unwin Hyman, 1988)

Bridges, L., *et al*, 'Regulating the Judicial Review Case Load', [2000] *Public Law*, 651

Brown Scott, J, ed., *The Classics of International Law* (New York: Oceana Publications, 1964)

Bunyan, T. ed., *Key Texts on Justice and Home Affairs in the EU Vol. 1 (1976–1993) From Trevi to Maastricht* (London: Statewatch, 1997)

Cahalan, P., *Belgian Refugee Relief in England during the Great War* (New York: Garland, 1982)

Castles, Crawley & Loughna, *States of Conflict: Causes and Patterns of Forced Migration to the EU and Policy Responses* (London: IPPR, 2003)

Castles, S., *Environmental change and forced migration: making sense of the debate* Working Paper No 70 (Geneva: UNHCR, October 2002)

Cesarani, D. & Kushner, T. eds., *The Internment of Aliens in Twentieth Century Britain* (London: Frank Cass, 1993)

Cesarani, D. ed., *The Making of Modern Anglo-Jewry* (Oxford: Basil Blackwell, 1990)

Chimni, B., *International Refugee Law – A Reader* (Sage, 2000)

Cholewinski, R., 'Enforced Destitution of Asylum Seekers in the UK' (1998) 10:3 *International Journal of Refugee Law*, 462

Cohen, R. ed., *Theories of Migration* (Cheltenham: Edward Elgar, 1996)

Cohen, S., *No One is Illegal: Asylum and Immigration Control Past and Present* (Stoke on Trent: Trentham Books, 2003)

Cohn, E.J., 'Legal Aspects of Internment', (1941) *Modern Law Review*, 200

Collinson, S., *Europe and International Migration* (London: Pinter Publishers for Royal Institute of International Affairs, 1994)

Colvin, M., 'Human rights and accountability after the Treaty of Amsterdam (1998) 2 *European Human Rights Law Review*

Craies, W., 'The Right of Aliens to Enter British Territory', (1890) 6 *LQR*, 27

Craig, P., *Administrative Law* (Sweet & Maxwell, 4th edition, 1999)

Crawley, H., *Breaking Down the Barriers – A Report on the Conduct of Asylum Interviews at Ports* (London: ILPA, 1999)

Crawley, H., *Refugees and Gender: Law and Process* (Bristol: Jordans, 2001)

Crawley, H., *Women as Asylum Seekers* (London: ILPA, 1997)

Cruz, A., *Carriers Liability in the Member States of the European Union* (Brussels: Churches Commission for Migrants in Europe, 1994)

Cunningham, W., *Alien Immigrants to England*, (London: Sonnenschein, 1897)

de Boigne, Comtesse, *Memoirs* (Heinemann, 1907)

de Chateaubriand, Vicomte F., *Mémoires D'Outre-tombe* (Paris, 1849–50)

de Schickler, Baron F., *Eglises du refuge en Angleterre* (Paris, 1892)

Duke & Marshall, *Home Office Research Study No. 142: Vietnamese Refugees since 1982* (London: HMSO, 1995)

Dummett & Nicol, *Subjects, Citizens, Aliens and Others* (London: Weidenfeld & Nicolson, 1990)

Dummett, Sir M., *On Immigration and Refugees* (Routledge, 2001)

Dunstan, D., *Distant Voices: CAB clients' Experience of Continuing Problems with the NASS* (London: CAB, October 2002)

ECRE, *The Promise of Protection: Progress towards A European Asylum Policy since Tampere* (ECRE, November 2001)

Edwards & Pijpers eds., *The Politics of the European Treaty Reform – The 1996 Intergovernmental Conference and Beyond* (London: Pinter, 1997)

Einarsen, T., 'The European Convention on Human Rights and the Notion of an Implied Right to *de facto* Asylum', (1990) 2:3 *International Journal of Refugee Law*, 361

Fabbricotti, A., 'The concept of inhuman or degrading treatment in international law and its application in asylum cases' (1998) 10:4 *International Journal of Refugee Law*, 637

Farbey, J., 'Joined-up government or loss of judicial powers? Part 5 of the Nationality, Immigration and Asylum Act 2002' (2003) 17:1 *International Journal of Refugee Law*, 36

Feller, E.,'Carrier Sanctions and International Law', (1989) 1 *International Journal of Refugee Law*, 48

Fenwick, H., 'The Anti-Terrorism, Crime and Security Act 2001: A Proportionate Response to September 11?' (2002) 65:5 *Modern Law Review*, 724

Ferris, E., *Refugees, Migrants and Human Rights in the Post-Cold War Era* (Switzerland: World Council of Churches, 1993)

Fiddick, J., *Immigration and Asylum*, Research Paper 99/16 (London: Home Affairs Section of House of Commons Library, February 19, 1999)

Fitzpatrick, J., 'Temporary protection of refugees: Elements of a formalized regime', (April 2000) 94 *American Journal of International Law*, 286

Fraser, C., *Control of Aliens in the British Commonwealth of Nations* (London: The Hogarth Press, 1940)

Gainer, B., *The Alien Invasion – the Origins of the Aliens Act of 1905* (London: Heinemann, 1972)

Galbraith, V.H. ed., *Anonimalle Chronicle 1333 to 1381*, (Manchester University Press, 1970)

Gallagher, D., 'The Evolution of the International Refugee System', (1989) 23:3 *International Migration Review*, 580

Garrard, J.A., 'Parallels of Protests: English Reactions to Jewish and Commonwealth Immigration', (1967–68) 9 *Race*, 49

Garry, H., 'Harmonisation of asylum law and policy within the EU: a human rights perspective' (2002) 20:2 *Netherlands Quarterly of Human Rights*, 163

Garvey, 'Toward a Reformulation of International Refugee Law' (1985) 26:2 *Harvard International Law Journal*, 483

Garvie, D., *Far From Home – The Housing of Asylum Seekers in Private Rented Accommodation* (London: Shelter, 2001)

Ghaleigh, N.S., *Immigration Detention and Human Rights: Deserving the Name of Democracy* (London: ARC)

Gillman, P., *'Collar the Lot!': How Britain Interned and Deported its Wartime Refugees* (London, 1980)

Goodwin-Gill, G., 'Asylum: The law and politics of change' (1995) 7:1 *International Journal of Refugee Law*, 12

Goodwin-Gill, G., '*Non-Refoulement* and the New Asylum Seekers', (1986) 26:4 *Virginia Journal of International Law*, 898

Goodwin-Gill, G., 'The Margin of interpretation: Different or disparate?' (1999) 11:4, *International Journal of Refugee Law*, 730

Goodwin-Gill, G., *The Refugee in International Law* (Oxford: Clarendon Press, 1996)

Gorlick, B., 'The Convention and the Committee against Torture: A Complementary Protection regime for Refugees', (1999) 11:3, *International Journal of Refugee Law*, 479

Gowlland-Debbas, V. ed., *The Problem of Refugees in the Light of Contemporary International Law Issues* (The Netherlands: Martinus Nijhoff, 1996)

Grahl-Madsen, A., *Territorial Asylum* (Sweden: Almquist & Wiksell International, 1980)

Grahl-Madsen, A., *The Status of Refugees in International Law* Vol. II (The Netherlands: A.W. Sijthoff-Leiden, 1972)

Grahl-Madsen, *The Status of Refugees in International Law* Vol. I (Netherlands: A.W. Sijthoff-Leyden, 1966)

Grant & Martin, *Immigration Law & Practice* (London: The Cobden Trust, 1982)

Greer, D., *The Incidence of the Emigration During the French Revolution* (Massachusetts: Peter Smith, 1951)

Grell, O.P., *Calvinist Exiles in Tudor and Stuart England* (Hampshire: Scolar Press, 1996)

Grotius, *De jure belli ac pacis*, Book II

Guild & Harlow eds., *Implementing Amsterdam – Immigration and Asylum Rights in EC Law* (Oxford: Hart, 2001)

Guild & Niessen, *The Developing Immigration and Asylum Policies of the EU* (The Hague: Kluwer Law, 1996)

Gwynn, R., *Huguenot Heritage – The History and Contribution of the Huguenots in Britain* (London: Routledge, 1985)

Hailbronner & Thiery, 'Schengen II and Dublin: responsibility for asylum applications in Europe', (1997) 34 *Common Market Law Review*, 957

Hailbronner, K., '*Non-Refoulement* and "Humanitarian" Refugees: Customary International law or Wishful Legal Thinking?', (1986) 26:4 *Virginia Journal of International Law*, 857

Hailbronner, K., 'Perspectives of a harmonization of the law of asylum after the Maastricht summit' (1992) 29:5 *Common Market Law Review*, 917

Hailbronner, K., 'The concept of "safe country" and expeditious asylum procedures: A western European perspective' (1993) 5:1 *International Journal of Refugee Law*, 31

Hailbronner, K., *Immigration and Asylum Law and Policy of the European Union* (The Hague: Kluwer Law International, 1999)

Hansen, R., 'Asylum policy in the EU' (2000) 14 *Georgetown Immigration law Journal*

Hansen, R., *Citizenship and Immigration in Post-war Britain* (Oxford: OUP, 2000)

Haque, R. *et al*, *Migrants in the UK: their characteristics and labour market outcomes and impacts*, RDS Occasional Paper No. 82 (London: Home Office, December 2002)

Harding, J., *The Uninvited* (London: Profile Books, 2000)

Harris, O'Boyle & Warbrick, *Law of the European Convention on Human Rights* (London: Butterworths, 1995)

Harrison, G.B., *The Elizabethan Journals – being a record of those things most talked of during the years 1591–1603* (London: Routledge & Kegan Paul Ltd.)

Harvey, A., *'The Risks of Getting it Wrong': the Asylum and Immigration Bill Session 1995–96 and the Determination of Special Adjudicators* (London: ARC, 1996).

Harvey, C., 'Talking about Refugee Law' (1999) 12:2 *Journal of Refugee Studies*, 101

Harvey, C., 'The European Regulation of asylum: Constructing a Model of Regional Solidarity? (1998) 4:4 *European Public Law*, 561

Harvey, C., *Seeking Asylum in the UK: Problems and Prospects* (London: Butterworths, 2000)

Hathaway & Dent, *Refugee Rights: Report on a Comparative Survey* (Toronto: York Lanes Press, 1995)

Hathaway & Harvey, 'Framing refugee protection in the new world disorder' (2001) 34 *Cornell International Law Journal*, 257

Hathaway & Neve, 'Making international refugee law relevant again: A proposal for collectivized and solution-oriented protection' (1997) 10 *Harvard Human Rights Journal*, 115

Hathaway, J. ed, *Reconceiving International Refugee Law* (The Netherlands: Kluwer Law International, 1997)

Hathaway, J., 'A Reconsideration of the Underlying Premise of Refugee Law' (1990) 31:1 *Harvard International Law Journal*, 129

Hathaway, J., 'International refugee law: the Michigan guidelines on the internal protection alternative' (1999) 21 *Michigan Journal of International Law*, 131

Hathaway, J., 'Reconceiving refugee law as human rights protection' (1991) 4:2 *Journal of Refugee Studies*, 113

Hathaway, J., 'The Evolution of Refugee Status in International Law: 1920–1950', (1994) 33 *International Comparative Law Quarterly*, 354

Hathaway, J., *The Law of Refugee Status* (Canada: Butterworths, 1991)

Haycraft, T., 'Alien Legislation and the Prerogative of the Crown', (1897) 13 *Law Quarterly review*, 165

Hayter, T., *Open Borders* (London: Pluto Press, 2000)

Helton, A.C., *The Price of Indifference – Refugees and Humanitarian Action in the New Century* (Oxford: OUP, 2002)

Henderson, M., *Best Practice Guide to Asylum Appeals* (London: ILPA, 1997)

Henriques, H., *The Jews and English Law* (London: Bibliophile Press, 1908)

Herzen, A., *My Past and Thoughts – The Memoirs of Alexander Herzen*, vol. III (London: Chatto & Windus, 1968)

Hirschfeld, G. ed., *Exile in Great Britain – Refugees from Hitler's Germany* (Leamington Spa: Berg, 1984)

Holborn, L., 'The Legal Status of Political Refugees, 1920–1938', (1938) 32:2 *American Journal of International Law*, 690

Holborn, L., *Refugees: A Problem of our Time*, Vol. I (Metuchen, N.J.: The Scarecrow Press, 1975)

Holborn, L., *The International Refugee Organisation: A Specialized Agency of the United Nations – Its History and Work 1946–1952* (London: OUP, 1956)

Holdsworth, W., *A History of English Law*, Vol. IX (Sweet & Maxwell/Methuen, 1966)

Holmes, C., *John Bull's Island – Immigration and British Society, 1871–1971* (London: Macmillan, 1994)

House of Commons Research Paper 00/32, *Human Rights in the EU: the Charter of Fundamental Rights*, March 20, 2000

Hughes & Liebaut eds., *Detention of Asylum Seekers in Europe: Analysis and Perspectives* (The Netherlands: Kluwer Law International, 1998)

Hunter, A., 'Between the domestic and the international: The role of the European Union in providing protection for unaccompanied refugee children in the United Kingdom', (2001) 3:3/4 *European Journal of Migration and Law*, 383

Hurwitz, A., 'The 1990 Dublin Convention: A comprehensive assessment', (1999) 11:4 *International Journal of Refugee Law*, 646

Huysmans, J., 'The European Union and the securitization of migration', (2000) 38:5 *Journal of Common Market Studies*, 751

Irvine of Lairg, Lord, 'Activism and Restraint: Human Rights and the Interpretative Process', (1999) 4 *European Human Rights Law Review*, 350

Irvine of Lairg, Lord, 'Judges and Decision-makers: The Theory and Practice of *Wednesbury* Review', [1996] *Public Law*, 59

Jackson, D., *Immigration Law and Practice* (London: Sweet & Maxwell, 1999)

Jackson, I., 'Ensuring that the exercise of UNHCR's traditional functions is maintained and reinforced in the 21st century', (2000) 12:4 *International Journal of Refugee Law*, 589

JCWI, *Immigration, Nationality & Asylum Law Handbook* (London: JCWI, 2002); ILPA, *Making an Asylum Application – A Best Practice Guide* (London: ILPA, May 2002)

Johnsson, A., 'UNHCR's protection role continually evolving' (1993) 92 *Refugees*, 15

Joly, D. ed., *Closing Doors: Global Changes in Asylum Regimes* (London: Macmillan, 2001)

Joly, D., *Haven or Hell? Asylum Policies and Refugees in Europe* London: Macmillan, 1996)

Joly, D., *Refugees – Asylum in Europe?* (London: Minority Rights Publications, 1992)

Jones, *Home Office Research Study No. 13: Vietnamese Refugees* (London: HMSO)

Jowell, Jeffrey & Lester, 'Beyond *Wednesbury*: Substantive Principles of Administrative Law', [1987] *Public Law*, 368

Juss, 'Toward a morally legitimate reform of refugee law: the uses of cultural jurisprudence', (1998) 11 *Harvard Human Rights Journal*, 336

Justice, ILPA & ARC, *Providing Protection – Towards Fair and Effective Asylum Procedures* (London: Justice/ILPA/ARC, 1997)

Keely, C., 'How Nation-States Create and Respond to Refugee Flows', (1996) 30:4 *International Migration Review*, 1057

Kelly, N., 'The Convention refugee definition and gender-based persecution: A decade's progress', (2001) 13:4 *International Journal of Refugee Law*, 559

Kerber, K., 'Temporary protection in the EU: a chronology' (1999) 14 *Georgetown Immigration Law Journal*, 35

Kidane, S., *Food, Shelter and Half a Chance* (London: BAAF, 2001)

Kiernan, V., 'Britons Old and New', in C. Holmes (ed.), *Immigrants and Minorities in British Society* (Allen & Unwin, 1978)

KPMG Peat Marwick, *Review of Asylum Appeals Procedure Final Report* (London: KPMG Peat Marwick, December 1994)

Kushner, T. & Knox, K., *Refugees in an Age of Genocide* (London: Frank Cass, 1999)

Lafitte, F., *The Internment of Aliens* (London: Penguin, 1940)

Lambert, H., 'Building a European asylum policy under the "First Pillar" of the consolidated Treaty establishing the EC' (1999) 11:2 *International Journal of Refugee Law*, 327

Lambert, H., *Seeking Asylum: Comparative Law and Practice in Selected European-Countries* (Martinus Mijhoff, 1995)

Lauterpacht, H., 'The Universal Declaration of Human Rights' (1948) 25 *British Yearbook of International Law*, 354

Lavenex, S., *Safe Third Countries – Extending EU Asylum and Immigration Policies to Central and Eastern Europe* (Hungary: CEU Press, 1999)

Legomsky, S., *Immigration and the Judiciary – Law and Politics in Britain and America* (Oxford: Clarendon Press, 1987)

Leigh, Leonard & Beyani, *Blackstone's Guide to the Asylum and immigration Act 1996* (London: Blackstone Press, 1996)

Lester of Herne Hill, Lord, 'Thirty years on: East African Asians case revisited' [2002] Spring *Public Law*, 52

Loescher & Milner, 'The missing link: the need for comprehensive engagement in regions of refugee origin' (2003) 79:3 *International Affairs*, 583

Loescher, G., *Beyond Charity – International Co-operation and the Global Refugee Crisis* (Oxford: OUP, 1993)

London, L., *Whitehall and the Jews 1933–1948 – British Immigration Policy and the Holocaust* (Cambridge: CUP, 2000)

Luqmani, J., 'Statutory review under the Nationality, Immigration and Asylum Act 2002, (May 2003) *Legal Action*, 24

MacDonald & Blake, *Immigration Law and Practice* (London: Butterworths, 1991)

Macdonald & Webber, *Macdonald's Immigration Law & Practice* (London: Butterworths, 2001)

MacDonald, I., *Immigration Law & Practice* (London: Butterworths, 1987)

Marrus, M., *The Unwanted – European Refugees in the Twentieth Century* (New York: Oxford University Press, 1985)

McKee, R., 'Within the meaning of the Act: Notes and queries on the Nationality, Immigration and Asylum Act 2002', (2003) 17:1 *Tolley's Journal of Immigration, Asylum and Nationality Law*, 8

Morgenstern, F., 'The Right of Asylum', (1949) 26 *British Yearbook of International Law*, 327

Morrison, J., *The Cost of Survival: The Trafficking of Refugees to the UK* (London: The Refugee Council, July 1998)

Morrison, J., *The Trafficking and Smuggling of Refugees: The End Game in European Asylum Policy?* (Geneva: UNHCR, July 2000)

Morse, A., *While Six Million died: A Chronicle of American Apathy* (New York: Random House, 1968)

Mosse, W. ed., *Second Chance – Two Centuries of German-speaking Jews in the United Kingdom* (Tübingen: J.C.B. Mohr (Paul Siebeck), 1991)

Nicholson & Twomey eds., *Current Issues of UK Asylum Law and Policy* (Aldershot: Ashgate, 1998)

Nicholson & Twomey eds., *Refugee Rights and Realities* (CUP, 1999)

Nicholson, F., 'Implementation of the Immigration (Carriers' Liability) Act 1987: Privatising Immigration Functions at the Expense of International Obligations?' (1997) 46 *International and Comparative Law Quarterly*, 586

Nicolson, C., *Strangers to England – Immigration to England 1100–1952* (London: Wayland Publishers, 1974)

Noll, G., 'Visions of the exceptional: Legal and theoretical issues raised by transit processing centres and protection zones' (2003) 5:3 *European Journal of Migration and Law*

Norris, M., '*Ex parte Smith*: irrationality and human rights' [1996] *Public Law*, 590

Nykänen, E., 'Protecting children? The European Convention on Human Rights and child asylum seekers' (2001) 3:3/4 *European Journal of Migration and Law*, 315

O'Higgins, P., 'Disguised Extradition: The Soblen Case' (1964) 27 *MLR*, 521

O'Higgins, P., 'The history of extradition in British practice, 1174–1794', (1964) 13 *Indian Yearbook of International Affairs*, 78

O'Keeffe, D., 'The emergence of a European immigration policy' (1995) 20:1 *European Law Review*, 20

O'Keeffe, D., 'The free movement of persons and the single market' (1992) 17:1 *European Law Review*, 3

Ogata, S., *et al*, *Towards a European Immigration Policy* (Brussels: The Philip Morris Institute, 1993)

Oxfam & Refugee Council, *Poverty and Asylum in the UK* (London: Oxfam/Refugee Council, 2002)

Peers, S., 'Immigration, asylum and the European Union Charter of Fundamental Rights' (2001) 3:2 *European Journal of Migration and Law*, 141

Peers, S., *EU Justice and Home Affairs Law* (London: Longman, 2000)

Peers, S., *Mind the Gap! Ineffective Member State Implementation of EU asylum Measures* (London: ILPA/Refugee Council, May 1998)

Peers, S., *The Amsterdam Proposals – The ILPA/MPG Proposed Directives in Immigration and Asylum* (London: ILPA/MPG, 2000)

Phuong, C., 'Enlarging Fortress Europe: EU accession, asylum, and immigration in candidate countries' (2003) 52 *International and Comparative Law Quarterly*, 641

Phuong, C., 'Persecution by non-state agents: comparative judicial interpretations of the 1951 Refugee Convention' (2002) 4:4 *European Journal of Migration and Law*, 521

Phuong, C., 'Persecution by third parties and European harmonisation of asylum policies' (2001) 16 *Georgetown Immigration Law Journal*, 81

Pirouet, L., *What Ever Happened to Asylum in Britain?: A Tale of Two Walls* (Berghahn Books, 2001)

Plender, R., 'International Human Rights Law on Asylum' in *Asylum Law* (London: IARLJ, 1995)

Pollock & Maitland, *The History of English Law before Edward I*, Vol.1 (Cambridge University Press, 1911)

Porter, B., *The Refugee Question in Mid-Victorian Politics* (Cambridge: Cambridge University Press, 1979)

Proudfoot, M., *European Refugees 1939–52 – A Study in Forced Population Movement* (London: Faber & Faber, 1956)

Robinson & Segrott, *Understanding the Decision-Making of Asylum Seekers*, Home Office Research Study 243, (London: Home Office RDSD, July 2002)

Robinson, V. ed., *The International Refugee Crisis: British and Canadian Responses* (Basingstoke: Macmillan/RSP, 1993)

Robinson, V., 'The Vietnamese reception and resettlement programme in the UK', (1985) 6 *Ethnic Groups*, 305

Roche, T.W.E., *The Key in the Lock – A History of Immigration Control in England from 1066 to the Present Day* (London: John Murray, 1969)

Rogers, I., 'From the Human Rights Act to the Charter: not another human rights instrument to consider', (2002) 3 *European Human Rights Law Review*, p. 343

Roth, C., *A History of the Jews* (Oxford: Clarendon Press, 1978)

Rudge, P., 'Reconciling State Interests with International Responsibilities: Asylum in North America and Western Europe' (1998) 10:1/2 *International Journal of Refugee Law*, 7

Ruff, A., 'The Immigration (Carriers' Liability) Act 1987: its Implications for Refugees and Airlines' (1989) 1:4 *International Journal of Refugee Law*, 481

Russell, S., *Most Vulnerable of All* (London: Amnesty International, 1999)

Rye, W., *England as seen by Foreigners in the days of Elizabeth and James the First* (London, 1865)

Salomon, K., *Refugees in the Cold War – Toward a New International Refugee Regime in the Early Postwar Era* (Lund: Lund University Press, 1991)

Scouloudi, I. ed., *Huguenots in Britain and their French Background, 1550–1800* (Hampshire: Macmillan Press, 1987)

Scoville, W.C., 'The Huguenots and the Diffusion of Technology. I', *Journal of Political Economy*, 60 (1952)

Scoville, W.C., *The Persecution of Huguenots and French Economic Development 1680–1720* (Berkeley and Los Angeles, 1960)

Sergeant, H., *Welcome to the Asylum – Immigration and Asylum in the UK* (London: Centre for Policy Studies, 2001)

Shah & Doebbler eds., *UK Asylum Law in its European Context* (London: Platinum & GEMS, 1999)

Shah, P., 'Refugees and safe third countries: United Kingdom, European and international aspects' (1995) 1:2 *European Public Law*, 259

Shah, P., *Refugees, Race and the Legal Concept of Asylum in Britain* (London: Cavendish, 2000)

Sherlock, A., 'Deportation of aliens and article 8 ECHR' (1998) *European Law Review*, 23 Supp HRs, 62

Sherman, A.J., *Island Refuge – Britain and Refugees from the Third Reich 1933–1939* (London: Paul Elek, 1973)

Sibley & Elias, *The Aliens Act and the Right of Asylum* (London: William Clowes & Sons, 1906)

Simpson, G., 'Asylum and Immigration in the EU after the Treaty of Amsterdam (1999) 5:1 *European Public Law*, 91

Simpson, J.H., *The Refugee Problem: Report of a Survey* (London: OUP, 1939)

Sjöberg, T., *The Powers and the Persecuted – The Refugee Problem and the Intergovern-mental Committee on Refugees* (Sweden: Lund University Press, 1991)

Skran, C., *Refugees in Inter-War Europe – The Emergence of a Regime* (New York: Clarendon Press, 1998)

Smiles, S., *The Huguenots: Their Settlements, Churches and Industries in England and Ireland* (London: John Murray, 1870)

Smithies & Fiddick, *Enoch Powell on Immigration* (London: Sphere Books, 1969)

Spencer, S. ed, *Strangers and Citizens: A Positive Approach to Migrants and Refugees* (London, IPPR/Rivers Oram Press, 1994)

Spijkerboer, T., *Gender and Refugee Status* (Ashgate, 2000)

Starmer, K., *European Human Rights Law – The Human Rights Act 1998 and the European Convention on Human Rights* (London: LAG, 1999)

Stevens, D. 'The migration of the Romanian Roma to the UK: a contextual study' (2003) 5.4 *European Journal of Migration and Law*

Stevens, D., 'Race relations and the changing face of United Kingdom asylum policy' (1992) 26:1&2 *Patterns of Prejudice*, 96

Stevens, D., 'Re-introduction of the United Kingdom Asylum Bill', (1993) 5:1 *International Journal of Refugee Law*, 91

Stevens, D., **'**The Asylum and Immigration Act 1996: Erosion of the Right to seek Asylum' (1998) 61 *Modern Law Review*, 207

Stevens, D., 'The Immigration and Asylum Act 1999: A missed opportunity?' (2001) 64:3 *Modern Law Review*, 413

Storey, 'Implications of Incorporation of the ECHR in the Immigration and Asylum Context: Some Challenges for Judicial Decision-making' (1998) 4 *European Human Rights Law Review*, 452

Storey, H., 'UK case law on the Internal Flight Alternative' (1997) 11:2 *Immigration and Nationality Law and Practice*, 7

Supperstone & O'Dempsey, *Supperstone & O'Dempsey on Immigration and Asylum* (London: FT Law & Tax, 1996)

Symes, M., *Caselaw on the Refugee Convention – The United Kingdom's Interpretation in the light of the International Authorities* (London: Refugee Legal Centre, 2000)

The Standing Committee of Experts in International Immigration, Refugee and Criminal Law, *A New Immigration Law for Europe? The 1992 London and 1993 Copenhagen Rules on Immigration* (Netherlands: Nederlands Centrum Buitenlanders, 1993)

Thomas, R., 'Asylum appeals overhauled again' [2003] Public Law, 260

Thomas, R., 'Asylum Seeker Support (2003) 10 Journal of Social Security Law, 163

Thomas, R., 'The impact of judicial review on Asylum' [2003] Autumn *Public Law*, 479

Thornberry, C., 'Dr. Soblen and the Alien Law of the United Kingdom', (1968) 12 *International Comparative Law Quarterly*, 467

Thornberry, C., 'Is the Non-surrender of Political Offenders Outdated?' (1963) 26 *MLR*, 555

Tomkins, A., 'Legislating against terror: the Anti-terrorism, Crime and Security Act 2001', [2002] Summer *Public Law*, 205

Troup, E., *The Home Office* (London: G.P. Putnam's Sons, 1925)

Tuitt, P., *False Images: The Law's Construction of the Refugee* (London: Pluto, 1996)

Turner, S.W. *et al*, 'Mental health of Kosovan Albanian refugees in the UK' (2003) 182 *The British Journal of Psychiatry*, 444

UNHCR, *Handbook on Procedures and Criteria for Determining Refugee Status* (Geneva, 1992)

UNHCR, *The State of the World's Refugees – Fifty Years of Humanitarian Action* (Oxford: OUP, 2000)

UNHCR, *The State of the World's Refugees* (New York: Penguin, 1993)

UNHCR, *The State of the World's Refugees 1997–98 – A Humanitarian Agenda* (Oxford: OUP, 1997)

Van den Wijngaert, C., *The political offence exception to extradition* The Netherlands: Kluwer, 1980)

Van Heuven Goedhart, G.J., 'The Problem of Refugees' (1953) I *Académie de Droit International Recueil des Cours*, 265

van Selm, J., *et al* eds., *The Refugee Convention at 50: a View from Forced Migration Studies* (USA: Lexington Books, 2003)

Veenkamp, Bentley & Buonfino, *People Flow: Managing Migration in a New European Commonwealth* (London: Demos, 2003)

Vernant, J., *The Refugee in the Post-War World* (London: Allen & Unwin, 1953)

Verschuren, Laird & Cumming, 'Rainfall and drought in equatorial east Africa during the past 1,100 years', (January 27, 2000) 403:6767 *Nature*, 410

Vevstad, V., *Refugee Protection – A European Challenge* (Norway: Tano Ashehoug, 1998)

Vincenzi, C., 'Aliens and the Judicial Review of Immigration Law' [1985] *Public Law*, 93

Wade and Forsyth, *Administrative Law* (Oxford: Clarendon Press, 7th edition, 1994)

Waldron, J., *Theories of Rights* (Oxford: OUP, 1984)

Walker, C., 'Armenian refugees: accidents of diplomacy or victims of ideology?', in Marrus & Bramwell eds., *Refugees in the Age of Total War* (London: Unwin Hyman, 1988)

Wallace, R., *Refugees and Asylum: A Community* Perspective (London: Butterworths, 1996)

Weis, P. ed., *The Refugee Convention 1951, The Travaux Preparatoires analysed, with a commentary by Dr Paul Weis* (Cambridge: Cambridge University Press, 1995)

Weis, P., 'The United Nations Declaration on Territorial Asylum', (1969) *Canadian Yearbook of International Law*,

Weiss, C., *History of the French Protestant Refugee* (Blackwood & Sons, 1854)

Williamson, L., 'A safe haven?: The development of British policy concerning unaccompanied refugee children 1933–93', (1995) 14:1 *Immigrants and Minorities*, 47

Willman, Knafler & Pierce, *A Guide to Legal and Welfare Rights – Support for Asylum Seekers* (London: Legal Action Group, 2001)

Wilson, F., *They came as Strangers – The Story of Refugees to Great Britain* (London: Hamish Hamilton, 1959)

Yungblut, L., *Strangers settled here amongst Us – Policies, Perceptions and the Presence of Aliens in Elizabethan England* (London: Routledge, 1996)

Zetter, R. *et al, An Assessment of the Impact of Asylum Policies in Europe 1990–2000*, Home Office Research Study 259 (London: Home Office RDSD, June 2003)

Zolberg, A. *et* al, *Escape from Violence – Conflict and the Refugee Crisis in the Developing World* (Oxford: OUP, 1989)

Index